Cryptography and Network Security, Fifth Edition

A tutorial and survey on network security technology. Each of the basic building blocks of network security, including conventional and public-key cryptography, authentication, and digital signatures, are covered. Thorough mathematical background for such algorithms as AES and RSA. The book covers important network security tools and applications, including S/MIME, IP Security, Kerberos, SSL/TLS, SET, and X509v3. In addition, methods for countering hackers and viruses are explored. **Second edition received the TAA award for the best Computer Science and Engineering Textbook of 1999.** ISBN 0-13-6097049

Network Security Essentials, Fourth Edition

A tutorial and survey on network security technology. The book covers important network security tools and applications, including S/MIME, IP Security, Kerberos, SSL/TLS, SET, and X509v3. In addition, methods for countering hackers and viruses arc explored.

Computer Security (with Lawrie Brown)

A comprehensive treatment of computer security technology, including algorithms, protocols, and applications. Covers cryptography, authentication, access control, database security, intrusion detection and prevention, malicious software, denial of service, firewalls, software security, physical security, human factors, auditing, legal and ethical aspects, and trusted systems. **Received the 2008 TAA award for the best Computer Science and Engineering Textbook of the year.** ISBN 0-13-600424-5

High-Speed Networks and Internets, Second Edition

A state-of-the art survey of high-speed networks. Topics covered include TCP congestion control, ATM traffic management, Internet traffic management, differentiated and integrated services, Internet routing protocols and multicast routing protocols, resource reservation and RSVP, and lossless and lossy compression. Examines important topic of self-similar data traffic. ISBN 0-13-03221-0

To my brilliant and brave wife,
Antigone Tricia, who has survived
the worst horrors imaginable.

CONTENTS

Online Resources x

Preface xi

About the Author xix

Chapter 0   Reader's and Instructor's Guide 1

0.1   Outline of this Book 2
0.2   Example Systems 2
0.3   A Roadmap for Readers and Instructors 3
0.4   Internet and Web Resources 4

PART 1 BACKGROUND 7

Chapter 1   Computer System Overview 7

1.1   Basic Elements 8
1.2   Evolution of the Microprocessor 10
1.3   Instruction Execution 11
1.4   Interrupts 14
1.5   The Memory Hierarchy 24
1.6   Cache Memory 27
1.7   Direct Memory Access 31
1.8   Multiprocessor and Multicore Organization 33
1.9   Recommended Reading and Web Sites 36
1.10   Key Terms, Review Questions, and Problems 37
1A   Performance Characteristics of Two-Level Memories 39

Chapter 2   Operating System Overview 46

2.1   Operating System Objectives and Functions 48
2.2   The Evolution of Operating Systems 52
2.3   Major Achievements 62
2.4   Developments Leading to Modern Operating Systems 71
2.5   Virtual Machines 74

2.6   OS Design Considerations for Multiprocessor and Multicore 77
2.7   Microsoft Windows Overview 80
2.8   Traditional UNIX Systems 90
2.9   Modern UNIX Systems 92
2.10   Linux 94
2.11   Linux VServer Virtual Machine Architecture 100
2.12   Recommended Reading and Web Sites 101
2.13   Key Terms, Review Questions, and Problems 103

PART 2 PROCESSES 106

Chapter 3   Process Description and Control 106

3.1   What Is a Process? 108
3.2   Process States 110
3.3   Process Description 126
3.4   Process Control 134
3.5   Execution of the Operating System 140
3.6   Security Issues 143
3.7   UNIX SVR4 Process Management 147
3.8   Summary 152
3.9   Recommended Reading 152
3.10   Key Terms, Review Questions, and Problems 153

Chapter 4   Threads 157

4.1   Processes and Threads 158
4.2   Types of Threads 164
4.3   Multicore and Multithreading 171
4.4   Windows 7 Thread and SMP Management 176
4.5   Solaris Thread and SMP Management 182
4.6   Linux Process and Thread Management 186
4.7   Mac OS X Grand Central Dispatch 189

4.8   Summary 192
4.9   Recommended Reading 192
4.10   Key Terms, Review Questions, and Problems 193

Chapter 5   Concurrency: Mutual Exclusion and Synchronization 198

5.1   Principles of Concurrency 201
5.2   Mutual Exclusion: Hardware Support 209
5.3   Semaphores 213
5.4   Monitors 226
5.5   Message Passing 233
5.6   Readers/Writers Problem 239
5.7   Summary 243
5.8   Recommended Reading 244
5.9   Key Terms, Review Questions, and Problems 245

Chapter 6   Concurrency: Deadlock and Starvation 258

6.1   Principles of Deadlock 259
6.2   Deadlock Prevention 268
6.3   Deadlock Avoidance 270
6.4   Deadlock Detection 276
6.5   An Integrated Deadlock Strategy 278
6.6   Dining Philosophers Problem 279
6.7   UNIX Concurrency Mechanisms 281
6.8   Linux Kernel Concurrency Mechanisms 285
6.9   Solaris Thread Synchronization Primitives 292
6.10   Windows 7 Concurrency Mechanisms 294
6.11   Summary 298
6.12   Recommended Reading 298
6.13   Key Terms, Review Questions, and Problems 299

PART 3 MEMORY 305

Chapter 7   Memory Management 305

7.1   Memory Management Requirements 307
7.2   Memory Partitioning 310

7.3   Paging 321
7.4   Segmentation 325
7.5   Security Issues 326
7.6   Summary 330
7.7   Recommended Reading 330
7.8   Key Terms, Review Questions, and Problems 331
7A   Loading and Linking 334

Chapter 8   Virtual Memory 340

8.1   Hardware and Control Structures 341
8.2   Operating System Software 360
8.3   UNIX and Solaris Memory Management 379
8.4   Linux Memory Management 384
8.5   Windows Memory Management 386
8.6   Summary 389
8.7   Recommended Reading and Web Sites 390
8.8   Key Terms, Review Questions, and Problems 391

PART 4 SCHEDULING 395

Chapter 9   Uniprocessor Scheduling 395

9.1   Types of Processor Scheduling 396
9.2   Scheduling Algorithms 400
9.3   Traditional UNIX Scheduling 422
9.4   Summary 424
9.5   Recommended Reading 425
9.6   Key Terms, Review Questions, and Problems 426

Chapter 10 Multiprocessor and Real-Time Scheduling 430

10.1   Multiprocessor Scheduling 431
10.2   Real-Time Scheduling 442
10.3   Linux Scheduling 457
10.4   UNIX SVR4 Scheduling 461
10.5   UNIX FreeBSD Scheduling 463
10.6   Windows Scheduling 466
10.7   Linux Virtual Machine Process Scheduling 468
10.8   Summary 469

10.9   Recommended Reading 470
10.10   Key Terms, Review Questions, and
        Problems 471

**PART 5 INPUT/OUTPUT AND
FILES 474**

**Chapter 11 I/O Management and Disk
        Scheduling 474**

11.1   I/O Devices 475
11.2   Organization of the I/O
        Function 477
11.3   Operating System Design Issues 480
11.4   I/O Buffering 483
11.5   Disk Scheduling 487
11.6   RAID 494
11.7   Disk Cache 502
11.8   UNIX SVR4 I/O 506
11.9   Linux I/O 509
11.10   Windows I/O 512
11.11   Summary 515
11.12   Recommended Reading 516
11.13   Key Terms, Review Questions, and
        Problems 517

Chapter 12 File Management 520

12.1   Overview 522
12.2   File Organization and Access 527
12.3   B-Trees 532
12.4   File Directories 535
12.5   File Sharing 540
12.6   Record Blocking 541
12.7   Secondary Storage
        Management 543
12.8   File System Security 551
12.9   UNIX File Management 553
12.10   Linux Virtual File System 560
12.11   Windows File System 564
12.12   Summary 569
12.13   Recommended Reading 570
12.14   Key Terms, Review Questions, and
        Problems 571

PART 6 EMBEDDED SYSTEMS 573

**Chapter 13 Embedded Operating
        Systems 573**

13.1   Embedded Systems 574
13.2   Characteristics of Embedded

        Operating Systems 576
13.3   eCos 579
13.4   TinyOS 594
13.5   Recommended Reading and
        Web Sites 603
13.6   Key Terms, Review Questions,
        and Problems 604

PART 7 COMPUTER SECURITY 607

**Chapter 14 Computer Security
        Threats 607**

14.1   Computer Security
        Concepts 608
14.2   Threats, Attacks, and Assets 610
14.3   Intruders 616
14.4   Malicious Software
        Overview 619
14.5   Viruses, Worms, and Bots 623
14.6   Rootkits 633
14.7   Recommended Reading and
        Web Sites 635
14.8   Key Terms, Review Questions,
        and Problems 636

**Chapter 15 Computer Security
        Techniques 639**

15.1   Authentication 640
15.2   Access Control 646
15.3   Intrusion Detection 653
15.4   Malware Defense 657
15.5   Dealing with Buffer Overflow
        Attacks 663
15.6   Windows 7 Security 667
15.7   Recommended Reading and
        Web Sites 672
15.8   Key Terms, Review Questions,
        and Problems 674

PART 8 DISTRIBUTED SYSTEMS 677

**Chapter 16 Distributed Processing, Client/
        Server, and Clusters 677**

16.1   Client/Server Computing 678
16.2   Service-Oriented
        Architecture 689
16.3   Distributed Message Passing 691
16.4   Remote Procedure Calls 695
16.5   Clusters 699

16.6 Windows Cluster Server 704

16.7 Beowulf and Linux Clusters 706

16.8 Summary 708

16.9 Recommended Reading and Web Sites 709

16.10 Key Terms, Review Questions, and Problems 710

APPENDICES

Appendix A   Topics in Concurrency A-1

A.1 Mutual Exclusion: Software Approaches A-2

A.2 Race Conditions and Semaphores A-8

A.3 A Barbershop Problem A-15

A.4 Problems A-21

Appendix B   Programming and Operating System Projects B-1

B.1 OS/161 B-2

B.2 Simulations B-3

B.3 Programming Projects B-4

B.4 Research Projects B-6

B.5 Reading/Report Assignments B-6

B.6 Writing Assignments B-6

B.7 Discussion Topics B-7

B.8 BACI B-7

Glossary 713

References 723

Index 743

ONLINE CHAPTERS AND APPENDICES[1]

Chapter 17 **Network Protocols 17-1**

17.1 The Need for a Protocol
Architecture 17-3

17.2 The TCP/IP Protocol
Architecture 17-6

17.3 Sockets 17-15

17.4 Linux Networking 17-21

17.5 Summary 17-22

17.6 Recommended Reading and Web
Sites 17-23

17.7 Key Terms, Review Questions, and
Problems 17-24

17A The Trivial File Transfer
Protocol 17-28

Chapter 18 **Distributed Process
Management 18-1**

18.1 Process Migration 18-2

18.2 Distributed Global States 18-10

18.3 Distributed Mutual
Exclusion 18-16

18.4 Distributed Deadlock 18-30

18.5 Summary 18-44

18.6 Recommended Reading 18-45

18.7 Key Terms, Review Questions, and
Problems 18-46

Chapter 19 **Overview of Probability
and Stochastic Processes 19-1**

19.1 Probability 19-2

19.2 Random Variables 19-8

19.3 Elementary Concepts of Stochastic Processes 19-14

19.4 Recommended Reading and Web
Sites 19-26

19.5 Key Terms, Review Questions, and
Problems 19-27

Chapter 20 **Queueing Analysis 20-1**

20.1 How Queues Behave—A Simple
Example 20-3

20.2 Why Queueing Analysis? 20-8

20.3 Queueing Models 20-10

20.4 Single-Server Queues 20-20

20.5 Multiserver Queues 20-22

20.6 Examples 20-24

20.7 Queues with Priorities 20-30

20.8 Networks of Queues 20-32

20.9 Other Queueing Models 20-37

20.10 Estimating Model
Parameters 20-38

20.11 Recommended Reading and Web
Sites 20-42

20.12 Key Terms, Review Questions, and
Problems 20-43

**Programming Project One   Developing
a Shell**

**Programming Project Two   The HOST
Dispatcher Shell**

Appendix C **Topics in Computer
Organization C-1**

C.1 Processor Registers C-2

C.2 Instruction Execution for I/O
Instructions C-6

C.3 I/O Communication
Techniques C-7

C.4 Hardware Performance
Issues for Multicore
Organization C-12

Appendix D **Object-Oriented
Design D-1**

D.1 Motivation D-2

D.2 Object-Oriented Concepts D-4

D.3 Benefits of Object-Oriented
Design D-9

D.4 CORBA D-11

D.5 Recommended Reading and
Web Site D-17

Appendix E **Amdahl's Law E-1**

Appendix F **Hash Tables F-1**

[1]Online chapters, appendices, and other documents are Premium Content, available via the access card
at the front of this book.

Appendix G   Response Time G-1

**Appendix H   Queueing System
              Concepts H-1**

H.1   The Single-Server Queue H-2
H.2   The Multiserver Queue H-4
H.3   Poisson Arrival Rate H-7

**Appendix I   The Complexity of
             Algorithms I-1**

Appendix J   Disk Storage Devices J-1

J.1   Magnetic Disk J-2
J.2   Optical Memory J-8

**Appendix K   Cryptographic
              Algorithms K-1**

K.1   Symmetric Encryption K-2
K.2   Public-Key Cryptography K-6
K.3   Secure Hash Functions K-10

Appendix L   Standards Organizations L-1

L.1   The Importance of Standards L-2
L.2   Standards and Regulation L-3
L.3   Standards-Setting Organizations L-4

**Appendix M   Sockets: A Programmer's
              Introduction M-1**

M.1   Sockets, Socket Descriptors, Ports,
          and Connections M-4

M.2   The Client/Server Model of
          Communication M-6
M.3   Sockets Elements M-8
M.4   Stream and Datagram
          Sockets M-28
M.5   Run-Time Program
          Control M-33
M.6   Remote Execution of a Windows
          Console Application M-38

**Appendix N   The International Reference
              Alphabet N-1**

**Appendix O   BACI: The Ben-Ari
              Concurrent Programming
              System O-1**

O.1   Introduction O-2
O.2   BACI O-3
O.3   Examples of BACI Programs O-7
O.4   BACI Projects O-11
O.5   Enhancements to the BACI
          System O-16

Appendix P   Procedure Control P-1

P.1   Stack Implementation P-2
P.2   Procedure Calls and Returns P-3
P.3   Reentrant Procedures P-4

ONLINE RESOURCES

Site	Location	Description
Companion Web Site	williamstallings.com/OS/ OS7e.html www.pearsonhighered.com/ stallings/	*Student Resources* button: Useful links and documents for students *Instructor Resources* button: Useful links and documents for instructors
Premium Web Content	www.pearsonhighered.com/ stallings/, click on Premium Web Content button and enter the student access code found on the card in the front of the book.	Online chapters, appendices, and other documents that supplement the book
Instructor Resource Center (IRC)	Pearsonhighered.com/ Stallings/, click on Instructor Resource button.	Solutions manual, projects manual, slides, and other useful documents
Computer Science Student Resource Site	computersciencestudent.com	Useful links and documents for computer science students

PREFACE

This book does not pretend to be a comprehensive record; but it aims at helping to disentangle from an immense mass of material the crucial issues and cardinal decisions. Throughout I have set myself to explain faithfully and to the best of my ability.

— *THE WORLD CRISIS*, WINSTON CHURCHILL

OBJECTIVES

This book is about the concepts, structure, and mechanisms of operating systems. Its purpose is to present, as clearly and completely as possible, the nature and characteristics of modern-day operating systems.

This task is challenging for several reasons. First, there is a tremendous range and variety of computer systems for which operating systems are designed. These include embedded systems, smart phones, single-user workstations and personal computers, medium-sized shared systems, large mainframe and supercomputers, and specialized machines such as real-time systems. The variety is not just in the capacity and speed of machines, but in applications and system support requirements as well. Second, the rapid pace of change that has always characterized computer systems continues with no letup. A number of key areas in operating system design are of recent origin, and research into these and other new areas continues.

In spite of this variety and pace of change, certain fundamental concepts apply consistently throughout. To be sure, the application of these concepts depends on the current state of technology and the particular application requirements. The intent of this book is to provide a thorough discussion of the fundamentals of operating system design and to relate these to contemporary design issues and to current directions in the development of operating systems.

EXAMPLE SYSTEMS

This text is intended to acquaint the reader with the design principles and implementation issues of contemporary operating systems. Accordingly, a purely conceptual or theoretical treatment would be inadequate. To illustrate the concepts and to tie them to real-world design choices that must be made, three operating systems have been chosen as running examples:

- **Windows 7:** A multitasking operating system for personal computers, workstations, and servers. This operating system incorporates many of the latest developments in operating system technology. In addition, Windows is one of the first important commercial operating systems to rely heavily on object-oriented design principles. This book covers the technology used in the most recent version of Windows, known as Windows 7.

- **UNIX:** A multiuser operating system, originally intended for minicomputers, but implemented on a wide range of machines from powerful microcomputers to supercomputers. Several flavors of UNIX are included as examples. FreeBSD is a widely used system that incorporates many state-of-the-art features. Solaris is a widely used commercial version of UNIX.

- **Linux:** An open-source version of UNIX that is now widely used.

These systems were chosen because of their relevance and representativeness. The discussion of the example systems is distributed throughout the text rather than assembled as a single chapter or appendix. Thus, during the discussion of concurrency, the concurrency mechanisms of each example system are described, and the motivation for the individual design choices is discussed. With this approach, the design concepts discussed in a given chapter are immediately reinforced with real-world examples.

INTENDED AUDIENCE

The book is intended for both an academic and a professional audience. As a textbook, it is intended as a one-semester undergraduate course in operating systems for computer science, computer engineering, and electrical engineering majors. It covers all of the core topics and most of the elective topics recommended in *Computer Science Curriculum 2008*, from the Joint Task Force on Computing Curricula of the IEEE Computer Society and the ACM, for the Undergraduate Program in Computer Science. The book also covers the operating systems topics recommended in the *Guidelines for Associate-Degree Curricula in Computer Science 2002*, also from the Joint Task Force on Computing Curricula of the IEEE Computer Society and the ACM. The book also serves as a basic reference volume and is suitable for self-study.

PLAN OF THE TEXT

The book is divided into eight parts (see Chapter 0 for an overview):

- Background
- Processes
- Memory
- Scheduling
- Input/output and files
- Embedded systems
- Security
- Distributed systems

The book includes a number of pedagogic features, including the use of animations and numerous figures and tables to clarify the discussion. Each chapter includes a list of key words, review questions, homework problems, suggestions for further reading, and recommended Web sites. The book also includes an extensive glossary, a list of frequently used acronyms, and a bibliography. In addition, a test bank is available to instructors.

WHAT'S NEW IN THE SEVENTH EDITION

In the 3 years since the sixth edition of this book was published, the field has seen continued innovations and improvements. In this new edition, I try to capture these changes while maintaining a broad and comprehensive coverage of the entire field. To begin the process of revision, the sixth edition of this book was extensively reviewed by a number of professors who teach the subject and by professionals working in the field. The result is that, in many places, the narrative has been clarified and tightened, and illustrations have been improved. Also, a number of new "field-tested" homework problems have been added.

Beyond these refinements to improve pedagogy and user friendliness, the technical content of the book has been updated throughout, to reflect the ongoing changes in this exciting field, and the instructor and student support has been expanded. The most noteworthy changes are as follows:

- **Windows 7:** Windows 7 is Microsoft's latest OS offering for PCs, workstations, and servers. The seventh edition provides details on Windows 7 internals in all of the key technology areas covered in this book, including process/thread management, scheduling, memory management, security, file systems, and I/O.

- **Multicore operating system issues:** The seventh edition now includes coverage of what has become the most prevalent new development in computer systems: the use of multiple processors on a single chip. At appropriate points in the book, operating system issues related to the use of a multicore organization are explored.

- **Virtual machines:** Chapter 2 now includes a section on virtual machines, which outlines the various approaches that have been implemented commercially.

- **New scheduling examples:** Chapter 10 now includes a discussion of the FreeBSD scheduling algorithm, designed for use with multiprocessor and multicore systems, and Linux VServer scheduling for a virtual machine environment.

- **Service-oriented architecture (SOA):** SOA is a form of client/server architecture that now enjoys widespread use in enterprise systems. SOA is now covered in Chapter 16.

- **Probability, statistics, and queueing analysis:** Two new chapters review key topics in these areas to provide background for OS performance analysis.

- **B-trees:** This is a technique for organizing indexes into files and databases that is commonly used in OS file systems, including those supported by

Mac OS X, Windows, and several Linux file systems. B-trees are now covered in Chapter 12.

- **Student study aids:** Each chapter now begins with a list of learning objectives. In addition, a chapter-by-chapter set of **review outlines** highlights key concepts that the student should concentrate on in each chapter.

- **OS/161:** OS/161 is an educational operating system that is becoming increasingly recognized as the teaching platform of choice. This new edition provides support for using OS/161 as an active learning component. See later in this Preface for details.

- **Sample syllabus:** The text contains more material than can be conveniently covered in one semester. Accordingly, instructors are provided with several sample syllabi that guide the use of the text within limited time (e.g., 16 weeks or 12 weeks). These samples are based on real-world experience by professors with the sixth edition.

With each new edition, it is a struggle to maintain a reasonable page count while adding new material. In part, this objective is realized by eliminating obsolete material and tightening the narrative. For this edition, chapters and appendices that are of less general interest have been moved online, as individual PDF files. This has allowed an expansion of material without the corresponding increase in size and price.

STUDENT RESOURCES

For this new edition, a tremendous amount of original supporting material has been made available online, in the following categories
The Companion Web site and student resource material can be reached through the Publisher's Web site www.pearsonhighered.com/stallings or by clicking on the button labeled "Book Info and More Instructor Resources" at the book's Companion Web site WilliamStallings.com/OS/OS7e.html. For this new edition, a tremendous amount of original supporting material has been made available online, in the following categories:

- **Homework problems and solutions:** To aid the student in understanding the material, a separate set of homework problems with solutions are available. These enable the students to test their understanding of the text.

- **Programming projects:** Two major programming projects, one to build a shell (or command line interpreter) and one to build a process dispatcher, are described.

- **Key papers:** Several dozen papers from the professional literature, many hard to find, are provided for further reading.

- **Supporting documents:** A variety of other useful documents are referenced in the text and provided online.

Premium Web Content
Purchasing this textbook new grants the reader 6 months of access to this online material. See the access card in the front of this book for details.

- **Online chapters:** To limit the size and cost of the book, four chapters of the book are provided in PDF format. The chapters are listed in this book's table of contents.

- **Online appendices:** There are numerous interesting topics that support material found in the text but whose inclusion is not warranted in the printed text. A total of 13 appendices cover these topics for the interested student. The appendices are listed in this book's table of contents.

INSTRUCTOR SUPPORT MATERIALS

Support materials are available at the Instructor Resource Center (IRC) for this textbook, which can be reached through the Publisher's Web site www.pearsonhighered.com/stallings or by clicking on the button labeled "Book Info and More Instructor Resources" at this book's Companion Web site WilliamStallings.com/OS/OS7e.html. To gain access to the IRC, please contact your local Pearson sales representative via pearsonhighered.com/educator/replocator/requestSalesRep.page or call Pearson Faculty Services at 1-800-526-0485. To support instructors, the following materials are provided:

- **Solutions manual:** Solutions to end-of-chapter Review Questions and Problems.

- **Projects manual:** Suggested project assignments for all of the project categories listed in the next section.

- **PowerPoint slides:** A set of slides covering all chapters, suitable for use in lecturing.

- **PDF files:** Reproductions of all figures and tables from the book.

- **Test bank:** A chapter-by-chapter set of questions.

- Links to Web sites for other courses being taught using this book.

- An Internet mailing list has been set up so that instructors using this book can exchange information, suggestions, and questions with each other and with the author. As soon as typos or other errors are discovered, an errata list for this book will be available at WilliamStallings.com. Sign-up information for this Internet mailing list.

- **Computer science student resource list:** A list of helpful links for computer science students and professionals is provided at ComputerScienceStudent.com, which provides documents, information, and useful links for computer science students and professionals.

- **Programming projects:** Two major programming projects, one to build a shell (or command line interpreter) and one to build a process dispatcher, are described in the online portion of this textbook. The IRC provides further information and step-by-step exercises for developing the programs. As an alternative, the instructor can assign a more extensive series of projects that cover many of the principles in the book. The student is provided with detailed instructions for doing each of the projects. In addition, there is a set of homework problems, which involve questions related to each project for the student to answer.

Projects and Other Student Exercises

For many instructors, an important component of an OS course is a project or set of projects by which the student gets hands-on experience to reinforce concepts from the text. This book provides an unparalleled degree of support for including a projects component in the course. In the online portion of the text, two major programming projects are defined. In addition, the instructor support materials available through Pearson not only include guidance on how to assign and structure the various projects but also includes a set of user's manuals for various project types plus specific assignments, all written especially for this book. Instructors can assign work in the following areas:

- **OS/161 projects:** Described below.
- **Simulation projects:** Described below.
- **Programming projects:** Described below.
- **Research projects:** A series of research assignments that instruct the student to research a particular topic on the Internet and write a report.
- **Reading/report assignments:** A list of papers that can be assigned for reading and writing a report, plus suggested assignment wording.
- **Writing assignments:** A list of writing assignments to facilitate learning the material.
- **Discussion topics:** These topics can be used in a classroom, chat room, or message board environment to explore certain areas in greater depth and to foster student collaboration.

In addition, information is provided on a software package known as BACI that serves as a framework for studying concurrency mechanisms.

This diverse set of projects and other student exercises enables the instructor to use the book as one component in a rich and varied learning experience and to tailor a course plan to meet the specific needs of the instructor and students. See Appendix B in this book for details.

OS/161

New to this edition is support for an active learning component based on OS/161. OS/161 is an educational operating system that is becoming increasingly recognized as the preferred teaching platform for OS internals. It aims to strike a balance between giving students experience in working on a real operating system and potentially overwhelming students with the complexity that exists in a fully fledged operating system, such as Linux. Compared to most deployed operating systems, OS/161 is quite small (approximately 20,000 lines of code and comments), and therefore it is much easier to develop an understanding of the entire code base.

The IRC includes:

1. A packaged set of html files that the instructor can upload to a course server for student access.

2. A getting-started manual to be handed out to students to help them begin using OS/161.

3. A set of exercises using OS/161, to be handed out to students.

4. Model solutions to each exercise for the instructor's use.

5. All of this will be cross-referenced with appropriate sections in the book, so that the student can read the textbook material and then do the corresponding OS/161 project.

Simulations for Students and Instructors

The IRC provides support for assigning projects based on a set of seven **simulations** that cover key areas of OS design. The student can use a set of simulation packages to analyze OS design features. The simulators are all written in Java and can be run either locally as a Java application or online through a browser. The IRC includes specific assignments to give to students, telling them specifically what they are to do and what results are expected.

Animations for Students and Instructors

This edition also incorporates animations. Animations provide a powerful tool for understanding the complex mechanisms of a modern OS. A total of 53 animations are used to illustrate key functions and algorithms in OS design. The animations are used for Chapters 3, 5, 6, 7, 8, 9, and 11. For access to the animations, click on the rotating globe at this book's Web site at WilliamStallings.com/OS/OS7e.html.

ACKNOWLEDGMENTS

This new edition has benefited from review by a number of people, who gave generously of their time and expertise. These include Samir Chettri (The University of Maryland, Baltimore County), Michael Rogers (Tennessee Technological University), Glenn Booker (Drexel University), Jeongkyu Lee (University of Bridgeport), Sanjiv Bhatia (University of Missouri, Baltimore County), Martin Barrett (East Tennessee State University), Lubomir Ivanov (Iona College), Bina Ramamurthy (University at Buffalo), Dean Kelley (Minnesota State University), Joel Weinstein (Northeastern University), all of whom reviewed most or all of the book.

Thanks also to the people who provided detailed reviews of a one or more chapters: John South (University of Dallas), Kevin Sanchez-Cherry (IT Security Specilist), Adri Jovin (PG Scholar,Department of IT, Anna University of Technology, Coimbatore), Thriveni Venkatesh (Professor Thriveni T K from GcMAT, Bangalore, India), Fernando Lichtschein (Instituto de Tecnología ORT Argentina), C. Annamala (Indian Institute of Technology Kharagpur),

Abdul-Rahman Mahmood (Independent IT & security consultant & Creator of AlphaPeeler crypto tool), and Abhilash V R (VVDN Technologies).

I would also like to thank Dave Probert, Architect in the Windows Core Kernel & Architecture team at Microsoft, for the review of the material on Windows Vista and for providing the comparisons of Linux and Vista; Tigran Aivazian, author of the Linux Kernel Internals document, which is part of the Linux Documentation Project, for the review of the material on Linux 2.6; Nick Garnett of eCosCentric, for the review of the material on eCos; and Philip Levis, one of the developers of TinyOS, for the review of the material on TinyOS.

Professor Andrew Peterson, Ioan Stefanovici, and OS instructors at the University of Toronto prepared the OS/161 supplements for the IRC.

Adam Critchley (University of Texas at San Antonio) developed the simulation exercises. Matt Sparks (University of Illinois at Urbana-Champaign) adapted a set of programming problems for use with this textbook.

Lawrie Brown of the Australian Defence Force Academy produced the material on buffer overflow attacks. Ching-Kuang Shene (Michigan Tech University) provided the examples used in the section on race conditions and reviewed the section. Tracy Camp and Keith Hellman, both at the Colorado School of Mines, developed a new set of homework problems. In addition, Fernando Ariel Gont contributed a number of homework problems; he also provided detailed reviews of all of the chapters.

I would also like to thank Bill Bynum (College of William and Mary) and Tracy Camp (Colorado School of Mines) for contributing Appendix O; Steve Taylor (Worcester Polytechnic Institute) for contributing the programming projects and reading/report assignments in the instructor's manual; and Professor Tan N. Nguyen (George Mason University) for contributing the research projects in the instruction manual. Ian G. Graham (Griffith University) contributed the two programming projects in the textbook. Oskars Rieksts (Kutztown University) generously allowed me to make use of his lecture notes, quizzes, and projects.

Finally, I would like to thank the many people responsible for the publication of the book, all of whom did their usual excellent job. This includes my editor Tracy Dunkelberger, her assistants Carole Snyder, Melinda Hagerty, and Allison Michael, and production manager Pat Brown. I also thank Shiny Rajesh and the production staff at Integra for another excellent and rapid job. Thanks also to the marketing and sales staffs at Pearson, without whose efforts this book would not be in your hands.

With all this assistance, little remains for which I can take full credit. However, I am proud to say that, with no help whatsoever, I selected all of the quotations.

ABOUT THE AUTHOR

William Stallings has made a unique contribution to understanding the broad sweep of technical developments in computer security, computer networking, and computer architecture. He has authored 17 titles, and, counting revised editions, a total of 42 books on various aspects of these subjects. His writings have appeared in numerous ACM and IEEE publications, including the *Proceedings of the IEEE* and *ACM Computing Reviews*.

He has 11 times received the award for the best Computer Science textbook of the year from the Text and Academic Authors Association.

In over 30 years in the field, he has been a technical contributor, technical manager, and an executive with several high-technology firms. He has designed and implemented both TCP/IP-based and OSI-based protocol suites on a variety of computers and operating systems, ranging from microcomputers to mainframes. As a consultant, he has advised government agencies, computer and software vendors, and major users on the design, selection, and use of networking software and products.

He has created and maintains the **Computer Science Student Resource Site** at http://www.computersciencestudent.com/. This site provides documents and links on a variety of subjects of general interest to computer science students (and professionals). He is a member of the editorial board of *Cryptologia*, a scholarly journal devoted to all aspects of cryptology.

Dr. Stallings holds a PhD from M.I.T. in Computer Science and a B.S. from Notre Dame in electrical engineering.

CHAPTER 0

READER'S AND INSTRUCTOR'S GUIDE

0.1 **Outline of This Book**

0.2 **Example Systems**

0.3 **A Roadmap for Readers and Instructors**

0.4 **Internet and Web Resources**
   Web Sites for This Book
   Other Web Sites
   USENET Newsgroups

These delightful records should have been my constant study.

THE IMPORTANCE OF BEING EARNEST, OSCAR WILDE

This book, with its accompanying Web site, covers a lot of material. Here we give the reader some basic background information.

0.1   OUTLINE OF THIS BOOK

The book is organized in eight parts:

Part One. Background: Provides an overview of computer architecture and organization, with emphasis on topics that relate to operating system (OS) design, plus an overview of the OS topics in remainder of the book.

Part Two. Processes: Presents a detailed analysis of processes, multithreading, symmetric multiprocessing (SMP), and microkernels. This part also examines the key aspects of concurrency on a single system, with emphasis on issues of mutual exclusion and deadlock.

Part Three. Memory: Provides a comprehensive survey of techniques for memory management, including virtual memory.

Part Four. Scheduling: Provides a comparative discussion of various approaches to process scheduling. Thread scheduling, SMP scheduling, and real-time scheduling are also examined.

Part Five. Input/Output and Files: Examines the issues involved in OS control of the I/O function. Special attention is devoted to disk I/O, which is the key to system performance. Also provides an overview of file management.

Part Six. Embedded Systems: Embedded systems far outnumber general-purpose computing systems and present a number of unique OS challenges. The chapter includes a discussion of common principles plus coverage of two example systems: TinyOS and eCos.

Part Seven. Security: Provides a survey of threats and mechanisms for providing computer and network security.

Part Eight. Distributed Systems: Examines the major trends in the networking of computer systems, including TCP/IP, client/server computing, and clusters. Also describes some of the key design areas in the development of distributed operating systems.

A number of online chapters and appendices cover additional topics relevant to the book.

0.2   EXAMPLE SYSTEMS

This text is intended to acquaint the reader with the design principles and implementation issues of contemporary operating systems. Accordingly, a purely conceptual or theoretical treatment would be inadequate. To illustrate the concepts and to tie them to real-world design choices that must be made, two operating systems have been chosen as running examples:

- **Windows:** A multitasking operating system designed to run on a variety of PCs, workstations, and servers. It is one of the few recent commercial operating systems that have essentially been designed from scratch. As such, it is in a position to incorporate in a clean fashion the latest developments in operating system technology. The current version, presented in this book, is Windows 7.
- **UNIX:** A multitasking operating system originally intended for minicomputers but implemented on a wide range of machines from powerful microcomputers to supercomputers. Included under this topic is Linux.

The discussion of the example systems is distributed throughout the text rather than assembled as a single chapter or appendix. Thus, during the discussion of concurrency, the concurrency mechanisms of each example system are described, and the motivation for the individual design choices is discussed. With this approach, the design concepts discussed in a given chapter are immediately reinforced with real-world examples.

The book also makes use of other example systems where appropriate, particularly in the chapter on embedded systems.

0.3 A ROADMAP FOR READERS AND INSTRUCTORS

It would be natural for the reader to question the particular ordering of topics presented in this book. For example, the topic of scheduling (Chapters 9 and 10) is closely related to those of concurrency (Chapters 5 and 6) and the general topic of processes (Chapter 3) and might reasonably be covered immediately after those topics.

The difficulty is that the various topics are highly interrelated. For example, in discussing virtual memory, it is useful to refer to the scheduling issues related to a page fault. Of course, it is also useful to refer to some memory management issues when discussing scheduling decisions. This type of example can be repeated endlessly: A discussion of scheduling requires some understanding of I/O management and vice versa.

Figure 0.1 suggests some of the important interrelationships between topics. The solid lines indicate very strong relationships, from the point of view of design and implementation decisions. Based on this diagram, it makes sense to begin with a basic discussion of processes, which we do in Chapter 3. After that, the order is somewhat arbitrary. Many treatments of operating systems bunch all of the material on processes at the beginning and then deal with other topics. This is certainly valid. However, the central significance of memory management, which I believe is of equal importance to process management, has led to a decision to present this material prior to an in-depth look at scheduling.

The ideal solution is for the student, after completing Chapters 1 through 3 in series, to read and absorb the following chapters in parallel: 4 followed by (optional) 5; 6 followed by 7; 8 followed by (optional) 9; 10. The remaining parts can

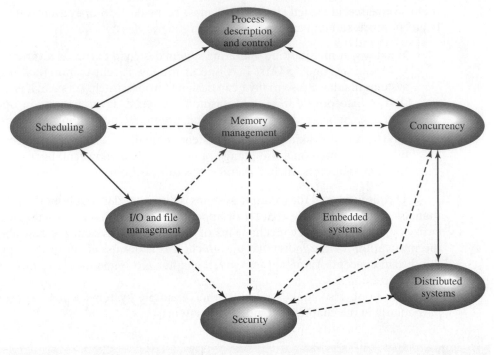

Figure 0.1   OS Topics

be done in any order. However, although the human brain may engage in parallel processing, the human student finds it impossible (and expensive) to work success-fully with four copies of the same book simultaneously open to four different chap-ters. Given the necessity for a linear ordering, I think that the ordering used in this book is the most effective.

A final word. Chapter 2, especially Section 2.3, provides a top-level view of all of the key concepts covered in later chapters. Thus, after reading Chapter 2, there is considerable flexibility in choosing the order in which to read the remaining chapters.

0.4   INTERNET AND WEB RESOURCES

There are a number of resources available on the Internet and the Web to support this book and for keeping up with developments in this field.

Web Sites for This Book

Three Web sites provide additional resources for students and instructors. A special Web page for this book is maintained at **WilliamStallings.com/OS/OS7e.html**. For students, this Web site includes a list of relevant links, organized by chapter, an errata sheet for the book, and links to the animations used throughout the book. For access to the animations, click on the rotating globe. There are also documents that introduce the C programming language for students who are not familiar with or need a refresher on this language For instructors, this Web site links to course pages by professors teaching from this book and provides a number of other useful documents and links.

There is also an access-controlled Web site, referred to as **Premium Content**, that provides a wealth of supporting material, including additional online chapters, additional online appendices, a set of homework problems with solutions, copies of a number of key papers in this field, and a number of other supporting documents. See the card at the front of this book for access information. Of particular note are the following online documents:

- **Pseudocode:** For those readers not comfortable with C, all of the algorithms are also reproduced in a Pascal-like pseudocode. This pseudocode language is intuitive and particularly easy to follow.

- **Windows 7, UNIX, and Linux descriptions:** As was mentioned, Windows and various flavors of UNIX are used as running case studies, with the discussion distributed throughout the text rather than assembled as a single chapter or appendix. Some readers would like to have all of this material in one place as a reference. Accordingly, all of the Windows, UNIX, and Linux material from the book is reproduced in three documents at the Web site.

Finally, additional material for instructors is available at the **Instructor Resource Center (IRC)** for this book. See Preface for details and access information.

As soon as any typos or other errors are discovered, an errata list for this book will be available at the Web site. Please report any errors that you spot. Errata sheets for my other books are at **WilliamStallings.com**.

I also maintain the Computer Science Student Resource Site, at **ComputerScienceStudent.com**. The purpose of this site is to provide documents, information, and links for computer science students and professionals. Links and documents are organized into six categories:

- **Math:** Includes a basic math refresher, a queueing analysis primer, a number system primer, and links to numerous math sites.

- **How-to:** Advice and guidance for solving homework problems, writing technical reports, and preparing technical presentations.

- **Research resources:** Links to important collections of papers, technical reports, and bibliographies.

- **Miscellaneous:** A variety of useful documents and links.

- **Computer science careers:** Useful links and documents for those considering a career in computer science.

- **Humor and other diversions:** You have to take your mind off your work once in a while.

Other Web Sites

There are numerous Web sites that provide information related to the topics of this book. In subsequent chapters, pointers to specific Web sites can be found in the *Recommended Reading and Web Sites* section. Because the URL for a particular Web site may change, I have not included URLs in the book. For all of the Web sites listed in the book, the appropriate link can be found at this book's Web site. Other links not mentioned in this book will be added to the Web site over time.

USENET Newsgroups

A number of USENET newsgroups are devoted to some aspect of operating systems or to a particular operating system. As with virtually all USENET groups, there is a high noise-to-signal ratio, but it is worth experimenting to see if any meet your needs. The most relevant are as follows:

- **comp.os.research:** The best group to follow. This is a moderated newsgroup that deals with research topics.
- **comp.os.misc:** A general discussion of OS topics.
- **comp.os.linux.development.system:** Linux discussion for developers.

PART 1 Background

CHAPTER 1

COMPUTER SYSTEM OVERVIEW

1.1   **Basic Elements**

1.2   **Evolution of the Microprocessor**

1.3   **Instruction Execution**

1.4   **Interrupts**
      Interrupts and the Instruction Cycle
      Interrupt Processing
      Multiple Interrupts

1.5   **The Memory Hierarchy**

1.6   **Cache Memory**
      Motivation
      Cache Principles
      Cache Design

1.7   **Direct Memory Access**

1.8   **Multiprocessor and Multicore Organization**
      Symmetric Multiprocessors
      Multicore Computers

1.9   **Recommended Reading and Web Sites**

1.10 **Key Terms, Review Questions, and Problems**

APPENDIX 1A   **Performance Characteristics of Two-Level Memories**
      Locality
      Operation of Two-Level Memory
      Performance

No artifact designed by man is so convenient for this kind of functional description as a digital computer. Almost the only ones of its properties that are detectable in its behavior are the organizational properties. Almost no interesting statement that one can make about on operating computer bears any particular relation to the specific nature of the hardware. A computer is an organization of elementary functional components in which, to a high approximation, only the function performed by those components is relevant to the behavior of the whole system.

THE SCIENCES OF THE ARTIFICIAL, HERBERT SIMON

LEARNING OBJECTIVES

After studying this chapter, you should be able to:

- Describe the basic elements of a computer system and their interrelationship.
- Explain the steps taken by a processor to execute an instruction.
- Understand the concept of interrupts and how and why a processor uses interrupts.
- List and describe the levels of a typical computer memory hierarchy.
- Explain the basic characteristics of multiprocessor and multicore organizations.
- Discuss the concept of locality and analyze the performance of a multilevel memory hierarchy.
- Understand the operation of a stack and its use to support procedure call and return.

An operating system (OS) exploits the hardware resources of one or more processors to provide a set of services to system users. The OS also manages secondary memory and I/O (input/output) devices on behalf of its users. Accordingly, it is important to have some understanding of the underlying computer system hardware before we begin our examination of operating systems.

This chapter provides an overview of computer system hardware. In most areas, the survey is brief, as it is assumed that the reader is familiar with this subject. However, several areas are covered in some detail because of their importance to topics covered later in the book. Further topics are covered in Appendix C.

1.1 BASIC ELEMENTS

At a top level, a computer consists of processor, memory, and I/O components, with one or more modules of each type. These components are interconnected in some fashion to achieve the main function of the computer, which is to execute programs. Thus, there are four main structural elements:

- **Processor:** Controls the operation of the computer and performs its data processing functions. When there is only one processor, it is often referred to as the **central processing unit** (CPU).

- **Main memory:** Stores data and programs. This memory is typically volatile; that is, when the computer is shut down, the contents of the memory are lost. In contrast, the contents of disk memory are retained even when the computer system is shut down. Main memory is also referred to as *real memory* or *primary memory*.
- **I/O modules:** Move data between the computer and its external environment. The external environment consists of a variety of devices, including secondary memory devices (e.g., disks), communications equipment, and terminals.
- **System bus:** Provides for communication among processors, main memory, and I/O modules.

Figure 1.1 depicts these top-level components. One of the processor's functions is to exchange data with memory. For this purpose, it typically makes use of two internal (to the processor) registers: a memory address register (MAR), which specifies the address in memory for the next read or write; and a memory buffer register (MBR), which contains the data to be written into memory or which receives

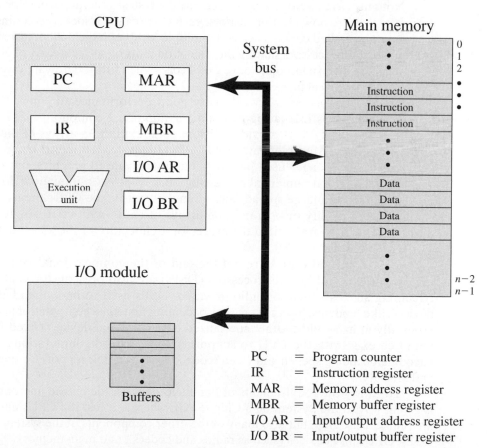

Figure 1.1   Computer Components: Top-Level View

the data read from memory. Similarly, an I/O address register (I/OAR) specifies a particular I/O device. An I/O buffer register (I/OBR) is used for the exchange of data between an I/O module and the processor.

A memory module consists of a set of locations, defined by sequentially numbered addresses. Each location contains a bit pattern that can be interpreted as either an instruction or data. An I/O module transfers data from external devices to processor and memory, and vice versa. It contains internal buffers for temporarily holding data until they can be sent on.

1.2   EVOLUTION OF THE MICROPROCESSOR

The hardware revolution that brought about desktop and handheld computing was the invention of the microprocessor, which contained a processor on a single chip. Though originally much slower than multichip processors, microprocessors have continually evolved to the point that they are now much faster for most computations due to the physics involved in moving information around in sub-nanosecond timeframes.

Not only have microprocessors become the fastest general purpose processors available, they are now multiprocessors; each chip (called a socket) contains multiple processors (called cores), each with multiple levels of large memory caches, and multiple logical processors sharing the execution units of each core. As of 2010, it is not unusual for even a laptop to have 2 or 4 cores, each with 2 hardware threads, for a total of 4 or 8 logical processors.

Although processors provide very good performance for most forms of computing, there is increasing demand for numerical computation. Graphical Processing Units (GPUs) provide efficient computation on arrays of data using Single-Instruction Multiple Data (SIMD) techniques pioneered in supercomputers. GPUs are no longer used just for rendering advanced graphics, but they are also used for general numerical processing, such as physics simulations for games or computations on large spreadsheets. Simultaneously, the CPUs themselves are gaining the capability of operating on arrays of data—with increasingly powerful vector units integrated into the processor architecture of the x86 and AMD64 families.

Processors and GPUs are not the end of the computational story for the modern PC. Digital Signal Processors (DSPs) are also present, for dealing with streaming signals—such as audio or video. DSPs used to be embedded in I/O devices, like modems, but they are now becoming first-class computational devices, especially in handhelds. Other specialized computational devices (fixed function units) co-exist with the CPU to support other standard computations, such as encoding/decoding speech and video (codecs), or providing support for encryption and security.

To satisfy the requirements of handheld devices, the classic microprocessor is giving way to the System on a Chip (SoC), where not just the CPUs and caches are on the same chip, but also many of the other components of the system, such as DSPs, GPUs, I/O devices (such as radios and codecs), and main memory.

1.3 INSTRUCTION EXECUTION

A program to be executed by a processor consists of a set of instructions stored in memory. In its simplest form, instruction processing consists of two steps: The processor reads (*fetches*) instructions from memory one at a time and executes each instruction. Program execution consists of repeating the process of instruction fetch and instruction execution. Instruction execution may involve several operations and depends on the nature of the instruction.

The processing required for a single instruction is called an *instruction cycle*. Using a simplified two-step description, the instruction cycle is depicted in Figure 1.2. The two steps are referred to as the *fetch stage* and the *execute stage.* Program execution halts only if the processor is turned off, some sort of unrecoverable error occurs, or a program instruction that halts the processor is encountered.

At the beginning of each instruction cycle, the processor fetches an instruction from memory. Typically, the program counter (PC) holds the address of the next instruction to be fetched. Unless instructed otherwise, the processor always increments the PC after each instruction fetch so that it will fetch the next instruction in sequence (i.e., the instruction located at the next higher memory address). For example, consider a simplified computer in which each instruction occupies one 16-bit word of memory. Assume that the program counter is set to location 300. The processor will next fetch the instruction at location 300. On succeeding instruction cycles, it will fetch instructions from locations 301, 302, 303, and so on. This sequence may be altered, as explained subsequently.

The fetched instruction is loaded into the instruction register (IR). The instruction contains bits that specify the action the processor is to take. The processor interprets the instruction and performs the required action. In general, these actions fall into four categories:

- **Processor-memory:** Data may be transferred from processor to memory or from memory to processor.
- **Processor-I/O:** Data may be transferred to or from a peripheral device by transferring between the processor and an I/O module.
- **Data processing:** The processor may perform some arithmetic or logic operation on data.
- **Control:** An instruction may specify that the sequence of execution be altered. For example, the processor may fetch an instruction from location 149, which

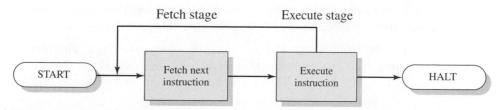

Figure 1.2   Basic Instruction Cycle

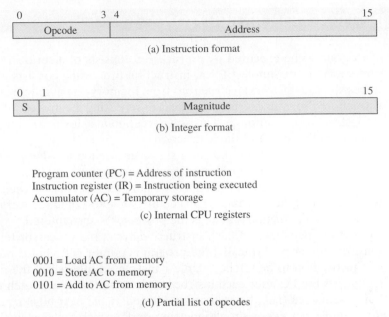

Figure 1.3   Characteristics of a Hypothetical Machine

specifies that the next instruction will be from location 182. The processor sets the program counter to 182. Thus, on the next fetch stage, the instruction will be fetched from location 182 rather than 150.

An instruction's execution may involve a combination of these actions.

Consider a simple example using a hypothetical processor that includes the characteristics listed in Figure 1.3. The processor contains a single data register, called the accumulator (AC). Both instructions and data are 16 bits long, and memory is organized as a sequence of 16-bit words. The instruction format provides 4 bits for the opcode, allowing as many as $2^4 = 16$ different opcodes (represented by a single hexadecimal[1] digit). The opcode defines the operation the processor is to perform. With the remaining 12 bits of the instruction format, up to $2^{12} = 4,096$ (4K) words of memory (denoted by three hexadecimal digits) can be directly addressed.

Figure 1.4 illustrates a partial program execution, showing the relevant portions of memory and processor registers. The program fragment shown adds the contents of the memory word at address 940 to the contents of the memory word at address 941 and stores the result in the latter location. Three instructions, which can be described as three fetch and three execute stages, are required:

1. The PC contains 300, the address of the first instruction. This instruction (the value 1940 in hexadecimal) is loaded into the IR and the PC is incremented. Note that this process involves the use of a memory address register (MAR)

---

[1]A basic refresher on number systems (decimal, binary, hexadecimal) can be found at the Computer Science Student Resource Site at ComputerScienceStudent.com.

Fetch stage   Execute stage

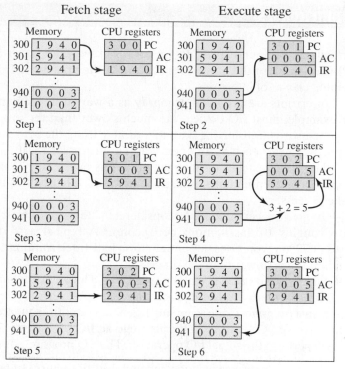

Figure 1.4   Example of Program Execution (contents
of memory and registers in hexadecimal)

and a memory buffer register (MBR). For simplicity, these intermediate registers are not shown.

2. The first 4 bits (first hexadecimal digit) in the IR indicate that the AC is to be loaded from memory. The remaining 12 bits (three hexadecimal digits) specify the address, which is 940.

3. The next instruction (5941) is fetched from location 301 and the PC is incremented.

4. The old contents of the AC and the contents of location 941 are added and the result is stored in the AC.

5. The next instruction (2941) is fetched from location 302 and the PC is incremented.

6. The contents of the AC are stored in location 941.

In this example, three instruction cycles, each consisting of a fetch stage and an execute stage, are needed to add the contents of location 940 to the contents of 941. With a more complex set of instructions, fewer instruction cycles would be needed. Most modern processors include instructions that contain more than one address. Thus the execution stage for a particular instruction may involve more than one reference to memory. Also, instead of memory references, an instruction may specify an I/O operation.

1.4 INTERRUPTS

Virtually all computers provide a mechanism by which other modules (I/O, memory) may interrupt the normal sequencing of the processor. Table 1.1 lists the most common classes of interrupts.

Interrupts are provided primarily as a way to improve processor utilization. For example, most I/O devices are much slower than the processor. Suppose that the processor is transferring data to a printer using the instruction cycle scheme of Figure 1.2. After each write operation, the processor must pause and remain idle until the printer catches up. The length of this pause may be on the order of many thousands or even millions of instruction cycles. Clearly, this is a very wasteful use of the processor.

To give a specific example, consider a PC that operates at 1 GHz, which would allow roughly 10^9 instructions per second.[2] A typical hard disk has a rotational speed of 7200 revolutions per minute for a half-track rotation time of 4 ms, which is 4 million times slower than the processor.

Figure 1.5a illustrates this state of affairs. The user program performs a series of WRITE calls interleaved with processing. The solid vertical lines represent segments of code in a program. Code segments 1, 2, and 3 refer to sequences of instructions that do not involve I/O. The WRITE calls are to an I/O routine that is a system utility and that will perform the actual I/O operation. The I/O program consists of three sections:

- A sequence of instructions, labeled 4 in the figure, to prepare for the actual I/O operation. This may include copying the data to be output into a special buffer and preparing the parameters for a device command.

- The actual I/O command. Without the use of interrupts, once this command is issued, the program must wait for the I/O device to perform the requested function (or periodically check the status, or poll, the I/O device). The program might wait by simply repeatedly performing a test operation to determine if the I/O operation is done.

- A sequence of instructions, labeled 5 in the figure, to complete the operation. This may include setting a flag indicating the success or failure of the operation.

Table 1.1 Classes of Interrupts

Program	Generated by some condition that occurs as a result of an instruction execution, such as arithmetic overflow, division by zero, attempt to execute an illegal machine instruction, and reference outside a user's allowed memory space.
Timer	Generated by a timer within the processor. This allows the operating system to perform certain functions on a regular basis.
I/O	Generated by an I/O controller, to signal normal completion of an operation or to signal a variety of error conditions.
Hardware failure	Generated by a failure, such as power failure or memory parity error.

---

[2]A discussion of the uses of numerical prefixes, such as giga and tera, is contained in a supporting document at the Computer Science Student Resource Site at ComputerScienceStudent.com.

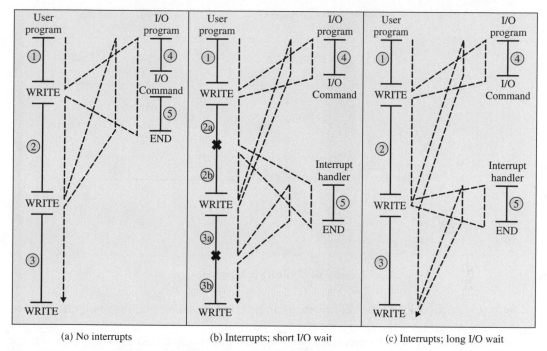

Figure 1.5   Program Flow of Control without and with Interrupts

The dashed line represents the path of execution followed by the processor; that is, this line shows the sequence in which instructions are executed. Thus, after the first WRITE instruction is encountered, the user program is interrupted and execution continues with the I/O program. After the I/O program execution is complete, execution resumes in the user program immediately following the WRITE instruction.

Because the I/O operation may take a relatively long time to complete, the I/O program is hung up waiting for the operation to complete; hence, the user program is stopped at the point of the WRITE call for some considerable period of time.

Interrupts and the Instruction Cycle

With interrupts, the processor can be engaged in executing other instructions while an I/O operation is in progress. Consider the flow of control in Figure 1.5b. As before, the user program reaches a point at which it makes a system call in the form of a WRITE call. The I/O program that is invoked in this case consists only of the preparation code and the actual I/O command. After these few instructions have been executed, control returns to the user program. Meanwhile, the external device is busy accepting data from computer memory and printing it. This I/O operation is conducted concurrently with the execution of instructions in the user program.

When the external device becomes ready to be serviced, that is, when it is ready to accept more data from the processor, the I/O module for that external device sends an *interrupt request* signal to the processor. The processor responds by suspending operation of the current program; branching off to a routine to service

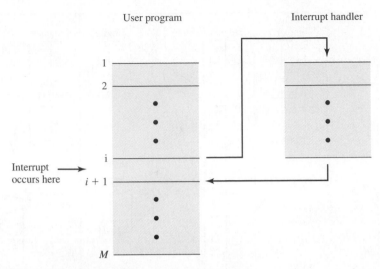

Figure 1.6   Transfer of Control via Interrupts

that particular I/O device, known as an interrupt handler; and resuming the original execution after the device is serviced. The points at which such interrupts occur are indicated by ✖ in Figure 1.5b. Note that an interrupt can occur at any point in the main program, not just at one specific instruction.

For the user program, an interrupt suspends the normal sequence of execution. When the interrupt processing is completed, execution resumes (Figure 1.6). Thus, the user program does not have to contain any special code to accommodate interrupts; the processor and the OS are responsible for suspending the user program and then resuming it at the same point.

To accommodate interrupts, an *interrupt stage* is added to the instruction cycle, as shown in Figure 1.7 (compare Figure 1.2). In the interrupt stage, the processor checks to see if any interrupts have occurred, indicated by the presence of an interrupt signal. If no interrupts are pending, the processor proceeds to the fetch stage and fetches the next instruction of the current program. If an interrupt is pending,

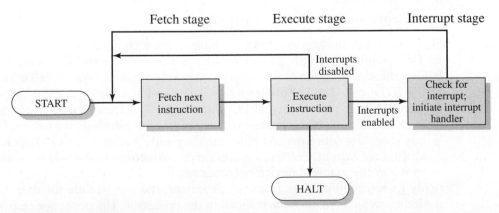

Figure 1.7   Instruction Cycle with Interrupts

the processor suspends execution of the current program and executes an *interrupt-handler* routine. The interrupt-handler routine is generally part of the OS. Typically, this routine determines the nature of the interrupt and performs whatever actions are needed. In the example we have been using, the handler determines which I/O module generated the interrupt and may branch to a program that will write more data out to that I/O module. When the interrupt-handler routine is completed, the processor can resume execution of the user program at the point of interruption.

It is clear that there is some overhead involved in this process. Extra instructions must be executed (in the interrupt handler) to determine the nature of the interrupt and to decide on the appropriate action. Nevertheless, because of the relatively large amount of time that would be wasted by simply waiting on an I/O operation, the processor can be employed much more efficiently with the use of interrupts.

To appreciate the gain in efficiency, consider Figure 1.8, which is a timing diagram based on the flow of control in Figures 1.5a and 1.5b. Figures 1.5b and 1.8

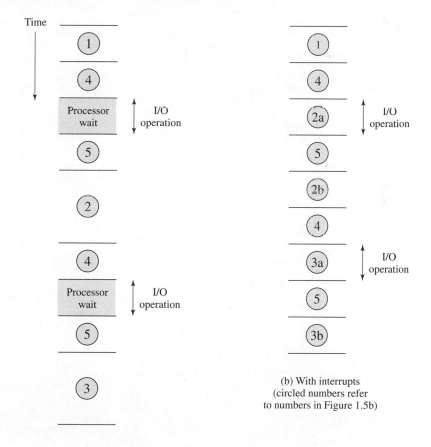

(a) Without interrupts
(circled numbers refer
to numbers in Figure 1.5a)

(b) With interrupts
(circled numbers refer
to numbers in Figure 1.5b)

Figure 1.8   Program Timing: Short I/O Wait

assume that the time required for the I/O operation is relatively short: less than the time to complete the execution of instructions between write operations in the user program. The more typical case, especially for a slow device such as a printer, is that the I/O operation will take much more time than executing a sequence of user instructions. Figure 1.5c indicates this state of affairs. In this case, the user program reaches the second WRITE call before the I/O operation spawned by the first call is complete. The result is that the user program is hung up at that point. When the preceding I/O operation is completed, this new WRITE call may be processed, and a new I/O operation may be started. Figure 1.9 shows the timing for this situation with and without the use of interrupts. We can see that there is still a gain in efficiency because part of the time during which the I/O operation is underway overlaps with the execution of user instructions.

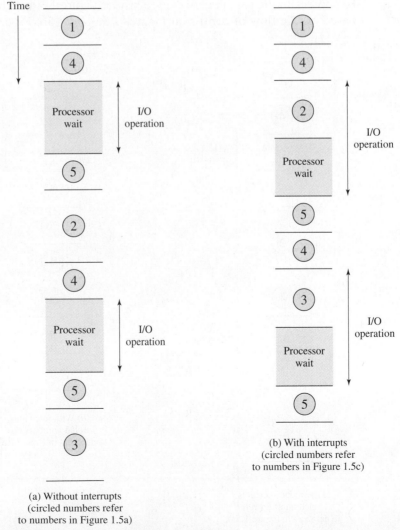

(a) Without interrupts
(circled numbers refer
to numbers in Figure 1.5a)

(b) With interrupts
(circled numbers refer
to numbers in Figure 1.5c)

Figure 1.9   Program Timing: Long I/O Wait

Interrupt Processing

An interrupt triggers a number of events, both in the processor hardware and in software. Figure 1.10 shows a typical sequence. When an I/O device completes an I/O operation, the following sequence of hardware events occurs:

1. The device issues an interrupt signal to the processor.

2. The processor finishes execution of the current instruction before responding to the interrupt, as indicated in Figure 1.7.

3. The processor tests for a pending interrupt request, determines that there is one, and sends an acknowledgment signal to the device that issued the interrupt. The acknowledgment allows the device to remove its interrupt signal.

4. The processor next needs to prepare to transfer control to the interrupt routine. To begin, it saves information needed to resume the current program at the point of interrupt. The minimum information required is the program status word[3] (PSW) and the location of the next instruction to be executed, which

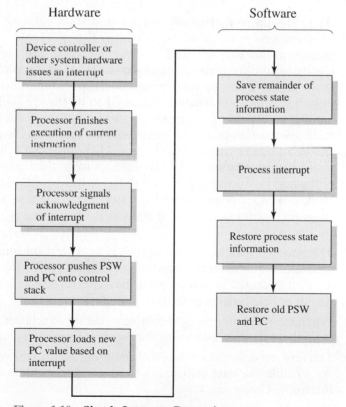

Figure 1.10   Simple Interrupt Processing

---

[3]The PSW contains status information about the currently running process, including memory usage information, condition codes, and other status information, such as an interrupt enable/disable bit and a kernel/user mode bit. See Appendix C for further discussion.

is contained in the program counter (PC). These can be pushed onto a control stack (see Appendix P).

5. The processor then loads the program counter with the entry location of the interrupt-handling routine that will respond to this interrupt. Depending on the computer architecture and OS design, there may be a single program, one for each type of interrupt, or one for each device and each type of interrupt. If there is more than one interrupt-handling routine, the processor must determine which one to invoke. This information may have been included in the original interrupt signal, or the processor may have to issue a request to the device that issued the interrupt to get a response that contains the needed information.

Once the program counter has been loaded, the processor proceeds to the next instruction cycle, which begins with an instruction fetch. Because the instruction fetch is determined by the contents of the program counter, control is transferred to the interrupt-handler program. The execution of this program results in the following operations:

6. At this point, the program counter and PSW relating to the interrupted program have been saved on the control stack. However, there is other information that is considered part of the state of the executing program. In particular, the contents of the processor registers need to be saved, because these registers may be used by the interrupt handler. So all of these values, plus any other state information, need to be saved. Typically, the interrupt handler will begin by saving the contents of all registers on the stack. Other state information that must be saved is discussed in Chapter 3. Figure 1.11a shows a simple example. In this case, a user program is interrupted after the instruction at location N. The contents of all of the registers plus the address of the next instruction ($N + 1$), a total of M words, are pushed onto the control stack. The stack pointer is updated to point to the new top of stack, and the program counter is updated to point to the beginning of the interrupt service routine.

7. The interrupt handler may now proceed to process the interrupt. This includes an examination of status information relating to the I/O operation or other event that caused an interrupt. It may also involve sending additional commands or acknowledgments to the I/O device.

8. When interrupt processing is complete, the saved register values are retrieved from the stack and restored to the registers (e.g., see Figure 1.11b).

9. The final act is to restore the PSW and program counter values from the stack. As a result, the next instruction to be executed will be from the previously interrupted program.

It is important to save all of the state information about the interrupted program for later resumption. This is because the interrupt is not a routine called from the program. Rather, the interrupt can occur at any time and therefore at any point in the execution of a user program. Its occurrence is unpredictable.

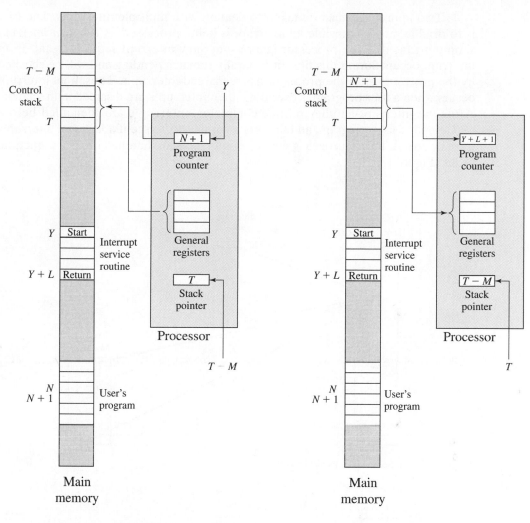

(a) Interrupt occurs after instruction
at location N

(b) Return from interrupt

Figure 1.11   Changes in Memory and Registers for an Interrupt

Multiple Interrupts

So far, we have discussed the occurrence of a single interrupt. Suppose, however, that one or more interrupts can occur while an interrupt is being processed. For example, a program may be receiving data from a communications line and printing results at the same time. The printer will generate an interrupt every time that it completes a print operation. The communication line controller will generate an interrupt every time a unit of data arrives. The unit could either be a single character or a block, depending on the nature of the communications discipline. In any case, it is possible for a communications interrupt to occur while a printer interrupt is being processed.

Two approaches can be taken to dealing with multiple interrupts. The first is to disable interrupts while an interrupt is being processed. A *disabled interrupt* simply means that the processor ignores any new interrupt request signal. If an interrupt occurs during this time, it generally remains pending and will be checked by the processor after the processor has reenabled interrupts. Thus, if an interrupt occurs when a user program is executing, then interrupts are disabled immediately. After the interrupt-handler routine completes, interrupts are reenabled before resuming the user program, and the processor checks to see if additional interrupts have occurred. This approach is simple, as interrupts are handled in strict sequential order (Figure 1.12a).

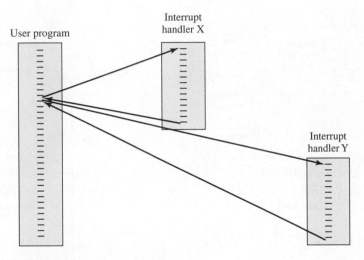

(a) Sequential interrupt processing

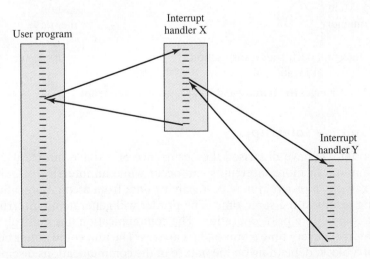

(b) Nested interrupt processing

Figure 1.12   Transfer of Control with Multiple Interrupts

The drawback to the preceding approach is that it does not take into account relative priority or time-critical needs. For example, when input arrives from the communications line, it may need to be absorbed rapidly to make room for more input. If the first batch of input has not been processed before the second batch arrives, data may be lost because the buffer on the I/O device may fill and overflow.

A second approach is to define priorities for interrupts and to allow an interrupt of higher priority to cause a lower-priority interrupt handler to be interrupted (Figure 1.12b). As an example of this second approach, consider a system with three I/O devices: a printer, a disk, and a communications line, with increasing priorities of 2, 4, and 5, respectively. Figure 1.13, based on an example in [TANE06], illustrates a possible sequence. A user program begins at $t = 0$. At $t = 10$, a printer interrupt occurs; user information is placed on the control stack and execution continues at the printer interrupt service routine (ISR). While this routine is still executing, at $t = 15$ a communications interrupt occurs. Because the communications line has higher priority than the printer, the interrupt request is honored. The printer ISR is interrupted, its state is pushed onto the stack, and execution continues at the communications ISR. While this routine is executing, a disk interrupt occurs ($t = 20$). Because this interrupt is of lower priority, it is simply held, and the communications ISR runs to completion.

When the communications ISR is complete ($t = 25$), the previous processor state is restored, which is the execution of the printer ISR. However, before even a single instruction in that routine can be executed, the processor honors the higher-priority disk interrupt and transfers control to the disk ISR. Only when that routine is complete ($t = 35$) is the printer ISR resumed. When that routine completes ($t = 40$), control finally returns to the user program.

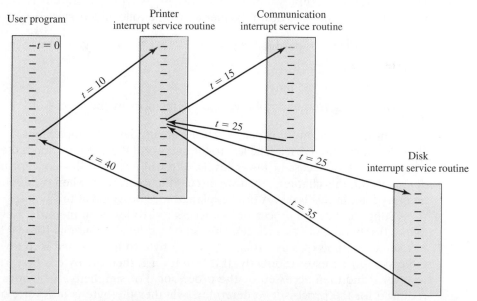

Figure 1.13   Example Time Sequence of Multiple Interrupts

1.5   THE MEMORY HIERARCHY

The design constraints on a computer's memory can be summed up by three questions: How much? How fast? How expensive?

The question of how much is somewhat open ended. If the capacity is there, applications will likely be developed to use it. The question of how fast is, in a sense, easier to answer. To achieve greatest performance, the memory must be able to keep up with the processor. That is, as the processor is executing instructions, we would not want it to have to pause waiting for instructions or operands. The final question must also be considered. For a practical system, the cost of memory must be reasonable in relationship to other components.

As might be expected, there is a trade-off among the three key characteristics of memory: namely, capacity, access time, and cost. A variety of technologies are used to implement memory systems, and across this spectrum of technologies, the following relationships hold:

- Faster access time, greater cost per bit
- Greater capacity, smaller cost per bit
- Greater capacity, slower access speed

The dilemma facing the designer is clear. The designer would like to use memory technologies that provide for large-capacity memory, both because the capacity is needed and because the cost per bit is low. However, to meet performance requirements, the designer needs to use expensive, relatively lower-capacity memories with fast access times.

The way out of this dilemma is to not rely on a single memory component or technology, but to employ a **memory hierarchy**. A typical hierarchy is illustrated in Figure 1.14. As one goes down the hierarchy, the following occur:

- **a.** Decreasing cost per bit
- **b.** Increasing capacity
- **c.** Increasing access time
- **d.** Decreasing frequency of access to the memory by the processor

Thus, smaller, more expensive, faster memories are supplemented by larger, cheaper, slower memories. The key to the success of this organization is the decreasing frequency of access at lower levels. We will examine this concept in greater detail later in this chapter, when we discuss the cache, and when we discuss virtual memory later in this book. A brief explanation is provided at this point.

Suppose that the processor has access to two levels of memory. Level 1 contains 1,000 bytes and has an access time of 0.1 μs; level 2 contains 100,000 bytes and has an access time of 1 μs. Assume that if a byte to be accessed is in level 1, then the processor accesses it directly. If it is in level 2, then the byte is first transferred to level 1 and then accessed by the processor. For simplicity, we ignore the time required for the processor to determine whether the byte is in level 1 or level 2.

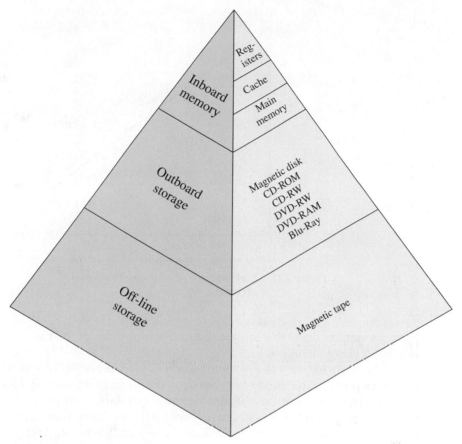

Figure 1.14   The Memory Hierarchy

Figure 1.15 shows the general shape of the curve that models this situation. The figure shows the average access time to a two-level memory as a function of the **hit ratio** H, where H is defined as the fraction of all memory accesses that are found in the faster memory (e.g., the cache), T_1 is the access time to level 1, and T_2 is the access time to level 2.[4] As can be seen, for high percentages of level 1 access, the average total access time is much closer to that of level 1 than that of level 2.

In our example, suppose 95% of the memory accesses are found in the cache ($H = 0.95$). Then the average time to access a byte can be expressed as

$$(0.95)\,(0.1\ \mu s) + (0.05)\,(0.1\ \mu s + 1\ \mu s) = 0.095 + 0.055 = 0.15\ \mu s$$

The result is close to the access time of the faster memory. So the strategy of using two memory levels works in principle, but only if conditions (a) through (d) in the preceding list apply. By employing a variety of technologies, a spectrum of

---

[4]If the accessed word is found in the faster memory, that is defined as a **hit**. A **miss** occurs if the accessed word is not found in the faster memory.

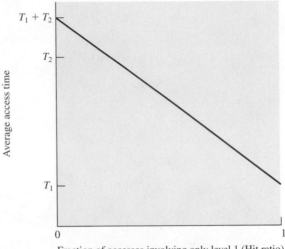

Figure 1.15   Performance of a Simple Two-Level Memory

memory systems exists that satisfies conditions (a) through (c). Fortunately, condition (d) is also generally valid.

The basis for the validity of condition (d) is a principle known as **locality of reference** [DENN68]. During the course of execution of a program, memory references by the processor, for both instructions and data, tend to cluster. Programs typically contain a number of iterative loops and subroutines. Once a loop or subroutine is entered, there are repeated references to a small set of instructions. Similarly, operations on tables and arrays involve access to a clustered set of data bytes. Over a long period of time, the clusters in use change, but over a short period of time, the processor is primarily working with fixed clusters of memory references.

Accordingly, it is possible to organize data across the hierarchy such that the percentage of accesses to each successively lower level is substantially less than that of the level above. Consider the two-level example already presented. Let level 2 memory contain all program instructions and data. The current clusters can be temporarily placed in level 1. From time to time, one of the clusters in level 1 will have to be swapped back to level 2 to make room for a new cluster coming in to level 1. On average, however, most references will be to instructions and data contained in level 1.

This principle can be applied across more than two levels of memory. The fastest, smallest, and most expensive type of memory consists of the registers internal to the processor. Typically, a processor will contain a few dozen such registers, although some processors contain hundreds of registers. Skipping down two levels, main memory is the principal internal memory system of the computer. Each location in main memory has a unique address, and most machine instructions refer to one or more main memory addresses. Main memory is usually extended with a higher-speed, smaller cache. The cache is not usually visible to the programmer or, indeed, to the processor. It is a device for staging the movement of data between main memory and processor registers to improve performance.

The three forms of memory just described are, typically, volatile and employ semiconductor technology. The use of three levels exploits the fact that semiconductor memory comes in a variety of types, which differ in speed and cost. Data are stored more permanently on external mass storage devices, of which the most common are hard disk and removable media, such as removable disk, tape, and optical storage. External, nonvolatile memory is also referred to as **secondary memory** or **auxiliary memory**. These are used to store program and data files, and are usually visible to the programmer only in terms of files and records, as opposed to individual bytes or words. A hard disk is also used to provide an extension to main memory known as virtual memory, which is discussed in Chapter 8.

Additional levels can be effectively added to the hierarchy in software. For example, a portion of main memory can be used as a buffer to temporarily hold data that are to be read out to disk. Such a technique, sometimes referred to as a disk cache (examined in detail in Chapter 11), improves performance in two ways:

- Disk writes are clustered. Instead of many small transfers of data, we have a few large transfers of data. This improves disk performance and minimizes processor involvement.
- Some data destined for write-out may be referenced by a program before the next dump to disk. In that case, the data are retrieved rapidly from the software cache rather than slowly from the disk.

Appendix 1A examines the performance implications of multilevel memory structures.

1.6 CACHE MEMORY

Although cache memory is invisible to the OS, it interacts with other memory management hardware. Furthermore, many of the principles used in virtual memory schemes (discussed in Chapter 8) are also applied in cache memory.

Motivation

On all instruction cycles, the processor accesses memory at least once, to fetch the instruction, and often one or more additional times, to fetch operands and/ or store results. The rate at which the processor can execute instructions is clearly limited by the memory cycle time (the time it takes to read one word from or write one word to memory). This limitation has been a significant problem because of the persistent mismatch between processor and main memory speeds: Over the years, processor speed has consistently increased more rapidly than memory access speed. We are faced with a trade-off among speed, cost, and size. Ideally, main memory should be built with the same technology as that of the processor registers, giving memory cycle times comparable to processor cycle times. This has always been too expensive a strategy. The solution is to exploit the principle of locality by providing a small, fast memory between the processor and main memory, namely the cache.

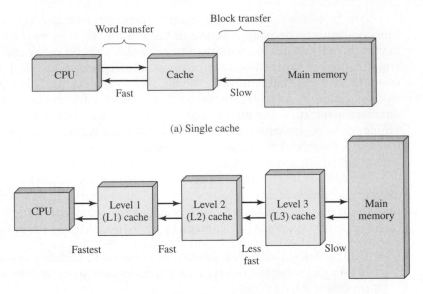

(a) Single cache

(b) Three-level cache organization

Figure 1.16   Cache and Main Memory

Cache Principles

Cache memory is intended to provide memory access time approaching that of the fastest memories available and at the same time support a large memory size that has the price of less expensive types of semiconductor memories. The concept is illustrated in Figure 1.16a. There is a relatively large and slow main memory together with a smaller, faster cache memory. The cache contains a copy of a portion of main memory. When the processor attempts to read a byte or word of memory, a check is made to determine if the byte or word is in the cache. If so, the byte or word is delivered to the processor. If not, a block of main memory, consisting of some fixed number of bytes, is read into the cache and then the byte or word is delivered to the processor. Because of the phenomenon of locality of reference, when a block of data is fetched into the cache to satisfy a single memory reference, it is likely that many of the near-future memory references will be to other bytes in the block.

Figure 1.16b depicts the use of multiple levels of cache. The L2 cache is slower and typically larger than the L1 cache, and the L3 cache is slower and typically larger than the L2 cache.

Figure 1.17 depicts the structure of a cache/main memory system. Main memory consists of up to 2^n addressable words, with each word having a unique n-bit address. For mapping purposes, this memory is considered to consist of a number of fixed-length **blocks** of K words each. That is, there are $M = 2^n/K$ blocks. Cache consists of C **slots** (also referred to as *lines*) of K words each, and the number of slots is considerably less than the number of main memory blocks $(C<<M)$.[5] Some subset of the blocks of main memory resides in the slots of the cache. If a word in a block

---

[5]The symbol $<<$ means *much less than*. Similarly, the symbol $>>$ means *much greater than*.

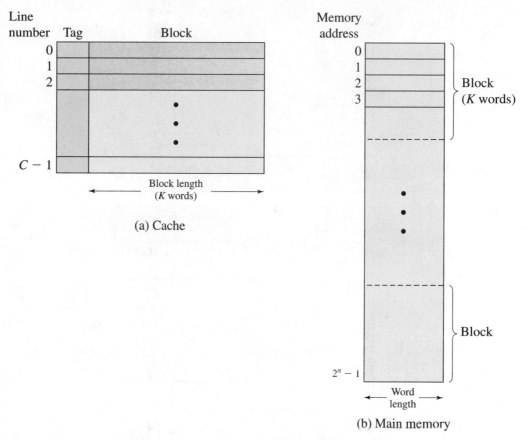

Figure 1.17   **Cache/Main-Memory Structure**

of memory that is not in the cache is read, that block is transferred to one of the slots of the cache. Because there are more blocks than slots, an individual slot cannot be uniquely and permanently dedicated to a particular block. Therefore, each slot includes a tag that identifies which particular block is currently being stored. The tag is usually some number of higher-order bits of the address and refers to all addresses that begin with that sequence of bits.

As a simple example, suppose that we have a 6-bit address and a 2-bit tag. The tag 01 refers to the block of locations with the following addresses: 010000, 010001, 010010, 010011, 010100, 010101, 010110, 010111, 011000, 011001, 011010, 011011, 011100, 011101, 011110, 011111.

Figure 1.18 illustrates the read operation. The processor generates the address, RA, of a word to be read. If the word is contained in the cache, it is delivered to the processor. Otherwise, the block containing that word is loaded into the cache and the word is delivered to the processor.

Cache Design

A detailed discussion of cache design is beyond the scope of this book. Key elements are briefly summarized here. We will see that similar design issues must be

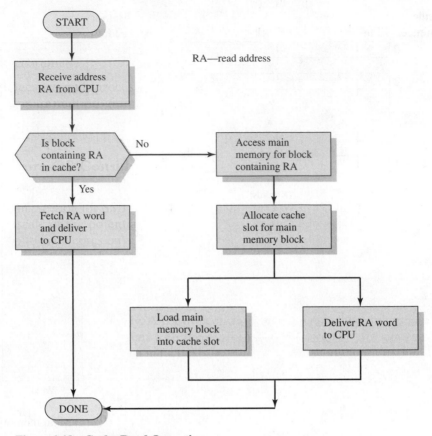

Figure 1.18   Cache Read Operation

addressed in dealing with virtual memory and disk cache design. They fall into the
following categories:

- Cache size
- Block size
- Mapping function
- Replacement algorithm
- Write policy
- Number of cache levels

We have already dealt with the issue of **cache size**. It turns out that reasonably small caches can have a significant impact on performance. Another size issue
is that of **block size**: the unit of data exchanged between cache and main memory.
As the block size increases from very small to larger sizes, the hit ratio will at first
increase because of the principle of locality: the high probability that data in the
vicinity of a referenced word are likely to be referenced in the near future. As the

block size increases, more useful data are brought into the cache. The hit ratio will begin to decrease, however, as the block becomes even bigger and the probability of using the newly fetched data becomes less than the probability of reusing the data that have to be moved out of the cache to make room for the new block.

When a new block of data is read into the cache, the **mapping function** determines which cache location the block will occupy. Two constraints affect the design of the mapping function. First, when one block is read in, another may have to be replaced. We would like to do this in such a way as to minimize the probability that we will replace a block that will be needed in the near future. The more flexible the mapping function, the more scope we have to design a replacement algorithm to maximize the hit ratio. Second, the more flexible the mapping function, the more complex is the circuitry required to search the cache to determine if a given block is in the cache.

The **replacement algorithm** chooses, within the constraints of the mapping function, which block to replace when a new block is to be loaded into the cache and the cache already has all slots filled with other blocks. We would like to replace the block that is least likely to be needed again in the near future. Although it is impossible to identify such a block, a reasonably effective strategy is to replace the block that has been in the cache longest with no reference to it. This policy is referred to as the least-recently-used (LRU) algorithm. Hardware mechanisms are needed to identify the least-recently-used block.

If the contents of a block in the cache are altered, then it is necessary to write it back to main memory before replacing it. The **write policy** dictates when the memory write operation takes place. At one extreme, the writing can occur every time that the block is updated. At the other extreme, the writing occurs only when the block is replaced. The latter policy minimizes memory write operations but leaves main memory in an obsolete state. This can interfere with multiple-processor operation and with direct memory access by I/O hardware modules.

Finally, it is now commonplace to have multiple levels of cache, labeled L1 (cache closest to the processor), L2, and in many cases a third level L3. A discussion of the performance benefits of multiple cache levels is beyond our scope; see [STAL10] for a discussion.

1.7 DIRECT MEMORY ACCESS

Three techniques are possible for I/O operations: programmed I/O, interrupt-driven I/O, and direct memory access (DMA). Before discussing DMA, we briefly define the other two techniques; see Appendix C for more detail.

When the processor is executing a program and encounters an instruction relating to I/O, it executes that instruction by issuing a command to the appropriate I/O module. In the case of **programmed I/O**, the I/O module performs the requested action and then sets the appropriate bits in the I/O status register but takes no further action to alert the processor. In particular, it does not interrupt the processor. Thus, after the I/O instruction is invoked, the processor must take some active role in determining when the I/O instruction is completed. For this purpose, the processor periodically checks the status of the I/O module until it finds that the operation is complete.

With programmed I/O, the processor has to wait a long time for the I/O module of concern to be ready for either reception or transmission of more data. The processor, while waiting, must repeatedly interrogate the status of the I/O module. As a result, the performance level of the entire system is severely degraded.

An alternative, known as **interrupt-driven I/O**, is for the processor to issue an I/O command to a module and then go on to do some other useful work. The I/O module will then interrupt the processor to request service when it is ready to exchange data with the processor. The processor then executes the data transfer, as before, and then resumes its former processing.

Interrupt-driven I/O, though more efficient than simple programmed I/O, still requires the active intervention of the processor to transfer data between memory and an I/O module, and any data transfer must traverse a path through the processor. Thus, both of these forms of I/O suffer from two inherent drawbacks:

1. The I/O transfer rate is limited by the speed with which the processor can test and service a device.

2. The processor is tied up in managing an I/O transfer; a number of instructions must be executed for each I/O transfer.

When large volumes of data are to be moved, a more efficient technique is required: **direct memory access (DMA).** The DMA function can be performed by a separate module on the system bus or it can be incorporated into an I/O module. In either case, the technique works as follows. When the processor wishes to read or write a block of data, it issues a command to the DMA module, by sending to the DMA module the following information:

- Whether a read or write is requested
- The address of the I/O device involved
- The starting location in memory to read data from or write data to
- The number of words to be read or written

The processor then continues with other work. It has delegated this I/O operation to the DMA module, and that module will take care of it. The DMA module transfers the entire block of data, one word at a time, directly to or from memory without going through the processor. When the transfer is complete, the DMA module sends an interrupt signal to the processor. Thus, the processor is involved only at the beginning and end of the transfer.

The DMA module needs to take control of the bus to transfer data to and from memory. Because of this competition for bus usage, there may be times when the processor needs the bus and must wait for the DMA module. Note that this is not an interrupt; the processor does not save a context and do something else. Rather, the processor pauses for one bus cycle (the time it takes to transfer one word across the bus). The overall effect is to cause the processor to execute more slowly during a DMA transfer when processor access to the bus is required. Nevertheless, for a multiple-word I/O transfer, DMA is far more efficient than interrupt-driven or programmed I/O.

1.8 MULTIPROCESSOR AND MULTICORE ORGANIZATION

Traditionally, the computer has been viewed as a sequential machine. Most computer programming languages require the programmer to specify algorithms as sequences of instructions. A processor executes programs by executing machine instructions in sequence and one at a time. Each instruction is executed in a sequence of operations (fetch instruction, fetch operands, perform operation, store results).

This view of the computer has never been entirely true. At the micro-operation level, multiple control signals are generated at the same time. Instruction pipelining, at least to the extent of overlapping fetch and execute operations, has been around for a long time. Both of these are examples of performing functions in parallel.

As computer technology has evolved and as the cost of computer hardware has dropped, computer designers have sought more and more opportunities for parallelism, usually to improve performance and, in some cases, to improve reliability. In this book, we examine the three most popular approaches to providing parallelism by replicating processors: symmetric multiprocessors (SMPs), multicore computers, and clusters. SMPs and multicore computers are discussed in this section; clusters are examined in Chapter 16.

Symmetric Multiprocessors

DEFINITION An SMP can be defined as a stand-alone computer system with the following characteristics:

1. There are two or more similar processors of comparable capability.
2. These processors share the same main memory and I/O facilities and are interconnected by a bus or other internal connection scheme, such that memory access time is approximately the same for each processor.
3. All processors share access to I/O devices, either through the same channels or through different channels that provide paths to the same device.
4. All processors can perform the same functions (hence the term *symmetric*).
5. The system is controlled by an integrated operating system that provides interaction between processors and their programs at the job, task, file, and data element levels.

Points 1 to 4 should be self-explanatory. Point 5 illustrates one of the contrasts with a loosely coupled multiprocessing system, such as a cluster. In the latter, the physical unit of interaction is usually a message or complete file. In an SMP, individual data elements can constitute the level of interaction, and there can be a high degree of cooperation between processes.

An SMP organization has a number of potential advantages over a uniprocessor organization, including the following:

- **Performance:** If the work to be done by a computer can be organized so that some portions of the work can be done in parallel, then a system with multiple processors will yield greater performance than one with a single processor of the same type.

- **Availability:** In a symmetric multiprocessor, because all processors can perform the same functions, the failure of a single processor does not halt the machine. Instead, the system can continue to function at reduced performance.
- **Incremental growth:** A user can enhance the performance of a system by adding an additional processor.
- **Scaling:** Vendors can offer a range of products with different price and performance characteristics based on the number of processors configured in the system.

It is important to note that these are potential, rather than guaranteed, benefits. The operating system must provide tools and functions to exploit the parallelism in an SMP system.

An attractive feature of an SMP is that the existence of multiple processors is transparent to the user. The operating system takes care of scheduling of tasks on individual processors and of synchronization among processors.

ORGANIZATION Figure 1.19 illustrates the general organization of an SMP. There are multiple processors, each of which contains its own control unit, arithmetic-logic unit, and registers. Each processor has access to a shared main memory and the I/O devices through some form of interconnection mechanism; a shared bus is a common facility. The processors can communicate with each other through memory (messages and status information left in shared address spaces). It may

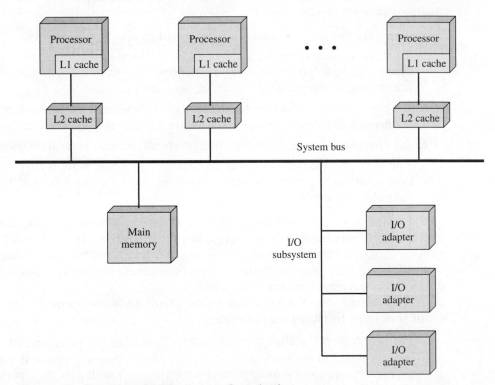

Figure 1.19   Symmetric Multiprocessor Organization

also be possible for processors to exchange signals directly. The memory is often organized so that multiple simultaneous accesses to separate blocks of memory are possible.

In modern computers, processors generally have at least one level of cache memory that is private to the processor. This use of cache introduces some new design considerations. Because each local cache contains an image of a portion of main memory, if a word is altered in one cache, it could conceivably invalidate a word in another cache. To prevent this, the other processors must be alerted that an update has taken place. This problem is known as the cache coherence problem and is typically addressed in hardware rather than by the OS.[6]

Multicore Computers

A **multicore** computer, also known as a **chip multiprocessor**, combines two or more processors (called cores) on a single piece of silicon (called a die). Typically, each core consists of all of the components of an independent processor, such as registers, ALU, pipeline hardware, and control unit, plus L1 instruction and data caches. In addition to the multiple cores, contemporary multicore chips also include L2 cache and, in some cases, L3 cache.

The motivation for the development of multicore computers can be summed up as follows. For decades, microprocessor systems have experienced a steady, usually exponential, increase in performance. This is partly due to hardware trends, such as an increase in clock frequency and the ability to put cache memory closer to the processor because of the increasing miniaturization of microcomputer components. Performance has also been improved by the increased complexity of processor design to exploit parallelism in instruction execution and memory access. In brief, designers have come up against practical limits in the ability to achieve greater performance by means of more complex processors. Designers have found that the best way to improve performance to take advantage of advances in hardware is to put multiple processors and a substantial amount of cache memory on a single chip. A detailed discussion of the rationale for this trend is beyond our scope, but is summarized in Appendix C.

An example of a multicore system is the Intel Core i7, which includes four x86 processors, each with a dedicated L2 cache, and with a shared L3 cache (Figure 1.20). One mechanism Intel uses to make its caches more effective is prefetching, in which the hardware examines memory access patterns and attempts to fill the caches speculatively with data that's likely to be requested soon.

The Core i7 chip supports two forms of external communications to other chips. The **DDR3 memory controller** brings the memory controller for the DDR (double data rate) main memory onto the chip. The interface supports three channels that are 8 bytes wide for a total bus width of 192 bits, for an aggregate data rate of up to 32 GB/s. With the memory controller on the chip, the Front Side Bus is eliminated. The **QuickPath Interconnect (QPI)** is a point-to-point link electrical interconnect specification. It enables high-speed communications among connected processor chips. The QPI link operates at 6.4 GT/s (transfers per second).

---

[6]A description of hardware-based cache coherency schemes is provided in [STAL10].

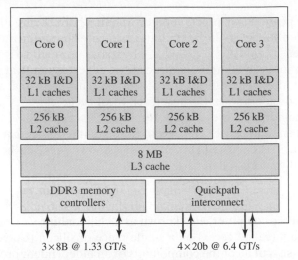

Figure 1.20   Intel Core i7 Block Diagram

At 16 bits per transfer, that adds up to 12.8 GB/s; and since QPI links involve dedicated bidirectional pairs, the total bandwidth is 25.6 GB/s.

1.9   RECOMMENDED READING AND WEB SITES

[STAL10] covers the topics of this chapter in detail. In addition, there are many other texts on computer organization and architecture. Among the more worthwhile texts are the following. [PATT09] is a comprehensive survey; [HENN07], by the same authors, is a more advanced text that emphasizes quantitative aspects of design.

[DENN05] looks at the history of the development and application of the locality principle, making for fascinating reading.

DENN05   Denning, P. "The Locality Principle." *Communications of the ACM*, July 2005.

HENN07   Hennessy, J., and Patterson, D. *Computer Architecture: A Quantitative Approach.* San Mateo, CA: Morgan Kaufmann, 2007.

PATT09   Patterson, D., and Hennessy, J. *Computer Organization and Design: The Hardware/Software Interface.* San Mateo, CA: Morgan Kaufmann, 2009.

STAL10   Stallings, W. *Computer Organization and Architecture, 8th ed.* Upper Saddle River, NJ: Prentice Hall, 2010.

Recommended Web sites:

- **WWW Computer Architecture Home Page:** A comprehensive index to information relevant to computer architecture researchers, including architecture groups and projects, technical organizations, literature, employment, and commercial information
- **CPU Info Center:** Information on specific processors, including technical papers, product information, and latest announcements

1.10 KEY TERMS, REVIEW QUESTIONS, AND PROBLEMS

Key Terms

address register	instruction register	program counter
cache memory	interrupt	programmed I/O
cache slot	interrupt-driven I/O	reentrant procedure
central processing unit	I/O module	register
data register	locality	secondary memory
direct memory access	main memory	spatial locality
hit ratio	multicore	stack
input/output	multiprocessor	system bus
instruction	processor	temporal locality
instruction cycle		

Review Questions

1.1. List and briefly define the four main elements of a computer.

1.2. Define the two main categories of processor registers.

1.3. In general terms, what are the four distinct actions that a machine instruction can specify?

1.4. What is an interrupt?

1.5. How are multiple interrupts dealt with?

1.6. What characteristics distinguish the various elements of a memory hierarchy?

1.7. What is cache memory?

1.8. What is the difference between a multiprocessor and a multicore system?

1.9. What is the distinction between spatial locality and temporal locality?

1.10. In general, what are the strategies for exploiting spatial locality and temporal locality?

Problems

1.1. Suppose the hypothetical processor of Figure 1.3 also has two I/O instructions:

$$0011 = \text{Load AC from I/O}$$
$$0111 = \text{Store AC to I/O}$$

In these cases, the 12-bit address identifies a particular external device. Show the program execution (using format of Figure 1.4) for the following program:

1. Load AC from device 5.
2. Add contents of memory location 940.
3. Store AC to device 6.

Assume that the next value retrieved from device 5 is 3 and that location 940 contains a value of 2.

1.2. The program execution of Figure 1.4 is described in the text using six steps. Expand this description to show the use of the MAR and MBR.

1.3. Consider a hypothetical 32-bit microprocessor having 32-bit instructions composed of two fields. The first byte contains the opcode and the remainder an immediate operand or an operand address.

  a. What is the maximum directly addressable memory capacity (in bytes)?

  b. Discuss the impact on the system speed if the microprocessor bus has

  1. a 32-bit local address bus and a 16-bit local data bus, or

  2. a 16-bit local address bus and a 16-bit local data bus.

  c. How many bits are needed for the program counter and the instruction register?

1.4. Consider a hypothetical microprocessor generating a 16-bit address (e.g., assume that the program counter and the address registers are 16 bits wide) and having a 16-bit data bus.

  a. What is the maximum memory address space that the processor can access directly if it is connected to a "16-bit memory"?

  b. What is the maximum memory address space that the processor can access directly if it is connected to an "8-bit memory"?

  c. What architectural features will allow this microprocessor to access a separate "I/O space"?

  d. If an input and an output instruction can specify an 8-bit I/O port number, how many 8-bit I/O ports can the microprocessor support? How many 16-bit I/O ports? Explain.

1.5. Consider a 32-bit microprocessor, with a 16-bit external data bus, driven by an 8-MHz input clock. Assume that this microprocessor has a bus cycle whose minimum duration equals four input clock cycles. What is the maximum data transfer rate across the bus that this microprocessor can sustain in bytes/s? To increase its performance, would it be better to make its external data bus 32 bits or to double the external clock frequency supplied to the microprocessor? State any other assumptions you make and explain. *Hint:* Determine the number of bytes that can be transferred per bus cycle.

1.6. Consider a computer system that contains an I/O module controlling a simple keyboard/printer Teletype. The following registers are contained in the CPU and connected directly to the system bus:

  INPR: Input Register, 8 bits
  OUTR: Output Register, 8 bits
  FGI: Input Flag, 1 bit
  FGO: Output Flag, 1 bit
  IEN: Interrupt Enable, 1 bit

Keystroke input from the Teletype and output to the printer are controlled by the I/O module. The Teletype is able to encode an alphanumeric symbol to an 8-bit word and decode an 8-bit word into an alphanumeric symbol. The Input flag is set when an 8-bit word enters the input register from the Teletype. The Output flag is set when a word is printed.

  a. Describe how the CPU, using the first four registers listed in this problem, can achieve I/O with the Teletype.

  b. Describe how the function can be performed more efficiently by also employing IEN.

1.7. In virtually all systems that include DMA modules, DMA access to main memory is given higher priority than processor access to main memory. Why?

1.8. A DMA module is transferring characters to main memory from an external device transmitting at 9600 bits per second (bps). The processor can fetch instructions at the rate of 1 million instructions per second. By how much will the processor be slowed down due to the DMA activity?

1.9. A computer consists of a CPU and an I/O device D connected to main memory M via a shared bus with a data bus width of one word. The CPU can execute a maximum of 106 instructions per second. An average instruction requires five processor cycles, three of which use the memory bus. A memory read or write operation uses one processor cycle. Suppose that the CPU is continuously executing "background" programs that require 95% of its instruction execution rate but not any I/O instructions.

Assume that one processor cycle equals one bus cycle. Now suppose that very large blocks of data are to be transferred between M and D.

    a. If programmed I/O is used and each one-word I/O transfer requires the CPU to execute two instructions, estimate the maximum I/O data transfer rate, in words per second, possible through D.

    b. Estimate the same rate if DMA transfer is used.

1.10. Consider the following code:

```
for (i = 0; i < 20; i++)
    for (j = 0; j < 10; j++)
        a[i] = a[i] * j
```

    a. Give one example of the spatial locality in the code.

    b. Give one example of the temporal locality in the code.

1.11. Generalize Equations (1.1) and (1.2) in Appendix 1A to n-level memory hierarchies.

1.12. Consider a memory system with the following parameters:

$$Tc = 100 \text{ ns} \quad Cc = 0.01 \text{ cents/bit}$$
$$Tm = 1{,}200 \text{ ns} \quad Cm = 0.001 \text{ cents/bit}$$

    a. What is the cost of 1 MByte of main memory?

    b. What is the cost of 1 MByte of main memory using cache memory technology?

    c. If the effective access time is 10% greater than the cache access time, what is the hit ratio H?

1.13. A computer has a cache, main memory, and a disk used for virtual memory. If a referenced word is in the cache, 20 ns are required to access it. If it is in main memory but not in the cache, 60 ns are needed to load it into the cache (this includes the time to originally check the cache), and then the reference is started again. If the word is not in main memory, 12 ms are required to fetch the word from disk, followed by 60 ns to copy it to the cache, and then the reference is started again. The cache hit ratio is 0.9 and the main-memory hit ratio is 0.6. What is the average time in ns required to access a referenced word on this system?

1.14. Suppose a stack is to be used by the processor to manage procedure calls and returns. Can the program counter be eliminated by using the top of the stack as a program counter?

APPENDIX 1A PERFORMANCE CHARACTERISTICS OF TWO-LEVEL MEMORIES

In this chapter, reference is made to a cache that acts as a buffer between main memory and processor, creating a two-level internal memory. This two-level architecture exploits a property known as locality to provide improved performance over a comparable one-level memory.

The main memory cache mechanism is part of the computer architecture, implemented in hardware and typically invisible to the OS. Accordingly, this mechanism is not pursued in this book. However, there are two other instances of a two-level memory approach that also exploit the property of locality and that are, at least partially, implemented in the OS: virtual memory and the disk cache (Table 1.2). These two topics are explored in Chapters 8 and 11, respectively. In this appendix, we look at some of the performance characteristics of two-level memories that are common to all three approaches.

Table 1.2 Characteristics of Two-Level Memories

	Main Memory Cache	Virtual Memory (Paging)	Disk Cache
Typical access time ratios	$5:1$	$10^6:1$	$10^6:1$
Memory management system	Implemented by special hardware	Combination of hardware and system software	System software
Typical block size	4 to 128 bytes	64 to 4096 bytes	64 to 4096 bytes
Access of processor to second level	Direct access	Indirect access	Indirect access

Locality

The basis for the performance advantage of a two-level memory is the principle of locality, referred to in Section 1.5. This principle states that memory references tend to cluster. Over a long period of time, the clusters in use change; but over a short period of time, the processor is primarily working with fixed clusters of memory references.

Intuitively, the principle of locality makes sense. Consider the following line of reasoning:

1. Except for branch and call instructions, which constitute only a small fraction of all program instructions, program execution is sequential. Hence, in most cases, the next instruction to be fetched immediately follows the last instruction fetched.

2. It is rare to have a long uninterrupted sequence of procedure calls followed by the corresponding sequence of returns. Rather, a program remains confined to a rather narrow window of procedure-invocation depth. Thus, over a short period of time references to instructions tend to be localized to a few procedures.

3. Most iterative constructs consist of a relatively small number of instructions repeated many times. For the duration of the iteration, computation is therefore confined to a small contiguous portion of a program.

4. In many programs, much of the computation involves processing data structures, such as arrays or sequences of records. In many cases, successive references to these data structures will be to closely located data items.

This line of reasoning has been confirmed in many studies. With reference to point (1), a variety of studies have analyzed the behavior of high-level language programs. Table 1.3 includes key results, measuring the appearance of various statement types during execution, from the following studies. The earliest study of programming language behavior, performed by Knuth [KNUT71], examined a collection of FORTRAN programs used as student exercises. Tanenbaum [TANE78] published measurements collected from over 300 procedures used in OS programs and written in a language that supports structured programming (SAL). Patterson and Sequin [PATT82] analyzed a set of measurements taken from compilers and programs for typesetting, computer-aided design (CAD), sorting, and file

Table 1.3 Relative Dynamic Frequency of High-Level Language Operations

Study Language Workload	[HUCK83] Pascal Scientific	[KNUT71] FORTRAN Student	[PATT82] Pascal System	[PATT82] C System	[TANE78] SAL System
Assign	74	67	45	38	42
Loop	4	3	5	3	4
Call	1	3	15	12	12
IF	20	11	29	43	36
GOTO	2	9	—	3	—
Other	—	7	6	1	6

comparison. The programming languages C and Pascal were studied. Huck [HUCK83] analyzed four programs intended to represent a mix of general-purpose scientific computing, including fast Fourier transform and the integration of systems of differential equations. There is good agreement in the results of this mixture of languages and applications that branching and call instructions represent only a fraction of statements executed during the lifetime of a program. Thus, these studies confirm assertion (1), from the preceding list.

With respect to assertion (2), studies reported in [PATT85] provide confirmation. This is illustrated in Figure 1.21, which shows call-return behavior. Each call is represented by the line moving down and to the right, and each return by the line moving up and to the right. In the figure, a *window* with depth equal to 5 is defined. Only a sequence of calls and returns with a net movement of 6 in either direction causes the window to move. As can be seen, the executing program can remain within a stationary window for long periods of time. A study by the same analysts of C and Pascal programs showed that a window of depth 8 would only need to shift on less than 1% of the calls or returns [TAMI83].

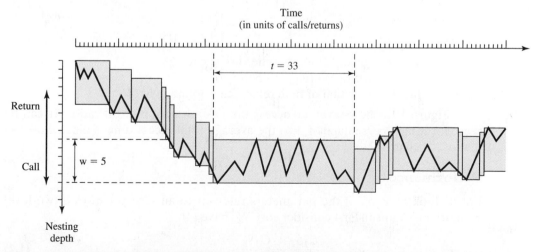

Figure 1.21 **Example Call-Return Behavior of a Program**

A distinction is made in the literature between spatial locality and temporal locality. **Spatial locality** refers to the tendency of execution to involve a number of memory locations that are clustered. This reflects the tendency of a processor to access instructions sequentially. Spatial location also reflects the tendency of a program to access data locations sequentially, such as when processing a table of data. **Temporal locality** refers to the tendency for a processor to access memory locations that have been used recently. For example, when an iteration loop is executed, the processor executes the same set of instructions repeatedly.

Traditionally, temporal locality is exploited by keeping recently used instruction and data values in cache memory and by exploiting a cache hierarchy. Spatial locality is generally exploited by using larger cache blocks and by incorporating prefetching mechanisms (fetching items whose use is expected) into the cache control logic. Recently, there has been considerable research on refining these techniques to achieve greater performance, but the basic strategies remain the same.

Operation of Two-Level Memory

The locality property can be exploited in the formation of a two-level memory. The upper-level memory (M1) is smaller, faster, and more expensive (per bit) than the lower-level memory (M2). M1 is used as a temporary store for part of the contents of the larger M2. When a memory reference is made, an attempt is made to access the item in M1. If this succeeds, then a quick access is made. If not, then a block of memory locations is copied from M2 to M1 and the access then takes place via M1. Because of locality, once a block is brought into M1, there should be a number of accesses to locations in that block, resulting in fast overall service.

To express the average time to access an item, we must consider not only the speeds of the two levels of memory but also the probability that a given reference can be found in M1. We have

$$T_s = H \times T_1 + (1 - H) \times (T_1 + T_2)$$
$$T_1 + (1 - H) \times T_2 \tag{1.1}$$

where

T_s = average (system) access time
T_1 = access time of M1 (e.g., cache, disk cache)
T_2 = access time of M2 (e.g., main memory, disk)
H = hit ratio (fraction of time reference is found in M1)

Figure 1.15 shows average access time as a function of hit ratio. As can be seen, for a high percentage of hits, the average total access time is much closer to that of M1 than M2.

Performance

Let us look at some of the parameters relevant to an assessment of a two-level memory mechanism. First consider cost. We have

$$C_s = \frac{C_1 S_1 + C_2 S_2}{S_1 + S_2} \tag{1.2}$$

where

C_s = average cost per bit for the combined two-level memory
C_1 = average cost per bit of upper-level memory M1
C_2 = average cost per bit of lower-level memory M2
S_1 = size of M1
S_2 = size of M2

We would like $C_s \approx C_2$. Given that $C_1 >> C_2$, this requires $S_1 << S_2$. Figure 1.22 shows the relationship.[7]

Next, consider access time. For a two-level memory to provide a significant performance improvement, we need to have T_s approximately equal to $T_1 \; T_s \approx T_1$. Given that T_1 is much less than $T_2 \; T_s >> T_1$, a hit ratio of close to 1 is needed.

So we would like M1 to be small to hold down cost, and large to improve the hit ratio and therefore the performance. Is there a size of M1 that satisfies both requirements to a reasonable extent? We can answer this question with a series of subquestions:

- What value of hit ratio is needed to satisfy the performance requirement?
- What size of M1 will assure the needed hit ratio?
- Does this size satisfy the cost requirement?

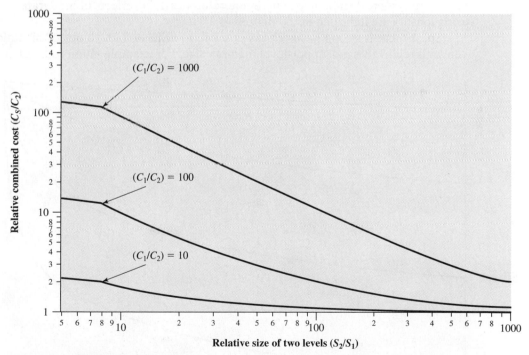

Figure 1.22   Relationship of Average Memory Cost to Relative Memory Size for a Two-Level Memory

[7]Note that both axes use a log scale. A basic review of log scales is in the math refresher document at the Computer Science Student Resource Site at ComputerScienceStudent.com.

To get at this, consider the quantity T_1/T_s, which is referred to as the *access efficiency*. It is a measure of how close average access time (T_s) is to M1 access time (T_1). From Equation (1.1),

$$\frac{T_1}{T_s} = \frac{1}{1 + (1 - H)\dfrac{T_2}{T_1}}$$ (1.3)

In Figure 1.23, we plot T_1/T_s as a function of the hit ratio H, with the quantity T_2/T_1 as a parameter. A hit ratio in the range of 0.8 to 0.9 would seem to be needed to satisfy the performance requirement.

We can now phrase the question about relative memory size more exactly. Is a hit ratio of 0.8 or higher reasonable for $S_1 << S_2$? This will depend on a number of factors, including the nature of the software being executed and the details of the design of the two-level memory. The main determinant is, of course, the degree of locality. Figure 1.24 suggests the effect of locality on the hit ratio. Clearly, if M1 is the same size as M2, then the hit ratio will be 1.0: All of the items in M2 are always stored also in M1. Now suppose that there is no locality; that is, references are completely random. In that case the hit ratio should be a strictly linear function of the relative memory size. For example, if M1 is half the size of M2, then at any time half of the items from M2 are also in M1 and the hit ratio will be 0.5. In practice, however, there is some degree of locality in the references. The effects of moderate and strong locality are indicated in the figure.

So, if there is strong locality, it is possible to achieve high values of hit ratio even with relatively small upper-level memory size. For example, numerous studies

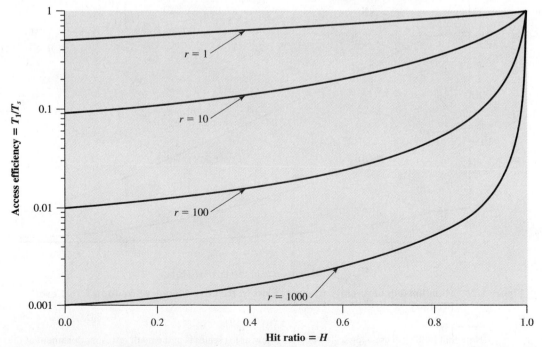

Figure 1.23   Access Efficiency as a Function of Hit Ratio ($r = T_2/T_1$)

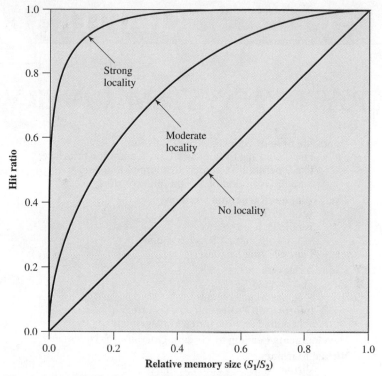

Figure 1.24   Hit Ratio as a Function of Relative Memory Size

have shown that rather small cache sizes will yield a hit ratio above 0.75 *regardless of the size of main memory* (e.g., [AGAR89], [PRZY88], [STRE83], and [SMIT82]). A cache in the range of 1K to 128K words is generally adequate, whereas main memory is now typically in the gigabyte range. When we consider virtual memory and disk cache, we will cite other studies that confirm the same phenomenon, namely that a relatively small M1 yields a high value of hit ratio because of locality.

This brings us to the last question listed earlier: Does the relative size of the two memories satisfy the cost requirement? The answer is clearly yes. If we need only a relatively small upper-level memory to achieve good performance, then the average cost per bit of the two levels of memory will approach that of the cheaper lower-level memory.

CHAPTER

OPERATING SYSTEM OVERVIEW

2.1 Operating System Objectives and Functions

The Operating System as a User/Computer Interface
The Operating System as Resource Manager
Ease of Evolution of an Operating System

2.2 The Evolution of Operating Systems

Serial Processing
Simple Batch Systems
Multiprogrammed Batch Systems
Time-Sharing Systems

2.3 Major Achievements

The Process
Memory Management
Information Protection and Security
Scheduling and Resource Management

2.4 Developments Leading to Modern Operating Systems

2.5 Virtual Machines

Virtual Machines and Virtualizing
Virtual Machine Architecture

2.6 OS Design Considerations for Multiprocessor and Multicore

Symmetric Multiprocessor OS Considerations
Multicore OS Considerations

2.7 Microsoft Windows Overview

History
The Modern OS
Architecture
Client/Server Model
Threads and SMP
Windows Objects
What Is New in Windows 7

2.8 Traditional Unix Systems

History
Description

2.9 Modern Unix Systems

System V Release 4 (SVR4)
BSD
Solaris 10

2.10 Linux

History
Modular Structure
Kernel Components

2.11 Linux Vserver Virtual Machine Architecture

2.12 Recommended Reading and Web Sites

2.13 Key Terms, Review Questions, and Problems

Operating systems are those programs that interface the machine with the applications programs. The main function of these systems is to dynamically allocate the shared system resources to the executing programs. As such, research in this area is clearly concerned with the management and scheduling of memory, processes, and other devices. But the interface with adjacent levels continues to shift with time. Functions that were originally part of the operating system have migrated to the hardware. On the other side, programmed functions extraneous to the problems being solved by the application programs are included in the operating system.

—*What Can Be Automated?: The Computer Science and Engineering Research Study*, MIT Press, 1980

LEARNING OBJECTIVES

After studying this chapter, you should be able to:

- Summarize, at a top level, the key functions of an operating system (OS).
- Discuss the evolution of operating systems for early simple batch systems to modern complex systems.
- Give a brief explanation of each of the major achievements in OS research, as defined in Section 2.3.
- Discuss the key design areas that have been instrumental in the development of modern operating systems.
- Define and discuss virtual machines and virtualization
- Understand the OS design issues raised by the introduction of multiprocessor and multicore organization.
- Understand the basic structure of Windows 7.
- Describe the essential elements of a traditional UNIX system.
- Explain the new features found in modern UNIX systems.
- Discuss Linux and its relationship to UNIX.

We begin our study of operating systems (OSs) with a brief history. This history is itself interesting and also serves the purpose of providing an overview of OS principles. The first section examines the objectives and functions of operating systems. Then we look at how operating systems have evolved from primitive batch systems to sophisticated multitasking, multiuser systems. The remainder of the chapter looks at the history and general characteristics of the two operating systems that serve as examples throughout this book. All of the material in this chapter is covered in greater depth later in the book.

2.1 OPERATING SYSTEM OBJECTIVES AND FUNCTIONS

An OS is a program that controls the execution of application programs and acts as an interface between applications and the computer hardware. It can be thought of as having three objectives:

- **Convenience:** An OS makes a computer more convenient to use.
- **Efficiency:** An OS allows the computer system resources to be used in an efficient manner.
- **Ability to evolve:** An OS should be constructed in such a way as to permit the effective development, testing, and introduction of new system functions without interfering with service.

Let us examine these three aspects of an OS in turn.

The Operating System as a User/Computer Interface

The hardware and software used in providing applications to a user can be viewed in a layered or hierarchical fashion, as depicted in Figure 2.1. The user of those applications, the end user, generally is not concerned with the details of computer hardware. Thus, the end user views a computer system in terms of a set of applications. An application can be expressed in a programming language and is developed by an application programmer. If one were to develop an application program as a set of machine instructions that is completely responsible for controlling the computer hardware, one would be faced with an overwhelmingly complex undertaking. To ease this chore, a set of system programs is provided. Some of these programs are referred to as utilities, or library programs. These implement frequently used functions that assist in program creation, the management of files, and the control of

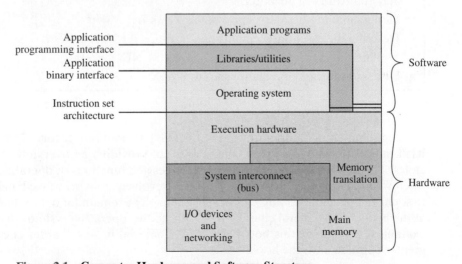

Figure 2.1   Computer Hardware and Software Structure

I/O devices. A programmer will make use of these facilities in developing an application, and the application, while it is running, will invoke the utilities to perform certain functions. The most important collection of system programs comprises the OS. The OS masks the details of the hardware from the programmer and provides the programmer with a convenient interface for using the system. It acts as mediator, making it easier for the programmer and for application programs to access and use those facilities and services.

Briefly, the OS typically provides services in the following areas:

- **Program development:** The OS provides a variety of facilities and services, such as editors and debuggers, to assist the programmer in creating programs. Typically, these services are in the form of utility programs that, while not strictly part of the core of the OS, are supplied with the OS and are referred to as application program development tools.

- **Program execution:** A number of steps need to be performed to execute a program. Instructions and data must be loaded into main memory, I/O devices and files must be initialized, and other resources must be prepared. The OS handles these scheduling duties for the user.

- **Access to I/O devices:** Each I/O device requires its own peculiar set of instructions or control signals for operation. The OS provides a uniform interface that hides these details so that programmers can access such devices using simple reads and writes.

- **Controlled access to files:** For file access, the OS must reflect a detailed understanding of not only the nature of the I/O device (disk drive, tape drive) but also the structure of the data contained in the files on the storage medium. In the case of a system with multiple users, the OS may provide protection mechanisms to control access to the files.

- **System access:** For shared or public systems, the OS controls access to the system as a whole and to specific system resources. The access function must provide protection of resources and data from unauthorized users and must resolve conflicts for resource contention.

- **Error detection and response:** A variety of errors can occur while a computer system is running. These include internal and external hardware errors, such as a memory error, or a device failure or malfunction; and various software errors, such as division by zero, attempt to access forbidden memory location, and inability of the OS to grant the request of an application. In each case, the OS must provide a response that clears the error condition with the least impact on running applications. The response may range from ending the program that caused the error, to retrying the operation, to simply reporting the error to the application.

- **Accounting:** A good OS will collect usage statistics for various resources and monitor performance parameters such as response time. On any system, this information is useful in anticipating the need for future enhancements and in tuning the system to improve performance. On a multiuser system, the information can be used for billing purposes.

Figure 2.1 also indicates three key interfaces in a typical computer system:

- **Instruction set architecture (ISA)**: The ISA defines the repertoire of machine language instructions that a computer can follow. This interface is the boundary between hardware and software. Note that both application programs and utilities may access the ISA directly. For these programs, a subset of the instruction repertoire is available (user ISA). The OS has access to additional machine language instructions that deal with managing system resources (system ISA).

- **Application binary interface (ABI)**: The ABI defines a standard for binary portability across programs. The ABI defines the system call interface to the operating system and the hardware resources and services available in a system through the user ISA.

- **Application programming interface (API)**: The API gives a program access to the hardware resources and services available in a system through the user ISA supplemented with high-level language (HLL) library calls. Any system calls are usually performed through libraries. Using an API enables application software to be ported easily, through recompilation, to other systems that support the same API.

The Operating System as Resource Manager

A computer is a set of resources for the movement, storage, and processing of data and for the control of these functions. The OS is responsible for managing these resources.

Can we say that it is the OS that controls the movement, storage, and processing of data? From one point of view, the answer is yes: By managing the computer's resources, the OS is in control of the computer's basic functions. But this control is exercised in a curious way. Normally, we think of a control mechanism as something external to that which is controlled, or at least as something that is a distinct and separate part of that which is controlled. (For example, a residential heating system is controlled by a thermostat, which is separate from the heat-generation and heat-distribution apparatus.) This is not the case with the OS, which as a control mechanism is unusual in two respects:

- The OS functions in the same way as ordinary computer software; that is, it is a program or suite of programs executed by the processor.

- The OS frequently relinquishes control and must depend on the processor to allow it to regain control.

Like other computer programs, the OS provides instructions for the processor. The key difference is in the intent of the program. The OS directs the processor in the use of the other system resources and in the timing of its execution of other programs. But in order for the processor to do any of these things, it must cease executing the OS program and execute other programs. Thus, the OS relinquishes control for the processor to do some "useful" work and then resumes control long enough to prepare the processor to do the next piece of work. The mechanisms involved in all this should become clear as the chapter proceeds.

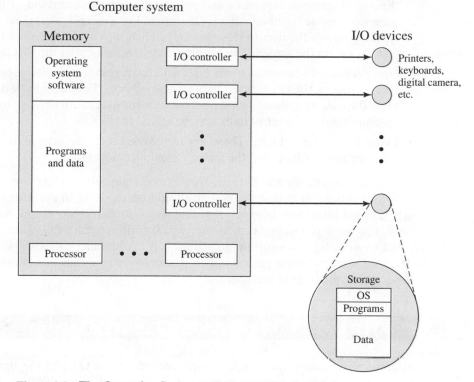

Figure 2.2   The Operating System as Resource Manager

Figure 2.2 suggests the main resources that are managed by the OS. A portion of the OS is in main memory. This includes the **kernel**, or **nucleus**, which contains the most frequently used functions in the OS and, at a given time, other portions of the OS currently in use. The remainder of main memory contains user programs and data. The memory management hardware in the processor and the OS jointly control the allocation of main memory, as we shall see. The OS decides when an I/O device can be used by a program in execution and controls access to and use of files. The processor itself is a resource, and the OS must determine how much processor time is to be devoted to the execution of a particular user program. In the case of a multiple-processor system, this decision must span all of the processors.

Ease of Evolution of an Operating System

A major OS will evolve over time for a number of reasons:

- **Hardware upgrades plus new types of hardware:** For example, early versions of UNIX and the Macintosh OS did not employ a paging mechanism because they were run on processors without paging hardware.[1] Subsequent versions of these operating systems were modified to exploit paging capabilities. Also,

---

[1]Paging is introduced briefly later in this chapter and is discussed in detail in Chapter 7.

the use of graphics terminals and page-mode terminals instead of line-at-a-time scroll mode terminals affects OS design. For example, a graphics terminal typically allows the user to view several applications at the same time through "windows" on the screen. This requires more sophisticated support in the OS.

- **New services:** In response to user demand or in response to the needs of system managers, the OS expands to offer new services. For example, if it is found to be difficult to maintain good performance for users with existing tools, new measurement and control tools may be added to the OS.

- **Fixes:** Any OS has faults. These are discovered over the course of time and fixes are made. Of course, the fix may introduce new faults.

The need to change an OS regularly places certain requirements on its design. An obvious statement is that the system should be modular in construction, with clearly defined interfaces between the modules, and that it should be well documented. For large programs, such as the typical contemporary OS, what might be referred to as straightforward modularization is inadequate [DENN80a]. That is, much more must be done than simply partitioning a program into modules. We return to this topic later in this chapter.

2.2 THE EVOLUTION OF OPERATING SYSTEMS

In attempting to understand the key requirements for an OS and the significance of the major features of a contemporary OS, it is useful to consider how operating systems have evolved over the years.

Serial Processing

With the earliest computers, from the late 1940s to the mid-1950s, the programmer interacted directly with the computer hardware; there was no OS. These computers were run from a console consisting of display lights, toggle switches, some form of input device, and a printer. Programs in machine code were loaded via the input device (e.g., a card reader). If an error halted the program, the error condition was indicated by the lights. If the program proceeded to a normal completion, the output appeared on the printer.

These early systems presented two main problems:

- **Scheduling:** Most installations used a hardcopy sign-up sheet to reserve computer time. Typically, a user could sign up for a block of time in multiples of a half hour or so. A user might sign up for an hour and finish in 45 minutes; this would result in wasted computer processing time. On the other hand, the user might run into problems, not finish in the allotted time, and be forced to stop before resolving the problem.

- **Setup time:** A single program, called a **job**, could involve loading the compiler plus the high-level language program (source program) into memory, saving the compiled program (object program) and then loading and linking together the object program and common functions. Each of these steps could involve mounting or dismounting tapes or setting up card decks. If an error occurred, the hapless user typically had to go back to the beginning of the setup sequence. Thus, a considerable amount of time was spent just in setting up the program to run.

This mode of operation could be termed *serial processing*, reflecting the fact that users have access to the computer in series. Over time, various system software tools were developed to attempt to make serial processing more efficient. These include libraries of common functions, linkers, loaders, debuggers, and I/O driver routines that were available as common software for all users.

Simple Batch Systems

Early computers were very expensive, and therefore it was important to maximize processor utilization. The wasted time due to scheduling and setup time was unacceptable.

To improve utilization, the concept of a batch OS was developed. It appears that the first batch OS (and the first OS of any kind) was developed in the mid-1950s by General Motors for use on an IBM 701 [WEIZ81]. The concept was subsequently refined and implemented on the IBM 704 by a number of IBM customers. By the early 1960s, a number of vendors had developed batch operating systems for their computer systems. IBSYS, the IBM OS for the 7090/7094 computers, is particularly notable because of its widespread influence on other systems.

The central idea behind the simple batch-processing scheme is the use of a piece of software known as the **monitor**. With this type of OS, the user no longer has direct access to the processor. Instead, the user submits the job on cards or tape to a computer operator, who batches the jobs together sequentially and places the entire batch on an input device, for use by the monitor. Each program is constructed to branch back to the monitor when it completes processing, at which point the monitor automatically begins loading the next program.

To understand how this scheme works, let us look at it from two points of view: that of the monitor and that of the processor.

- **Monitor point of view:** The monitor controls the sequence of events. For this to be so, much of the monitor must always be in main memory and available for execution (Figure 2.3). That portion is referred to as the **resident monitor**. The rest of the monitor consists of utilities and common functions that are loaded as subroutines to the user program at the beginning of any job that requires them. The monitor reads in jobs one at a time from the input device (typically a card reader or magnetic tape drive). As it is read in, the current job is placed in the user program area, and control is passed to this job. When the job is completed, it returns control to the monitor, which immediately reads in the next job. The results of each job are sent to an output device, such as a printer, for delivery to the user.

- **Processor point of view:** At a certain point, the processor is executing instructions from the portion of main memory containing the monitor. These instructions cause the next job to be read into another portion of main

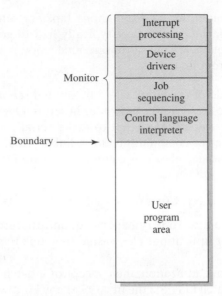

Figure 2.3   Memory Layout for a Resident Monitor

memory. Once a job has been read in, the processor will encounter a branch instruction in the monitor that instructs the processor to continue execution at the start of the user program. The processor will then execute the instructions in the user program until it encounters an ending or error condition. Either event causes the processor to fetch its next instruction from the monitor program. Thus the phrase "control is passed to a job" simply means that the processor is now fetching and executing instructions in a user program, and "control is returned to the monitor" means that the processor is now fetching and executing instructions from the monitor program.

The monitor performs a scheduling function: A batch of jobs is queued up, and jobs are executed as rapidly as possible, with no intervening idle time. The monitor improves job setup time as well. With each job, instructions are included in a primitive form of **job control language (JCL)**. This is a special type of programming language used to provide instructions to the monitor. A simple example is that of a user submitting a program written in the programming language FORTRAN plus some data to be used by the program. All FORTRAN instructions and data are on a separate punched card or a separate record on tape. In addition to FORTRAN and data lines, the job includes job control instructions, which are denoted by the beginning $. The overall format of the job looks like this:

```
$JOB
$FTN
   •
   •           }        FORTRAN instructions
   •
```

```
$LOAD
$RUN
  •
  •        Data
  •
$END
```

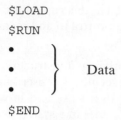

To execute this job, the monitor reads the $FTN line and loads the appropriate language compiler from its mass storage (usually tape). The compiler translates the user's program into object code, which is stored in memory or mass storage. If it is stored in memory, the operation is referred to as "compile, load, and go." If it is stored on tape, then the $LOAD instruction is required. This instruction is read by the monitor, which regains control after the compile operation. The monitor invokes the loader, which loads the object program into memory (in place of the compiler) and transfers control to it. In this manner, a large segment of main memory can be shared among different subsystems, although only one such subsystem could be executing at a time.

During the execution of the user program, any input instruction causes one line of data to be read. The input instruction in the user program causes an input routine that is part of the OS to be invoked. The input routine checks to make sure that the program does not accidentally read in a JCL line. If this happens, an error occurs and control transfers to the monitor. At the completion of the user job, the monitor will scan the input lines until it encounters the next JCL instruction. Thus, the system is protected against a program with too many or too few data lines.

The monitor, or batch OS, is simply a computer program. It relies on the ability of the processor to fetch instructions from various portions of main memory to alternately seize and relinquish control. Certain other hardware features are also desirable:

- **Memory protection:** While the user program is executing, it must not alter the memory area containing the monitor. If such an attempt is made, the processor hardware should detect an error and transfer control to the monitor. The monitor would then abort the job, print out an error message, and load in the next job.

- **Timer:** A timer is used to prevent a single job from monopolizing the system. The timer is set at the beginning of each job. If the timer expires, the user program is stopped, and control returns to the monitor.

- **Privileged instructions:** Certain machine level instructions are designated privileged and can be executed only by the monitor. If the processor encounters such an instruction while executing a user program, an error occurs causing control to be transferred to the monitor. Among the privileged instructions are I/O instructions, so that the monitor retains control of all I/O devices. This prevents, for example, a user program from accidentally reading job control instructions from the next job. If a user program wishes to perform I/O, it must request that the monitor perform the operation for it.

- **Interrupts:** Early computer models did not have this capability. This feature gives the OS more flexibility in relinquishing control to and regaining control from user programs.

Considerations of memory protection and privileged instructions lead to the concept of modes of operation. A user program executes in a **user mode**, in which certain areas of memory are protected from the user's use and in which certain instructions may not be executed. The monitor executes in a system mode, or what has come to be called **kernel mode**, in which privileged instructions may be executed and in which protected areas of memory may be accessed.

Of course, an OS can be built without these features. But computer vendors quickly learned that the results were chaos, and so even relatively primitive batch operating systems were provided with these hardware features.

With a batch OS, processor time alternates between execution of user programs and execution of the monitor. There have been two sacrifices: Some main memory is now given over to the monitor and some processor time is consumed by the monitor. Both of these are forms of overhead. Despite this overhead, the simple batch system improves utilization of the computer.

Multiprogrammed Batch Systems

Even with the automatic job sequencing provided by a simple batch OS, the processor is often idle. The problem is that I/O devices are slow compared to the processor. Figure 2.4 details a representative calculation. The calculation concerns a program that processes a file of records and performs, on average, 100 machine instructions per record. In this example, the computer spends over 96% of its time waiting for I/O devices to finish transferring data to and from the file. Figure 2.5a illustrates this situation, where we have a single program, referred to as uniprogramming. The processor spends a certain amount of time executing, until it reaches an I/O instruction. It must then wait until that I/O instruction concludes before proceeding.

This inefficiency is not necessary. We know that there must be enough memory to hold the OS (resident monitor) and one user program. Suppose that there is room for the OS and two user programs. When one job needs to wait for I/O, the processor can switch to the other job, which is likely not waiting for I/O (Figure 2.5b). Furthermore, we might expand memory to hold three, four, or more programs and switch among all of them (Figure 2.5c). The approach is known as **multiprogramming**, or **multitasking**. It is the central theme of modern operating systems.

Read one record from file	15 μs
Execute 100 instructions	1 μs
Write one record to file	15 μs
Total	31 μs
Percent CPU Utilization $= \dfrac{1}{31} = 0.032 = 3.2\%$	

Figure 2.4 System Utilization Example

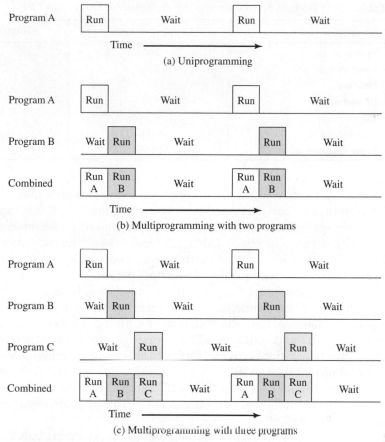

Figure 2.5   Multiprogramming Example

To illustrate the benefit of multiprogramming, we give a simple example. Consider a computer with 250 Mbytes of available memory (not used by the OS), a disk, a terminal, and a printer. Three programs, JOB1, JOB2, and JOB3, are submitted for execution at the same time, with the attributes listed in Table 2.1. We assume minimal processor requirements for JOB2 and JOB3 and continuous disk and printer use by JOB3. For a simple batch environment, these jobs will be executed in sequence. Thus, JOB1 completes in 5 minutes. JOB2 must wait until

Table 2.1   Sample Program Execution Attributes

	JOB1	**JOB2**	**JOB3**
Type of job	Heavy compute	Heavy I/O	Heavy I/O
Duration	5 min	15 min	10 min
Memory required	50 M	100 M	75 M
Need disk?	No	No	Yes
Need terminal?	No	Yes	No
Need printer?	No	No	Yes

Table 2.2 Effects of Multiprogramming on Resource Utilization

	Uniprogramming	Multiprogramming
Processor use	20%	40%
Memory use	33%	67%
Disk use	33%	67%
Printer use	33%	67%
Elapsed time	30 min	15 min
Throughput	6 jobs/hr	12 jobs/hr
Mean response time	18 min	10 min

the 5 minutes are over and then completes 15 minutes after that. JOB3 begins after 20 minutes and completes at 30 minutes from the time it was initially submitted. The average resource utilization, throughput, and response times are shown in the uniprogramming column of Table 2.2. Device-by-device utilization is illustrated in Figure 2.6a. It is evident that there is gross underutilization for all resources when averaged over the required 30-minute time period.

Now suppose that the jobs are run concurrently under a multiprogramming OS. Because there is little resource contention between the jobs, all three can run in nearly minimum time while coexisting with the others in the computer (assuming that JOB2 and JOB3 are allotted enough processor time to keep their input and output operations active). JOB1 will still require 5 minutes to complete, but at the end of that time, JOB2 will be one-third finished and JOB3 half finished. All three jobs will have finished within 15 minutes. The improvement is evident when examining the multiprogramming column of Table 2.2, obtained from the histogram shown in Figure 2.6b.

As with a simple batch system, a multiprogramming batch system must rely on certain computer hardware features. The most notable additional feature that is useful for multiprogramming is the hardware that supports I/O interrupts and DMA (direct memory access). With interrupt-driven I/O or DMA, the processor can issue an I/O command for one job and proceed with the execution of another job while the I/O is carried out by the device controller. When the I/O operation is complete, the processor is interrupted and control is passed to an interrupt-handling program in the OS. The OS will then pass control to another job.

Multiprogramming operating systems are fairly sophisticated compared to single-program, or **uniprogramming**, systems. To have several jobs ready to run, they must be kept in main memory, requiring some form of **memory management**. In addition, if several jobs are ready to run, the processor must decide which one to run, this decision requires an algorithm for scheduling. These concepts are discussed later in this chapter.

Time–Sharing Systems

With the use of multiprogramming, batch processing can be quite efficient. However, for many jobs, it is desirable to provide a mode in which the user interacts directly with the computer. Indeed, for some jobs, such as transaction processing, an interactive mode is essential.

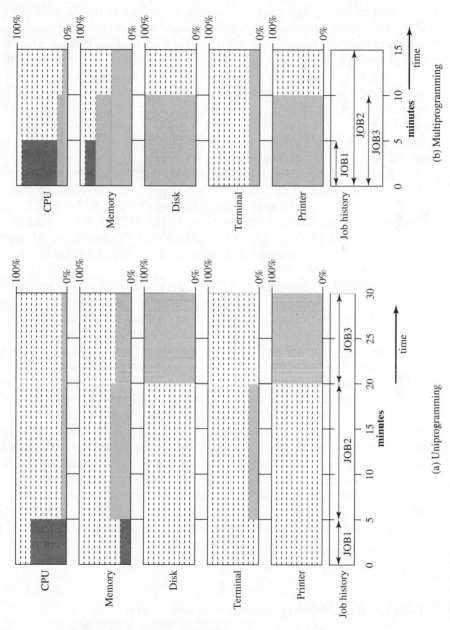

(a) Uniprogramming

(b) Multiprogramming

Figure 2.6 Utilization Histograms

59

Today, the requirement for an interactive computing facility can be, and often is, met by the use of a dedicated personal computer or workstation. That option was not available in the 1960s, when most computers were big and costly. Instead, time sharing was developed.

Just as multiprogramming allows the processor to handle multiple batch jobs at a time, multiprogramming can also be used to handle multiple interactive jobs. In this latter case, the technique is referred to as **time sharing**, because processor time is shared among multiple users. In a time-sharing system, multiple users simultaneously access the system through terminals, with the OS interleaving the execution of each user program in a short burst or quantum of computation. Thus, if there are n users actively requesting service at one time, each user will only see on the average $1/n$ of the effective computer capacity, not counting OS overhead. However, given the relatively slow human reaction time, the response time on a properly designed system should be similar to that on a dedicated computer.

Both batch processing and time sharing use multiprogramming. The key differences are listed in Table 2.3.

One of the first time-sharing operating systems to be developed was the Compatible Time-Sharing System (CTSS) [CORB62], developed at MIT by a group known as Project MAC (Machine-Aided Cognition, or Multiple-Access Computers). The system was first developed for the IBM 709 in 1961 and later transferred to an IBM 7094.

Compared to later systems, CTSS is primitive. The system ran on a computer with 32,000 36-bit words of main memory, with the resident monitor consuming 5000 of that. When control was to be assigned to an interactive user, the user's program and data were loaded into the remaining 27,000 words of main memory. A program was always loaded to start at the location of the 5000th word; this simplified both the monitor and memory management. A system clock generated interrupts at a rate of approximately one every 0.2 seconds. At each clock interrupt, the OS regained control and could assign the processor to another user. This technique is known as **time slicing**. Thus, at regular time intervals, the current user would be preempted and another user loaded in. To preserve the old user program status for later resumption, the old user programs and data were written out to disk before the new user programs and data were read in. Subsequently, the old user program code and data were restored in main memory when that program was next given a turn.

To minimize disk traffic, user memory was only written out when the incoming program would overwrite it. This principle is illustrated in Figure 2.7. Assume that there are four interactive users with the following memory requirements, in words:

- JOB1: 15,000
- JOB2: 20,000

Table 2.3 Batch Multiprogramming versus Time Sharing

	Batch Multiprogramming	**Time Sharing**
Principal objective	Maximize processor use	Minimize response time
Source of directives to operating system	Job control language commands provided with the job	Commands entered at the terminal

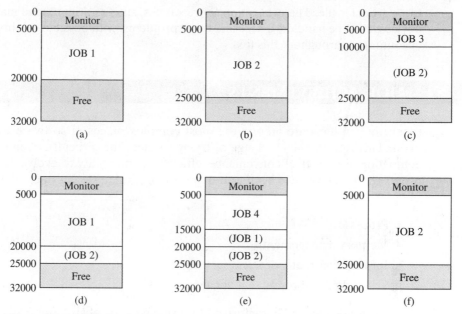

Figure 2.7   CTSS Operation

- JOB3: 5000
- JOB4: 10,000

Initially, the monitor loads JOB1 and transfers control to it (a). Later, the monitor decides to transfer control to JOB2. Because JOB2 requires more memory than JOB1, JOB1 must be written out first, and then JOB2 can be loaded (b). Next, JOB3 is loaded in to be run. However, because JOB3 is smaller than JOB2, a portion of JOB2 can remain in memory, reducing disk write time (c). Later, the monitor decides to transfer control back to JOB1. An additional portion of JOB2 must be written out when JOB1 is loaded back into memory (d). When JOB4 is loaded, part of JOB1 and the portion of JOB2 remaining in memory are retained (e). At this point, if either JOB1 or JOB2 is activated, only a partial load will be required. In this example, it is JOB2 that runs next. This requires that JOB4 and the remaining resident portion of JOB1 be written out and that the missing portion of JOB2 be read in (f).

The CTSS approach is primitive compared to present-day time sharing, but it was effective. It was extremely simple, which minimized the size of the monitor. Because a job was always loaded into the same locations in memory, there was no need for relocation techniques at load time (discussed subsequently). The technique of only writing out what was necessary minimized disk activity. Running on the 7094, CTSS supported a maximum of 32 users.

Time sharing and multiprogramming raise a host of new problems for the OS. If multiple jobs are in memory, then they must be protected from interfering with each other by, for example, modifying each other's data. With multiple interactive users, the file system must be protected so that only authorized users have access to a particular file. The contention for resources, such as printers and mass storage devices, must be handled. These and other problems, with possible solutions, will be encountered throughout this text.

2.3   MAJOR ACHIEVEMENTS

Operating systems are among the most complex pieces of software ever developed. This reflects the challenge of trying to meet the difficult and in some cases competing objectives of convenience, efficiency, and ability to evolve. [DENN80a] proposes that there have been four major theoretical advances in the development of operating systems:

* Processes
* Memory management
* Information protection and security
* Scheduling and resource management

Each advance is characterized by principles, or abstractions, developed to meet difficult practical problems. Taken together, these five areas span many of the key design and implementation issues of modern operating systems. The brief review of these five areas in this section serves as an overview of much of the rest of the text.

The Process

Central to the design of operating systems is the concept of *process*. This term was first used by the designers of Multics in the 1960s [DALE68]. It is a somewhat more general term than *job*. Many definitions have been given for the term *process*, including

* A program in execution
* An instance of a program running on a computer
* The entity that can be assigned to and executed on a processor
* A unit of activity characterized by a single sequential thread of execution, a current state, and an associated set of system resources

This concept should become clearer as we proceed.

Three major lines of computer system development created problems in timing and synchronization that contributed to the development of the concept of the process: multiprogramming batch operation, time sharing, and real-time transaction systems. As we have seen, multiprogramming was designed to keep the processor and I/O devices, including storage devices, simultaneously busy to achieve maximum efficiency. The key mechanism is this: In response to signals indicating the completion of I/O transactions, the processor is switched among the various programs residing in main memory.

A second line of development was general-purpose time sharing. Here, the key design objective is to be responsive to the needs of the individual user and yet, for cost reasons, be able to support many users simultaneously. These goals are compatible because of the relatively slow reaction time of the user. For example, if a typical user needs an average of 2 seconds of processing time per minute, then close to 30 such users should be able to share the same system without noticeable interference. Of course, OS overhead must be factored into such calculations.

A third important line of development has been real-time transaction processing systems. In this case, a number of users are entering queries or updates against a database. An example is an airline reservation system. The key difference between the transaction processing system and the time-sharing system is that the former is limited to one or a few applications, whereas users of a time-sharing system can engage in program development, job execution, and the use of various applications. In both cases, system response time is paramount.

The principal tool available to system programmers in developing the early multiprogramming and multiuser interactive systems was the interrupt. The activity of any job could be suspended by the occurrence of a defined event, such as an I/O completion. The processor would save some sort of context (e.g., program counter and other registers) and branch to an interrupt-handling routine, which would determine the nature of the interrupt, process the interrupt, and then resume user processing with the interrupted job or some other job.

The design of the system software to coordinate these various activities turned out to be remarkably difficult. With many jobs in progress at any one time, each of which involved numerous steps to be performed in sequence, it became impossible to analyze all of the possible combinations of sequences of events. In the absence of some systematic means of coordination and cooperation among activities, programmers resorted to ad hoc methods based on their understanding of the environment that the OS had to control. These efforts were vulnerable to subtle programming errors whose effects could be observed only when certain relatively rare sequences of actions occurred. These errors were difficult to diagnose because they needed to be distinguished from application software errors and hardware errors. Even when the error was detected, it was difficult to determine the cause, because the precise conditions under which the errors appeared were very hard to reproduce. In general terms, there are four main causes of such errors [DENN80a]:

- **Improper synchronization:** It is often the case that a routine must be suspended awaiting an event elsewhere in the system. For example, a program that initiates an I/O read must wait until the data are available in a buffer before proceeding. In such cases, a signal from some other routine is required. Improper design of the signaling mechanism can result in signals being lost or duplicate signals being received.

- **Failed mutual exclusion:** It is often the case that more than one user or program will attempt to make use of a shared resource at the same time. For example, two users may attempt to edit the same file at the same time. If these accesses are not controlled, an error can occur. There must be some sort of mutual exclusion mechanism that permits only one routine at a time to perform an update against the file. The implementation of such mutual exclusion is difficult to verify as being correct under all possible sequences of events.

- **Nondeterminate program operation:** The results of a particular program normally should depend only on the input to that program and not on the activities of other programs in a shared system. But when programs share memory, and their execution is interleaved by the processor, they may interfere with each other by overwriting common memory areas in unpredictable ways. Thus, the order in which various programs are scheduled may affect the outcome of any particular program.

- **Deadlocks:** It is possible for two or more programs to be hung up waiting for each other. For example, two programs may each require two I/O devices to perform some operation (e.g., disk to tape copy). One of the programs has seized control of one of the devices and the other program has control of the other device. Each is waiting for the other program to release the desired resource. Such a deadlock may depend on the chance timing of resource allocation and release.

What is needed to tackle these problems is a systematic way to monitor and control the various programs executing on the processor. The concept of the process provides the foundation. We can think of a process as consisting of three components:

- An executable program
- The associated data needed by the program (variables, work space, buffers, etc.)
- The execution context of the program

This last element is essential. The **execution context**, or **process state**, is the internal data by which the OS is able to supervise and control the process. This internal information is separated from the process, because the OS has information not permitted to the process. The context includes all of the information that the OS needs to manage the process and that the processor needs to execute the process properly. The context includes the contents of the various processor registers, such as the program counter and data registers. It also includes information of use to the OS, such as the priority of the process and whether the process is waiting for the completion of a particular I/O event.

Figure 2.8 indicates a way in which processes may be managed. Two processes, A and B, exist in portions of main memory. That is, a block of memory is allocated to each process that contains the program, data, and context information. Each process is recorded in a process list built and maintained by the OS. The process list contains one entry for each process, which includes a pointer to the location of the block of memory that contains the process. The entry may also include part or all of the execution context of the process. The remainder of the execution context is stored elsewhere, perhaps with the process itself (as indicated in Figure 2.8) or frequently in a separate region of memory. The process index register contains the index into the process list of the process currently controlling the processor. The program counter points to the next instruction in that process to be executed. The base and limit registers define the region in memory occupied

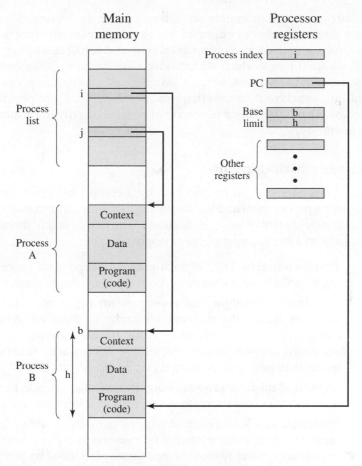

Figure 2.8   Typical Process Implementation

by the process: The base register is the starting address of the region of memory and the limit is the size of the region (in bytes or words). The program counter and all data references are interpreted relative to the base register and must not exceed the value in the limit register. This prevents interprocess interference.

In Figure 2.8, the process index register indicates that process B is executing. Process A was previously executing but has been temporarily interrupted. The contents of all the registers at the moment of A's interruption were recorded in its execution context. Later, the OS can perform a process switch and resume execution of process A. The process switch consists of storing the context of B and restoring the context of A. When the program counter is loaded with a value pointing into A's program area, process A will automatically resume execution.

Thus, the process is realized as a data structure. A process can either be executing or awaiting execution. The entire **state** of the process at any instant is contained in its context. This structure allows the development of powerful techniques for ensuring coordination and cooperation among processes. New features can be designed and incorporated into the OS (e.g., priority) by expanding the context to include any new information needed to support the feature. Throughout this book, we will see a number of examples where this process structure is employed to solve the problems raised by multiprogramming and resource sharing.

A final point, which we introduce briefly here, is the concept of **thread**. In essence, a single process, which is assigned certain resources, can be broken up into multiple, concurrent threads that execute cooperatively to perform the work of the process. This introduces a new level of parallel activity to be managed by the hardware and software.

Memory Management

The needs of users can be met best by a computing environment that supports modular programming and the flexible use of data. System managers need efficient and orderly control of storage allocation. The OS, to satisfy these requirements, has five principal storage management responsibilities:

- **Process isolation:** The OS must prevent independent processes from interfering with each other's memory, both data and instructions.
- **Automatic allocation and management:** Programs should be dynamically allocated across the memory hierarchy as required. Allocation should be transparent to the programmer. Thus, the programmer is relieved of concerns relating to memory limitations, and the OS can achieve efficiency by assigning memory to jobs only as needed.
- **Support of modular programming:** Programmers should be able to define program modules, and to create, destroy, and alter the size of modules dynamically.
- **Protection and access control:** Sharing of memory, at any level of the memory hierarchy, creates the potential for one program to address the memory space of another. This is desirable when sharing is needed by particular applications. At other times, it threatens the integrity of programs and even of the OS itself. The OS must allow portions of memory to be accessible in various ways by various users.
- **Long-term storage:** Many application programs require means for storing information for extended periods of time, after the computer has been powered down.

Typically, operating systems meet these requirements with virtual memory and file system facilities. The file system implements a long-term store, with information stored in named objects, called files. The file is a convenient concept for the programmer and is a useful unit of access control and protection for the OS.

Virtual memory is a facility that allows programs to address memory from a logical point of view, without regard to the amount of main memory physically available. Virtual memory was conceived to meet the requirement of having multiple user jobs reside in main memory concurrently, so that there would not be a hiatus between the execution of successive processes while one process was written out to secondary store and the successor process was read in. Because processes vary in size, if the processor switches among a number of processes it is difficult to pack them compactly into main memory. Paging systems were introduced, which allow processes to be comprised of a number of fixed-size blocks, called pages. A program references a word by means of a **virtual address** consisting of a page number and an offset within the page. Each page of a process may be located anywhere in main memory. The paging system provides for a dynamic mapping between the virtual address used in the program and a **real address**, or physical address, in main memory.

With dynamic mapping hardware available, the next logical step was to eliminate the requirement that all pages of a process reside in main memory simultaneously. All the pages of a process are maintained on disk. When a process is executing, some of its pages are in main memory. If reference is made to a page that is not in main memory, the memory management hardware detects this and arranges for the missing page to be loaded. Such a scheme is referred to as **virtual memory** and is depicted in Figure 2.9.

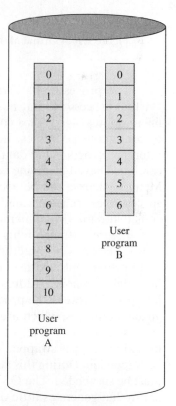

A.1			
	A.0	A.2	
	A.5		
B.0	B.1	B.2	B.3
		A.7	
	A.9		
		A.8	
	B.5	B.6	

Main memory

Main memory consists of a number of fixed-length frames, each equal to the size of a page. For a program to execute, some or all of its pages must be in main memory.

Disk

Secondary memory (disk) can hold many fixed-length pages. A user program consists of some number of pages. Pages for all programs plus the operating system are on disk, as are files.

Figure 2.9   Virtual Memory Concepts

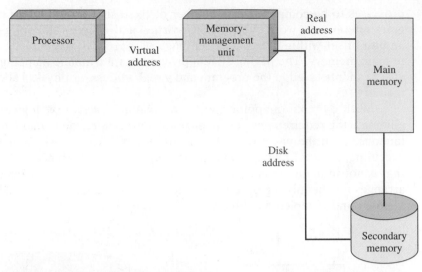

Figure 2.10   Virtual Memory Addressing

The processor hardware, together with the OS, provides the user with a "virtual processor" that has access to a virtual memory. This memory may be a linear address space or a collection of segments, which are variable-length blocks of contiguous addresses. In either case, programming language instructions can reference program and data locations in the virtual memory area. Process isolation can be achieved by giving each process a unique, nonoverlapping virtual memory. Memory sharing can be achieved by overlapping portions of two virtual memory spaces. Files are maintained in a long-term store. Files and portions of files may be copied into the virtual memory for manipulation by programs.

Figure 2.10 highlights the addressing concerns in a virtual memory scheme. Storage consists of directly addressable (by machine instructions) main memory and lower-speed auxiliary memory that is accessed indirectly by loading blocks into main memory. Address translation hardware (memory management unit) is interposed between the processor and memory. Programs reference locations using virtual addresses, which are mapped into real main memory addresses. If a reference is made to a virtual address not in real memory, then a portion of the contents of real memory is swapped out to auxiliary memory and the desired block of data is swapped in. During this activity, the process that generated the address reference must be suspended. The OS designer needs to develop an address translation mechanism that generates little overhead and a storage allocation policy that minimizes the traffic between memory levels.

Information Protection and Security

The growth in the use of time-sharing systems and, more recently, computer networks has brought with it a growth in concern for the protection of information. The nature of the threat that concerns an organization will vary greatly depending on the circumstances. However, there are some general-purpose tools that can be built into computers and operating systems that support a variety of protection and security mechanisms. In general, we are concerned with the problem of controlling access to computer systems and the information stored in them.

Much of the work in security and protection as it relates to operating systems can be roughly grouped into four categories:

- **Availability:** Concerned with protecting the system against interruption.
- **Confidentiality:** Assures that users cannot read data for which access is unauthorized.
- **Data integrity:** Protection of data from unauthorized modification.
- **Authenticity:** Concerned with the proper verification of the identity of users and the validity of messages or data.

Scheduling and Resource Management

A key responsibility of the OS is to manage the various resources available to it (main memory space, I/O devices, processors) and to schedule their use by the various active processes. Any resource allocation and scheduling policy must consider three factors:

- **Fairness:** Typically, we would like all processes that are competing for the use of a particular resource to be given approximately equal and fair access to that resource. This is especially so for jobs of the same class, that is, jobs of similar demands.
- **Differential responsiveness:** On the other hand, the OS may need to discriminate among different classes of jobs with different service requirements. The OS should attempt to make allocation and scheduling decisions to meet the total set of requirements. The OS should also make these decisions dynamically. For example, if a process is waiting for the use of an I/O device, the OS may wish to schedule that process for execution as soon as possible to free up the device for later demands from other processes.
- **Efficiency:** The OS should attempt to maximize throughput, minimize response time, and, in the case of time sharing, accommodate as many users as possible. These criteria conflict; finding the right balance for a particular situation is an ongoing problem for OS research.

Scheduling and resource management are essentially operations-research problems and the mathematical results of that discipline can be applied. In addition, measurement of system activity is important to be able to monitor performance and make adjustments.

Figure 2.11 suggests the major elements of the OS involved in the scheduling of processes and the allocation of resources in a multiprogramming environment. The OS maintains a number of queues, each of which is simply a list of processes waiting for some resource. The short-term queue consists of processes that are in main memory (or at least an essential minimum portion of each is in main memory) and are ready to run as soon as the processor is made available. Any one of these processes could use the processor next. It is up to the short-term scheduler, or

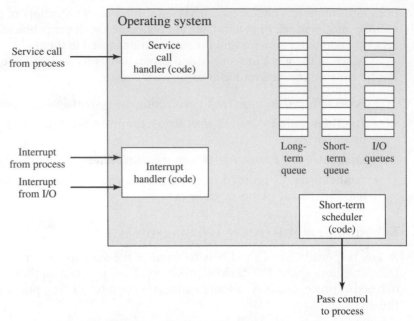

Figure 2.11   Key Elements of an Operating System for Multiprogramming

dispatcher, to pick one. A common strategy is to give each process in the queue some time in turn; this is referred to as a **round-robin** technique. In effect, the round-robin technique employs a circular queue. Another strategy is to assign priority levels to the various processes, with the scheduler selecting processes in priority order.

The long-term queue is a list of new jobs waiting to use the processor. The OS adds jobs to the system by transferring a process from the long-term queue to the short-term queue. At that time, a portion of main memory must be allocated to the incoming process. Thus, the OS must be sure that it does not overcommit memory or processing time by admitting too many processes to the system. There is an I/O queue for each I/O device. More than one process may request the use of the same I/O device. All processes waiting to use each device are lined up in that device's queue. Again, the OS must determine which process to assign to an available I/O device.

The OS receives control of the processor at the interrupt handler if an interrupt occurs. A process may specifically invoke some OS service, such as an I/O device handler by means of a service call. In this case, a service call handler is the entry point into the OS. In any case, once the interrupt or service call is handled, the short-term scheduler is invoked to pick a process for execution.

The foregoing is a functional description; details and modular design of this portion of the OS will differ in various systems. Much of the research and development effort in operating systems has been directed at picking algorithms and data structures for this function that provide fairness, differential responsiveness, and efficiency.

2.4 DEVELOPMENTS LEADING TO MODERN OPERATING SYSTEMS

Over the years, there has been a gradual evolution of OS structure and capabilities. However, in recent years a number of new design elements have been introduced into both new operating systems and new releases of existing operating systems that create a major change in the nature of operating systems. These modern operating systems respond to new developments in hardware, new applications, and new security threats. Among the key hardware drivers are multiprocessor systems, greatly increased processor speed, high-speed network attachments, and increasing size and variety of memory storage devices. In the application arena, multimedia applications, Internet and Web access, and client/server computing have influenced OS design. With respect to security, Internet access to computers has greatly increased the potential threat and increasingly sophisticated attacks, such as viruses, worms, and hacking techniques, have had a profound impact on OS design.

The rate of change in the demands on operating systems requires not just modifications and enhancements to existing architectures but new ways of organizing the OS. A wide range of different approaches and design elements has been tried in both experimental and commercial operating systems, but much of the work fits into the following categories:

- Microkernel architecture
- Multithreading
- Symmetric multiprocessing
- Distributed operating systems
- Object-oriented design

Most operating systems, until recently, featured a large **monolithic kernel**. Most of what is thought of as OS functionality is provided in these large kernels, including scheduling, file system, networking, device drivers, memory management, and more. Typically, a monolithic kernel is implemented as a single process, with all elements sharing the same address space. A **microkernel architecture** assigns only a few essential functions to the kernel, including address spaces, interprocess communication (IPC), and basic scheduling. Other OS services are provided by processes, sometimes called servers, that run in user mode and are treated like any other application by the microkernel. This approach decouples kernel and server development. Servers may be customized to specific application or environment requirements. The microkernel approach simplifies implementation, provides flexibility, and is well suited to a distributed environment. In essence, a microkernel interacts with local and remote server processes in the same way, facilitating construction of distributed systems.

Multithreading is a technique in which a process, executing an application, is divided into threads that can run concurrently. We can make the following distinction:

- **Thread:** A dispatchable unit of work. It includes a processor context (which includes the program counter and stack pointer) and its own data area for a stack (to enable subroutine branching). A thread executes sequentially and is interruptable so that the processor can turn to another thread.

- **Process:** A collection of one or more threads and associated system resources (such as memory containing both code and data, open files, and devices). This corresponds closely to the concept of a program in execution. By breaking a single application into multiple threads, the programmer has great control over the modularity of the application and the timing of application-related events.

Multithreading is useful for applications that perform a number of essentially independent tasks that do not need to be serialized. An example is a database server that listens for and processes numerous client requests. With multiple threads running within the same process, switching back and forth among threads involves less processor overhead than a major process switch between different processes. Threads are also useful for structuring processes that are part of the OS kernel as described in subsequent chapters.

Symmetric multiprocessing (SMP) is a term that refers to a computer hardware architecture (described in Chapter 1) and also to the OS behavior that exploits that architecture. The OS of an SMP schedules processes or threads across all of the processors. SMP has a number of potential advantages over uniprocessor architecture, including the following:

- **Performance:** If the work to be done by a computer can be organized so that some portions of the work can be done in parallel, then a system with multiple processors will yield greater performance than one with a single processor of the same type. This is illustrated in Figure 2.12. With multiprogramming, only one process can execute at a time; meanwhile all other processes are waiting for the processor. With multiprocessing, more than one process can be running simultaneously, each on a different processor.

- **Availability:** In a symmetric multiprocessor, because all processors can perform the same functions, the failure of a single processor does not halt the system. Instead, the system can continue to function at reduced performance.

- **Incremental growth:** A user can enhance the performance of a system by adding an additional processor.

- **Scaling:** Vendors can offer a range of products with different price and performance characteristics based on the number of processors configured in the system.

It is important to note that these are potential, rather than guaranteed, benefits. The OS must provide tools and functions to exploit the parallelism in an SMP system.

Multithreading and SMP are often discussed together, but the two are independent facilities. Even on a uniprocessor system, multithreading is useful for structuring applications and kernel processes. An SMP system is useful even for nonthreaded processes, because several processes can run in parallel. However, the two facilities complement each other and can be used effectively together.

An attractive feature of an SMP is that the existence of multiple processors is transparent to the user. The OS takes care of scheduling of threads or processes on

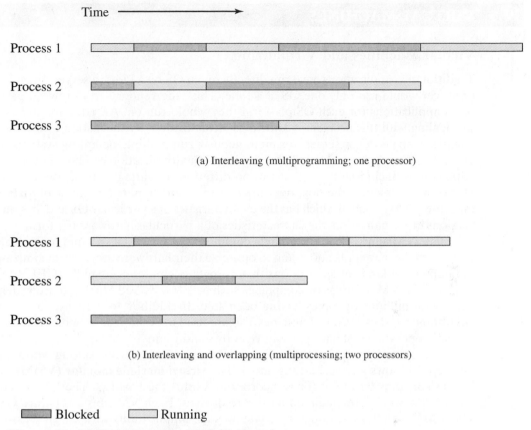

(a) Interleaving (multiprogramming; one processor)

(b) Interleaving and overlapping (multiprocessing; two processors)

■■■ Blocked   ▭ Running

Figure 2.12   Multiprogramming and Multiprocessing

individual processors and of synchronization among processors. This book discusses the scheduling and synchronization mechanisms used to provide the single-system appearance to the user. A different problem is to provide the appearance of a single system for a cluster of separate computers—a multicomputer system. In this case, we are dealing with a collection of entities (computers), each with its own main memory, secondary memory, and other I/O modules. A **distributed operating system** provides the illusion of a single main memory space and a single secondary memory space, plus other unified access facilities, such as a distributed file system. Although clusters are becoming increasingly popular, and there are many cluster products on the market, the state of the art for distributed operating systems lags that of uniprocessor and SMP operating systems. We examine such systems in Part Eight.

Another innovation in OS design is the use of object-oriented technologies. **Object-oriented design** lends discipline to the process of adding modular extensions to a small kernel. At the OS level, an object-based structure enables programmers to customize an OS without disrupting system integrity. Object orientation also eases the development of distributed tools and full-blown distributed operating systems.

2.5   VIRTUAL MACHINES

Virtual Machines and Virtualizing

Traditionally, applications have run directly on an OS on a PC or a server. Each PC or server would run only one OS at a time. Thus, the vendor had to rewrite parts of its applications for each OS/platform they would run on. An effective strategy for dealing with this problem is known as **virtualization**. Virtualization technology enables a single PC or server to simultaneously run multiple operating systems or multiple sessions of a single OS. A machine with virtualization can host numerous applications, including those that run on different operating systems, on a single platform. In essence, the host operating system can support a number of **virtual machines (VM)**, each of which has the characteristics of a particular OS and, in some versions of virtualization, the characteristics of a particular hardware platform.

The VM approach is becoming a common way for businesses and individuals to deal with legacy applications and to optimize their hardware usage by maximizing the number of kinds of applications that a single computer can handle [GEER09]. Commercial VM offerings by companies such as VMware and Microsoft are widely used, with millions of copies having been sold. In addition to their use in server environments, these VM technologies also are used in desktop environments to run multiple operating systems, typically Windows and Linux.

The specific architecture of the VM approach varies among vendors. Figure 2.13 shows a typical arrangement. The **virtual machine monitor (VMM)**, or **hypervisor**, runs on top of (or is incorporated into) the host OS. The VMM supports VMs, which are emulated hardware devices. Each VM runs a separate OS. The VMM handles each operating system's communications with the processor, the storage medium, and the network. To execute programs, the VMM hands off the processor control to a virtual OS on a VM. Most VMs use virtualized network

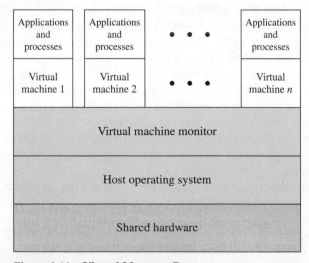

Figure 2.13   Virtual Memory Concept

connections to communicate with one another, when such communication is needed. Key to the success of this approach is that the VMM provides a layer between software environments and the underlying hardware and host OS that is programmable, transparent to the software above it, and makes efficient use of the hardware below it.

Virtual Machine Architecture[2]

Recall from Section 2.1 (see Figure 2.1) the discussion of the application programming interface, the application binary interface, and the instruction set architecture. Let us use these interface concepts to clarify the meaning of *machine* in the term *virtual machine*. Consider a process executing a compiled application program. From the perspective of the **process**, the machine on which it executes consists of the virtual memory space assigned to the process, the processor registers it may use, the user-level machine instructions it may execute, and the OS system calls it may invoke for I/O. Thus the **ABI** defines the machine as seen by a process.

From the perspective of an **application**, the machine characteristics are specified by high-level language capabilities, and OS and system library calls. Thus, the **API** defines the machine for an application.

For the **operating system**, the machine hardware defines the system that supports the operation of the OS and the numerous processes that execute concurrently. These processes share a file system and other I/O resources. The system allocates real memory and I/O resources to the processes and allows the processes to interact with their resources. From the OS perspective, therefore, it is the **ISA** that provides the interface between the system and machine.

With these considerations in mind, we can consider two architectural approaches to implementing virtual machines: process VMs and system VMs.

PROCESS VIRTUAL MACHINE In essence, a process VM presents an ABI to an application process, translates a set of OS and user-level instructions composing one platform to those of another (Figure 2.14a). A process VM is a virtual platform for executing a single process. As such, the process VM is created when the process is created and terminated when the process is terminated.

In order to provide cross-platform portability, a common implementation of the process VM architecture is as part of an overall HLL application environment. The resulting ABI does not correspond to any specific machine. Instead, the ABI specification is designed to easily support a given HLL or set of HLLs and to be easily portable to a variety of ISAs. The HLL VM includes a front-end compiler that generates a virtual binary code for execution or interpretation. This code can then be executed on any machine that has the process VM implemented.

Two widely used examples of this approach are the Java VM architecture and the Microsoft Common Language Infrastructure, which is the foundation of the .NET framework.

---

[2]Much of the discussion that follows is based on [SMIT05].

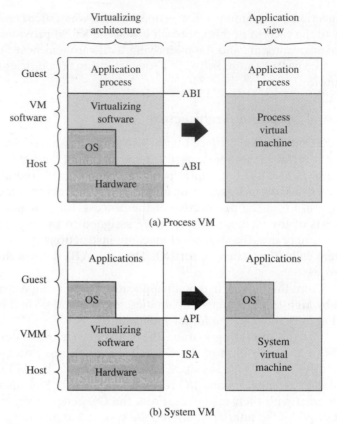

Figure 2.14   Process and System Virtual Machines

SYSTEM VIRTUAL MACHINE   In a system VM, virtualizing software translates the ISA used by one hardware platform to that of another. Note in Figure 2.14a that the virtualizing software in the process VM approach makes use of the services of the host OS, while in the system VM approach there is logically no separate host OS, rather the host system OS incorporates the VM capability. In the system VM case, the virtualizing software is host to a number of guest operating systems, with each VM including its own OS. The VMM emulates the hardware ISA so that the guest software can potentially execute a different ISA from the one implemented on the host.

With the system VM approach, a single hardware platform can support multiple, isolated guest OS environments simultaneously. This approach provides a number of benefits, including application portability, support of legacy systems without the need to maintain legacy hardware, and security by means of isolation of each guest OS environment from the other guest environments.

A variant on the architecture shown in Figure 2.14b is referred to as a *hosted VM*. In this case, the VMM is built on top of an existing host OS. The VMM relies on the host OS to provide device drivers and other lower-level services. An example of a hosted VM is the VMware GSX server.

2.6 OS DESIGN CONSIDERATIONS FOR MULTIPROCESSOR AND MULTICORE

Symmetric Multiprocessor OS Considerations

In an SMP system, the kernel can execute on any processor, and typically each processor does self-scheduling from the pool of available processes or threads. The kernel can be constructed as multiple processes or multiple threads, allowing portions of the kernel to execute in parallel. The SMP approach complicates the OS. The OS designer must deal with the complexity due to sharing resources (like data structures) and coordinating actions (like accessing devices) from multiple parts of the OS executing at the same time. Techniques must be employed to resolve and synchronize claims to resources.

An SMP operating system manages processor and other computer resources so that the user may view the system in the same fashion as a multiprogramming uniprocessor system. A user may construct applications that use multiple processes or multiple threads within processes without regard to whether a single processor or multiple processors will be available. Thus, a multiprocessor OS must provide all the functionality of a multiprogramming system plus additional features to accommodate multiple processors. The key design issues include the following:

- **Simultaneous concurrent processes or threads:** Kernel routines need to be reentrant to allow several processors to execute the same kernel code simultaneously. With multiple processors executing the same or different parts of the kernel, kernel tables and management structures must be managed properly to avoid data corruption or invalid operations.

- **Scheduling:** Any processor may perform scheduling, which complicates the task of enforcing a scheduling policy and assuring that corruption of the scheduler data structures is avoided. If kernel-level multithreading is used, then the opportunity exists to schedule multiple threads from the same process simultaneously on multiple processors. Multiprocessor scheduling is examined in Chapter 10.

- **Synchronization:** With multiple active processes having potential access to shared address spaces or shared I/O resources, care must be taken to provide effective synchronization. Synchronization is a facility that enforces mutual exclusion and event ordering. A common synchronization mechanism used in multiprocessor operating systems is locks, described in Chapter 5.

- **Memory management:** Memory management on a multiprocessor must deal with all of the issues found on uniprocessor computers and is discussed in Part Three. In addition, the OS needs to exploit the available hardware parallelism to achieve the best performance. The paging mechanisms on different processors must be coordinated to enforce consistency when several processors share a page or segment and to decide on page replacement. The reuse of physical pages is the biggest problem of concern; that is, it must be guaranteed that a physical page can no longer be accessed with its old contents before the page is put to a new use.

- **Reliability and fault tolerance:** The OS should provide graceful degradation in the face of processor failure. The scheduler and other portions of the OS must recognize the loss of a processor and restructure management tables accordingly.

Because multiprocessor OS design issues generally involve extensions to solutions to multiprogramming uniprocessor design problems, we do not treat multiprocessor operating systems separately. Rather, specific multiprocessor issues are addressed in the proper context throughout this book.

Multicore OS Considerations

The considerations for multicore systems include all the design issues discussed so far in this section for SMP systems. But additional concerns arise. The issue is one of the scale of the potential parallelism. Current multicore vendors offer systems with up to eight cores on a single chip. With each succeeding processor technology generation, the number of cores and the amount of shared and dedicated cache memory increases, so that we are now entering the era of "many-core" systems.

The design challenge for a many-core multicore system is to efficiently harness the multicore processing power and intelligently manage the substantial on-chip resources efficiently. A central concern is how to match the inherent parallelism of a many-core system with the performance requirements of applications. The potential for parallelism in fact exists at three levels in contemporary multicore system. First, there is hardware parallelism within each core processor, known as instruction level parallelism, which may or may not be exploited by application programmers and compilers. Second, there is the potential for multiprogramming and multithreaded execution within each processor. Finally, there is the potential for a single application to execute in concurrent processes or threads across multiple cores. Without strong and effective OS support for the last two types of parallelism just mentioned, hardware resources will not be efficiently used.

In essence, then, since the advent of multicore technology, OS designers have been struggling with the problem of how best to extract parallelism from computing workloads. A variety of approaches are being explored for next-generation operating systems. We introduce two general strategies in this section and consider some details in later chapters.

PARALLELISM WITHIN APPLICATIONS Most applications can, in principle, be subdivided into multiple tasks that can execute in parallel, with these tasks then being implemented as multiple processes, perhaps each with multiple threads. The difficulty is that the developer must decide how to split up the application work into independently executable tasks. That is, the developer must decide what pieces can or should be executed asynchronously or in parallel. It is primarily the compiler and the programming language features that support the parallel programming design process. But, the OS can support this design process, at minimum, by efficiently allocating resources among parallel tasks as defined by the developer.

Perhaps the most effective initiative to support developers is implemented in the latest release of the UNIX-based Mac OS X operating system. Mac OS X 10.6 includes a multicore support capability known as Grand Central Dispatch (GCD).

GCD does not help the developer decide how to break up a task or application into separate concurrent parts. But once a developer has identified something that can be split off into a separate task, GCD makes it as easy and noninvasive as possible to actually do so.

In essence, GCD is a thread pool mechanism, in which the OS maps tasks onto threads representing an available degree of concurrency (plus threads for blocking on I/O). Windows also has a thread pool mechanism (since 2000), and thread pools have been heavily used in server applications for years. What is new in GCD is the extension to programming languages to allow anonymous functions (called blocks) as a way of specifying tasks. GCD is hence not a major evolutionary step. Nevertheless, it is a new and valuable tool for exploiting the available parallelism of a multicore system.

One of Apple's slogans for GCD is "islands of serialization in a sea of concurrency." That captures the practical reality of adding more concurrency to run-of-the-mill desktop applications. Those islands are what isolate developers from the thorny problems of simultaneous data access, deadlock, and other pitfalls of multithreading. Developers are encouraged to identify functions of their applications that would be better executed off the main thread, even if they are made up of several sequential or otherwise partially interdependent tasks. GCD makes it easy to break off the entire unit of work while maintaining the existing order and dependencies between subtasks. In later chapters, we look at some of the details of GCD.

VIRTUAL MACHINE APPROACH An alternative approach is to recognize that with the ever-increasing number of cores on a chip, the attempt to multiprogram individual cores to support multiple applications may be a misplaced use of resources [JACK10]. If instead, we allow one or more cores to be dedicated to a particular process and then leave the processor alone to devote its efforts to that process, we avoid much of the overhead of task switching and scheduling decisions. The multicore OS could then act as a hypervisor that makes a high-level decision to allocate cores to applications but does little in the way of resource allocation beyond that.

The reasoning behind this approach is as follows. In the early days of computing, one program was run on a single processor. With multiprogramming, each application is given the illusion that it is running on a dedicated processor. Multiprogramming is based on the concept of a process, which is an abstraction of an execution environment. To manage processes, the OS requires protected space, free from user and program interference. For this purpose, the distinction between kernel mode and user mode was developed. In effect, kernel mode and user mode abstracted the processor into two processors. With all these virtual processors, however, come struggles over who gets the attention of the real processor. The overhead of switching between all these processors starts to grow to the point where responsiveness suffers, especially when multiple cores are introduced. But with many-core systems, we can consider dropping the distinction between kernel and user mode. In this approach, the OS acts more like a hypervisor. The programs themselves take on many of the duties of resource management. The OS assigns an application a processor and some memory, and the program itself, using metadata generated by the compiler, would best know how to use these resources.

2.7   MICROSOFT WINDOWS OVERVIEW

History

The story of Windows begins with a very different OS, developed by Microsoft for the first IBM personal computer and referred to as MS-DOS. The initial version, MS-DOS 1.0, was released in August 1981. It consisted of 4000 lines of assembly language source code and ran in 8 Kbytes of memory using the Intel 8086 microprocessor.

The IBM PC was an important stage in a continuing revolution in computing that has expanded computing from the data center of the 1960s, to the departmental minicomputer of the 1970s, and to the desktop in the 1980s. The revolution has continued with computing moving into the briefcase in the 1990s, and into our pockets during the most recent decade.

Microsoft's initial OS ran a single application at a time, using a command line interface to control the system. It took a long time for Microsoft to develop a true GUI interface for the PC; on their third try they succeeded. The 16-bit Windows 3.0 shipped in 1990 and instantly became successful, selling a million copies in six months. Windows 3.0 was implemented as a layer on top of MS-DOS and suffered from the limitations of that primitive system. Five years later, Microsoft shipped a 32-bit version, Windows 95, which was also very successful and led to the development of additional versions: Windows 98 and Windows Me.

Meanwhile, it had become clear to Microsoft that the MS-DOS platform could not sustain a truly modern OS. In 1989 Microsoft hired Dave Cutler, who had developed the very successful RSX-11M and VAX/VMS operating systems at Digital Equipment Corporation. Cutler's charter was to develop a modern OS, which was portable to architectures other than the Intel x86 family, and yet compatible with the OS/2 system that Microsoft was jointly developing with IBM, as well as the portable UNIX standard, POSIX. This system was christened NT (New Technology).

The first version of Windows NT (3.1) was released in 1993, with the same GUI as Windows 3.1, the follow-on to Windows 3.0. However, NT 3.1 was a new 32-bit OS with the ability to support older DOS and Windows applications as well as provide OS/2 support. Several versions of NT 3.x followed with support for additional hardware platforms. In 1996, Microsoft released NT 4.0 with the same user interface as Windows 95. In 2000, Microsoft introduced the next major upgrade of the NT OS: Windows 2000. The underlying Executive and Kernel architecture is fundamentally the same as in NT 3.1, but new features have been added. The emphasis in Windows 2000 was the addition of services and functions to support distributed processing. The central element of Windows 2000's new features was Active Directory, which is a distributed directory service able to map names of arbitrary objects to any kind of information about those objects. Windows 2000 also added the plug-and-play and power-management facilities that were already in Windows 98, the successor to Windows 95. These features are particularly important for laptop computers.

In 2001, a new desktop version of NT was released, known as Windows XP. The goal of Windows XP was to finally replace the versions of Windows based on MS-DOS with an OS based on NT. In 2007, Microsoft shipped Windows Vista for the desktop and a short time later, Windows Server 2008. In 2009, they shipped

Windows 7 and Windows Server 2008 R2. Despite the difference in naming, the client and server versions of these systems use many of the same files, but with additional features and capabilities enabled for servers.

Over the years, NT has attempted to support multiple processor architectures; the Intel i860 was the original target for NT as well as the x86. Subsequently, NT added support for the Digital Alpha architecture, the PowerPC, and the MIPS. Later came the Intel IA64 (Itanium) and the 64-bit version of the x86, based on the AMD64 processor architecture. Windows 7 supports only x86 and AMD64. Windows Server 2008 R2 supports only AMD64 and IA64—but Microsoft has announced that it will end support for IA64 in future releases. All the other processor architectures have failed in the market, and today only the x86, AMD64, and ARM architectures are viable. Microsoft's support for ARM is limited to their Windows CE OS, which runs on phones and handheld devices. Windows CE has little relationship to the NT-based Windows that runs on slates, netbooks/laptops, desktops, and servers.

Microsoft has announced that it is developing a version of NT that targets cloud computing: Windows Azure. Azure includes a number of features that are specific to the requirements of public and private clouds. Though it is closely related to Windows Server, it does not share files in the same way that the Windows client and server versions do.

The Modern OS

Modern operating systems, such as today's Windows and UNIX (with all its flavors like Solaris, Linux, and MacOS X), must exploit the capabilities of all the billions of transistors on each silicon chip. They must work with multiple 32-bit and 64-bit CPUs, with adjunct GPUs, DSPs, and fixed function units. They must provide support for sophisticated input/output (multiple touch-sensitive displays, cameras, microphones, biometric and other sensors) and handle a variety of data challenges (streaming media, photos, scientific number crunching, search queries)—all while giving a human being a responsive, real-time experience with the computing system.

To handle these requirements, the computer cannot be doing only one thing at a time. Unlike the early days of the PC, when the OS ran a single application at a time, hundreds of activities are taking place to provide the modern computing experience. The OS can no longer just switch to the application and step away until it is needed; it must aggressively manage the system and coordinate between all the competing computations that are taking place often simultaneously on the multiple CPUs, GPUs, and DSPs that may be present in a modern computing environment. Thus all modern operating systems have multitasking capability, even though they may be acting on behalf of only a single human being (called the user).

Windows is a sophisticated multitasking OS, designed to manage the complexity of the modern computing environment, provide a rich platform for application developers, and support a rich set of experiences for users. Like Solaris, Windows is designed to have the features that enterprises need, while at the same time Windows, like MacOS, provides the simplicity and ease-of-use that consumers require. In the following sections we will present an overview of the fundamental structure and capabilities of Windows.

Architecture

Figure 2.15 illustrates the overall structure of Windows 7; all releases of Windows based on NT have essentially the same structure at this level of detail.

As with virtually all operating systems, Windows separates application-oriented software from the core OS software. The latter, which includes the Executive, the Kernel, device drivers, and the hardware abstraction layer, runs in kernel mode. Kernel mode software has access to system data and to the hardware. The remaining software, running in user mode, has limited access to system data.

OPERATING SYSTEM ORGANIZATION Windows has a highly modular architecture. Each system function is managed by just one component of the OS. The rest of the OS and all applications access that function through the responsible component using standard interfaces. Key system data can only be accessed through the appropriate

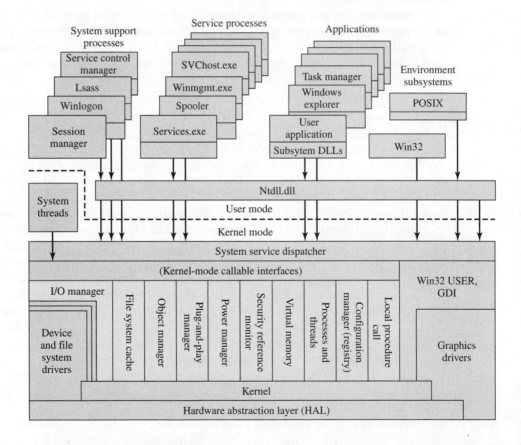

Lsass = local security authentication server   Colored area indicates Executive
POSIX = portable operating system interface
GDI = graphics device interface
DLL = dynamic link libraries

Figure 2.15   Windows and Windows Vista Architecture [RUSS11]

function. In principle, any module can be removed, upgraded, or replaced without rewriting the entire system or its standard application program interfaces (APIs).

The kernel-mode components of Windows are the following:

- **Executive:** Contains the core OS services, such as memory management, process and thread management, security, I/O, and interprocess communication.

- **Kernel:** Controls execution of the processors. The Kernel manages thread scheduling, process switching, exception and interrupt handling, and multiprocessor synchronization. Unlike the rest of the Executive and the user level, the Kernel's own code does not run in threads.

- **Hardware abstraction layer (HAL):** Maps between generic hardware commands and responses and those unique to a specific platform. It isolates the OS from platform-specific hardware differences. The HAL makes each computer's system bus, direct memory access (DMA) controller, interrupt controller, system timers, and memory controller look the same to the Executive and Kernel components. It also delivers the support needed for SMP, explained subsequently.

- **Device drivers:** Dynamic libraries that extend the functionality of the Executive. These include hardware device drivers that translate user I/O function calls into specific hardware device I/O requests and software components for implementing file systems, network protocols, and any other system extensions that need to run in kernel mode.

- **Windowing and graphics system:** Implements the GUI functions, such as dealing with windows, user interface controls, and drawing.

The Windows Executive includes components for specific system functions and provides an API for user-mode software. Following is a brief description of each of the Executive modules:

- **I/O manager:** Provides a framework through which I/O devices are accessible to applications, and is responsible for dispatching to the appropriate device drivers for further processing. The I/O manager implements all the Windows I/O APIs and enforces security and naming for devices, network protocols, and file systems (using the object manager). Windows I/O is discussed in Chapter 11.

- **Cache manager:** Improves the performance of file-based I/O by causing recently referenced file data to reside in main memory for quick access, and deferring disk writes by holding the updates in memory for a short time before sending them to the disk in more efficient batches.

- **Object manager:** Creates, manages, and deletes Windows Executive objects that are used to represent resources such as processes, threads, and synchronization objects. It enforces uniform rules for retaining, naming, and setting the security of objects. The object manager also creates the entries in each processes' handle table, which consist of access control information and a pointer to the object. Windows objects are discussed later in this section.

- **Plug-and-play manager:** Determines which drivers are required to support a particular device and loads those drivers.

- **Power manager:** Coordinates power management among various devices and can be configured to reduce power consumption by shutting down idle devices, putting the processor to sleep, and even writing all of memory to disk and shutting off power to the entire system.

- **Security reference monitor:** Enforces access-validation and audit-generation rules. The Windows object-oriented model allows for a consistent and uniform view of security, right down to the fundamental entities that make up the Executive. Thus, Windows uses the same routines for access validation and for audit checks for all protected objects, including files, processes, address spaces, and I/O devices. Windows security is discussed in Chapter 15.

- **Virtual memory manager:** Manages virtual addresses, physical memory, and the paging files on disk. Controls the memory management hardware and data structures which map virtual addresses in the process's address space to physical pages in the computer's memory. Windows virtual memory management is described in Chapter 8.

- **Process/thread manager:** Creates, manages, and deletes process and thread objects. Windows process and thread management are described in Chapter 4.

- **Configuration manager:** Responsible for implementing and managing the system registry, which is the repository for both system-wide and per-user settings of various parameters.

- **Advanced local procedure call (ALPC) facility:** Implements an efficient cross-process procedure call mechanism for communication between local processes implementing services and subsystems. Similar to the remote procedure call (RPC) facility used for distributed processing.

USER-MODE PROCESSES   Four basic types of user-mode processes are supported by Windows:

- **Special system processes:** User-mode services needed to manage the system, such as the session manager, the authentication subsystem, the service manager, and the logon process.

- **Service processes:** The printer spooler, the event logger, user-mode components that cooperate with device drivers, various network services, and many, many others. Services are used by both Microsoft and external software developers to extend system functionality as they are the only way to run background user-mode activity on a Windows system.

- **Environment subsystems:** Provide different OS personalities (environments). The supported subsystems are Win32 and POSIX. Each environment subsystem includes a subsystem process shared among all applications using the subsystem and dynamic link libraries (DLLs) that convert the user application calls to ALPC calls on the subsystem process, and/or native Windows calls.

- **User applications:** Executables (EXEs) and DLLs that provide the functionality users run to make use of the system. EXEs and DLLs are generally targeted at a specific environment subsystem; although some of the programs that are provided as part of the OS use the native system interfaces (NT API). There is also support for running 32-bit programs on 64-bit systems.

Windows is structured to support applications written for multiple OS personalities. Windows provides this support using a common set of kernel mode components that underlie the OS environment subsystems. The implementation of each environment subsystem includes a separate process, which contains the shared data structures, privileges, and Executive object handles needed to implement a particular personality. The process is started by the Windows Session Manager when the first application of that type is started. The subsystem process runs as a system user, so the Executive will protect its address space from processes run by ordinary users.

An environment subsystem provides a graphical or command-line user interface that defines the look and feel of the OS for a user. In addition, each subsystem provides the API for that particular environment. This means that applications created for a particular operating environment need only be recompiled to run on Windows. Because the OS interface that they see is the same as that for which they were written, the source code does not need to be modified.

Client/Server Model

The Windows OS services, the environment subsystems, and the applications are structured using the client/server computing model, which is a common model for distributed computing and which is discussed in Part Six. This same architecture can be adopted for use internally to a single system, as is the case with Windows.

The native NT API is a set of kernel-based services which provide the core abstractions used by the system, such as processes, threads, virtual memory, I/O, and communication. Windows provides a far richer set of services by using the client/server model to implement functionality in user-mode processes. Both the environment subsystems and the Windows user-mode services are implemented as processes that communicate with clients via RPC. Each server process waits for a request from a client for one of its services (e.g., memory services, process creation services, or networking services). A client, which can be an application program or another server program, requests a service by sending a message. The message is routed through the Executive to the appropriate server. The server performs the requested operation and returns the results or status information by means of another message, which is routed through the Executive back to the client.

Advantages of a client/server architecture include the following:

- It simplifies the Executive. It is possible to construct a variety of APIs implemented in user-mode servers without any conflicts or duplications in the Executive. New APIs can be added easily.

- It improves reliability. Each new server runs outside of the kernel, with its own partition of memory, protected from other servers. A single server can fail without crashing or corrupting the rest of the OS.

- It provides a uniform means for applications to communicate with services via RPCs without restricting flexibility. The message-passing process is hidden from the client applications by function stubs, which are small pieces of code which wrap the RPC call. When an application makes an API call to an environment subsystem or a service, the stub in the client application packages the parameters for the call and sends them as a message to the server process that implements the call.

- It provides a suitable base for distributed computing. Typically, distributed computing makes use of a client/server model, with remote procedure calls implemented using distributed client and server modules and the exchange of messages between clients and servers. With Windows, a local server can pass a message on to a remote server for processing on behalf of local client applications. Clients need not know whether a request is being serviced locally or remotely. Indeed, whether a request is serviced locally or remotely can change dynamically based on current load conditions and on dynamic configuration changes.

Threads and SMP

Two important characteristics of Windows are its support for threads and for symmetric multiprocessing (SMP), both of which were introduced in Section 2.4. [RUSS11] lists the following features of Windows that support threads and SMP:

- OS routines can run on any available processor, and different routines can execute simultaneously on different processors.
- Windows supports the use of multiple threads of execution within a single process. Multiple threads within the same process may execute on different processors simultaneously.
- Server processes may use multiple threads to process requests from more than one client simultaneously.
- Windows provides mechanisms for sharing data and resources between processes and flexible interprocess communication capabilities.

Windows Objects

Though the core of Windows is written in C, the design principles followed draw heavily on the concepts of object-oriented design. This approach facilitates the sharing of resources and data among processes and the protection of resources from unauthorized access. Among the key object-oriented concepts used by Windows are the following:

- **Encapsulation:** An object consists of one or more items of data, called attributes, and one or more procedures that may be performed on those data, called services. The only way to access the data in an object is by invoking one of the object's services. Thus, the data in the object can easily be protected from unauthorized use and from incorrect use (e.g., trying to execute a nonexecutable piece of data).
- **Object class and instance:** An object class is a template that lists the attributes and services of an object and defines certain object characteristics. The OS can create specific instances of an object class as needed. For example, there is a single process object class and one process object for every currently active process. This approach simplifies object creation and management.
- **Inheritance:** Although the implementation is hand coded, the Executive uses inheritance to extend object classes by adding new features. Every Executive

class is based on a base class which specifies virtual methods that support creating, naming, securing, and deleting objects. Dispatcher objects are Executive objects that inherit the properties of an event object, so they can use common synchronization methods. Other specific object types, such as the device class, allow classes for specific devices to inherit from the base class, and add additional data and methods.

- **Polymorphism:** Internally, Windows uses a common set of API functions to manipulate objects of any type; this is a feature of polymorphism, as defined in Appendix D. However, Windows is not completely polymorphic because there are many APIs that are specific to a single object type.

The reader unfamiliar with object-oriented concepts should review Appendix D.

Not all entities in Windows are objects. Objects are used in cases where data are intended for user mode access or when data access is shared or restricted. Among the entities represented by objects are files, processes, threads, semaphores, timers, and graphical windows. Windows creates and manages all types of objects in a uniform way, via the object manager. The object manager is responsible for creating and destroying objects on behalf of applications and for granting access to an object's services and data.

Each object within the Executive, sometimes referred to as a kernel object (to distinguish from user-level objects not of concern to the Executive), exists as a memory block allocated by the kernel and is directly accessible only by kernel mode components. Some elements of the data structure (e.g., object name, security parameters, usage count) are common to all object types, while other elements are specific to a particular object type (e.g., a thread object's priority). Because these object data structures are in the part of each process's address space accessible only by the kernel, it is impossible for an application to reference these data structures and read or write them directly. Instead, applications manipulate objects indirectly through the set of object manipulation functions supported by the Executive. When an object is created, the application that requested the creation receives back a handle for the object. In essence, a handle is an index into a per-process Executive table containing a pointer to the referenced object. This handle can then be used by any thread within the same process to invoke Win32 functions that work with objects, or can be duplicated into other processes.

Objects may have security information associated with them, in the form of a Security Descriptor (SD). This security information can be used to restrict access to the object based on contents of a token object which describes a particular user. For example, a process may create a named semaphore object with the intent that only certain users should be able to open and use that semaphore. The SD for the semaphore object can list those users that are allowed (or denied) access to the semaphore object along with the sort of access permitted (read, write, change, etc.).

In Windows, objects may be either named or unnamed. When a process creates an unnamed object, the object manager returns a handle to that object, and the handle is the only way to refer to it. Handles can be inherited by child processes, or duplicated between processes. Named objects are also given a name that other unrelated processes can use to obtain a handle to the object. For example, if proc-

Table 2.4 Windows Kernel Control Objects

Asynchronous Procedure Call	Used to break into the execution of a specified thread and to cause a procedure to be called in a specified processor mode.
Deferred Procedure Call	Used to postpone interrupt processing to avoid delaying hardware interrupts. Also used to implement timers and interprocessor communication.
Interrupt	Used to connect an interrupt source to an interrupt service routine by means of an entry in an Interrupt Dispatch Table (IDT). Each processor has an IDT that is used to dispatch interrupts that occur on that processor.
Process	Represents the virtual address space and control information necessary for the execution of a set of thread objects. A process contains a pointer to an address map, a list of ready threads containing thread objects, a list of threads belonging to the process, the total accumulated time for all threads executing within the process, and a base priority.
Thread	Represents thread objects, including scheduling priority and quantum, and which processors the thread may run on.
Profile	Used to measure the distribution of run time within a block of code. Both user and system code can be profiled.

ess A wishes to synchronize with process B, it could create a named event object and pass the name of the event to B. Process B could then open and use that event object. However, if A simply wished to use the event to synchronize two threads within itself, it would create an unnamed event object, because there is no need for other processes to be able to use that event.

There are two categories of objects used by Windows for synchronizing the use of the processor:

- **Dispatcher objects:** The subset of Executive objects which threads can wait on to control the dispatching and synchronization of thread-based system operations. These are described in Chapter 6.

- **Control objects:** Used by the Kernel component to manage the operation of the processor in areas not managed by normal thread scheduling. Table 2.4 lists the Kernel control objects.

Windows is not a full-blown object-oriented OS. It is not implemented in an object-oriented language. Data structures that reside completely within one Executive component are not represented as objects. Nevertheless, Windows illustrates the power of object-oriented technology and represents the increasing trend toward the use of this technology in OS design.

What Is New in Windows 7

The core architecture of Windows has been very stable; however, at each release there are new features and improvements made even at the lower levels of the system. Many of the changes in Windows are not visible in the features themselves, but in the performance and stability of the system. These are due to changes in the engineering behind Windows. Other improvements are due to new features, or improvements to existing features:

- **Engineering improvements:** The performance of hundreds of key scenarios, such as opening a file from the GUI, are tracked and continuously character-ized to identify and fix problems. The system is now built in layers which can be separately tested, improving modularity and reducing complexity.

- **Performance improvements:** The amount of memory required has been reduced, both for clients and servers. The VMM is more aggressive about limiting the memory use of runaway processes (see Section 8.5). Background processes can arrange to start upon an event trigger, such as a plugging in a camera, rather than running continuously.

- **Reliability improvements:** The user-mode heap is more tolerant of memory allocation errors by C/C++ programmers, such as continuing to use memory after it is freed. Programs that make such errors are detected and the heap allocation policies are modified for that program to defer freeing memory and avoid corruption of the program's data.

- **Energy efficiency:** Many improvements have been made to the energy effi-ciency of Windows. On servers, unused processors can be "parked," reducing their energy use. All Windows systems are more efficient in how the timers work; avoiding timer interrupts and the associated background activity allows the processors to remain idle longer, which allows modern processors to con-sume less energy. Windows accomplishes this by coalescing timer interrupts into batches.

- **Security:** Windows 7 builds on the security features in Windows Vista, which added integrity levels to the security model, provided BitLocker volume encryption (see Section 15.6), and limited privileged actions by ordinary users. BitLocker is now easier to set up and use, and privileged actions result in many fewer annoying GUI pop-ups.

- **Thread improvements:** The most interesting Windows 7 changes were in the Kernel. The number of logical CPUs available on each system is growing dramatically. Previous versions of Windows limited the number of CPUs to 64, because of the bitmasks used to represent values like processor affinity (see Section 4.4). Windows 7 can support hundreds of CPUs. To ensure that the performance of the system scaled with the number of CPUs, major improvements were made to the Kernel-scheduling code to break apart locks and reduce contention. As the number of available CPUs increase, new programming environments are being developed to support the finer-grain parallelism than is available with threads. Windows 7 supports a form of User-Mode Scheduling which separates the user-mode and kernel-mode portions of threads, allowing the user-mode portions to yield the CPU without enter-ing the Kernel scheduler. Finally, Windows Server 2008 R2 introduced Dynamic Fair Share Scheduling (DFSS) to allow multiuser servers to limit how much one user can interfere with another. DFSS keeps a user with 20 running threads from getting twice as much processor time as a user with only 10 running threads.

2.8 TRADITIONAL UNIX SYSTEMS

History

The history of UNIX is an oft-told tale and will not be repeated in great detail here. Instead, we provide a brief summary.

UNIX was initially developed at Bell Labs and became operational on a PDP-7 in 1970. Some of the people involved at Bell Labs had also participated in the time-sharing work being done at MIT's Project MAC. That project led to the development of first CTSS and then Multics. Although it is common to say that the original UNIX was a scaled-down version of Multics, the developers of UNIX actually claimed to be more influenced by CTSS [RITC78]. Nevertheless, UNIX incorporated many ideas from Multics.

Work on UNIX at Bell Labs, and later elsewhere, produced a series of versions of UNIX. The first notable milestone was porting the UNIX system from the PDP-7 to the PDP-11. This was the first hint that UNIX would be an OS for all computers. The next important milestone was the rewriting of UNIX in the programming language C. This was an unheard-of strategy at the time. It was generally felt that something as complex as an OS, which must deal with time-critical events, had to be written exclusively in assembly language. Reasons for this attitude include the following:

- Memory (both RAM and secondary store) was small and expensive by today's standards, so effective use was important. This included various techniques for overlaying memory with different code and data segments, and self-modifying code.

- Even though compilers had been available since the 1950s, the computer industry was generally skeptical of the quality of automatically generated code. With resource capacity small, efficient code, both in terms of time and space, was essential.

- Processor and bus speeds were relatively slow, so saving clock cycles could make a substantial difference in execution time.

The C implementation demonstrated the advantages of using a high-level language for most if not all of the system code. Today, virtually all UNIX implementations are written in C.

These early versions of UNIX were popular within Bell Labs. In 1974, the UNIX system was described in a technical journal for the first time [RITC74]. This spurred great interest in the system. Licenses for UNIX were provided to commercial institutions as well as universities. The first widely available version outside Bell Labs was Version 6, in 1976. The follow-on Version 7, released in 1978, is the ancestor of most modern UNIX systems. The most important of the non-AT&T systems to be developed was done at the University of California at Berkeley, called UNIX BSD (Berkeley Software Distribution), running first on PDP and then VAX computers. AT&T continued to develop and refine the system. By 1982, Bell Labs had combined several AT&T variants of UNIX into a single system, marketed commercially as UNIX System III. A number of features was later added to the OS to produce UNIX System V.

Description

Figure 2.16 provides a general description of the classic UNIX architecture. The underlying hardware is surrounded by the OS software. The OS is often called the system kernel, or simply the kernel, to emphasize its isolation from the user and applications. It is the UNIX kernel that we will be concerned with in our use of UNIX as an example in this book. UNIX also comes equipped with a number of user services and interfaces that are considered part of the system. These can be grouped into the shell, other interface software, and the components of the C compiler (compiler, assembler, loader). The layer outside of this consists of user applications and the user interface to the C compiler.

A closer look at the kernel is provided in Figure 2.17. User programs can invoke OS services either directly or through library programs. The system call interface is the boundary with the user and allows higher-level software to gain access to specific kernel functions. At the other end, the OS contains primitive routines that interact directly with the hardware. Between these two interfaces, the system is divided into two main parts, one concerned with process control and the other concerned with file management and I/O. The process control subsystem is responsible for memory management, the scheduling and dispatching of processes, and the synchronization and interprocess communication of processes. The file system exchanges data between memory and external devices either as a stream of characters or in blocks. To achieve this, a variety of device drivers are used. For block-oriented transfers, a disk cache approach is used: A system buffer in main memory is interposed between the user address space and the external device.

The description in this subsection has dealt with what might be termed *traditional UNIX systems*; [VAHA96] uses this term to refer to System V Release 3 (SVR3), 4.3BSD, and earlier versions. The following general statements may be

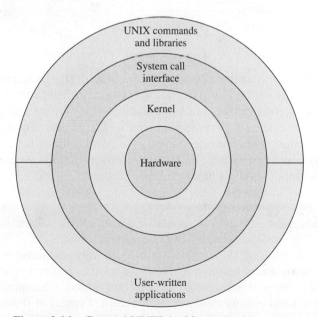

Figure 2.16   General UNIX Architecture

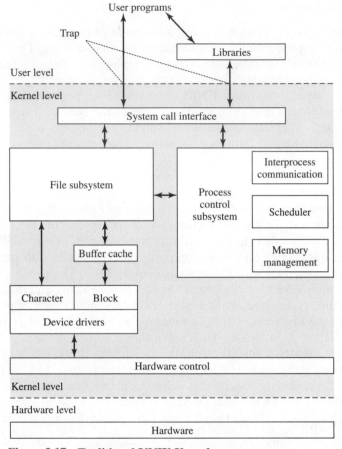

Figure 2.17   Traditional UNIX Kernel

made about a traditional UNIX system. It is designed to run on a single processor and lacks the ability to protect its data structures from concurrent access by multiple processors. Its kernel is not very versatile, supporting a single type of file system, process scheduling policy, and executable file format. The traditional UNIX kernel is not designed to be extensible and has few facilities for code reuse. The result is that, as new features were added to the various UNIX versions, much new code had to be added, yielding a bloated and unmodular kernel.

2.9   MODERN UNIX SYSTEMS

As UNIX evolved, the number of different implementations proliferated, each providing some useful features. There was a need to produce a new implementation that unified many of the important innovations, added other modern OS design features, and produced a more modular architecture. Typical of the modern UNIX kernel is the architecture depicted in Figure 2.18. There is a small core of facilities, written in

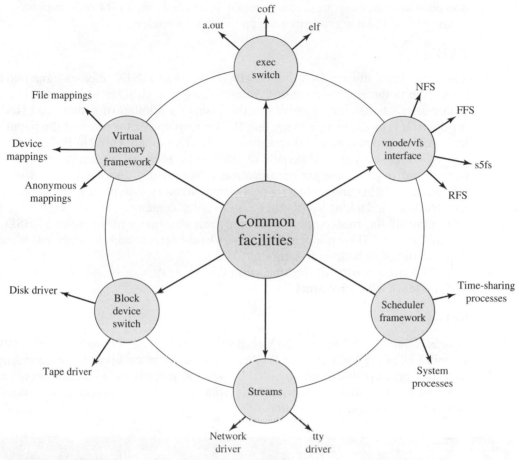

Figure 2.18   Modern UNIX Kernel

a modular fashion, that provide functions and services needed by a number of OS processes. Each of the outer circles represents functions and an interface that may be implemented in a variety of ways.

We now turn to some examples of modern UNIX systems.

System V Release 4 (SVR4)

SVR4, developed jointly by AT&T and Sun Microsystems, combines features from SVR3, 4.3BSD, Microsoft Xenix System V, and SunOS. It was almost a total rewrite of the System V kernel and produced a clean, if complex, implementation. New features in the release include real-time processing support, process scheduling classes, dynamically allocated data structures, virtual memory management, virtual file system, and a preemptive kernel.

SVR4 draws on the efforts of both commercial and academic designers and was developed to provide a uniform platform for commercial UNIX deployment. It has succeeded in this objective and is perhaps the most important UNIX variant. It incorporates most of the important features ever developed on any UNIX system and does so in an integrated, commercially viable fashion. SVR4 runs on processors ranging from 32-bit microprocessors up to supercomputers.

BSD

The Berkeley Software Distribution (BSD) series of UNIX releases have played a key role in the development of OS design theory. 4.xBSD is widely used in academic installations and has served as the basis of a number of commercial UNIX products. It is probably safe to say that BSD is responsible for much of the popularity of UNIX and that most enhancements to UNIX first appeared in BSD versions.

4.4BSD was the final version of BSD to be released by Berkeley, with the design and implementation organization subsequently dissolved. It is a major upgrade to 4.3BSD and includes a new virtual memory system, changes in the kernel structure, and a long list of other feature enhancements.

One of the most widely used and best documented versions of BSD is FreeBSD. FreeBSD is popular for Internet-based servers and firewalls and is used in a number of embedded systems.

The latest version of the Macintosh OS, Mac OS X, is based on FreeBSD 5.0 and the Mach 3.0 microkernel.

Solaris 10

Solaris is Sun's SVR4-based UNIX release, with the latest version being 10. Solaris provides all of the features of SVR4 plus a number of more advanced features, such as a fully preemptable, multithreaded kernel, full support for SMP, and an object-oriented interface to file systems. Solaris is the most widely used and most successful commercial UNIX implementation.

2.10 LINUX

History

Linux started out as a UNIX variant for the IBM PC (Intel 80386) architecture. Linus Torvalds, a Finnish student of computer science, wrote the initial version. Torvalds posted an early version of Linux on the Internet in 1991. Since then, a number of people, collaborating over the Internet, have contributed to the development of Linux, all under the control of Torvalds. Because Linux is free and the source code is available, it became an early alternative to other UNIX workstations, such as those offered by Sun Microsystems and IBM. Today, Linux is a full-featured UNIX system that runs on all of these platforms and more, including Intel Pentium and Itanium, and the Motorola/IBM PowerPC.

Key to the success of Linux has been the availability of free software packages under the auspices of the Free Software Foundation (FSF). FSF's goal is stable, platform-independent software that is free, high quality, and embraced by the user community. FSF's GNU project[3] provides tools for software developers, and the

---

[3]GNU is a recursive acronym for *GNU's Not Unix*. The GNU project is a free software set of packages and tools for developing a UNIX-like operating system; it is often used with the Linux kernel.

GNU Public License (GPL) is the FSF seal of approval. Torvalds used GNU tools in developing his kernel, which he then released under the GPL. Thus, the Linux distributions that you see today are the product of FSF's GNU project, Torvald's individual effort, and the efforts of many collaborators all over the world.

In addition to its use by many individual programmers, Linux has now made significant penetration into the corporate world. This is not only because of the free software, but also because of the quality of the Linux kernel. Many talented programmers have contributed to the current version, resulting in a technically impressive product. Moreover, Linux is highly modular and easily configured. This makes it easy to squeeze optimal performance from a variety of hardware platforms. Plus, with the source code available, vendors can tweak applications and utilities to meet specific requirements. Throughout this book, we will provide details of Linux kernel internals based on the most recent version, Linux 2.6.

Modular Structure

Most UNIX kernels are monolithic. Recall from earlier in this chapter that a monolithic kernel is one that includes virtually all of the OS functionality in one large block of code that runs as a single process with a single address space. All the functional components of the kernel have access to all of its internal data structures and routines. If changes are made to any portion of a typical monolithic OS, all the modules and routines must be relinked and reinstalled and the system rebooted before the changes can take effect. As a result, any modification, such as adding a new device driver or file system function, is difficult. This problem is especially acute for Linux, for which development is global and done by a loosely associated group of independent programmers.

Although Linux does not use a microkernel approach, it achieves many of the potential advantages of this approach by means of its particular modular architecture. Linux is structured as a collection of modules, a number of which can be automatically loaded and unloaded on demand. These relatively independent blocks are referred to as **loadable modules** [GOYE99]. In essence, a module is an object file whose code can be linked to and unlinked from the kernel at runtime. Typically, a module implements some specific function, such as a file system, a device driver, or some other feature of the kernel's upper layer. A module does not execute as its own process or thread, although it can create kernel threads for various purposes as necessary. Rather, a module is executed in kernel mode on behalf of the current process.

Thus, although Linux may be considered monolithic, its modular structure overcomes some of the difficulties in developing and evolving the kernel.

The Linux loadable modules have two important characteristics:

- **Dynamic linking:** A kernel module can be loaded and linked into the kernel while the kernel is already in memory and executing. A module can also be unlinked and removed from memory at any time.

- **Stackable modules:** The modules are arranged in a hierarchy. Individual modules serve as libraries when they are referenced by client modules higher up in the hierarchy, and as clients when they reference modules further down.

Dynamic linking [FRAN97] facilitates configuration and saves kernel memory. In Linux, a user program or user can explicitly load and unload kernel modules using the insmod and rmmod commands. The kernel itself monitors the need for particular functions and can load and unload modules as needed. With stackable modules, dependencies between modules can be defined. This has two benefits:

1. Code common to a set of similar modules (e.g., drivers for similar hardware) can be moved into a single module, reducing replication.

2. The kernel can make sure that needed modules are present, refraining from unloading a module on which other running modules depend, and loading any additional required modules when a new module is loaded.

Figure 2.19 is an example that illustrates the structures used by Linux to manage modules. The figure shows the list of kernel modules after only two modules have been loaded: FAT and VFAT. Each module is defined by two tables, the module table and the symbol table. The module table includes the following elements:

- ***next:** Pointer to the following module. All modules are organized into a linked list. The list begins with a pseudomodule (not shown in Figure 2.19).
- ***name:** Pointer to module name
- **size:** Module size in memory pages
- **usecount:** Module usage counter. The counter is incremented when an operation involving the module's functions is started and decremented when the operation terminates.

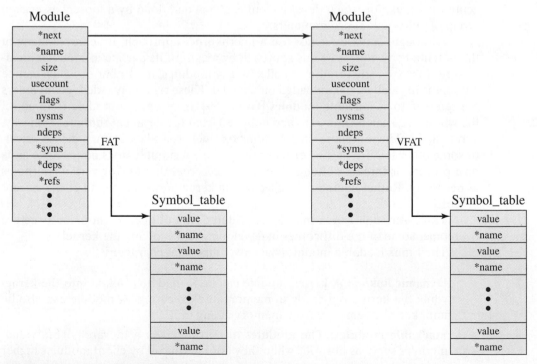

Figure 2.19 **Example List of Linux Kernel Modules**

- **flags:** Module flags
- **nsyms:** Number of exported symbols
- **ndeps:** Number of referenced modules
- ***syms:** Pointer to this module's symbol table.
- ***deps:** Pointer to list of modules that are referenced by this module.
- ***refs:** Pointer to list of modules that use this module.

The symbol table defines those symbols controlled by this module that are used elsewhere.

Figure 2.19 shows that the VFAT module was loaded after the FAT module and that the VFAT module is dependent on the FAT module.

Kernel Components

Figure 2.20, taken from [MOSB02], shows the main components of the Linux kernel as implemented on an IA-64 architecture (e.g., Intel Itanium). The figure shows several processes running on top of the kernel. Each box indicates a separate process, while each squiggly line with an arrowhead represents a thread of execution.[4] The kernel itself consists of an interacting collection of components, with arrows

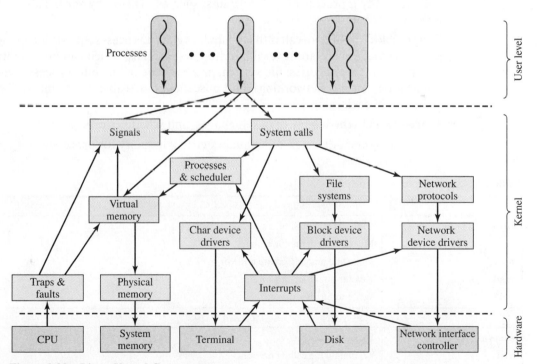

Figure 2.20   Linux Kernel Components

---

[4]In Linux, there is no distinction between the concepts of processes and threads. However, multiple threads in Linux can be grouped together in such a way that, effectively, you can have a single process comprising multiple threads. These matters are discussed in Chapter 4.

Table 2.5 Some Linux Signals

SIGHUP	Terminal hangup	SIGCONT	Continue
SIGQUIT	Keyboard quit	SIGTSTP	Keyboard stop
SIGTRAP	Trace trap	SIGTTOU	Terminal write
SIGBUS	Bus error	SIGXCPU	CPU limit exceeded
SIGKILL	Kill signal	SIGVTALRM	Virtual alarm clock
SIGSEGV	Segmentation violation	SIGWINCH	Window size unchanged
SIGPIPT	Broken pipe	SIGPWR	Power failure
SIGTERM	Termination	SIGRTMIN	First real-time signal
SIGCHLD	Child status unchanged	SIGRTMAX	Last real-time signal

indicating the main interactions. The underlying hardware is also depicted as a set of components with arrows indicating which kernel components use or control which hardware components. All of the kernel components, of course, execute on the processor but, for simplicity, these relationships are not shown.

Briefly, the principal kernel components are the following:

- **Signals:** The kernel uses signals to call into a process. For example, signals are used to notify a process of certain faults, such as division by zero. Table 2.5 gives a few examples of signals.

- **System calls:** The system call is the means by which a process requests a specific kernel service. There are several hundred system calls, which can be roughly grouped into six categories: file system, process, scheduling, interprocess communication, socket (networking), and miscellaneous. Table 2.6 defines a few examples in each category.

- **Processes and scheduler:** Creates, manages, and schedules processes.

- **Virtual memory:** Allocates and manages virtual memory for processes.

Table 2.6 Some Linux System Calls

File system Related	
close	Close a file descriptor.
link	Make a new name for a file.
open	Open and possibly create a file or device.
read	Read from file descriptor.
write	Write to file descriptor.
Process Related	
execve	Execute program.
exit	Terminate the calling process.
getpid	Get process identification.
setuid	Set user identity of the current process.
prtrace	Provides a means by which a parent process may observe and control the execution of another process, and examine and change its core image and registers.

Table 2.6 (*continued*)

Scheduling Related	
sched_getparam	Set the scheduling parameters associated with the scheduling policy for the process identified by `pid`.
sched_get_priority_max	Return the maximum priority value that can be used with the scheduling algorithm identified by `policy`.
sched_setscheduler	Set both the scheduling policy (e.g., FIFO) and the associated parameters for the process `pid`.
sched_rr_get_interval	Write into the timespec structure pointed to by the parameter `tp` the round-robin time quantum for the process `pid`.
sched_yield	A process can relinquish the processor voluntarily without blocking via this system call. The process will then be moved to the end of the queue for its static priority and a new process gets to run.

Interprocess Communication (IPC) Related	
msgrcv	A message buffer structure is allocated to receive a message. The system call then reads a message from the message queue specified by msqid into the newly created message buffer.
semctl	Perform the control operation specified by `cmd` on the semaphore set `semid`.
semop	Perform operations on selected members of the semaphore set `semid`.
shmat	Attach the shared memory segment identified by `semid` to the data segment of the calling process.
shmctl	Allow the user to receive information on a shared memory segment; set the owner, group, and permissions of a shared memory segment; or destroy a segment.

Socket (networking) Related	
bind	Assigns the local IP address and port for a socket. Returns 0 for success and −1 for error.
connect	Establish a connection between the given socket and the remote socket associated with sockaddr.
gethostname	Return local host name.
send	Send the bytes contained in buffer pointed to by *msg over the given socket.
setsockopt	Set the options on a socket

Miscellaneous	
create_module	Attempt to create a loadable module entry and reserve the kernel memory that will be needed to hold the module.
fsync	Copy all in-core parts of a file to disk, and waits until the device reports that all parts are on stable storage.
query_module	Request information related to loadable modules from the kernel.
time	Return the time in seconds since January 1, 1970.
vhangup	Simulate a hangup on the current terminal. This call arranges for other users to have a "clean" tty at login time.

- **File systems:** Provides a global, hierarchical namespace for files, directories, and other file related objects and provides file system functions.

- **Network protocols:** Supports the Sockets interface to users for the TCP/IP protocol suite.

- **Character device drivers:** Manages devices that require the kernel to send or receive data one byte at a time, such as terminals, modems, and printers.

- **Block device drivers:** Manages devices that read and write data in blocks, such as various forms of secondary memory (magnetic disks, CD-ROMs, etc.).

- **Network device drivers:** Manages network interface cards and communications ports that connect to network devices, such as bridges and routers.

- **Traps and faults:** Handles traps and faults generated by the processor, such as a memory fault.

- **Physical memory:** Manages the pool of page frames in real memory and allocates pages for virtual memory.

- **Interrupts:** Handles interrupts from peripheral devices.

2.11 LINUX VSERVER VIRTUAL MACHINE ARCHITECTURE

Linux VServer is an open-source, fast, lightweight approach to implementing virtual machines on a Linux server [SOLT07, LIGN05]. Only a single copy of the Linux kernel is involved. VServer consists of a relatively modest modification to the kernel plus a small set of OS userland[5] tools. The VServer Linux kernel supports a number of separate *virtual servers*. The kernel manages all system resources and tasks, including process scheduling, memory, disk space, and processor time. This is closer in concept to the process VM rather than the system VM of Figure 2.14.

Each virtual server is isolated from the others using Linux kernel capabilities. This provides security and makes it easy to set up multiple virtual machines on a single platform. The isolation involves four elements: chroot, chcontext, chbind, and capabilities.

The **chroot** command is a UNIX or Linux command to make the root directory (/) become something other than its default for the lifetime of the current process. It can only be run by privileged users and is used to give a process (commonly a network server such as FTP or HTTP) access to a restricted portion of the file system. This command provides **file system isolation**. All commands executed by the virtual server can only affect files that start with the defined root for that server.

The **chcontext** Linux utility allocates a new security context and executes commands in that context. The usual or *hosted* security context is the context 0. This context has the same privileges as the root user (UID 0): This context can see and kill other tasks in the other contexts. Context number 1 is used to view

---

[5]The term *userland* refers to all application software that runs in user space rather than kernel space. *OS userland* usually refers to the various programs and libraries that the operating system uses to interact with the kernel: software that performs input/output, manipulates file system objects, etc.

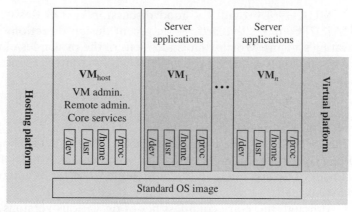

Figure 2.21   Linux VServer Architecture

other contexts but cannot affect them. All other contexts provide complete isolation: Processes from one context can neither see nor interact with processes from another context. This provides the ability to run similar contexts on the same computer without any interaction possible at the application level. Thus, each virtual server has its own execution context that provides **process isolation**.

The **chbind** utility executes a command, and locks the resulting process and its children into using a specific IP address. Once called, all packets sent out by this virtual server through the system's network interface are assigned the sending IP address derived from the argument given to chbind. This system call provides **network isolation**: Each virtual server uses a separate and distinct IP address. Incoming traffic intended for one virtual server cannot be accessed by other virtual servers.

Finally, each virtual server is assigned a set of **capabilities**. The concept of capabilities, as used in Linux, refers to a partitioning of the privileges available to a root user, such as the ability to read files or to trace processes owned by another user. Thus, each virtual server can be assigned a limited subset of the root user's privileges. This provides **root isolation**. VServer can also set resource limits, such as limits to the amount of virtual memory a process may use.

Figure 2.21, based on [SOLT07], shows the general architecture of Linux VServer. VServer provides a shared, virtualized OS image, consisting of a root file system, and a shared set of system libraries and kernel services. Each VM can be booted, shut down, and rebooted independently. Figure 2.21 shows three groupings of software running on the computer system. The **hosting platform** includes the shared OS image and a privileged host VM, whose function is to monitor and manage the other VMs. The **virtual platform** creates virtual machines and is the view of the system seen by the **applications** running on the individual VMs.

2.12 RECOMMENDED READING AND WEB SITES

[BRIN01] is an excellent collection of papers covering major advances in OS design over the years. [SWAI07] is a provocative and interesting short article on the future of operating systems.

[MUKH96] provides a good discussion of OS design issues for SMPs. [CHAP97] contains five articles on recent design directions for multiprocessor operating systems. Worthwhile discussions of the principles of microkernel design are contained in [LIED95] and [LIED96]; the latter focuses on performance issues.

[LI10] and [SMIT05] provide good treatments of virtual machines.

An excellent treatment of UNIX internals, which provides a comparative analysis of a number of variants, is [VAHA96]. For UNIX SVR4, [GOOD94] provides a definitive treatment, with ample technical detail. For the popular open-source FreeBSD, [MCKU05] is highly recommended. [MCDO07] provides a good treatment of Solaris internals. Good treatments of Linux internals are [LOVE10] and [MAUE08].

Although there are countless books on various versions of Windows, there is remarkably little material available on Windows internals. The book to read is [RUSS11].

BRIN01 Brinch Hansen, P. *Classic Operating Systems: From Batch Processing to Distributed Systems.* New York: Springer-Verlag, 2001.

CHAP97 Chapin, S., and Maccabe, A., eds. "Multiprocessor Operating Systems: Harnessing the Power." special issue of *IEEE Concurrency*, April–June 1997.

GOOD94 Goodheart, B., and Cox, J. *The Magic Garden Explained: The Internals of UNIX System V Release 4.* Englewood Cliffs, NJ: Prentice Hall, 1994.

LOVE10 Love, R. *Linux Kernel Development.* Upper Saddle River, NJ: Addison-Wesley, 2010.

LI10 Li, Y.; Li, W.; and Jiang, C. "A Survey of Virtual Machine Systems: Current Technology and Future Trends." *Proceedings, Third International Symposium on Electronic Commerce and Security*, 2010.

LIED95 Liedtke, J. "On μ-Kernel Construction." *Proceedings of the Fifteenth ACM Symposium on Operating Systems Principles*, December 1995.

LIED96 Liedtke, J. "Toward Real Microkernels." *Communications of the ACM*, September 1996.

MAUE08 Mauerer, W. *Professional Linux Kernel Architecture.* New York: Wiley, 2008.

MCDO07 McDougall, R., and Mauro, J. *Solaris Internals: Solaris 10 and OpenSolaris Kernel Architecture.* Palo Alto, CA: Sun Microsystems Press, 2007.

MCKU05 McKusick, M., and Neville-Neil, J. *The Design and Implementation of the FreeBSD Operating System.* Reading, MA: Addison-Wesley, 2005.

MUKH96 Mukherjee, B., and Karsten, S. "Operating Systems for Parallel Machines." In *Parallel Computers: Theory and Practice.* Edited by T. Casavant, P. Tvrkik, and F. Plasil. Los Alamitos, CA: IEEE Computer Society Press, 1996.

RUSS11 Russinovich, M.; Solomon, D.; and Ionescu, A. *Windows Internals: Covering Windows 7 and Windows Server 2008 R2.* Redmond, WA: Microsoft Press, 2011.

SMIT05 Smith, J., and Nair, R. "The Architecture of Virtual Machines." *Computer*, May 2005.

SWAI07 Swaine, M. "Wither Operating Systems?" *Dr. Dobb's Journal*, March 2007.

VAHA96 Vahalia, U. *UNIX Internals: The New Frontiers.* Upper Saddle River, NJ: Prentice Hall, 1996.

Recommended Web sites:

- **The Operating System Resource Center:** A useful collection of documents and papers on a wide range of OS topics.
- **Operating System Technical Comparison:** Includes a substantial amount of information on a variety of operating systems.
- **ACM Special Interest Group on Operating Systems:** Information on SIGOPS publications and conferences.
- **IEEE Technical Committee on Operating Systems and Application Environments:** Includes an online newsletter and links to other sites.
- **The comp.os.research FAQ:** Lengthy and worthwhile FAQ covering OS design issues.
- **UNIX Guru Universe:** Excellent source of UNIX information.
- **Linux Documentation Project:** The name describes the site.
- **IBM's Linux Website:** Provides a wide range of technical and user information on Linux. Much of it is devoted to IBM products but there is a lot of useful general technical information.
- **Windows Development:** Good source of information on Windows internals.

2.13 KEY TERMS, REVIEW QUESTIONS, AND PROBLEMS

Key Terms

batch processing	multiprogramming	round robin
batch system	multitasking	scheduling
execution context	multithreading	serial processing
interrupt	nucleus	symmetric multiprocessing
job	operating system	task
job control language	physical address	thread
kernel	privileged instruction	time sharing
memory management	process	time-sharing system
microkernel	process state	uniprogramming
monitor	real address	virtual address
monolithic kernel	resident monitor	virtual machine
multiprogrammed batch system		

Review Questions

2.1 What are three objectives of an OS design?

2.2 What is the kernel of an OS?

2.3 What is multiprogramming?

2.4 What is a process?

2.5 How is the execution context of a process used by the OS?

2.6 List and briefly explain five storage management responsibilities of a typical OS.

2.7 Explain the distinction between a real address and a virtual address.

2.8 Describe the round-robin scheduling technique.

2.9 Explain the difference between a monolithic kernel and a microkernel.

2.10 What is multithreading?

2.11 List the key design issues for an SMP operating system.

Problems

2.1 Suppose that we have a multiprogrammed computer in which each job has identical characteristics. In one computation period, T, for a job, half the time is spent in I/O and the other half in processor activity. Each job runs for a total of N periods. Assume that a simple round-robin scheduling is used, and that I/O operations can overlap with processor operation. Define the following quantities:

- Turnaround time = actual time to complete a job
- Throughput = average number of jobs completed per time period T
- Processor utilization = percentage of time that the processor is active (not waiting)

Compute these quantities for one, two, and four simultaneous jobs, assuming that the period T is distributed in each of the following ways:

a. I/O first half, processor second half

b. I/O first and fourth quarters, processor second and third quarter

2.2 An I/O-bound program is one that, if run alone, would spend more time waiting for I/O than using the processor. A processor-bound program is the opposite. Suppose a short-term scheduling algorithm favors those programs that have used little processor time in the recent past. Explain why this algorithm favors I/O-bound programs and yet does not permanently deny processor time to processor-bound programs.

2.3 Contrast the scheduling policies you might use when trying to optimize a time-sharing system with those you would use to optimize a multiprogrammed batch system.

2.4 What is the purpose of system calls, and how do system calls relate to the OS and to the concept of dual-mode (kernel-mode and user-mode) operation?

2.5 In IBM's mainframe OS, OS/390, one of the major modules in the kernel is the System Resource Manager. This module is responsible for the allocation of resources among address spaces (processes). The SRM gives OS/390 a degree of sophistication unique among operating systems. No other mainframe OS, and certainly no other type of OS, can match the functions performed by SRM. The concept of resource includes processor, real memory, and I/O channels. SRM accumulates statistics pertaining to utilization of processor, channel, and various key data structures. Its purpose is to provide optimum performance based on performance monitoring and analysis. The installation sets forth various performance objectives, and these serve as guidance to the SRM, which dynamically modifies installation and job performance characteristics based on system utilization. In turn, the SRM provides reports that enable the trained operator to refine the configuration and parameter settings to improve user service.

This problem concerns one example of SRM activity. Real memory is divided into equal-sized blocks called frames, of which there may be many thousands. Each frame can hold a block of virtual memory referred to as a page. SRM receives control approximately 20 times per second and inspects each and every page frame. If the page has not been referenced or changed, a counter is incremented by 1. Over time, SRM averages these numbers to determine the average number of seconds that a page frame in the system goes untouched. What might be the purpose of this and what action might SRM take?

2.6 A multiprocessor with eight processors has 20 attached tape drives. There is a large number of jobs submitted to the system that each require a maximum of four tape drives to complete execution. Assume that each job starts running with only three tape drives for a long period before requiring the fourth tape drive for a short period toward the end of its operation. Also assume an endless supply of such jobs.

a. Assume the scheduler in the OS will not start a job unless there are four tape drives available. When a job is started, four drives are assigned immediately and are not released until the job finishes. What is the maximum number of jobs that can be in progress at once? What are the maximum and minimum number of tape drives that may be left idle as a result of this policy?

b. Suggest an alternative policy to improve tape drive utilization and at the same time avoid system deadlock. What is the maximum number of jobs that can be in progress at once? What are the bounds on the number of idling tape drives?

PART 2 Processes

CHAPTER 3

PROCESS DESCRIPTION AND CONTROL

3.1 What Is a Process?
Background
Processes and Process Control Blocks

3.2 Process States
A Two-State Process Model
The Creation and Termination of Processes
A Five-State Model
Suspended Processes

3.3 Process Description
Operating System Control Structures
Process Control Structures

3.4 Process Control
Modes of Execution
Process Creation
Process Switching

3.5 Execution of the Operating System
Nonprocess Kernel
Execution within User Processes
Process-Based Operating System

3.6 Security Issues
System Access Threats
Countermeasures

3.7 UNIX SVR4 Process Management
Process States
Process Description
Process Control

3.8 Summary

3.9 Recommended Reading

3.10 Key Terms, Review Questions, and Problems

The concept of process is fundamental to the structure of modern computer operating systems. Its evolution in analyzing problems of synchronization, deadlock, and scheduling in operating systems has been a major intellectual contribution of computer science.

WHAT CAN BE AUTOMATED?: THE COMPUTER SCIENCE AND ENGINEERING
RESEARCH STUDY, MIT PRESS, 1980

LEARNING OBJECTIVES

After studying this chapter, you should be able to:

- Define the term *process* and explain the relationship between processes and process control blocks.
- Explain the concept of a process state and discuss the state transitions the processes undergo.
- List and describe the purpose of the data structures and data structure elements used by an OS to manage processes.
- Assess the requirements for process control by the OS.
- Understand the issues involved in the execution of OS code.
- Assess the key security issues that relate to operating systems.
- Describe the process management scheme for UNIX SVR4.

All multiprogramming operating systems, from single-user systems such as Windows for end users to mainframe systems such as IBM's mainframe operating system, z/OS, which can support thousands of users, are built around the concept of the process. Most requirements that the OS must meet can be expressed with reference to processes:

- The OS must interleave the execution of multiple processes, to maximize processor utilization while providing reasonable response time.
- The OS must allocate resources to processes in conformance with a specific policy (e.g., certain functions or applications are of higher priority) while at the same time avoiding deadlock.[1]
- The OS may be required to support interprocess communication and user creation of processes, both of which may aid in the structuring of applications.

We begin with an examination of the way in which the OS represents and controls processes. Then, the chapter discusses process states, which characterize the behavior of processes. Then we look at the data structures that the OS uses to manage processes. These include data structures to represent the state of each

---

[1]Deadlock is examined in Chapter 6. As a simple example, deadlock occurs if two processes need the same two resources to continue and each has ownership of one. Unless some action is taken, each process will wait indefinitely for the missing resource.

process and data structures that record other characteristics of processes that the OS needs to achieve its objectives. Next, we look at the ways in which the OS uses these data structures to control process execution. Finally, we discuss process management in UNIX SVR4. Chapter 4 provides more modern examples of process management.

This chapter occasionally refers to virtual memory. Much of the time, we can ignore this concept in dealing with processes, but at certain points in the discussion, virtual memory considerations are pertinent. Virtual memory is previewed in Chapter 2 and discussed in detail in Chapter 8. A set of animations that illustrate concepts in this chapter is available online. Click on the rotating globe at this book's Web site at WilliamStallings.com/OS/OS7e.html for access.

3.1 WHAT IS A PROCESS?

Background

Before defining the term *process*, it is useful to summarize some of the concepts introduced in Chapters 1 and 2:

1. A computer platform consists of a collection of hardware resources, such as the processor, main memory, I/O modules, timers, disk drives, and so on.

2. Computer applications are developed to perform some task. Typically, they accept input from the outside world, perform some processing, and generate output.

3. It is inefficient for applications to be written directly for a given hardware platform. The principal reasons for this are as follows:

   a. Numerous applications can be developed for the same platform. Thus, it makes sense to develop common routines for accessing the computer's resources.

   b. The processor itself provides only limited support for multiprogramming. Software is needed to manage the sharing of the processor and other resources by multiple applications at the same time.

   c. When multiple applications are active at the same time, it is necessary to protect the data, I/O use, and other resource use of each application from the others.

4. The OS was developed to provide a convenient, feature-rich, secure, and consistent interface for applications to use. The OS is a layer of software between the applications and the computer hardware (Figure 2.1) that supports applications and utilities.

5. We can think of the OS as providing a uniform, abstract representation of resources that can be requested and accessed by applications. Resources include main memory, network interfaces, file systems, and so on. Once the OS has created these resource abstractions for applications to use, it must also manage their use. For example, an OS may permit resource sharing and resource protection.

Now that we have the concepts of applications, system software, and resources, we are in a position to discuss how the OS can, in an orderly fashion, manage the execution of applications so that

- Resources are made available to multiple applications.
- The physical processor is switched among multiple applications so all will appear to be progressing.
- The processor and I/O devices can be used efficiently.

The approach taken by all modern operating systems is to rely on a model in which the execution of an application corresponds to the existence of one or more processes.

Processes and Process Control Blocks

Recall from Chapter 2 that we suggested several definitions of the term *process*, including

- A program in execution
- An instance of a program running on a computer
- The entity that can be assigned to and executed on a processor
- A unit of activity characterized by the execution of a sequence of instructions, a current state, and an associated set of system resources

We can also think of a process as an entity that consists of a number of elements. Two essential elements of a process are **program code** (which may be shared with other processes that are executing the same program) and a **set of data** associated with that code. Let us suppose that the processor begins to execute this program code, and we refer to this executing entity as a process. At any given point in time, *while the program is executing*, this process can be uniquely characterized by a number of elements, including the following:

- **Identifier:** A unique identifier associated with this process, to distinguish it from all other processes.
- **State:** If the process is currently executing, it is in the running state.
- **Priority:** Priority level relative to other processes.
- **Program counter:** The address of the next instruction in the program to be executed.
- **Memory pointers:** Includes pointers to the program code and data associated with this process, plus any memory blocks shared with other processes.
- **Context data:** These are data that are present in registers in the processor while the process is executing.
- **I/O status information:** Includes outstanding I/O requests, I/O devices (e.g., disk drives) assigned to this process, a list of files in use by the process, and so on.
- **Accounting information:** May include the amount of processor time and clock time used, time limits, account numbers, and so on.

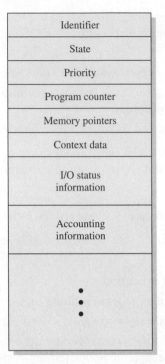

Figure 3.1 Simplified Process Control Block

The information in the preceding list is stored in a data structure, typically called a **process control block** (Figure 3.1), that is created and managed by the OS. The significant point about the process control block is that it contains sufficient information so that it is possible to interrupt a running process and later resume execution as if the interruption had not occurred. The process control block is the key tool that enables the OS to support multiple processes and to provide for multiprocessing. When a process is interrupted, the current values of the program counter and the processor registers (context data) are saved in the appropriate fields of the corresponding process control block, and the state of the process is changed to some other value, such as *blocked* or *ready* (described subsequently). The OS is now free to put some other process in the running state. The program counter and context data for this process are loaded into the processor registers and this process now begins to execute.

Thus, we can say that a process consists of program code and associated data plus a process control block. For a single-processor computer, at any given time, at most one process is executing and that process is in the *running* state.

3.2 PROCESS STATES

As just discussed, for a program to be executed, a process, or task, is created for that program. From the processor's point of view, it executes instructions from its repertoire in some sequence dictated by the changing values in the program counter

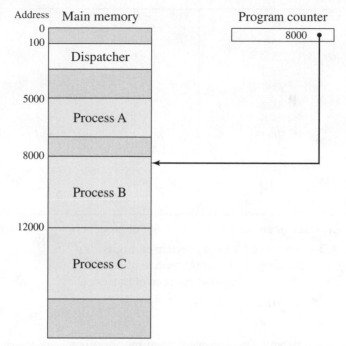

**Figure 3.2 Snapshot of Example Execution (Figure 3.4)
at Instruction Cycle 13**

register. Over time, the program counter may refer to code in different programs that are part of different processes. From the point of view of an individual program, its execution involves a sequence of instructions within that program.

We can characterize the behavior of an individual process by listing the sequence of instructions that execute for that process. Such a listing is referred to as a **trace** of the process. We can characterize behavior of the processor by showing how the traces of the various processes are interleaved.

Let us consider a very simple example. Figure 3.2 shows a memory layout of three processes. To simplify the discussion, we assume no use of virtual memory; thus all three processes are represented by programs that are fully loaded in main memory. In addition, there is a small **dispatcher** program that switches the processor from one process to another. Figure 3.3 shows the traces of each of the processes during the early part of their execution. The first 12 instructions executed in processes A and C are shown. Process B executes four instructions, and we assume that the fourth instruction invokes an I/O operation for which the process must wait.

Now let us view these traces from the processor's point of view. Figure 3.4 shows the interleaved traces resulting from the first 52 instruction cycles (for convenience, the instruction cycles are numbered). In this figure, the shaded areas represent code executed by the dispatcher. The same sequence of instructions is executed by the dispatcher in each instance because the same functionality of the dispatcher is being executed. We assume that the OS only allows a process to continue execution for a maximum of six instruction cycles, after which it is interrupted;

5000	8000	12000
5001	8001	12001
5002	8002	12002
5003	8003	12003
5004		12004
5005		12005
5006		12006
5007		12007
5008		12008
5009		12009
5010		12010
5011		12011

(a) Trace of process A   (b) Trace of process B   (c) Trace of process C

5000 = Starting address of program of process A
8000 = Starting address of program of process B
12000 = Starting address of program of process C

Figure 3.3   Traces of Processes of Figure 3.2

this prevents any single process from monopolizing processor time. As Figure 3.4 shows, the first six instructions of process A are executed, followed by a time-out and the execution of some code in the dispatcher, which executes six instructions before turning control to process B.[2] After four instructions are executed, process B requests an I/O action for which it must wait. Therefore, the processor stops executing process B and moves on, via the dispatcher, to process C. After a time-out, the processor moves back to process A. When this process times out, process B is still waiting for the I/O operation to complete, so the dispatcher moves on to process C again.

A Two–State Process Model

The operating system's principal responsibility is controlling the execution of processes; this includes determining the interleaving pattern for execution and allocating resources to processes. The first step in designing an OS to control processes is to describe the behavior that we would like the processes to exhibit.

We can construct the simplest possible model by observing that, at any time, a process is either being executed by a processor or not. In this model, a process may be in one of two states: Running or Not Running, as shown in Figure 3.5a. When the OS creates a new process, it creates a process control block for the process and enters that process into the system in the Not Running state. The process exists, is known to the OS, and is waiting for an opportunity to execute. From time to time, the currently running process will be interrupted and the dispatcher portion of the OS will select some other process to run. The former process moves from the

---

[2]The small number of instructions executed for the processes and the dispatcher are unrealistically low; they are used in this simplified example to clarify the discussion.

1	5000		27	12004
2	5001		28	12005
3	5002		----------------------Time-out	
4	5003		29	100
5	5004		30	101
6	5005		31	102
----------------------Time-out			32	103
7	100		33	104
8	101		34	105
9	102		35	5006
10	103		36	5007
11	104		37	5008
12	105		38	5009
13	8000		39	5010
14	8001		40	5011
15	8002		----------------------Time-out	
16	8003		41	100
----------------------I/O request			42	101
17	100		43	102
18	101		44	103
19	102		45	104
20	103		46	105
21	104		47	12006
22	105		48	12007
23	12000		49	12008
24	12001		50	12009
25	12002		51	12010
26	12003		52	12011
			----------------------Time-out	

100 = Starting address of dispatcher program

Shaded areas indicate execution of dispatcher process;
first and third columns count instruction cycles;
second and fourth columns show address of instruction being executed

Figure 3.4 Combined Trace of Processes of Figure 3.2

Running state to the Not Running state, and one of the other processes moves to the Running state.

From this simple model, we can already begin to appreciate some of the design elements of the OS. Each process must be represented in some way so that the OS can keep track of it. That is, there must be some information relating to each process, including current state and location in memory; this is the process control block. Processes that are not running must be kept in some sort of queue, waiting their turn to execute. Figure 3.5b suggests a structure. There is a single queue in which each entry is a pointer to the process control block of a particular process. Alternatively,

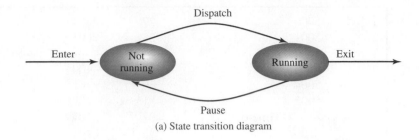

(a) State transition diagram

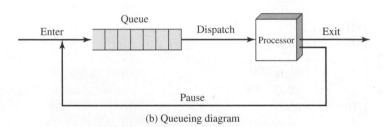

(b) Queueing diagram

Figure 3.5   Two-State Process Model

the queue may consist of a linked list of data blocks, in which each block represents one process; we will explore this latter implementation subsequently.

We can describe the behavior of the dispatcher in terms of this queueing diagram. A process that is interrupted is transferred to the queue of waiting processes. Alternatively, if the process has completed or aborted, it is discarded (exits the system). In either case, the dispatcher takes another process from the queue to execute.

The Creation and Termination of Processes

Before refining our simple two-state model, it will be useful to discuss the creation and termination of processes; ultimately, and regardless of the model of process behavior that is used, the life of a process is bounded by its creation and termination.

PROCESS CREATION   When a new process is to be added to those currently being managed, the OS builds the data structures that are used to manage the process and allocates address space in main memory to the process. We describe these data structures in Section 3.3. These actions constitute the creation of a new process.

Four common events lead to the creation of a process, as indicated in Table 3.1. In a batch environment, a process is created in response to the submission of a job. In an interactive environment, a process is created when a new user attempts to log on. In both cases, the OS is responsible for the creation of the new process. An OS may also create a process on behalf of an application. For example, if a user requests that a file be printed, the OS can create a process that will manage the printing. The requesting process can thus proceed independently of the time required to complete the printing task.

Table 3.1 Reasons for Process Creation

New batch job	The OS is provided with a batch job control stream, usually on tape or disk. When the OS is prepared to take on new work, it will read the next sequence of job control commands.
Interactive log-on	A user at a terminal logs on to the system.
Created by OS to provide a service	The OS can create a process to perform a function on behalf of a user program, without the user having to wait (e.g., a process to control printing).
Spawned by existing process	For purposes of modularity or to exploit parallelism, a user program can dictate the creation of a number of processes.

Traditionally, the OS created all processes in a way that was transparent to the user or application program, and this is still commonly found with many contemporary operating systems. However, it can be useful to allow one process to cause the creation of another. For example, an application process may generate another process to receive data that the application is generating and to organize those data into a form suitable for later analysis. The new process runs in parallel to the original process and is activated from time to time when new data are available. This arrangement can be very useful in structuring the application. As another example, a server process (e.g., print server, file server) may generate a new process for each request that it handles. When the OS creates a process at the explicit request of another process, the action is referred to as **process spawning**.

When one process spawns another, the former is referred to as the **parent process,** and the spawned process is referred to as the **child process.** Typically, the "related" processes need to communicate and cooperate with each other. Achieving this cooperation is a difficult task for the programmer; this topic is discussed in Chapter 5.

PROCESS TERMINATION Table 3.2 summarizes typical reasons for process termination. Any computer system must provide a means for a process to indicate its completion. A batch job should include a Halt instruction or an explicit OS service call for termination. In the former case, the Halt instruction will generate an interrupt to alert the OS that a process has completed. For an interactive application, the action of the user will indicate when the process is completed. For example, in a time-sharing system, the process for a particular user is to be terminated when the user logs off or turns off his or her terminal. On a personal computer or workstation, a user may quit an application (e.g., word processing or spreadsheet). All of these actions ultimately result in a service request to the OS to terminate the requesting process.

Additionally, a number of error and fault conditions can lead to the termination of a process. Table 3.2 lists some of the more commonly recognized conditions.[3]

Finally, in some operating systems, a process may be terminated by the process that created it or when the parent process is itself terminated.

---

[3]A forgiving operating system might, in some cases, allow the user to recover from a fault without terminating the process. For example, if a user requests access to a file and that access is denied, the operating system might simply inform the user that access is denied and allow the process to proceed.

Table 3.2 Reasons for Process Termination

Normal completion	The process executes an OS service call to indicate that it has completed running.
Time limit exceeded	The process has run longer than the specified total time limit. There are a number of possibilities for the type of time that is measured. These include total elapsed time ("wall clock time"), amount of time spent executing, and, in the case of an interactive process, the amount of time since the user last provided any input.
Memory unavailable	The process requires more memory than the system can provide.
Bounds violation	The process tries to access a memory location that it is not allowed to access.
Protection error	The process attempts to use a resource such as a file that it is not allowed to use, or it tries to use it in an improper fashion, such as writing to a read-only file.
Arithmetic error	The process tries a prohibited computation, such as division by zero, or tries to store numbers larger than the hardware can accommodate.
Time overrun	The process has waited longer than a specified maximum for a certain event to occur.
I/O failure	An error occurs during input or output, such as inability to find a file, failure to read or write after a specified maximum number of tries (when, for example, a defective area is encountered on a tape), or invalid operation (such as reading from the line printer).
Invalid instruction	The process attempts to execute a nonexistent instruction (often a result of branching into a data area and attempting to execute the data).
Privileged instruction	The process attempts to use an instruction reserved for the operating system.
Data misuse	A piece of data is of the wrong type or is not initialized.
Operator or OS intervention	For some reason, the operator or the operating system has terminated the process (e.g., if a deadlock exists).
Parent termination	When a parent terminates, the operating system may automatically terminate all of the offspring of that parent.
Parent request	A parent process typically has the authority to terminate any of its offspring.

A Five-State Model

If all processes were always ready to execute, then the queueing discipline suggested by Figure 3.5b would be effective. The queue is a first-in-first-out list and the processor operates in **round-robin** fashion on the available processes (each process in the queue is given a certain amount of time, in turn, to execute and then returned to the queue, unless blocked). However, even with the simple example that we have described, this implementation is inadequate: Some processes in the Not Running state are ready to execute, while others are blocked, waiting for an I/O operation to complete. Thus, using a single queue, the dispatcher could not just select the process at the oldest end of the queue. Rather, the dispatcher would have to scan the list looking for the process that is not blocked and that has been in the queue the longest.

A more natural way to handle this situation is to split the Not Running state into two states: Ready and Blocked. This is shown in Figure 3.6. For good measure,

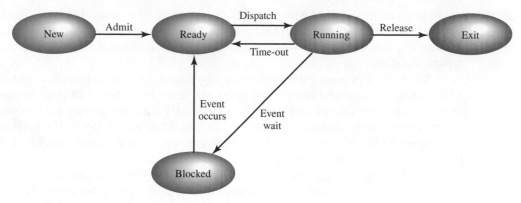

Figure 3.6   Five-State Process Model

we have added two additional states that will prove useful. The five states in this new diagram are:

- **Running:** The process that is currently being executed. For this chapter, we will assume a computer with a single processor, so at most one process at a time can be in this state.

- **Ready:** A process that is prepared to execute when given the opportunity.

- **Blocked/Waiting:**[4] A process that cannot execute until some event occurs, such as the completion of an I/O operation.

- **New:** A process that has just been created but has not yet been admitted to the pool of executable processes by the OS. Typically, a new process has not yet been loaded into main memory, although its process control block has been created.

- **Exit:** A process that has been released from the pool of executable processes by the OS, either because it halted or because it aborted for some reason.

The New and Exit states are useful constructs for process management. The New state corresponds to a process that has just been defined. For example, if a new user attempts to log on to a time-sharing system or a new batch job is submitted for execution, the OS can define a new process in two stages. First, the OS performs the necessary housekeeping chores. An identifier is associated with the process. Any tables that will be needed to manage the process are allocated and built. At this point, the process is in the New state. This means that the OS has performed the necessary actions to create the process but has not committed itself to the execution of the process. For example, the OS may limit the number of processes that may be in the system for reasons of performance or main memory limitation. While a process is in the new state, information concerning the process that is needed by the OS is maintained in control tables in main memory. However, the process itself is

---

[4]*Waiting* is a frequently used alternative term for *Blocked* as a process state. Generally, we will use *Blocked*, but the terms are interchangeable.

not in main memory. That is, the code of the program to be executed is not in main memory, and no space has been allocated for the data associated with that program. While the process is in the New state, the program remains in secondary storage, typically disk storage.[5]

Similarly, a process exits a system in two stages. First, a process is terminated when it reaches a natural completion point, when it aborts due to an unrecoverable error, or when another process with the appropriate authority causes the process to abort. Termination moves the process to the exit state. At this point, the process is no longer eligible for execution. The tables and other information associated with the job are temporarily preserved by the OS, which provides time for auxiliary or support programs to extract any needed information. For example, an accounting program may need to record the processor time and other resources utilized by the process for billing purposes. A utility program may need to extract information about the history of the process for purposes related to performance or utilization analysis. Once these programs have extracted the needed information, the OS no longer needs to maintain any data relating to the process and the process is deleted from the system.

Figure 3.6 indicates the types of events that lead to each state transition for a process; the possible transitions are as follows:

- **Null → New:** A new process is created to execute a program. This event occurs for any of the reasons listed in Table 3.1.

- **New → Ready:** The OS will move a process from the New state to the Ready state when it is prepared to take on an additional process. Most systems set some limit based on the number of existing processes or the amount of virtual memory committed to existing processes. This limit assures that there are not so many active processes as to degrade performance.

- **Ready → Running:** When it is time to select a process to run, the OS chooses one of the processes in the Ready state. This is the job of the scheduler or dispatcher. Scheduling is explored in Part Four.

- **Running → Exit:** The currently running process is terminated by the OS if the process indicates that it has completed, or if it aborts. See Table 3.2.

- **Running → Ready:** The most common reason for this transition is that the running process has reached the maximum allowable time for uninterrupted execution; virtually all multiprogramming operating systems impose this type of time discipline. There are several other alternative causes for this transition, which are not implemented in all operating systems. Of particular importance is the case in which the OS assigns different levels of priority to different processes. Suppose, for example, that process A is running at a given priority level, and process B, at a higher priority level, is blocked. If the OS learns that the event upon which process B has been waiting has occurred, moving B to a ready state, then it can interrupt process A and dispatch process B. We

---

[5]In the discussion in this paragraph, we ignore the concept of virtual memory. In systems that support virtual memory, when a process moves from New to Ready, its program code and data are loaded into virtual memory. Virtual memory was briefly discussed in Chapter 2 and is examined in detail in Chapter 8.

say that the OS has **preempted** process A.[6] Finally, a process may voluntarily release control of the processor. An example is a background process that performs some accounting or maintenance function periodically.

- **Running → Blocked:** A process is put in the Blocked state if it requests something for which it must wait. A request to the OS is usually in the form of a system service call; that is, a call from the running program to a procedure that is part of the operating system code. For example, a process may request a service from the OS that the OS is not prepared to perform immediately. It can request a resource, such as a file or a shared section of virtual memory, that is not immediately available. Or the process may initiate an action, such as an I/O operation, that must be completed before the process can continue. When processes communicate with each other, a process may be blocked when it is waiting for another process to provide data or waiting for a message from another process.

- **Blocked → Ready:** A process in the Blocked state is moved to the Ready state when the event for which it has been waiting occurs.

- **Ready → Exit:** For clarity, this transition is not shown on the state diagram. In some systems, a parent may terminate a child' process at any time. Also, if a parent terminates, all child processes associated with that parent may be terminated.

- **Blocked → Exit:** The comments under the preceding item apply.

Returning to our simple example, Figure 3.7 shows the transition of each process among the states. Figure 3.8a suggests the way in which a queueing discipline might be implemented with two queues: a Ready queue and a Blocked queue. As each process is admitted to the system, it is placed in the Ready queue. When it is time for the OS to choose another process to run, it selects one from the Ready

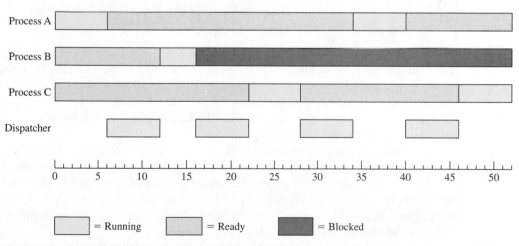

Figure 3.7   Process States for the Trace of Figure 3.4

---

[6]In general, the term *preemption* is defined to be the reclaiming of a resource from a process before the process has finished using it. In this case, the resource is the processor itself. The process is executing and could continue to execute, but is preempted so that another process can be executed.

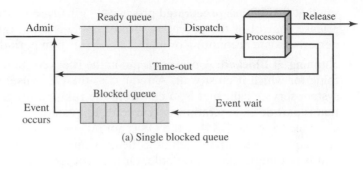

(a) Single blocked queue

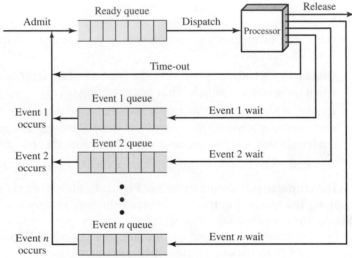

(b) Multiple blocked queues

Figure 3.8   Queueing Model for Figure 3.6

queue. In the absence of any priority scheme, this can be a simple first-in-first-out queue. When a running process is removed from execution, it is either terminated or placed in the Ready or Blocked queue, depending on the circumstances. Finally, when an event occurs, any process in the Blocked queue that has been waiting on that event only is moved to the Ready queue.

This latter arrangement means that, when an event occurs, the OS must scan the entire blocked queue, searching for those processes waiting on that event. In a large OS, there could be hundreds or even thousands of processes in that queue. Therefore, it would be more efficient to have a number of queues, one for each event. Then, when the event occurs, the entire list of processes in the appropriate queue can be moved to the Ready state (Figure 3.8b).

One final refinement: If the dispatching of processes is dictated by a priority scheme, then it would be convenient to have a number of Ready queues, one for each priority level. The OS could then readily determine which is the highest-priority ready process that has been waiting the longest.

Suspended Processes

THE NEED FOR SWAPPING   The three principal states just described (Ready, Running, Blocked) provide a systematic way of modeling the behavior of processes and guide the implementation of the OS. Some operating systems are constructed using just these three states.

However, there is good justification for adding other states to the model. To see the benefit of these new states, consider a system that does not employ virtual memory. Each process to be executed must be loaded fully into main memory. Thus, in Figure 3.8b, all of the processes in all of the queues must be resident in main memory.

Recall that the reason for all of this elaborate machinery is that I/O activities are much slower than computation and therefore the processor in a uniprogramming system is idle most of the time. But the arrangement of Figure 3.8b does not entirely solve the problem. It is true that, in this case, memory holds multiple processes and that the processor can move to another process when one process is blocked. But the processor is so much faster than I/O that it will be common for all of the processes in memory to be waiting for I/O. Thus, even with multiprogramming, a processor could be idle most of the time.

What to do? Main memory could be expanded to accommodate more processes. But there are two flaws in this approach. First, there is a cost associated with main memory, which, though small on a per-byte basis, begins to add up as we get into the gigabytes of storage. Second, the appetite of programs for memory has grown as fast as the cost of memory has dropped. So larger memory results in larger processes, not more processes.

Another solution is swapping, which involves moving part or all of a process from main memory to disk. When none of the processes in main memory is in the Ready state, the OS swaps one of the blocked processes out on to disk into a suspend queue. This is a queue of existing processes that have been temporarily kicked out of main memory, or suspended. The OS then brings in another process from the suspend queue, or it honors a new-process request. Execution then continues with the newly arrived process.

Swapping, however, is an I/O operation, and therefore there is the potential for making the problem worse, not better. But because disk I/O is generally the fastest I/O on a system (e.g., compared to tape or printer I/O), swapping will usually enhance performance.

With the use of swapping as just described, one other state must be added to our process behavior model (Figure 3.9a): the Suspend state. When all of the processes in main memory are in the Blocked state, the OS can suspend one process by putting it in the Suspend state and transferring it to disk. The space that is freed in main memory can then be used to bring in another process.

When the OS has performed a swapping-out operation, it has two choices for selecting a process to bring into main memory: It can admit a newly created process or it can bring in a previously suspended process. It would appear that the preference should be to bring in a previously suspended process, to provide it with service rather than increasing the total load on the system.

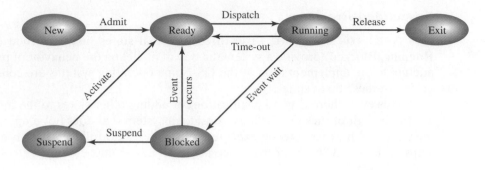

(a) With one suspend state

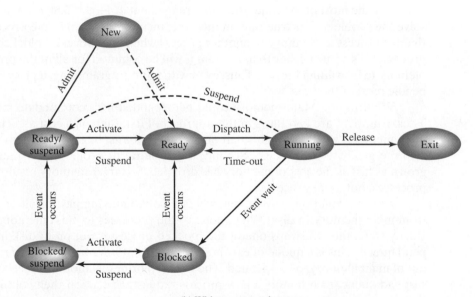

(b) With two suspend states

Figure 3.9   Process State Transition Diagram with Suspend States

But this line of reasoning presents a difficulty. All of the processes that have been suspended were in the Blocked state at the time of suspension. It clearly would not do any good to bring a blocked process back into main memory, because it is still not ready for execution. Recognize, however, that each process in the Suspend state was originally blocked on a particular event. When that event occurs, the process is not blocked and is potentially available for execution.

Therefore, we need to rethink this aspect of the design. There are two independent concepts here: whether a process is waiting on an event (blocked or not) and whether a process has been swapped out of main memory (suspended or not). To accommodate this 2 × 2 combination, we need four states:

- **Ready:** The process is in main memory and available for execution
- **Blocked:** The process is in main memory and awaiting an event.

- **Blocked/Suspend:** The process is in secondary memory and awaiting an event.
- **Ready/Suspend:** The process is in secondary memory but is available for execution as soon as it is loaded into main memory.

Before looking at a state transition diagram that encompasses the two new suspend states, one other point should be mentioned. The discussion so far has assumed that virtual memory is not in use and that a process is either all in main memory or all out of main memory. With a virtual memory scheme, it is possible to execute a process that is only partially in main memory. If reference is made to a process address that is not in main memory, then the appropriate portion of the process can be brought in. The use of virtual memory would appear to eliminate the need for explicit swapping, because any desired address in any desired process can be moved in or out of main memory by the memory management hardware of the processor. However, as we shall see in Chapter 8, the performance of a virtual memory system can collapse if there is a sufficiently large number of active processes, all of which are partially in main memory. Therefore, even in a virtual memory system, the OS will need to swap out processes explicitly and completely from time to time in the interests of performance.

Let us look now, in Figure 3.9b, at the state transition model that we have developed. (The dashed lines in the figure indicate possible but not necessary transitions.) Important new transitions are the following:

- **Blocked → Blocked/Suspend:** If there are no ready processes, then at least one blocked process is swapped out to make room for another process that is not blocked. This transition can be made even if there are ready processes available, if the OS determines that the currently running process or a ready process that it would like to dispatch requires more main memory to maintain adequate performance.
- **Blocked/Suspend → Ready/Suspend:** A process in the Blocked/Suspend state is moved to the Ready/Suspend state when the event for which it has been waiting occurs. Note that this requires that the state information concerning suspended processes must be accessible to the OS.
- **Ready/Suspend → Ready:** When there are no ready processes in main memory, the OS will need to bring one in to continue execution. In addition, it might be the case that a process in the Ready/Suspend state has higher priority than any of the processes in the Ready state. In that case, the OS designer may dictate that it is more important to get at the higher-priority process than to minimize swapping.
- **Ready → Ready/Suspend:** Normally, the OS would prefer to suspend a blocked process rather than a ready one, because the ready process can now be executed, whereas the blocked process is taking up main memory space and cannot be executed. However, it may be necessary to suspend a ready process if that is the only way to free up a sufficiently large block of main memory. Also, the OS may choose to suspend a lower–priority ready process rather than a higher–priority blocked process if it believes that the blocked process will be ready soon.

Several other transitions that are worth considering are the following:

- **New → Ready/Suspend and New → Ready:** When a new process is created, it can either be added to the Ready queue or the Ready/Suspend queue. In either case, the OS must create a process control block and allocate an address space to the process. It might be preferable for the OS to perform these housekeeping duties at an early time, so that it can maintain a large pool of processes that are not blocked. With this strategy, there would often be insufficient room in main memory for a new process; hence the use of the (New → Ready/Suspend) transition. On the other hand, we could argue that a just-in-time philosophy of creating processes as late as possible reduces OS overhead and allows that OS to perform the process-creation duties at a time when the system is clogged with blocked processes anyway.

- **Blocked/Suspend → Blocked:** Inclusion of this transition may seem to be poor design. After all, if a process is not ready to execute and is not already in main memory, what is the point of bringing it in? But consider the following scenario: A process terminates, freeing up some main memory. There is a process in the (Blocked/Suspend) queue with a higher priority than any of the processes in the (Ready/Suspend) queue and the OS has reason to believe that the blocking event for that process will occur soon. Under these circumstances, it would seem reasonable to bring a blocked process into main memory in preference to a ready process.

- **Running → Ready/Suspend:** Normally, a running process is moved to the Ready state when its time allocation expires. If, however, the OS is preempting the process because a higher-priority process on the Blocked/Suspend queue has just become unblocked, the OS could move the running process directly to the (Ready/Suspend) queue and free some main memory.

- **Any State → Exit:** Typically, a process terminates while it is running, either because it has completed or because of some fatal fault condition. However, in some operating systems, a process may be terminated by the process that created it or when the parent process is itself terminated. If this is allowed, then a process in any state can be moved to the Exit state.

OTHER USES OF SUSPENSION   So far, we have equated the concept of a suspended process with that of a process that is not in main memory. A process that is not in main memory is not immediately available for execution, whether or not it is awaiting an event.

We can generalize the concept of a suspended process. Let us define a suspended process as having the following characteristics:

1. The process is not immediately available for execution.
2. The process may or may not be waiting on an event. If it is, this blocked condition is independent of the suspend condition, and occurrence of the blocking event does not enable the process to be executed immediately.

Table 3.3 Reasons for Process Suspension

Swapping	The OS needs to release sufficient main memory to bring in a process that is ready to execute.
Other OS reason	The OS may suspend a background or utility process or a process that is suspected of causing a problem.
Interactive user request	A user may wish to suspend execution of a program for purposes of debugging or in connection with the use of a resource.
Timing	A process may be executed periodically (e.g., an accounting or system monitoring process) and may be suspended while waiting for the next time interval.
Parent process request	A parent process may wish to suspend execution of a descendent to examine or modify the suspended process, or to coordinate the activity of various descendants.

3. The process was placed in a suspended state by an agent: either itself, a parent process, or the OS, for the purpose of preventing its execution.

4. The process may not be removed from this state until the agent explicitly orders the removal.

Table 3.3 lists some reasons for the suspension of a process. One reason that we have discussed is to provide memory space either to bring in a Ready/Suspended process or to increase the memory allocated to other Ready processes. The OS may have other motivations for suspending a process. For example, an auditing or tracing process may be employed to monitor activity on the system; the process may be used to record the level of utilization of various resources (processor, memory, channels) and the rate of progress of the user processes in the system. The OS, under operator control, may turn this process on and off from time to time. If the OS detects or suspects a problem, it may suspend a process. One example of this is deadlock, which is discussed in Chapter 6. As another example, a problem is detected on a communications line, and the operator has the OS suspend the process that is using the line while some tests are run.

Another set of reasons concerns the actions of an interactive user. For example, if a user suspects a bug in the program, he or she may debug the program by suspending its execution, examining and modifying the program or data, and resuming execution. Or there may be a background process that is collecting trace or accounting statistics, which the user may wish to be able to turn on and off.

Timing considerations may also lead to a swapping decision. For example, if a process is to be activated periodically but is idle most of the time, then it should be swapped out between uses. A program that monitors utilization or user activity is an example.

Finally, a parent process may wish to suspend a descendent process. For example, process A may spawn process B to perform a file read. Subsequently, process B encounters an error in the file read procedure and reports this to process A. Process A suspends process B to investigate the cause.

In all of these cases, the activation of a suspended process is requested by the agent that initially requested the suspension.

3.3 PROCESS DESCRIPTION

The OS controls events within the computer system. It schedules and dispatches processes for execution by the processor, allocates resources to processes, and responds to requests by user processes for basic services. Fundamentally, we can think of the OS as that entity that manages the use of system resources by processes.

This concept is illustrated in Figure 3.10. In a multiprogramming environment, there are a number of processes (P_1,..., P_n) that have been created and exist in virtual memory. Each process, during the course of its execution, needs access to certain system resources, including the processor, I/O devices, and main memory. In the figure, process P_1 is running; at least part of the process is in main memory, and it has control of two I/O devices. Process P_2 is also in main memory but is blocked waiting for an I/O device allocated to P_1. Process P_n has been swapped out and is therefore suspended.

We explore the details of the management of these resources by the OS on behalf of the processes in later chapters. Here we are concerned with a more fundamental question: What information does the OS need to control processes and manage resources for them?

Operating System Control Structures

If the OS is to manage processes and resources, it must have information about the current status of each process and resource. The universal approach to providing this information is straightforward: The OS constructs and maintains tables of information about each entity that it is managing. A general idea of the scope of this effort is indicated in Figure 3.11, which shows four different types of tables maintained by the OS: memory, I/O, file, and process. Although the details will differ from one OS to another, fundamentally, all operating systems maintain information in these four categories.

Memory tables are used to keep track of both main (real) and secondary (virtual) memory. Some of main memory is reserved for use by the OS; the remainder is available for use by processes. Processes are maintained on secondary memory using some sort of virtual memory or simple swapping mechanism. The memory tables must include the following information:

- The allocation of main memory to processes
- The allocation of secondary memory to processes

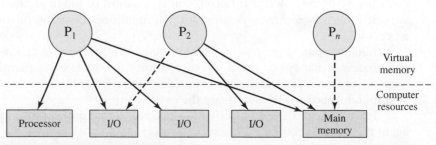

Figure 3.10 **Processes and Resources (resource allocation at one snapshot in time)**

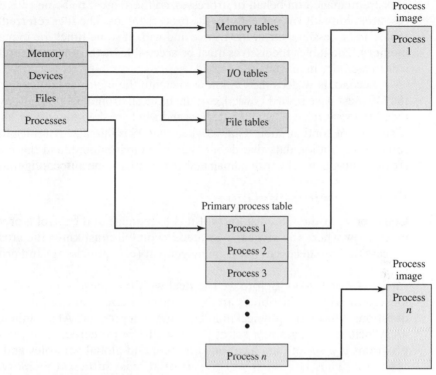

Figure 3.11   General Structure of Operating System Control Tables

- Any protection attributes of blocks of main or virtual memory, such as which processes may access certain shared memory regions
- Any information needed to manage virtual memory

We examine the information structures for memory management in detail in Part Three.

I/O tables are used by the OS to manage the I/O devices and channels of the computer system. At any given time, an I/O device may be available or assigned to a particular process. If an I/O operation is in progress, the OS needs to know the status of the I/O operation and the location in main memory being used as the source or destination of the I/O transfer. I/O management is examined in Chapter 11.

The OS may also maintain **file tables**. These tables provide information about the existence of files, their location on secondary memory, their current status, and other attributes. Much, if not all, of this information may be maintained and used by a file management system, in which case the OS has little or no knowledge of files. In other operating systems, much of the detail of file management is managed by the OS itself. This topic is explored in Chapter 12.

Finally, the OS must maintain **process tables** to manage processes. The remainder of this section is devoted to an examination of the required process tables. Before proceeding to this discussion, two additional points should be made. First, although Figure 3.11 shows four distinct sets of tables, it should be clear that these tables must be linked or cross-referenced in some fashion. Memory, I/O, and files are managed on behalf of processes, so there must be some reference to these resources, directly or indirectly, in the process tables. The files referred to in the file tables are accessible via an I/O device and will, at some times, be in main or virtual memory. The tables themselves must be accessible by the OS and therefore are subject to memory management.

Second, how does the OS know to create the tables in the first place? Clearly, the OS must have some knowledge of the basic environment, such as how much main memory exists, what are the I/O devices and what are their identifiers, and so on. This is an issue of configuration. That is, when the OS is initialized, it must have access to some configuration data that define the basic environment, and these data must be created outside the OS, with human assistance or by some autoconfiguration software.

Process Control Structures

Consider what the OS must know if it is to manage and control a process. First, it must know where the process is located; second, it must know the attributes of the process that are necessary for its management (e.g., process ID and process state).

PROCESS LOCATION   Before we can deal with the questions of where a process is located or what its attributes are, we need to address an even more fundamental question: What is the physical manifestation of a process? At a minimum, a process must include a program or set of programs to be executed. Associated with these programs is a set of data locations for local and global variables and any defined constants. Thus, a process will consist of at least sufficient memory to hold the programs and data of that process. In addition, the execution of a program typically involves a stack (see Appendix P) that is used to keep track of procedure calls and parameter passing between procedures. Finally, each process has associated with it a number of attributes that are used by the OS for process control. Typically, the collection of attributes is referred to as a *process control block*.[7] We can refer to this collection of program, data, stack, and attributes as the **process image** (Table 3.4).

The location of a process image will depend on the memory management scheme being used. In the simplest case, the process image is maintained as a

Table 3.4   Typical Elements of a Process Image

User Data
The modifiable part of the user space. May include program data, a user stack area, and programs that may be modified.
User Program
The program to be executed.
Stack
Each process has one or more last-in-first-out (LIFO) stacks associated with it. A stack is used to store parameters and calling addresses for procedure and system calls.
Process Control Block
Data needed by the OS to control the process (see Table 3.5).

---

[7]Other commonly used names for this data structure are *task control block*, *process descriptor*, and *task descriptor*.

contiguous, or continuous, block of memory. This block is maintained in secondary memory, usually disk. So that the OS can manage the process, at least a small portion of its image must be maintained in main memory. To execute the process, the entire process image must be loaded into main memory or at least virtual memory. Thus, the OS needs to know the location of each process on disk and, for each such process that is in main memory, the location of that process in main memory. We saw a slightly more complex variation on this scheme with the CTSS OS, in Chapter 2. With CTSS, when a process is swapped out, part of the process image may remain in main memory. Thus, the OS must keep track of which portions of the image of each process are still in main memory.

Modern operating systems presume paging hardware that allows noncontiguous physical memory to support partially resident processes.[8] At any given time, a portion of a process image may be in main memory, with the remainder in secondary memory.[9] Therefore, process tables maintained by the OS must show the location of each page of each process image.

Figure 3.11 depicts the structure of the location information in the following way. There is a primary process table with one entry for each process. Each entry contains, at least, a pointer to a process image. If the process image contains multiple blocks, this information is contained directly in the primary process table or is available by cross-reference to entries in memory tables. Of course, this depiction is generic; a particular OS will have its own way of organizing the location information.

PROCESS ATTRIBUTES A sophisticated multiprogramming system requires a great deal of information about each process. As was explained, this information can be considered to reside in a process control block. Different systems will organize this information in different ways, and several examples of this appear at the end of this chapter and the next. For now, let us simply explore the type of information that might be of use to an OS without considering in any detail how that information is organized.

Table 3.5 lists the typical categories of information required by the OS for each process. You may be somewhat surprised at the quantity of information required. As you gain a greater appreciation of the responsibilities of the OS, this list should appear more reasonable.

We can group the process control block information into three general categories:

- Process identification
- Processor state information
- Process control information

---

[8]A brief overview of the concepts of pages, segments, and virtual memory is provided in the subsection on memory management in Section 2.3.

[9]This brief discussion slides over some details. In particular, in a system that uses virtual memory, all of the process image for an active process is always in secondary memory. When a portion of the image is loaded into main memory, it is copied rather than moved. Thus, the secondary memory retains a copy of all segments and/or pages. However, if the main memory portion of the image is modified, the secondary copy will be out of date until the main memory portion is copied back onto disk.

Table 3.5 Typical Elements of a Process Control Block

Process Identification

Identifiers

Numeric identifiers that may be stored with the process control block include

- Identifier of this process
- Identifier of the process that created this process (parent process)
- User identifier

Processor State Information

User-Visible Registers

A user-visible register is one that may be referenced by means of the machine language that the processor executes while in user mode. Typically, there are from 8 to 32 of these registers, although some RISC implementations have over 100.

Control and Status Registers

These are a variety of processor registers that are employed to control the operation of the processor. These include

- **Program counter:** Contains the address of the next instruction to be fetched
- **Condition codes:** Result of the most recent arithmetic or logical operation (e.g., sign, zero, carry, equal, overflow)
- **Status information:** Includes interrupt enabled/disabled flags, execution mode

Stack Pointers

Each process has one or more last-in-first-out (LIFO) system stacks associated with it. A stack is used to store parameters and calling addresses for procedure and system calls. The stack pointer points to the top of the stack.

Process Control Information

Scheduling and State Information

This is information that is needed by the operating system to perform its scheduling function. Typical items of information:

- **Process state:** Defines the readiness of the process to be scheduled for execution (e.g., running, ready, waiting, halted).
- **Priority:** One or more fields may be used to describe the scheduling priority of the process. In some systems, several values are required (e.g., default, current, highest-allowable).
- **Scheduling-related information:** This will depend on the scheduling algorithm used. Examples are the amount of time that the process has been waiting and the amount of time that the process executed the last time it was running.
- **Event:** Identity of event the process is awaiting before it can be resumed.

Data Structuring

A process may be linked to other process in a queue, ring, or some other structure. For example, all processes in a waiting state for a particular priority level may be linked in a queue. A process may exhibit a parent–child (creator–created) relationship with another process. The process control block may contain pointers to other processes to support these structures.

Interprocess Communication

Various flags, signals, and messages may be associated with communication between two independent processes. Some or all of this information may be maintained in the process control block.

Process Privileges

Processes are granted privileges in terms of the memory that may be accessed and the types of instructions that may be executed. In addition, privileges may apply to the use of system utilities and services.

Memory Management

This section may include pointers to segment and/or page tables that describe the virtual memory assigned to this process.

Resource Ownership and Utilization

Resources controlled by the process may be indicated, such as opened files. A history of utilization of the processor or other resources may also be included; this information may be needed by the scheduler.

With respect to **process identification**, in virtually all operating systems, each process is assigned a unique numeric identifier, which may simply be an index into the primary process table (Figure 3.11); otherwise there must be a mapping that allows the OS to locate the appropriate tables based on the process identifier. This identifier is useful in several ways. Many of the other tables controlled by the OS may use process identifiers to cross-reference process tables. For example, the memory tables may be organized so as to provide a map of main memory with an indication of which process is assigned to each region. Similar references will appear in I/O and file tables. When processes communicate with one another, the process identifier informs the OS of the destination of a particular communication. When processes are allowed to create other processes, identifiers indicate the parent and descendents of each process.

In addition to these process identifiers, a process may be assigned a user identifier that indicates the user responsible for the job.

Processor state information consists of the contents of processor registers. While a process is running, of course, the information is in the registers. When a process is interrupted, all of this register information must be saved so that it can be restored when the process resumes execution. The nature and number of registers involved depend on the design of the processor. Typically, the register set will include user-visible registers, control and status registers, and stack pointers. These are described in Chapter 1.

Of particular note, all processor designs include a register or set of registers, often known as the program status word (PSW), that contains status information. The PSW typically contain condition codes plus other status information. A good example of a processor status word is that on Intel x86 processors, referred to as the EFLAGS register (shown in Figure 3.12 and Table 3.6). This structure is used by any OS (including UNIX and Windows) running on an x86 processor.

The third major category of information in the process control block can be called, for want of a better name, **process control information**. This is the additional information needed by the OS to control and coordinate the various active processes. The last part of Table 3.5 indicates the scope of this information. As

ID	= Identification flag	DF	= Direction flag
VIP	= Virtual interrupt pending	IF	= Interrupt enable flag
VIF	= Virtual interrupt flag	TF	= Trap flag
AC	= Alignment check	SF	= Sign flag
VM	= Virtual 8086 mode	ZF	= Zero flag
RF	= Resume flag	AF	= Auxiliary carry flag
NT	= Nested task flag	PF	= Parity flag
IOPL	= I/O privilege level	CF	= Carry flag
OF	= Overflow flag		

Figure 3.12   x86 EFLAGS Register

Table 3.6   Pentium EFLAGS Register Bits

Control Bits

AC (Alignment check)
Set if a word or doubleword is addressed on a nonword or non-doubleword boundary.

ID (Identification flag)
If this bit can be set and cleared, this processor supports the CPUID instruction. This instruction provides information about the vendor, family, and model.

RF (Resume flag)
Allows the programmer to disable debug exceptions so that the instruction can be restarted after a debug exception without immediately causing another debug exception.

IOPL (I/O privilege level)
When set, causes the processor to generate an exception on all accesses to I/O devices during protected mode operation.

DF (Direction flag)
Determines whether string processing instructions increment or decrement the 16-bit half-registers SI and DI (for 16-bit operations) or the 32-bit registers ESI and EDI (for 32-bit operations).

IF (Interrupt enable flag)
When set, the processor will recognize external interrupts.

TF (Trap flag)
When set, causes an interrupt after the execution of each instruction. This is used for debugging.

Operating Mode Bits

NT (Nested task flag)
Indicates that the current task is nested within another task in protected mode operation.

VM (Virtual 8086 mode)
Allows the programmer to enable or disable virtual 8086 mode, which determines whether the processor runs as an 8086 machine.

VIP (Virtual interrupt pending)
Used in virtual 8086 mode to indicate that one or more interrupts are awaiting service.

VIF (Virtual interrupt flag)
Used in virtual 8086 mode instead of IF.

Condition Codes

AF (Auxiliary carry flag)
Represents carrying or borrowing between half-bytes of an 8-bit arithmetic or logic operation using the AL register.

CF (Carry flag)
Indicates carrying out or borrowing into the leftmost bit position following an arithmetic operation. Also modified by some of the shift and rotate operations.

OF (Overflow flag)
Indicates an arithmetic overflow after an addition or subtraction.

PF (Parity flag)
Parity of the result of an arithmetic or logic operation. 1 indicates even parity; 0 indicates odd parity.

SF (Sign flag)
Indicates the sign of the result of an arithmetic or logic operation.

ZF (Zero flag)
Indicates that the result of an arithmetic or logic operation is 0.

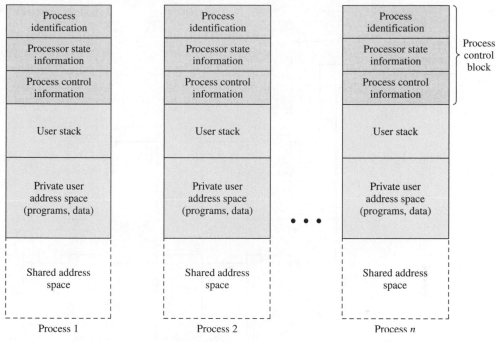

Figure 3.13   User Processes in Virtual Memory

we examine the details of operating system functionality in succeeding chapters, the need for the various items on this list should become clear.

Figure 3.13 suggests the structure of process images in virtual memory. Each process image consists of a process control block, a user stack, the private address space of the process, and any other address space that the process shares with other processes. In the figure, each process image appears as a contiguous range of addresses. In an actual implementation, this may not be the case; it will depend on the memory management scheme and the way in which control structures are organized by the OS.

As indicated in Table 3.5, the process control block may contain structuring information, including pointers that allow the linking of process control blocks. Thus, the queues that were described in the preceding section could be implemented as linked lists of process control blocks. For example, the queueing structure of Figure 3.8a could be implemented as suggested in Figure 3.14.

THE ROLE OF THE PROCESS CONTROL BLOCK   The process control block is the most important data structure in an OS. Each process control block contains all of the information about a process that is needed by the OS. The blocks are read and/or modified by virtually every module in the OS, including those involved with scheduling, resource allocation, interrupt processing, and performance monitoring and analysis. One can say that the set of process control blocks defines the state of the OS.

This brings up an important design issue. A number of routines within the OS will need access to information in process control blocks. The provision of direct

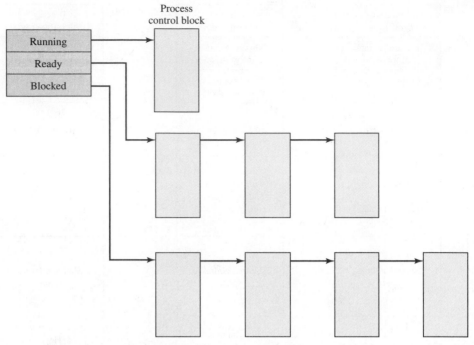

Figure 3.14 Process List Structures

access to these tables is not difficult. Each process is equipped with a unique ID, and this can be used as an index into a table of pointers to the process control blocks. The difficulty is not access but rather protection. Two problems present themselves:

- A bug in a single routine, such as an interrupt handler, could damage process control blocks, which could destroy the system's ability to manage the affected processes.
- A design change in the structure or semantics of the process control block could affect a number of modules in the OS.

These problems can be addressed by requiring all routines in the OS to go through a handler routine, the only job of which is to protect process control blocks, and which is the sole arbiter for reading and writing these blocks. The trade-off in the use of such a routine involves performance issues and the degree to which the remainder of the system software can be trusted to be correct.

3.4 PROCESS CONTROL

Modes of Execution

Before continuing with our discussion of the way in which the OS manages processes, we need to distinguish between the mode of processor execution normally associated with the OS and that normally associated with user programs. Most processors support at least two modes of execution. Certain instructions can only be executed in the more-privileged mode. These would include reading or altering a control register, such as the program status word; primitive I/O instructions; and instructions that relate to memory management. In addition, certain regions of memory can only be accessed in the more-privileged mode.

The less-privileged mode is often referred to as the **user mode,** because user programs typically would execute in this mode. The more-privileged mode is referred to as the **system mode, control mode,** or **kernel mode.** This last term refers to the kernel of the OS, which is that portion of the OS that encompasses the important system functions. Table 3.7 lists the functions typically found in the kernel of an OS.

The reason for using two modes should be clear. It is necessary to protect the OS and key operating system tables, such as process control blocks, from interference by user programs. In the kernel mode, the software has complete control of the processor and all its instructions, registers, and memory. This level of control is not necessary and for safety is not desirable for user programs.

Two questions arise: How does the processor know in which mode it is to be executing and how is the mode changed? Regarding the first question, typically there is a bit in the program status word (PSW) that indicates the mode of execution. This bit is changed in response to certain events. Typically, when a user makes a call to an operating system service or when an interrupt triggers execution of an operating system routine, the mode is set to the kernel mode and, upon return from the service to the user process, the mode is set to user mode. As an example, consider the Intel Itanium processor, which implements the 64-bit IA-64 architecture. The processor has a processor status register (psr) that includes a 2-bit cpl (current privilege level) field. Level 0 is the most privileged level, while level 3 is the least privileged level. Most operating systems, such as Linux, use level 0 for the kernel and one other level

Table 3.7   Typical Functions of an Operating System Kernel

Process Management
• Process creation and termination
• Process scheduling and dispatching
• Process switching
• Process synchronization and support for interprocess communication
• Management of process control blocks
Memory Management
• Allocation of address space to processes
• Swapping
• Page and segment management
I/O Management
• Buffer management
• Allocation of I/O channels and devices to processes
Support Functions
• Interrupt handling
• Accounting
• Monitoring

for user mode. When an interrupt occurs, the processor clears most of the bits in the psr, including the cpl field. This automatically sets the cpl to level 0. At the end of the interrupt-handling routine, the final instruction that is executed is irt (interrupt return). This instruction causes the processor to restore the psr of the interrupted program, which restores the privilege level of that program. A similar sequence occurs when an application places a system call. For the Itanium, an application places a system call by placing the system call identifier and the system call arguments in a predefined area and then executing a special instruction that has the effect of interrupting execution at the user level and transferring control to the kernel.

Process Creation

In Section 3.2, we discussed the events that lead to the creation of a new process. Having discussed the data structures associated with a process, we are now in a position to describe briefly the steps involved in actually creating the process.

Once the OS decides, for whatever reason (Table 3.1), to create a new process, it can proceed as follows:

1. **Assign a unique process identifier to the new process.** At this time, a new entry is added to the primary process table, which contains one entry per process.

2. **Allocate space for the process.** This includes all elements of the process image. Thus, the OS must know how much space is needed for the private user address space (programs and data) and the user stack. These values can be assigned by default based on the type of process, or they can be set based on user request at job creation time. If a process is spawned by another process, the parent process can pass the needed values to the OS as part of the process-creation request. If any existing address space is to be shared by this new process, the appropriate linkages must be set up. Finally, space for a process control block must be allocated.

3. **Initialize the process control block.** The process identification portion contains the ID of this process plus other appropriate IDs, such as that of the parent process. The processor state information portion will typically be initialized with most entries zero, except for the program counter (set to the program entry point) and system stack pointers (set to define the process stack boundaries). The process control information portion is initialized based on standard default values plus attributes that have been requested for this process. For example, the process state would typically be initialized to Ready or Ready/ Suspend. The priority may be set by default to the lowest priority unless an explicit request is made for a higher priority. Initially, the process may own no resources (I/O devices, files) unless there is an explicit request for these or unless they are inherited from the parent.

4. **Set the appropriate linkages.** For example, if the OS maintains each scheduling queue as a linked list, then the new process must be put in the Ready or Ready/Suspend list.

5. **Create or expand other data structures.** For example, the OS may maintain an accounting file on each process to be used subsequently for billing and/or performance assessment purposes.

Process Switching

On the face of it, the function of process switching would seem to be straightforward. At some time, a running process is interrupted and the OS assigns another process to the Running state and turns control over to that process. However, several design issues are raised. First, what events trigger a process switch? Another issue is that we must recognize the distinction between mode switching and process switching. Finally, what must the OS do to the various data structures under its control to achieve a process switch?

WHEN TO SWITCH PROCESSES   A process switch may occur any time that the OS has gained control from the currently running process. Table 3.8 suggests the possible events that may give control to the OS.

First, let us consider system interrupts. Actually, we can distinguish, as many systems do, two kinds of system interrupts, one of which is simply referred to as an interrupt, and the other as a trap. The former is due to some sort of event that is external to and independent of the currently running process, such as the completion of an I/O operation. The latter relates to an error or exception condition generated within the currently running process, such as an illegal file access attempt. With an ordinary **interrupt,** control is first transferred to an interrupt handler, which does some basic housekeeping and then branches to an OS routine that is concerned with the particular type of interrupt that has occurred. Examples include the following:

- **Clock interrupt:** The OS determines whether the currently running process has been executing for the maximum allowable unit of time, referred to as a **time slice**. That is, a time slice is the maximum amount of time that a process can execute before being interrupted. If so, this process must be switched to a Ready state and another process dispatched.

- **I/O interrupt:** The OS determines what I/O action has occurred. If the I/O action constitutes an event for which one or more processes are waiting, then the OS moves all of the corresponding blocked processes to the Ready state (and Blocked/Suspend processes to the Ready/Suspend state). The OS must then decide whether to resume execution of the process currently in the Running state or to preempt that process for a higher-priority Ready process.

- **Memory fault:** The processor encounters a virtual memory address reference for a word that is not in main memory. The OS must bring in the block

Table 3.8   Mechanisms for Interrupting the Execution of a Process

Mechanism	Cause	Use
Interrupt	External to the execution of the current instruction	Reaction to an asynchronous external event
Trap	Associated with the execution of the current instruction	Handling of an error or an exception condition
Supervisor call	Explicit request	Call to an operating system function

(page or segment) of memory containing the reference from secondary memory to main memory. After the I/O request is issued to bring in the block of memory, the process with the memory fault is placed in a blocked state; the OS then performs a process switch to resume execution of another process. After the desired block is brought into memory, that process is placed in the Ready state.

With a **trap,** the OS determines if the error or exception condition is fatal. If so, then the currently running process is moved to the Exit state and a process switch occurs. If not, then the action of the OS will depend on the nature of the error and the design of the OS. It may attempt some recovery procedure or simply notify the user. It may do a process switch or resume the currently running process.

Finally, the OS may be activated by a **supervisor call** from the program being executed. For example, a user process is running and an instruction is executed that requests an I/O operation, such as a file open. This call results in a transfer to a routine that is part of the operating system code. The use of a system call may place the user process in the Blocked state.

MODE SWITCHING   In Chapter 1, we discussed the inclusion of an interrupt stage as part of the instruction cycle. Recall that, in the interrupt stage, the processor checks to see if any interrupts are pending, indicated by the presence of an interrupt signal. If no interrupts are pending, the processor proceeds to the fetch stage and fetches the next instruction of the current program in the current process. If an interrupt is pending, the processor does the following:

1. It sets the program counter to the starting address of an interrupt handler program.
2. It switches from user mode to kernel mode so that the interrupt processing code may include privileged instructions.

The processor now proceeds to the fetch stage and fetches the first instruction of the interrupt handler program, which will service the interrupt. At this point, typically, the context of the process that has been interrupted is saved into that process control block of the interrupted program.

One question that may now occur to you is, What constitutes the context that is saved? The answer is that it must include any information that may be altered by the execution of the interrupt handler and that will be needed to resume the program that was interrupted. Thus, the portion of the process control block that was referred to as processor state information must be saved. This includes the program counter, other processor registers, and stack information.

Does anything else need to be done? That depends on what happens next. The interrupt handler is typically a short program that performs a few basic tasks related to an interrupt. For example, it resets the flag or indicator that signals the presence of an interrupt. It may send an acknowledgment to the entity that issued the interrupt, such as an I/O module. And it may do some basic housekeeping relating to the effects of the event that caused the interrupt. For example, if the interrupt relates to an I/O event, the interrupt handler will check for an error condition. If an error has occurred, the interrupt handler may send a signal to the process that originally requested the I/O operation. If the interrupt is by the clock, then the handler will hand control over to the dispatcher, which will want to pass control to another process because the time slice allotted to the currently running process has expired.

What about the other information in the process control block? If this interrupt is to be followed by a switch to another process, then some work will need to be done. However, in most operating systems, the occurrence of an interrupt does not necessarily mean a process switch. It is possible that, after the interrupt handler has executed, the currently running process will resume execution. In that case, all that is necessary is to save the processor state information when the interrupt occurs and restore that information when control is returned to the program that was running. Typically, the saving and restoring functions are performed in hardware.

CHANGE OF PROCESS STATE   It is clear, then, that the mode switch is a concept distinct from that of the process switch.[10] A mode switch may occur without changing the state of the process that is currently in the Running state. In that case, the context saving and subsequent restoral involve little overhead. However, if the currently running process is to be moved to another state (Ready, Blocked, etc.), then the OS must make substantial changes in its environment. The steps involved in a full process switch are as follows:

1. Save the context of the processor, including program counter and other registers.
2. Update the process control block of the process that is currently in the Running state. This includes changing the state of the process to one of the other states (Ready; Blocked; Ready/Suspend; or Exit). Other relevant fields must also be updated, including the reason for leaving the Running state and accounting information.
3. Move the process control block of this process to the appropriate queue (Ready; Blocked on Event *i*; Ready/Suspend).
4. Select another process for execution; this topic is explored in Part Four.
5. Update the process control block of the process selected. This includes changing the state of this process to Running.
6. Update memory management data structures. This may be required, depending on how address translation is managed; this topic is explored in Part Three.
7. Restore the context of the processor to that which existed at the time the selected process was last switched out of the Running state, by loading in the previous values of the program counter and other registers.

Thus, the process switch, which involves a state change, requires more effort than a mode switch.

---

[10]The term *context switch* is often found in OS literature and textbooks. Unfortunately, although most of the literature uses this term to mean what is here called a process switch, other sources use it to mean a mode switch or even a thread switch (defined in the next chapter). To avoid ambiguity, the term is not used in this book.

3.5 EXECUTION OF THE OPERATING SYSTEM

In Chapter 2, we pointed out two intriguing facts about operating systems:

- The OS functions in the same way as ordinary computer software in the sense that the OS is a set of programs executed by the processor.
- The OS frequently relinquishes control and depends on the processor to restore control to the OS.

If the OS is just a collection of programs and if it is executed by the processor just like any other program, is the OS a process? If so, how is it controlled? These interesting questions have inspired a number of design approaches. Figure 3.15 illustrates a range of approaches that are found in various contemporary operating systems.

Nonprocess Kernel

One traditional approach, common on many older operating systems, is to execute the kernel of the OS outside of any process (Figure 3.15a). With this approach, when the currently running process is interrupted or issues a supervisor call, the mode context of this process is saved and control is passed to the kernel. The OS has its own region of memory to use and its own system stack for controlling procedure calls and returns. The OS can perform any desired functions and restore the context of the interrupted process, which causes execution to resume in the interrupted

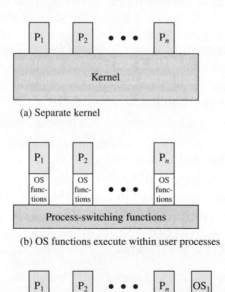

(a) Separate kernel

(b) OS functions execute within user processes

(c) OS functions execute as separate processes

Figure 3.15 Relationship between Operating System and User Processes

user process. Alternatively, the OS can complete the function of saving the environment of the process and proceed to schedule and dispatch another process. Whether this happens depends on the reason for the interruption and the circumstances at the time.

In any case, the key point here is that the concept of process is considered to apply only to user programs. The operating system code is executed as a separate entity that operates in privileged mode.

Execution within User Processes

An alternative that is common with operating systems on smaller computers (PCs, workstations) is to execute virtually all OS software in the context of a user process. The view is that the OS is primarily a collection of routines that the user calls to perform various functions, executed within the environment of the user's process. This is illustrated in Figure 3.15b. At any given point, the OS is managing n process images. Each image includes not only the regions illustrated in Figure 3.13, but also program, data, and stack areas for kernel programs.

Figure 3.16 suggests a typical process image structure for this strategy. A separate kernel stack is used to manage calls/returns while the process is in kernel mode.

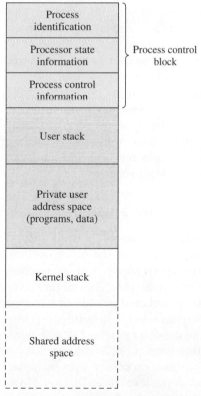

Figure 3.16   Process Image: Operating System Executes within User Space

Operating system code and data are in the shared address space and are shared by all user processes.

When an interrupt, trap, or supervisor call occurs, the processor is placed in kernel mode and control is passed to the OS. To pass control from a user program to the OS, the mode context is saved and a mode switch takes place to an operating system routine. However, execution continues within the current user process. Thus, a process switch is not performed, just a mode switch within the same process.

If the OS, upon completion of its work, determines that the current process should continue to run, then a mode switch resumes the interrupted program within the current process. This is one of the key advantages of this approach: A user program has been interrupted to employ some operating system routine, and then resumed, and all of this has occurred without incurring the penalty of two process switches. If, however, it is determined that a process switch is to occur rather than returning to the previously executing program, then control is passed to a process-switching routine. This routine may or may not execute in the current process, depending on system design. At some point, however, the current process has to be placed in a nonrunning state and another process designated as the running process. During this phase, it is logically most convenient to view execution as taking place outside of all processes.

In a way, this view of the OS is remarkable. Simply put, at certain points in time, a process will save its state information, choose another process to run from among those that are ready, and relinquish control to that process. The reason this is not an arbitrary and indeed chaotic situation is that during the critical time, the code that is executed in the user process is shared operating system code and not user code. Because of the concept of user mode and kernel mode, the user cannot tamper with or interfere with the operating system routines, even though they are executing in the user's process environment. This further reminds us that there is a distinction between the concepts of process and program and that the relationship between the two is not one to one. Within a process, both a user program and operating system programs may execute, and the operating system programs that execute in the various user processes are identical.

Process–Based Operating System

Another alternative, illustrated in Figure 3.15c, is to implement the OS as a collection of system processes. As in the other options, the software that is part of the kernel executes in a kernel mode. In this case, however, major kernel functions are organized as separate processes. Again, there may be a small amount of process-switching code that is executed outside of any process.

This approach has several advantages. It imposes a program design discipline that encourages the use of a modular OS with minimal, clean interfaces between the modules. In addition, some noncritical operating system functions are conveniently implemented as separate processes. For example, we mentioned earlier a monitor program that records the level of utilization of various resources (processor, memory, channels) and the rate of progress of the user processes in the system. Because this program does not provide a particular service to any active process, it can only be invoked by the OS. As a process, the function can run at an assigned priority level and be interleaved with other processes under dispatcher control. Finally, implementing the OS as a set of processes is useful in a multiprocessor or multicomputer environment, in which some of the operating system services can be shipped out to dedicated processors, improving performance.

3.6 SECURITY ISSUES

An OS associates a set of privileges with each process. These privileges dictate what resources the process may access, including regions of memory, files, privileged system instructions, and so on. Typically, a process that executes on behalf of a user has the privileges that the OS recognizes for that user. A system or utility process may have privileges assigned at configuration time.

On a typical system, the highest level of privilege is referred to as administrator, supervisor, or root access.[11] Root access provides access to all the functions and services of the operating system. With root access, a process has complete control of the system and can add or change programs and files, monitor other processes, send and receive network traffic, and alter privileges.

A key security issue in the design of any OS is to prevent, or at least detect, attempts by a user or a piece of malicious software (malware) from gaining unauthorized privileges on the system and, in particular, from gaining root access. In this section, we briefly summarize the threats and countermeasures related to this security issue. Part Seven provides more detail.

System Access Threats

System access threats fall into two general categories: intruders and malicious software.

INTRUDERS   One of the most common threats to security is the intruder (the other is viruses), often referred to as a hacker or cracker. In an important early study of intrusion, Anderson [ANDE80] identified three classes of intruders:

- **Masquerader:** An individual who is not authorized to use the computer and who penetrates a system's access controls to exploit a legitimate user's account
- **Misfeasor:** A legitimate user who accesses data, programs, or resources for which such access is not authorized, or who is authorized for such access but misuses his or her privileges
- **Clandestine user:** An individual who seizes supervisory control of the system and uses this control to evade auditing and access controls or to suppress audit collection

The masquerader is likely to be an outsider; the misfeasor generally is an insider; and the clandestine user can be either an outsider or an insider.

Intruder attacks range from the benign to the serious. At the benign end of the scale, there are many people who simply wish to explore internets and see what is

---

[11]On UNIX systems, the administrator, or *superuser*, account is called root; hence the term *root access.*

out there. At the serious end are individuals who are attempting to read privileged data, perform unauthorized modifications to data, or disrupt the system.

The objective of the intruder is to gain access to a system or to increase the range of privileges accessible on a system. Most initial attacks use system or software vulnerabilities that allow a user to execute code that opens a back door into the system. Intruders can get access to a system by exploiting attacks such as buffer overflows on a program that runs with certain privileges. We introduce buffer overflow attacks in Chapter 7.

Alternatively, the intruder attempts to acquire information that should have been protected. In some cases, this information is in the form of a user password. With knowledge of some other user's password, an intruder can log in to a system and exercise all the privileges accorded to the legitimate user.

MALICIOUS SOFTWARE   Perhaps the most sophisticated types of threats to computer systems are presented by programs that exploit vulnerabilities in computing systems. Such threats are referred to as **malicious software**, or **malware**. In this context, we are concerned with threats to application programs as well as utility programs, such as editors and compilers, and kernel-level programs.

Malicious software can be divided into two categories: those that need a host program, and those that are independent. The former, referred to as **parasitic**, are essentially fragments of programs that cannot exist independently of some actual application program, utility, or system program. Viruses, logic bombs, and backdoors are examples. The latter are self-contained programs that can be scheduled and run by the operating system. Worms and bot programs are examples.

We can also differentiate between those software threats that do not replicate and those that do. The former are programs or fragments of programs that are activated by a trigger. Examples are logic bombs, backdoors, and bot programs. The latter consists of either a program fragment or an independent program that, when executed, may produce one or more copies of itself to be activated later on the same system or some other system. Viruses and worms are examples.

Malicious software can be relatively harmless or may perform one or more of a number of harmful actions, including destroying files and data in main memory, bypassing controls to gain privileged access, and providing a means for intruders to bypass access controls.

Countermeasures

INTRUSION DETECTION   RFC 2828 (*Internet Security Glossary*) defines intrusion detection as follows: A security service that monitors and analyzes system events for the purpose of finding, and providing real-time or near real-time warning of, attempts to access system resources in an unauthorized manner.

Intrusion detection systems (IDSs) can be classified as follows:

- **Host-based IDS:** Monitors the characteristics of a single host and the events occurring within that host for suspicious activity
- **Network-based IDS:** Monitors network traffic for particular network segments or devices and analyzes network, transport, and application protocols to identify suspicious activity

An IDS comprises three logical components:

- **Sensors:** Sensors are responsible for collecting data. The input for a sensor may be any part of a system that could contain evidence of an intrusion. Types of input to a sensor include network packets, log files, and system call traces. Sensors collect and forward this information to the analyzer.

- **Analyzers:** Analyzers receive input from one or more sensors or from other analyzers. The analyzer is responsible for determining if an intrusion has occurred. The output of this component is an indication that an intrusion has occurred. The output may include evidence supporting the conclusion that an intrusion occurred. The analyzer may provide guidance about what actions to take as a result of the intrusion.

- **User interface:** The user interface to an IDS enables a user to view output from the system or control the behavior of the system. In some systems, the user interface may equate to a manager, director, or console component.

Intrusion detection systems are typically designed to detect human intruder behavior as well as malicious software behavior.

AUTHENTICATION In most computer security contexts, user authentication is the fundamental building block and the primary line of defense. User authentication is the basis for most types of access control and for user accountability. RFC 2828 defines user authentication as follows:

The process of verifying an identity claimed by or for a system entity. An authentication process consists of two steps:

- **Identification step:** Presenting an identifier to the security system. (Identifiers should be assigned carefully, because authenticated identities are the basis for other security services, such as access control service.)
- **Verification step:** Presenting or generating authentication information that corroborates the binding between the entity and the identifier.

For example, user Alice Toklas could have the user identifier ABTOKLAS. This information needs to be stored on any server or computer system that Alice wishes to use and could be known to system administrators and other users. A typical item of authentication information associated with this user ID is a password, which is kept secret (known only to Alice and to the system). If no one is able to obtain or guess Alice's password, then the combination of Alice's user ID and password enables administrators to set up Alice's access permissions and audit her activity. Because Alice's ID is not secret, system users can send her e-mail, but because her password is secret, no one can pretend to be Alice.

In essence, identification is the means by which a user provides a claimed identity to the system; user authentication is the means of establishing the validity of the claim.

There are four general means of authenticating a user's identity, which can be used alone or in combination:

- **Something the individual knows:** Examples include a password, a personal identification number (PIN), or answers to a prearranged set of questions.
- **Something the individual possesses:** Examples include electronic keycards, smart cards, and physical keys. This type of authenticator is referred to as a *token.*
- **Something the individual is (static biometrics):** Examples include recognition by fingerprint, retina, and face.
- **Something the individual does (dynamic biometrics):** Examples include recognition by voice pattern, handwriting characteristics, and typing rhythm.

All of these methods, properly implemented and used, can provide secure user authentication. However, each method has problems. An adversary may be able to guess or steal a password. Similarly, an adversary may be able to forge or steal a token. A user may forget a password or lose a token. Further, there is a significant administrative overhead for managing password and token information on systems and securing such information on systems. With respect to biometric authenticators, there are a variety of problems, including dealing with false positives and false negatives, user acceptance, cost, and convenience.

ACCESS CONTROL   Access control implements a security policy that specifies who or what (e.g., in the case of a process) may have access to each specific system resource and the type of access that is permitted in each instance.

An access control mechanism mediates between a user (or a process executing on behalf of a user) and system resources, such as applications, operating systems, firewalls, routers, files, and databases. The system must first authenticate a user seeking access. Typically, the authentication function determines whether the user is permitted to access the system at all. Then the access control function determines if the specific requested access by this user is permitted. A security administrator maintains an authorization database that specifies what type of access to which resources is allowed for this user. The access control function consults this database to determine whether to grant access. An auditing function monitors and keeps a record of user accesses to system resources.

FIREWALLS   Firewalls can be an effective means of protecting a local system or network of systems from network-based security threats while at the same time affording access to the outside world via wide area networks and the Internet. Traditionally, a firewall is a dedicated computer that interfaces with computers outside a network and has special security precautions built into it in order to protect sensitive files on computers within the network. It is used to service outside network, especially Internet, connections and dial-in lines. Personal firewalls that are implemented in hardware or software, and associated with a single workstation or PC, are also common.

[BELL94] lists the following design goals for a firewall:

1. All traffic from inside to outside, and vice versa, must pass through the firewall. This is achieved by physically blocking all access to the local network except via the firewall. Various configurations are possible, as explained later in this chapter.

2. Only authorized traffic, as defined by the local security policy, will be allowed to pass. Various types of firewalls are used, which implement various types of security policies.

3. The firewall itself is immune to penetration. This implies the use of a hardened system with a secured operating system. Trusted computer systems are suitable for hosting a firewall and often required in government applications.

3.7   UNIX SVR4 PROCESS MANAGEMENT

UNIX System V makes use of a simple but powerful process facility that is highly visible to the user. UNIX follows the model of Figure 3.15b, in which most of the OS executes within the environment of a user process. UNIX uses two categories of processes: system processes and user processes. System processes run in kernel mode and execute operating system code to perform administrative and housekeeping functions, such as allocation of memory and process swapping. User processes operate in user mode to execute user programs and utilities and in kernel mode to execute instructions that belong to the kernel. A user process enters kernel mode by issuing a system call, when an exception (fault) is generated, or when an interrupt occurs.

Process States

A total of nine process states are recognized by the UNIX SVR4 operating system; these are listed in Table 3.9 and a state transition diagram is shown in Figure 3.17

Table 3.9   UNIX Process States

User Running	Executing in user mode.
Kernel Running	Executing in kernel mode.
Ready to Run, in Memory	Ready to run as soon as the kernel schedules it.
Asleep in Memory	Unable to execute until an event occurs; process is in main memory (a blocked state).
Ready to Run, Swapped	Process is ready to run, but the swapper must swap the process into main memory before the kernel can schedule it to execute.
Sleeping, Swapped	The process is awaiting an event and has been swapped to secondary storage (a blocked state).
Preempted	Process is returning from kernel to user mode, but the kernel preempts it and does a process switch to schedule another process.
Created	Process is newly created and not yet ready to run.
Zombie	Process no longer exists, but it leaves a record for its parent process to collect.

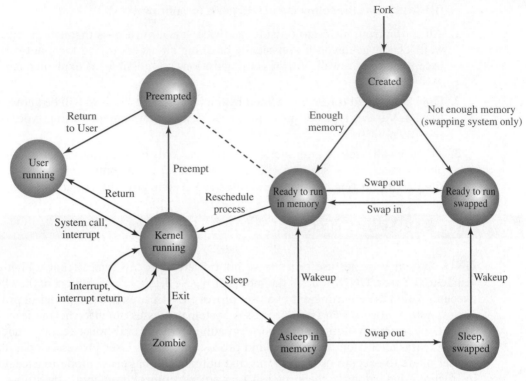

Figure 3.17   UNIX Process State Transition Diagram

(based on figure in [BACH86]). This figure is similar to Figure 3.9b, with the two UNIX sleeping states corresponding to the two blocked states. The differences are as follows:

- UNIX employs two Running states to indicate whether the process is executing in user mode or kernel mode.

- A distinction is made between the two states: (Ready to Run, in Memory) and (Preempted). These are essentially the same state, as indicated by the dotted line joining them. The distinction is made to emphasize the way in which the preempted state is entered. When a process is running in kernel mode (as a result of a supervisor call, clock interrupt, or I/O interrupt), there will come a time when the kernel has completed its work and is ready to return control to the user program. At this point, the kernel may decide to preempt the current process in favor of one that is ready and of higher priority. In that case, the current process moves to the preempted state. However, for purposes of dispatching, those processes in the Preempted state and those in the (Ready to Run, in Memory) state form one queue.

Preemption can only occur when a process is about to move from kernel mode to user mode. While a process is running in kernel mode, it may not be preempted. This makes UNIX unsuitable for real-time processing. Chapter 10 discusses the requirements for real-time processing.

Two processes are unique in UNIX. Process 0 is a special process that is created when the system boots; in effect, it is predefined as a data structure loaded at boot time. It is the swapper process. In addition, process 0 spawns process 1, referred to as the init process; all other processes in the system have process 1 as an ancestor. When a new interactive user logs on to the system, it is process 1 that creates a user process for that user. Subsequently, the user process can create child processes in a branching tree, so that any particular application can consist of a number of related processes.

Process Description

A process in UNIX is a rather complex set of data structures that provide the OS with all of the information necessary to manage and dispatch processes. Table 3.10 summarizes the elements of the process image, which are organized into three parts: user-level context, register context, and system-level context.

The **user-level context** contains the basic elements of a user's program and can be generated directly from a compiled object file. The user's program is separated into text and data areas; the text area is read-only and is intended to hold the program's instructions. While the process is executing, the processor uses the user stack area for procedure calls and returns and parameter passing. The shared memory area is a data area that is shared with other processes. There is only one physical copy of a shared memory area, but, by the use of virtual memory, it appears

Table 3.10   UNIX Process Image

User-Level Context	
Process text	Executable machine instructions of the program
Process data	Data accessible by the program of this process
User stack	Contains the arguments, local variables, and pointers for functions executing in user mode
Shared memory	Memory shared with other processes, used for interprocess communication
Register Context	
Program counter	Address of next instruction to be executed; may be in kernel or user memory space of this process
Processor status register	Contains the hardware status at the time of preemption; contents and format are hardware dependent
Stack pointer	Points to the top of the kernel or user stack, depending on the mode of operation at the time or preemption
General-purpose registers	Hardware dependent
System-Level Context	
Process table entry	Defines state of a process; this information is always accessible to the operating system
U (user) area	Process control information that needs to be accessed only in the context of the process
Per process region table	Defines the mapping from virtual to physical addresses; also contains a permission field that indicates the type of access allowed the process: read-only, read-write, or read-execute
Kernel stack	Contains the stack frame of kernel procedures as the process executes in kernel mode

Table 3.11 UNIX Process Table Entry

Process status	Current state of process.
Pointers	To U area and process memory area (text, data, stack).
Process size	Enables the operating system to know how much space to allocate the process.
User identifiers	The **real user ID** identifies the user who is responsible for the running process. The **effective user ID** may be used by a process to gain temporary privileges associated with a particular program; while that program is being executed as part of the process, the process operates with the effective user ID.
Process identifiers	ID of this process; ID of parent process. These are set up when the process enters the Created state during the fork system call.
Event descriptor	Valid when a process is in a sleeping state; when the event occurs, the process is transferred to a ready-to-run state.
Priority	Used for process scheduling.
Signal	Enumerates signals sent to a process but not yet handled.
Timers	Include process execution time, kernel resource utilization, and user-set timer used to send alarm signal to a process.
P_link	Pointer to the next link in the ready queue (valid if process is ready to execute).
Memory status	Indicates whether process image is in main memory or swapped out. If it is in memory, this field also indicates whether it may be swapped out or is temporarily locked into main memory.

to each sharing process that the shared memory region is in its address space. When a process is not running, the processor status information is stored in the **register context** area.

The **system-level context** contains the remaining information that the OS needs to manage the process. It consists of a static part, which is fixed in size and stays with a process throughout its lifetime, and a dynamic part, which varies in size through the life of the process. One element of the static part is the process table entry. This is actually part of the process table maintained by the OS, with one entry per process. The process table entry contains process control information that is accessible to the kernel at all times; hence, in a virtual memory system, all process table entries are maintained in main memory. Table 3.11 lists the contents of a process table entry. The user area, or U area, contains additional process control information that is needed by the kernel when it is executing in the context of this process; it is also used when paging processes to and from memory. Table 3.12 shows the contents of this table.

The distinction between the process table entry and the U area reflects the fact that the UNIX kernel always executes in the context of some process. Much of the time, the kernel will be dealing with the concerns of that process. However, some of the time, such as when the kernel is performing a scheduling algorithm preparatory to dispatching another process, it will need access to information about other processes. The information in a process table can be accessed when the given process is not the current one.

The third static portion of the system-level context is the per process region table, which is used by the memory management system. Finally, the kernel stack is

Table 3.12   UNIX U Area

Process table pointer	Indicates entry that corresponds to the U area.
User identifiers	Real and effective user IDs. Used to determine user privileges.
Timers	Record time that the process (and its descendants) spent executing in user mode and in kernel mode.
Signal-handler array	For each type of signal defined in the system, indicates how the process will react to receipt of that signal (exit, ignore, execute specified user function).
Control terminal	Indicates login terminal for this process, if one exists.
Error field	Records errors encountered during a system call.
Return value	Contains the result of system calls.
I/O parameters	Describe the amount of data to transfer, the address of the source (or target) data array in user space, and file offsets for I/O.
File parameters	Current directory and current root describe the file system environment of the process.
User file descriptor table	Records the files the process has opened.
Limit fields	Restrict the size of the process and the size of a file it can write.
Permission modes fields	Mask mode settings on files the process creates.

the dynamic portion of the system-level context. This stack is used when the process is executing in kernel mode and contains the information that must be saved and restored as procedure calls and interrupts occur.

Process Control

Process creation in UNIX is made by means of the kernel system call, `fork( )`. When a process issues a fork request, the OS performs the following functions [BACH86]:

1. It allocates a slot in the process table for the new process.
2. It assigns a unique process ID to the child process.
3. It makes a copy of the process image of the parent, with the exception of any shared memory.
4. It increments counters for any files owned by the parent, to reflect that an additional process now also owns those files.
5. It assigns the child process to the Ready to Run state.
6. It returns the ID number of the child to the parent process, and a 0 value to the child process.

All of this work is accomplished in kernel mode in the parent process. When the kernel has completed these functions it can do one of the following, as part of the dispatcher routine:

- Stay in the parent process. Control returns to user mode at the point of the fork call of the parent.

- Transfer control to the child process. The child process begins executing at the same point in the code as the parent, namely at the return from the fork call.

- Transfer control to another process. Both parent and child are left in the Ready to Run state.

It is perhaps difficult to visualize this method of process creation because both parent and child are executing the same passage of code. The difference is this: When the return from the fork occurs, the return parameter is tested. If the value is zero, then this is the child process, and a branch can be executed to the appropriate user program to continue execution. If the value is nonzero, then this is the parent process, and the main line of execution can continue.

3.8   SUMMARY

The most fundamental concept in a modern OS is the process. The principal function of the OS is to create, manage, and terminate processes. While processes are active, the OS must see that each is allocated time for execution by the processor, coordinate their activities, manage conflicting demands, and allocate system resources to processes.

To perform its process management functions, the OS maintains a description of each process, or process image, which includes the address space within which the process executes, and a process control block. The latter contains all of the information that is required by the OS to manage the process, including its current state, resources allocated to it, priority, and other relevant data.

During its lifetime, a process moves among a number of states. The most important of these are Ready, Running, and Blocked. A ready process is one that is not currently executing but that is ready to be executed as soon as the OS dispatches it. The running process is that process that is currently being executed by the processor. In a multiple-processor system, more than one process can be in this state. A blocked process is waiting for the completion of some event, such as an I/O operation.

A running process is interrupted either by an interrupt, which is an event that occurs outside the process and that is recognized by the processor, or by executing a supervisor call to the OS. In either case, the processor performs a mode switch, transferring control to an operating system routine. The OS, after it has completed necessary work, may resume the interrupted process or switch to some other process.

3.9   RECOMMENDED READING

Good descriptions of UNIX process management are found in [GOOD94] and [GRAY97]. [NEHM75] is an interesting discussion of process states and the operating system primitives needed for process dispatching.

GOOD94 Goodheart, B., and Cox, J. *The Magic Garden Explained: The Internals of UNIX System V Release 4.* Englewood Cliffs, NJ: Prentice Hall, 1994.

GRAY97 Gray, J. *Interprocess Communications in UNIX: The Nooks and Crannies.* Upper Saddle River, NJ: Prentice Hall, 1997.

NEHM75 Nehmer, J. "Dispatcher Primitives for the Construction of Operating System Kernels." *Acta Informatica*, vol. 5, 1975.

3.10 KEY TERMS, REVIEW QUESTIONS, AND PROBLEMS

Key Terms

blocked state	privileged mode	suspend state
child process	process	swapping
exit state	process control block	system mode
interrupt	process image	task
kernel mode	process switch	trace
mode switch	program status word	trap
new state	ready state	user mode
parent process	round robin	
preempt	running state	

Review Questions

3.1 What is an instruction trace?

3.2 What common events lead to the creation of a process?

3.3 For the processing model of Figure 3.6, briefly define each state.

3.4 What does it mean to preempt a process?

3.5 What is swapping and what is its purpose?

3.6 Why does Figure 3.9b have two blocked states?

3.7 List four characteristics of a suspended process.

3.8 For what types of entities does the OS maintain tables of information for management purposes?

3.9 List three general categories of information in a process control block.

3.10 Why are two modes (user and kernel) needed?

3.11 What are the steps performed by an OS to create a new process?

3.12 What is the difference between an interrupt and a trap?

3.13 Give three examples of an interrupt.

3.14 What is the difference between a mode switch and a process switch?

Problems

3.1 The following state transition table is a simplified model of process management, with the labels representing transitions between states of READY, RUN, BLOCKED, and NONRESIDENT.

	READY	RUN	BLOCKED	NONRESIDENT
READY	–	1	–	5
RUN	2	–	3	–
BLOCKED	4	–	–	6

Give an example of an event that can cause each of the above transitions. Draw a diagram if that helps.

3.2 Assume that at time 5 no system resources are being used except for the processor and memory. Now consider the following events:

At time 5: P1 executes a command to read from disk unit 3.
At time 15: P5's time slice expires.
At time 18: P7 executes a command to write to disk unit 3.
At time 20: P3 executes a command to read from disk unit 2.
At time 24: P5 executes a command to write to disk unit 3.
At time 28: P5 is swapped out.
At time 33: An interrupt occurs from disk unit 2: P3's read is complete.
At time 36: An interrupt occurs from disk unit 3: P1's read is complete.
At time 38: P8 terminates.
At time 40: An interrupt occurs from disk unit 3: P5's write is complete.
At time 44: P5 is swapped back in.
At time 48: An interrupt occurs from disk unit 3: P7's write is complete.

For each time 22, 37, and 47, identify which state each process is in. If a process is blocked, further identify the event on which is it blocked.

3.3 Figure 3.9b contains seven states. In principle, one could draw a transition between any two states, for a total of 42 different transitions.

a. List all of the possible transitions and give an example of what could cause each transition.

b. List all of the impossible transitions and explain why.

3.4 For the seven-state process model of Figure 3.9b, draw a queueing diagram similar to that of Figure 3.8b.

3.5 Consider the state transition diagram of Figure 3.9b. Suppose that it is time for the OS to dispatch a process and that there are processes in both the Ready state and the Ready/Suspend state, and that at least one process in the Ready/Suspend state has higher scheduling priority than any of the processes in the Ready state. Two extreme policies are as follows: (1) Always dispatch from a process in the Ready state, to minimize swapping, and (2) always give preference to the highest-priority process, even though that may mean swapping when swapping is not necessary. Suggest an intermediate policy that tries to balance the concerns of priority and performance.

3.6 Table 3.13 shows the process states for the VAX/VMS operating system.

a. Can you provide a justification for the existence of so many distinct wait states?

b. Why do the following states not have resident and swapped-out versions: Page Fault Wait, Collided Page Wait, Common Event Wait, Free Page Wait, and Resource Wait?

c. Draw the state transition diagram and indicate the action or occurrence that causes each transition.

3.7 The VAX/VMS operating system makes use of four processor access modes to facilitate the protection and sharing of system resources among processes. The access mode determines

- **Instruction execution privileges:** What instructions the processor may execute
- **Memory access privileges:** Which locations in virtual memory the current instruction may access

Table 3.13 VAX/VMS Process States

Process State	Process Condition
Currently Executing	Running process.
Computable (resident)	Ready and resident in main memory.
Computable (outswapped)	Ready, but swapped out of main memory.
Page Fault Wait	Process has referenced a page not in main memory and must wait for the page to be read in.
Collided Page Wait	Process has referenced a shared page that is the cause of an existing page fault wait in another process, or a private page that is in the process of being read in or written out.
Common Event Wait	Waiting for shared event flag (event flags are single-bit interprocess signaling mechanisms).
Free Page Wait	Waiting for a free page in main memory to be added to the collection of pages in main memory devoted to this process (the working set of the process).
Hibernate Wait (resident)	Process puts itself in a wait state.
Hibernate Wait (outswapped)	Hibernating process is swapped out of main memory.
Local Event Wait (resident)	Process in main memory and waiting for local event flag (usually I/O completion).
Local Event Wait (outswapped)	Process in local event wait is swapped out of main memory.
Suspended Wait (resident)	Process is put into a wait state by another process.
Suspended Wait (outswapped)	Suspended process is swapped out of main memory.
Resource Wait	Process waiting for miscellaneous system resource.

The four modes are as follows:

- **Kernel:** Executes the kernel of the VMS operating system, which includes memory management, interrupt handling, and I/O operations
- **Executive:** Executes many of the OS service calls, including file and record (disk and tape) management routines
- **Supervisor:** Executes other OS services, such as responses to user commands
- **User:** Executes user programs, plus utilities such as compilers, editors, linkers, and debuggers

A process executing in a less-privileged mode often needs to call a procedure that executes in a more-privileged mode; for example, a user program requires an operating system service. This call is achieved by using a change-mode (CHM) instruction, which causes an interrupt that transfers control to a routine at the new access mode. A return is made by executing the REI (return from exception or interrupt) instruction.

    a. A number of operating systems have two modes, kernel and user. What are the advantages and disadvantages of providing four modes instead of two?

    b. Can you make a case for even more than four modes?

3.8 The VMS scheme discussed in the preceding problem is often referred to as a ring protection structure, as illustrated in Figure 3.18. Indeed, the simple kernel/user scheme, as described in Section 3.3, is a two-ring structure. [SILB04] points out a problem with this approach:

> The main disadvantage of the ring (hierarchical) structure is that it does not allow us to enforce the need-to-know principle. In particular, if an object must

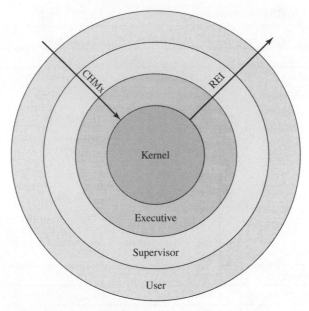

Figure 3.18   VAX/VMS Access Modes

be accessible in domain Dj but not accessible in domain Di, then we must have $j < i$. But this means that every segment accessible in Di is also accessible in Dj.

Explain clearly what the problem is that is referred to in the preceding quote.

3.9   Figure 3.8b suggests that a process can only be in one event queue at a time.

    a. Is it possible that you would want to allow a process to wait on more than one event at the same time? Provide an example.

    b. In that case, how would you modify the queueing structure of the figure to support this new feature?

3.10   In a number of early computers, an interrupt caused the register values to be stored in fixed locations associated with the given interrupt signal. Under what circumstances is this a practical technique? Explain why it is inconvenient in general.

3.11   In Section 3.4, it was stated that UNIX is unsuitable for real-time applications because a process executing in kernel mode may not be preempted. Elaborate.

3.12   You have executed the following C program:

```
main ()
{  int pid;
pid = fork ();
printf ("%d \n", pid);
}
```

What are the possible outputs, assuming the fork succeeded?

CHAPTER 4

THREADS

4.1 Processes and Threads
Multithreading
Thread Functionality

4.2 Types of Threads
User-Level and Kernel-Level Threads
Other Arrangements

4.3 Multicore and Multithreading
Performance of Software on Multicore
Application Example: Valve Game Software

4.4 Windows 7 Thread and SMP Management
Process and Thread Objects
Multithreading
Thread States
Support for OS Subsystems
Symmetric Multiprocessing Support

4.5 Solaris Thread and SMP Management
Multithreaded Architecture
Motivation
Process Structure
Thread Execution
Interrupts as Threads

4.6 Linux Process and Thread Management
Linux Tasks
Linux Threads

4.7 Mac OS X Grand Central Dispatch

4.8 Summary

4.9 Recommended Reading

4.10 Key Terms, Review Questions, and Problems

The basic idea is that the several components in any complex system will perform particular subfunctions that contribute to the overall function.

—*THE SCIENCES OF THE ARTIFICIAL*, HERBERT SIMON

LEARNING OBJECTIVES

After studying this chapter, you should be able to:

- Understand the distinction between process and thread.
- Describe the basic design issues for threads.
- Explain the difference between user-level threads and kernel-level threads.
- Describe the thread management facility in Windows 7.
- Describe the thread management facility in Solaris.
- Describe the thread management facility in Linux.

This chapter examines some more advanced concepts related to process management, which are found in a number of contemporary operating systems. We show that the concept of process is more complex and subtle than presented so far and in fact embodies two separate and potentially independent concepts: one relating to resource ownership and another relating to execution. This distinction has led to the development, in many operating systems, of a construct known as the **thread**.

4.1 PROCESSES AND THREADS

The discussion so far has presented the concept of a process as embodying two characteristics:

- **Resource ownership:** A process includes a virtual address space to hold the process image; recall from Chapter 3 that the process image is the collection of program, data, stack, and attributes defined in the process control block. From time to time, a process may be allocated control or ownership of resources, such as main memory, I/O channels, I/O devices, and files. The OS performs a protection function to prevent unwanted interference between processes with respect to resources.
- **Scheduling/execution:** The execution of a process follows an execution path (trace) through one or more programs (e.g., Figure 1.5). This execution may be interleaved with that of other processes. Thus, a process has an execution state (Running, Ready, etc.) and a dispatching priority and is the entity that is scheduled and dispatched by the OS.

Some thought should convince the reader that these two characteristics are independent and could be treated independently by the OS. This is done in a number of operating systems, particularly recently developed systems. To distinguish the two characteristics, the unit of dispatching is usually referred to as a thread or **lightweight process**, while the unit of resource ownership is usually referred to as a **process** or **task**.[1]

Multithreading

Multithreading refers to the ability of an OS to support multiple, concurrent paths of execution within a single process. The traditional approach of a single thread of execution per process, in which the concept of a thread is not recognized, is referred to as a single-threaded approach. The two arrangements shown in the left half of Figure 4.1 are single-threaded approaches. MS-DOS is an example of an OS that supports a single user process and a single thread. Other operating systems, such as some variants of UNIX, support multiple user processes but only support one thread per process. The right half of Figure 4.1 depicts multithreaded approaches. A Java run-time environment is an example of a system of one process with multiple threads. Of interest in this section is the use of multiple processes, each of which supports multiple threads. This approach is taken in Windows, Solaris, and many modern versions of UNIX, among others. In this section we give a general description

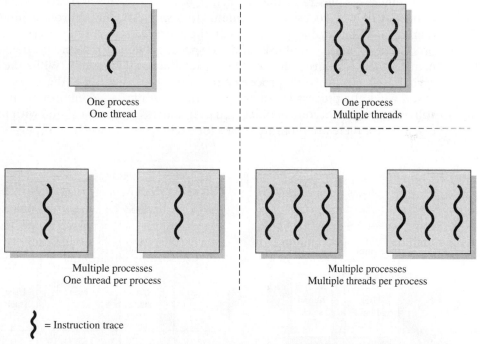

$\}$ = Instruction trace

Figure 4.1 Threads and Processes [ANDE97]

---

[1]Alas, even this degree of consistency is not maintained. In IBM's mainframe operating systems, the concepts of address space and task, respectively, correspond roughly to the concepts of process and thread that we describe in this section. Also, in the literature, the term *lightweight process* is used as either (1) equivalent to the term *thread*, (2) a particular type of thread known as a kernel-level thread, or (3) in the case of Solaris, an entity that maps user-level threads to kernel-level threads.

of multithreading; the details of the Windows, Solaris, and Linux approaches are discussed later in this chapter.

In a multithreaded environment, a process is defined as the unit of resource allocation and a unit of protection. The following are associated with processes:

- A virtual address space that holds the process image
- Protected access to processors, other processes (for interprocess communication), files, and I/O resources (devices and channels)

Within a process, there may be one or more threads, each with the following:

- A thread execution state (Running, Ready, etc.)
- A saved thread context when not running; one way to view a thread is as an independent program counter operating within a process
- An execution stack
- Some per-thread static storage for local variables
- Access to the memory and resources of its process, shared with all other threads in that process

Figure 4.2 illustrates the distinction between threads and processes from the point of view of process management. In a single-threaded process model (i.e., there is no distinct concept of thread), the representation of a process includes its process control block and user address space, as well as user and kernel stacks to manage the call/return behavior of the execution of the process. While the process is running, it controls the processor registers. The contents of these registers are saved when the process is not running. In a multithreaded environment, there is still a single process control block and user address space associated with the process, but now there are separate stacks for each thread, as well as a separate control

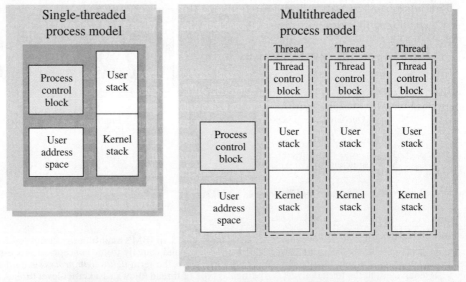

Figure 4.2   Single-Threaded and Multithreaded Process Models

block for each thread containing register values, priority, and other thread-related state information.

Thus, all of the threads of a process share the state and resources of that process. They reside in the same address space and have access to the same data. When one thread alters an item of data in memory, other threads see the results if and when they access that item. If one thread opens a file with read privileges, other threads in the same process can also read from that file.

The key benefits of threads derive from the performance implications:

1. It takes far less time to create a new thread in an existing process than to create a brand-new process. Studies done by the Mach developers show that thread creation is ten times faster than process creation in UNIX [TEVA87].

2. It takes less time to terminate a thread than a process.

3. It takes less time to switch between two threads within the same process than to switch between processes.

4. Threads enhance efficiency in communication between different executing programs. In most operating systems, communication between independent processes requires the intervention of the kernel to provide protection and the mechanisms needed for communication. However, because threads within the same process share memory and files, they can communicate with each other without invoking the kernel.

Thus, if there is an application or function that should be implemented as a set of related units of execution, it is far more efficient to do so as a collection of threads rather than a collection of separate processes.

An example of an application that could make use of threads is a file server. As each new file request comes in, a new thread can be spawned for the file management program. Because a server will handle many requests, many threads will be created and destroyed in a short period. If the server runs on a multiprocessor computer, then multiple threads within the same process can be executing simultaneously on different processors. Further, because processes or threads in a file server must share file data and therefore coordinate their actions, it is faster to use threads and shared memory than processes and message passing for this coordination.

The thread construct is also useful on a single processor to simplify the structure of a program that is logically doing several different functions.

[LETW88] gives four examples of the uses of threads in a single-user multi-processing system:

- **Foreground and background work:** For example, in a spreadsheet program, one thread could display menus and read user input, while another thread executes user commands and updates the spreadsheet. This arrangement often increases the perceived speed of the application by allowing the program to prompt for the next command before the previous command is complete.

- **Asynchronous processing:** Asynchronous elements in the program can be implemented as threads. For example, as a protection against power failure, one can design a word processor to write its random access memory (RAM) buffer to disk once every minute. A thread can be created whose sole job is periodic backup and that schedules itself directly with the OS; there is no need for fancy code in the main program to provide for time checks or to coordinate input and output.

- **Speed of execution:** A multithreaded process can compute one batch of data while reading the next batch from a device. On a multiprocessor system, multiple threads from the same process may be able to execute simultaneously. Thus, even though one thread may be blocked for an I/O operation to read in a batch of data, another thread may be executing.
- **Modular program structure:** Programs that involve a variety of activities or a variety of sources and destinations of input and output may be easier to design and implement using threads.

In an OS that supports threads, scheduling and dispatching is done on a thread basis; hence, most of the state information dealing with execution is maintained in thread-level data structures. There are, however, several actions that affect all of the threads in a process and that the OS must manage at the process level. For example, suspension involves swapping the address space of one process out of main memory to make room for the address space of another process. Because all threads in a process share the same address space, all threads are suspended at the same time. Similarly, termination of a process terminates all threads within that process.

Thread Functionality

Like processes, threads have execution states and may synchronize with one another. We look at these two aspects of thread functionality in turn.

THREAD STATES As with processes, the key states for a thread are Running, Ready, and Blocked. Generally, it does not make sense to associate suspend states with threads because such states are process-level concepts. In particular, if a process is swapped out, all of its threads are necessarily swapped out because they all share the address space of the process.

There are four basic thread operations associated with a change in thread state [ANDE04]:

- **Spawn:** Typically, when a new process is spawned, a thread for that process is also spawned. Subsequently, a thread within a process may spawn another thread within the same process, providing an instruction pointer and arguments for the new thread. The new thread is provided with its own register context and stack space and placed on the ready queue.
- **Block:** When a thread needs to wait for an event, it will block (saving its user registers, program counter, and stack pointers). The processor may now turn to the execution of another ready thread in the same or a different process.
- **Unblock:** When the event for which a thread is blocked occurs, the thread is moved to the Ready queue.
- **Finish:** When a thread completes, its register context and stacks are deallocated.

A significant issue is whether the blocking of a thread results in the blocking of the entire process. In other words, if one thread in a process is blocked, does this prevent the running of any other thread in the same process even if that other thread is in a ready state? Clearly, some of the flexibility and power of threads is lost if the one blocked thread blocks an entire process.

We return to this issue subsequently in our discussion of user-level versus kernel-level threads, but for now let us consider the performance benefits of threads that do not block an entire process. Figure 4.3 (based on one in [KLEI96]) shows a program that performs two remote procedure calls (RPCs)[2] to two different hosts to obtain a combined result. In a single-threaded program, the results are obtained in sequence, so the program has to wait for a response from each server in turn. Rewriting the program to use a separate thread for each RPC results in a substantial speedup. Note that if this program operates on a uniprocessor, the requests must be generated sequentially and the results processed in sequence; however, the program waits concurrently for the two replies.

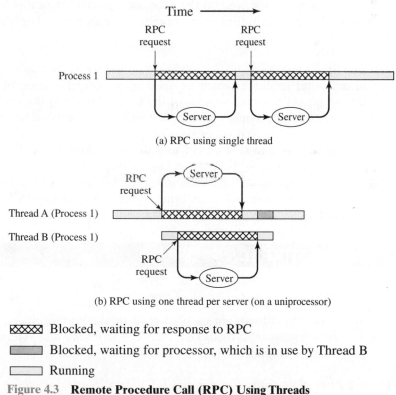

(a) RPC using single thread

(b) RPC using one thread per server (on a uniprocessor)

Blocked, waiting for response to RPC

Blocked, waiting for processor, which is in use by Thread B

Running

Figure 4.3   Remote Procedure Call (RPC) Using Threads

---

[2]An RPC is a technique by which two programs, which may execute on different machines, interact using procedure call/return syntax and semantics. Both the called and calling program behave as if the partner program were running on the same machine. RPCs are often used for client/server applications and are discussed in Chapter 16.

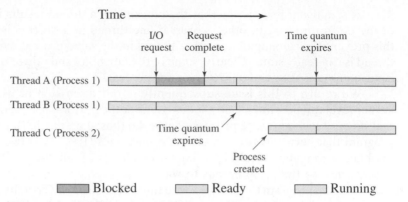

Figure 4.4 Multithreading Example on a Uniprocessor

On a uniprocessor, multiprogramming enables the interleaving of multiple threads within multiple processes. In the example of Figure 4.4, three threads in two processes are interleaved on the processor. Execution passes from one thread to another either when the currently running thread is blocked or when its time slice is exhausted.[3]

THREAD SYNCHRONIZATION   All of the threads of a process share the same address space and other resources, such as open files. Any alteration of a resource by one thread affects the environment of the other threads in the same process. It is therefore necessary to synchronize the activities of the various threads so that they do not interfere with each other or corrupt data structures. For example, if two threads each try to add an element to a doubly linked list at the same time, one element may be lost or the list may end up malformed.

The issues raised and the techniques used in the synchronization of threads are, in general, the same as for the synchronization of processes. These issues and techniques are the subject of Chapters 5 and 6.

4.2 TYPES OF THREADS

User–Level and Kernel–Level Threads

There are two broad categories of thread implementation: user-level threads (ULTs) and kernel-level threads (KLTs).[4] The latter are also referred to in the literature as *kernel-supported threads* or *lightweight processes*.

USER-LEVEL THREADS   In a pure ULT facility, all of the work of thread management is done by the application and the kernel is not aware of the existence of threads. Figure 4.5a illustrates the pure ULT approach. Any application can be

---

[3]In this example, thread C begins to run after thread A exhausts its time quantum, even though thread B is also ready to run. The choice between B and C is a scheduling decision, a topic covered in Part Four.
[4]The acronyms ULT and KLT are not widely used but are introduced for conciseness.

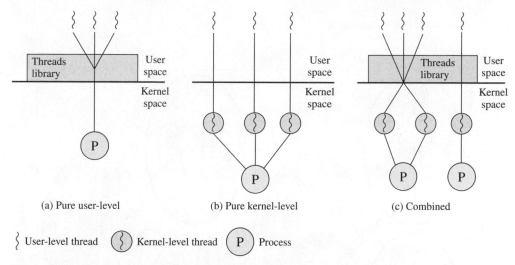

Figure 4.5   User-Level and Kernel-Level Threads

programmed to be multithreaded by using a threads library, which is a package of routines for ULT management. The threads library contains code for creating and destroying threads, for passing messages and data between threads, for scheduling thread execution, and for saving and restoring thread contexts.

By default, an application begins with a single thread and begins running in that thread. This application and its thread are allocated to a single process managed by the kernel. At any time that the application is running (the process is in the Running state), the application may spawn a new thread to run within the same process. Spawning is done by invoking the spawn utility in the threads library. Control is passed to that utility by a procedure call. The threads library creates a data structure for the new thread and then passes control to one of the threads within this process that is in the Ready state, using some scheduling algorithm. When control is passed to the library, the context of the current thread is saved, and when control is passed from the library to a thread, the context of that thread is restored. The context essentially consists of the contents of user registers, the program counter, and stack pointers.

All of the activity described in the preceding paragraph takes place in user space and within a single process. The kernel is unaware of this activity. The kernel continues to schedule the process as a unit and assigns a single execution state (Ready, Running, Blocked, etc.) to that process. The following examples should clarify the relationship between thread scheduling and process scheduling. Suppose that process B is executing in its thread 2; the states of the process and two ULTs that are part of the process are shown in Figure 4.6a. Each of the following is a possible occurrence:

1. The application executing in thread 2 makes a system call that blocks B. For example, an I/O call is made. This causes control to transfer to the kernel. The kernel invokes the I/O action, places process B in the Blocked state, and switches to another process. Meanwhile, according to the data structure maintained by

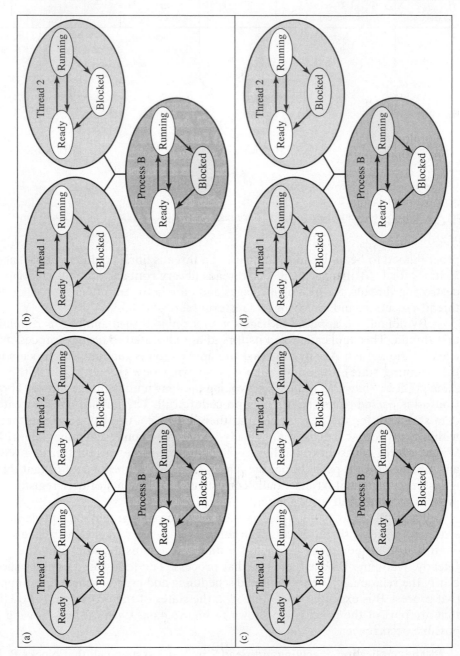

Figure 4.6   Examples of the Relationships between User-Level Thread States and Process States

the threads library, thread 2 of process B is still in the Running state. It is important to note that thread 2 is not actually running in the sense of being executed on a processor; but it is perceived as being in the Running state by the threads library. The corresponding state diagrams are shown in Figure 4.6b.

2. A clock interrupt passes control to the kernel, and the kernel determines that the currently running process (B) has exhausted its time slice. The kernel places process B in the Ready state and switches to another process. Meanwhile, according to the data structure maintained by the threads library, thread 2 of process B is still in the Running state. The corresponding state diagrams are shown in Figure 4.6c.

3. Thread 2 has reached a point where it needs some action performed by thread 1 of process B. Thread 2 enters a Blocked state and thread 1 transitions from Ready to Running. The process itself remains in the Running state. The corresponding state diagrams are shown in Figure 4.6d.

In cases 1 and 2 (Figures 4.6b and 4.6c), when the kernel switches control back to process B, execution resumes in thread 2. Also note that a process can be interrupted, either by exhausting its time slice or by being preempted by a higher-priority process, while it is executing code in the threads library. Thus, a process may be in the midst of a thread switch from one thread to another when interrupted. When that process is resumed, execution continues within the threads library, which completes the thread switch and transfers control to another thread within that process.

There are a number of advantages to the use of ULTs instead of KLTs, including the following:

1. Thread switching does not require kernel mode privileges because all of the thread management data structures are within the user address space of a single process. Therefore, the process does not switch to the kernel mode to do thread management. This saves the overhead of two mode switches (user to kernel; kernel back to user).

2. Scheduling can be application specific. One application may benefit most from a simple round-robin scheduling algorithm, while another might benefit from a priority-based scheduling algorithm. The scheduling algorithm can be tailored to the application without disturbing the underlying OS scheduler.

3. ULTs can run on any OS. No changes are required to the underlying kernel to support ULTs. The threads library is a set of application-level functions shared by all applications.

There are two distinct disadvantages of ULTs compared to KLTs:

1. In a typical OS, many system calls are blocking. As a result, when a ULT executes a system call, not only is that thread blocked, but also all of the threads within the process are blocked.

2. In a pure ULT strategy, a multithreaded application cannot take advantage of multiprocessing. A kernel assigns one process to only one processor at a time. Therefore, only a single thread within a process can execute at a time. In effect, we have application-level multiprogramming within a single process.

While this multiprogramming can result in a significant speedup of the application, there are applications that would benefit from the ability to execute portions of code simultaneously.

There are ways to work around these two problems. For example, both problems can be overcome by writing an application as multiple processes rather than multiple threads. But this approach eliminates the main advantage of threads: Each switch becomes a process switch rather than a thread switch, resulting in much greater overhead.

Another way to overcome the problem of blocking threads is to use a technique referred to as **jacketing**. The purpose of jacketing is to convert a blocking system call into a nonblocking system call. For example, instead of directly calling a system I/O routine, a thread calls an application-level I/O jacket routine. Within this jacket routine is code that checks to determine if the I/O device is busy. If it is, the thread enters the Blocked state and passes control (through the threads library) to another thread. When this thread later is given control again, the jacket routine checks the I/O device again.

KERNEL-LEVEL THREADS   In a pure KLT facility, all of the work of thread management is done by the kernel. There is no thread management code in the application level, simply an application programming interface (API) to the kernel thread facility. Windows is an example of this approach.

Figure 4.5b depicts the pure KLT approach. The kernel maintains context information for the process as a whole and for individual threads within the process. Scheduling by the kernel is done on a thread basis. This approach overcomes the two principal drawbacks of the ULT approach. First, the kernel can simultaneously schedule multiple threads from the same process on multiple processors. Second, if one thread in a process is blocked, the kernel can schedule another thread of the same process. Another advantage of the KLT approach is that kernel routines themselves can be multithreaded.

The principal disadvantage of the KLT approach compared to the ULT approach is that the transfer of control from one thread to another within the same process requires a mode switch to the kernel. To illustrate the differences, Table 4.1 shows the results of measurements taken on a uniprocessor VAX computer running a UNIX-like OS. The two benchmarks are as follows: Null Fork, the time to create, schedule, execute, and complete a process/thread that invokes the null procedure (i.e., the overhead of forking a process/thread); and Signal-Wait, the time for a process/thread to signal a waiting process/thread and then wait on a condition (i.e., the overhead of synchronizing two processes/threads together). We see that there is an order of magnitude or more of difference between ULTs and KLTs and similarly between KLTs and processes.

Table 4.1   Thread and Process Operation Latencies (μs)

Operation	User-Level Threads	Kernel-Level Threads	Processes
Null Fork	34	948	11,300
Signal Wait	37	441	1,840

Thus, on the face of it, while there is a significant speedup by using KLT multithreading compared to single-threaded processes, there is an additional significant speedup by using ULTs. However, whether or not the additional speedup is realized depends on the nature of the applications involved. If most of the thread switches in an application require kernel mode access, then a ULT-based scheme may not perform much better than a KLT-based scheme.

COMBINED APPROACHES Some operating systems provide a combined ULT/ KLT facility (Figure 4.5c). In a combined system, thread creation is done completely in user space, as is the bulk of the scheduling and synchronization of threads within an application. The multiple ULTs from a single application are mapped onto some (smaller or equal) number of KLTs. The programmer may adjust the number of KLTs for a particular application and processor to achieve the best overall results.

In a combined approach, multiple threads within the same application can run in parallel on multiple processors, and a blocking system call need not block the entire process. If properly designed, this approach should combine the advantages of the pure ULT and KLT approaches while minimizing the disadvantages.

Solaris is a good example of an OS using this combined approach. The current Solaris version limits the ULT/KLT relationship to be one-to-one.

Other Arrangements

As we have said, the concepts of resource allocation and dispatching unit have traditionally been embodied in the single concept of the process—that is, as a 1 : 1 relationship between threads and processes. Recently, there has been much interest in providing for multiple threads within a single process, which is a many-to-one relationship. However, as Table 4.2 shows, the other two combinations have also been investigated, namely, a many-to-many relationship and a one-to-many relationship.

MANY-TO-MANY RELATIONSHIP The idea of having a many-to-many relationship between threads and processes has been explored in the experimental operating system TRIX [PAZZ92, WARD80]. In TRIX, there are the concepts of domain

Table 4.2 Relationship between Threads and Processes

Threads: Processes	Description	Example Systems
1:1	Each thread of execution is a unique process with its own address space and resources.	Traditional UNIX implementations
M:1	A process defines an address space and dynamic resource ownership. Multiple threads may be created and executed within that process.	Windows NT, Solaris, Linux, OS/2, OS/390, MACH
1:M	A thread may migrate from one process environment to another. This allows a thread to be easily moved among distinct systems.	Ra (Clouds), Emerald
M:N	Combines attributes of M:1 and 1:M cases.	TRIX

and thread. A domain is a static entity, consisting of an address space and "ports" through which messages may be sent and received. A thread is a single execution path, with an execution stack, processor state, and scheduling information.

As with the multithreading approaches discussed so far, multiple threads may execute in a single domain, providing the efficiency gains discussed earlier. However, it is also possible for a single user activity, or application, to be performed in multiple domains. In this case, a thread exists that can move from one domain to another.

The use of a single thread in multiple domains seems primarily motivated by a desire to provide structuring tools for the programmer. For example, consider a program that makes use of an I/O subprogram. In a multiprogramming environment that allows user-spawned processes, the main program could generate a new process to handle I/O and then continue to execute. However, if the future progress of the main program depends on the outcome of the I/O operation, then the main program will have to wait for the other I/O program to finish. There are several ways to implement this application:

1. The entire program can be implemented as a single process. This is a reasonable and straightforward solution. There are drawbacks related to memory management. The process as a whole may require considerable main memory to execute efficiently, whereas the I/O subprogram requires a relatively small address space to buffer I/O and to handle the relatively small amount of program code. Because the I/O program executes in the address space of the larger program, either the entire process must remain in main memory during the I/O operation or the I/O operation is subject to swapping. This memory management effect would also exist if the main program and the I/O subprogram were implemented as two threads in the same address space.

2. The main program and I/O subprogram can be implemented as two separate processes. This incurs the overhead of creating the subordinate process. If the I/O activity is frequent, one must either leave the subordinate process alive, which consumes management resources, or frequently create and destroy the subprogram, which is inefficient.

3. Treat the main program and the I/O subprogram as a single activity that is to be implemented as a single thread. However, one address space (domain) could be created for the main program and one for the I/O subprogram. Thus, the thread can be moved between the two address spaces as execution proceeds. The OS can manage the two address spaces independently, and no process creation overhead is incurred. Furthermore, the address space used by the I/O subprogram could also be shared by other simple I/O programs.

The experiences of the TRIX developers indicate that the third option has merit and may be the most effective solution for some applications.

ONE-TO-MANY RELATIONSHIP In the field of distributed operating systems (designed to control distributed computer systems), there has been interest in the concept of a thread as primarily an entity that can move among address spaces.[5] A notable example of this research is the Clouds operating system, and especially its kernel, known as Ra [DASG92]. Another example is the Emerald system [STEE95].

A thread in Clouds is a unit of activity from the user's perspective. A process is a virtual address space with an associated process control block. Upon creation, a thread starts executing in a process by invoking an entry point to a program in that process. Threads may move from one address space to another and actually span computer boundaries (i.e., move from one computer to another). As a thread moves, it must carry with it certain information, such as the controlling terminal, global parameters, and scheduling guidance (e.g., priority).

The Clouds approach provides an effective way of insulating both users and programmers from the details of the distributed environment. A user's activity may be represented as a single thread, and the movement of that thread among computers may be dictated by the OS for a variety of system-related reasons, such as the need to access a remote resource, and load balancing.

4.3 MULTICORE AND MULTITHREADING

The use of a multicore system to support a single application with multiple threads, such as might occur on a workstation, a video-game console, or a personal computer running a processor-intense application, raises issues of performance and application design. In this section, we first look at some of the performance implications of a multithreaded application on a multicore system and then describe a specific example of an application designed to exploit multicore capabilities.

Performance of Software on Multicore

The potential performance benefits of a multicore organization depend on the ability to effectively exploit the parallel resources available to the application. Let us focus first on a single application running on a multicore system. Amdahl's law (see Appendix E) states that:

$$\text{Speedup} = \frac{\text{time to execute program on a single processor}}{\text{time to execute program on } N \text{ parallel processors}} = \frac{1}{(1-f) + \dfrac{f}{N}}$$

The law assumes a program in which a fraction $(1 - f)$ of the execution time involves code that is inherently serial and a fraction f that involves code that is infinitely parallelizable with no scheduling overhead.

This law appears to make the prospect of a multicore organization attractive. But as Figure 4.7a shows, even a small amount of serial code has a noticeable impact. If only 10% of the code is inherently serial ($f = 0.9$), running the program on a multicore system with eight processors yields a performance gain of only a factor of 4.7. In addition, software typically incurs overhead as a result of communication

---

[5]The movement of processes or threads among address spaces, or thread migration, on different machines has become a hot topic in recent years. Chapter 18 explores this topic.

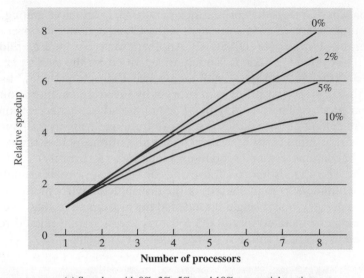

(a) Speedup with 0%, 2%, 5%, and 10% sequential portions

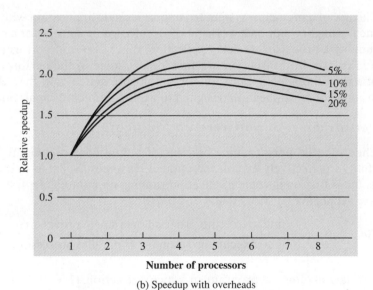

(b) Speedup with overheads

Figure 4.7 **Performance Effect of Multiple Cores**

and distribution of work to multiple processors and cache coherence overhead. This results in a curve where performance peaks and then begins to degrade because of the increased burden of the overhead of using multiple processors. Figure 4.7b, from [MCDO07], is a representative example.

However, software engineers have been addressing this problem and there are numerous applications in which it is possible to effectively exploit a multicore system. [MCDO07] reports on a set of database applications, in which great attention

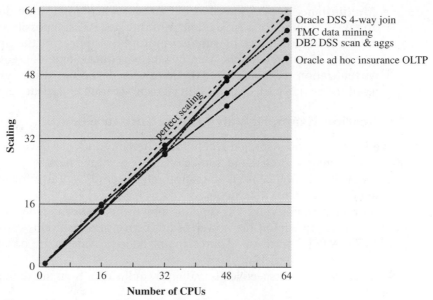

Figure 4.8   Scaling of Database Workloads on Multiple-Processor Hardware

was paid to reducing the serial fraction within hardware architectures, operating systems, middleware, and the database application software. Figure 4.8 shows the result. As this example shows, database management systems and database applications are one area in which multicore systems can be used effectively. Many kinds of servers can also effectively use the parallel multicore organization, because servers typically handle numerous relatively independent transactions in parallel.

In addition to general-purpose server software, a number of classes of applications benefit directly from the ability to scale throughput with the number of cores. [MCDO06] lists the following examples:

- **Multithreaded native applications:** Multithreaded applications are characterized by having a small number of highly threaded processes. Examples of threaded applications include Lotus Domino or Siebel CRM (Customer Relationship Manager).

- **Multiprocess applications:** Multiprocess applications are characterized by the presence of many single-threaded processes. Examples of multiprocess applications include the Oracle database, SAP, and PeopleSoft.

- **Java applications:** Java applications embrace threading in a fundamental way. Not only does the Java language greatly facilitate multithreaded applications, but the Java Virtual Machine is a multithreaded process that provides scheduling and memory management for Java applications. Java applications that can benefit directly from multicore resources include application servers such as Sun's Java Application Server, BEA's Weblogic, IBM's Websphere, and the open-source Tomcat application server. All applications that use a Java 2 Platform, Enterprise Edition (J2EE platform) application server can immediately benefit from multicore technology.

- **Multiinstance applications:** Even if an individual application does not scale to take advantage of a large number of threads, it is still possible to gain from multicore architecture by running multiple instances of the application in parallel. If multiple application instances require some degree of isolation, virtualization technology (for the hardware of the operating system) can be used to provide each of them with its own separate and secure environment.

Application Example: Valve Game Software

Valve is an entertainment and technology company that has developed a number of popular games, as well as the Source engine, one of the most widely played game engines available. Source is an animation engine used by Valve for its games and licensed for other game developers.

In recent years, Valve has reprogrammed the Source engine software to use multithreading to exploit the power of multicore processor chips from Intel and AMD [REIM06]. The revised Source engine code provides more powerful support for Valve games such as Half Life 2.

From Valve's perspective, threading granularity options are defined as follows [HARR06]:

- **Coarse threading:** Individual modules, called systems, are assigned to individual processors. In the Source engine case, this would mean putting rendering on one processor, AI (artificial intelligence) on another, physics on another, and so on. This is straightforward. In essence, each major module is single threaded and the principal coordination involves synchronizing all the threads with a timeline thread.

- **Fine-grained threading:** Many similar or identical tasks are spread across multiple processors. For example, a loop that iterates over an array of data can be split up into a number of smaller parallel loops in individual threads that can be scheduled in parallel.

- **Hybrid threading:** This involves the selective use of fine-grained threading for some systems and single threading for other systems.

Valve found that through coarse threading, it could achieve up to twice the performance across two processors compared to executing on a single processor. But this performance gain could only be achieved with contrived cases. For real-world gameplay, the improvement was on the order of a factor of 1.2. Valve also found that effective use of fine-grained threading was difficult. The time per work unit can be variable, and managing the timeline of outcomes and consequences involved complex programming.

Valve found that a hybrid threading approach was the most promising and would scale the best, as multicore systems with 8 or 16 processors became available. Valve identified systems that operate very effectively being permanently assigned to a single processor. An example is sound mixing, which has little user interaction, is not constrained by the frame configuration of windows, and works on its own set of data. Other modules, such as scene rendering, can be organized into a number of threads so that the module can execute on a single processor but achieve greater performance as it is spread out over more and more processors.

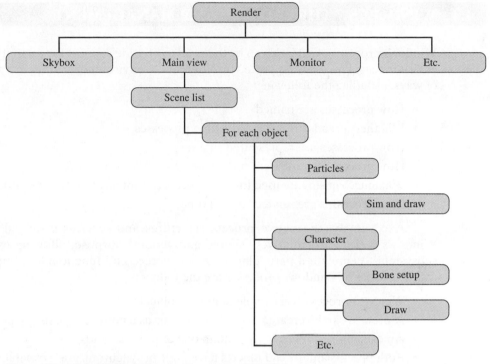

Figure 4.9   Hybrid Threading for Rendering Module

Figure 4.9 illustrates the thread structure for the rendering module. In this hier-archical structure, higher-level threads spawn lower-level threads as needed. The rendering module relies on a critical part of the Source engine, the world list, which is a database representation of the visual elements in the game's world. The first task is to determine what are the areas of the world that need to be rendered. The next task is to determine what objects are in the scene as viewed from multiple angles. Then comes the processor-intensive work. The rendering module has to work out the rendering of each object from multiple points of view, such as the player's view, the view of TV monitors, and the point of view of reflections in water.

Some of the key elements of the threading strategy for the rendering module are listed in [LEON07] and include the following:

- Construct scene-rendering lists for multiple scenes in parallel (e.g., the world and its reflection in water).
- Overlap graphics simulation.
- Compute character bone transformations for all characters in all scenes in parallel.
- Allow multiple threads to draw in parallel.

The designers found that simply locking key databases, such as the world list, for a thread was too inefficient. Over 95% of the time, a thread is trying to read from a data set, and only 5% of the time at most is spent in writing to a data set. Thus, a concurrency mechanism known as the single-writer-multiple-readers model works effectively.

4.4   WINDOWS 7 THREAD AND SMP MANAGEMENT

Windows process design is driven by the need to provide support for a variety of OS environments. Processes supported by different OS environments differ in a number of ways, including the following:

- How processes are named
- Whether threads are provided within processes
- How processes are represented
- How process resources are protected
- What mechanisms are used for interprocess communication and synchronization
- How processes are related to each other

Accordingly, the native process structures and services provided by the Windows Kernel are relatively simple and general purpose, allowing each OS subsystem to emulate a particular process structure and functionality. Important characteristics of Windows processes are the following:

- Windows processes are implemented as objects.
- A process can be created as new process, or as a copy of an existing process.
- An executable process may contain one or more threads.
- Both process and thread objects have built-in synchronization capabilities.

Figure 4.10, based on one in [RUSS11], illustrates the way in which a process relates to the resources it controls or uses. Each process is assigned a security access

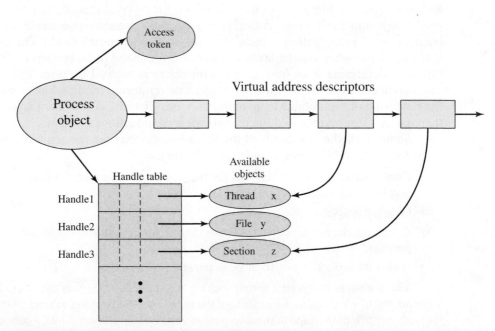

Figure 4.10   **A Windows Process and Its Resources**

token, called the primary token of the process. When a user first logs on, Windows creates an access token that includes the security ID for the user. Every process that is created by or runs on behalf of this user has a copy of this access token. Windows uses the token to validate the user's ability to access secured objects or to perform restricted functions on the system and on secured objects. The access token controls whether the process can change its own attributes. In this case, the process does not have a handle opened to its access token. If the process attempts to open such a handle, the security system determines whether this is permitted and therefore whether the process may change its own attributes.

Also related to the process is a series of blocks that define the virtual address space currently assigned to this process. The process cannot directly modify these structures but must rely on the virtual memory manager, which provides a memory-allocation service for the process.

Finally, the process includes an object table, with handles to other objects known to this process. Figure 4.10 shows a single thread. In addition, the process has access to a file object and to a section object that defines a section of shared memory.

Process and Thread Objects

The object-oriented structure of Windows facilitates the development of a general-purpose process facility. Windows makes use of two types of process-related objects: processes and threads. A process is an entity corresponding to a user job or application that owns resources, such as memory and open files. A thread is a dispatchable unit of work that executes sequentially and is interruptible, so that the processor can turn to another thread.

Each Windows process is represented by an object whose general structure is shown in Figure 4.11a. Each process is defined by a number of attributes and encapsulates a number of actions, or services, that it may perform. A process will perform a service when called upon through a set of published interface methods. When Windows creates a new process, it uses the object class, or type, defined for the Windows process as a template to generate a new object instance. At the time of creation, attribute values are assigned. Table 4.3 gives a brief definition of each of the object attributes for a process object.

A Windows process must contain at least one thread to execute. That thread may then create other threads. In a multiprocessor system, multiple threads from the same process may execute in parallel. Figure 4.11b depicts the object structure for a thread object, and Table 4.4 defines the thread object attributes. Note that some of the attributes of a thread resemble those of a process. In those cases, the thread attribute value is derived from the process attribute value. For example, the *thread processor affinity* is the set of processors in a multiprocessor system that may execute this thread; this set is equal to or a subset of the *process processor affinity*.

Note that one of the attributes of a thread object is context, which contains the values of the processor registers when the thread last ran. This information enables threads to be suspended and resumed. Furthermore, it is possible to alter the behavior of a thread by altering its context while it is suspended.

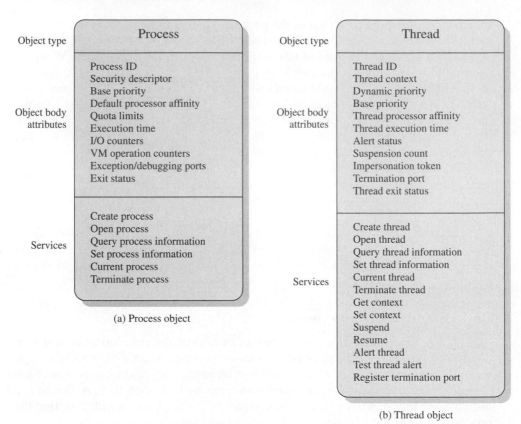

Object type	Process		Object type	Thread
Object body attributes	Process ID Security descriptor Base priority Default processor affinity Quota limits Execution time I/O counters VM operation counters Exception/debugging ports Exit status		Object body attributes	Thread ID Thread context Dynamic priority Base priority Thread processor affinity Thread execution time Alert status Suspension count Impersonation token Termination port Thread exit status
Services	Create process Open process Query process information Set process information Current process Terminate process		Services	Create thread Open thread Query thread information Set thread information Current thread Terminate thread Get context Set context Suspend Resume Alert thread Test thread alert Register termination port

(a) Process object

(b) Thread object

Figure 4.11   Windows Process and Thread Objects

Table 4.3   Windows Process Object Attributes

Process ID	A unique value that identifies the process to the operating system.
Security descriptor	Describes who created an object, who can gain access to or use the object, and who is denied access to the object.
Base priority	A baseline execution priority for the process's threads.
Default processor affinity	The default set of processors on which the process's threads can run.
Quota limits	The maximum amount of paged and nonpaged system memory, paging file space, and processor time a user's processes can use.
Execution time	The total amount of time all threads in the process have executed.
I/O counters	Variables that record the number and type of I/O operations that the process's threads have performed.
VM operation counters	Variables that record the number and types of virtual memory operations that the process's threads have performed.
Exception/debugging ports	Interprocess communication channels to which the process manager sends a message when one of the process's threads causes an exception. Normally, these are connected to environment subsystem and debugger processes, respectively.
Exit status	The reason for a process's termination.

Table 4.4   Windows Thread Object Attributes

Thread ID	A unique value that identifies a thread when it calls a server.
Thread context	The set of register values and other volatile data that defines the execution state of a thread.
Dynamic priority	The thread's execution priority at any given moment.
Base priority	The lower limit of the thread's dynamic priority.
Thread processor affinity	The set of processors on which the thread can run, which is a subset or all of the processor affinity of the thread's process.
Thread execution time	The cumulative amount of time a thread has executed in user mode and in kernel mode.
Alert status	A flag that indicates whether a waiting thread may execute an asynchronous procedure call.
Suspension count	The number of times the thread's execution has been suspended without being resumed.
Impersonation token	A temporary access token allowing a thread to perform operations on behalf of another process (used by subsystems).
Termination port	An interprocess communication channel to which the process manager sends a message when the thread terminates (used by subsystems).
Thread exit status	The reason for a thread's termination.

Multithreading

Windows supports concurrency among processes because threads in different processes may execute concurrently (appear to run at the same time). Moreover, multiple threads within the same process may be allocated to separate processors and execute simultaneously (actually run at the same time). A multithreaded process achieves concurrency without the overhead of using multiple processes. Threads within the same process can exchange information through their common address space and have access to the shared resources of the process. Threads in different processes can exchange information through shared memory that has been set up between the two processes.

An object-oriented multithreaded process is an efficient means of implementing a server application. For example, one server process can service a number of clients concurrently.

Thread States

An existing Windows thread is in one of six states (Figure 4.12):

- **Ready:** A ready thread may be scheduled for execution. The Kernel dispatcher keeps track of all ready threads and schedules them in priority order.
- **Standby:** A standby thread has been selected to run next on a particular processor. The thread waits in this state until that processor is made available. If the standby thread's priority is high enough, the running thread on that

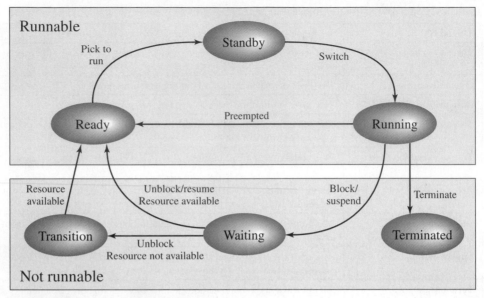

Figure 4.12   Windows Thread States

processor may be preempted in favor of the standby thread. Otherwise, the standby thread waits until the running thread blocks or exhausts its time slice.

- **Running:** Once the Kernel dispatcher performs a thread switch, the standby thread enters the Running state and begins execution and continues execution until it is preempted by a higher-priority thread, exhausts its time slice, blocks, or terminates. In the first two cases, it goes back to the Ready state.

- **Waiting:** A thread enters the Waiting state when (1) it is blocked on an event (e.g., I/O), (2) it voluntarily waits for synchronization purposes, or (3) an environment subsystem directs the thread to suspend itself. When the waiting condition is satisfied, the thread moves to the Ready state if all of its resources are available.

- **Transition:** A thread enters this state after waiting if it is ready to run but the resources are not available. For example, the thread's stack may be paged out of memory. When the resources are available, the thread goes to the Ready state.

- **Terminated:** A thread can be terminated by itself, by another thread, or when its parent process terminates. Once housekeeping chores are completed, the thread is removed from the system, or it may be retained by the Executive[6] for future reinitialization.

---

[6]The Windows Executive is described in Chapter 2. It contains the base operating system services, such as memory management, process and thread management, security, I/O, and interprocess communication.

Support for OS Subsystems

The general-purpose process and thread facility must support the particular process and thread structures of the various OS environments. It is the responsibility of each OS subsystem to exploit the Windows process and thread features to emulate the process and thread facilities of its corresponding OS. This area of process/thread management is complicated, and we give only a brief overview here.

Process creation begins with a request for a new process from an application. The application issues a create-process request to the corresponding protected subsystem, which passes the request to the Executive. The Executive creates a process object and returns a handle for that object to the subsystem. When Windows creates a process, it does not automatically create a thread. In the case of Win32, a new process must always be created with an initial thread. Therefore, for the Win32 subsystem calls the Windows process manager again to create a thread for the new process, receiving a thread handle back from Windows. The appropriate thread and process information are then returned to the application. In the case of POSIX, threads are not supported. Therefore, the POSIX subsystem obtains a thread for the new process from Windows so that the process may be activated but returns only process information to the application. The fact that the POSIX process is implemented using both a process and a thread from the Windows Executive is not visible to the application.

When a new process is created by the Executive, the new process inherits many of its attributes from the creating process. However, in the Win32 environment, this process creation is done indirectly. An application client process issues its process creation request to the Win32 subsystem; then the subsystem in turn issues a process request to the Windows executive. Because the desired effect is that the new process inherits characteristics of the client process and not of the server process, Windows enables the subsystem to specify the parent of the new process. The new process then inherits the parent's access token, quota limits, base priority, and default processor affinity.

Symmetric Multiprocessing Support

Windows supports SMP hardware configurations. The threads of any process, including those of the executive, can run on any processor. In the absence of affinity restrictions, explained in the next paragraph, the kernel dispatcher assigns a ready thread to the next available processor. This assures that no processor is idle or is executing a lower-priority thread when a higher-priority thread is ready. Multiple threads from the same process can be executing simultaneously on multiple processors.

As a default, the kernel dispatcher uses the policy of **soft affinity** in assigning threads to processors: The dispatcher tries to assign a ready thread to the same processor it last ran on. This helps reuse data still in that processor's memory caches from the previous execution of the thread. It is possible for an application to restrict its thread execution only to certain processors (**hard affinity**).

4.5 SOLARIS THREAD AND SMP MANAGEMENT

Solaris implements multilevel thread support designed to provide considerable flexibility in exploiting processor resources.

Multithreaded Architecture

Solaris makes use of four separate thread-related concepts:

- **Process:** This is the normal UNIX process and includes the user's address space, stack, and process control block.
- **User-level threads:** Implemented through a threads library in the address space of a process, these are invisible to the OS. A user-level thread (ULT)[7] is a user-created unit of execution within a process.
- **Lightweight processes:** A lightweight process (LWP) can be viewed as a mapping between ULTs and kernel threads. Each LWP supports ULT and maps to one kernel thread. LWPs are scheduled by the kernel independently and may execute in parallel on multiprocessors.
- **Kernel threads:** These are the fundamental entities that can be scheduled and dispatched to run on one of the system processors.

Figure 4.13 illustrates the relationship among these four entities. Note that there is always exactly one kernel thread for each LWP. An LWP is visible within a process to the application. Thus, LWP data structures exist within their respective process address space. At the same time, each LWP is bound to a single dispatchable kernel thread, and the data structure for that kernel thread is maintained within the kernel's address space.

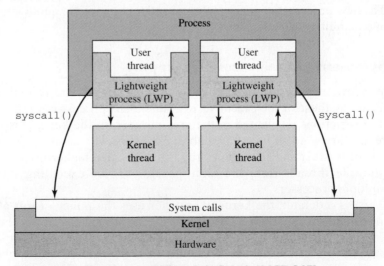

Figure 4.13   Processes and Threads in Solaris [MCDO07]

---

[7]Again, the acronym ULT is unique to this book and is not found in the Solaris literature.

A process may consist of a single ULT bound to a single LWP. In this case, there is a single thread of execution, corresponding to a traditional UNIX process. When concurrency is not required within a single process, an application uses this process structure. If an application requires concurrency, its process contains multiple threads, each bound to a single LWP, which in turn are each bound to a single kernel thread.

In addition, there are kernel threads that are not associated with LWPs. The kernel creates, runs, and destroys these kernel threads to execute specific system functions. The use of kernel threads rather than kernel processes to implement system functions reduces the overhead of switching within the kernel (from a process switch to a thread switch).

Motivation

The three-level thread structure (ULT, LWP, kernel thread) in Solaris is intended to facilitate thread management by the OS and to provide a clean interface to applications. The ULT interface can be a standard thread library. A defined ULT maps onto a LWP, which is managed by the OS and which has defined states of execution, defined subsequently. An LWP is bound to a kernel thread with a one-to-one correspondence in execution states. Thus, concurrency and execution are managed at the level of the kernel thread.

In addition, an application has access to hardware through an application programming interface consisting of system calls. The API allows the user to invoke kernel services to perform privileged tasks on behalf of the calling process, such as read or write a file, issue a control command to a device, create a new process or thread, allocate memory for the process to use, and so on.

Process Structure

Figure 4.14 compares, in general terms, the process structure of a traditional UNIX system with that of Solaris. On a typical UNIX implementation, the process structure includes the process ID; the user IDs; a signal dispatch table, which the kernel uses to decide what to do when sending a signal to a process; file descriptors, which describe the state of files in use by this process; a memory map, which defines the address space for this process; and a processor state structure, which includes the kernel stack for this process. Solaris retains this basic structure but replaces the processor state block with a list of structures containing one data block for each LWP.

The LWP data structure includes the following elements:

- An LWP identifier
- The priority of this LWP and hence the kernel thread that supports it
- A signal mask that tells the kernel which signals will be accepted
- Saved values of user-level registers (when the LWP is not running)
- The kernel stack for this LWP, which includes system call arguments, results, and error codes for each call level
- Resource usage and profiling data
- Pointer to the corresponding kernel thread
- Pointer to the process structure

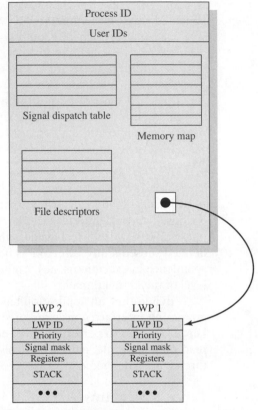

Figure 4.14   Process Structure in Traditional UNIX and Solaris [LEWI96]

Thread Execution

Figure 4.15 shows a simplified view of both thread execution states. These states reflect the execution status of both a kernel thread and the LWP bound to it. As mentioned, some kernel threads are not associated with an LWP; the same execution diagram applies. The states are as follows:

- **RUN:** The thread is runnable; that is, the thread is ready to execute.
- **ONPROC:** The thread is executing on a processor.
- **SLEEP:** The thread is blocked.
- **STOP:** The thread is stopped.
- **ZOMBIE:** The thread has terminated.
- **FREE:** Thread resources have been released and the thread is awaiting removal from the OS thread data structure.

A thread moves from ONPROC to RUN if it is preempted by a higher-priority thread or because of time slicing. A thread moves from ONPROC to SLEEP if it

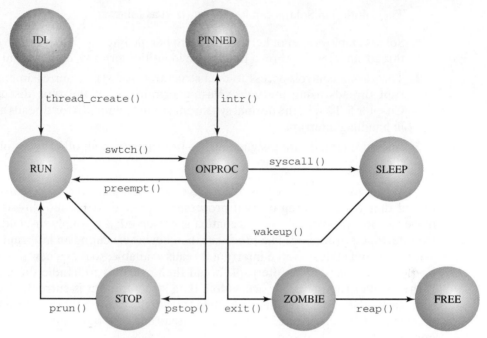

Figure 4.15   Solaris Thread States

is blocked and must await an event to return the RUN state. Blocking occurs if the thread invokes a system call and must wait for the system service to be performed. A thread enters the STOP state if its process is stopped; this might be done for debugging purposes.

Interrupts as Threads

Most operating systems contain two fundamental forms of concurrent activity: processes and interrupts. Processes (or threads) cooperate with each other and manage the use of shared data structures by means of a variety of primitives that enforce mutual exclusion (only one process at a time can execute certain code or access certain data) and that synchronize their execution. Interrupts are synchronized by preventing their handling for a period of time. Solaris unifies these two concepts into a single model, namely kernel threads and the mechanisms for scheduling and executing kernel threads. To do this, interrupts are converted to kernel threads.

The motivation for converting interrupts to threads is to reduce overhead. Interrupt handlers often manipulate data shared by the rest of the kernel. Therefore, while a kernel routine that accesses such data is executing, interrupts must be blocked, even though most interrupts will not affect that data. Typically, the way this is done is for the routine to set the interrupt priority level higher to block interrupts and then lower the priority level after access is completed. These operations take time. The problem is magnified on a multiprocessor system. The kernel must protect more objects and may need to block interrupts on all processors.

The solution in Solaris can be summarized as follows:

1. Solaris employs a set of kernel threads to handle interrupts. As with any kernel thread, an interrupt thread has its own identifier, priority, context, and stack.

2. The kernel controls access to data structures and synchronizes among interrupt threads using mutual exclusion primitives, of the type discussed in Chapter 5. That is, the normal synchronization techniques for threads are used in handling interrupts.

3. Interrupt threads are assigned higher priorities than all other types of kernel threads.

When an interrupt occurs, it is delivered to a particular processor and the thread that was executing on that processor is pinned. A pinned thread cannot move to another processor and its context is preserved; it is simply suspended until the interrupt is processed. The processor then begins executing an interrupt thread. There is a pool of deactivated interrupt threads available, so that a new thread creation is not required. The interrupt thread then executes to handle the interrupt. If the handler routine needs access to a data structure that is currently locked in some fashion for use by another executing thread, the interrupt thread must wait for access to that data structure. An interrupt thread can only be preempted by another interrupt thread of higher priority.

Experience with Solaris interrupt threads indicates that this approach provides superior performance to the traditional interrupt-handling strategy [KLEI95].

4.6 LINUX PROCESS AND THREAD MANAGEMENT

Linux Tasks

A process, or task, in Linux is represented by a `task_struct` data structure. The `task_struct` data structure contains information in a number of categories:

- **State:** The execution state of the process (executing, ready, suspended, stopped, zombie). This is described subsequently.

- **Scheduling information:** Information needed by Linux to schedule processes. A process can be normal or real time and has a priority. Real-time processes are scheduled before normal processes, and within each category, relative priorities can be used. A counter keeps track of the amount of time a process is allowed to execute.

- **Identifiers:** Each process has a unique process identifier and also has user and group identifiers. A group identifier is used to assign resource access privileges to a group of processes.

- **Interprocess communication:** Linux supports the IPC mechanisms found in UNIX SVR4, described in Chapter 6.

- **Links:** Each process includes a link to its parent process, links to its siblings (processes with the same parent), and links to all of its children.

- **Times and timers:** Includes process creation time and the amount of processor time so far consumed by the process. A process may also have associated one or more interval timers. A process defines an interval timer by means of a system call; as a result, a signal is sent to the process when the timer expires. A timer may be single use or periodic.

- **File system:** Includes pointers to any files opened by this process, as well as pointers to the current and the root directories for this process.

- **Address space:** Defines the virtual address space assigned to this process.

- **Processor-specific context:** The registers and stack information that constitute the context of this process.

Figure 4.16 shows the execution states of a process. These are as follows:

- **Running:** This state value corresponds to two states. A Running process is either executing or it is ready to execute.

- **Interruptible:** This is a blocked state, in which the process is waiting for an event, such as the end of an I/O operation, the availability of a resource, or a signal from another process.

- **Uninterruptible:** This is another blocked state. The difference between this and the Interruptible state is that in an Uninterruptible state, a process is waiting directly on hardware conditions and therefore will not handle any signals.

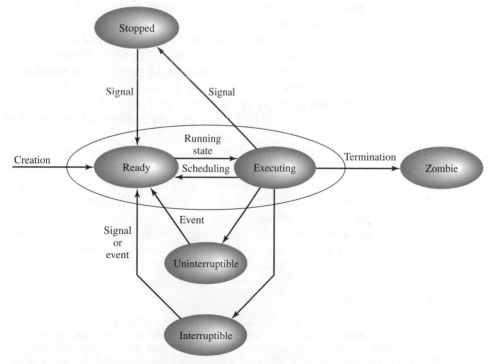

Figure 4.16   Linux Process/Thread Model

- **Stopped:** The process has been halted and can only resume by positive action from another process. For example, a process that is being debugged can be put into the Stopped state.
- **Zombie:** The process has been terminated but, for some reason, still must have its task structure in the process table.

Linux Threads

Traditional UNIX systems support a single thread of execution per process, while modern UNIX systems typically provide support for multiple kernel-level threads per process. As with traditional UNIX systems, older versions of the Linux kernel offered no support for multithreading. Instead, applications would need to be written with a set of user-level library functions, the most popular of which is known as *pthread (POSIX thread) libraries*, with all of the threads mapping into a single kernel-level process.[8] We have seen that modern versions of UNIX offer kernel-level threads. Linux provides a unique solution in that it does not recognize a distinction between threads and processes. Using a mechanism similar to the lightweight processes of Solaris, user-level threads are mapped into kernel-level processes. Multiple user-level threads that constitute a single user-level process are mapped into Linux kernel-level processes that share the same group ID. This enables these processes to share resources such as files and memory and to avoid the need for a context switch when the scheduler switches among processes in the same group.

A new process is created in Linux by copying the attributes of the current process. A new process can be *cloned* so that it shares resources, such as files, signal handlers, and virtual memory. When the two processes share the same virtual memory, they function as threads within a single process. However, no separate type of data structure is defined for a thread. In place of the usual fork() command, processes are created in Linux using the clone() command. This command includes a set of flags as arguments, defined in Table 4.5. The traditional fork() system call is implemented by Linux as a clone() system call with all of the clone flags cleared.

When the Linux kernel performs a switch from one process to another, it checks whether the address of the page directory of the current process is the same as that of the to-be-scheduled process. If they are, then they are sharing the same address space, so that a context switch is basically just a jump from one location of code to another location of code.

Although cloned processes that are part of the same process group can share the same memory space, they cannot share the same user stacks. Thus the clone() call creates separate stack spaces for each process.

---

[8]POSIX (Portable Operating Systems based on UNIX) is an IEEE API standard that includes a standard for a thread API. Libraries implementing the POSIX Threads standard are often named *Pthreads*. Pthreads are most commonly used on UNIX-like POSIX systems such as Linux and Solaris, but Microsoft Windows implementations also exist.

Table 4.5   Linux clone () flags

CLONE_CLEARID	Clear the task ID.
CLONE_DETACHED	The parent does not want a SIGCHLD signal sent on exit.
CLONE_FILES	Share the table that identifies the open files.
CLONE_FS	Share the table that identifies the root directory and the current working directory, as well as the value of the bit mask used to mask the initial file permissions of a new file.
CLONE_IDLETASK	Set PID to zero, which refers to an idle task. The idle task is employed when all available tasks are blocked waiting for resources.
CLONE_NEWNS	Create a new namespace for the child.
CLONE_PARENT	Caller and new task share the same parent process.
CLONE_PTRACE	If the parent process is being traced, the child process will also be traced.
CLONE_SETTID	Write the TID back to user space.
CLONE_SETTLS	Create a new TLS for the child.
CLONE_SIGHAND	Share the table that identifies the signal handlers.
CLONE_SYSVSEM	Share System V SEM_UNDO semantics.
CLONE_THREAD	Insert this process into the same thread group of the parent. If this flag is true, it implicitly enforces CLONE_PARENT.
CLONE_VFORK	If set, the parent does not get scheduled for execution until the child invokes the *execve()* system call.
CLONE_VM	Share the address space (memory descriptor and all page tables).

4.7 MAC OS X GRAND CENTRAL DISPATCH

As was mentioned in Chapter 2, Mac OS X Grand Central Dispatch (GCD) provides a pool of available threads. Designers can designate portions of applications, called blocks, that can be dispatched independently and run concurrently. The OS will provide as much concurrency as possible based on the number of cores available and the thread capacity of the system. Although other operating systems have implemented thread pools, GCD provides a qualitative improvement in ease of use and efficiency.

A block is a simple extension to C or other languages, such as C++. The purpose of defining a block is to define a self-contained unit of work, including code plus data. Here is a simple example of a block definition:

```
x = ^{ printf("hello world\n"); }
```

A block is denoted by a caret at the start of the function, which is enclosed in curly brackets. The above block definition defines x as a way of calling the function, so that invoking the function x() would print the words *hello world*.

Blocks enable the programmer to encapsulate complex functions, together with their arguments and data, so that they can easily be referenced and passed around in a program, much like a variable.[9] Symbolically:

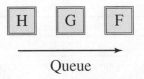

Blocks are scheduled and dispatched by means of queues. The application makes use of system queues provided by GCD and may also set up private queues. Blocks are put onto a queue as they are encountered during program execution. GCD then uses those queues to describe concurrency, serialization, and callbacks. Queues are lightweight user-space data structures, which generally makes them far more efficient than manually managing threads and locks. For example, this queue has three blocks:

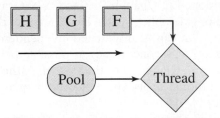

Depending on the queue and how it is defined, GCD either treats these blocks as potentially concurrent activities, or treats them as serial activities. In either case, blocks are dispatched on a first-in-first-out basis. If this is a concurrent queue, then the dispatcher assigns F to a thread as soon as one is available, then G, then H. If this is a serial queue, the dispatcher assigns F to a thread, and then only assigns G to a thread after F has completed. The use of predefined threads saves the cost of creating a new thread for each request, reducing the latency associated with processing a block. Thread pools are automatically sized by the system to maximize the performance of the applications using GCD while minimizing the number of idle or competing threads.

In addition to scheduling blocks directly, the application can associate a single block and queue with an event source, such as a timer, network socket, or file descriptor. Every time the source issues an event, the block is scheduled if it is not

---

[9]Much of the material in the remainder of this section is based on [APPL09].

already running. This allows rapid response without the expense of polling or "parking a thread" on the event source.

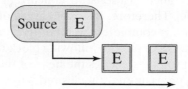

An example from [SIRA09] indicates the ease of using GCD. Consider a document-based application with a button that, when clicked, will analyze the current document and display some interesting statistics about it. In the common case, this analysis should execute in under a second, so the following code is used to connect the button with an action:

```
- (Inaction)analyzeDocument:(NSButton *)sender
{
    NSDictionary *stats = [myDoc analyze];
    [myModel setDict:stats];
    [myStatsView setNeedsDisplay:YES];
    [stats release];
}
```

The first line of the function body analyzes the document, the second line updates the application's internal state, and the third line tells the application that the statistics view needs to be updated to reflect this new state. This code, which follows a common pattern, is executed in the main thread. The design is acceptable so long as the analysis does not take too long, because after the user clicks the button, the main thread of the application needs to handle that user input as fast as possible so it can get back to the main event loop to process the next user action. But if the user opens a very large or complex document, the analyze step may take an unacceptably long amount of time. A developer may be reluctant to alter the code to meet this unlikely event, which may involve application-global objects, thread management, callbacks, argument marshalling, context objects, new variables, and so on. But with GCD, a modest addition to the code produces the desired result:

```
- (IBAction)analyzeDocument:(NSButton *)sender
    {dispatch_async(dispatch_get_global_queue(0, 0), ^{
        NSDictionary *stats = [myDoc analyze];
        dispatch_async(dispatch_get_main_queue(), ^{
            [myModel setDict:stats];
            [myStatsView setNeedsDisplay:YES];
            [stats release];
        });
    });
}
```

All functions in GCD begin with `dispatch_`. The outer `dispatch_async()` call puts a task on a global concurrent queue. This tells the OS that the block can be assigned to a separate concurrent queue, off the main queue, and executed in parallel. Therefore, the main thread of execution is not delayed. When the analyze function is complete, the inner `dispatch_async()` call is encountered. This directs the OS to put the following block of code at the end of the main queue, to be executed when it reaches the head of the queue. So, with very little work on the part of the programmer, the desired requirement is met.

4.8   SUMMARY

Some operating systems distinguish the concepts of process and thread, the former related to resource ownership and the latter related to program execution. This approach may lead to improved efficiency and coding convenience. In a multithreaded system, multiple concurrent threads may be defined within a single process. This may be done using either user-level threads or kernel-level threads. User-level threads are unknown to the OS and are created and managed by a threads library that runs in the user space of a process. User-level threads are very efficient because a mode switch is not required to switch from one thread to another. However, only a single user-level thread within a process can execute at a time, and if one thread blocks, the entire process is blocked. Kernel-level threads are threads within a process that are maintained by the kernel. Because they are recognized by the kernel, multiple threads within the same process can execute in parallel on a multiprocessor and the blocking of a thread does not block the entire process. However, a mode switch is required to switch from one thread to another.

4.9   RECOMMENDED READING

[LEWI96] and [KLEI96] provide good overviews of thread concepts and a discussion of programming strategies; the former focuses more on concepts and the latter more on programming, but both provide useful coverage of both topics. [PHAM96] discusses the Windows NT thread facility in depth. Good coverage of UNIX threads concepts is found in [ROBB04].

KLEI96   Kleiman, S., Shah, D., and Smallders, B. *Programming with Threads.* Upper Saddle River, NJ: Prentice Hall, 1996.

LEWI96   Lewis, B., and Berg, D. *Threads Primer.* Upper Saddle River, NJ: Prentice Hall, 1996.

PHAM96   Pham, T., and Garg, P. *Multithreaded Programming with Windows NT.* Upper Saddle River, NJ: Prentice Hall, 1996.

ROBB04   Robbins, K., and Robbins, S. *UNIX Systems Programming: Communication, Concurrency, and Threads.* Upper Saddle River, NJ: Prentice Hall, 2004.

4.10 KEY TERMS, REVIEW QUESTIONS, AND PROBLEMS

Key Terms

kernel-level thread	multithreading	task
lightweight process	port	thread
message	process	user-level thread

Review Questions

4.1 Table 3.5 lists typical elements found in a process control block for an unthreaded OS. Of these, which should belong to a thread control block and which should belong to a process control block for a multithreaded system?

4.2 List reasons why a mode switch between threads may be cheaper than a mode switch between processes.

4.3 What are the two separate and potentially independent characteristics embodied in the concept of process?

4.4 Give four general examples of the use of threads in a single-user multiprocessing system.

4.5 What resources are typically shared by all of the threads of a process?

4.6 List three advantages of ULTs over KLTs.

4.7 List two disadvantages of ULTs compared to KLTs.

4.8 Define jacketing.

Problems

4.1 It was pointed out that two advantages of using multiple threads within a process are that (1) less work is involved in creating a new thread within an existing process than in creating a new process, and (2) communication among threads within the same process is simplified. Is it also the case that a mode switch between two threads within the same process involves less work than a mode switch between two threads in different processes?

4.2 In the discussion of ULTs versus KLTs, it was pointed out that a disadvantage of ULTs is that when a ULT executes a system call, not only is that thread blocked, but also all of the threads within the process are blocked. Why is that so?

4.3 OS/2 is an obsolete OS for PCs from IBM. In OS/2, what is commonly embodied in the concept of process in other operating systems is split into three separate types of entities: session, processes, and threads. A session is a collection of one or more processes associated with a user interface (keyboard, display, and mouse). The session represents an interactive user application, such as a word processing program or a spreadsheet. This concept allows the personal-computer user to open more than one application, giving each one or more windows on the screen. The OS must keep track of which window, and therefore which session, is active, so that keyboard and mouse input are routed to the appropriate session. At any time, one session is in foreground mode, with other sessions in background mode. All keyboard and mouse input is directed to one of the processes of the foreground session, as dictated by the applications. When a session is in foreground mode, a process performing video output sends it directly to the hardware video buffer and thence to the user's screen. When the session is moved to the background, the hardware video buffer is saved to a logical video buffer for that session. While a session is in background, if any of the threads of any of the processes of that session executes and produces screen output, that output is directed to the logical video buffer. When the session returns to foreground, the screen is updated to reflect the current contents of the logical video buffer for the new foreground session.

There is a way to reduce the number of process-related concepts in OS/2 from three to two. Eliminate sessions, and associate the user interface (keyboard, mouse, and screen) with processes. Thus, one process at a time is in foreground mode. For further structuring, processes can be broken up into threads.

a. What benefits are lost with this approach?
b. If you go ahead with this modification, where do you assign resources (memory, files, etc.): at the process or thread level?

4.4 Consider an environment in which there is a one-to-one mapping between user-level threads and kernel-level threads that allows one or more threads within a process to issue blocking system calls while other threads continue to run. Explain why this model can make multithreaded programs run faster than their single-threaded counterparts on a uniprocessor computer.

4.5 If a process exits and there are still threads of that process running, will they continue to run?

4.6 The OS/390 mainframe operating system is structured around the concepts of address space and task. Roughly speaking, a single address space corresponds to a single application and corresponds more or less to a process in other operating systems. Within an address space, a number of tasks may be generated and execute concurrently; this corresponds roughly to the concept of multithreading. Two data structures are key to managing this task structure. An address space control block (ASCB) contains information about an address space needed by OS/390 whether or not that address space is executing. Information in the ASCB includes dispatching priority, real and virtual memory allocated to this address space, the number of ready tasks in this address space, and whether each is swapped out. A task control block (TCB) represents a user program in execution. It contains information needed for managing a task within an address space, including processor status information, pointers to programs that are part of this task, and task execution state. ASCBs are global structures maintained in system memory, while TCBs are local structures maintained within their address space. What is the advantage of splitting the control information into global and local portions?

4.7 Many current language specifications, such as for C and C++, are inadequate for multithreaded programs. This can have an impact on compilers and the correctness of code, as this problem illustrates. Consider the following declarations and function definition:

```
int global_positives = 0;
typedef struct list {
    struct list *next;
    double val;
} * list;
```

```
void count_positives(list l)
{
    list p;
    for (p = l; p; p = p -> next)
        if (p -> val > 0.0)
            ++global_positives;
}
```

Now consider the case in which thread A performs

```
count_positives(<list containing only negative values>);
```

while thread B performs

```
++global_positives;
```

a. What does the function do?

b. The C language only addresses single-threaded execution. Does the use of two parallel threads create any problems or potential problems? *- not in this case as thread A does not effect global-pos*

4.8 But some existing optimizing compilers (including gcc, which tends to be relatively conservative) will "optimize" count_positives to something similar to

```
void count_positives(list l)
{
    list p;
    register int r;
    r = global_positives;
    for (p = l; p; p = p -> next)
        if (p -> val > 0.0) ++r;
    global_positives = r;
}
```

will always update your c[..] race condition potentially causing with thread B

What problem or potential problem occurs with this compiled version of the program if threads A and B are executed concurrently?

4.9 Consider the following code using the POSIX Pthreads API:

```
thread2.c
#include <pthread.h>
#include <stdlib.h>
#include <unistd.h>
#include <stdio.h>
int myglobal;
    void *thread_function(void *arg) {
        int i,j;
        for ( i=0; i<20; i++ ) {
            j=myglobal;
            j=j+1;
            printf(".");
            fflush(stdout);
            sleep(1);
            myglobal=j;
        }
```

```
                    return NULL;
        }
        int main(void) {
            pthread_t mythread;
            int i;
            if ( pthread_create( &mythread, NULL, thread_function,
                NULL) ) {
                printf(ldquo;error creating thread.");
                abort();
            }
        for ( i=0; i<20; i++) {
            myglobal=myglobal+1;
            printf("o");
            fflush(stdout);
            sleep(1);
        }
        if ( pthread_join ( mythread, NULL ) ) {
            printf("error joining thread.");
            abort();
        }
        printf("\nmyglobal equals %d\n",myglobal);
        exit(0);
        }
```

In main() we first declare a variable called mythread, which has a type of pthread_t. This is essentially an ID for a thread. Next, the if statement creates a thread associated with mythread. The call pthread_create() returns zero on success and a nonzero value on failure. The third argument of pthread_create() is the name of a function that the new thread will execute when it starts. When this thread_function() returns, the thread terminates. Meanwhile, the main program itself defines a thread, so that there are two threads executing. The pthread_join function enables the main thread to wait until the new thread completes.

a. What does this program accomplish? *increments myglobal 20 x each thread (2 thread)*

b. Here is the output from the executed program:

```
$ ./thread2
..o.o.o.o.oo.o.o.o.o.o.o.o.o.o..o.o.o.o.o    multiplies
myglobal equals 21                  race condition occurs
```

Is this the output you would expect? If not, what has gone wrong?

4.10 The Solaris documentation states that a ULT may yield to another thread of the same priority. Isn't it possible that there will be a runnable thread of higher priority and that therefore the yield function should result in yielding to a thread of the same or higher priority?

4.11 In Solaris 9 and Solaris 10, there is a one-to-one mapping between ULTs and LWPs. In Solaris 8, a single LWP supports one or more ULTs.

a. What is the possible benefit of allowing a many-to-one mapping of ULTs to LWPs?

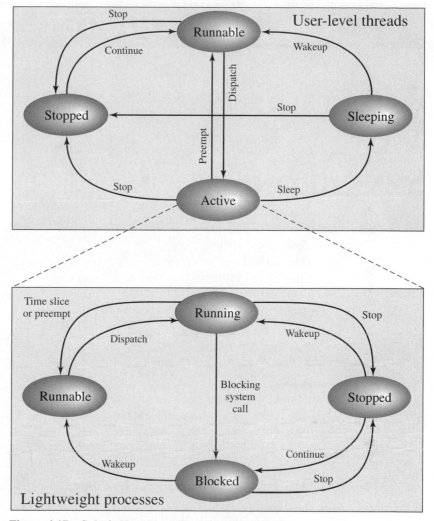

Figure 4.17   Solaris User-Level Thread and LWP States

b. In Solaris 8, the thread execution state of a ULT is distinct from that of its LWP. Explain why.

c. Figure 4.17 shows the state transition diagrams for a ULT and its associated LWP in Solaris 8 and 9. Explain the operation of the two diagrams and their relationships.

4.12. Explain the rationale for the Uninterruptible state in Linux.

will not handle any signals except from hardware
eg. device driver searching for corresponding hardware
cannot be interrupted until process completion or
hardware could be left in unpredictable state

CHAPTER 5

CONCURRENCY: MUTUAL EXCLUSION AND SYNCHRONIZATION

5.1 Principles of Concurrency
   A Simple Example
   Race Condition
   Operating System Concerns
   Process Interaction
   Requirements for Mutual Exclusion

5.2 Mutual Exclusion: Hardware Support
   Interrupt Disabling
   Special Machine Instructions

5.3 Semaphores
   Mutual Exclusion
   The Producer/Consumer Problem
   Implementation of Semaphores

5.4 Monitors
   Monitor with Signal
   Alternate Model of Monitors with Notify and Broadcast

5.5 Message Passing
   Synchronization
   Addressing
   Message Format
   Queueing Discipline
   Mutual Exclusion

5.6 Readers/Writers Problem
   Readers Have Priority
   Writers Have Priority

5.7 Summary

5.8 Recommended Reading

5.9 Key Terms, Review Questions, and Problems

> *Designing correct routines for controlling concurrent activities proved to be one of the most difficult aspects of systems programming. The ad hoc techniques used by programmers of early multiprogramming and real-time systems were always vulnerable to subtle programming errors whose effects could be observed only when certain relatively rare sequences of actions occurred. The errors are particularly difficult to locate, since the precise conditions under which they appear are very hard to reproduce.*
>
> —*The Computer Science and Engineering Research Study*, MIT Press, 1980

LEARNING OBJECTIVES

After studying this chapter, you should be able to:

- Discuss basic concepts related to concurrency, such as race conditions, OS concerns, and mutual exclusion requirements.
- Understand hardware approaches to supporting mutual exclusion.
- Define and explain semaphores.
- Define and explain monitors.
- Define and explain monitors.
- Explain the readers/writers problem.

The central themes of operating system design are all concerned with the management of processes and threads:

- **Multiprogramming:** The management of multiple processes within a uniprocessor system
- **Multiprocessing:** The management of multiple processes within a multiprocessor
- **Distributed processing:** The management of multiple processes executing on multiple, distributed computer systems. The recent proliferation of clusters is a prime example of this type of system.

Fundamental to all of these areas, and fundamental to OS design, is concurrency. Concurrency encompasses a host of design issues, including communication among processes, sharing of and competing for resources (such as memory, files, and I/O access), synchronization of the activities of multiple processes, and allocation of processor time to processes. We shall see that these issues arise not just in multiprocessing and distributed processing environments but even in single-processor multiprogramming systems.

Concurrency arises in three different contexts:

- **Multiple applications:** Multiprogramming was invented to allow processing time to be dynamically shared among a number of active applications.
- **Structured applications:** As an extension of the principles of modular design and structured programming, some applications can be effectively programmed as a set of concurrent processes.

- **Operating system structure:** The same structuring advantages apply to systems programs, and we have seen that operating systems are themselves often implemented as a set of processes or threads.

Because of the importance of this topic, four chapters and an appendix focus on concurrency-related issues. Chapters 5 and 6 deal with concurrency in multiprogramming and multiprocessing systems. Chapters 16 and 18 examine concurrency issues related to distributed processing.

This chapter begins with an introduction to the concept of concurrency and the implications of the execution of multiple concurrent processes.[1] We find that the basic requirement for support of concurrent processes is the ability to enforce mutual exclusion; that is, the ability to exclude all other processes from a course of action while one process is granted that ability. Next, we examine some hardware mechanisms that can support mutual exclusion. Then we look at solutions that do not involve busy waiting and that can be supported either by the OS or enforced by language compilers. We examine three approaches: semaphores, monitors, and message passing.

Two classic problems in concurrency are used to illustrate the concepts and compare the approaches presented in this chapter. The producer/consumer problem is introduced in Section 5.3 and used as a running example. The chapter closes with the readers/writers problem.

Our discussion of concurrency continues in Chapter 6, and we defer a discussion of the concurrency mechanisms of our example systems until the end of that chapter. Appendix A covers additional topics on concurrency. Table 5.1 lists some key terms related to concurrency. A set of animations that illustrate concepts in this chapter is available online. Click on the rotating globe at this book's Web site at WilliamStallings.com/OS/OS7e.html for access.

Table 5.1   Some Key Terms Related to Concurrency

atomic operation	A function or action implemented as a sequence of one or more instructions that appears to be indivisible; that is, no other process can see an intermediate state or interrupt the operation. The sequence of instruction is guaranteed to execute as a group, or not execute at all, having no visible effect on system state. Atomicity guarantees isolation from concurrent processes.
critical section	A section of code within a process that requires access to shared resources and that must not be executed while another process is in a corresponding section of code.
deadlock	A situation in which two or more processes are unable to proceed because each is waiting for one of the others to do something.
livelock	A situation in which two or more processes continuously change their states in response to changes in the other process(es) without doing any useful work.
mutual exclusion	The requirement that when one process is in a critical section that accesses shared resources, no other process may be in a critical section that accesses any of those shared resources.
race condition	A situation in which multiple threads or processes read and write a shared data item and the final result depends on the relative timing of their execution.
starvation	A situation in which a runnable process is overlooked indefinitely by the scheduler; although it is able to proceed, it is never chosen.

---

[1]For simplicity, we generally refer to the concurrent execution of *processes*. In fact, as we have seen in the preceding chapter, in some systems the fundamental unit of concurrency is a thread rather than a process.

5.1 PRINCIPLES OF CONCURRENCY

In a single-processor multiprogramming system, processes are interleaved in time to yield the appearance of simultaneous execution (Figure 2.12a). Even though actual parallel processing is not achieved, and even though there is a certain amount of overhead involved in switching back and forth between processes, interleaved execution provides major benefits in processing efficiency and in program structuring. In a multiple-processor system, it is possible not only to interleave the execution of multiple processes but also to overlap them (Figure 2.12b).

At first glance, it may seem that interleaving and overlapping represent fundamentally different modes of execution and present different problems. In fact, both techniques can be viewed as examples of concurrent processing, and both present the same problems. In the case of a uniprocessor, the problems stem from a basic characteristic of multiprogramming systems: The relative speed of execution of processes cannot be predicted. It depends on the activities of other processes, the way in which the OS handles interrupts, and the scheduling policies of the OS. The following difficulties arise:

1. The sharing of global resources is fraught with peril. For example, if two processes both make use of the same global variable and both perform reads and writes on that variable, then the order in which the various reads and writes are executed is critical. An example of this problem is shown in the following subsection.

2. It is difficult for the OS to manage the allocation of resources optimally. For example, process A may request use of, and be granted control of, a particular I/O channel and then be suspended before using that channel. It may be undesirable for the OS simply to lock the channel and prevent its use by other processes; indeed this may lead to a deadlock condition, as described in Chapter 6.

3. It becomes very difficult to locate a programming error because results are typically not deterministic and reproducible (e.g., see [LEBL87, CARR89, SHEN02] for a discussion of this point).

All of the foregoing difficulties present themselves in a multiprocessor system as well, because here too the relative speed of execution of processes is unpredictable. A multiprocessor system must also deal with problems arising from the simultaneous execution of multiple processes. Fundamentally, however, the problems are the same as those for uniprocessor systems. This should become clear as the discussion proceeds.

A Simple Example

Consider the following procedure:

```
void echo()
{
    chin = getchar();
    chout = chin;
    putchar(chout);
}
```

This procedure shows the essential elements of a program that will provide a character echo procedure; input is obtained from a keyboard one keystroke at a time. Each input character is stored in variable chin. It is then transferred to variable chout and sent to the display. Any program can call this procedure repeatedly to accept user input and display it on the user's screen.

Now consider that we have a single-processor multiprogramming system supporting a single user. The user can jump from one application to another, and each application uses the same keyboard for input and the same screen for output. Because each application needs to use the procedure echo, it makes sense for it to be a shared procedure that is loaded into a portion of memory global to all applications. Thus, only a single copy of the echo procedure is used, saving space.

The sharing of main memory among processes is useful to permit efficient and close interaction among processes. However, such sharing can lead to problems. Consider the following sequence:

1. Process P1 invokes the echo procedure and is interrupted immediately after getchar returns its value and stores it in chin. At this point, the most recently entered character, x, is stored in variable chin.

2. Process P2 is activated and invokes the echo procedure, which runs to conclusion, inputting and then displaying a single character, y, on the screen.

3. Process P1 is resumed. By this time, the value x has been overwritten in chin and therefore lost. Instead, chin contains y, which is transferred to chout and displayed.

Thus, the first character is lost and the second character is displayed twice. The essence of this problem is the shared global variable, chin. Multiple processes have access to this variable. If one process updates the global variable and then is interrupted, another process may alter the variable before the first process can use its value. Suppose, however, that we permit only one process at a time to be in that procedure. Then the foregoing sequence would result in the following:

1. Process P1 invokes the echo procedure and is interrupted immediately after the conclusion of the input function. At this point, the most recently entered character, x, is stored in variable chin.

2. Process P2 is activated and invokes the echo procedure. However, because P1 is still inside the echo procedure, although currently suspended, P2 is blocked from entering the procedure. Therefore, P2 is suspended awaiting the availability of the echo procedure.

3. At some later time, process P1 is resumed and completes execution of echo. The proper character, x, is displayed.

4. When P1 exits echo, this removes the block on P2. When P2 is later resumed, the echo procedure is successfully invoked.

This example shows that it is necessary to protect shared global variables (and other shared global resources) and that the only way to do that is to control the code that accesses the variable. If we impose the discipline that only one process at a time may enter echo and that once in echo the procedure must run to completion before it is available for another process, then the type of error just discussed will not occur. How that discipline may be imposed is a major topic of this chapter.

This problem was stated with the assumption that there was a single-processor, multiprogramming OS. The example demonstrates that the problems of concurrency occur even when there is a single processor. In a multiprocessor system, the same problems of protected shared resources arise, and the same solution works. First, suppose that there is no mechanism for controlling access to the shared global variable:

1. Processes P1 and P2 are both executing, each on a separate processor. Both processes invoke the echo procedure.

2. The following events occur; events on the same line take place in parallel:

```
       Process P1              Process P2
   •                       •
   chin = getchar();       •
   •                       chin = getchar();
   chout = chin;           chout = chin;
   putchar(chout);         •
   •                       putchar(chout);
   •                       •
```

The result is that the character input to P1 is lost before being displayed, and the character input to P2 is displayed by both P1 and P2. Again, let us add the capability of enforcing the discipline that only one process at a time may be in echo. Then the following sequence occurs:

1. Processes P1 and P2 are both executing, each on a separate processor. P1 invokes the echo procedure.

2. While P1 is inside the echo procedure, P2 invokes echo. Because P1 is still inside the echo procedure (whether P1 is suspended or executing), P2 is blocked from entering the procedure. Therefore, P2 is suspended awaiting the availability of the echo procedure.

3. At a later time, process P1 completes execution of echo, exits that procedure, and continues executing. Immediately upon the exit of P1 from echo, P2 is resumed and begins executing echo.

In the case of a uniprocessor system, the reason we have a problem is that an interrupt can stop instruction execution anywhere in a process. In the case of a multiprocessor system, we have that same condition and, in addition, a problem can be caused because two processes may be executing simultaneously and both trying to access the same global variable. However, the solution to both types of problem is the same: control access to the shared resource.

Race Condition

A race condition occurs when multiple processes or threads read and write data items so that the final result depends on the order of execution of instructions in the multiple processes. Let us consider two simple examples.

As a first example, suppose that two processes, P1 and P2, share the global variable a. At some point in its execution, P1 updates a to the value 1, and at some point in its execution, P2 updates a to the value 2. Thus, the two tasks are in a race to write variable a. In this example, the "loser" of the race (the process that updates last) determines the final value of a.

For our second example, consider two process, P3 and P4, that share global variables b and c, with initial values b = 1 and c = 2. At some point in its execution, P3 executes the assignment b = b + c, and at some point in its execution, P4 executes the assignment c = b + c. Note that the two processes update different variables. However, the final values of the two variables depend on the order in which the two processes execute these two assignments. If P3 executes its assignment statement first, then the final values are b = 3 and c = 5. If P4 executes its assignment statement first, then the final values are b = 4 and c = 3.

Appendix A includes a discussion of race conditions using semaphores as an example.

Operating System Concerns

What design and management issues are raised by the existence of concurrency? We can list the following concerns:

1. The OS must be able to keep track of the various processes. This is done with the use of process control blocks and was described in Chapter 4.

2. The OS must allocate and deallocate various resources for each active process. At times, multiple processes want access to the same resource. These resources include

   - **Processor time:** This is the scheduling function, discussed in Part Four.
   - **Memory:** Most operating systems use a virtual memory scheme. The topic is addressed in Part Three.
   - **Files:** Discussed in Chapter 12.
   - **I/O devices:** Discussed in Chapter 11.

3. The OS must protect the data and physical resources of each process against unintended interference by other processes. This involves techniques that relate to memory, files, and I/O devices. A general treatment of protection is found in Part Seven.

4. The functioning of a process, and the output it produces, must be independent of the speed at which its execution is carried out relative to the speed of other concurrent processes. This is the subject of this chapter.

To understand how the issue of speed independence can be addressed, we need to look at the ways in which processes can interact.

Process Interaction

We can classify the ways in which processes interact on the basis of the degree to which they are aware of each other's existence. Table 5.2 lists three possible degrees of awareness plus the consequences of each:

- **Processes unaware of each other:** These are independent processes that are not intended to work together. The best example of this situation is the multiprogramming of multiple independent processes. These can either be batch jobs or interactive sessions or a mixture. Although the processes are not working together, the OS needs to be concerned about **competition** for resources. For example, two independent applications may both want to access the same disk or file or printer. The OS must regulate these accesses.

- **Processes indirectly aware of each other:** These are processes that are not necessarily aware of each other by their respective process IDs but that share access to some object, such as an I/O buffer. Such processes exhibit **cooperation** in sharing the common object.

- **Processes directly aware of each other:** These are processes that are able to communicate with each other by process ID and that are designed to work jointly on some activity. Again, such processes exhibit **cooperation**.

Conditions will not always be as clear-cut as suggested in Table 5.2. Rather, several processes may exhibit aspects of both competition and cooperation. Nevertheless, it is productive to examine each of the three items in the preceding list separately and determine their implications for the OS.

Table 5.2   Process Interaction

Degree of Awareness	Relationship	Influence that One Process Has on the Other	Potential Control Problems
Processes unaware of each other	Competition	• Results of one process independent of the action of others • Timing of process may be affected	• Mutual exclusion • Deadlock (renewable resource) • Starvation
Processes indirectly aware of each other (e.g., shared object)	Cooperation by sharing	• Results of one process may depend on information obtained from others • Timing of process may be affected	• Mutual exclusion • Deadlock (renewable resource) • Starvation • Data coherence
Processes directly aware of each other (have communication primitives available to them)	Cooperation by communication	• Results of one process may depend on information obtained from others • Timing of process may be affected	• Deadlock (consumable resource) • Starvation

COMPETITION AMONG PROCESSES FOR RESOURCES Concurrent processes come into conflict with each other when they are competing for the use of the same resource. In its pure form, we can describe the situation as follows. Two or more processes need to access a resource during the course of their execution. Each process is unaware of the existence of other processes, and each is to be unaffected by the execution of the other processes. It follows from this that each process should leave the state of any resource that it uses unaffected. Examples of resources include I/O devices, memory, processor time, and the clock.

There is no exchange of information between the competing processes. However, the execution of one process may affect the behavior of competing processes. In particular, if two processes both wish access to a single resource, then one process will be allocated that resource by the OS, and the other will have to wait. Therefore, the process that is denied access will be slowed down. In an extreme case, the blocked process may never get access to the resource and hence will never terminate successfully.

In the case of competing processes three control problems must be faced. First is the need for **mutual exclusion**. Suppose two or more processes require access to a single nonsharable resource, such as a printer. During the course of execution, each process will be sending commands to the I/O device, receiving status information, sending data, and/or receiving data. We will refer to such a resource as a **critical resource**, and the portion of the program that uses it as a **critical section** of the program. It is important that only one program at a time be allowed in its critical section. We cannot simply rely on the OS to understand and enforce this restriction because the detailed requirements may not be obvious. In the case of the printer, for example, we want any individual process to have control of the printer while it prints an entire file. Otherwise, lines from competing processes will be interleaved.

The enforcement of mutual exclusion creates two additional control problems. One is that of **deadlock**. For example, consider two processes, P1 and P2, and two resources, R1 and R2. Suppose that each process needs access to both resources to perform part of its function. Then it is possible to have the following situation: the OS assigns R1 to P2, and R2 to P1. Each process is waiting for one of the two resources. Neither will release the resource that it already owns until it has acquired the other resource and performed the function requiring both resources. The two processes are deadlocked.

A final control problem is **starvation**. Suppose that three processes (P1, P2, P3) each require periodic access to resource R. Consider the situation in which P1 is in possession of the resource, and both P2 and P3 are delayed, waiting for that resource. When P1 exits its critical section, either P2 or P3 should be allowed access to R. Assume that the OS grants access to P3 and that P1 again requires access before P3 completes its critical section. If the OS grants access to P1 after P3 has finished, and subsequently alternately grants access to P1 and P3, then P2 may indefinitely be denied access to the resource, even though there is no deadlock situation.

Control of competition inevitably involves the OS because it is the OS that allocates resources. In addition, the processes themselves will need to be able to

```
    /* PROCESS 1 */              /* PROCESS 2 */                  /* PROCESS n */

void P1                     void P2                          void Pn
{                           {                                {
  while (true) {              while (true) {                   while (true) {
    /* preceding code */;       /* preceding code */;            /* preceding code */;
    entercritical (Ra);         entercritical (Ra);      • • •   entercritical (Ra);
    /* critical section */;     /* critical section */;          /* critical section */;
    exitcritical (Ra);          exitcritical (Ra);              exitcritical (Ra);
    /* following code */;       /* following code */;            /* following code */;
  }                           }                                }
}                           }                                }
```

Figure 5.1   Illustration of Mutual Exclusion

express the requirement for mutual exclusion in some fashion, such as locking a resource prior to its use. Any solution will involve some support from the OS, such as the provision of the locking facility. Figure 5.1 illustrates the mutual exclusion mechanism in abstract terms. There are *n* processes to be executed concurrently. Each process includes (1) a critical section that operates on some resource Ra, and (2) additional code preceding and following the critical section that does not involve access to Ra. Because all processes access the same resource Ra, it is desired that only one process at a time be in its critical section. To enforce mutual exclusion, two functions are provided: entercritical and exitcritical. Each function takes as an argument the name of the resource that is the subject of competition. Any process that attempts to enter its critical section while another process is in its critical section, for the same resource, is made to wait.

It remains to examine specific mechanisms for providing the functions entercritical and exitcritical. For the moment, we defer this issue while we consider the other cases of process interaction.

COOPERATION AMONG PROCESSES BY SHARING   The case of cooperation by sharing covers processes that interact with other processes without being explicitly aware of them. For example, multiple processes may have access to shared variables or to shared files or databases. Processes may use and update the shared data without reference to other processes but know that other processes may have access to the same data. Thus the processes must cooperate to ensure that the data they share are properly managed. The control mechanisms must ensure the integrity of the shared data.

Because data are held on resources (devices, memory), the control problems of mutual exclusion, deadlock, and starvation are again present. The only difference is that data items may be accessed in two different modes, reading and writing, and only writing operations must be mutually exclusive.

However, over and above these problems, a new requirement is introduced: that of data coherence. As a simple example, consider a bookkeeping application in which various data items may be updated. Suppose two items of data a and b are to be maintained in the relationship $a = b$. That is, any program that updates one value must also update the other to maintain the relationship. Now consider the following two processes:

```
P1:
        a = a + 1;
        b = b + 1;
P2:
        b = 2 * b;
        a = 2 * a;
```

If the state is initially consistent, each process taken separately will leave the shared data in a consistent state. Now consider the following concurrent execution sequence, in which the two processes respect mutual exclusion on each individual data item (a and b):

```
        a = a + 1;
        b = 2 * b;
        b = b + 1;
        a = 2 * a;
```

At the end of this execution sequence, the condition $a = b$ no longer holds. For example, if we start with $a = b = 1$, at the end of this execution sequence we have $a = 4$ and $b = 3$. The problem can be avoided by declaring the entire sequence in each process to be a critical section.

Thus, we see that the concept of critical section is important in the case of cooperation by sharing. The same abstract functions of `entercritical` and `exitcritical` discussed earlier (Figure 5.1) can be used here. In this case, the argument for the functions could be a variable, a file, or any other shared object. Furthermore, if critical sections are used to provide data integrity, then there may be no specific resource or variable that can be identified as an argument. In that case, we can think of the argument as being an identifier that is shared among concurrent processes to identify critical sections that must be mutually exclusive.

COOPERATION AMONG PROCESSES BY COMMUNICATION   In the first two cases that we have discussed, each process has its own isolated environment that does not include the other processes. The interactions among processes are indirect. In both cases, there is a sharing. In the case of competition, they are sharing resources without being aware of the other processes. In the second case, they are sharing values, and although each process is not explicitly aware of the other processes, it is aware of the need to maintain data integrity. When processes cooperate by communication, however, the various processes participate in a common effort that links all of the processes. The communication provides a way to synchronize, or coordinate, the various activities.

Typically, communication can be characterized as consisting of messages of some sort. Primitives for sending and receiving messages may be provided as part of the programming language or provided by the OS kernel.

Because nothing is shared between processes in the act of passing messages, mutual exclusion is not a control requirement for this sort of cooperation. However, the problems of deadlock and starvation are still present. As an example of deadlock, two processes may be blocked, each waiting for a communication from the other. As an example of starvation, consider three processes, P1, P2, and P3, that exhibit the following behavior. P1 is repeatedly attempting to communicate with either P2 or P3, and P2 and P3 are both attempting to communicate with P1. A sequence could arise in which P1 and P2 exchange information repeatedly, while P3 is blocked waiting for a communication from P1. There is no deadlock, because P1 remains active, but P3 is starved.

Requirements for Mutual Exclusion

Any facility or capability that is to provide support for mutual exclusion should meet the following requirements:

1. Mutual exclusion must be enforced: Only one process at a time is allowed into its critical section, among all processes that have critical sections for the same resource or shared object.

2. A process that halts in its noncritical section must do so without interfering with other processes.

3. It must not be possible for a process requiring access to a critical section to be delayed indefinitely: no deadlock or starvation.

4. When no process is in a critical section, any process that requests entry to its critical section must be permitted to enter without delay.

5. No assumptions are made about relative process speeds or number of processors.

6. A process remains inside its critical section for a finite time only.

There are a number of ways in which the requirements for mutual exclusion can be satisfied. One approach is to leave the responsibility with the processes that wish to execute concurrently. Processes, whether they are system programs or application programs, would be required to coordinate with one another to enforce mutual exclusion, with no support from the programming language or the OS. We can refer to these as software approaches. Although this approach is prone to high processing overhead and bugs, it is nevertheless useful to examine such approaches to gain a better understanding of the complexity of concurrent processing. This topic is covered in Appendix A. A second approach involves the use of special-purpose machine instructions. These have the advantage of reducing overhead but nevertheless will be shown to be unattractive as a general-purpose solution; they are covered in Section 5.2. A third approach is to provide some level of support within the OS or a programming language. Three of the most important such approaches are examined in Sections 5.3 through 5.5.

5.2 MUTUAL EXCLUSION: HARDWARE SUPPORT

In this section, we look at several interesting hardware approaches to mutual exclusion.

Interrupt Disabling

In a uniprocessor system, concurrent processes cannot have overlapped execution; they can only be interleaved. Furthermore, a process will continue to run until it invokes an OS service or until it is interrupted. Therefore, to guarantee mutual exclusion, it is sufficient to prevent a process from being interrupted. This capability can be provided in the form of primitives defined by the OS kernel for disabling and enabling interrupts. A process can then enforce mutual exclusion in the following way (compare Figure 5.1):

```
while (true) {
    /* disable interrupts */;
    /* critical section */;
    /* enable interrupts */;
    /* remainder */;
}
```

Because the critical section cannot be interrupted, mutual exclusion is guaranteed. The price of this approach, however, is high. The efficiency of execution could be noticeably degraded because the processor is limited in its ability to interleave processes. Another problem is that this approach will not work in a multiprocessor architecture. When the computer includes more than one processor, it is possible (and typical) for more than one process to be executing at a time. In this case, disabled interrupts do not guarantee mutual exclusion.

Special Machine Instructions

In a multiprocessor configuration, several processors share access to a common main memory. In this case, there is not a master/slave relationship; rather the processors behave independently in a peer relationship. There is no interrupt mechanism between processors on which mutual exclusion can be based.

At the hardware level, as was mentioned, access to a memory location excludes any other access to that same location. With this as a foundation, processor designers have proposed several machine instructions that carry out two actions atomically,[2] such as reading and writing or reading and testing, of a single memory location with one instruction fetch cycle. During execution of the instruction, access to the memory location is blocked for any other instruction referencing that location.

In this section, we look at two of the most commonly implemented instructions. Others are described in [RAYN86] and [STON93].

COMPARE&SWAP INSTRUCTION   The compare&swap instruction, also called a compare and exchange instruction, can be defined as follows [HERL90]:

---

[2] The term *atomic* means that the instruction is treated as a single step that cannot be interrupted.

```
int compare_and_swap (int *word, int testval, int newval)
{
    int oldval;
    oldval = *word
    if (oldval == testval) *word = newval;
    return oldval;
}
```

This version of the instruction checks a memory location (*word) against a test value (testval). If the memory location's current value is testval, it is replaced with newval; otherwise it is left unchanged. The old memory value is always returned; thus, the memory location has been updated if the returned value is the same as the test value. This atomic instruction therefore has two parts: A **compare** is made between a memory value and a test value; if the values are the same, a **swap** occurs. The entire compare&swap function is carried out atomically—that is, it is not subject to interruption.

Another version of this instruction returns a Boolean value: true if the swap occurred; false otherwise. Some version of this instruction is available on nearly all processor families (x86, IA64, sparc, IBM z series, etc.), and most operating systems use this instruction for support of concurrency.

Figure 5.2a shows a mutual exclusion protocol based on the use of this instruction.[3] A shared variable bolt is initialized to 0. The only process that may enter its critical section is one that finds bolt equal to 0. All other processes attempting

```
/* program mutualexclusion */
const int n = /* number of processes */;
int bolt;
void P(int i)
{
    while (true) {
        while (compare_and_swap(bolt, 0, 1) == 1)
            /* do nothing */;
        /* critical section */;
        bolt = 0;
        /* remainder */;
    }
}
void main()
{
    bolt = 0;
    parbegin (P(1), P(2), ... ,P(n));
}
```

```
/* program mutualexclusion */
int const n = /* number of processes */;
int bolt;
void P(int i)
{
    int keyi = 1;
    while (true) {
        do exchange (&keyi, &bolt)
        while (keyi != 0);
        /* critical section */;
        bolt = 0;
        /* remainder */;
    }
}
void main()
{
    bolt = 0;
    parbegin (P(1), P(2), ..., P(n));
}
```

(a) Compare and swap instruction   (b) Exchange instruction

Figure 5.2   Hardware Support for Mutual Exclusion

---

[3]The construct **parbegin** (P1, P2, ..., Pn) means the following: suspend the execution of the main program; initiate concurrent execution of procedures P1, P2, ..., Pn; when all of P1, P2, ..., Pn have terminated, resume the main program.

to enter their critical section go into a busy waiting mode. The term **busy waiting,** or **spin waiting,** refers to a technique in which a process can do nothing until it gets permission to enter its critical section but continues to execute an instruction or set of instructions that tests the appropriate variable to gain entrance. When a process leaves its critical section, it resets *bolt* to 0; at this point one and only one of the waiting processes is granted access to its critical section. The choice of process depends on which process happens to execute the `compare&swap` instruction next.

EXCHANGE INSTRUCTION   The exchange instruction can be defined as follows:

```
void exchange (int *register, int *memory)
{
    int temp;
    temp = *memory;
    *memory = *register;
    *register = temp;
}
```

The instruction exchanges the contents of a register with that of a memory location. Both the Intel IA-32 architecture (Pentium) and the IA-64 architecture (Itanium) contain an XCHG instruction.

Figure 5.2b shows a mutual exclusion protocol based on the use of an exchange instruction. A shared variable *bolt* is initialized to 0. Each process uses a local variable *key* that is initialized to 1. The only process that may enter its critical section is one that finds *bolt* equal to 0. It excludes all other processes from the critical section by setting *bolt* to 1. When a process leaves its critical section, it resets *bolt* to 0, allowing another process to gain access to its critical section.

Note that the following expression always holds because of the way in which the variables are initialized and because of the nature of the exchange algorithm:

$$bolt + \sum_i key_i = n$$

If *bolt* = 0, then no process is in its critical section. If *bolt* = 1, then exactly one process is in its critical section, namely the process whose *key* value equals 0.

PROPERTIES OF THE MACHINE-INSTRUCTION APPROACH   The use of a special machine instruction to enforce mutual exclusion has a number of advantages:

- It is applicable to any number of processes on either a single processor or multiple processors sharing main memory.
- It is simple and therefore easy to verify.
- It can be used to support multiple critical sections; each critical section can be defined by its own variable.

There are some serious disadvantages:

- **Busy waiting is employed:** Thus, while a process is waiting for access to a critical section, it continues to consume processor time.

- **Starvation is possible:** When a process leaves a critical section and more than one process is waiting, the selection of a waiting process is arbitrary. Thus, some process could indefinitely be denied access.

- **Deadlock is possible:** Consider the following scenario on a single-processor system. Process P1 executes the special instruction (e.g., `compare&swap`, `exchange`) and enters its critical section. P1 is then interrupted to give the processor to P2, which has higher priority. If P2 now attempts to use the same resource as P1, it will be denied access because of the mutual exclusion mechanism. Thus, it will go into a busy waiting loop. However, P1 will never be dispatched because it is of lower priority than another ready process, P2.

Because of the drawbacks of both the software and hardware solutions, we need to look for other mechanisms.

5.3 SEMAPHORES

We now turn to OS and programming language mechanisms that are used to provide concurrency. Table 5.3 summarizes mechanisms in common use. We begin, in this section, with semaphores. The next two sections discuss monitors and message passing. The other mechanisms in Table 5.3 are discussed when treating specific OS examples, in Chapters 6 and 13.

Table 5.3 Common Concurrency Mechanisms

Semaphore	An integer value used for signaling among processes. Only three operations may be performed on a semaphore, all of which are atomic: initialize, decrement, and increment. The decrement operation may result in the blocking of a process, and the increment operation may result in the unblocking of a process. Also known as a **counting semaphore** or a **general semaphore.**
Binary Semaphore	A semaphore that takes on only the values 0 and 1.
Mutex	Similar to a binary semaphore. A key difference between the two is that the process that locks the mutex (sets the value to zero) must be the one to unlock it (sets the value to 1).
Condition Variable	A data type that is used to block a process or thread until a particular condition is true.
Monitor	A programming language construct that encapsulates variables, access procedures, and initialization code within an abstract data type. The monitor's variable may only be accessed via its access procedures and only one process may be actively accessing the monitor at any one time. The access procedures are *critical sections*. A monitor may have a queue of processes that are waiting to access it.
Event Flags	A memory word used as a synchronization mechanism. Application code may associate a different event with each bit in a flag. A thread can wait for either a single event or a combination of events by checking one or multiple bits in the corresponding flag. The thread is blocked until all of the required bits are set (AND) or until at least one of the bits is set (OR).
Mailboxes/Messages	A means for two processes to exchange information and that may be used for synchronization.
Spinlocks	Mutual exclusion mechanism in which a process executes in an infinite loop waiting for the value of a lock variable to indicate availability.

The first major advance in dealing with the problems of concurrent processes came in 1965 with Dijkstra's treatise [DIJK65]. Dijkstra was concerned with the design of an OS as a collection of cooperating sequential processes and with the development of efficient and reliable mechanisms for supporting cooperation. These mechanisms can just as readily be used by user processes if the processor and OS make the mechanisms available.

The fundamental principle is this: Two or more processes can cooperate by means of simple signals, such that a process can be forced to stop at a specified place until it has received a specific signal. Any complex coordination requirement can be satisfied by the appropriate structure of signals. For signaling, special variables called semaphores are used. To transmit a signal via semaphore s, a process executes the primitive semSignal(s). To receive a signal via semaphore s, a process executes the primitive semWait(s); if the corresponding signal has not yet been transmitted, the process is suspended until the transmission takes place.[4]

To achieve the desired effect, we can view the semaphore as a variable that has an integer value upon which only three operations are defined:

1. A semaphore may be initialized to a nonnegative integer value.

2. The semWait operation decrements the semaphore value. If the value becomes negative, then the process executing the semWait is blocked. Otherwise, the process continues execution.

3. The semSignal operation increments the semaphore value. If the resulting value is less than or equal to zero, then a process blocked by a semWait operation, if any, is unblocked.

Other than these three operations, there is no way to inspect or manipulate semaphores.

We explain these operations as follows. To begin, the semaphore has a zero or positive value. If the value is positive, that value equals the number of processes that can issue a wait and immediately continue to execute. If the value is zero, either by initialization or because a number of processes equal to the initial semaphore value have issued a wait, the next process to issue a wait is blocked, and the semaphore value goes negative. Each subsequent wait drives the semaphore value further into minus territory. The negative value equals the number of processes waiting to be unblocked. Each signal unblocks one of the waiting processes when the semaphore value is negative.

[DOWN08] points out three interesting consequences of the semaphore definition:

- In general, there is no way to know before a process decrements a semaphore whether it will block or not.

---

[4]In Dijkstra's original paper and in much of the literature, the letter P is used for semWait and the letter V for semSignal; these are the initials of the Dutch words for test (*proberen*) and increment (*verhogen*). In some of the literature, the terms wait and signal are used. This book uses semWait and semSignal for clarity, and to avoid confusion with similar wait and signal operations in monitors, discussed subsequently

```
struct semaphore {
      int count;
      queueType queue;
};
void semWait(semaphore s)
{
      s.count--;
      if (s.count < 0) {
        /* place this process in s.queue */;
        /* block this process */;
      }
}
void semSignal(semaphore s)
{
      s.count++;
      if (s.count<= 0) {
        /* remove a process P from s.queue */;
        /* place process P on ready list */;
      }
}
```

Figure 5.3   A Definition of Semaphore Primitives

- After a process increments a semaphore and another process gets woken up, both processes continue running concurrently. There is no way to know which process, if either, will continue immediately on a uniprocessor system.

- When you signal a semaphore, you don't necessarily know whether another process is waiting, so the number of unblocked processes may be zero or one.

Figure 5.3 suggests a more formal definition of the primitives for semaphores. The semWait and semSignal primitives are assumed to be atomic. A more restricted version, known as the **binary semaphore**, is defined in Figure 5.4. A binary semaphore may only take on the values 0 and 1 and can be defined by the following three operations:

1. A binary semaphore may be initialized to 0 or 1.
2. The semWaitB operation checks the semaphore value. If the value is zero, then the process executing the semWaitB is blocked. If the value is one, then the value is changed to zero and the process continues execution.
3. The semSignalB operation checks to see if any processes are blocked on this semaphore (semaphore value equals 0). If so, then a process blocked by a semWaitB operation is unblocked. If no processes are blocked, then the value of the semaphore is set to one.

In principle, it should be easier to implement the binary semaphore, and it can be shown that it has the same expressive power as the general semaphore (see Problem 5.16). To contrast the two types of semaphores, the nonbinary semaphore is often referred to as either a **counting semaphore** or a **general semaphore**.

A concept related to the binary semaphore is the **mutex**. A key difference between the two is that the process that locks the mutex (sets the value to zero)

```
struct binary_semaphore {
      enum {zero, one} value;
      queueType queue;
};
void semWaitB(binary_semaphore s)
{
      if (s.value == one)
            s.value = zero;
      else {
                  /* place this process in s.queue */;
                  /* block this process */;
      }
}
void semSignalB(semaphore s)
{
      if (s.queue is empty())
            s.value = one;
      else {
                  /* remove a process P from s.queue */;
                  /* place process P on ready list */;
      }
}
```

Figure 5.4   A Definition of Binary Semaphore Primitives

must be the one to unlock it (sets the value to 1). In contrast, it is possible for one process to lock a binary semaphore and for another to unlock it.[5]

For both counting semaphores and binary semaphores, a queue is used to hold processes waiting on the semaphore. The question arises of the order in which processes are removed from such a queue. The fairest removal policy is first-in-first-out (FIFO): The process that has been blocked the longest is released from the queue first; a semaphore whose definition includes this policy is called a **strong semaphore**. A semaphore that does not specify the order in which processes are removed from the queue is a **weak semaphore**. Figure 5.5, based on one in [DENN84], is an example of the operation of a strong semaphore. Here processes A, B, and C depend on a result from process D. Initially (1), A is running; B, C, and D are ready; and the semaphore count is 1, indicating that one of D's results is available. When A issues a semWait instruction on semaphore s, the semaphore decrements to 0, and A can continue to execute; subsequently it rejoins the ready queue. Then B runs (2), eventually issues a semWait instruction, and is blocked, allowing D to run (3). When D completes a new result, it issues a semSignal instruction, which allows B to move to the ready queue (4). D rejoins the ready queue and C begins to run (5) but is blocked when it issues a semWait instruction. Similarly, A and B run and are blocked on the semaphore, allowing D to resume execution (6). When D has a result, it issues a semSignal, which transfers C to the ready queue. Later cycles of D will release A and B from the Blocked state.

---

[5]In some of the literature, and in some textbooks, no distinction is made between a mutex and a binary semaphore. However, in practice, a number of operating systems, such as Linux, Windows, and Solaris offer a mutex facility which conforms to the definition in this book.

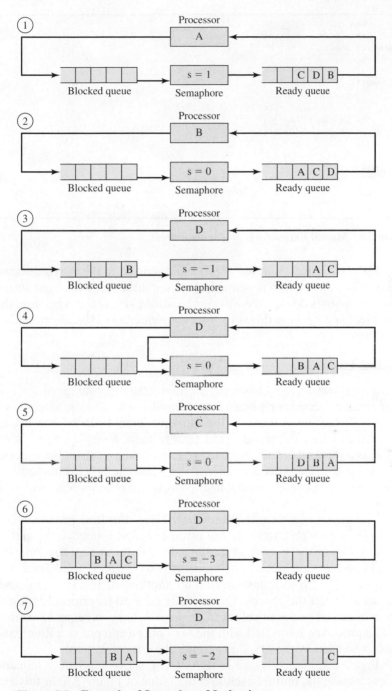

Figure 5.5   Example of Semaphore Mechanism

```
/* program mutualexclusion */
const int n = /* number of processes */;
semaphore s = 1;
void P(int i)
{
    while (true) {
        semWait(s);
        /* critical section */;
        semSignal(s);
        /* remainder */;
    }
}
void main()
{
    parbegin (P(1), P(2),…, P(n));
}
```

Figure 5.6   Mutual Exclusion Using Semaphores

For the mutual exclusion algorithm discussed in the next subsection and illustrated in Figure 5.6, strong semaphores guarantee freedom from starvation, while weak semaphores do not. We will assume strong semaphores because they are more convenient and because this is the form of semaphore typically provided by operating systems.

Mutual Exclusion

Figure 5.6 shows a straightforward solution to the mutual exclusion problem using a semaphore s (compare Figure 5.1). Consider n processes, identified in the array $P(i)$, all of which need access to the same resource. Each process has a critical section used to access the resource. In each process, a semWait(s) is executed just before its critical section. If the value of s becomes negative, the process is blocked. If the value is 1, then it is decremented to 0 and the process immediately enters its critical section; because s is no longer positive, no other process will be able to enter its critical section.

The semaphore is initialized to 1. Thus, the first process that executes a semWait will be able to enter the critical section immediately, setting the value of s to 0. Any other process attempting to enter the critical section will find it busy and will be blocked, setting the value of s to –1. Any number of processes may attempt entry; each such unsuccessful attempt results in a further decrement of the value of s. When the process that initially entered its critical section departs, s is incremented and one of the blocked processes (if any) is removed from the queue of blocked processes associated with the semaphore and put in a Ready state. When it is next scheduled by the OS, it may enter the critical section.

Figure 5.7, based on one in [BACO03], shows a possible sequence for three processes using the mutual exclusion discipline of Figure 5.6. In this example three processes (A, B, C) access a shared resource protected by the semaphore *lock*. Process A executes semWait(*lock*); because the semaphore has a value of 1 at the time of the semWait operation, A can immediately enter its critical section and the semaphore takes on the value 0. While A is in its critical section, both B and C

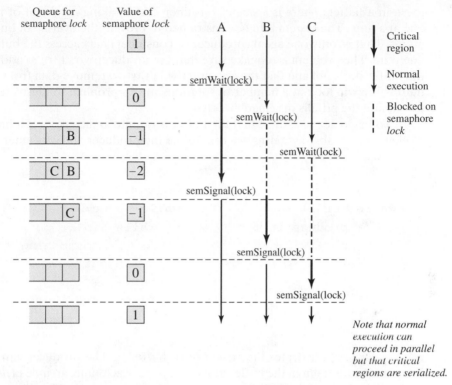

Figure 5.7   Processes Accessing Shared Data Protected by a Semaphore

perform a semWait operation and are blocked pending the availability of the semaphore. When A exits its critical section and performs semSignal(lock), B, which was the first process in the queue, can now enter its critical section.

The program of Figure 5.6 can equally well handle a requirement that more than one process be allowed in its critical section at a time. This requirement is met simply by initializing the semaphore to the specified value. Thus, at any time, the value of *s.count* can be interpreted as follows:

- *s.count* $\geq$ 0: *s.count* is the number of processes that can execute semWait(*s*) without suspension (if no semSignal(*s*) is executed in the meantime). Such situations will allow semaphores to support synchronization as well as mutual exclusion.

- *s.count* < 0: The magnitude of *s.count* is the number of processes suspended in *s.queue*.

The Producer/Consumer Problem

We now examine one of the most common problems faced in concurrent processing: the producer/consumer problem. The general statement is this: There are one or more producers generating some type of data (records, characters) and placing these in a buffer. There is a single consumer that is taking items out of the buffer one at a time. The system is to be constrained to prevent the overlap of buffer operations. That is, only one agent (producer or consumer) may access the buffer at any one time. The problem is to make sure that the producer won't try to add data into the buffer if it's full and that the consumer won't try to remove data from an empty buffer. We will look at a number of solutions to this problem to illustrate both the power and the pitfalls of semaphores.

To begin, let us assume that the buffer is infinite and consists of a linear array of elements. In abstract terms, we can define the producer and consumer functions as follows:

```
producer:                        consumer:
while (true) {                   while (true) {
    /* produce item v */;            while (in <= out)
    b[in] = v;                           /* do nothing */;
    in++;                            w = b[out];
}                                    out++;
                                     /* consume item w */;
                                 }
```

Figure 5.8 illustrates the structure of buffer b. The producer can generate items and store them in the buffer at its own pace. Each time, an index (*in*) into the buffer is incremented. The consumer proceeds in a similar fashion but must make sure that it does not attempt to read from an empty buffer. Hence, the consumer makes sure that the producer has advanced beyond it (*in> out*) before proceeding.

Let us try to implement this system using binary semaphores. Figure 5.9 is a first attempt. Rather than deal with the indices *in* and *out*, we can simply keep track of the number of items in the buffer, using the integer variable *n* (= *in* – *out*). The semaphore s is used to enforce mutual exclusion; the semaphore delay is used to force the consumer to semWait if the buffer is empty.

This solution seems rather straightforward. The producer is free to add to the buffer at any time. It performs semWaitB(s) before appending and semSignalB(s) afterward to prevent the consumer or any other producer from

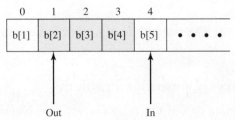

Out   In

Note: Shaded area indicates portion of buffer that is occupied

Figure 5.8   Infinite Buffer for the Producer/Consumer Problem

```
/* program producerconsumer */
      int n;
      binary_semaphore s = 1, delay = 0;
      void producer()
      {
            while (true) {
                  produce();
                  semWaitB(s);
                  append();
                  n++;
                  if (n==1) semSignalB(delay);
                  semSignalB(s);
            }
      }
      void consumer()
      {
            semWaitB(delay);
            while (true) {
                  semWaitB(s);
                  take();
                  n--;
                  semSignalB(s);
                  consume();
                  if (n==0) semWaitB(delay);
            }
      }
      void main()
      {
            n = 0;
            parbegin (producer, consumer);
      }
```

Figure 5.9   An Incorrect Solution to the Infinite-Buffer Producer/Consumer Problem Using Binary Semaphores

accessing the buffer during the append operation. Also, while in the critical section, the producer increments the value of *n*. If *n* = 1, then the buffer was empty just prior to this append, so the producer performs semSignalB(delay) to alert the consumer of this fact. The consumer begins by waiting for the first item to be produced, using semWaitB(delay). It then takes an item and decrements *n* in its critical section. If the producer is able to stay ahead of the consumer (a common situation), then the consumer will rarely block on the semaphore delay because *n* will usually be positive. Hence both producer and consumer run smoothly.

There is, however, a flaw in this program. When the consumer has exhausted the buffer, it needs to reset the delay semaphore so that it will be forced to wait until the producer has placed more items in the buffer. This is the purpose of the statement: **if** n == 0 semWaitB(delay). Consider the scenario outlined in Table 5.4. In line 14, the consumer fails to execute the semWaitB operation. The consumer did indeed exhaust the buffer and set *n* to 0 (line 8), but the producer has incremented *n* before the consumer can test it in line 14. The result is a semSignalB not matched by a prior semWaitB. The value of –1 for *n* in line 20 means that the consumer has consumed an item from the buffer that does not exist. It would not do simply to move the conditional statement inside the critical section of the consumer because this could lead to deadlock (e.g., after line 8 of Table 5.4).

Table 5.4 Possible Scenario for the Program of Figure 5.9

	Producer	Consumer	s	n	Delay
1			1	0	0
2	semWaitB(s)		0	0	0
3	n++		0	1	0
4	**if** (n==1) (semSignalB(delay))		0	1	1
5	semSignalB(s)		1	1	1
6		semWaitB(delay)	1	1	0
7		semWaitB(s)	0	1	0
8		n--	0	0	0
9		semSignalB(s)	1	0	0
10	semWaitB(s)		0	0	0
11	n++		0	1	0
12	**if** (n==1) (semSignalB(delay))		0	1	1
13	semSignalB(s)		1	1	1
14		**if** (n==0) (semWaitB(delay))	1	1	1
15		semWaitB(s)	0	1	1
16		n--	0	0	1
17		semSignalB(s)	1	0	1
18		**if** (n==0) (semWaitB(delay))	1	0	0
19		semWaitB(s)	0	0	0
20		n--	0	–1	0
21		semSignalB(s)	1	–1	0

Note: White areas represent the critical section controlled by semaphore s.

A fix for the problem is to introduce an auxiliary variable that can be set in the consumer's critical section for use later on. This is shown in Figure 5.10. A careful trace of the logic should convince you that deadlock can no longer occur.

A somewhat cleaner solution can be obtained if general semaphores (also called counting semaphores) are used, as shown in Figure 5.11. The variable n is now a semaphore. Its value still is equal to the number of items in the buffer. Suppose now that in transcribing this program, a mistake is made and the operations semSignal(s) and semSignal(n) are interchanged. This would require that the semSignal(n) operation be performed in the producer's critical section without interruption by the consumer or another producer. Would this affect

```
/* program producerconsumer */
    int n;
    binary_semaphore s = 1, delay = 0;
    void producer()
    {
        while (true) {
            produce();
            semWaitB(s);
            append();
            n++;
            if (n==1) semSignalB(delay);
            semSignalB(s);
        }
    }
    void consumer()
    {
        int m; /* a local variable */
        semWaitB(delay);
        while (true) {
            semWaitB(s);
            take();
            n--;
            m = n;
            semSignalB(s);
            consume();
            if (m==0) semWaitB(delay);
        }
    }
    void main()
    {
        n = 0;
        parbegin (producer, consumer);
    }
```

Figure 5.10   A Correct Solution to the Infinite-Buffer Producer/Consumer Problem Using Binary Semaphores

the program? No, because the consumer must wait on both semaphores before proceeding in any case.

Now suppose that the semWait(n) and semWait(s) operations are accidentally reversed. This produces a serious, indeed a fatal, flaw. If the consumer ever enters its critical section when the buffer is empty (*n.count* = 0), then no producer can ever append to the buffer and the system is deadlocked. This is a good example of the subtlety of semaphores and the difficulty of producing correct designs.

Finally, let us add a new and realistic restriction to the producer/consumer problem: namely, that the buffer is finite. The buffer is treated as a circular storage (Figure 5.12), and pointer values must be expressed modulo the size of the buffer. The following relationships hold:

Block on:	Unblock on:
Producer: insert in full buffer	Consumer: item inserted
Consumer: remove from empty buffer	Producer: item removed

```
/* program producerconsumer */
    semaphore n = 0, s = 1;
    void producer()
    {
        while (true) {
            produce();
            semWait(s);
            append();
            semSignal(s);
            semSignal(n);
        }
    }
    void consumer()
    {
        while (true) {
            semWait(n);
            semWait(s);
            take();
            semSignal(s);
            consume();
        }
    }
    void main()
    {
        parbegin (producer, consumer);
    }
```

Figure 5.11   A Solution to the Infinite-Buffer Producer/Consumer Problem Using Semaphores

The producer and consumer functions can be expressed as follows (variable *in* and *out* are initialized to 0 and *n* is the size of the buffer):

```
producer:                        consumer:
while (true) {                   while (true) {
    /* produce item v */             while (in == out)
    while ((in + 1) % n == out)          /* do nothing */;
        /* do nothing */;            w = b[out];
    b[in] = v;                       out = (out + 1) % n;
    in = (in + 1) % n;              /* consume item w */;
}                                }
```

Figure 5.13 shows a solution using general semaphores. The semaphore *e* has been added to keep track of the number of empty spaces.

Another instructive example in the use of semaphores is the barbershop problem, described in Appendix A. Appendix A also includes additional examples of the problem of race conditions when using semaphores.

Implementation of Semaphores

As was mentioned earlier, it is imperative that the semWait and semSignal operations be implemented as atomic primitives. One obvious way is to implement them

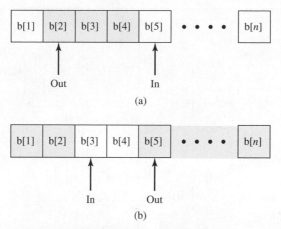

Figure 5.12 Finite Circular Buffer for the Producer/Consumer Problem

in hardware or firmware. Failing this, a variety of schemes have been suggested. The essence of the problem is one of mutual exclusion: Only one process at a time may manipulate a semaphore with either a semWait or semSignal operation. Thus, any of the software schemes, such as Dekker's algorithm or Peterson's algorithm (Appendix A), could be used; this would entail a substantial processing overhead.

```
/* program boundedbuffer */
    const int sizeofbuffer = /* buffer size */;
    semaphore s = 1, n = 0, e = sizeofbuffer;
    void producer()
    {
        while (true) {
            produce();
            semWait(e);
            semWait(s);
            append();
            semSignal(s);
            semSignal(n);
        }
    }
    void consumer()
    {
        while (true) {
            semWait(n);
            semWait(s);
            take();
            semSignal(s);
            semSignal(e);
            consume();
        }
    }
    void main()
    {
            parbegin (producer, consumer);
    }
```

Figure 5.13   A Solution to the Bounded-Buffer Producer/Consumer Problem Using Semaphores

```
semWait(s)
{
    while (compare_and_swap(s.flag, 0 , 1) == 1)
        /* do nothing */;
    s.count--;
    if (s.count < 0) {
        /* place this process in s.queue*/;
        /* block this process (must also set
s.flag to 0) */;
    }
    s.flag = 0;
}

semSignal(s)
{
    while (compare_and_swap(s.flag, 0 , 1) == 1)
        /* do nothing */;
    s.count++;
    if (s.count<= 0) {
        /* remove a process P from s.queue */;
        /* place process P on ready list */;
    }
    s.flag = 0;
}
```

```
semWait(s)
{
    inhibit interrupts;
    s.count--;
    if (s.count < 0) {
        /* place this process in s.queue */;
        /* block this process and allow inter-
rupts*/;
    }
    else
        allow interrupts;
}

semSignal(s)
{
    inhibit interrupts;
    s.count++;
    if (s.count<= 0) {
        /* remove a process P from s.queue */;
        /* place process P on ready list */;
    }
    allow interrupts;
}
```

(a) Compare and Swap Instruction   (b) Interrupts

Figure 5.14   Two Possible Implementations of Semaphores

Another alternative is to use one of the hardware-supported schemes for mutual exclusion. For example, Figure 5.14a shows the use of a `compare&swap` instruction. In this implementation, the semaphore is again a structure, as in Figure 5.3, but now includes a new integer component, *s.flag*. Admittedly, this involves a form of busy waiting. However, the `semWait` and `semSignal` operations are relatively short, so the amount of busy waiting involved should be minor.

For a single-processor system, it is possible to inhibit interrupts for the duration of a `semWait` or `semSignal` operation, as suggested in Figure 5.14b. Once again, the relatively short duration of these operations means that this approach is reasonable.

5.4   MONITORS

Semaphores provide a primitive yet powerful and flexible tool for enforcing mutual exclusion and for coordinating processes. However, as Figure 5.9 suggests, it may be difficult to produce a correct program using semaphores. The difficulty is that `semWait` and `semSignal` operations may be scattered throughout a program and it is not easy to see the overall effect of these operations on the semaphores they affect.

The monitor is a programming-language construct that provides equivalent functionality to that of semaphores and that is easier to control. The concept was first formally defined in [HOAR74]. The monitor construct has been implemented in a number of programming languages, including Concurrent Pascal, Pascal-Plus, Modula-2, Modula-3, and Java. It has also been implemented as a program library. This allows programmers to put a monitor lock on any object. In particular, for something like a linked list, you may want to lock all linked lists with one lock, or have one lock for each list, or have one lock for each element of each list.

We begin with a look at Hoare's version and then examine a refinement.

Monitor with Signal

A monitor is a software module consisting of one or more procedures, an initialization sequence, and local data. The chief characteristics of a monitor are the following:

1. The local data variables are accessible only by the monitor's procedures and not by any external procedure.

2. A process enters the monitor by invoking one of its procedures.

3. Only one process may be executing in the monitor at a time; any other processes that have invoked the monitor are blocked, waiting for the monitor to become available.

The first two characteristics are reminiscent of those for objects in object-oriented software. Indeed, an object-oriented OS or programming language can readily implement a monitor as an object with special characteristics.

By enforcing the discipline of one process at a time, the monitor is able to provide a mutual exclusion facility. The data variables in the monitor can be accessed by only one process at a time. Thus, a shared data structure can be protected by placing it in a monitor. If the data in a monitor represent some resource, then the monitor provides a mutual exclusion facility for accessing the resource.

To be useful for concurrent processing, the monitor must include synchronization tools. For example, suppose a process invokes the monitor and, while in the monitor, must be blocked until some condition is satisfied. A facility is needed by which the process is not only blocked but releases the monitor so that some other process may enter it. Later, when the condition is satisfied and the monitor is again available, the process needs to be resumed and allowed to reenter the monitor at the point of its suspension.

A monitor supports synchronization by the use of **condition variables** that are contained within the monitor and accessible only within the monitor. Condition variables are a special data type in monitors, which are operated on by two functions:

- cwait(c): Suspend execution of the calling process on condition *c*. The monitor is now available for use by another process.

- csignal(c): Resume execution of some process blocked after a cwait on the same condition. If there are several such processes, choose one of them; if there is no such process, do nothing.

Note that monitor *wait* and *signal* operations are different from those for the semaphore. If a process in a monitor signals and no task is waiting on the condition variable, the signal is lost.

Figure 5.15 illustrates the structure of a monitor. Although a process can enter the monitor by invoking any of its procedures, we can think of the monitor as having a single entry point that is guarded so that only one process may be in the monitor at a time. Other processes that attempt to enter the monitor join a queue of

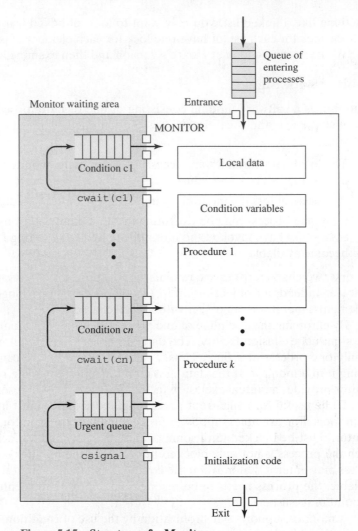

Figure 5.15   Structure of a Monitor

processes blocked waiting for monitor availability. Once a process is in the monitor, it may temporarily block itself on condition *x* by issuing `cwait(x)`; it is then placed in a queue of processes waiting to reenter the monitor when the condition changes, and resume execution at the point in its program following the `cwait(x)` call.

If a process that is executing in the monitor detects a change in the condition variable x, it issues `csignal(x)`, which alerts the corresponding condition queue that the condition has changed.

As an example of the use of a monitor, let us return to the bounded-buffer producer/consumer problem. Figure 5.16 shows a solution using a monitor. The monitor module, `boundedbuffer`, controls the buffer used to store and retrieve characters. The monitor includes two condition variables (declared with the construct **cond**): *notfull* is true when there is room to add at least one character to the buffer, and *notempty* is true when there is at least one character in the buffer.

```
/* program producerconsumer */
monitor boundedbuffer;
char buffer [N];                                    /* space for N items */
int nextin, nextout;                                /* buffer pointers */
int count;                                    /* number of items in buffer */
cond notfull, notempty;         /* condition variables for synchronization */

void append (char x)
{
    if (count == N) cwait(notfull);        /* buffer is full; avoid overflow */
    buffer[nextin] = x;
    nextin = (nextin + 1) % N;
    count++;
    /* one more item in buffer */
    csignal (nonempty);                           /*resume any waiting consumer */
}
void take (char x)
{
    if (count == 0) cwait(notempty);       /* buffer is empty; avoid underflow */
    x = buffer[nextout];
    nextout = (nextout + 1) % N;
    count--;                                       /* one fewer item in buffer */
    csignal (notfull);                        /* resume any waiting producer */
}
{                                                       /* monitor body */
    nextin = 0; nextout = 0; count = 0;         /* buffer initially empty */
}
```

```
void producer()
{
    char x;
    while (true) {
    produce(x);
    append(x);
    }
]
void consumer()
{
    char x;
    while (true) {
    take(x);
    consume(x);
    }
}
void main()
{
    parbegin (producer, consumer);
}
```

Figure 5.16   A Solution to the Bounded-Buffer Producer/Consumer Problem Using a Monitor

A producer can add characters to the buffer only by means of the procedure append inside the monitor; the producer does not have direct access to *buffer*. The procedure first checks the condition *notfull* to determine if there is space available in the buffer. If not, the process executing the monitor is blocked on that condition. Some other process (producer or consumer) may now enter the monitor. Later, when the buffer is no longer full, the blocked process may be removed from the queue, reactivated, and resume processing. After placing a character in the buffer, the process signals the *notempty* condition. A similar description can be made of the consumer function.

This example points out the division of responsibility with monitors compared to semaphores. In the case of monitors, the monitor construct itself enforces mutual exclusion: It is not possible for both a producer and a consumer simultaneously to access the buffer. However, the programmer must place the appropriate cwait and csignal primitives inside the monitor to prevent processes from depositing items in a full buffer or removing them from an empty one. In the case of semaphores, both mutual exclusion and synchronization are the responsibility of the programmer.

Note that in Figure 5.16, a process exits the monitor immediately after executing the csignal function. If the csignal does not occur at the end of the procedure, then, in Hoare's proposal, the process issuing the signal is blocked to make the monitor available and placed in a queue until the monitor is free. One possibility at this point would be to place the blocked process in the entrance queue, so that it would have to compete for access with other processes that had not yet entered the monitor. However, because a process blocked on a csignal function has already partially performed its task in the monitor, it makes sense to give this process precedence over newly entering processes by setting up a separate urgent queue (Figure 5.15). One language that uses monitors, Concurrent Pascal, requires that csignal only appear as the last operation executed by a monitor procedure.

If there are no processes waiting on condition x, then the execution of csignal(x) has no effect.

As with semaphores, it is possible to make mistakes in the synchronization function of monitors. For example, if either of the csignal functions in the boundedbuffer monitor are omitted, then processes entering the corresponding condition queue are permanently hung up. The advantage that monitors have over semaphores is that all of the synchronization functions are confined to the monitor. Therefore, it is easier to verify that the synchronization has been done correctly and to detect bugs. Furthermore, once a monitor is correctly programmed, access to the protected resource is correct for access from all processes. In contrast, with semaphores, resource access is correct only if all of the processes that access the resource are programmed correctly.

Alternate Model of Monitors with Notify and Broadcast

Hoare's definition of monitors [HOAR74] requires that if there is at least one process in a condition queue, a process from that queue runs immediately when another process issues a csignal for that condition. Thus, the process issuing the csignal must either immediately exit the monitor or be blocked on the monitor.

There are two drawbacks to this approach:

1. If the process issuing the csignal has not finished with the monitor, then two additional process switches are required: one to block this process and another to resume it when the monitor becomes available.

2. Process scheduling associated with a signal must be perfectly reliable. When a csignal is issued, a process from the corresponding condition queue must be activated immediately and the scheduler must ensure that no other process

enters the monitor before activation. Otherwise, the condition under which the process was activated could change. For example, in Figure 5.16, when a `csignal(notempty)` is issued, a process from the `notempty` queue must be activated before a new consumer enters the monitor. Another example: a producer process may append a character to an empty buffer and then fail before signaling; any processes in the `notempty` queue would be permanently hung up.

Lampson and Redell developed a different definition of monitors for the language Mesa [LAMP80]. Their approach overcomes the problems just listed and supports several useful extensions. The Mesa monitor structure is also used in the Modula-3 systems programming language [NELS91]. In Mesa, the `csignal` primitive is replaced by `cnotify`, with the following interpretation: When a process executing in a monitor executes `cnotify(x)`, it causes the *x* condition queue to be notified, but the signaling process continues to execute. The result of the notification is that the process at the head of the condition queue will be resumed at some convenient future time when the monitor is available. However, because there is no guarantee that some other process will not enter the monitor before the waiting process, the waiting process must recheck the condition. For example, the procedures in the `boundedbuffer` monitor would now have the code of Figure 5.17.

The **if** statements are replaced by **while** loops. Thus, this arrangement results in at least one extra evaluation of the condition variable. In return, however, there are no extra process switches, and no constraints on when the waiting process must run after a `cnotify`.

One useful refinement that can be associated with the `cnotify` primitive is a watchdog timer associated with each condition primitive. A process that has been waiting for the maximum timeout interval will be placed in a Ready state regardless of whether the condition has been notified. When activated, the process checks the condition and continues if the condition is satisfied. The timeout prevents the indefinite starvation of a process in the event that some other process fails before signaling a condition.

```
void append (char x)
{
        while (count == N) cwait(notfull);       /* buffer is full; avoid overflow */
        buffer[nextin] = x;
        nextin = (nextin + 1) % N;
        count++;                                        /* one more item in buffer */
        cnotify(notempty);                       /* notify any waiting consumer */
}

void take (char x)
{
        while (count == 0) cwait(notempty);      /* buffer is empty; avoid underflow */
        x = buffer[nextout];
        nextout = (nextout + 1) % N);
        count--;                                       /* one fewer item in buffer */
        cnotify(notfull);                        /* notify any waiting producer */
}
```

Figure 5.17   Bounded-Buffer Monitor Code for Mesa Monitor

With the rule that a process is notified rather than forcibly reactivated, it is possible to add a `cbroadcast` primitive to the repertoire. The broadcast causes all processes waiting on a condition to be placed in a Ready state. This is convenient in situations where a process does not know how many other processes should be reactivated. For example, in the producer/consumer program, suppose that both the `append` and the `take` functions can apply to variable length blocks of characters. In that case, if a producer adds a block of characters to the buffer, it need not know how many characters each waiting consumer is prepared to consume. It simply issues a `cbroadcast` and all waiting processes are alerted to try again.

In addition, a broadcast can be used when a process would have difficulty figuring out precisely which other process to reactivate. A good example is a memory manager. The manager has j bytes free; a process frees up an additional k bytes, but it does not know which waiting process can proceed with a total of $k + j$ bytes. Hence it uses broadcast, and all processes check for themselves if there is enough memory free.

An advantage of Lampson/Redell monitors over Hoare monitors is that the Lampson/Redell approach is less prone to error. In the Lampson/Redell approach, because each procedure checks the monitor variable after being signaled, with the use of the **while** construct, a process can signal or broadcast incorrectly without causing an error in the signaled program. The signaled program will check the relevant variable and, if the desired condition is not met, continue to wait.

Another advantage of the Lampson/Redell monitor is that it lends itself to a more modular approach to program construction. For example, consider the implementation of a buffer allocator. There are two levels of conditions to be satisfied for cooperating sequential processes:

1. Consistent data structures. Thus, the monitor enforces mutual exclusion and completes an input or output operation before allowing another operation on the buffer.

2. Level 1, plus enough memory for this process to complete its allocation request.

In the Hoare monitor, each signal conveys the level 1 condition but also carries the implicit message, "I have freed enough bytes for your particular allocate call to work now." Thus, the signal implicitly carries the level 2 condition. If the programmer later changes the definition of the level 2 condition, it will be necessary to reprogram all signaling processes. If the programmer changes the assumptions made by any particular waiting process (i.e., waiting for a slightly different level 2 invariant), it may be necessary to reprogram all signaling processes. This is unmodular and likely to cause synchronization errors (e.g., wake up by mistake) when the code is modified. The programmer has to remember to modify all procedures in the monitor every time a small change is made to the level 2 condition. With a Lampson/Redell monitor, a broadcast ensures the level 1 condition and carries a hint that level 2 might hold; each process should check the level 2 condition itself. If a change is made in the level 2 condition in either a waiter or a signaler, there is no possibility of erroneous wakeup because each procedure checks its own level 2 condition. Therefore, the level 2 condition can be hidden within each procedure. With the Hoare monitor, the level 2 condition must be carried from the waiter into the code of every signaling process, which violates data abstraction and interprocedural modularity principles.

5.5   MESSAGE PASSING

When processes interact with one another, two fundamental requirements must be satisfied: synchronization and communication. Processes need to be synchronized to enforce mutual exclusion; cooperating processes may need to exchange information. One approach to providing both of these functions is message passing. Message passing has the further advantage that it lends itself to implementation in distributed systems as well as in shared-memory multiprocessor and uniprocessor systems.

Message-passing systems come in many forms. In this section, we provide a general introduction that discusses features typically found in such systems. The actual function of message passing is normally provided in the form of a pair of primitives:

```
send (destination, message)
receive (source, message)
```

This is the minimum set of operations needed for processes to engage in message passing. A process sends information in the form of a *message* to another process designated by a *destination*. A process receives information by executing the receive primitive, indicating the *source* and the *message*.

A number of design issues relating to message-passing systems are listed in Table 5.5, and examined in the remainder of this section.

Table 5.5   Design Characteristics of Message Systems for Interprocess Communication and Synchronization

Synchronization	Format
Send	Content
blocking	Length
nonblocking	fixed
Receive	variable
blocking	
nonblocking	**Queueing Discipline**
test for arrival	FIFO
	Priority
Addressing	
Direct	
send	
receive	
explicit	
implicit	
Indirect	
static	
dynamic	
ownership	

Synchronization

The communication of a message between two processes implies some level of synchronization between the two: The receiver cannot receive a message until it has been sent by another process. In addition, we need to specify what happens to a process after it issues a `send` or `receive` primitive.

Consider the `send` primitive first. When a `send` primitive is executed in a process, there are two possibilities: Either the sending process is blocked until the message is received, or it is not. Similarly, when a process issues a `receive` primitive, there are two possibilities:

1. If a message has previously been sent, the message is received and execution continues.

2. If there is no waiting message, then either (a) the process is blocked until a message arrives, or (b) the process continues to execute, abandoning the attempt to receive.

Thus, both the sender and receiver can be blocking or nonblocking. Three combinations are common, although any particular system will usually have only one or two combinations implemented:

- **Blocking send, blocking receive:** Both the sender and receiver are blocked until the message is delivered; this is sometimes referred to as a *rendezvous*. This combination allows for tight synchronization between processes.

- **Nonblocking send, blocking receive:** Although the sender may continue on, the receiver is blocked until the requested message arrives. This is probably the most useful combination. It allows a process to send one or more messages to a variety of destinations as quickly as possible. A process that must receive a message before it can do useful work needs to be blocked until such a message arrives. An example is a server process that exists to provide a service or resource to other processes.

- **Nonblocking send, nonblocking receive:** Neither party is required to wait.

The nonblocking `send` is more natural for many concurrent programming tasks. For example, if it is used to request an output operation, such as printing, it allows the requesting process to issue the request in the form of a message and then carry on. One potential danger of the nonblocking `send` is that an error could lead to a situation in which a process repeatedly generates messages. Because there is no blocking to discipline the process, these messages could consume system resources, including processor time and buffer space, to the detriment of other processes and the OS. Also, the nonblocking `send` places the burden on the programmer to determine that a message has been received: Processes must employ reply messages to acknowledge receipt of a message.

For the `receive` primitive, the blocking version appears to be more natural for many concurrent programming tasks. Generally, a process that requests a message will need the expected information before proceeding. However, if a message is lost, which can happen in a distributed system, or if a process fails before it sends an anticipated message, a receiving process could be blocked indefinitely. This problem can be solved by the use of the nonblocking `receive`. However, the danger of this approach is that if a message is sent after a process has already executed a matching `receive`, the message will be lost. Other possible approaches are to allow a process to test whether a message is waiting before issuing a `receive` and allow a process to specify more than one source in a `receive` primitive. The latter approach is useful if a process is waiting for messages from more than one source and can proceed if any of these messages arrive.

Addressing

Clearly, it is necessary to have a way of specifying in the `send` primitive which process is to receive the message. Similarly, most implementations allow a receiving process to indicate the source of a message to be received.

The various schemes for specifying processes in `send` and `receive` primitives fall into two categories: direct addressing and indirect addressing. With **direct addressing**, the `send` primitive includes a specific identifier of the destination process. The `receive` primitive can be handled in one of two ways. One possibility is to require that the process explicitly designate a sending process. Thus, the process must know ahead of time from which process a message is expected. This will often be effective for cooperating concurrent processes. In other cases, however, it is impossible to specify the anticipated source process. An example is a printer-server process, which will accept a print request message from any other process. For such applications, a more effective approach is the use of implicit addressing. In this case, the *source* parameter of the `receive` primitive possesses a value returned when the receive operation has been performed.

The other general approach is **indirect addressing**. In this case, messages are not sent directly from sender to receiver but rather are sent to a shared data structure consisting of queues that can temporarily hold messages. Such queues are generally referred to as *mailboxes*. Thus, for two processes to communicate, one process sends a message to the appropriate mailbox and the other process picks up the message from the mailbox.

A strength of the use of indirect addressing is that, by decoupling the sender and receiver, it allows for greater flexibility in the use of messages. The relationship between senders and receivers can be one to one, many to one, one to many, or many to many (Figure 5.18). A **one-to-one** relationship allows a private communications link to be set up between two processes. This insulates their interaction from erroneous interference from other processes. A **many-to-one** relationship is useful for client/server interaction; one process provides service to a number of other processes. In this case, the mailbox is often referred to as a *port*. A **one-to-many** relationship allows for one sender and multiple receivers; it is useful for applications where a message or some information is to be broadcast to a set of processes. A **many-to-many** relationship allows multiple server processes to provide concurrent service to multiple clients.

The association of processes to mailboxes can be either static or dynamic. Ports are often statically associated with a particular process; that is, the port is created and assigned to the process permanently. Similarly, a one-to-one relationship is typically defined statically and permanently. When there are many senders,

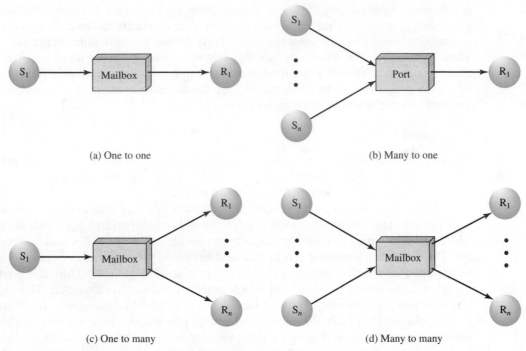

(a) One to one   (b) Many to one

(c) One to many   (d) Many to many

Figure 5.18   Indirect Process Communication

the association of a sender to a mailbox may occur dynamically. Primitives such as `connect` and `disconnect` may be used for this purpose.

A related issue has to do with the ownership of a mailbox. In the case of a port, it is typically owned by and created by the receiving process. Thus, when the process is destroyed, the port is also destroyed. For the general mailbox case, the OS may offer a create-mailbox service. Such mailboxes can be viewed either as being owned by the creating process, in which case they terminate with the process, or as being owned by the OS, in which case an explicit command will be required to destroy the mailbox.

Message Format

The format of the message depends on the objectives of the messaging facility and whether the facility runs on a single computer or on a distributed system. For some operating systems, designers have preferred short, fixed-length messages to minimize processing and storage overhead. If a large amount of data is to be passed, the data can be placed in a file and the message then simply references that file. A more flexible approach is to allow variable-length messages.

Figure 5.19 shows a typical message format for operating systems that support variable-length messages. The message is divided into two parts: a header, which contains information about the message, and a body, which contains the actual contents of the message. The header may contain an identification of the source and intended destination of the message, a length field, and a type field to discriminate among various types of messages. There may also be additional control information,

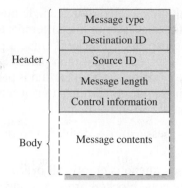

Figure 5.19 General Message Format

such as a pointer field so that a linked list of messages can be created; a sequence number, to keep track of the number and order of messages passed between source and destination; and a priority field.

Queueing Discipline

The simplest queueing discipline is first-in-first-out, but this may not be sufficient if some messages are more urgent than others. An alternative is to allow the specifying of message priority, on the basis of message type or by designation by the sender. Another alternative is to allow the receiver to inspect the message queue and select which message to receive next.

Mutual Exclusion

Figure 5.20 shows one way in which message passing can be used to enforce mutual exclusion (compare Figures 5.1, 5.2, and 5.6). We assume the use of the blocking `receive` primitive and the nonblocking `send` primitive. A set of concurrent processes share a mailbox, `box`, which can be used by all processes to send and receive.

```
/* program mutualexclusion */
const int n = /* number of process */
void P(int i)
{
    message msg;
    while (true) {
        receive (box, msg);
        /* critical section */;
        send (box, msg);
        /* remainder */;
    }
}
void main()
{
    create mailbox (box);
    send (box, null);
    parbegin (P(1), P(2),…, P(n));
```

Figure 5.20 Mutual Exclusion Using Messages

The mailbox is initialized to contain a single message with null content. A process wishing to enter its critical section first attempts to receive a message. If the mailbox is empty, then the process is blocked. Once a process has acquired the message, it performs its critical section and then places the message back into the mailbox. Thus, the message functions as a token that is passed from process to process.

The preceding solution assumes that if more than one process performs the receive operation concurrently, then:

- If there is a message, it is delivered to only one process and the others are blocked, or
- If the message queue is empty, all processes are blocked; when a message is available, only one blocked process is activated and given the message.

These assumptions are true of virtually all message-passing facilities.

As an example of the use of message passing, Figure 5.21 is a solution to the bounded-buffer producer/consumer problem. Using the basic mutual-exclusion power of message passing, the problem could have been solved with an algorithmic structure similar to that of Figure 5.13. Instead, the program of Figure 5.21 takes advantage of the ability of message passing to be used to pass data in addition to signals. Two mailboxes are used. As the producer generates data, it is sent as messages to the mailbox mayconsume. As long as there is at least one message in that mailbox, the consumer can consume. Hence mayconsume serves as the buffer; the data in the buffer are organized as a queue of messages. The "size" of the buffer is

```
const int
    capacity = /* buffering capacity */ ;
    null = /* empty message */ ;
int i;
void producer()
{   message pmsg;
    while (true) {
      receive (mayproduce,pmsg);
      pmsg = produce();
      send (mayconsume,pmsg);
    }
}
void consumer()
{   message cmsg;
    while (true) {
      receive (mayconsume,cmsg);
      consume (cmsg);
      send (mayproduce,null);
    }
}
void main()
{
    create_mailbox (mayproduce);
    create_mailbox (mayconsume);
    for (int i = 1;i<= capacity;i++) send (mayproduce,null);
    parbegin (producer,consumer);
}
```

Figure 5.21   A Solution to the Bounded-Buffer Producer/Consumer Problem Using Messages

determined by the global variable `capacity`. Initially, the mailbox `mayproduce` is filled with a number of null messages equal to the capacity of the buffer. The number of messages in `mayproduce` shrinks with each production and grows with each consumption.

This approach is quite flexible. There may be multiple producers and consumers, as long as all have access to both mailboxes. The system may even be distributed, with all producer processes and the `mayproduce` mailbox at one site and all the consumer processes and the `mayconsume` mailbox at another.

5.6 READERS/WRITERS PROBLEM

In dealing with the design of synchronization and concurrency mechanisms, it is useful to be able to relate the problem at hand to known problems and to be able to test any solution in terms of its ability to solve these known problems. In the literature, several problems have assumed importance and appear frequently, both because they are examples of common design problems and because of their educational value. One such problem is the producer/consumer problem, which has already been explored. In this section, we look at another classic problem: the readers/writers problem.

The readers/writers problem is defined as follows: There is a data area shared among a number of processes. The data area could be a file, a block of main memory, or even a bank of processor registers. There are a number of processes that only read the data area (readers) and a number that only write to the data area (writers). The conditions that must be satisfied are as follows:

1. Any number of readers may simultaneously read the file.
2. Only one writer at a time may write to the file.
3. If a writer is writing to the file, no reader may read it.

Thus, readers are processes that are not required to exclude one another and writers are processes that are required to exclude all other processes, readers and writers alike.

Before proceeding, let us distinguish this problem from two others: the general mutual exclusion problem and the producer/consumer problem. In the readers/writers problem readers do not also write to the data area, nor do writers read the data area while writing. A more general case, which includes this case, is to allow any of the processes to read or write the data area. In that case, we can declare any portion of a process that accesses the data area to be a critical section and impose the general mutual exclusion solution. The reason for being concerned with the more restricted case is that more efficient solutions are possible for this case and that the less efficient solutions to the general problem are unacceptably slow. For example, suppose that the shared area is a library catalog. Ordinary users of the library read the catalog to locate a book. One or more librarians are able to update the catalog. In the general solution, every access to the catalog would be treated as a critical section, and users would be forced to read the catalog one at a time. This would clearly impose intolerable delays. At the same time, it is important to prevent writers from interfering with each other and it is also required to prevent reading while writing is in progress to prevent the access of inconsistent information.

Can the producer/consumer problem be considered simply a special case of the readers/writers problem with a single writer (the producer) and a single reader (the consumer)? The answer is no. The producer is not just a writer. It must read queue pointers to determine where to write the next item, and it must determine if the buffer is full. Similarly, the consumer is not just a reader, because it must adjust the queue pointers to show that it has removed a unit from the buffer.

We now examine two solutions to the problem.

Readers Have Priority

Figure 5.22 is a solution using semaphores, showing one instance each of a reader and a writer; the solution does not change for multiple readers and writers. The writer process is simple. The semaphore wsem is used to enforce mutual exclusion. As long as one writer is accessing the shared data area, no other writers and no readers may access it. The reader process also makes use of wsem to enforce mutual exclusion. However, to allow multiple readers, we require that, when there are no readers reading, the first reader that attempts to read should wait on wsem. When

```
/* program readersandwriters */
int readcount;
semaphore x = 1,wsem = 1;
void reader()
{
    while (true){
      semWait (x);
      readcount++;
      if(readcount == 1)
          semWait (wsem);
      semSignal (x);
      READUNIT();
      semWait (x);
      readcount--;
      if(readcount == 0)
          semSignal (wsem);
      semSignal (x);
      }
}
void writer()
{
    while (true){
      semWait (wsem);
      WRITEUNIT();
      semSignal (wsem);
      }
}

void main()
{
    readcount = 0;
    parbegin (reader,writer);
}
```

Figure 5.22   **A Solution to the Readers/Writers Problem Using Semaphore: Readers Have Priority**

there is already at least one reader reading, subsequent readers need not wait before entering. The global variable `readcount` is used to keep track of the number of readers, and the semaphore x is used to assure that `readcount` is updated properly.

Writers Have Priority

In the previous solution, readers have priority. Once a single reader has begun to access the data area, it is possible for readers to retain control of the data area as long as there is at least one reader in the act of reading. Therefore, writers are subject to starvation.

Figure 5.23 shows a solution that guarantees that no new readers are allowed access to the data area once at least one writer has declared a desire to write. For

```
/* program readersandwriters */
int readcount,writecount;
void reader()
{
    while (true){
        semWait (z);
            semWait (rsem);
                semWait (x);
                        readcount++;
                        if (readcount == 1)
                                semWait (wsem);
                        semSignal (x);
                semSignal (rsem);
            semSignal (z);
            READUNIT();
            semWait (x);
                readcount--;
                if (readcount == 0) semSignal (wsem);
            semSignal (x);
    }
}
void writer ()
{
    while (true){
        semWait (y);
            writecount++;
            if (writecount == 1)
                semWait (rsem);
        semSignal (y);
        semWait (wsem);
        WRITEUNIT();
        semSignal (wsem);
        semWait (y);
            writecount;
            if (writecount == 0) semSignal (rsem);
        semSignal (y);
    }
}
void main()
{
    readcount = writecount = 0;
    parbegin (reader, writer);
}
```

Figure 5.23 A Solution to the Readers/Writers Problem Using Semaphore: Writers Have Priority

Table 5.6   State of the Process Queues for Program of Figure 5.23

Readers only in the system	• *wsem* set • no queues
Writers only in the system	• *wsem* and *rsem* set • writers queue on *wsem*
Both readers and writers with read first	• *wsem* set by reader • *rsem* set by writer • all writers queue on *wsem* • one reader queues on *rsem* • other readers queue on *z*
Both readers and writers with write first	• *wsem* set by writer • *rsem* set by writer • writers queue on *wsem* • one reader queues on *rsem* • other readers queue on *z*

writers, the following semaphores and variables are added to the ones already defined:

- A semaphore rsem that inhibits all readers while there is at least one writer desiring access to the data area
- A variable writecount that controls the setting of rsem
- A semaphore y that controls the updating of writecount

For readers, one additional semaphore is needed. A long queue must not be allowed to build up on rsem; otherwise writers will not be able to jump the queue. Therefore, only one reader is allowed to queue on rsem, with any additional readers queueing on semaphore z, immediately before waiting on rsem. Table 5.6 summarizes the possibilities.

An alternative solution, which gives writers priority and which is implemented using message passing, is shown in Figure 5.24. In this case, there is a controller process that has access to the shared data area. Other processes wishing to access the data area send a request message to the controller, are granted access with an "OK" reply message, and indicate completion of access with a "finished" message. The controller is equipped with three mailboxes, one for each type of message that it may receive.

The controller process services write request messages before read request messages to give writers priority. In addition, mutual exclusion must be enforced. To do this the variable *count* is used, which is initialized to some number greater than the maximum possible number of readers. In this example, we use a value of 100. The action of the controller can be summarized as follows:

- If *count* > 0, then no writer is waiting and there may or may not be readers active. Service all "finished" messages first to clear active readers. Then service write requests and then read requests.
- If *count* = 0, then the only request outstanding is a write request. Allow the writer to proceed and wait for a "finished" message.

```
void reader(int i)                   void controller()
{                                    {
   message rmsg;                        while (true)
      while (true) {                     {
         rmsg = i;                          if (count > 0) {
         send (readrequest, rmsg);             if (!empty (finished)) {
         receive (mbox[i], rmsg);                 receive (finished, msg);
         READUNIT ();                             count++;
         rmsg = i;                             }
         send (finished, rmsg);                else if (!empty (writerequest)) {
      }                                           receive (writerequest, msg);
}                                                 writer_id = msg.id;
void writer(int j)                                count = count - 100;
{                                              }
   message rmsg;                               else if (!empty (readrequest)) {
   while(true) {                                  receive (readrequest, msg);
      rmsg = j;                                    count--;
      send (writerequest, rmsg);                   send (msg.id, "OK");
      receive (mbox[j], rmsg);                  }
      WRITEUNIT ();                          }
      rmsg = j;                              if (count == 0) {
      send (finished, rmsg);                    send (writer_id, "OK");
   }                                            receive (finished, msg);
}                                              count = 100;
                                            }
                                            while (count < 0) {
                                               receive (finished, msg);
                                               count++;
                                            }
                                          }
                                       }
```

Figure 5.24 A Solution to the Readers/Writers Problem Using Message Passing

- If *count* < 0, then a writer has made a request and is being made to wait to clear all active readers. Therefore, only "finished" messages should be serviced.

5.7 SUMMARY

The central themes of modern operating systems are multiprogramming, multiprocessing, and distributed processing. Fundamental to these themes, and fundamental to the technology of OS design, is concurrency. When multiple processes are executing concurrently, either actually in the case of a multiprocessor system or virtually in the case of a single-processor multiprogramming system, issues of conflict resolution and cooperation arise.

Concurrent processes may interact in a number of ways. Processes that are unaware of each other may nevertheless compete for resources, such as processor time or access to I/O devices. Processes may be indirectly aware of one another because they share access to a common object, such as a block of main memory or a file. Finally, processes may be directly aware of each other and cooperate by the exchange of information. The key issues that arise in these interactions are mutual exclusion and deadlock.

Mutual exclusion is a condition in which there is a set of concurrent processes, only one of which is able to access a given resource or perform a given function at any time. Mutual exclusion techniques can be used to resolve conflicts, such as competition for resources, and to synchronize processes so that they can cooperate. An example of the latter is the producer/consumer model, in which one process is putting data into a buffer and one or more processes are extracting data from that buffer.

One approach to supporting mutual exclusion involves the use of special-purpose machine instructions. This approach reduces overhead but is still inefficient because it uses busy waiting.

Another approach to supporting mutual exclusion is to provide features within the OS. Two of the most common techniques are semaphores and message facilities. Semaphores are used for signaling among processes and can be readily used to enforce a mutual-exclusion discipline. Messages are useful for the enforcement of mutual exclusion and also provide an effective means of interprocess communication.

5.8   RECOMMENDED READING

The misnamed *Little Book of Semaphores* (291 pages) [DOWN08] provides numerous examples of the uses of semaphores; available free online.

[ANDR83] surveys many of the mechanisms described in this chapter. [BEN82] provides a very clear and even entertaining discussion of concurrency, mutual exclusion, semaphores, and other related topics. A more formal treatment, expanded to include distributed systems, is contained in [BEN06]. [AXFO88] is another readable and useful treatment; it also contains a number of problems with worked-out solutions. [RAYN86] is a comprehensive and lucid collection of algorithms for mutual exclusion, covering software (e.g., Dekker) and hardware approaches, as well as semaphores and messages. [HOAR85] is a very readable classic that presents a formal approach to defining sequential processes and concurrency. [LAMP86] is a lengthy formal treatment of mutual exclusion. [RUDO90] is a useful aid in understanding concurrency. [BACO03] is a well-organized treatment of concurrency. [BIRR89] provides a good practical introduction to programming using concurrency. [BUHR95] is an exhaustive survey of monitors. [KANG98] is an instructive analysis of 12 different scheduling policies for the readers/writers problem.

ANDR83   Andrews, G., and Schneider, F. "Concepts and Notations for Concurrent Programming." *Computing Surveys*, March 1983.

AXFO88   Axford, T. *Concurrent Programming: Fundamental Techniques for Real-Time and Parallel Software Design.* New York: Wiley, 1988.

BACO03   Bacon, J., and Harris, T. *Operating Systems: Concurrent and Distributed Software Design.* Reading, MA: Addison-Wesley, 2003.

BEN82   Ben-Ari, M. *Principles of Concurrent Programming.* Englewood Cliffs, NJ: Prentice Hall, 1982.

BEN06   Ben-Ari, M. *Principles of Concurrent and Distributed Programming*. Harlow, England: Addison-Wesley, 2006.

BIRR89   Birrell, A. *An Introduction to Programming with Threads*. SRC Research Report 35, Compaq Systems Research Center, Palo Alto, CA, January 1989. Available at http://www.research.compaq.com/SRC

BUHR95   Buhr, P., and Fortier, M. "Monitor Classification." *ACM Computing Surveys*, March 1995.

DOWN08   Downey, A. *The Little Book of Semaphores*. www.greenteapress.com /semaphores/

HOAR85   Hoare, C. *Communicating Sequential Processes*. Englewood Cliffs, NJ: Prentice-Hall, 1985.

KANG98   Kang, S., and Lee, J. "Analysis and Solution of Non-Preemptive Policies for Scheduling Readers and Writers." *Operating Systems Review*, July 1998.

LAMP86   Lamport, L. "The Mutual Exclusion Problem." *Journal of the ACM*, April 1986.

RAYN86   Raynal, M. *Algorithms for Mutual Exclusion*. Cambridge, MA: MIT Press, 1986.

RUDO90   Rudolph, B. "Self-Assessment Procedure XXI: Concurrency." *Communications of the ACM*, May 1990.

5.9   KEY TERMS, REVIEW QUESTIONS, AND PROBLEMS

Key Terms

atomic	critical resource	nonblocking
binary semaphore	critical section	race condition
blocking	deadlock	semaphore
busy waiting	general semaphore	spin waiting
concurrency	message passing	starvation
concurrent processes	monitor	strong semaphore
coroutine	mutual exclusion	weak semaphore
counting semaphore	mutex	

Review Questions

5.1   List four design issues for which the concept of concurrency is relevant.

5.2   What are three contexts in which concurrency arises?

5.3   What is the basic requirement for the execution of concurrent processes?

5.4   List three degrees of awareness between processes and briefly define each.

5.5   What is the distinction between competing processes and cooperating processes?

5.6   List the three control problems associated with competing processes and briefly define each.

5.7   List the requirements for mutual exclusion.

5.8   What operations can be performed on a semaphore?

5.9   What is the difference between binary and general semaphores?

5.10   What is the difference between strong and weak semaphores?

5.11   What is a monitor?

5.12   What is the distinction between *blocking* and *nonblocking* with respect to messages?

5.13   What conditions are generally associated with the readers/writers problem?

Problems

 5.1   At the beginning of Section 5.1, it is stated that multiprogramming and multiprocessing present the same problems, with respect to concurrency. This is true as far as it goes. However, cite two differences in terms of concurrency between multiprogramming and multiprocessing.

5.2   Processes and threads provide a powerful structuring tool for implementing programs that would be much more complex as simple sequential programs. An earlier construct that is instructive to examine is the coroutine. The purpose of this problem is to introduce coroutines and compare them to processes. Consider this simple problem from [CONW63]:

Read 80-column cards and print them on 125-character lines, with the following changes. After every card image an extra blank is inserted, and every adjacent pair of asterisks (**) on a card is replaced by the character.

a.   Develop a solution to this problem as an ordinary sequential program. You will find that the program is tricky to write. The interactions among the various elements of the program are uneven because of the conversion from a length of 80 to 125; furthermore, the length of the card image, after conversion, will vary depending on the number of double asterisk occurrences. One way to improve clarity, and to minimize the potential for bugs, is to write the application as three separate procedures. The first procedure reads in card images, pads each image with a blank, and writes a stream of characters to a temporary file. After all of the cards have been read, the second procedure reads the temporary file, does the character substitution, and writes out a second temporary file. The third procedure reads the stream of characters from the second temporary file and prints lines of 125 characters each.

b.   The sequential solution is unattractive because of the overhead of I/O and temporary files. Conway proposed a new form of program structure, the coroutine, that allows the application to be written as three programs connected by one-character buffers (Figure 5.25). In a traditional **procedure**, there is a master/slave relationship between the called and calling procedure. The calling procedure may execute a call from any point in the procedure; the called procedure is begun at its entry point and returns to the calling procedure at the point of call. The **coroutine** exhibits a more symmetric relationship. As each call is made, execution takes up from the last active point in the called procedure. Because there is no sense in which a calling procedure is "higher" than the called, there is no return. Rather, any coroutine can pass control to any other coroutine with a resume command. The first time a coroutine is invoked, it is "resumed" at its entry point. Subsequently, the coroutine is reactivated at the point of its own last resume command. Note that only one coroutine in a program can be in execution at one time and that the transition points are explicitly defined in the code, so this is not an example of concurrent processing. Explain the operation of the program in Figure 5.25.

c.   The program does not address the termination condition. Assume that the I/O routine READCARD returns the value true if it has placed an 80-character image in *inbuf*; otherwise it returns false. Modify the program to include this contingency. Note that the last printed line may therefore contain less than 125 characters.

d.   Rewrite the solution as a set of three processes using semaphores.

```
char rs, sp;                              void squash()
char inbuf[80], outbuf[125] ;             {
void read()                                   while (true) {
{                                                 if (rs != "*") {
    while (true) {                                    sp = rs;
        READCARD (inbuf);                             RESUME print;
        for (int i=0; i < 80; i++){               }
            rs = inbuf [i];                       else{
            RESUME squash                             RESUME read;
        }                                             if (rs == "*") {
        rs = " ";                                         sp = " ";
        RESUME squash;                                    RESUME print;
    }                                                 }
}                                                     else {
void print()                                              sp = "*";
{                                                         RESUME print;
    while (true) {                                        sp = rs;
        for (int j = 0; j < 125; j++){                    RESUME print;
            outbuf [j] = sp;                          }
            RESUME squash                         }
        }                                         RESUME read;
        OUTPUT (outbuf);                      }
    }                                     }
}
```

Figure 5.25   **An Application of Coroutines**

5.3 Consider the following program:

```
        P1: {                             P2:{
        shared int. x;                    shared int x;
        x = 10;                           x = 10;
        while (1) {                       while ( 1 ) {
            x = x - 1;                        x = x - 1;
            x = x + 1;                        x = x + 1;
            if (x != 10)                      if (x!-10)
                printf("x is %d",x)                printf("x is %d",x)
        }                                 }
    }                                 }
}                                 }
```

Note that the scheduler in a uniprocessor system would implement pseudo-parallel execution of these two concurrent processes by interleaving their instructions, without restriction on the order of the interleaving.

a. Show a sequence (i.e., trace the sequence of interleavings of statements) such that the statement "x is 10" is printed.

b. Show a sequence such that the statement "x is 8" is printed. You should remember that the increment/decrements at the source language level are not done atomically, that is, the assembly language code:

```
LD    R0,X   /* load R0 from memory location x */
INCR  R0     /* increment R0 */
STO   R0,X   /* store the incremented value back in X */
```

implements the single C increment instruction (x = x + 1).

5.4 Consider the following program:

```
const int n = 50;
int tally;
void total()
{
    int count;
    for (count = 1; count<= n; count++){
        tally++;
    }
}
void main()
{
    tally = 0;
    parbegin (total (), total ());
    write (tally);
}
```

a. Determine the proper lower bound and upper bound on the final value of the shared variable *tally* output by this concurrent program. Assume processes can execute at any relative speed and that a value can only be incremented after it has been loaded into a register by a separate machine instruction.

b. Suppose that an arbitrary number of these processes are permitted to execute in parallel under the assumptions of part (a). What effect will this modification have on the range of final values of *tally*?

5.5 Is busy waiting always less efficient (in terms of using processor time) than a blocking wait? Explain.

5.6 Consider the following program:

```
boolean blocked [2];
int turn;
void P (int id)
{
  while (true) {
      blocked[id] = true;
      while (turn != id) {
          while (blocked[1-id])
              /* do nothing */;
          turn = id;
      }
      /* critical section */
      blocked[id] = false;
      /* remainder */
  }
}
void main()
{
  blocked[0] = false;
  blocked[1] = false;
  turn = 0;
  parbegin (P(0), P(1));
}
```

This software solution to the mutual exclusion problem for two processes is proposed in [HYMA66]. Find a counterexample that demonstrates that this solution is incorrect. It is interesting to note that even the *Communications of the ACM* was fooled on this one.

5.7 A software approach to mutual exclusion is Lamport's **bakery algorithm** [LAMP74], so called because it is based on the practice in bakeries and other shops in which every customer receives a numbered ticket on arrival, allowing each to be served in turn. The algorithm is as follows:

```
boolean choosing[n];
int number[n];
while (true) {
   choosing[i] = true;
   number[i] = 1 + getmax(number[], n);
   choosing[i] = false;
   for (int j = 0; j < n; j++){
     while (choosing[j]) { };
     while ((number[j] != 0) && (number[j],j) < (number[i],i)) { };
   }
   /* critical section */
   number [i] = 0;
   /* remainder */
}
```

The arrays *choosing* and *number* are initialized to false and 0, respectively. The ith element of each array may be read and written by process i but only read by other processes. The notation $(a, b) < (c, d)$ is defined as:

$$(a < c) \text{ or } (a = c \text{ and } b < d)$$

a. Describe the algorithm in words.
b. Show that this algorithm avoids deadlock.
c. Show that it enforces mutual exclusion.

5.8 Now consider a version of the bakery algorithm without the variable `choosing`. Then we have

```
1 int number[n];
2 while (true) {
3    number[i] = 1 + getmax(number[], n);   /* get max of all tickets assigned */
4    for (int j = 0; j < n; j++){
5      while ((number[j] != 0) && (number[j],j) < (number[i],i)) { };
6    }
7    /* critical section */
8    number [i] = 0;
9    /* remainder */
10 }
```

Does this version violate mutual exclusion? Explain why or why not.

5.9 Consider the following program which provides a software approach to mutual exclusion:

> **integer array** control [1 :N]; **integer** k
>
> where $1 \le k \le N$, and each element of "control" is either 0, 1,
> or 2. All elements of "control" are initially zero; the initial value
> of k is immaterial.

The program of the ith process ($1 \le i \le N$) is

```
begin integer j;
L0: control [i] := 1;
LI: for j:=k step 1 until N, 1 step 1 until k do
      begin
          if j = i then goto L2;
```

```
                    if control [j] ≠ 0 then goto L1
               end;
     L2: control [i] := 2;
          for j := 1 step 1 until N do
               if j ≠ i and control [j] = 2 then goto L0;
     L3: if control [k] ≠ 0 and k ≠ i then goto L0;
     L4: k := i;
          critical section;
     L5: for j := k step 1 until N, 1 step 1 until k do
          if j ≠ k and control [j] ≠ 0 then
             begin
                k := j;
                   goto L6
             end;
     L6: control [i] := 0;
     L7: remainder of cycle;
          goto L0;
     end
```

This is referred to as the Eisenberg-McGuire algorithm. Explain its operation and its key features.

5.10 Consider the first instance of the statement `bolt = 0` in Figure 5.2b.

  a. Achieve the same result using the `exchange` instruction.

  b. Which method is preferable?

5.11 When a special machine instruction is used to provide mutual exclusion in the fashion of Figure 5.2, there is no control over how long a process must wait before being granted access to its critical section. Devise an algorithm that uses the `compare&swap` instruction but that guarantees that any process waiting to enter its critical section will do so within $n - 1$ turns, where n is the number of processes that may require access to the critical section and a "turn" is an event consisting of one process leaving the critical section and another process being granted access.

5.12 Consider the following definition of semaphores:

```
     void semWait(s)
     {
         if (s.count > 0) {
           s.count--;
         }
         else {
           place this process in s.queue;
           block;
         }
     }
     void semSignal (s)
     {
         if (there is at least one process blocked on
             semaphore s) {
             remove a process P from s.queue;
             place process P on ready list;
         }
         else
             s.count++;
     }
```

Compare this set of definitions with that of Figure 5.3. Note one difference: With the preceding definition, a semaphore can never take on a negative value. Is there any difference in the effect of the two sets of definitions when used in programs? That is, could you substitute one set for the other without altering the meaning of the program?

5.13 Consider a sharable resource with the following characteristics: (1) As long as there are fewer than three processes using the resource, new processes can start using it right away. (2) Once there are three process using the resource, all three must leave before any new processes can begin using it. We realize that counters are needed to keep track of how many processes are waiting and active, and that these counters are themselves shared resources that must be protected with mutual exclusion. So we might create the following solution:

```
1   semaphore mutex = 1, block = 0;       /* share variables: semaphores, */
2   int active = 0, waiting = 0;                     /* counters, and */
3   boolean must_wait = false;                    /* state information */
4
5   semWait(mutex);                        /* Enter the mutual exclusion */
6   if(must_wait) {                     /* If there are (or were) 3, then */
7       ++waiting;                     /* we must wait, but we must leave */
8       semSignal(mutex);                 /* the mutual exclusion first */
9       semWait(block);           /* Wait for all current users to depart */
10      SemWait(mutex);                   /* Reenter the mutual exclusion */
11      --waiting;                     /* and update the waiting count */
12  }
13  ++active;                     /* Update active count, and remember */
14  must_wait - active -- 3;                  /* if the count reached 3 */
15  semSignal(mutex);                     /* Leave the mutual exclusion */
16
17  /* critical section */
18
19  semWait(mutex);                        /* Enter mutual exclusion */
20  --active;                          /* and update the active count */
21  if(active == 0) {                          /* Last one to leave? */
22      int n;
23      if (waiting < 3) n = waiting;
24      else n = 3;                          /* If so, unblock up to 3 */
25      while( n > 0 ) {                       /* waiting processes */
26          semSignal(block);
27          --n;
28      }
29  must_wait = false;               /* All active processes have left */
30  }
31  semSignal(mutex);                     /* Leave the mutual exclusion */
```

The solution appears to do everything right: All accesses to the shared variables are protected by mutual exclusion, processes do not block themselves while in the mutual exclusion, new processes are prevented from using the resource if there are (or were) three active users, and the last process to depart unblocks up to three waiting processes.

a. The program is nevertheless incorrect. Explain why.
b. Suppose we change the if in line 6 to a while. Does this solve any problem in the program? Do any difficulties remain?

5.14   Now consider this correct solution to the preceding problem:

```
1    semaphore mutex = 1, block = 0;          /* share variables: semaphores, */
2    int active = 0, waiting = 0;                    /* counters, and */
3    boolean must_wait = false;                        /* state information */
4
5    semWait(mutex);                            /* Enter the mutual exclusion */
6    if(must_wait) {                        /* If there are (or were) 3, then */
7        ++waiting;                        /* we must wait, but we must leave */
8        semSignal(mutex);                    /* the mutual exclusion first */
9        semWait(block);            /* Wait for all current users to depart */
10   } else {
11       ++active;                            /* Update active count, and */
12       must_wait = active == 3;     /* remember if the count reached 3 */
13       semSignal(mutex);                    /* Leave mutual exclusion */
14   }
15
16   /* critical section */
17
18   semWait(mutex);                              /* Enter mutual exclusion */
19   --active;                             /* and update the active count */
20   if(active == 0) {                              /* Last one to leave? */
21       int n;
22       if (waiting < 3) n = waiting;
23       else n = 3;                /* If so, see how many processes to unblock */
24       waiting -= n;             /* Deduct this number from waiting count */
25       active = n;                    /* and set active to this number */
26       while( n > 0 ) {                    /* Now unblock the processes */
27           semSignal(block);                        /* one by one */
28           --n;
29       }
30       must_wait = active == 3;             /* Remember if the count is 3 */
31   }
32   semSignal(mutex);                       /* Leave the mutual exclusion */
```

a. Explain how this program works and why it is correct.

b. This solution does not completely prevent newly arriving processes from cutting in line but it does make it less likely. Give an example of cutting in line.

c. This program is an example of a general design pattern that is a uniform way to implement solutions to many concurrency problems using semaphores. It has been referred to as the **I'll Do It For You** pattern. Describe the pattern.

5.15   Now consider another correct solution to the preceding problem:

```
1    semaphore mutex = 1, block = 0;          /* share variables: semaphores, */
2    int active = 0, waiting = 0;                    /* counters, and */
3    boolean must_wait = false;                        /* state information */
4
5    semWait(mutex);                            /* Enter the mutual exclusion */
6    if(must_wait) {                        /* If there are (or were) 3, then */
7        ++waiting;                        /* we must wait, but we must leave */
8        semSignal(mutex);                    /* the mutual exclusion first */
9        semWait(block);            /* Wait for all current users to depart */
10       --waiting;            /* We've got the mutual exclusion; update count */
11   }
12   ++active;                       /* Update active count, and remember */
13   must_wait = active == 3;                    /* if the count reached 3 */
```

```
14 if(waiting > 0 && !must_wait)               /* If there are others waiting */
15     semSignal(block);;                       /* and we don't yet have 3 active, */
16                                               /* unblock a waiting process */
17 else semSignal(mutex);                       /* otherwise open the mutual exclusion */
18
19 /* critical section */
20
21 semWait(mutex);                              /* Enter mutual exclusion */
22 --active;                                    /* and update the active count */
23 if(active == 0)                              /* If last one to leave? */
24     must_wait = false;                       /* set up to let new processes enter */
25 if(waiting == 0 && !must_wait)               /* If there are others waiting */
26     semSignal(block);;                       /* and we don't have 3 active, */
27                                               /* unblock a waiting process */
28 else semSignal(mutex);                       /* otherwise open the mutual exclusion */
```

a. Explain how this program works and why it is correct.

b. Does this solution differ from the preceding one in terms of the number of processes that can be unblocked at a time? Explain.

c. This program is an example of a general design pattern that is a uniform way to implement solutions to many concurrency problems using semaphores. It has been referred to as the **Pass The Baton** pattern. Describe the pattern.

5.16 It should be possible to implement general semaphores using binary semaphores. We can use the operations semWaitB and semSignalB and two binary semaphores, delay and mutex. Consider the following:

```
void semWait(semaphore s)
{
    semWaitB(mutex);
    s--;
    if (s < 0) {
        semSignalB(mutex);
        semWaitB(delay);
    }
    else SemsignalB(mutex);
}
void semSignal(semaphore s);
{
    semWaitB(mutex);
    s++;
    if (s <= 0)
        semSignalB(delay);
    else semSignalB(mutex);
}
```

Initially, s is set to the desired semaphore value. Each semWait operation decrements s, and each semSignal operation increments s. The binary semaphore mutex, which is initialized to 1, assures that there is mutual exclusion for the updating of s. The binary semaphore delay, which is initialized to 0, is used to block processes.

There is a flaw in the preceding program. Demonstrate the flaw and propose a change that will fix it. *Hint:* Suppose two processes each call semWait(s) when s is initially 0, and after the first has just performed semSignalB(mutex) but not performed semWaitB(delay), the second call to semWait(s) proceeds to the same point. All that you need to do is move a single line of the program.

5.17 In 1978, Dijkstra put forward the conjecture that there was no solution to the mutual exclusion problem avoiding starvation, applicable to an unknown but finite number of processes, using a finite number of weak semaphores. In 1979, J. M. Morris refuted this conjecture by publishing an algorithm using three weak semaphores. The behavior of the algorithm can be described as follows: If one or several process are waiting in a `semWait(S)` operation and another process is executing `semSignal(S)`, the value of the semaphore S is not modified and one of the waiting processes is unblocked independently of `semWait(S)`. Apart from the three semaphores, the algorithm uses two nonnegative integer variables as counters of the number of processes in certain sections of the algorithm. Thus, semaphores A and B are initialized to 1, while semaphore M and counters NA and NM are initialized to 0. The mutual exclusion semaphore B protects access to the shared variable NA. A process attempting to enter its critical section must cross two barriers represented by semaphores A and M. Counters NA and NM, respectively, contain the number of processes ready to cross barrier A and those having already crossed barrier A but not yet barrier M. In the second part of the protocol, the NM processes blocked at M will enter their critical sections one by one, using a cascade technique similar to that used in the first part. Define an algorithm that conforms to this description.

5.18 The following problem was once used on an exam:

> Jurassic Park consists of a dinosaur museum and a park for safari riding. There are m passengers and n single-passenger cars. Passengers wander around the museum for a while, then line up to take a ride in a safari car. When a car is available, it loads the one passenger it can hold and rides around the park for a random amount of time. If the n cars are all out riding passengers around, then a passenger who wants to ride waits; if a car is ready to load but there are no waiting passengers, then the car waits. Use semaphores to synchronize the m passenger processes and the n car processes.

The following skeleton code was found on a scrap of paper on the floor of the exam room. Grade it for correctness. Ignore syntax and missing variable declarations. Remember that P and V correspond to `semWait` and `semSignal`.

```
resource Jurassic_Park()
  sem car_avail := 0, car_taken := 0, car_filled := 0, passenger_released := 0
  process passenger(i := 1 to num_passengers)
    do true -> nap(int(random(1000*wander_time)))
      P(car_avail); V(car_taken); P(car_filled)
      P(passenger_released)
    od
  end passenger

  process car(j := 1 to num_cars)
    do true -> V(car_avail); P(car_taken); V(car_filled)
    nap(int(random(1000*ride_time)))
    V(passenger_released)
    od
    end car
end Jurassic_Park
```

5.19 In the commentary on Figure 5.9 and Table 5.4, it was stated that "it would not do simply to move the conditional statement inside the critical section (controlled by s) of the consumer because this could lead to deadlock." Demonstrate this with a table similar to Table 5.4.

5.20 Consider the solution to the infinite-buffer producer/consumer problem defined in Figure 5.10. Suppose we have the (common) case in which the producer and consumer are running at roughly the same speed. The scenario could be:

Producer: append; `semSignal`; produce; ... ; append; `semSignal`; produce; ...
Consumer: consume; ... ; take; `semWait`; consume; ... ; take; `semWait`; ...

The producer always manages to append a new element to the buffer and signal during the consumption of the previous element by the consumer. The producer is always appending to an empty buffer and the consumer is always taking the sole item in the buffer. Although the consumer never blocks on the semaphore, a large number of calls to the semaphore mechanism is made, creating considerable overhead.

Construct a new program that will be more efficient under these circumstances. *Hints:* Allow n to have the value -1, which is to mean that not only is the buffer empty but that the consumer has detected this fact and is going to block until the producer supplies fresh data. The solution does not require the use of the local variable m found in Figure 5.10.

5.21 Consider Figure 5.13. Would the meaning of the program change if the following were interchanged?

a. semWait(e);semWait(s)
b. semSignal(s);semSignal(n)
c. semWait(n);semWait(s)
d. semSignal(s);semSignal(e)

5.22 The following pseudocode is a correct implementation of the producer/consumer problem with a bounded buffer:

```
item[3] buffer; // initially empty
semaphore empty; // initialized to +3
semaphore full; // initialized to 0
binary_semaphore mutex; // initialized to 1
```

void producer() { ...	void consumer() { ...
while (true) {	while (true) {
item = produce();	c1: wait(full);
p1: wait(empty);	/ wait(mutex);
/ wait(mutex);	c2: item = take();
p2: append(item);	\ signal(mutex);
\ signal(mutex);	c3: signal(empty);
p3: signal(full);	consume(item);
}	}
}	}

Labels p1, p2, p3 and c1, c2, c3 refer to the lines of code shown above (p2 and c2 each cover three lines of code). Semaphores empty and full are linear semaphores that can take unbounded negative and positive values. There are multiple producer processes, referred to as Pa, Pb, Pc, etc., and multiple consumer processes, referred to as Ca, Cb, Cc, etc. Each semaphore maintains a FIFO (first-in-first-out) queue of blocked processes. In the scheduling chart below, each line represents the state of the buffer and semaphores after the scheduled execution has occurred. To simplify, we assume that scheduling is such that processes are never interrupted while executing a given portion of code p1, or p2, ..., or c3. Your task is to complete the following chart.

Scheduled Step of Execution	full's State and Queue	Buffer	empty's State and Queue
Initialization	full = 0	OOO	empty = +3
Ca executes c1	full = –1 (Ca)	OOO	empty = +3
Cb executes c1	full = –2 (Ca, Cb)	OOO	empty = +3

Scheduled Step of Execution	full's State and Queue	Buffer	empty's State and Queue
Pa executes p1	full = –2 (Ca, Cb)	OOO	empty = +2
Pa executes p2	full = –2 (Ca, Cb)	X OO	empty = +2
Pa executes p3	full = –1 (Cb) Ca	X OO	empty = +2
Ca executes c2	full = –1 (Cb)	OOO	empty = +2
Ca executes c3	full = –1 (Cb)	OOO	empty = +3
Pb executes p1	full =		empty =
Pa executes p1	full =		empty =
Pa executes __	full =		empty =
Pb executes __	full =		empty =
Pb executes __	full =		empty =
Pc executes p1	full =		empty =
Cb executes __	full =		empty =
Pc executes __	full =		empty =
Cb executes __	full =		empty =
Pa executes __	full =		empty =
Pb executes p1-p3	full =		empty =
Pc executes __	full =		empty =
Pa executes p1	full =		empty =
Pd executes p1	full =		empty =
Ca executes c1-c3	full =		empty =
Pa executes __	full =		empty =
Cc executes c1-c2	full =		empty =
Pa executes __	full =		empty =
Cc executes c3	full =		empty =
Pd executes p2-p3	full =		empty =

5.23 This problem demonstrates the use of semaphores to coordinate three types of processes.[6] Santa Claus sleeps in his shop at the North Pole and can only be wakened by either (1) all nine reindeer being back from their vacation in the South Pacific, or (2) some of the elves having difficulties making toys; to allow Santa to get some sleep, the elves can only wake him when three of them have problems. When three elves are having their problems solved, any other elves wishing to visit Santa must wait for those elves to return. If Santa wakes up to find three elves waiting at his shop's door, along with the last reindeer having come back from the tropics, Santa has decided that the elves can wait until after Christmas, because it is more important to get his sleigh ready. (It is assumed that the reindeer do not want to leave the tropics, and therefore they stay there until the last possible moment.) The last reindeer to arrive must get Santa while the others wait in a warming hut before being harnessed to the sleigh. Solve this problem using semaphores.

5.24 Show that message passing and semaphores have equivalent functionality by
   a. Implementing message passing using semaphores. *Hint:* Make use of a shared buffer area to hold mailboxes, each one consisting of an array of message slots.
   b. Implementing a semaphore using message passing. *Hint:* Introduce a separate synchronization process.

---

[6] I am grateful to John Trono of St. Michael's College in Vermont for supplying this problem.

5.25 Explain what is the problem with this implementation of the one-writer many-readers problem?

```
int readcount;                  // shared and initialized to 0
Semaphore mutex, wrt;           // shared and initialized to 1;

// Writer :                     // Readers :
                                semWait(mutex);
                                readcount := readcount + 1;
semWait(wrt);                   if readcount == 1 then semWait(wrt);
/* Writing performed*/          semSignal(mutex);
semSignal(wrt);                 /*reading performed*/
                                semWait(mutex);
                                readcount := readcount - 1;
                                if readcount == 0 then Up(wrt);
                                semSignal(mutex);
```

CHAPTER 6

CONCURRENCY: DEADLOCK AND STARVATION

6.1 Principles of Deadlock
Reusable Resources
Consumable Resources
Resource Allocation Graphs
The Conditions for Deadlock

6.2 Deadlock Prevention
Mutual Exclusion
Hold and Wait
No Preemption
Circular Wait

6.3 Deadlock Avoidance
Process Initiation Denial
Resource Allocation Denial

6.4 Deadlock Detection
Deadlock Detection Algorithm
Recovery

6.5 An Integrated Deadlock Strategy

6.6 Dining Philosophers Problem
Solution Using Semaphores
Solution Using a Monitor

6.7 UNIX Concurrency Mechanisms

6.8 Linux Kernel Concurrency Mechanisms

6.9 Solaris Thread Synchronization Primitives

6.10 Windows 7 Concurrency Mechanisms

6.11 Summary

6.12 Recommended Reading

6.13 Key Terms, Review Questions, and Problems

When two trains approach each other at a crossing, both shall come to a full stop and neither shall start up again until the other has gone.

STATUTE PASSED BY THE KANSAS STATE LEGISLATURE, EARLY IN THE 20TH CENTURY
—*A TREASURY OF RAILROAD FOLKLORE,*
B. A. BOTKIN AND ALVIN F. HARLOW

LEARNING OBJECTIVES

After studying this chapter, you should be able to:

- List and explain the conditions for deadlock.
- Define deadlock prevention and describe deadlock prevention strategies related to each of the conditions for deadlock.
- Explain the difference between deadlock prevention and deadlock avoidance.
- Understand two approaches to deadlock avoidance.
- Explain the fundamental difference in approach between deadlock detection and deadlock prevention or avoidance.
- Understand how an integrated deadlock strategy can be designed.
- Analyze the dining philosophers problem.
- Explain the concurrency and synchronization methods used in UNIX, Linux, Solaris, and Windows 7.

This chapter examines two problems that plague all efforts to support concurrent processing: deadlock and starvation. We begin with a discussion of the underlying principles of deadlock and the related problem of starvation. Then we examine the three common approaches to dealing with deadlock: prevention, detection, and avoidance. We then look at one of the classic problems used to illustrate both synchronization and deadlock issues: the dining philosophers problem.

As with Chapter 5, the discussion in this chapter is limited to a consideration of concurrency and deadlock on a single system. Measures to deal with distributed deadlock problems are assessed in Chapter 18. An animation illustrating deadlock is available online. Click on the rotating globe at WilliamStallings.com/OS/OS7e.html for access.

6.1 PRINCIPLES OF DEADLOCK

Deadlock can be defined as the *permanent* blocking of a set of processes that either compete for system resources or communicate with each other. A set of processes is deadlocked when each process in the set is blocked awaiting an event (typically the freeing up of some requested resource) that can only be triggered by another blocked process in the set. Deadlock is permanent because none of the events is ever triggered. Unlike other problems in concurrent process management, there is no efficient solution in the general case.

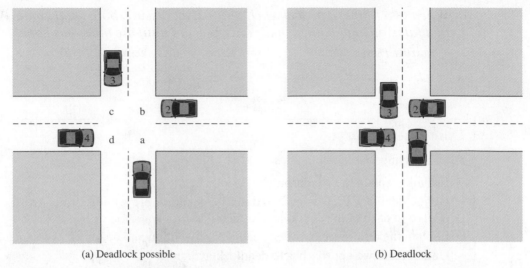

(a) Deadlock possible   (b) Deadlock

Figure 6.1   Illustration of Deadlock

All deadlocks involve conflicting needs for resources by two or more processes. A common example is the traffic deadlock. Figure 6.1a shows a situation in which four cars have arrived at a four-way stop intersection at approximately the same time. The four quadrants of the intersection are the resources over which control is needed. In particular, if all four cars wish to go straight through the intersection, the resource requirements are as follows:

- Car 1, traveling north, needs quadrants a and b.
- Car 2 needs quadrants b and c.
- Car 3 needs quadrants c and d.
- Car 4 needs quadrants d and a.

The rule of the road in the United States is that a car at a four-way stop should defer to a car immediately to its right. This rule works if there are only two or three cars at the intersection. For example, if only the northbound and westbound cars arrive at the intersection, the northbound car will wait and the westbound car proceeds. However, if all four cars arrive at about the same time and all four follow the rule, each will refrain from entering the intersection. This causes a potential deadlock. It is only a potential deadlock, because the necessary resources are available for any of the cars to proceed. If one car eventually chooses to proceed, it can do so.

However, if all four cars ignore the rules and proceed (cautiously) into the intersection at the same time, then each car seizes one resource (one quadrant) but cannot proceed because the required second resource has already been seized by another car. This is an actual deadlock.

Let us now look at a depiction of deadlock involving processes and computer resources. Figure 6.2 (based on one in [BACO03]), which we refer to as a **joint progress diagram**, illustrates the progress of two processes competing for two

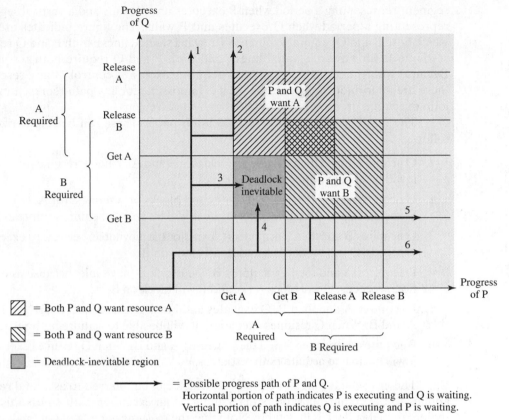

Figure 6.2 Example of Deadlock

resources. Each process needs exclusive use of both resources for a certain period of time. Two processes, P and Q, have the following general form:

Process P	**Process Q**
• • •	• • •
Get A	Get B
• • •	• • •
Get B	Get A
• • •	• • •
Release A	Release B
• • •	• • •
Release B	Release A
• • •	• • •

In Figure 6.2, the *x*-axis represents progress in the execution of P and the *y*-axis represents progress in the execution of Q. The joint progress of the two processes is therefore represented by a path that progresses from the origin in a northeasterly direction. For a uniprocessor system, only one process at a time may execute, and the path consists of alternating horizontal and vertical segments, with a horizontal segment representing a period when P executes and Q waits and a vertical segment representing a period when Q executes and P waits. The figure indicates areas in which both P and Q require resource A (upward slanted lines); both P and Q require resource B (downward slanted lines); and both P and Q require both resources. Because we assume that each process requires exclusive control of any resource, these are all forbidden regions; that is, it is impossible for any path representing the joint execution progress of P and Q to enter these regions.

The figure shows six different execution paths. These can be summarized as follows:

1. Q acquires B and then A and then releases B and A. When P resumes execution, it will be able to acquire both resources.

2. Q acquires B and then A. P executes and blocks on a request for A. Q releases B and A. When P resumes execution, it will be able to acquire both resources.

3. Q acquires B and then P acquires A. Deadlock is inevitable, because as execution proceeds, Q will block on A and P will block on B.

4. P acquires A and then Q acquires B. Deadlock is inevitable, because as execution proceeds, Q will block on A and P will block on B.

5. P acquires A and then B. Q executes and blocks on a request for B. P releases A and B. When Q resumes execution, it will be able to acquire both resources.

6. P acquires A and then B and then releases A and B. When Q resumes execution, it will be able to acquire both resources.

The gray-shaded area of Figure 6.2, which can be referred to as a **fatal region**, applies to the commentary on paths 3 and 4. If an execution path enters this fatal region, then deadlock is inevitable. Note that the existence of a fatal region depends on the logic of the two processes. However, deadlock is only inevitable if the joint progress of the two processes creates a path that enters the fatal region.

Whether or not deadlock occurs depends on both the dynamics of the execution and on the details of the application. For example, suppose that P does not need both resources at the same time so that the two processes have the following form:

Process P	**Process Q**
• • •	• • •
Get A	Get B
• • •	• • •
Release A	Get A
• • •	• • •
Get B	Release B
• • •	• • •
Release B	Release A
• • •	• • •

This situation is reflected in Figure 6.3. Some thought should convince you that regardless of the relative timing of the two processes, deadlock cannot occur.

As shown, the joint progress diagram can be used to record the execution history of two processes that share resources. In cases where more than two processes

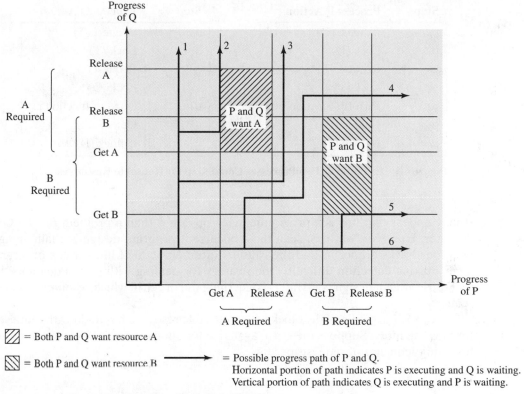

Figure 6.3   Example of No Deadlock [BACO03]

may compete for the same resource, a higher-dimensional diagram would be required. The principles concerning fatal regions and deadlock would remain the same.

Reusable Resources

Two general categories of resources can be distinguished: reusable and consumable. A reusable resource is one that can be safely used by only one process at a time and is not depleted by that use. Processes obtain resource units that they later release for reuse by other processes. Examples of reusable resources include processors; I/O channels; main and secondary memory; devices; and data structures such as files, databases, and semaphores.

As an example of deadlock involving reusable resources, consider two processes that compete for exclusive access to a disk file D and a tape drive T. The programs engage in the operations depicted in Figure 6.4. Deadlock occurs if each process holds one resource and requests the other. For example, deadlock occurs if the multiprogramming system interleaves the execution of the two processes as follows:

$$p_0 \; p_1 \; q_0 \; q_1 \; p_2 \; q_2$$

Step	Process P Action	Step	Process Q Action
p_0	Request (D)	q_0	Request (T)
p_1	Lock (D)	q_1	Lock (T)
p_2	Request (T)	q_2	Request (D)
p_3	Lock (T)	q_3	Lock (D)
p_4	Perform function	q_4	Perform function
p_5	Unlock (D)	q_5	Unlock (T)
p_6	Unlock (T)	q_6	Unlock (D)

Figure 6.4 Example of Two Processes Competing for Reusable Resources

It may appear that this is a programming error rather than a problem for the OS designer. However, we have seen that concurrent program design is challenging. Such deadlocks do occur, and the cause is often embedded in complex program logic, making detection difficult. One strategy for dealing with such a deadlock is to impose system design constraints concerning the order in which resources can be requested.

Another example of deadlock with a reusable resource has to do with requests for main memory. Suppose the space available for allocation is 200 Kbytes, and the following sequence of requests occurs:

P1	P2
...	...
Request 80 Kbytes;	Request 70 Kbytes;
...	...
Request 60 Kbytes;	Request 80 Kbytes;

Deadlock occurs if both processes progress to their second request. If the amount of memory to be requested is not known ahead of time, it is difficult to deal with this type of deadlock by means of system design constraints. The best way to deal with this particular problem is, in effect, to eliminate the possibility by using virtual memory, which is discussed in Chapter 8.

Consumable Resources

A consumable resource is one that can be created (produced) and destroyed (consumed). Typically, there is no limit on the number of consumable resources of a particular type. An unblocked producing process may create any number of such resources. When a resource is acquired by a consuming process, the resource ceases to exist. Examples of consumable resources are interrupts, signals, messages, and information in I/O buffers.

As an example of deadlock involving consumable resources, consider the following pair of processes, in which each process attempts to receive a message from the other process and then send a message to the other process:

P1	P2
...	...
Receive (P2);	Receive (P1);
...	...
Send (P2, M1);	Send (P1, M2);

Deadlock occurs if the Receive is blocking (i.e., the receiving process is blocked until the message is received). Once again, a design error is the cause of the deadlock. Such errors may be quite subtle and difficult to detect. Furthermore, it may take a rare combination of events to cause the deadlock; thus a program

Table 6.1   Summary of Deadlock Detection, Prevention, and Avoidance Approaches for Operating Systems [ISLO80]

Approach	Resource Allocation Policy	Different Schemes	Major Advantages	Major Disadvantages
Prevention	Conservative; undercommits resources	Requesting all resources at once	• Works well for processes that perform a single burst of activity • No preemption necessary	• Inefficient • Delays process initiation • Future resource requirements must be known by processes
		Preemption	• Convenient when applied to resources whose state can be saved and restored easily	• Preempts more often than necessary
		Resource ordering	• Feasible to enforce via compile-time checks • Needs no run-time computation since problem is solved in system design	• Disallows incremental resource requests
Avoidance	Midway between that of detection and prevention	Manipulate to find at least one safe path	• No preemption necessary	• Future resource requirements must be known by OS • Processes can be blocked for long periods
Detection	Very liberal; requested resources are granted where possible	Invoke periodically to test for deadlock	• Never delays process initiation • Facilitates online handling	• Inherent preemption losses

could be in use for a considerable period of time, even years, before the deadlock actually occurs.

There is no single effective strategy that can deal with all types of deadlock. Table 6.1 summarizes the key elements of the most important approaches that have been developed: prevention, avoidance, and detection. We examine each of these in turn, after first introducing resource allocation graphs and then discussing the conditions for deadlock.

Resource Allocation Graphs

A useful tool in characterizing the allocation of resources to processes is the **resource allocation graph**, introduced by Holt [HOLT72]. The resource allocation graph is a directed graph that depicts a state of the system of resources and processes, with each process and each resource represented by a node. A graph edge directed from a process to a resource indicates a resource that has been requested by the process but not yet granted (Figure 6.5a). Within a resource node, a dot is shown for each instance of that resource. Examples of resource types that may have multiple instances are I/O devices that are allocated by a resource management module in the OS. A graph edge directed from a reusable resource node dot to a process indicates a request that has been granted (Figure 6.5b); that is, the process

(a) Resource is requested   (b) Resource is held

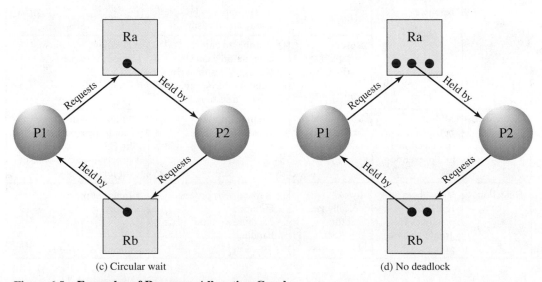

(c) Circular wait   (d) No deadlock

Figure 6.5   Examples of Resource Allocation Graphs

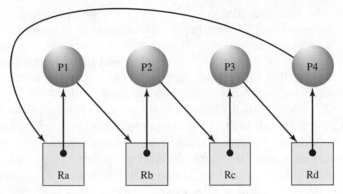

Figure 6.6   Resource Allocation Graph for Figure 6.1b

has been assigned one unit of that resource. A graph edge directed from a consumable resource node dot to a process indicates that the process is the producer of that resource.

Figure 6.5c shows an example deadlock. There is only one unit each of resources Ra and Rb. Process P1 holds Rb and requests Ra, while P2 holds Ra but requests Rb. Figure 6.5d has the same topology as Figure 6.5c, but there is no deadlock because multiple units of each resource are available.

The resource allocation graph of Figure 6.6 corresponds to the deadlock situation in Figure 6.1b. Note that in this case, we do not have a simple situation in which two processes each have one resource the other needs. Rather, in this case, there is a circular chain of processes and resources that results in deadlock.

The Conditions for Deadlock

Three conditions of policy must be present for a deadlock to be possible:

1. **Mutual exclusion.** Only one process may use a resource at a time. No process may access a resource unit that has been allocated to another process.

2. **Hold and wait.** A process may hold allocated resources while awaiting assignment of other resources.

3. **No preemption.** No resource can be forcibly removed from a process holding it.

In many ways these conditions are quite desirable. For example, mutual exclusion is needed to ensure consistency of results and the integrity of a database. Similarly, preemption should not be done arbitrarily. For example, when data resources are involved, preemption must be supported by a rollback recovery mechanism, which restores a process and its resources to a suitable previous state from which the process can eventually repeat its actions.

The first three conditions are necessary but not sufficient for a deadlock to exist. For deadlock to actually take place, a fourth condition is required:

4. **Circular wait.** A closed chain of processes exists, such that each process holds at least one resource needed by the next process in the chain (e.g., Figure 6.5c and Figure 6.6).

The fourth condition is, actually, a potential consequence of the first three. That is, given that the first three conditions exist, a sequence of events may occur that lead to an unresolvable circular wait. The unresolvable circular wait is in fact the definition of deadlock. The circular wait listed as condition 4 is unresolvable because the first three conditions hold. Thus, the four conditions, taken together, constitute necessary and sufficient conditions for deadlock.[1]

To clarify this discussion, it is useful to return to the concept of the joint progress diagram, such as the one shown in Figure 6.2. Recall that we defined a fatal region as one such that once the processes have progressed into that region, those processes will deadlock. A fatal region exists only if all of the first three conditions listed above are met. If one or more of these conditions are not met, there is no fatal region and deadlock cannot occur. Thus, these are necessary conditions for deadlock. For deadlock to occur, there must not only be a fatal region, but also a sequence of resource requests that has led into the fatal region. If a circular wait condition occurs, then in fact the fatal region has been entered. Thus, all four conditions listed above are sufficient for deadlock. To summarize,

Possibility of Deadlock	Existence of Deadlock
1. Mutual exclusion	**1.** Mutual exclusion
2. No preemption	**2.** No preemption
3. Hold and wait	**3.** Hold and wait
	4. Circular wait

Three general approaches exist for dealing with deadlock. First, one can **prevent** deadlock by adopting a policy that eliminates one of the conditions (conditions 1 through 4). Second, one can **avoid** deadlock by making the appropriate dynamic choices based on the current state of resource allocation. Third, one can attempt to **detect** the presence of deadlock (conditions 1 through 4 hold) and take action to recover. We discuss each of these approaches in turn.

6.2 DEADLOCK PREVENTION

The strategy of deadlock prevention is, simply put, to design a system in such a way that the possibility of deadlock is excluded. We can view deadlock prevention methods as falling into two classes. An indirect method of deadlock prevention is to prevent the occurrence of one of the three necessary conditions listed previously (items 1 through 3). A direct method of deadlock prevention is to prevent the occurrence of a circular wait (item 4). We now examine techniques related to each of the four conditions.

---

[1]Virtually all textbooks simply list these four conditions as the conditions needed for deadlock, but such a presentation obscures some of the subtler issues. Item 4, the circular wait condition, is fundamentally different from the other three conditions. Items 1 through 3 are policy decisions, while item 4 is a circumstance that might occur depending on the sequencing of requests and releases by the involved processes. Linking circular wait with the three necessary conditions leads to inadequate distinction between prevention and avoidance. See [SHUB90] and [SHUB03] for a discussion.

Mutual Exclusion

In general, the first of the four listed conditions cannot be disallowed. If access to a resource requires mutual exclusion, then mutual exclusion must be supported by the OS. Some resources, such as files, may allow multiple accesses for reads but only exclusive access for writes. Even in this case, deadlock can occur if more than one process requires write permission.

Hold and Wait

The hold-and-wait condition can be prevented by requiring that a process request all of its required resources at one time and blocking the process until all requests can be granted simultaneously. This approach is inefficient in two ways. First, a process may be held up for a long time waiting for all of its resource requests to be filled, when in fact it could have proceeded with only some of the resources. Second, resources allocated to a process may remain unused for a considerable period, during which time they are denied to other processes. Another problem is that a process may not know in advance all of the resources that it will require.

There is also the practical problem created by the use of modular programming or a multithreaded structure for an application. An application would need to be aware of all resources that will be requested at all levels or in all modules to make the simultaneous request.

No Preemption

This condition can be prevented in several ways. First, if a process holding certain resources is denied a further request, that process must release its original resources and, if necessary, request them again together with the additional resource. Alternatively, if a process requests a resource that is currently held by another process, the OS may preempt the second process and require it to release its resources. This latter scheme would prevent deadlock only if no two processes possessed the same priority.

This approach is practical only when applied to resources whose state can be easily saved and restored later, as is the case with a processor.

Circular Wait

The circular-wait condition can be prevented by defining a linear ordering of resource types. If a process has been allocated resources of type R, then it may subsequently request only those resources of types following R in the ordering.

To see that this strategy works, let us associate an index with each resource type. Then resource R_i precedes R_j in the ordering if $i < j$. Now suppose that two processes, A and B, are deadlocked because A has acquired R_i and requested R_j, and B has acquired R_j and requested R_i. This condition is impossible because it implies $i < j$ and $j < i$.

As with hold-and-wait prevention, circular-wait prevention may be inefficient, slowing down processes and denying resource access unnecessarily.

6.3 DEADLOCK AVOIDANCE

An approach to solving the deadlock problem that differs subtly from deadlock prevention is deadlock avoidance.[2] In **deadlock prevention**, we constrain resource requests to prevent at least one of the four conditions of deadlock. This is either done indirectly, by preventing one of the three necessary policy conditions (mutual exclusion, hold and wait, no preemption), or directly, by preventing circular wait. This leads to inefficient use of resources and inefficient execution of processes. **Deadlock avoidance**, on the other hand, allows the three necessary conditions but makes judicious choices to assure that the deadlock point is never reached. As such, avoidance allows more concurrency than prevention. With deadlock avoidance, a decision is made dynamically whether the current resource allocation request will, if granted, potentially lead to a deadlock. Deadlock avoidance thus requires knowledge of future process resource requests.

In this section, we describe two approaches to deadlock avoidance:

- Do not start a process if its demands might lead to deadlock.
- Do not grant an incremental resource request to a process if this allocation might lead to deadlock.

Process Initiation Denial

Consider a system of n processes and m different types of resources. Let us define the following vectors and matrices:

Resource = $\mathbf{R} = (R_1, R_2, \dots, R_m)$	Total amount of each resource in the system
Available = $\mathbf{V} = (V_1, V_2, \dots, V_m)$	Total amount of each resource not allocated to any process
Claim = $\mathbf{C} = \begin{pmatrix} C_{11} & C_{12} & \dots & C_{1m} \\ C_{21} & C_{22} & \dots & C_{2m} \\ \vdots & \vdots & \vdots & \vdots \\ C_{n1} & C_{n2} & \dots & C_{nm} \end{pmatrix}$	C_{ij} = requirement of process i for resource j
Allocation = $\mathbf{A} = \begin{pmatrix} A_{11} & A_{12} & \dots & A_{1m} \\ A_{21} & A_{22} & \dots & A_{2m} \\ \vdots & \vdots & \vdots & \vdots \\ A_{n1} & A_{n2} & \dots & A_{nm} \end{pmatrix}$	A_{ij} = current allocation to process i of resource j

The matrix Claim gives the maximum requirement of each process for each resource, with one row dedicated to each process. This information must be

---

[2]The term *avoidance* is a bit confusing. In fact, one could consider the strategies discussed in this section to be examples of deadlock prevention because they indeed prevent the occurrence of a deadlock.

declared in advance by a process for deadlock avoidance to work. Similarly, the matrix Allocation gives the current allocation to each process. The following relationships hold:

1. $R_j = V_j + \sum_{i=1}^{n} A_{ij},$ for all j All resources are either available or allocated.

2. $C_{ij} \leq R_j,$ for all i,j,   No process can claim more than the total amount of resources in the system.

3. $A_{ij} \leq C_{ij},$ for all i,j,   No process is allocated more resources of any type than the process originally claimed to need.

With these quantities defined, we can define a deadlock avoidance policy that refuses to start a new process if its resource requirements might lead to deadlock. Start a new process P_{n+1} only if

$$R_j \geq C_{(n+1)j} + \sum_{i=1}^{n} C_{ij} \quad \text{for all } j$$

That is, a process is only started if the maximum claim of all current processes plus those of the new process can be met. This strategy is hardly optimal, because it assumes the worst: that all processes will make their maximum claims together.

Resource Allocation Denial

The strategy of resource allocation denial, referred to as the **banker's algorithm**,[3] was first proposed in [DIJK65]. Let us begin by defining the concepts of state and safe state. Consider a system with a fixed number of processes and a fixed number of resources. At any time a process may have zero or more resources allocated to it. The **state** of the system reflects the current allocation of resources to processes. Thus, the state consists of the two vectors, Resource and Available, and the two matrices, Claim and Allocation, defined earlier. A **safe state** is one in which there is at least one sequence of resource allocations to processes that does not result in a deadlock (i.e., all of the processes can be run to completion). An **unsafe state** is, of course, a state that is not safe.

The following example illustrates these concepts. Figure 6.7a shows the state of a system consisting of four processes and three resources. The total amount of resources R1, R2, and R3 are 9, 3, and 6 units, respectively. In the current state allocations have been made to the four processes, leaving 1 unit of R2

---

[3]Dijkstra used this name because of the analogy of this problem to one in banking, with customers who wish to borrow money corresponding to processes and the money to be borrowed corresponding to resources. Stated as a banking problem, the bank has a limited reserve of money to lend and a list of customers, each with a line of credit. A customer may choose to borrow against the line of credit a portion at a time, and there is no guarantee that the customer will make any repayment until after having taken out the maximum amount of loan. The banker can refuse a loan to a customer if there is a risk that the bank will have insufficient funds to make further loans that will permit the customers to repay eventually.

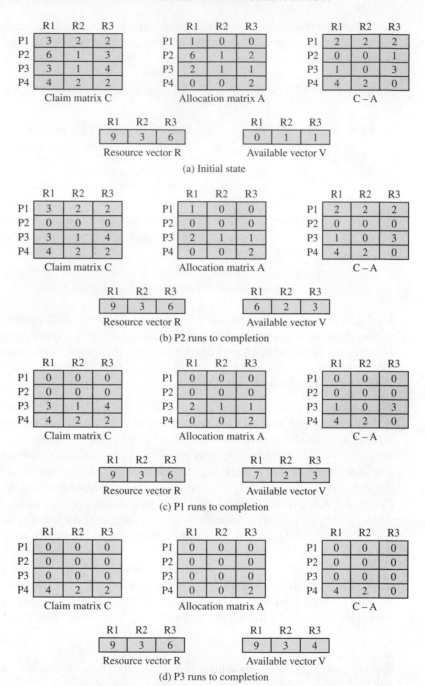

Figure 6.7 **Determination of a Safe State**

and 1 unit of R3 available. Is this a safe state? To answer this question, we ask an intermediate question: Can any of the four processes be run to completion with the resources available? That is, can the difference between the maximum requirement and current allocation for any process be met with the available resources? In terms of the matrices and vectors introduced earlier, the condition to be met for process i is:

$$C_{ij} - A_{ij} \leq V_j, \quad \text{for all } j$$

Clearly, this is not possible for P1, which has only 1 unit of R1 and requires 2 more units of R1, 2 units of R2, and 2 units of R3. However, by assigning one unit of R3 to process P2, P2 has its maximum required resources allocated and can run to completion. Let us assume that this is accomplished. When P2 completes, its resources can be returned to the pool of available resources. The resulting state is shown in Figure 6.7b. Now we can ask again if any of the remaining processes can be completed. In this case, each of the remaining processes could be completed. Suppose we choose P1, allocate the required resources, complete P1, and return all of P1's resources to the available pool. We are left in the state shown in Figure 6.7c. Next, we can complete P3, resulting in the state of Figure 6.7d. Finally, we can complete P4. At this point, all of the processes have been run to completion. Thus, the state defined by Figure 6.7a is a safe state.

These concepts suggest the following deadlock avoidance strategy, which ensures that the system of processes and resources is always in a safe state. When a process makes a request for a set of resources, assume that the request is granted, update the system state accordingly, and then determine if the result is a safe state. If so, grant the request and, if not, block the process until it is safe to grant the request.

Consider the state defined in Figure 6.8a. Suppose P2 makes a request for one additional unit of R1 and one additional unit of R3. If we assume the request is granted, then the resulting state is that of Figure 6.7a. We have already seen that this is a safe state; therefore, it is safe to grant the request. Now let us return to the state of Figure 6.8a and suppose that P1 makes the request for one additional unit each of R1 and R3; if we assume that the request is granted, we are left in the state of Figure 6.8b. Is this a safe state? The answer is no, because each process will need at least one additional unit of R1, and there are none available. Thus, on the basis of deadlock avoidance, the request by P1 should be denied and P1 should be blocked.

It is important to point out that Figure 6.8b is not a deadlocked state. It merely has the potential for deadlock. It is possible, for example, that if P1 were run from this state it would subsequently release one unit of R1 and one unit of R3 prior to needing these resources again. If that happened, the system would return to a safe state. Thus, the deadlock avoidance strategy does not predict deadlock with certainty; it merely anticipates the possibility of deadlock and assures that there is never such a possibility.

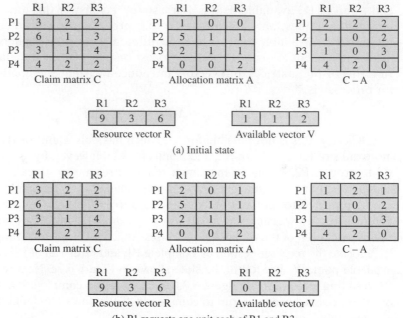

(a) Initial state

(b) P1 requests one unit each of R1 and R3

Figure 6.8   Determination of an Unsafe State

Figure 6.9 gives an abstract version of the deadlock avoidance logic. The main algorithm is shown in part (b). With the state of the system defined by the data structure state, request[*] is a vector defining the resources requested by process i. First, a check is made to assure that the request does not exceed the original claim of the process. If the request is valid, the next step is to determine if it is possible to fulfill the request (i.e., there are sufficient resources available). If it is not possible, then the process is suspended. If it is possible, the final step is to determine if it is safe to fulfill the request. To do this, the resources are tentatively assigned to process i to form newstate. Then a test for safety is made using the algorithm in Figure 6.9c.

Deadlock avoidance has the advantage that it is not necessary to preempt and rollback processes, as in deadlock detection, and is less restrictive than deadlock prevention. However, it does have a number of restrictions on its use:

- The maximum resource requirement for each process must be stated in advance.
- The processes under consideration must be independent; that is, the order in which they execute must be unconstrained by any synchronization requirements.
- There must be a fixed number of resources to allocate.
- No process may exit while holding resources.

```
struct state {
      int resource[m];
      int available[m];
      int claim[n][m];
      int alloc[n][m];
}
```

(a) Global data structures

```
if (alloc [i,*] + request [*] > claim [i,*])
    <error>;                            /* total request > claim*/
else if (request [*] > available [*])
    <suspend process>;
else {                                  /* simulate alloc */
    <define newstate by:
    alloc [i,*] = alloc [i,*] + request [*];
    available [*] = available [*] - request [*]>;
}
if (safe (newstate))
    <carry out allocation>;
else {
    <restore original state>;
    <suspend process>;
}
```

(b) Resource alloc algorithm

```
boolean safe (state S) {
    int currentavail[m];
    process rest[<number of processes>];
    currentavail = available;
    rest = {all processes};
    possible = true;
    while (possible) {
        <find a process Pk in rest such that
            claim [k,*] - alloc [k,*]<= currentavail;
        if (found) {                 /* simulate execution of Pk */
            currentavail = currentavail + alloc [k,*];
            rest = rest - {Pk};
        }
        else possible = false;
    }
    return (rest == null);
}
```

(c) Test for safety algorithm (banker's algorithm)

Figure 6.9   Deadlock Avoidance Logic

6.4 DEADLOCK DETECTION

Deadlock prevention strategies are very conservative; they solve the problem of deadlock by limiting access to resources and by imposing restrictions on processes. At the opposite extreme, deadlock detection strategies do not limit resource access or restrict process actions. With deadlock detection, requested resources are granted to processes whenever possible. Periodically, the OS performs an algorithm that allows it to detect the circular wait condition described earlier in condition (4) and illustrated in Figure 6.6.

Deadlock Detection Algorithm

A check for deadlock can be made as frequently as each resource request or, less frequently, depending on how likely it is for a deadlock to occur. Checking at each resource request has two advantages: It leads to early detection, and the algorithm is relatively simple because it is based on incremental changes to the state of the system. On the other hand, such frequent checks consume considerable processor time.

A common algorithm for deadlock detection is one described in [COFF71]. The Allocation matrix and Available vector described in the previous section are used. In addition, a request matrix $\mathbf{Q}$ is defined such that Qij represents the amount of resources of type j requested by process i. The algorithm proceeds by marking processes that are not deadlocked. Initially, all processes are unmarked. Then the following steps are performed:

1. Mark each process that has a row in the Allocation matrix of all zeros.
2. Initialize a temporary vector $\mathbf{W}$ to equal the Available vector.
3. Find an index i such that process i is currently unmarked and the ith row of $\mathbf{Q}$ is less than or equal to $\mathbf{W}$. That is, $Q_{ik} \leq W_k$, for $1 \leq k \leq m$. If no such row is found, terminate the algorithm.
4. If such a row is found, mark process i and add the corresponding row of the allocation matrix to $\mathbf{W}$. That is, set $W_k = W_k + A_{ik}$, for $1 \leq k \leq m$. Return to step 3.

A deadlock exists if and only if there are unmarked processes at the end of the algorithm. Each unmarked process is deadlocked. The strategy in this algorithm is to find a process whose resource requests can be satisfied with the available resources, and then assume that those resources are granted and that the process runs to completion and releases all of its resources. The algorithm then looks for another process to satisfy. Note that this algorithm does not guarantee to prevent deadlock; that will depend on the order in which future requests are granted. All that it does is determine if deadlock currently exists.

We can use Figure 6.10 to illustrate the deadlock detection algorithm. The algorithm proceeds as follows:

1. Mark P4, because P4 has no allocated resources.
2. Set $\mathbf{W} = (0\,0\,0\,0\,1)$.

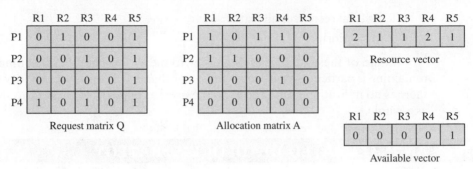

Figure 6.10   **Example for Deadlock Detection**

3. The request of process P3 is less than or equal to **W**, so mark P3 and set

$$\mathbf{W} = \mathbf{W} + (0\ 0\ 0\ 1\ 0) = (0\ 0\ 0\ 1\ 1).$$

4. No other unmarked process has a row in **Q** that is less than or equal to **W**. Therefore, terminate the algorithm.

The algorithm concludes with P1 and P2 unmarked, indicating that these processes are deadlocked.

Recovery

Once deadlock has been detected, some strategy is needed for recovery. The following are possible approaches, listed in order of increasing sophistication:

1. Abort all deadlocked processes. This is, believe it or not, one of the most common, if not the most common, solution adopted in operating systems.
2. Back up each deadlocked process to some previously defined checkpoint, and restart all processes. This requires that rollback and restart mechanisms be built in to the system. The risk in this approach is that the original deadlock may recur. However, the nondeterminancy of concurrent processing may ensure that this does not happen.
3. Successively abort deadlocked processes until deadlock no longer exists. The order in which processes are selected for abortion should be on the basis of some criterion of minimum cost. After each abortion, the detection algorithm must be reinvoked to see whether deadlock still exists.
4. Successively preempt resources until deadlock no longer exists. As in (3), a cost-based selection should be used, and reinvocation of the detection algorithm is required after each preemption. A process that has a resource preempted from it must be rolled back to a point prior to its acquisition of that resource.

For (3) and (4), the selection criteria could be one of the following. Choose the process with the

- least amount of processor time consumed so far
- least amount of output produced so far
- most estimated time remaining

- least total resources allocated so far
- lowest priority

Some of these quantities are easier to measure than others. Estimated time remaining is particularly suspect. Also, other than by means of the priority measure, there is no indication of the "cost" to the user, as opposed to the cost to the system as a whole.

6.5 AN INTEGRATED DEADLOCK STRATEGY

As Table 6.1 suggests, there are strengths and weaknesses to all of the strategies for dealing with deadlock. Rather than attempting to design an OS facility that employs only one of these strategies, it might be more efficient to use different strategies in different situations. [HOWA73] suggests one approach:

- Group resources into a number of different resource classes.
- Use the linear ordering strategy defined previously for the prevention of circular wait to prevent deadlocks between resource classes.
- Within a resource class, use the algorithm that is most appropriate for that class.

As an example of this technique, consider the following classes of resources:

- **Swappable space:** Blocks of memory on secondary storage for use in swapping processes
- **Process resources:** Assignable devices, such as tape drives, and files
- **Main memory:** Assignable to processes in pages or segments
- **Internal resources:** Such as I/O channels

The order of the preceding list represents the order in which resources are assigned. The order is a reasonable one, considering the sequence of steps that a process may follow during its lifetime. Within each class, the following strategies could be used:

- **Swappable space:** Prevention of deadlocks by requiring that all of the required resources that may be used be allocated at one time, as in the hold-and-wait prevention strategy. This strategy is reasonable if the maximum storage requirements are known, which is often the case. Deadlock avoidance is also a possibility.
- **Process resources:** Avoidance will often be effective in this category, because it is reasonable to expect processes to declare ahead of time the resources that they will require in this class. Prevention by means of resource ordering within this class is also possible.
- **Main memory:** Prevention by preemption appears to be the most appropriate strategy for main memory. When a process is preempted, it is simply swapped to secondary memory, freeing space to resolve the deadlock.
- **Internal resources:** Prevention by means of resource ordering can be used.

6.6 DINING PHILOSOPHERS PROBLEM

We now turn to the dining philosophers problem, introduced by Dijkstra [DIJK71]. Five philosophers live in a house, where a table is laid for them. The life of each philosopher consists principally of thinking and eating, and through years of thought, all of the philosophers had agreed that the only food that contributed to their thinking efforts was spaghetti. Due to a lack of manual skill, each philosopher requires two forks to eat spaghetti.

The eating arrangements are simple (Figure 6.11): a round table on which is set a large serving bowl of spaghetti, five plates, one for each philosopher, and five forks. A philosopher wishing to eat goes to his or her assigned place at the table and, using the two forks on either side of the plate, takes and eats some spaghetti. The problem: Devise a ritual (algorithm) that will allow the philosophers to eat. The algorithm must satisfy mutual exclusion (no two philosophers can use the same fork at the same time) while avoiding deadlock and starvation (in this case, the term has literal as well as algorithmic meaning!).

This problem may not seem important or relevant in itself. However, it does illustrate basic problems in deadlock and starvation. Furthermore, attempts to develop solutions reveal many of the difficulties in concurrent programming (e.g., see [GING90]). In addition, the dining philosophers problem can be seen as representative of problems dealing with the coordination of shared resources, which may

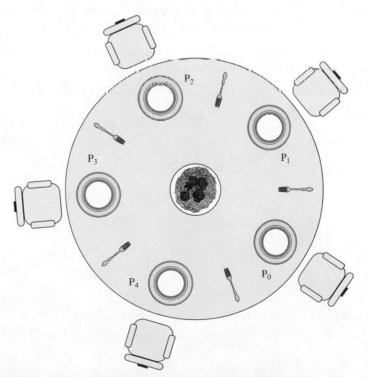

Figure 6.11   Dining Arrangement for Philosophers

occur when an application includes concurrent threads of execution. Accordingly, this problem is a standard test case for evaluating approaches to synchronization.

Solution Using Semaphores

Figure 6.12 suggests a solution using semaphores. Each philosopher picks up first the fork on the left and then the fork on the right. After the philosopher is finished eating, the two forks are replaced on the table. This solution, alas, leads to deadlock: If all of the philosophers are hungry at the same time, they all sit down, they all pick up the fork on their left, and they all reach out for the other fork, which is not there. In this undignified position, all philosophers starve.

To overcome the risk of deadlock, we could buy five additional forks (a more sanitary solution!) or teach the philosophers to eat spaghetti with just one fork. As another approach, we could consider adding an attendant who only allows four philosophers at a time into the dining room. With at most four seated philosophers, at least one philosopher will have access to two forks. Figure 6.13 shows such a solution, again using semaphores. This solution is free of deadlock and starvation.

Solution Using a Monitor

Figure 6.14 shows a solution to the dining philosophers problem using a monitor. A vector of five condition variables is defined, one condition variable per fork. These condition variables are used to enable a philosopher to wait for the availability of a fork. In addition, there is a Boolean vector that records the availability status of each fork (true means the fork is available). The monitor consists of two procedures. The get_forks procedure is used by a philosopher to seize his or her left and

```
/* program   diningphilosophers */
semaphore fork [5] = {1};
int i;
void philosopher (int i)
{
      while (true) {
            think();
            wait (fork[i]);
            wait (fork [(i+1) mod 5]);
            eat();
            signal(fork [(i+1) mod 5]);
            signal(fork[i]);
      }
}
void main()
{
      parbegin (philosopher (0), philosopher (1),
            philosopher (2),     philosopher (3),
            philosopher (4));
}
```

Figure 6.12   **A First Solution to the Dining Philosophers Problem**

```
/* program   diningphilosophers */
semaphore fork[5] = {1};
semaphore room = {4};
int i;
void philosopher (int i)
{
    while (true) {
        think();
        wait (room);
        wait (fork[i]);
        wait (fork [(i+1) mod 5]);
        eat();
        signal (fork [(i+1) mod 5]);
        signal (fork[i]);
        signal (room);
    }
}
void main()
{
    parbegin (philosopher (0), philosopher (1),
        philosopher (2), philosopher (3),
        philosopher (4));
}
```

Figure 6.13   A Second Solution to the Dining Philosophers Problem

right forks. If either fork is unavailable, the philosopher process is queued on the appropriate condition variable. This enables another philosopher process to enter the monitor. The `release-forks` procedure is used to make two forks available. Note that the structure of this solution is similar to that of the semaphore solution proposed in Figure 6.12. In both cases, a philosopher seizes first the left fork and then the right fork. Unlike the semaphore solution, this monitor solution does not suffer from deadlock, because only one process at a time may be in the monitor. For example, the first philosopher process to enter the monitor is guaranteed that it can pick up the right fork after it picks up the left fork before the next philosopher to the right has a chance to seize its left fork, which is this philosopher's right fork.

6.7 UNIX CONCURRENCY MECHANISMS

UNIX provides a variety of mechanisms for interprocessor communication and synchronization. Here, we look at the most important of these:

- Pipes
- Messages
- Shared memory
- Semaphores
- Signals

```
monitor dining_controller;
cond ForkReady[5];    /* condition variable for synchronization */
boolean fork[5] = {true};   /* availability status of each fork */

void get_forks(int pid)   /* pid is the philosopher id number */
{
   int left = pid;
   int right = (++pid) % 5;
   /*grant the left fork*/
   if (!fork(left)
      cwait(ForkReady[left]); /* queue on condition variable */
   fork(left) = false;
   /*grant the right fork*/
   if (!fork(right)
      cwait(ForkReady(right); /* queue on condition variable */
   fork(right) = false:
}
void release_forks(int pid)
{
   int left = pid;
   int right = (++pid) % 5;
   /*release the left fork*/
   if (empty(ForkReady[left])/*no one is waiting for this fork */
      fork(left) = true;
   else               /* awaken a process waiting on this fork */
      csignal(ForkReady[left]);
   /*release the right fork*/
   if (empty(ForkReady[right])/*no one is waiting for this fork */
      fork(right) = true;
   else               /* awaken a process waiting on this fork */
      csignal(ForkReady[right]);
}
```

```
void philosopher[k=0 to 4]    /* the five philosopher clients */
{
   while (true) {
     <think>;
     get_forks(k);   /* client requests two forks via monitor */
     <eat spaghetti>;
     release_forks(k);/* client releases forks via the monitor */
   }
}
```

Figure 6.14   **A Solution to the Dining Philosophers Problem Using a Monitor**

Pipes, messages, and shared memory can be used to communicate data between processes, whereas semaphores and signals are used to trigger actions by other processes.

Pipes

One of the most significant contributions of UNIX to the development of operating systems is the pipe. Inspired by the concept of coroutines [RITC84], a pipe is a circular buffer allowing two processes to communicate on the producer–consumer model. Thus, it is a first-in-first-out queue, written by one process and read by another.

When a pipe is created, it is given a fixed size in bytes. When a process attempts to write into the pipe, the write request is immediately executed if there is sufficient room; otherwise the process is blocked. Similarly, a reading process is blocked if it attempts to read more bytes than are currently in the pipe; otherwise the read request is immediately executed. The OS enforces mutual exclusion: that is, only one process can access a pipe at a time.

There are two types of pipes: named and unnamed. Only related processes can share unnamed pipes, while either related or unrelated processes can share named pipes.

Messages

A message is a block of bytes with an accompanying type. UNIX provides `msgsnd` and `msgrcv` system calls for processes to engage in message passing. Associated with each process is a message queue, which functions like a mailbox.

The message sender specifies the type of message with each message sent, and this can be used as a selection criterion by the receiver. The receiver can either retrieve messages in first-in-first-out order or by type. A process will block when trying to send a message to a full queue. A process will also block when trying to read from an empty queue. If a process attempts to read a message of a certain type and fails because no message of that type is present, the process is not blocked.

Shared Memory

The fastest form of interprocess communication provided in UNIX is shared memory. This is a common block of virtual memory shared by multiple processes. Processes read and write shared memory using the same machine instructions they use to read and write other portions of their virtual memory space. Permission is read-only or read-write for a process, determined on a per-process basis. Mutual exclusion constraints are not part of the shared-memory facility but must be provided by the processes using the shared memory.

Semaphores

The semaphore system calls in UNIX System V are a generalization of the `semWait` and `semSignal` primitives defined in Chapter 5; several operations can be performed simultaneously and the increment and decrement operations can be values greater than 1. The kernel does all of the requested operations atomically; no other process may access the semaphore until all operations have completed.

A semaphore consists of the following elements:

- Current value of the semaphore
- Process ID of the last process to operate on the semaphore
- Number of processes waiting for the semaphore value to be greater than its current value
- Number of processes waiting for the semaphore value to be zero

Associated with the semaphore are queues of processes blocked on that semaphore.

Semaphores are actually created in sets, with a semaphore set consisting of one or more semaphores. There is a `semctl` system call that allows all of the semaphore values in the set to be set at the same time. In addition, there is a `sem_op` system call that takes as an argument a list of semaphore operations, each defined on one of the semaphores in a set. When this call is made, the kernel performs the indicated operations one at a time. For each operation, the actual function is specified by the value `sem_op`. The following are the possibilities:

- If `sem_op` is positive, the kernel increments the value of the semaphore and awakens all processes waiting for the value of the semaphore to increase.
- If `sem_op` is 0, the kernel checks the semaphore value. If the semaphore value equals 0, the kernel continues with the other operations on the list. Otherwise, the kernel increments the number of processes waiting for this semaphore to be 0 and suspends the process to wait for the event that the value of the semaphore equals 0.
- If `sem_op` is negative and its absolute value is less than or equal to the semaphore value, the kernel adds `sem_op` (a negative number) to the semaphore value. If the result is 0, the kernel awakens all processes waiting for the value of the semaphore to equal 0.
- If `sem_op` is negative and its absolute value is greater than the semaphore value, the kernel suspends the process on the event that the value of the semaphore increases.

This generalization of the semaphore provides considerable flexibility in performing process synchronization and coordination.

Signals

A signal is a software mechanism that informs a process of the occurrence of asynchronous events. A signal is similar to a hardware interrupt but does not employ priorities. That is, all signals are treated equally; signals that occur at the same time are presented to a process one at a time, with no particular ordering.

Processes may send each other signals, or the kernel may send signals internally. A signal is delivered by updating a field in the process table for the process to which the signal is being sent. Because each signal is maintained as a single bit, signals of a given type cannot be queued. A signal is processed just after a process wakes up to run or whenever the process is preparing to return from a system call. A process may respond to a signal by performing some default action (e.g., termination), executing a signal-handler function, or ignoring the signal.

Table 6.2 lists signals defined for UNIX SVR4.

Table 6.2   UNIX Signals

Value	Name	Description
01	SIGHUP	Hang up; sent to process when kernel assumes that the user of that process is doing no useful work
02	SIGINT	Interrupt
03	SIGQUIT	Quit; sent by user to induce halting of process and production of core dump
04	SIGILL	Illegal instruction
05	SIGTRAP	Trace trap; triggers the execution of code for process tracing
06	SIGIOT	IOT instruction
07	SIGEMT	EMT instruction
08	SIGFPE	Floating-point exception
09	SIGKILL	Kill; terminate process
10	SIGBUS	Bus error
11	SIGSEGV	Segmentation violation; process attempts to access location outside its virtual address space
12	SIGSYS	Bad argument to system call
13	SIGPIPE	Write on a pipe that has no readers attached to it
14	SIGALRM	Alarm clock; issued when a process wishes to receive a signal after a period of time
15	SIGTERM	Software termination
16	SIGUSR1	User-defined signal 1
17	SIGUSR2	User-defined signal 2
18	SIGCHLD	Death of a child
19	SIGPWR	Power failure

6.8   LINUX KERNEL CONCURRENCY MECHANISMS

Linux includes all of the concurrency mechanisms found in other UNIX systems, such as SVR4, including pipes, messages, shared memory, and signals. In addition, Linux 2.6 includes a rich set of concurrency mechanisms specifically intended for use when a thread is executing in kernel mode. That is, these are mechanisms used within the kernel to provide concurrency in the execution of kernel code. This section examines the Linux kernel concurrency mechanisms.

Atomic Operations

Linux provides a set of operations that guarantee atomic operations on a variable. These operations can be used to avoid simple race conditions. An atomic operation executes without interruption and without interference. On a uniprocessor system, a thread performing an atomic operation cannot be interrupted once the operation has started until the operation is finished. In addition, on a multiprocessor system, the variable being operated on is locked from access by other threads until this operation is completed.

Two types of atomic operations are defined in Linux: integer operations, which operate on an integer variable, and bitmap operations, which operate on one bit in a bitmap (Table 6.3). These operations must be implemented on any architecture that implements Linux. For some architectures, there are corresponding assembly language instructions for the atomic operations. On other architectures, an operation that locks the memory bus is used to guarantee that the operation is atomic.

For **atomic integer operations**, a special data type is used, `atomic_t`. The atomic integer operations can be used only on this data type, and no other operations

Table 6.3   Linux Atomic Operations

Atomic Integer Operations	
`ATOMIC_INIT (int i)`	At declaration: initialize an atomic_t to i
`int atomic_read(atomic_t *v)`	Read integer value of v
`void atomic_set(atomic_t *v, int i)`	Set the value of v to integer i
`void atomic_add(int i, atomic_t *v)`	Add i to v
`void atomic_sub(int i, atomic_t *v)`	Subtract i from v
`void atomic_inc(atomic_t *v)`	Add 1 to v
`void atomic_dec(atomic_t *v)`	Subtract 1 from v
`int atomic_sub_and_test(int i, atomic_t *v)`	Subtract i from v; return 1 if the result is zero; return 0 otherwise
`int atomic_add_negative(int i, atomic_t *v)`	Add i to v; return 1 if the result is negative; return 0 otherwise (used for implementing semaphores)
`int atomic_dec_and_test(atomic_t *v)`	Subtract 1 from v; return 1 if the result is zero; return 0 otherwise
`int atomic_inc_and_test(atomic_t *v)`	Add 1 to v; return 1 if the result is zero; return 0 otherwise
Atomic Bitmap Operations	
`void set_bit(int nr, void *addr)`	Set bit nr in the bitmap pointed to by addr
`void clear_bit(int nr, void *addr)`	Clear bit nr in the bitmap pointed to by addr
`void change_bit(int nr, void *addr)`	Invert bit nr in the bitmap pointed to by addr
`int test_and_set_bit(int nr, void *addr)`	Set bit nr in the bitmap pointed to by addr; return the old bit value
`int test_and_clear_bit(int nr, void *addr)`	Clear bit nr in the bitmap pointed to by addr; return the old bit value
`int test_and_change_bit(int nr, void *addr)`	Invert bit nr in the bitmap pointed to by addr; return the old bit value
`int test_bit(int nr, void *addr)`	Return the value of bit nr in the bitmap pointed to by addr

are allowed on this data type. [LOVE04] lists the following advantages for these restrictions:

1. The atomic operations are never used on variables that might in some circumstances be unprotected from race conditions.
2. Variables of this data type are protected from improper use by nonatomic operations.
3. The compiler cannot erroneously optimize access to the value (e.g., by using an alias rather than the correct memory address).
4. This data type serves to hide architecture-specific differences in its implementation.

A typical use of the atomic integer data type is to implement counters.

The **atomic bitmap operations** operate on one of a sequence of bits at an arbitrary memory location indicated by a pointer variable. Thus, there is no equivalent to the `atomic_t` data type needed for atomic integer operations.

Atomic operations are the simplest of the approaches to kernel synchronization. More complex locking mechanisms can be built on top of them.

Spinlocks

The most common technique used for protecting a critical section in Linux is the spinlock. Only one thread at a time can acquire a spinlock. Any other thread attempting to acquire the same lock will keep trying (spinning) until it can acquire the lock. In essence a spinlock is built on an integer location in memory that is checked by each thread before it enters its critical section. If the value is 0, the thread sets the value to 1 and enters its critical section. If the value is nonzero, the thread continually checks the value until it is zero. The spinlock is easy to implement but has the disadvantage that locked-out threads continue to execute in a busy-waiting mode. Thus spinlocks are most effective in situations where the wait time for acquiring a lock is expected to be very short, say on the order of less than two context changes.

The basic form of use of a spinlock is the following:

```
spin_lock(&lock)
/* critical section */
spin_unlock(&lock)
```

BASIC SPINLOCKS   The basic spinlock (as opposed to the reader–writer spinlock explained subsequently) comes in four flavors (Table 6.4):

- **Plain:** If the critical section of code is not executed by interrupt handlers or if the interrupts are disabled during the execution of the critical section, then the plain spinlock can be used. It does not affect the interrupt state on the processor on which it is run.
- **_irq:** If interrupts are always enabled, then this spinlock should be used.
- **_irqsave:** If it is not known if interrupts will be enabled or disabled at the time of execution, then this version should be used. When a lock is acquired, the current state of interrupts on the local processor is saved, to be restored when the lock is released.

Table 6.4   Linux Spinlocks

`void spin_lock(spinlock_t *lock)`	Acquires the specified lock, spinning if needed until it is available
`void spin_lock_irq(spinlock_t *lock)`	Like spin_lock, but also disables interrupts on the local processor
`void spin_lock_irqsave(spinlock_t *lock, unsigned long flags)`	Like spin_lock_irq, but also saves the current interrupt state in flags
`void spin_lock_bh(spinlock_t *lock)`	Like spin_lock, but also disables the execution of all bottom halves
`void spin_unlock(spinlock_t *lock)`	Releases given lock
`void spin_unlock_irq(spinlock_t *lock)`	Releases given lock and enables local interrupts
`void spin_unlock_irqrestore(spinlock_t *lock, unsigned long flags)`	Releases given lock and restores local interrupts to given previous state
`void spin_unlock_bh(spinlock_t *lock)`	Releases given lock and enables bottom halves
`void spin_lock_init(spinlock_t *lock)`	Initializes given spinlock
`int spin_trylock(spinlock_t *lock)`	Tries to acquire specified lock; returns nonzero if lock is currently held and zero otherwise
`int spin_is_locked(spinlock_t *lock)`	Returns nonzero if lock is currently held and zero otherwise

- **_bh:** When an interrupt occurs, the minimum amount of work necessary is performed by the corresponding interrupt handler. A piece of code, called the *bottom half*, performs the remainder of the interrupt-related work, allowing the current interrupt to be enabled as soon as possible. The _bh spinlock is used to disable and then enable bottom halves to avoid conflict with the protected critical section.

The plain spinlock is used if the programmer knows that the protected data is not accessed by an interrupt handler or bottom half. Otherwise, the appropriate nonplain spinlock is used.

Spinlocks are implemented differently on a uniprocessor system versus a multiprocessor system. For a uniprocessor system, the following considerations apply. If kernel preemption is turned off, so that a thread executing in kernel mode cannot be interrupted, then the locks are deleted at compile time; they are not needed. If kernel preemption is enabled, which does permit interrupts, then the spinlocks again compile away (i.e., no test of a spinlock memory location occurs) but are simply implemented as code that enables/disables interrupts. On a multiple processor system, the spinlock is compiled into code that does in fact test the spinlock location. The use of the spinlock mechanism in a program allows it to be independent of whether it is executed on a uniprocessor or multiprocessor system.

READER–WRITER SPINLOCK   The reader–writer spinlock is a mechanism that allows a greater degree of concurrency within the kernel than the basic spinlock. The reader–writer spinlock allows multiple threads to have simultaneous access to the same data structure for reading only but gives exclusive access to the spinlock for a thread that intends to update the data structure. Each reader–writer spinlock consists of a 24-bit reader counter and an unlock flag, with the following interpretation:

Counter	Flag	Interpretation
0	1	The spinlock is released and available for use
0	0	Spinlock has been acquired for writing by one thread
$n\ (n > 0)$	0	Spinlock has been acquired for reading by n threads
$n\ (n > 0)$	1	Not valid

As with the basic spinlock, there are plain, `_irq`, and `_irqsave` versions of the reader–writer spinlock.

Note that the reader–writer spinlock favors readers over writers. If the spinlock is held for readers, then so long as there is at least one reader, the spinlock cannot be preempted by a writer. Furthermore, new readers may be added to the spinlock even while a writer is waiting.

Semaphores

At the user level, Linux provides a semaphore interface corresponding to that in UNIX SVR4. Internally, Linux provides an implementation of semaphores for its own use. That is, code that is part of the kernel can invoke kernel semaphores. These kernel semaphores cannot be accessed directly by the user program via system calls. They are implemented as functions within the kernel and are thus more efficient than user-visible semaphores.

Linux provides three types of semaphore facilities in the kernel: binary semaphores, counting semaphores, and reader–writer semaphores.

BINARY AND COUNTING SEMAPHORES The binary and counting semaphores defined in Linux 2.6 (Table 6.5) have the same functionality as described for such semaphores in Chapter 5. The function names down and up are used for the functions referred to in Chapter 5 as `semWait` and `semSignal`, respectively.

A counting semaphore is initialized using the `sema_init` function, which gives the semaphore a name and assigns an initial value to the semaphore. Binary semaphores, called MUTEXes in Linux, are initialized using the `init_MUTEX` and `init_MUTEX_LOCKED` functions, which initialize the semaphore to 1 or 0, respectively.

Linux provides three versions of the down (`semWait`) operation.

1. The down function corresponds to the traditional `semWait` operation. That is, the thread tests the semaphore and blocks if the semaphore is not available. The thread will awaken when a corresponding up operation on this semaphore occurs. Note that this function name is used for an operation on either a counting semaphore or a binary semaphore.

2. The `down_interruptible` function allows the thread to receive and respond to a kernel signal while being blocked on the down operation. If the thread is woken up by a signal, the `down_interruptible` function increments the count value of the semaphore and returns an error code known in

Linux as -EINTR. This alerts the thread that the invoked semaphore function has aborted. In effect, the thread has been forced to "give up" the semaphore. This feature is useful for device drivers and other services in which it is convenient to override a semaphore operation.

3. The down_trylock function makes it possible to try to acquire a semaphore without being blocked. If the semaphore is available, it is acquired. Otherwise, this function returns a nonzero value without blocking the thread.

READER–WRITER SEMAPHORES   The reader–writer semaphore divides users into readers and writers; it allows multiple concurrent readers (with no writers) but only a single writer (with no concurrent readers). In effect, the semaphore functions as a counting semaphore for readers but a binary semaphore (MUTEX) for writers. Table 6.5 shows the basic reader–writer semaphore operations. The reader–writer semaphore uses uninterruptible sleep, so there is only one version of each of the down operations.

Table 6.5   Linux Semaphores

Traditional Semaphores	
void sema_init(struct semaphore *sem, int count)	Initializes the dynamically created semaphore to the given count
void init_MUTEX(struct semaphore *sem)	Initializes the dynamically created semaphore with a count of 1 (initially unlocked)
void init_MUTEX_LOCKED(struct semaphore *sem)	Initializes the dynamically created semaphore with a count of 0 (initially locked)
void down(struct semaphore *sem)	Attempts to acquire the given semaphore, entering uninterruptible sleep if semaphore is unavailable
int down_interruptible(struct semaphore *sem)	Attempts to acquire the given semaphore, entering interruptible sleep if semaphore is unavailable; returns-EINTR value if a signal other than the result of an up operation is received
int down_trylock(struct semaphore *sem)	Attempts to acquire the given semaphore, and returns a nonzero value if semaphore is unavailable
void up(struct semaphore *sem)	Releases the given semaphore
Reader–Writer Semaphores	
void init_rwsem(struct rw_semaphore, *rwsem)	Initializes the dynamically created semaphore with a count of 1
void down_read(struct rw_semaphore, *rwsem)	Down operation for readers
void up_read(struct rw_semaphore, *rwsem)	Up operation for readers
void down_write(struct rw_semaphore, *rwsem)	Down operation for writers
void up_write(struct rw_semaphore, *rwsem)	Up operation for writers

Barriers

In some architectures, compilers and/or the processor hardware may reorder memory accesses in source code to optimize performance. These reorderings are done to optimize the use of the instruction pipeline in the processor. The reordering algorithms contain checks to ensure that data dependencies are not violated. For example, the code:

```
a = 1;
b = 1;
```

may be reordered so that memory location b is updated before memory location a is updated. However, the code:

```
a = 1;
b = a;
```

will not be reordered. Even so, there are occasions when it is important that reads or writes are executed in the order specified because of use of the information that is made by another thread or a hardware device.

To enforce the order in which instructions are executed, Linux provides the memory barrier facility. Table 6.6 lists the most important functions that are defined for this facility. The rmb() operation insures that no reads occur across the barrier defined by the place of the rmb() in the code. Similarly, the wmb() operation insures that no writes occur across the barrier defined by the place of the wmb() in the code. The mb() operation provides both a load and store barrier.

Two important points to note about the barrier operations:

1. The barriers relate to machine instructions, namely loads and stores. Thus the higher-level language instruction a = b involves both a load (read) from location b and a store (write) to location a.

2. The rmb, wmb, and mb operations dictate the behavior of both the compiler and the processor. In the case of the compiler, the barrier operation dictates that the compiler not reorder instructions during the compile process. In the case of the processor, the barrier operation dictates that any instructions pending in the pipeline before the barrier must be committed for execution before any instructions encountered after the barrier.

Table 6.6 Linux Memory Barrier Operations

rmb()	Prevents loads from being reordered across the barrier
wmb()	Prevents stores from being reordered across the barrier
mb()	Prevents loads and stores from being reordered across the barrier
Barrier()	Prevents the compiler from reordering loads or stores across the barrier
smp_rmb()	On SMP, provides a rmb() and on UP provides a barrier()
smp_wmb()	On SMP, provides a wmb() and on UP provides a barrier()
smp_mb()	On SMP, provides a mb() and on UP provides a barrier()

Note: SMP = symmetric multiprocessor;
UP = uniprocessor

The `barrier()` operation is a lighter-weight version of the `mb()` operation, in that it only controls the compiler's behavior. This would be useful if it is known that the processor will not perform undesirable reorderings. For example, the Intel x86 processors do not reorder writes.

The `smp_rmb`, `smp_wmb`, and `smp_mb` operations provide an optimization for code that may be compiled on either a uniprocessor (UP) or a symmetric multiprocessor (SMP). These instructions are defined as the usual memory barriers for an SMP, but for a UP, they are all treated only as compiler barriers. The `smp_` operations are useful in situations in which the data dependencies of concern will only arise in an SMP context.

6.9 SOLARIS THREAD SYNCHRONIZATION PRIMITIVES

In addition to the concurrency mechanisms of UNIX SVR4, Solaris supports four thread synchronization primitives:

- Mutual exclusion (mutex) locks
- Semaphores
- Multiple readers, single writer (readers/writer) locks
- Condition variables

Solaris implements these primitives within the kernel for kernel threads; they are also provided in the threads library for user-level threads. Figure 6.15 shows the data structures for these primitives. The initialization functions for the primitives fill in some of the data members. Once a synchronization object is created, there are essentially only two operations that can be performed: enter (acquire lock) and release (unlock). There are no mechanisms in the kernel or the threads library to enforce mutual exclusion or to prevent deadlock. If a thread attempts to access a piece of data or code that is supposed to be protected but does not use the appropriate synchronization primitive, then such access occurs. If a thread locks an object and then fails to unlock it, no kernel action is taken.

All of the synchronization primitives require the existence of a hardware instruction that allows an object to be tested and set in one atomic operation.

Mutual Exclusion Lock

A mutex is used to ensure that only one thread at a time can access the resource protected by the mutex. The thread that locks the mutex must be the one that unlocks it. A thread attempts to acquire a mutex lock by executing the `mutex_enter` primitive. If `mutex_enter` cannot set the lock (because it is already set by another thread), the blocking action depends on type-specific information stored in the mutex object. The default blocking policy is a spinlock: A blocked thread polls the status of the lock while executing in a busy waiting loop. An interrupt-based blocking mechanism is optional. In this latter case, the mutex includes a `turnstile id` that identifies a queue of threads sleeping on this lock.

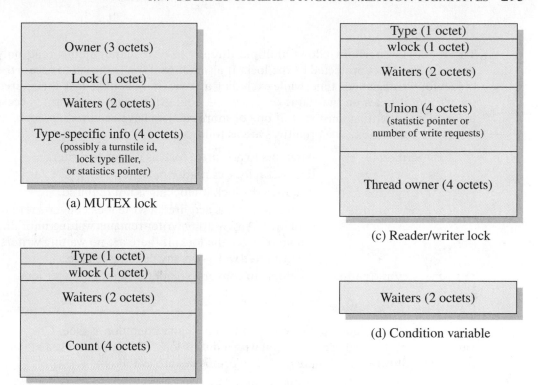

Figure 6.15   Solaris Synchronization Data Structures

The operations on a mutex lock are:

`mutex_enter()`	Acquires the lock, potentially blocking if it is already held
`mutex_exit()`	Releases the lock, potentially unblocking a waiter
`mutex_tryenter()`	Acquires the lock if it is not already held

The `mutex_tryenter()` primitive provides a nonblocking way of performing the mutual exclusion function. This enables the programmer to use a busy-wait approach for user-level threads, which avoids blocking the entire process because one thread is blocked.

Semaphores

Solaris provides classic counting semaphores, with the following primitives:

`sema_p()`	Decrements the semaphore, potentially blocking the thread
`sema_v()`	Increments the semaphore, potentially unblocking a waiting thread
`sema_tryp()`	Decrements the semaphore if blocking is not required

Again, the `sema_tryp()` primitive permits busy waiting.

Readers/Writer Lock

The readers/writer lock allows multiple threads to have simultaneous read-only access to an object protected by the lock. It also allows a single thread to access the object for writing at one time, while excluding all readers. When the lock is acquired for writing it takes on the status of `write lock`: All threads attempting access for reading or writing must wait. If one or more readers have acquired the lock, its status is `read lock`. The primitives are as follows:

`rw_enter()`	Attempts to acquire a lock as reader or writer.
`rw_exit()`	Releases a lock as reader or writer.
`rw_tryenter()`	Acquires the lock if blocking is not required.
`rw_downgrade()`	A thread that has acquired a write lock converts it to a read lock. Any waiting writer remains waiting until this thread releases the lock. If there are no waiting writers, the primitive wakes up any pending readers.
`rw_tryupgrade()`	Attempts to convert a reader lock into a writer lock.

Condition Variables

A condition variable is used to wait until a particular condition is true. Condition variables must be used in conjunction with a mutex lock. This implements a monitor of the type illustrated in Figure 6.14. The primitives are as follows:

`cv_wait()`	Blocks until the condition is signaled
`cv_signal()`	Wakes up one of the threads blocked in `cv_wait()`
`cv_broadcast()`	Wakes up all of the threads blocked in `cv_wait()`

`cv_wait()` releases the associated mutex before blocking and reacquires it before returning. Because reacquisition of the mutex may be blocked by other threads waiting for the mutex, the condition that caused the wait must be retested. Thus, typical usage is as follows:

```
mutex_enter(&m)
* *
while (some_condition) {
  cv_wait(&cv, &m);
}
* *
mutex_exit(&m);
```

This allows the condition to be a complex expression, because it is protected by the mutex.

6.10 WINDOWS 7 CONCURRENCY MECHANISMS

Windows provides synchronization among threads as part of the object architecture. The most important methods of synchronization are Executive dispatcher objects, user–mode critical sections, slim reader–writer locks, condition variables, and lock-free operations. Dispatcher objects make use of wait functions. We first describe wait functions and then look at the synchronization methods.

Wait Functions

The wait functions allow a thread to block its own execution. The wait functions do not return until the specified criteria have been met. The type of wait function determines the set of criteria used. When a wait function is called, it checks whether the wait criteria have been met. If the criteria have not been met, the calling thread enters the wait state. It uses no processor time while waiting for the criteria to be met.

The most straightforward type of wait function is one that waits on a single object. The WaitForSingleObject function requires a handle to one synchronization object. The function returns when one of the following occurs:

- The specified object is in the signaled state.
- The time-out interval elapses. The time-out interval can be set to INFINITE to specify that the wait will not time out.

Dispatcher Objects

The mechanism used by the Windows Executive to implement synchronization facilities is the family of dispatcher objects, which are listed with brief descriptions in Table 6.7.

Table 6.7 Windows Synchronization Objects

Object Type	Definition	Set to Signaled State When	Effect on Waiting Threads
Notification event	An announcement that a system event has occurred	Thread sets the event	All released
Synchronization event	An announcement that a system event has occurred.	Thread sets the event	One thread released
Mutex	A mechanism that provides mutual exclusion capabilities; equivalent to a binary semaphore	Owning thread or other thread releases the mutex	One thread released
Semaphore	A counter that regulates the number of threads that can use a resource	Semaphore count drops to zero	All released
Waitable timer	A counter that records the passage of time	Set time arrives or time interval expires	All released
File	An instance of an opened file or I/O device	I/O operation completes	All released
Process	A program invocation, including the address space and resources required to run the program	Last thread terminates	All released
Thread	An executable entity within a process	Thread terminates	All released

Note: Shaded rows correspond to objects that exist for the sole purpose of synchronization.

The first five object types in the table are specifically designed to support synchronization. The remaining object types have other uses but also may be used for synchronization.

Each dispatcher object instance can be in either a signaled or unsignaled state. A thread can be blocked on an object in an unsignaled state; the thread is released when the object enters the signaled state. The mechanism is straightforward: A thread issues a wait request to the Windows Executive, using the handle of the synchronization object. When an object enters the signaled state, the Windows Executive releases one or all of the thread objects that are waiting on that dispatcher object.

The **event object** is useful in sending a signal to a thread indicating that a particular event has occurred. For example, in overlapped input and output, the system sets a specified event object to the signaled state when the overlapped operation has been completed. The **mutex object** is used to enforce mutually exclusive access to a resource, allowing only one thread object at a time to gain access. It therefore functions as a binary semaphore. When the mutex object enters the signaled state, only one of the threads waiting on the mutex is released. Mutexes can be used to synchronize threads running in different processes. Like mutexes, **semaphore objects** may be shared by threads in multiple processes. The Windows semaphore is a counting semaphore. In essence, the **waitable timer object** signals at a certain time and/or at regular intervals.

Critical Sections

Critical sections provide a synchronization mechanism similar to that provided by mutex objects, except that critical sections can be used only by the threads of a single process. Event, mutex, and semaphore objects can also be used in a single-process application, but critical sections provide a much faster, more efficient mechanism for mutual-exclusion synchronization.

The process is responsible for allocating the memory used by a critical section. Typically, this is done by simply declaring a variable of type CRITICAL_SECTION. Before the threads of the process can use it, initialize the critical section by using the InitializeCriticalSection function.

A thread uses the EnterCriticalSection or TryEnterCriticalSection function to request ownership of a critical section. It uses the LeaveCriticalSection function to release ownership of a critical section. If the critical section is currently owned by another thread, EnterCriticalSection waits indefinitely for ownership. In contrast, when a mutex object is used for mutual exclusion, the wait functions accept a specified time-out interval. The TryEnterCriticalSection function attempts to enter a critical section without blocking the calling thread.

Critical sections use a sophisticated algorithm when trying to acquire the mutex. If the system is a multiprocessor, the code will attempt to acquire a spinlock. This works well in situations where the critical section is acquired for only a short time. Effectively the spinlock optimizes for the case where the thread that currently owns the critical section is executing on another processor. If the spinlock cannot be acquired within a reasonable number of iterations, a dispatcher object is used to block the thread so that the Kernel can dispatch another thread onto the processor.

The dispatcher object is only allocated as a last resort. Most critical sections are needed for correctness, but in practice are rarely contended. By lazily allocating the dispatcher object the system saves significant amounts of kernel virtual memory.

Slim Read–Writer Locks and Condition Variables

Windows Vista added a user mode reader–writer. Like critical sections, the reader–writer lock enters the kernel to block only after attempting to use a spinlock. It is *slim* in the sense that it normally only requires allocation of a single pointer-sized piece of memory.

To use an SRW lock, a process declares a variable of type SRWLOCK and a calls `InitializeSRWLock` to initialize it. Threads call `AcquireSRWLockExclusive` or `AcquireSRWLockShared` to acquire the lock and `ReleaseSRWLockExclusive` or `ReleaseSRWLockShared` to release it.

Windows also has condition variables. The process must declare a `CONDITION_VARIABLE` and initialize it in some thread by calling `InitializeConditionVariable`. Condition variables can be used with either critical sections or SRW locks, so there are two methods, `SleepConditionVariableCS` and `SleepConditionVariableSRW`, which sleep on the specified condition and releases the specified lock as an atomic operation.

There are two wake methods, `WakeConditionVariable` and `Wake AllConditionVariable`, which wake one or all of the sleeping threads, respectively. Condition variables are used as follows:

1. Acquire exclusive lock
2. While (predicate() == FALSE) SleepConditionVariable()
3. Perform the protected operation
4. Release the lock

Lock-free Synchronization

Windows also relies heavily on interlocked operations for synchronization. Interlocked operations use hardware facilities to guarantee that memory locations can be read, modified, and written in a single atomic operation. Examples include `InterlockedIncrement` and `InterlockedCompareExchange`; the latter allows a memory location to be updated only if it hasn't changed values since being read.

Many of the synchronization primitives use interlocked operations within their implementation, but these operations are also available to programmers for situations where they want to synchronize without taking a software lock. These so-called *lock-free* synchronization primitives have the advantage that a thread can never be switched away from a processor, say at the end of its timeslice, while still holding a lock. Thus they cannot block another thread from running.

More complex lock-free primitives can be built out of the interlocked operations, most notably Windows SLists, which provide a lock-free LIFO queue. SLists are managed using functions like `InterlockedPushEntrySList` and `InterlockedPopEntrySList`.

6.11 SUMMARY

Deadlock is the blocking of a set of processes that either compete for system resources or communicate with each other. The blockage is permanent unless the OS takes some extraordinary action, such as killing one or more processes or forcing one or more processes to backtrack. Deadlock may involve reusable resources or consumable resources. A reusable resource is one that is not depleted or destroyed by use, such as an I/O channel or a region of memory. A consumable resource is one that is destroyed when it is acquired by a process; examples include messages and information in I/O buffers.

There are three general approaches to dealing with deadlock: prevention, detection, and avoidance. Deadlock prevention guarantees that deadlock will not occur, by assuring that one of the necessary conditions for deadlock is not met. Deadlock detection is needed if the OS is always willing to grant resource requests; periodically, the OS must check for deadlock and take action to break the deadlock. Deadlock avoidance involves the analysis of each new resource request to determine if it could lead to deadlock, and granting it only if deadlock is not possible.

6.12 RECOMMENDED READING

The classic paper on deadlocks, [HOLT72], is still well worth a read, as is [COFF71]. Another good survey is [ISLO80]. [CORB96] is a thorough treatment of deadlock detection. [DIMI98] is a nice overview of deadlocks. Two papers by Levine [LEVI03a, LEVI03b] clarify some of the concepts used in discussions of deadlock. [SHUB03] is a useful overview of deadlock. [ABRA06] describes a deadlock detection package.

The concurrency mechanisms in UNIX SVR4, Linux, and Solaris 2 are well covered in [GRAY97], [LOVE10], and [MCDO07], respectively. [HALL10] is a thorough treatment of UNIX concurrency and interprocess communication mechanisms.

ABRA06 Abramson, T. "Detecting Potential Deadlocks." *Dr. Dobb's Journal*, January 2006.

COFF71 Coffman, E., Elphick, M., and Shoshani, A. "System Deadlocks." *Computing Surveys*, June 1971.

CORB96 Corbett, J. "Evaluating Deadlock Detection Methods for Concurrent Software." *IEEE Transactions on Software Engineering*, March 1996.

DIMI98 Dimitoglou, G. "Deadlocks and Methods for Their Detection, Prevention, and Recovery in Modern Operating Systems." *Operating Systems Review*, July 1998.

GRAY97 Gray, J. *Interprocess Communications in UNIX: The Nooks and Crannies.* Upper Saddle River, NJ: Prentice Hall, 1997.

HALL10 Hall, B. Beej's Guide to Unix IPC. 2010. Document available in premium content section for this book.

HOLT72 Holt, R. "Some Deadlock Properties of Computer Systems." *Computing Surveys*, September 1972.

ISLO80 Isloor, S., and Marsland, T. "The Deadlock Problem: An Overview." *Computer*, September 1980.

LEVI03a Levine, G. "Defining Deadlock." *Operating Systems Review*, January 2003.

LEVI03b Levine, G. "Defining Deadlock with Fungible Resources." *Operating Systems Review*, July 2003.

LOVE10 Love, R. *Linux Kernel Development.* Upper Saddle River, NJ: Addison-Wesley, 2010.

MCDO07 McDougall, R., and Mauro, J. *Solaris Internals: Solaris 10 and OpenSolaris Kernel Architecture.* Palo Alto, CA: Sun Microsystems Press, 2007.

SHUB03 Shub, C. "A Unified Treatment of Deadlock." *Journal of Computing in Small Colleges*, October 2003. Available through the ACM digital library.

6.13 KEY TERMS, REVIEW QUESTIONS, AND PROBLEMS

Key Terms

banker's algorithm	deadlock prevention	pipe
circular wait	hold and wait	preemption
consumable resource	joint progress diagram	resource allocation graph
deadlock	memory barrier	reusable resource
deadlock avoidance	message	spinlock
deadlock detection	mutual exclusion	starvation

Review Questions

6.1 Give examples of reusable and consumable resources.

6.2 What are the three conditions that must be present for deadlock to be possible?

6.3 What are the four conditions that create deadlock?

6.4 How can the hold-and-wait condition be prevented?

6.5 List two ways in which the no-preemption condition can be prevented.

6.6 How can the circular wait condition be prevented?

6.7 What is the difference among deadlock avoidance, detection, and prevention?

Problems

6.1 Show that the four conditions of deadlock apply to Figure 6.1a.

6.2 Show how each of the techniques of prevention, avoidance, and detection can be applied to Figure 6.1.

6.3 For Figure 6.3, provide a narrative description of each of the six depicted paths, similar to the description of the paths of Figure 6.2 provided in Section 6.1.

6.4 It was stated that deadlock cannot occur for the situation reflected in Figure 6.3. Justify that statement.

6.5 Given the following state for the Banker's Algorithm.

6 processes P0 through P5

4 resource types: A (15 instances); B (6 instances)

C (9 instances); D (10 instances)

Snapshot at time T0:

Available

A	B	C	D
6	3	5	4

Process	Current allocation				Maximum demand			
	A	B	C	D	A	B	C	D
P0	2	0	2	1	9	5	5	5
P1	0	1	1	1	2	2	3	3
P2	4	1	0	2	7	5	4	4
P3	1	0	0	1	3	3	3	2
P4	1	1	0	0	5	2	2	1
P5	1	0	1	1	4	4	4	4

a. Verify that the Available array has been calculated correctly.
b. Calculate the Need matrix.
c. Show that the current state is safe, that is, show a safe sequence of processes. In addition, to the sequence show how the Available (working array) changes as each process terminates.
d. Given the request (3,2,3,3) from Process P5. Should this request be granted? Why or why not?

6.6 In the code below, three processes are competing for six resources labeled A to F.
a. Using a resource allocation graph (Figures 6.5 and 6.6), show the possibility of a deadlock in this implementation.
b. Modify the order of some of the get requests to prevent the possibility of any deadlock. You cannot move requests across procedures, only change the order inside each procedure. Use a resource allocation graph to justify your answer.

```
void P0()                    void P1()                    void P2()
{                            {                            {
  while (true) {               while (true) {               while (true) {
    get(A);                      get(D);                      get(C);
    get(B);                      get(E);                      get(F);
    get(C);                      get(B);                      get(D);
    // critical region:          // critical region:          // critical region:
    // use A, B, C              // use D, E, B               // use C, F, D
    release(A);                  release(D);                  release(C);
    release(B);                  release(E);                  release(F);
    release(C);                  release(B);                  release(D);
  }                            }                            }
}                            }                            }
```

6.7 A spooling system (Figure 6.16) consists of an input process I, a user process P, and an output process O connected by two buffers. The processes exchange data in

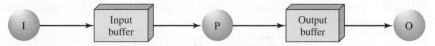

Figure 6.16   A Spooling System

blocks of equal size. These blocks are buffered on a disk using a floating boundary between the input and the output buffers, depending on the speed of the processes. The communication primitives used ensure that the following resource constraint is satisfied:

$$i + o \leq \max$$

where

max = maximum number of blocks on disk
i = number of input blocks on disk
o = number of output blocks on disk

The following is known about the processes:

1. As long as the environment supplies data, process I will eventually input it to the disk (provided disk space becomes available).
2. As long as input is available on the disk, process P will eventually consume it and output a finite amount of data on the disk for each block input (provided disk space becomes available).
3. As long as output is available on the disk, process O will eventually consume it.

Show that this system can become deadlocked.

6.8 Suggest an additional resource constraint that will prevent the deadlock in Problem 6.7 but still permit the boundary between input and output buffers to vary in accordance with the present needs of the processes.

6.9 In the THE multiprogramming system [DIJK68], a drum (precursor to the disk for secondary storage) is divided into input buffers, processing areas, and output buffers, with floating boundaries, depending on the speed of the processes involved. The current state of the drum can be characterized by the following parameters:

max = maximum number of pages on drum
i = number of input pages on drum
p = number of processing pages on drum
o = number of output pages on drum
$reso$ = minimum number of pages reserved for output
$resp$ = minimum number of pages reserved for processing

Formulate the necessary resource constraints that guarantee that the drum capacity is not exceeded and that a minimum number of pages is reserved permanently for output and processing.

6.10 In the THE multiprogramming system, a page can make the following state transitions:

1. empty $\rightarrow$ input buffer   (input production)
2. input buffer $\rightarrow$ processing area   (input consumption)
3. processing area $\rightarrow$ output buffer   (output production)
4. output buffer $\rightarrow$ empty   (output consumption)
5. empty $\rightarrow$ processing area   (procedure call)
6. processing area $\rightarrow$ empty   (procedure return)

a. Define the effect of these transitions in terms of the quantities i, o, and p.
b. Can any of them lead to a deadlock if the assumptions made in Problem 6.6 about input processes, user processes, and output processes hold?

6.11 Consider a system with a total of 150 units of memory, allocated to three processes as shown:

Process	Max	Hold
1	70	45
2	60	40
3	60	15

Apply the banker's algorithm to determine whether it would be safe to grant each of the following requests. If yes, indicate a sequence of terminations that could be guaranteed possible. If no, show the reduction of the resulting allocation table.

a. A fourth process arrives, with a maximum memory need of 60 and an initial need of 25 units.

b. A fourth process arrives, with a maximum memory need of 60 and an initial need of 35 units.

6.12 Evaluate the banker's algorithm for its usefulness in an OS.

6.13 A pipeline algorithm is implemented so that a stream of data elements of type T produced by a process P_0 passes through a sequence of processes $P_1, P_2, ..., P_{n-1}$, which operates on the elements in that order.

a. Define a generalized message buffer that contains all the partially consumed data elements and write an algorithm for process Pi $(0 \le i \le n-1)$, of the form

repeat
    receive from predecessor;
    consume element;
    send to successor:

forever

Assume P_0 receives input elements sent by P_{n-1}. The algorithm should enable the processes to operate directly on messages stored in the buffer so that copying is unnecessary.

b. Show that the processes cannot be deadlocked with respect to the common buffer.

6.14 Suppose the following two processes, foo and bar are executed concurrently and share the semaphore variables S and R (each initialized to 1) and the integer variable x (initialized to 0).

```
void foo( ) {                    void bar( ) {
    do {                             do {
        semWait(S);                      semWait(R);
        semWait(R);                      semWait(S);
        x++;                             x--;
        semSignal(S);                    semSignal(S;
        SemSignal(R);                    SemSignal(R);
    } while (1);                     } while (1);
}                                }
```

a. Can the concurrent execution of these two processes result in one or both being blocked forever? If yes, give an execution sequence in which one or both are blocked forever.

b. Can the concurrent execution of these two processes result in the indefinite postponement of one of them? If yes, give an execution sequence in which one is indefinitely postponed.

6.15 Consider a system consisting of four processes and a single resource. The current state of the claim and allocation matrices are:

$$C = \begin{pmatrix} 3 \\ 2 \\ 9 \\ 7 \end{pmatrix} \quad A = \begin{pmatrix} 1 \\ 1 \\ 3 \\ 2 \end{pmatrix}$$

What is the minimum number of units of the resource needed to be available for this state to be safe?

6.16 Consider the following ways of handling deadlock: (1) banker's algorithm, (2) detect deadlock and kill thread, releasing all resources, (3) reserve all resources in advance, (4) restart thread and release all resources if thread needs to wait, (5) resource ordering, and (6) detect deadlock and roll back thread's actions.

    a. One criterion to use in evaluating different approaches to deadlock is which approach permits the greatest concurrency. In other words, which approach allows the most threads to make progress without waiting when there is no deadlock? Give a rank order from 1 to 6 for each of the ways of handling deadlock just listed, where 1 allows the greatest degree of concurrency. Comment on your ordering.

    b. Another criterion is efficiency; in other words, which requires the least processor overhead. Rank order the approaches from 1 to 6, with 1 being the most efficient, assuming that deadlock is a very rare event. Comment on your ordering. Does your ordering change if deadlocks occur frequently?

6.17 Comment on the following solution to the dining philosophers problem. A hungry philosopher first picks up his left fork; if his right fork is also available, he picks up his right fork and starts eating; otherwise he puts down his left fork again and repeats the cycle.

6.18 Suppose that there are two types of philosophers. One type always picks up his left fork first (a "lefty"), and the other type always picks up his right fork first (a "righty"). The behavior of a lefty is defined in Figure 6.12. The behavior of a righty is as follows:

```
begin
  repeat
        think;
        wait ( fork[ (i+1) mod 5] );
        wait ( fork[i] );
        eat;
        signal ( fork[i] );
        signal ( fork[ (i+1) mod 5] );
    forever
  end;
```

Prove the following:

    a. Any seating arrangement of lefties and righties with at least one of each avoids deadlock.

    b. Any seating arrangement of lefties and righties with at least one of each prevents starvation.

6.19 Figure 6.17 shows another solution to the dining philosophers problem using monitors. Compare to Figure 6.14 and report your conclusions.

6.20 In Table 6.3, some of the Linux atomic operations do not involve two accesses to a variable, such as `atomic_read(atomic_t *v)`. A simple read operation is obviously atomic in any architecture. Therefore, why is this operation added to the repertoire of atomic operations?

6.21 Consider the following fragment of code on a Linux system.

```
read_lock(&mr_rwlock);
write_lock(&mr_rwlock);
```

Where `mr_rwlock` is a reader–writer lock. What is the effect of this code?

```
monitor dining_controller;
enum states {thinking, hungry, eating} state[5];
cond needFork[5]                              /* condition variable */

void get_forks(int pid)          /* pid is the philosopher id number */
{
    state[pid] = hungry;                     /* announce that I'm hungry */
    if (state[(pid+1) % 5] == eating || (state[(pid-1) % 5] == eating)
    cwait(needFork[pid]);        /* wait if either neighbor is eating */
    state[pid] = eating;    /* proceed if neither neighbor is eating */
}

void release_forks(int pid)
{
    state[pid] = thinking;
    /* give right (higher) neighbor a chance to eat */
    if (state[(pid+1) % 5] == hungry) && (state[(pid+2)
    % 5]) != eating)
    csignal(needFork[pid+1]);
    /* give left (lower) neighbor a chance to eat */
    else if (state[(pid-1) % 5] == hungry) && (state[(pid-2)
    % 5]) != eating)
    csignal(needFork[pid-1]);
}

void philosopher[k=0 to 4]                /* the five philosopher clients */
{
    while (true) {
      <think>;
      get_forks(k);              /* client requests two forks via monitor */
      <eat spaghetti>;
      release_forks(k);          /* client releases forks via the monitor */
    }
}
```

Figure 6.17   **Another Solution to the Dining Philosophers Problem Using a Monitor**

6.22   The two variables a and b have initial values of 1 and 2, respectively. The following
        code is for a Linux system:

Thread 1	Thread 2
a = 3;	—
mb();	—
b = 4;	c = b;
—	rmb();
—	d = a;

What possible errors are avoided by the use of the memory barriers?

PART 3 Memory

CHAPTER 7

MEMORY MANAGEMENT

7.1 Memory Management Requirements
Relocation
Protection
Sharing
Logical Organization
Physical Organization

7.2 Memory Partitioning
Fixed Partitioning
Dynamic Partitioning
Buddy System
Relocation

7.3 Paging

7.4 Segmentation

7.5 Security Issues
Buffer Overflow Attacks
Defending against Buffer Overflows

7.6 Summary

7.7 Recommended Reading

7.8 Key Terms, Review Questions, and Problems

APPENDIX 7A   Loading and Linking

I cannot guarantee that I carry all the facts in my mind. Intense mental concentration has a curious way of blotting out what has passed. Each of my cases displaces the last, and Mlle. Carère has blurred my recollection of Baskerville Hall. Tomorrow some other little problem may be submitted to my notice which will in turn dispossess the fair French lady and the infamous Upwood.

—THE HOUND OF THE BASKERVILLES,
ARTHUR CONAN DOYLE.

LEARNING OBJECTIVES

After studying this chapter, you should be able to:

- Discuss the principal requirements for memory management.
- Understand the reason for memory partitioning and explain the various techniques that are used.
- Understand and explain the concept of paging.
- Understand and explain the concept of segmentation.
- Assess the relative advantages of paging and segmentation.
- Summarize key security issues related to memory management.
- Describe the concepts of loading and linking.

In a uniprogramming system, main memory is divided into two parts: one part for the operating system (resident monitor, kernel) and one part for the program currently being executed. In a multiprogramming system, the "user" part of memory must be further subdivided to accommodate multiple processes. The task of subdivision is carried out dynamically by the operating system and is known as **memory management**.

Effective memory management is vital in a multiprogramming system. If only a few processes are in memory, then for much of the time all of the processes will be waiting for I/O and the processor will be idle. Thus memory needs to be allocated to ensure a reasonable supply of ready processes to consume available processor time.

We begin with the requirements that memory management is intended to satisfy. Next, we discuss a variety of simple schemes that have been used for memory management

Table 7.1 introduces some key terms for our discussion. A set of animations that illustrate concepts in this chapter is available online. Click on the rotating globe at WilliamStallings.com/OS/OS7e.html for access.

Table 7.1 Memory Management Terms

Frame	A fixed-length block of main memory.
Page	A fixed-length block of data that resides in secondary memory (such as disk). A page of data may temporarily be copied into a frame of main memory.
Segment	A variable-length block of data that resides in secondary memory. An entire segment may temporarily be copied into an available region of main memory (segmentation) or the segment may be divided into pages which can be individually copied into main memory (combined segmentation and paging).

7.1 MEMORY MANAGEMENT REQUIREMENTS

While surveying the various mechanisms and policies associated with memory management, it is helpful to keep in mind the requirements that memory management is intended to satisfy. These requirements include the following:

- Relocation
- Protection
- Sharing
- Logical organization
- Physical organization

Relocation

In a multiprogramming system, the available main memory is generally shared among a number of processes. Typically, it is not possible for the programmer to know in advance which other programs will be resident in main memory at the time of execution of his or her program. In addition, we would like to be able to swap active processes in and out of main memory to maximize processor utilization by providing a large pool of ready processes to execute. Once a program is swapped out to disk, it would be quite limiting to specify that when it is next swapped back in, it must be placed in the same main memory region as before. Instead, we may need to **relocate** the process to a different area of memory.

Thus, we cannot know ahead of time where a program will be placed, and we must allow for the possibility that the program may be moved about in main memory due to swapping. These facts raise some technical concerns related to addressing, as illustrated in Figure 7.1. The figure depicts a process image. For simplicity, let us assume that the process image occupies a contiguous region of main memory. Clearly, the operating system will need to know the location of process control information and of the execution stack, as well as the entry point to begin execution of the program for this process. Because the operating system is managing memory and is responsible for bringing this process into main memory, these addresses are easy to come by. In addition, however, the processor must deal with memory

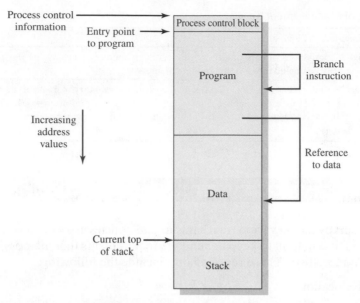

Figure 7.1   Addressing Requirements for a Process

references within the program. Branch instructions contain an address to reference the instruction to be executed next. Data reference instructions contain the address of the byte or word of data referenced. Somehow, the processor hardware and operating system software must be able to translate the memory references found in the code of the program into actual physical memory addresses, reflecting the current location of the program in main memory.

Protection

Each process should be protected against unwanted interference by other processes, whether accidental or intentional. Thus, programs in other processes should not be able to reference memory locations in a process for reading or writing purposes without permission. In one sense, satisfaction of the relocation requirement increases the difficulty of satisfying the protection requirement. Because the location of a program in main memory is unpredictable, it is impossible to check absolute addresses at compile time to assure protection. Furthermore, most programming languages allow the dynamic calculation of addresses at run time (e.g., by computing an array subscript or a pointer into a data structure). Hence all memory references generated by a process must be checked at run time to ensure that they refer only to the memory space allocated to that process. Fortunately, we shall see that mechanisms that support relocation also support the protection requirement.

Normally, a user process cannot access any portion of the operating system, neither program nor data. Again, usually a program in one process cannot branch to an instruction in another process. Without special arrangement, a program in one process cannot access the data area of another process. The processor must be able to abort such instructions at the point of execution.

Note that the memory protection requirement must be satisfied by the processor (hardware) rather than the operating system (software). This is because the OS cannot anticipate all of the memory references that a program will make. Even if such anticipation were possible, it would be prohibitively time consuming to screen each program in advance for possible memory-reference violations. Thus, it is only possible to assess the permissibility of a memory reference (data access or branch) at the time of execution of the instruction making the reference. To accomplish this, the processor hardware must have that capability.

Sharing

Any protection mechanism must have the flexibility to allow several processes to access the same portion of main memory. For example, if a number of processes are executing the same program, it is advantageous to allow each process to access the same copy of the program rather than have its own separate copy. Processes that are cooperating on some task may need to share access to the same data structure. The memory management system must therefore allow controlled access to shared areas of memory without compromising essential protection. Again, we will see that the mechanisms used to support relocation support sharing capabilities.

Logical Organization

Almost invariably, main memory in a computer system is organized as a linear, or one-dimensional, address space, consisting of a sequence of bytes or words. Secondary memory, at its physical level, is similarly organized. While this organization closely mirrors the actual machine hardware, it does not correspond to the way in which programs are typically constructed. Most programs are organized into modules, some of which are unmodifiable (read only, execute only) and some of which contain data that may be modified. If the operating system and computer hardware can effectively deal with user programs and data in the form of modules of some sort, then a number of advantages can be realized:

1. Modules can be written and compiled independently, with all references from one module to another resolved by the system at run time.

2. With modest additional overhead, different degrees of protection (read only, execute only) can be given to different modules.

3. It is possible to introduce mechanisms by which modules can be shared among processes. The advantage of providing sharing on a module level is that this corresponds to the user's way of viewing the problem, and hence it is easy for the user to specify the sharing that is desired.

The tool that most readily satisfies these requirements is segmentation, which is one of the memory management techniques explored in this chapter.

Physical Organization

As we discussed in Section 1.5, computer memory is organized into at least two levels, referred to as main memory and secondary memory. Main memory provides fast access at relatively high cost. In addition, main memory is volatile; that is, it does not provide permanent storage. Secondary memory is slower and cheaper than main memory and is usually not volatile. Thus secondary memory of large capacity can be provided for long-term storage of programs and data, while a smaller main memory holds programs and data currently in use.

In this two-level scheme, the organization of the flow of information between main and secondary memory is a major system concern. The responsibility for this flow could be assigned to the individual programmer, but this is impractical and undesirable for two reasons:

1. The main memory available for a program plus its data may be insufficient. In that case, the programmer must engage in a practice known as **overlaying**, in which the program and data are organized in such a way that various modules can be assigned the same region of memory, with a main program responsible for switching the modules in and out as needed. Even with the aid of compiler tools, overlay programming wastes programmer time.

2. In a multiprogramming environment, the programmer does not know at the time of coding how much space will be available or where that space will be.

It is clear, then, that the task of moving information between the two levels of memory should be a system responsibility. This task is the essence of memory management.

7.2   MEMORY PARTITIONING

The principal operation of memory management is to bring processes into main memory for execution by the processor. In almost all modern multiprogramming systems, this involves a sophisticated scheme known as virtual memory. Virtual memory is, in turn, based on the use of one or both of two basic techniques: segmentation and paging. Before we can look at these virtual memory techniques, we must prepare the ground by looking at simpler techniques that do not involve virtual memory (Table 7.2 summarizes all the techniques examined in this chapter and the next). One of these techniques, partitioning, has been used in several variations in some now-obsolete operating systems. The other two techniques, simple paging and simple segmentation, are not used by themselves. However, it will clarify the discussion of virtual memory if we look first at these two techniques in the absence of virtual memory considerations.

Fixed Partitioning

In most schemes for memory management, we can assume that the OS occupies some fixed portion of main memory and that the rest of main memory is available for use by multiple processes. The simplest scheme for managing this available memory is to partition it into regions with fixed boundaries.

PARTITION SIZES   Figure 7.2 shows examples of two alternatives for fixed partitioning. One possibility is to make use of equal-size partitions. In this case, any process whose size is less than or equal to the partition size can be loaded into

Table 7.2 Memory Management Techniques

Technique	Description	Strengths	Weaknesses
Fixed Partitioning	Main memory is divided into a number of static partitions at system generation time. A process may be loaded into a partition of equal or greater size.	Simple to implement; little operating system overhead.	Inefficient use of memory due to internal fragmentation; maximum number of active processes is fixed.
Dynamic Partitioning	Partitions are created dynamically, so that each process is loaded into a partition of exactly the same size as that process.	No internal fragmentation; more efficient use of main memory.	Inefficient use of processor due to the need for compaction to counter external fragmentation.
Simple Paging	Main memory is divided into a number of equal-size frames. Each process is divided into a number of equal-size pages of the same length as frames. A process is loaded by loading all of its pages into available, not necessarily contiguous, frames.	No external fragmentation.	A small amount of internal fragmentation.
Simple Segmentation	Each process is divided into a number of segments. A process is loaded by loading all of its segments into dynamic partitions that need not be contiguous.	No internal fragmentation; improved memory utilization and reduced overhead compared to dynamic partitioning.	External fragmentation.
Virtual Memory Paging	As with simple paging, except that it is not necessary to load all of the pages of a process. Nonresident pages that are needed are brought in later automatically.	No external fragmentation; higher degree of multiprogramming; large virtual address space.	Overhead of complex memory management.
Virtual Memory Segmentation	As with simple segmentation, except that it is not necessary to load all of the segments of a process. Nonresident segments that are needed are brought in later automatically.	No internal fragmentation, higher degree of multiprogramming; large virtual address space; protection and sharing support.	Overhead of complex memory management.

any available partition. If all partitions are full and no process is in the Ready or Running state, the operating system can swap a process out of any of the partitions and load in another process, so that there is some work for the processor.

There are two difficulties with the use of equal-size fixed partitions:

- A program may be too big to fit into a partition. In this case, the programmer must design the program with the use of overlays so that only a portion of the program need be in main memory at any one time. When a module is needed

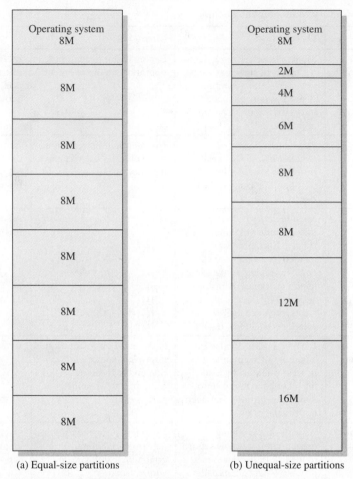

(a) Equal-size partitions   (b) Unequal-size partitions

Figure 7.2   Example of Fixed Partitioning of a 64-Mbyte Memory

that is not present, the user's program must load that module into the program's partition, overlaying whatever programs or data are there.

- Main memory utilization is extremely inefficient. Any program, no matter how small, occupies an entire partition. In our example, there may be a program whose length is less than 2 Mbytes; yet it occupies an 8-Mbyte partition whenever it is swapped in. This phenomenon, in which there is wasted space internal to a partition due to the fact that the block of data loaded is smaller than the partition, is referred to as **internal fragmentation**.

Both of these problems can be lessened, though not solved, by using unequal-size partitions (Figure 7.2b). In this example, programs as large as 16 Mbytes can be accommodated without overlays. Partitions smaller than 8 Mbytes allow smaller programs to be accommodated with less internal fragmentation.

PLACEMENT ALGORITHM   With equal-size partitions, the placement of processes in memory is trivial. As long as there is any available partition, a process can be loaded into that partition. Because all partitions are of equal size, it does not matter which partition is used. If all partitions are occupied with processes that are not ready to run, then one of these processes must be swapped out to make room for a new process. Which one to swap out is a scheduling decision; this topic is explored in Part Four.

With unequal-size partitions, there are two possible ways to assign processes to partitions. The simplest way is to assign each process to the smallest partition within which it will fit.[1] In this case, a scheduling queue is needed for each partition, to hold swapped-out processes destined for that partition (Figure 7.3a). The advantage of this approach is that processes are always assigned in such a way as to minimize wasted memory within a partition (internal fragmentation).

Although this technique seems optimum from the point of view of an individual partition, it is not optimum from the point of view of the system as a whole. In Figure 7.2b, for example, consider a case in which there are no processes with a size between 12 and 16M at a certain point in time. In that case, the 16M partition will remain unused, even though some smaller process could have been assigned to it. Thus, a preferable approach would be to employ a single queue for all processes (Figure 7.3b). When it is time to load a process into main memory, the smallest available partition that will hold the process is selected. If all partitions are occupied, then a swapping decision must be made. Preference might be given to swapping out of the smallest partition that will hold the incoming process. It is also possible to

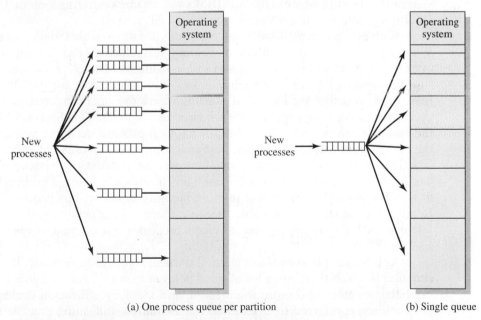

(a) One process queue per partition   (b) Single queue

Figure 7.3   Memory Assignment for Fixed Partitioning

---

[1]This assumes that one knows the maximum amount of memory that a process will require. This is not always the case. If it is not known how large a process may become, the only alternatives are an overlay scheme or the use of virtual memory.

consider other factors, such as priority, and a preference for swapping out blocked processes versus ready processes.

The use of unequal-size partitions provides a degree of flexibility to fixed partitioning. In addition, it can be said that fixed-partitioning schemes are relatively simple and require minimal OS software and processing overhead. However, there are disadvantages:

- The number of partitions specified at system generation time limits the number of active (not suspended) processes in the system.

- Because partition sizes are preset at system generation time, small jobs will not utilize partition space efficiently. In an environment where the main storage requirement of all jobs is known beforehand, this may be reasonable, but in most cases, it is an inefficient technique.

The use of fixed partitioning is almost unknown today. One example of a successful operating system that did use this technique was an early IBM mainframe operating system, OS/MFT (Multiprogramming with a Fixed Number of Tasks).

Dynamic Partitioning

To overcome some of the difficulties with fixed partitioning, an approach known as dynamic partitioning was developed. Again, this approach has been supplanted by more sophisticated memory management techniques. An important operating system that used this technique was IBM's mainframe operating system, OS/MVT (Multiprogramming with a Variable Number of Tasks).

With dynamic partitioning, the partitions are of variable length and number. When a process is brought into main memory, it is allocated exactly as much memory as it requires and no more. An example, using 64 Mbytes of main memory, is shown in Figure 7.4. Initially, main memory is empty, except for the OS (a). The first three processes are loaded in, starting where the operating system ends and occupying just enough space for each process (b, c, d). This leaves a "hole" at the end of memory that is too small for a fourth process. At some point, none of the processes in memory is ready. The operating system swaps out process 2 (e), which leaves sufficient room to load a new process, process 4 (f). Because process 4 is smaller than process 2, another small hole is created. Later, a point is reached at which none of the processes in main memory is ready, but process 2, in the Ready-Suspend state, is available. Because there is insufficient room in memory for process 2, the operating system swaps process 1 out (g) and swaps process 2 back in (h).

As this example shows, this method starts out well, but eventually it leads to a situation in which there are a lot of small holes in memory. As time goes on, memory becomes more and more fragmented, and memory utilization declines. This phenomenon is referred to as **external fragmentation**, indicating that the memory that is external to all partitions becomes increasingly fragmented. This is in contrast to internal fragmentation, referred to earlier.

One technique for overcoming external fragmentation is **compaction**: From time to time, the OS shifts the processes so that they are contiguous and so that all of the free memory is together in one block. For example, in Figure 7.4h, compaction

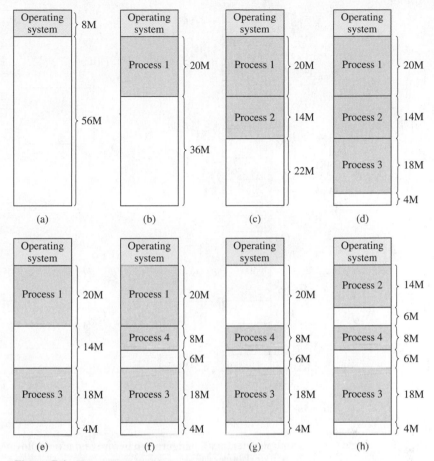

Figure 7.4   The Effect of Dynamic Partitioning

will result in a block of free memory of length 16M. This may well be sufficient to load in an additional process. The difficulty with compaction is that it is a time-consuming procedure and wasteful of processor time. Note that compaction implies the need for a dynamic relocation capability. That is, it must be possible to move a program from one region to another in main memory without invalidating the memory references in the program (see Appendix 7A).

PLACEMENT ALGORITHM   Because memory compaction is time consuming, the OS designer must be clever in deciding how to assign processes to memory (how to plug the holes). When it is time to load or swap a process into main memory, and if there is more than one free block of memory of sufficient size, then the operating system must decide which free block to allocate.

Three placement algorithms that might be considered are best-fit, first-fit, and next-fit. All, of course, are limited to choosing among free blocks of main memory that are equal to or larger than the process to be brought in. **Best-fit** chooses the block that is closest in size to the request. **First-fit** begins to scan memory from the

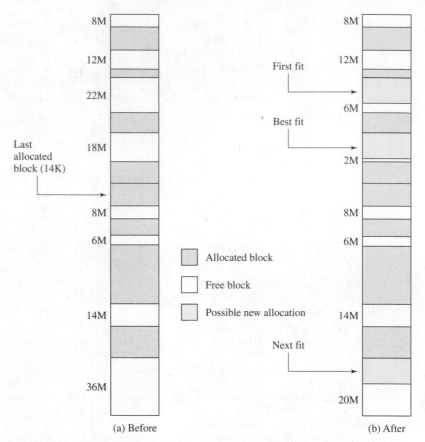

Figure 7.5   Example Memory Configuration before and after Allocation of 16-Mbyte Block

beginning and chooses the first available block that is large enough. **Next-fit** begins to scan memory from the location of the last placement, and chooses the next available block that is large enough.

Figure 7.5a shows an example memory configuration after a number of placement and swapping-out operations. The last block that was used was a 22-Mbyte block from which a 14-Mbyte partition was created. Figure 7.5b shows the difference between the best-, first-, and next-fit placement algorithms in satisfying a 16-Mbyte allocation request. Best-fit will search the entire list of available blocks and make use of the 18-Mbyte block, leaving a 2-Mbyte fragment. First-fit results in a 6-Mbyte fragment, and next-fit results in a 20-Mbyte fragment.

Which of these approaches is best will depend on the exact sequence of process swappings that occurs and the size of those processes. However, some general comments can be made (see also [BREN89], [SHOR75], and [BAYS77]). The first-fit algorithm is not only the simplest but usually the best and fastest as well. The next-fit algorithm tends to produce slightly worse results than the first-fit. The next-fit algorithm will more frequently lead to an allocation from a free block at the end of memory. The result is that the largest block of free memory, which usually appears at the end of the memory space, is quickly broken up into small fragments. Thus, compaction may be required more frequently with next-fit. On the other hand, the first-fit algorithm may litter the front end with small free partitions that need to be searched over on each subsequent first-fit pass. The best-fit algorithm, despite its name, is usually the worst performer. Because this algorithm looks for the smallest block that will satisfy the requirement, it guarantees that the fragment left behind is as small as possible. Although each memory request always wastes the smallest amount of memory, the result is that main memory is quickly littered by blocks too small to satisfy memory allocation requests. Thus, memory compaction must be done more frequently than with the other algorithms.

REPLACEMENT ALGORITHM In a multiprogramming system using dynamic partitioning, there will come a time when all of the processes in main memory are in a blocked state and there is insufficient memory, even after compaction, for an additional process. To avoid wasting processor time waiting for an active process to become unblocked, the OS will swap one of the processes out of main memory to make room for a new process or for a process in a Ready-Suspend state. Therefore, the operating system must choose which process to replace. Because the topic of replacement algorithms will be covered in some detail with respect to various virtual memory schemes, we defer a discussion of replacement algorithms until then.

Buddy System

Both fixed and dynamic partitioning schemes have drawbacks. A fixed partitioning scheme limits the number of active processes and may use space inefficiently if there is a poor match between available partition sizes and process sizes. A dynamic partitioning scheme is more complex to maintain and includes the overhead of compaction. An interesting compromise is the buddy system ([KNUT97], [PETE77]).

In a buddy system, memory blocks are available of size 2^K words, $L \leq K \leq U$, where

2^L = smallest size block that is allocated

2^U = largest size block that is allocated; generally 2^U is the size of the entire memory available for allocation

To begin, the entire space available for allocation is treated as a single block of size 2^U. If a request of size s such that $2^{U-1} < s \leq 2^U$ is made, then the entire block is allocated. Otherwise, the block is split into two equal buddies of size 2^{U-1}. If $2^{U-2} < s \leq 2^{U-1}$, then the request is allocated to one of the two buddies. Otherwise, one of the buddies is split in half again. This process continues until the smallest block greater than or equal to s is generated and allocated to the request. At any time, the buddy system maintains a list of holes (unallocated blocks) of each size 2^i. A hole may be removed from the $(i + 1)$ list by splitting it in half to create two buddies of size 2^i in the i list. Whenever a pair of buddies on the i list both become unallocated, they are removed from that list and coalesced into a single block on the $(i + 1)$

list. Presented with a request for an allocation of size k such that $2^{i-1} < k \le 2^i$, the following recursive algorithm is used to find a hole of size 2^i:

```
void get_hole(int i)
{
  if (i == (U + 1)) <failure>;
  if (<i_list empty>) {
    get_hole(i + 1);
    <split hole into buddies>;
    <put buddies on i_list>;
  }
  <take first hole on i_list>;
}
```

Figure 7.6 gives an example using a 1-Mbyte initial block. The first request, A, is for 100 Kbytes, for which a 128K block is needed. The initial block is divided into two 512K buddies. The first of these is divided into two 256K buddies, and the first of these is divided into two 128K buddies, one of which is allocated to A. The next request, B, requires a 256K block. Such a block is already available and is allocated. The process continues with splitting and coalescing occurring as needed. Note that when E is released, two 128K buddies are coalesced into a 256K block, which is immediately coalesced with its buddy.

Figure 7.7 shows a binary tree representation of the buddy allocation immediately after the Release B request. The leaf nodes represent the current partitioning of the memory. If two buddies are leaf nodes, then at least one must be allocated; otherwise they would be coalesced into a larger block.

1-Mbyte block	1M			
Request 100K	A = 128K | 128K	256K	512K	
Request 240K	A = 128K | 128K	B = 256K	512K	
Request 64K	A = 128K | C = 64K | 64K	B = 256K	512K	
Request 256K	A = 128K | C = 64K | 64K	B = 256K	D = 256K	256K
Release B	A = 128K | C = 64K | 64K	256K	D = 256K	256K
Release A	128K | C = 64K | 64K	256K	D = 256K	256K
Request 75K	E = 128K | C = 64K | 64K	256K	D = 256K	256K
Release C	E = 128K | 128K	256K	D = 256K	256K
Release E	512K		D = 256K	256K
Release D	1M			

Figure 7.6   Example of Buddy System

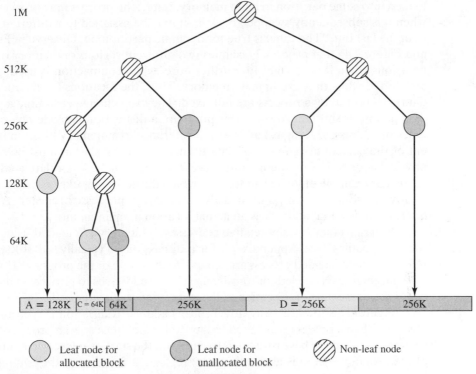

Figure 7.7   Tree Representation of Buddy System

The buddy system is a reasonable compromise to overcome the disadvantages of both the fixed and variable partitioning schemes, but in contemporary operating systems, virtual memory based on paging and segmentation is superior. However, the buddy system has found application in parallel systems as an efficient means of allocation and release for parallel programs (e.g., see [JOHN92]). A modified form of the buddy system is used for UNIX kernel memory allocation (described in Chapter 8).

Relocation

Before we consider ways of dealing with the shortcomings of partitioning, we must clear up one loose end, which relates to the placement of processes in memory. When the fixed partition scheme of Figure 7.3a is used, we can expect that a process will always be assigned to the same partition. That is, whichever partition is selected when a new process is loaded will always be used to swap that process back into memory after it has been swapped out. In that case, a simple relocating loader, such as is described in Appendix 7A, can be used: When the process is first loaded, all relative memory references in the code are replaced by absolute main memory addresses, determined by the base address of the loaded process.

In the case of equal-size partitions (Figure 7.2), and in the case of a single process queue for unequal-size partitions (Figure 7.3b), a process may occupy different partitions during the course of its life. When a process image is first created, it is loaded into some partition in main memory. Later, the process may be swapped out; when it is subsequently swapped back in, it may be assigned to a different partition than the last time. The same is true for dynamic partitioning. Observe in Figure 7.4c and Figure 7.4h that process 2 occupies two different regions of memory on the two occasions when it is brought in. Furthermore, when compaction is used, processes are shifted while they are in main memory. Thus, the locations (of instructions and data) referenced by a process are not fixed. They will change each time a process is swapped in or shifted. To solve this problem, a distinction is made among several types of addresses. A **logical address** is a reference to a memory location independent of the current assignment of data to memory; a translation must be made to a physical address before the memory access can be achieved. A **relative address** is a particular example of logical address, in which the address is expressed as a location relative to some known point, usually a value in a processor register. A **physical address**, or absolute address, is an actual location in main memory.

Programs that employ relative addresses in memory are loaded using dynamic run-time loading (see Appendix 7A for a discussion). Typically, all of the memory references in the loaded process are relative to the origin of the program. Thus a hardware mechanism is needed for translating relative addresses to physical main memory addresses at the time of execution of the instruction that contains the reference.

Figure 7.8 shows the way in which this address translation is typically accomplished. When a process is assigned to the Running state, a special processor register, sometimes called the base register, is loaded with the starting address in main memory of the program. There is also a "bounds" register that indicates the ending location

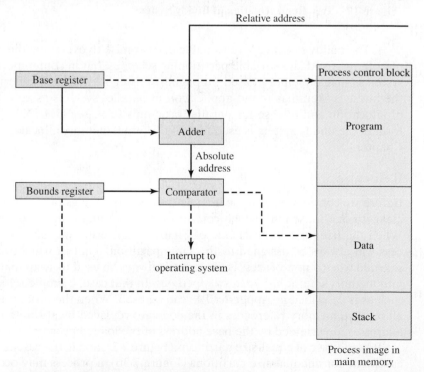

Figure 7.8   Hardware Support for Relocation

of the program; these values must be set when the program is loaded into memory or when the process image is swapped in. During the course of execution of the process, relative addresses are encountered. These include the contents of the instruction register, instruction addresses that occur in branch and call instructions, and data addresses that occur in load and store instructions. Each such relative address goes through two steps of manipulation by the processor. First, the value in the base register is added to the relative address to produce an absolute address. Second, the resulting address is compared to the value in the bounds register. If the address is within bounds, then the instruction execution may proceed. Otherwise, an interrupt is generated to the operating system, which must respond to the error in some fashion.

The scheme of Figure 7.8 allows programs to be swapped in and out of memory during the course of execution. It also provides a measure of protection: Each process image is isolated by the contents of the base and bounds registers and safe from unwanted accesses by other processes.

7.3 PAGING

Both unequal fixed-size and variable-size partitions are inefficient in the use of memory; the former results in internal fragmentation, the latter in external fragmentation. Suppose, however, that main memory is partitioned into equal fixed-size chunks that are relatively small, and that each process is also divided into small fixed-size chunks of the same size. Then the chunks of a process, known as **pages,** could be assigned to available chunks of memory, known as **frames,** or page frames. We show in this section that the wasted space in memory for each process is due to internal fragmentation consisting of only a fraction of the last page of a process. There is no external fragmentation.

Figure 7.9 illustrates the use of pages and frames. At a given point in time, some of the frames in memory are in use and some are free. A list of free frames is maintained by the OS. Process A, stored on disk, consists of four pages. When it is time to load this process, the OS finds four free frames and loads the four pages of process A into the four frames (Figure 7.9b). Process B, consisting of three pages, and process C, consisting of four pages, are subsequently loaded. Then process B is suspended and is swapped out of main memory. Later, all of the processes in main memory are blocked, and the OS needs to bring in a new process, process D, which consists of five pages.

Now suppose, as in this example, that there are not sufficient unused contiguous frames to hold the process. Does this prevent the operating system from loading D? The answer is no, because we can once again use the concept of logical address. A simple base address register will no longer suffice. Rather, the operating system maintains a **page table** for each process. The page table shows the frame location for each page of the process. Within the program, each logical address consists of a page number and an offset within the page. Recall that in the case of simple partition, a logical address is the location of a word relative to the beginning of the program; the processor translates that into a physical address. With paging, the logical-to-physical address translation is still done by processor hardware. Now the processor must know how to access the page table of the current process. Presented with a logical

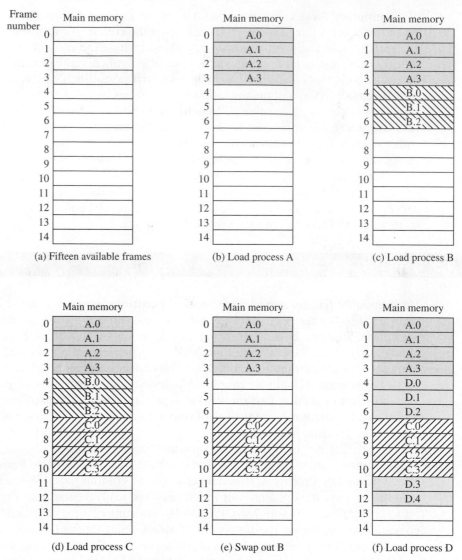

Figure 7.9 **Assignment of Process to Free Frames**

address (page number, offset), the processor uses the page table to produce a physical address (frame number, offset).

Continuing our example, the five pages of process D are loaded into frames 4, 5, 6, 11, and 12. Figure 7.10 shows the various page tables at this time. A page table contains one entry for each page of the process, so that the table is easily indexed by the page number (starting at page 0). Each page table entry contains the number of the frame in main memory, if any, that holds the corresponding page. In addition, the OS maintains a single free-frame list of all the frames in main memory that are currently unoccupied and available for pages.

Thus we see that simple paging, as described here, is similar to fixed partitioning. The differences are that, with paging, the partitions are rather small; a

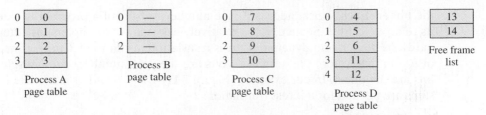

Figure 7.10 Data Structures for the Example of Figure 7.9 at Time Epoch (f)

program may occupy more than one partition; and these partitions need not be contiguous.

To make this paging scheme convenient, let us dictate that the page size, hence the frame size, must be a power of 2. With the use of a page size that is a power of 2, it is easy to demonstrate that the relative address, which is defined with reference to the origin of the program, and the logical address, expressed as a page number and offset, are the same. An example is shown in Figure 7.11. In this example, 16-bit addresses are used, and the page size is 1K = 1,024 bytes. The relative address 1502, in binary form, is 0000010111011110. With a page size of 1K, an offset field of 10 bits is needed, leaving 6 bits for the page number. Thus a program can consist of a maximum of $2^6 = 64$ pages of 1K bytes each. As Figure 7.11b shows, relative address 1502 corresponds to an offset of 478 (0111011110) on page 1 (000001), which yields the same 16-bit number, 0000010111011110.

The consequences of using a page size that is a power of 2 are twofold. First, the logical addressing scheme is transparent to the programmer, the assembler, and

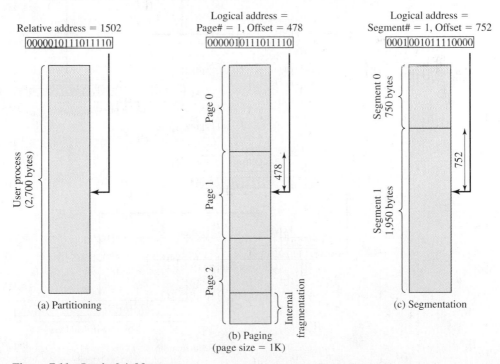

Figure 7.11 Logical Addresses

the linker. Each logical address (page number, offset) of a program is identical to its relative address. Second, it is a relatively easy matter to implement a function in hardware to perform dynamic address translation at run time. Consider an address of $n + m$ bits, where the leftmost n bits are the page number and the rightmost m bits are the offset. In our example (Figure 7.11b), $n = 6$ and $m = 10$. The following steps are needed for address translation:

- Extract the page number as the leftmost n bits of the logical address.
- Use the page number as an index into the process page table to find the frame number, k.
- The starting physical address of the frame is $k \times 2_m$, and the physical address of the referenced byte is that number plus the offset. This physical address need not be calculated; it is easily constructed by appending the frame number to the offset.

In our example, we have the logical address 0000010111011110, which is page number 1, offset 478. Suppose that this page is residing in main memory frame 6 = binary 000110. Then the physical address is frame number 6, offset 478 = 0001100111011110 (Figure 7.12a).

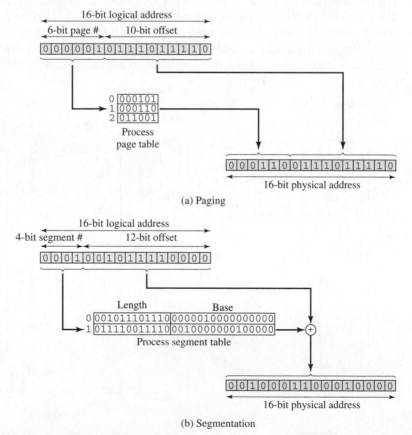

(a) Paging

(b) Segmentation

Figure 7.12   Examples of Logical-to-Physical Address Translation

To summarize, with simple paging, main memory is divided into many small equal-size frames. Each process is divided into frame-size pages. Smaller processes require fewer pages; larger processes require more. When a process is brought in, all of its pages are loaded into available frames, and a page table is set up. This approach solves many of the problems inherent in partitioning.

7.4 SEGMENTATION

A user program can be subdivided using segmentation, in which the program and its associated data are divided into a number of **segments**. It is not required that all segments of all programs be of the same length, although there is a maximum segment length. As with paging, a logical address using segmentation consists of two parts, in this case a segment number and an offset.

Because of the use of unequal-size segments, segmentation is similar to dynamic partitioning. In the absence of an overlay scheme or the use of virtual memory, it would be required that all of a program's segments be loaded into memory for execution. The difference, compared to dynamic partitioning, is that with segmentation a program may occupy more than one partition, and these partitions need not be contiguous. Segmentation eliminates internal fragmentation but, like dynamic partitioning, it suffers from external fragmentation. However, because a process is broken up into a number of smaller pieces, the external fragmentation should be less.

Whereas paging is invisible to the programmer, segmentation is usually visible and is provided as a convenience for organizing programs and data. Typically, the programmer or compiler will assign programs and data to different segments. For purposes of modular programming, the program or data may be further broken down into multiple segments. The principal inconvenience of this service is that the programmer must be aware of the maximum segment size limitation.

Another consequence of unequal-size segments is that there is no simple relationship between logical addresses and physical addresses. Analogous to paging, a simple segmentation scheme would make use of a segment table for each process and a list of free blocks of main memory. Each segment table entry would have to give the starting address in main memory of the corresponding segment. The entry should also provide the length of the segment, to assure that invalid addresses are not used. When a process enters the Running state, the address of its segment table is loaded into a special register used by the memory management hardware. Consider an address of $n + m$ bits, where the leftmost n bits are the segment number and the rightmost m bits are the offset. In our example (Figure 7.11c), $n = 4$ and $m = 12$. Thus the maximum segment size is $2^{12} = 4096$. The following steps are needed for address translation:

- Extract the segment number as the leftmost n bits of the logical address.
- Use the segment number as an index into the process segment table to find the starting physical address of the segment.
- Compare the offset, expressed in the rightmost m bits, to the length of the segment. If the offset is greater than or equal to the length, the address is invalid.

- The desired physical address is the sum of the starting physical address of the segment plus the offset.

In our example, we have the logical address 0001001011110000, which is segment number 1, offset 752. Suppose that this segment is residing in main memory starting at physical address 0010000000100000. Then the physical address is 0010000000100000 + 001011110000 = 0010001100010000 (Figure 7.12b).

To summarize, with simple segmentation, a process is divided into a number of segments that need not be of equal size. When a process is brought in, all of its segments are loaded into available regions of memory, and a segment table is set up.

7.5   SECURITY ISSUES

Main memory and virtual memory are system resources subject to security threats and for which security countermeasures need to be taken. The most obvious security requirement is the prevention of unauthorized access to the memory contents of processes. If a process has not declared a portion of its memory to be sharable, then no other process should have access to the contents of that portion of memory. If a process declares that a portion of memory may be shared by other designated processes, then the security service of the OS must ensure that only the designated processes have access. The security threats and countermeasures discussed in Chapter 3 are relevant to this type of memory protection.

In this section, we summarize another threat that involves memory protection. Part Seven provides more detail.

Buffer Overflow Attacks

One serious security threat related to memory management remains to be introduced: **buffer overflow**, also known as a **buffer overrun**, which is defined in the NIST (National Institute of Standards and Technology) *Glossary of Key Information Security Terms* as follows:

> **buffer overrun:** A condition at an interface under which more input can be placed into a buffer or data-holding area than the capacity allocated, overwriting other information. Attackers exploit such a condition to crash a system or to insert specially crafted code that allows them to gain control of the system.

A buffer overflow can occur as a result of a programming error when a process attempts to store data beyond the limits of a fixed-sized buffer and consequently overwrites adjacent memory locations. These locations could hold other program variables or parameters or program control flow data such as return addresses and pointers to previous stack frames. The buffer could be located on the stack, in the heap, or in the data section of the process. The consequences of this error include corruption of data used by the program, unexpected transfer of control in the program, possibly memory access violations, and very likely eventual program termination. When done deliberately as part of an attack on a system, the transfer of control could be to code of the attacker's choosing, resulting in the ability to execute arbitrary code with the privileges of the attacked process. Buffer overflow attacks are one of the most prevalent and dangerous types of security attacks.

To illustrate the basic operation of a common type of buffer overflow, known as **stack overflow**, consider the C main function given in Figure 7.13a. This contains three variables (`valid`, `str1`, and `str2`),[2] whose values will typically be saved in adjacent memory locations. Their order and location depends on the type of variable (local or global), the language and compiler used, and the target machine architecture. For this example, we assume that they are saved in consecutive memory locations, from highest to lowest, as shown in Figure 7.14.[3] This is typically the case for local variables in a C function on common processor architectures such as the Intel Pentium family. The purpose of the code fragment is to call the function `next_tag(str1)` to copy into `str1` some expected tag value.

```
int main(int argc, char *argv[]) {
    int valid = FALSE;
    char str1[8];
    char str2[8];

    next_tag(str1);
    gets(str2);
    if (strncmp(str1, str2, 8) == 0)
        valid = TRUE;
    printf("buffer1: str1(%s), str2(%s), valid(%d)\n", str1, str2, valid);
}
```

(a) Basic buffer overflow C code

```
$ cc -g -o buffer1 buffer1.c
$ ./buffer1
START
buffer1: str1(START), str2(START), valid(1)
$ ./buffer1
EVILINPUTVALUE
buffer1: str1(TVALUE), str2(EVILINPUTVALUE), valid(0)
$ ./buffer1
BADINPUTBADINPUT
buffer1: str1(BADINPUT), str2(BADINPUTBADINPUT), valid(1)
```

(b) Basic buffer overflow example runs

Figure 7.13   Basic Buffer Overflow Example

---

[2]In this example, the flag variable is saved as an integer rather than a Boolean. This is done both because it is the classic C style and to avoid issues of word alignment in its storage. The buffers are deliberately small to accentuate the buffer overflow issue being illustrated.

[3]Address and data values are specified in hexadecimal in this and related figures. Data values are also shown in ASCII where appropriate.

Memory Address	Before gets (str2)	After gets (str2)	Contains Value of
. . . .	. . . .	. . . .	
bffffbf4	34fcffbf 4 . . .	34fcffbf 3 . . .	argv
bffffbf0	01000000	01000000	argc
bffffbec	c6bd0340 . . . @	c6bd0340 . . . @	return addr
bffffbe8	08fcffbf	08fcffbf	old base ptr
bffffbe4	00000000	01000000	valid
bffffbe0	80640140 . d . @	00640140 . d . @	
bffffbdc	54001540 T . . @	4e505554 N P U T	str1[4-7]
bffffbd8	53544152 S T A R	42414449 B A D I	str1[0-3]
bffffbd4	00850408	4e505554 N P U T	str2[4-7]
bffffbd0	30561540 0 v . @	42414449 B A D I	str2[0-3]
. . . .	. . . .	. . . .	

Figure 7.14 Basic Buffer Overflow Stack Values

Let's assume this will be the string START. It then reads the next line from the standard input for the program using the C library gets() function, and then compares the string read with the expected tag. If the next line did indeed contain just the string START, this comparison would succeed, and the variable valid would be set to TRUE.[4] This case is shown in the first of the three example program runs in Figure 7.13b. Any other input tag would leave it with the value FALSE. Such a code fragment might be used to parse some structured network protocol interaction or formatted text file.

The problem with this code exists because the traditional C library gets() function does not include any checking on the amount of data copied. It reads the next line of text from the program's standard input up until the first newline[5] character occurs and copies it into the supplied buffer followed by the NULL terminator

---

[4]In C the logical values FALSE and TRUE are simply integers with the values 0 and 1 (or indeed any nonzero value), respectively. Symbolic defines are often used to map these symbolic names to their underlying value, as was done in this program.

[5]The newline (NL) or linefeed (LF) character is the standard end of line terminator for UNIX systems, and hence for C, and is the character with the ASCII value 0x0a.

used with C strings.[6] If more than seven characters are present on the input line, when read in they will (along with the terminating NULL character) require more room than is available in the str2 buffer. Consequently, the extra characters will overwrite the values of the adjacent variable, str1 in this case. For example, if the input line contained EVILINPUTVALUE, the result will be that str1 will be over-written with the characters TVALUE, and str2 will use not only the eight characters allocated to it but seven more from str1 as well. This can be seen in the second example run in Figure 7.13b. The overflow has resulted in corruption of a variable not directly used to save the input. Because these strings are not equal, valid also retains the value FALSE. Further, if 16 or more characters were input, additional memory locations would be overwritten.

The preceding example illustrates the basic behavior of a buffer overflow. At its simplest, any unchecked copying of data into a buffer could result in corruption of adjacent memory locations, which may be other variables, or possibly program control addresses and data. Even this simple example could be taken further. Knowing the structure of the code processing it, an attacker could arrange for the overwritten value to set the value in str1 equal to the value placed in str2, resulting in the subsequent comparison succeeding. For example, the input line could be the string BADINPUTBADINPUT. This results in the comparison succeeding, as shown in the third of the three example program runs in Figure 7.13b, and illustrated in Figure 7.14, with the values of the local variables before and after the call to gets(). Note also that the terminating NULL for the input string was written to the memory location following str1. This means the flow of control in the program will continue as if the expected tag was found, when in fact the tag read was something completely different. This will almost certainly result in program behavior that was not intended. How serious this is depends very much on the logic in the attacked program. One dangerous possibility occurs if instead of being a tag, the values in these buffers were an expected and supplied password needed to access privileged features. If so, the buffer overflow provides the attacker with a means of accessing these features without actually knowing the correct password.

To exploit any type of buffer overflow, such as those we have illustrated here, the attacker needs:

1. To identify a buffer overflow vulnerability in some program that can be triggered using externally sourced data under the attackers control, and

2. To understand how that buffer will be stored in the processes memory, and hence the potential for corrupting adjacent memory locations and potentially altering the flow of execution of the program.

Identifying vulnerable programs may be done by inspection of program source, tracing the execution of programs as they process oversized input, or using tools such as *fuzzing*, which we discuss in Part Seven, to automatically identify potentially

---

[6]Strings in C are stored in an array of characters and terminated with the NULL character, which has the ASCII value 0x00. Any remaining locations in the array are undefined, and typically contain whatever value was previously saved in that area of memory. This can be clearly seen in the value in the variable str2 in the "Before" column of Figure 7.14.

vulnerable programs. What the attacker does with the resulting corruption of memory varies considerably, depending on what values are being overwritten.

Defending against Buffer Overflows

Finding and exploiting a stack buffer overflow is not that difficult. The large number of exploits over the previous couple of decades clearly illustrates this. There is consequently a need to defend systems against such attacks by either preventing them or at least detecting and aborting such attacks. Countermeasures can be broadly classified into two categories:

- Compile-time defenses, which aim to harden programs to resist attacks in new programs
- Run-time defenses, which aim to detect and abort attacks in existing programs

While suitable defenses have been known for a couple of decades, the very large existing base of vulnerable software and systems hinders their deployment. Hence the interest in run-time defenses, which can be deployed in operating systems and updates and can provide some protection for existing vulnerable programs.

7.6 SUMMARY

One of the most important and complex tasks of an operating system is memory management. Memory management involves treating main memory as a resource to be allocated to and shared among a number of active processes. To use the processor and the I/O facilities efficiently, it is desirable to maintain as many processes in main memory as possible. In addition, it is desirable to free programmers from size restrictions in program development.

The basic tools of memory management are paging and segmentation. With paging, each process is divided into relatively small, fixed-size pages. Segmentation provides for the use of pieces of varying size. It is also possible to combine segmentation and paging in a single memory management scheme.

7.7 RECOMMENDED READING

Because partitioning has been supplanted by virtual memory techniques, most OS books offer only cursory coverage. One of the more complete and interesting treatments is in [MILE92]. A thorough discussion of partitioning strategies is found in [KNUT97].

The topics of linking and loading are covered in many books on program development, computer architecture, and operating systems. A particularly detailed treatment is [BECK97]. [CLAR98] also contains a good discussion. A thorough practical discussion of this topic, with numerous OS examples, is [LEVI00].

BECK97   Beck, L. *System Software*. Reading, MA: Addison-Wesley, 1997.

CLAR98   Clarke, D., and Merusi, D. *System Software Programming: The Way Things Work*. Upper Saddle River, NJ: Prentice Hall, 1998.

KNUT97   Knuth, D. *The Art of Computer Programming, Volume 1: Fundamental Algorithms*. Reading, MA: Addison-Wesley, 1997.

LEVI00   Levine, J. *Linkers and Loaders*. San Francisco: Morgan Kaufmann, 2000.

MILE92   Milenkovic, M. *Operating Systems: Concepts and Design*. New York: McGraw-Hill, 1992.

7.8   KEY TERMS, REVIEW QUESTIONS, AND PROBLEMS

Key Terms

absolute loading	linkage editor	physical address
buddy system	linking	physical organization
compaction	loading	protection
dynamic linking	logical address	relative address
dynamic partitioning	logical organization	relocatable loading
dynamic run-time loading	memory management	relocation
external fragmentation	page	segment
fixed partitioning	page table	segmentation
frame	paging	sharing
internal fragmentation	partitioning	

Review Questions

7.1   What requirements is memory management intended to satisfy?

7.2   Why is the capability to relocate processes desirable?

7.3   Why is it not possible to enforce memory protection at compile time?

7.4   What are some reasons to allow two or more processes to all have access to a particular region of memory?

7.5   In a fixed-partitioning scheme, what are the advantages of using unequal-size partitions?

7.6   What is the difference between internal and external fragmentation?

7.7   What are the distinctions among logical, relative, and physical addresses?

7.8   What is the difference between a page and a frame?

7.9   What is the difference between a page and a segment?

Problems

7.1   In Section 2.3, we listed five objectives of memory management, and in Section 7.1, we listed five requirements. Argue that each list encompasses all of the concerns addressed in the other.

7.2 Consider a fixed partitioning scheme with equal-size partitions of 2^{16} bytes and a total main memory size of 2^{24} bytes. A process table is maintained that includes a pointer to a partition for each resident process. How many bits are required for the pointer?

7.3 Consider a dynamic partitioning scheme. Show that, on average, the memory contains half as many holes as segments.

7.4 To implement the various placement algorithms discussed for dynamic partitioning (Section 7.2), a list of the free blocks of memory must be kept. For each of the three methods discussed (best-fit, first-fit, next-fit), what is the average length of the search?

7.5 Another placement algorithm for dynamic partitioning is referred to as worst-fit. In this case, the largest free block of memory is used for bringing in a process.
   a. Discuss the pros and cons of this method compared to first-, next-, and best-fit.
   b. What is the average length of the search for worst-fit?

7.6 This diagram shows an example of memory configuration under dynamic partitioning, after a number of placement and swapping-out operations have been carried out. Addresses go from left to right; gray areas indicate blocks occupied by processes; white areas indicate free memory blocks. The last process placed is 2-Mbyte and is marked with an X. Only one process was swapped out after that.

   a. What was the maximum size of the swapped out process?
   b. What was the size of the free block just before it was partitioned by X?
   c. A new 3-Mbyte allocation request must be satisfied next. Indicate the intervals of memory where a partition will be created for the new process under the following four placement algorithms: best-fit, first-fit, next-fit, worst-fit. For each algorithm, draw a horizontal segment under the memory strip and label it clearly.

7.7 A 1-Mbyte block of memory is allocated using the buddy system.
   a. Show the results of the following sequence in a figure similar to Figure 7.6: Request 70; Request 35; Request 80; Return A; Request 60; Return B; Return D; Return C.
   b. Show the binary tree representation following Return B.

7.8 Consider a buddy system in which a particular block under the current allocation has an address of 011011110000.
   a. If the block is of size 4, what is the binary address of its buddy?
   b. If the block is of size 16, what is the binary address of its buddy?

7.9 Let $\text{buddy}_k(x)$ = address of the buddy of the block of size 2^k whose address is x. Write a general expression for $\text{buddy}_k(x)$.

7.10 The Fibonacci sequence is defined as follows:

$$F_0 = 0, \quad F_1 = 1, \quad F_{n+2} = F_{n+1} + F_n, \quad n \geq 0$$

   a. Could this sequence be used to establish a buddy system?
   b. What would be the advantage of this system over the binary buddy system described in this chapter?

7.11 During the course of execution of a program, the processor will increment the contents of the instruction register (program counter) by one word after each instruction fetch, but will alter the contents of that register if it encounters a branch or call instruction that causes execution to continue elsewhere in the program. Now consider Figure 7.8. There are two alternatives with respect to instruction addresses:
   • Maintain a relative address in the instruction register and do the dynamic address translation using the instruction register as input. When a successful branch or call is encountered, the relative address generated by that branch or call is loaded into the instruction register.
   • Maintain an absolute address in the instruction register. When a successful branch or call is encountered, dynamic address translation is employed, with the results stored in the instruction register.
   Which approach is preferable?

7.12 Consider a simple paging system with the following parameters: 2^{32} bytes of physical memory; page size of 2^{10} bytes; 2^{16} pages of logical address space.
   a. How many bits are in a logical address?
   b. How many bytes in a frame?
   c. How many bits in the physical address specify the frame?
   d. How many entries in the page table?
   e. How many bits in each page table entry? Assume each page table entry contains a valid/invalid bit.

7.13 Write the binary translation of the logical address 0001010010111010 under the following hypothetical memory management schemes, and explain your answer:
   a. a paging system with a 256-address page size, using a page table in which the frame number happens to be four times smaller than the page number
   b. a segmentation system with a 1K-address maximum segment size, using a segment table in which bases happen to be regularly placed at real addresses: $22 + 4{,}096 \times$ segment #

7.14 Consider a simple segmentation system that has the following segment table:

Starting Address	Length (bytes)
660	248
1,752	422
222	198
996	604

For each of the following logical addresses, determine the physical address or indicate if a segment fault occurs:
   a. 0, 198
   b. 2, 156
   c. 1, 530
   d. 3, 444
   e. 0, 222

7.15 Consider a memory in which contiguous segments S_1, S_2,...,S_n are placed in their order of creation from one end of the store to the other, as suggested by the following figure:

S_1	S_2	$\bullet\ \bullet\ \bullet$	S_n	Hole

When segment S_{n+1} is being created, it is placed immediately after segment S_n even though some of the segments S1, S2,...,S_n may already have been deleted. When the boundary between segments (in use or deleted) and the hole reaches the other end of the memory, the segments in use are compacted.
   a. Show that the fraction of time F spent on compacting obeys the following inequality:

$$F \geq \frac{1 - f}{1 + kf} \qquad \text{where} \quad k = \frac{t}{2s} - 1$$

where
   s = average length of a segment, in words
   t = average lifetime of a segment, in memory references
   f = fraction of the memory that is unused under equilibrium conditions

   Hint: Find the average speed at which the boundary crosses the memory and assume that the copying of a single word requires at least two memory references.
   b. Find F for $f = 0.2$, $t = 1{,}000$, and $s = 50$.

APPENDIX 7A LOADING AND LINKING

The first step in the creation of an active process is to load a program into main memory and create a process image (Figure 7.15). Figure 7.16 depicts a scenario typical for most systems. The application consists of a number of compiled or assembled modules in object-code form. These are linked to resolve any references between modules. At the same time, references to library routines are resolved. The library routines themselves may be incorporated into the program or referenced as shared code that must be supplied by the operating system at run time. In this appendix, we summarize the key features of linkers and loaders. For clarity in the presentation, we begin with a description of the loading task when a single program module is involved; no linking is required.

Loading

In Figure 7.16, the loader places the load module in main memory starting at location x. In loading the program, the addressing requirement illustrated in Figure 7.1 must be satisfied. In general, three approaches can be taken:

- Absolute loading
- Relocatable loading
- Dynamic run-time loading

ABSOLUTE LOADING   An absolute loader requires that a given load module always be loaded into the same location in main memory. Thus, in the load module presented to the loader, all address references must be to specific, or absolute, main

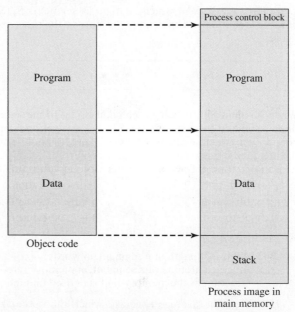

Object code

Process control block

Program

Data

Stack

Process image in
main memory

Figure 7.15   The Loading Function

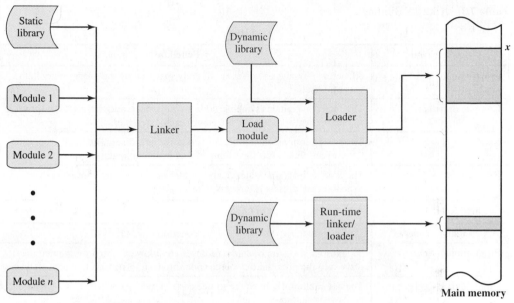

Figure 7.16   A Linking and Loading Scenario

memory addresses. For example, if x in Figure 7.16 is location 1024, then the first word in a load module destined for that region of memory has address 1024.

The assignment of specific address values to memory references within a program can be done either by the programmer or at compile or assembly time (Table 7.3a). There are several disadvantages to the former approach. First, every programmer would have to know the intended assignment strategy for placing modules into main memory. Second, if any modifications are made to the program that involve insertions or deletions in the body of the module, then all of the addresses will have to be altered. Accordingly, it is preferable to allow memory references within programs to be expressed symbolically and then resolve those symbolic references at the time of compilation or assembly. This is illustrated in Figure 7.17. Every reference to an instruction or item of data is initially represented by a symbol. In preparing the module for input to an absolute loader, the assembler or compiler will convert all of these references to specific addresses (in this example, for a module to be loaded starting at location 1024), as shown in Figure 7.17b.

RELOCATABLE LOADING   The disadvantage of binding memory references to specific addresses prior to loading is that the resulting load module can only be placed in one region of main memory. However, when many programs share main memory, it may not be desirable to decide ahead of time into which region of memory a particular module should be loaded. It is better to make that decision at load time. Thus we need a load module that can be located anywhere in main memory.

To satisfy this new requirement, the assembler or compiler produces not actual main memory addresses (absolute addresses) but addresses that are relative to some known point, such as the start of the program. This technique is illustrated in Figure 7.17c. The start of the load module is assigned the relative address 0, and

Table 7.3 Address Binding

(a) Loader

Binding Time	Function
Programming time	All actual physical addresses are directly specified by the programmer in the program itself.
Compile or assembly time	The program contains symbolic address references, and these are converted to actual physical addresses by the compiler or assembler.
Load time	The compiler or assembler produces relative addresses. The loader translates these to absolute addresses at the time of program loading.
Run time	The loaded program retains relative addresses. These are converted dynamically to absolute addresses by processor hardware.

(b) Linker

Linkage Time	Function
Programming time	No external program or data references are allowed. The programmer must place into the program the source code for all subprograms that are referenced.
Compile or assembly time	The assembler must fetch the source code of every subroutine that is referenced and assemble them as a unit.
Load module creation	All object modules have been assembled using relative addresses. These modules are linked together and all references are restated relative to the origin of the final load module.
Load time	External references are not resolved until the load module is to be loaded into main memory. At that time, referenced dynamic link modules are appended to the load module, and the entire package is loaded into main or virtual memory.
Run time	External references are not resolved until the external call is executed by the processor. At that time, the process is interrupted and the desired module is linked to the calling program.

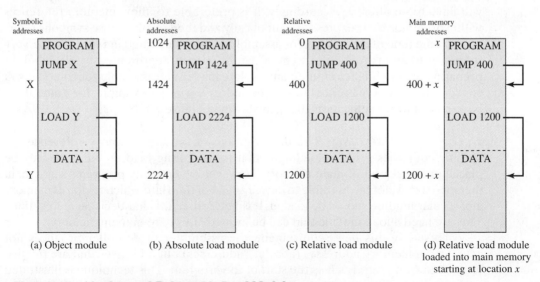

(a) Object module   (b) Absolute load module   (c) Relative load module   (d) Relative load module loaded into main memory starting at location x

Figure 7.17 Absolute and Relocatable Load Modules

all other memory references within the module are expressed relative to the beginning of the module.

With all memory references expressed in relative format, it becomes a simple task for the loader to place the module in the desired location. If the module is to be loaded beginning at location x, then the loader must simply add x to each memory reference as it loads the module into memory. To assist in this task, the load module must include information that tells the loader where the address references are and how they are to be interpreted (usually relative to the program origin, but also possibly relative to some other point in the program, such as the current location). This set of information is prepared by the compiler or assembler and is usually referred to as the relocation dictionary.

DYNAMIC RUN-TIME LOADING   Relocatable loaders are common and provide obvious benefits relative to absolute loaders. However, in a multiprogramming environment, even one that does not depend on virtual memory, the relocatable loading scheme is inadequate. We have referred to the need to swap process images in and out of main memory to maximize the utilization of the processor. To maximize main memory utilization, we would like to be able to swap the process image back into different locations at different times. Thus, a program, once loaded, may be swapped out to disk and then swapped back in at a different location. This would be impossible if memory references had been bound to absolute addresses at the initial load time.

The alternative is to defer the calculation of an absolute address until it is actually needed at run time. For this purpose, the load module is loaded into main memory with all memory references in relative form (Figure 7.17c). It is not until an instruction is actually executed that the absolute address is calculated. To assure that this function does not degrade performance, it must be done by special processor hardware rather than software. This hardware is described in Section 7.2.

Dynamic address calculation provides complete flexibility. A program can be loaded into any region of main memory. Subsequently, the execution of the program can be interrupted and the program can be swapped out of main memory, to be later swapped back in at a different location.

Linking

The function of a linker is to take as input a collection of object modules and produce a load module, consisting of an integrated set of program and data modules, to be passed to the loader. In each object module, there may be address references to locations in other modules. Each such reference can only be expressed symbolically in an unlinked object module. The linker creates a single load module that is the contiguous joining of all of the object modules. Each intramodule reference must be changed from a symbolic address to a reference to a location within the overall load module. For example, module A in Figure 7.18a contains a procedure invocation of module B. When these modules are combined in the load module, this symbolic reference to module B is changed to a specific reference to the location of the entry point of B within the load module.

LINKAGE EDITOR   The nature of this address linkage will depend on the type of load module to be created and when the linkage occurs (Table 7.3b). If, as is

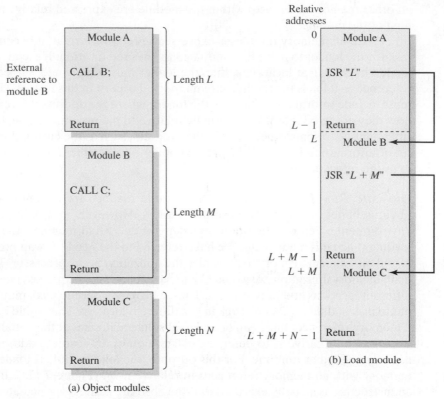

(a) Object modules

(b) Load module

Figure 7.18   The Linking Function

usually the case, a relocatable load module is desired, then linkage is usually done in the following fashion. Each compiled or assembled object module is created with references relative to the beginning of the object module. All of these modules are put together into a single relocatable load module with all references relative to the origin of the load module. This module can be used as input for relocatable loading or dynamic run-time loading.

A linker that produces a relocatable load module is often referred to as a linkage editor. Figure 7.18 illustrates the linkage editor function.

DYNAMIC LINKER   As with loading, it is possible to defer some linkage functions. The term *dynamic linking* is used to refer to the practice of deferring the linkage of some external modules until after the load module has been created. Thus, the load module contains unresolved references to other programs. These references can be resolved either at load time or run time.

For *load-time dynamic linking* (involving upper dynamic library in Figure 7.16), the following steps occur. The load module (application module) to be loaded is read into memory. Any reference to an external module (target module) causes the loader to find the target module, load it, and alter the reference to a relative address in memory from the beginning of the application module. There are several advantages to this approach over what might be called static linking:

- It becomes easier to incorporate changed or upgraded versions of the target module, which may be an operating system utility or some other general-purpose routine. With static linking, a change to such a supporting module would require the relinking of the entire application module. Not only is this inefficient, but it may be impossible in some circumstances. For example, in the personal computer field, most commercial software is released in load module form; source and object versions are not released.

- Having target code in a dynamic link file paves the way for automatic code sharing. The operating system can recognize that more than one application is using the same target code because it loaded and linked that code. It can use that information to load a single copy of the target code and link it to both applications, rather than having to load one copy for each application.

- It becomes easier for independent software developers to extend the functionality of a widely used operating system such as Linux. A developer can come up with a new function that may be useful to a variety of applications and package it as a dynamic link module.

With **run-time dynamic linking** (involving lower dynamic library in Figure 7.16), some of the linking is postponed until execution time. External references to target modules remain in the loaded program. When a call is made to the absent module, the operating system locates the module, loads it, and links it to the calling module. Such modules are typically shareable. In the Windows environment, these are call dynamic-link libraries (DLLs). Thus, if one process is already making use of a dynamically-linked shared module, then that module is in main memory and a new process can simply link to the already-loaded module.

The use of DLLs can lead to a problem commonly referred to as **DLL hell**. DLL hell occurs if two or more processes are sharing a DLL module but expect different versions of the module. For example, an application or system function might be reinstalled and bring in with it an older version of a DLL file.

We have seen that dynamic loading allows an entire load module to be moved around; however, the structure of the module is static, being unchanged throughout the execution of the process and from one execution to the next. However, in some cases, it is not possible to determine prior to execution which object modules will be required. This situation is typified by transaction-processing applications, such as an airline reservation system or a banking application. The nature of the transaction dictates which program modules are required, and they are loaded as appropriate and linked with the main program. The advantage of the use of such a dynamic linker is that it is not necessary to allocate memory for program units unless those units are referenced. This capability is used in support of segmentation systems.

One additional refinement is possible: An application need not know the names of all the modules or entry points that may be called. For example, a charting program may be written to work with a variety of plotters, each of which is driven by a different driver package. The application can learn the name of the plotter that is currently installed on the system from another process or by looking it up in a configuration file. This allows the user of the application to install a new plotter that did not exist at the time the application was written.

CHAPTER 8

VIRTUAL MEMORY

8.1 Hardware and Control Structures
Locality and Virtual Memory
Paging
Segmentation
Combined Paging and Segmentation
Protection and Sharing

8.2 Operating System Software
Fetch Policy
Placement Policy
Replacement Policy
Resident Set Management
Cleaning Policy
Load Control

8.3 UNIX and Solaris Memory Management
Paging System
Kernel Memory Allocator

8.4 Linux Memory Management
Linux Virtual Memory
Kernel Memory Allocation

8.5 Windows Memory Management
Windows Virtual Address Map
Windows Paging

8.6 Summary

8.7 Recommended Reading and Web Sites

8.8 Key Terms, Review Questions, and Problems

You're gonna need a bigger boat.

—STEVEN SPIELBERG, *JAWS*, 1975

LEARNING OBJECTIVES

After studying this chapter, you should be able to:

- Define virtual memory.
- Describe the hardware and control structures that support virtual memory.
- Describe the various OS mechanisms used to implement virtual memory.
- Describe the virtual memory management mechanisms in UNIX, Linux, and Windows 7.

Chapter 7 introduced the concepts of paging and segmentation and analyzed their shortcomings. We now move to a discussion of virtual memory. An analysis of this topic is complicated by the fact that memory management is a complex interrelationship between processor hardware and operating system software. We focus first on the hardware aspect of virtual memory, looking at the use of paging, segmentation, and combined paging and segmentation. Then we look at the issues involved in the design of a virtual memory facility in operating systems.

Table 8.1 defines some key terms related to virtual memory. A set of animations that illustrate concepts in this chapter is available online. Click on the rotating globe at WilliamStallings.com/OS/OS7e.html for access.

8.1 HARDWARE AND CONTROL STRUCTURES

Comparing simple paging and simple segmentation, on the one hand, with fixed and dynamic partitioning, on the other, we see the foundation for a fundamental breakthrough in memory management. Two characteristics of paging and segmentation are the keys to this breakthrough:

Table 8.1 Virtual Memory Terminology

Virtual memory	A storage allocation scheme in which secondary memory can be addressed as though it were part of main memory. The addresses a program may use to reference memory are distinguished from the addresses the memory system uses to identify physical storage sites, and program-generated addresses are translated automatically to the corresponding machine addresses. The size of virtual storage is limited by the addressing scheme of the computer system and by the amount of secondary memory available and not by the actual number of main storage locations.
Virtual address	The address assigned to a location in virtual memory to allow that location to be accessed as though it were part of main memory.
Virtual address space	The virtual storage assigned to a process.
Address space	The range of memory addresses available to a process.
Real address	The address of a storage location in main memory.

1. All memory references within a process are logical addresses that are dynamically translated into physical addresses at run time. This means that a process may be swapped in and out of main memory such that it occupies different regions of main memory at different times during the course of execution.

2. A process may be broken up into a number of pieces (pages or segments) and these pieces need not be contiguously located in main memory during execution. The combination of dynamic run-time address translation and the use of a page or segment table permits this.

Now we come to the breakthrough. *If the preceding two characteristics are present, then it is not necessary that all of the pages or all of the segments of a process be in main memory during execution.* If the piece (segment or page) that holds the next instruction to be fetched and the piece that holds the next data location to be accessed are in main memory, then at least for a time execution may proceed.

Let us consider how this may be accomplished. For now, we can talk in general terms, and we will use the term *piece* to refer to either page or segment, depending on whether paging or segmentation is employed. Suppose that it is time to bring a new process into memory. The OS begins by bringing in only one or a few pieces, to include the initial program piece and the initial data piece to which those instructions refer. The portion of a process that is actually in main memory at any time is called the **resident set** of the process. As the process executes, things proceed smoothly as long as all memory references are to locations that are in the resident set. Using the segment or page table, the processor always is able to determine whether this is so. If the processor encounters a logical address that is not in main memory, it generates an interrupt indicating a memory access fault. The OS puts the interrupted process in a blocking state. For the execution of this process to proceed later, the OS must bring into main memory the piece of the process that contains the logical address that caused the access fault. For this purpose, the OS issues a disk I/O read request. After the I/O request has been issued, the OS can dispatch another process to run while the disk I/O is performed. Once the desired piece has been brought into main memory, an I/O interrupt is issued, giving control back to the OS, which places the affected process back into a Ready state.

It may immediately occur to you to question the efficiency of this maneuver, in which a process may be executing and have to be interrupted for no other reason than that you have failed to load in all of the needed pieces of the process. For now, let us defer consideration of this question with the assurance that efficiency is possible. Instead, let us ponder the implications of our new strategy. There are two implications, the second more startling than the first, and both lead to improved system utilization:

1. **More processes may be maintained in main memory.** Because we are only going to load some of the pieces of any particular process, there is room for more processes. This leads to more efficient utilization of the processor because it is more likely that at least one of the more numerous processes will be in a Ready state at any particular time.

2. **A process may be larger than all of main memory.** One of the most fundamental restrictions in programming is lifted. Without the scheme we have been discussing, a programmer must be acutely aware of how much memory is available. If the program being written is too large, the programmer must devise ways to

structure the program into pieces that can be loaded separately in some sort of overlay strategy. With virtual memory based on paging or segmentation, that job is left to the OS and the hardware. As far as the programmer is concerned, he or she is dealing with a huge memory, the size associated with disk storage. The OS automatically loads pieces of a process into main memory as required.

Because a process executes only in main memory, that memory is referred to as **real memory.** But a programmer or user perceives a potentially much larger memory—that which is allocated on disk. This latter is referred to as **virtual memory.** Virtual memory allows for very effective multiprogramming and relieves the user of the unnecessarily tight constraints of main memory. Table 8.2 summarizes characteristics of paging and segmentation, with and without the use of virtual memory.

Table 8.2 Characteristics of Paging and Segmentation

Simple Paging	Virtual Memory Paging	Simple Segmentation	Virtual Memory Segmentation
Main memory partitioned into small fixed-size chunks called frames	Main memory partitioned into small fixed-size chunks called frames	Main memory not partitioned	Main memory not partitioned
Program broken into pages by the compiler or memory management system	Program broken into pages by the compiler or memory management system	Program segments specified by the programmer to the compiler (i.e., the decision is made by the programmer)	Program segments specified by the programmer to the compiler (i.e., the decision is made by the programmer)
Internal fragmentation within frames	Internal fragmentation within frames	No internal fragmentation	No internal fragmentation
No external fragmentation	No external fragmentation	External fragmentation	External fragmentation
Operating system must maintain a page table for each process showing which frame each page occupies	Operating system must maintain a page table for each process showing which frame each page occupies	Operating system must maintain a segment table for each process showing the load address and length of each segment	Operating system must maintain a segment table for each process showing the load address and length of each segment
Operating system must maintain a free frame list	Operating system must maintain a free frame list	Operating system must maintain a list of free holes in main memory	Operating system must maintain a list of free holes in main memory
Processor uses page number, offset to calculate absolute address	Processor uses page number, offset to calculate absolute address	Processor uses segment number, offset to calculate absolute address	Processor uses segment number, offset to calculate absolute address
All the pages of a process must be in main memory for process to run, unless overlays are used	Not all pages of a process need be in main memory frames for the process to run. Pages may be read in as needed	All the segments of a process must be in main memory for process to run, unless overlays are used	Not all segments of a process need be in main memory for the process to run. Segments may be read in as needed
	Reading a page into main memory may require writing a page out to disk		Reading a segment into main memory may require writing one or more segments out to disk

Locality and Virtual Memory

The benefits of virtual memory are attractive, but is the scheme practical? At one time, there was considerable debate on this point, but experience with numerous operating systems has demonstrated beyond doubt that virtual memory does work. Accordingly, virtual memory, based on either paging or paging plus segmentation, has become an essential component of contemporary operating systems.

To understand the key issue and why virtual memory was a matter of much debate, let us examine again the task of the OS with respect to virtual memory. Consider a large process, consisting of a long program plus a number of arrays of data. Over any short period of time, execution may be confined to a small section of the program (e.g., a subroutine) and access to perhaps only one or two arrays of data. If this is so, then it would clearly be wasteful to load in dozens of pieces for that process when only a few pieces will be used before the program is suspended and swapped out. We can make better use of memory by loading in just a few pieces. Then, if the program branches to an instruction or references a data item on a piece not in main memory, a fault is triggered. This tells the OS to bring in the desired piece.

Thus, at any one time, only a few pieces of any given process are in memory, and therefore more processes can be maintained in memory. Furthermore, time is saved because unused pieces are not swapped in and out of memory. However, the OS must be clever about how it manages this scheme. In the steady state, practically all of main memory will be occupied with process pieces, so that the processor and OS have direct access to as many processes as possible. Thus, when the OS brings one piece in, it must throw another out. If it throws out a piece just before it is used, then it will just have to go get that piece again almost immediately. Too much of this leads to a condition known as **thrashing**: The system spends most of its time swapping pieces rather than executing instructions. The avoidance of thrashing was a major research area in the 1970s and led to a variety of complex but effective algorithms. In essence, the OS tries to guess, based on recent history, which pieces are least likely to be used in the near future.

This reasoning is based on belief in the **principle of locality**, which was introduced in Chapter 1 (see especially Appendix 1A). To summarize, the principle of locality states that program and data references within a process tend to cluster. Hence, the assumption that only a few pieces of a process will be needed over a short period of time is valid. Also, it should be possible to make intelligent guesses about which pieces of a process will be needed in the near future, which avoids thrashing.

One way to confirm the principle of locality is to look at the performance of processes in a virtual memory environment. Figure 8.1 is a rather famous diagram that dramatically illustrates the principle of locality [HATF72]. Note that, during the lifetime of the process, references are confined to a subset of pages.

Thus we see that the principle of locality suggests that a virtual memory scheme may work. For virtual memory to be practical and effective, two ingredients are needed. First, there must be hardware support for the paging and/or segmentation scheme to be employed. Second, the OS must include software for managing the movement of pages and/or segments between secondary memory and main memory. In this section, we examine the hardware aspect and look at the

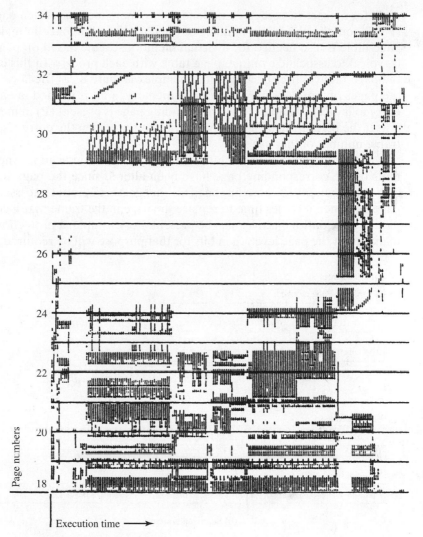

Page numbers

Execution time ⟶

Figure 8.1 Paging Behavior

necessary control structures, which are created and maintained by the OS but are used by the memory management hardware. An examination of the OS issues is provided in the next section.

Paging

The term *virtual memory* is usually associated with systems that employ paging, although virtual memory based on segmentation is also used and is discussed next. The use of paging to achieve virtual memory was first reported for the Atlas computer [KILB62] and soon came into widespread commercial use.

In the discussion of simple paging, we indicated that each process has its own page table, and when all of its pages are loaded into main memory, the page table for a process is created and loaded into main memory. Each page table entry (PTE) contains the frame number of the corresponding page in main memory. A page table is also needed for a virtual memory scheme based on paging. Again, it is typical to associate a unique page table with each process. In this case, however, the page table entries become more complex (Figure 8.2a). Because only some of the pages of a process may be in main memory, a bit is needed in each page table entry to indicate whether the corresponding page is present (P) in main memory or not. If the bit indicates that the page is in memory, then the entry also includes the frame number of that page.

The page table entry includes a modify (M) bit, indicating whether the contents of the corresponding page have been altered since the page was last loaded into main memory. If there has been no change, then it is not necessary to write the page out when it comes time to replace the page in the frame that it currently occupies. Other control bits may also be present. For example, if protection or sharing is managed at the page level, then bits for that purpose will be required.

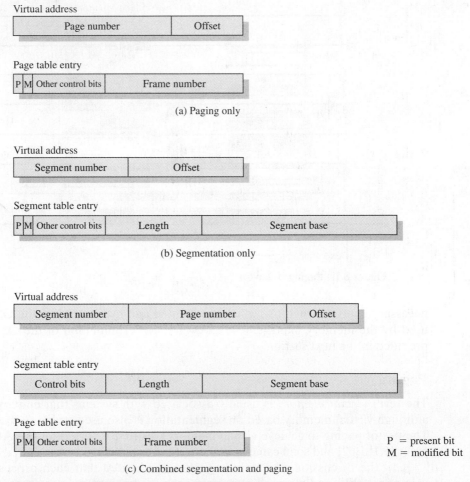

P = present bit
M = modified bit

Figure 8.2 Typical Memory Management Formats

PAGE TABLE STRUCTURE   The basic mechanism for reading a word from memory involves the translation of a virtual, or logical, address, consisting of page number and offset, into a physical address, consisting of frame number and offset, using a page table. Because the page table is of variable length, depending on the size of the process, we cannot expect to hold it in registers. Instead, it must be in main memory to be accessed. Figure 8.3 suggests a hardware implementation. When a particular process is running, a register holds the starting address of the page table for that process. The page number of a virtual address is used to index that table and look up the corresponding frame number. This is combined with the offset portion of the virtual address to produce the desired real address. Typically, the page number field is longer than the frame number field ($n > m$).

In most systems, there is one page table per process. But each process can occupy huge amounts of virtual memory. For example, in the VAX architecture, each process can have up to $2^{31} = 2$ Gbytes of virtual memory. Using $2^9 = 512$-byte pages means that as many as 2^{22} page table entries are required *per process*. Clearly, the amount of memory devoted to page tables alone could be unacceptably high. To overcome this problem, most virtual memory schemes store page tables in virtual memory rather than real memory. This means that page tables are subject to paging just as other pages are. When a process is running, at least a part of its page table must be in main memory, including the page table entry of the currently executing page. Some processors make use of a two-level scheme to organize large page tables. In this scheme, there is a page directory, in which each entry points to a page table. Thus, if the length of the page directory is X, and if the maximum length of a page table is Y, then a process can

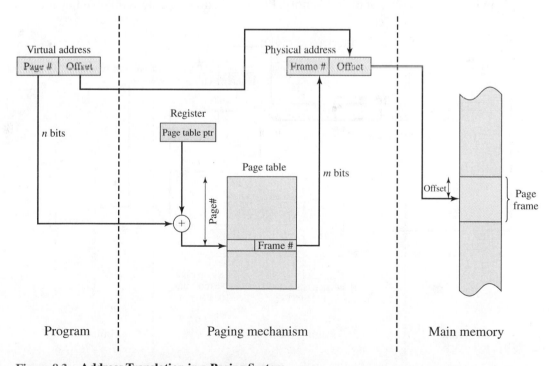

Figure 8.3   Address Translation in a Paging System

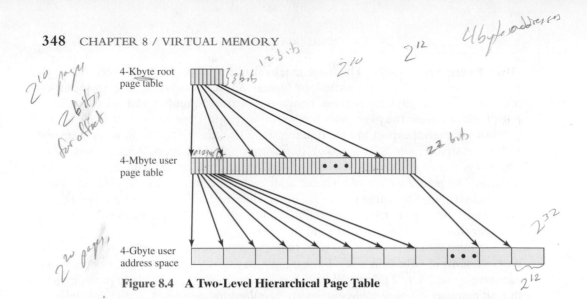

Figure 8.4   A Two-Level Hierarchical Page Table

consist of up to $X \times Y$ pages. Typically, the maximum length of a page table is restricted to be equal to one page. For example, the Pentium processor uses this approach.

Figure 8.4 shows an example of a two-level scheme typical for use with a 32-bit address. If we assume byte-level addressing and 4-Kbyte (2^{12}) pages, then the 4-Gbyte (2^{32}) virtual address space is composed of 2^{20} pages. If each of these pages is mapped by a 4-byte page table entry, we can create a user page table composed of 2^{20} PTEs requiring 4 Mbytes (2^{22}). This huge user page table, occupying 2^{10} pages, can be kept in virtual memory and mapped by a root page table with 2^{10} PTEs occupying 4 Kbytes (2^{12}) of main memory. Figure 8.5 shows the steps involved in address

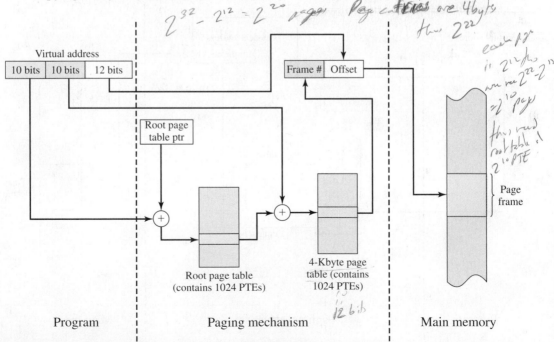

Figure 8.5   Address Translation in a Two-Level Paging System

translation for this scheme. The root page always remains in main memory. The first 10 bits of a virtual address are used to index into the root page to find a PTE for a page of the user page table. If that page is not in main memory, a page fault occurs. If that page is in main memory, then the next 10 bits of the virtual address index into the user PTE page to find the PTE for the page that is referenced by the virtual address.

INVERTED PAGE TABLE A drawback of the type of page tables that we have been discussing is that their size is proportional to that of the virtual address space.

An alternative approach to the use of one or multiple-level page tables is the use of an **inverted page table** structure. Variations on this approach are used on the PowerPC, UltraSPARC, and the IA-64 architecture. An implementation of the Mach operating system on the RT-PC also uses this technique.

In this approach, the page number portion of a virtual address is mapped into a hash value using a simple hashing function.[1] The hash value is a pointer to the inverted page table, which contains the page table entries. There is one entry in the inverted page table for each real memory page frame rather than one per virtual page. Thus, a fixed proportion of real memory is required for the tables regardless of the number of processes or virtual pages supported. Because more than one virtual address may map into the same hash table entry, a chaining technique is used for managing the overflow. The hashing technique results in chains that are typically short—between one and two entries. The page table's structure is called *inverted* because it indexes page table entries by frame number rather than by virtual page number.

Figure 8.6 shows a typical implementation of the inverted page table approach. For a physical memory size of 2^m frames, the inverted page table contains 2^m entries, so that the ith entry refers to frame i. Each entry in the page table includes the following:

- **Page number:** This is the page number portion of the virtual address.
- **Process identifier:** The process that owns this page. The combination of page number and process identifier identify a page within the virtual address space of a particular process.
- **Control bits:** This field includes flags, such as valid, referenced, and modified; and protection and locking information.
- **Chain pointer:** This field is null (perhaps indicated by a separate bit) if there are no chained entries for this entry. Otherwise, the field contains the index value (number between 0 and $2^m - 1$) of the next entry in the chain.

In this example, the virtual address includes an n-bit page number, with $n > m$. The hash function maps the n-bit page number into an m-bit quantity, which is used to index into the inverted page table.

TRANSLATION LOOKASIDE BUFFER In principle, every virtual memory reference can cause two physical memory accesses: one to fetch the appropriate page table entry and one to fetch the desired data. Thus, a straightforward virtual memory

---

[1]See Appendix F for a discussion of hashing.

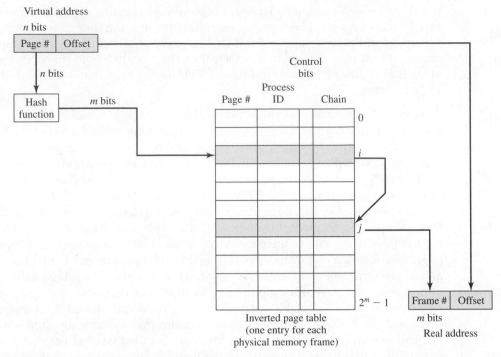

Figure 8.6   Inverted Page Table Structure

scheme would have the effect of doubling the memory access time. To overcome this problem, most virtual memory schemes make use of a special high-speed cache for page table entries, usually called a **translation lookaside buffer (TLB)**. This cache functions in the same way as a memory cache (see Chapter 1) and contains those page table entries that have been most recently used. The organization of the resulting paging hardware is illustrated in Figure 8.7. Given a virtual address, the processor will first examine the TLB. If the desired page table entry is present (*TLB hit*), then the frame number is retrieved and the real address is formed. If the desired page table entry is not found (*TLB miss*), then the processor uses the page number to index the process page table and examine the corresponding page table entry. If the "present bit" is set, then the page is in main memory, and the processor can retrieve the frame number from the page table entry to form the real address. The processor also updates the TLB to include this new page table entry. Finally, if the present bit is not set, then the desired page is not in main memory and a memory access fault, called a **page fault**, is issued. At this point, we leave the realm of hardware and invoke the OS, which loads the needed page and updates the page table.

Figure 8.8 is a flowchart that shows the use of the TLB. The flowchart shows that if the desired page is not in main memory, a page fault interrupt causes the page fault handling routine to be invoked. To keep the flowchart simple, the fact that the OS may dispatch another process while disk I/O is underway is not shown. By the principle of locality, most virtual memory references will be to locations in

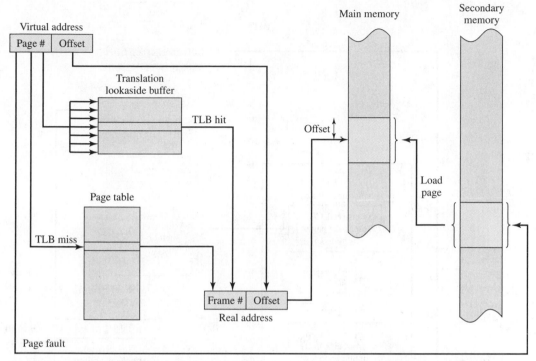

Figure 8.7   Use of a Translation Lookaside Buffer

recently used pages. Therefore, most references will involve page table entries in the cache. Studies of the VAX TLB have shown that this scheme can significantly improve performance [CLAR85, SATY81].

There are a number of additional details concerning the actual organization of the TLB. Because the TLB contains only some of the entries in a full page table, we cannot simply index into the TLB based on page number. Instead, each entry in the TLB must include the page number as well as the complete page table entry. The processor is equipped with hardware that allows it to interrogate simultaneously a number of TLB entries to determine if there is a match on page number. This technique is referred to as **associative mapping** and is contrasted with the direct mapping, or indexing, used for lookup in the page table in Figure 8.9. The design of the TLB also must consider the way in which entries are organized in the TLB and which entry to replace when a new entry is brought in. These issues must be considered in any hardware cache design. This topic is not pursued here; the reader may consult a treatment of cache design for further details (e.g., [STAL10]).

Finally, the virtual memory mechanism must interact with the cache system (not the TLB cache, but the main memory cache). This is illustrated in Figure 8.10. A virtual address will generally be in the form of a page number, offset. First, the memory system consults the TLB to see if the matching page table entry is present. If it is, the real (physical) address is generated by combining the frame number with the offset. If not, the entry is accessed from a page table. Once the real address is

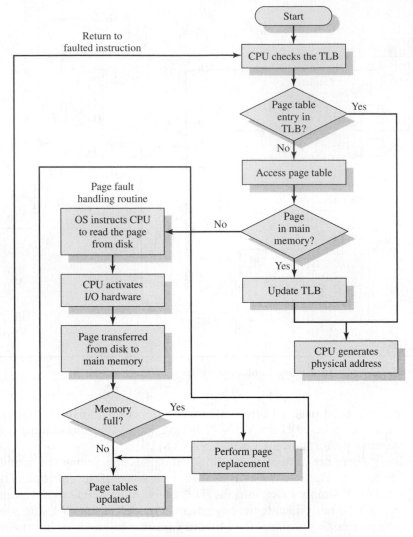

Figure 8.8   Operation of Paging and Translation Lookaside Buffer (TLB)

generated, which is in the form of a tag[2] and a remainder, the cache is consulted to see if the block containing that word is present. If so, it is returned to the CPU. If not, the word is retrieved from main memory.

The reader should be able to appreciate the complexity of the CPU hardware involved in a single memory reference. The virtual address is translated into a real address. This involves reference to a page table entry, which may be in the TLB, in main memory, or on disk. The referenced word may be in cache, main memory, or on disk. If the referenced word is only on disk, the page containing the word must

---

[2]See Figure 1.17. Typically, a tag is just the leftmost bits of the real address. Again, for a more detailed discussion of caches, see [STAL10].

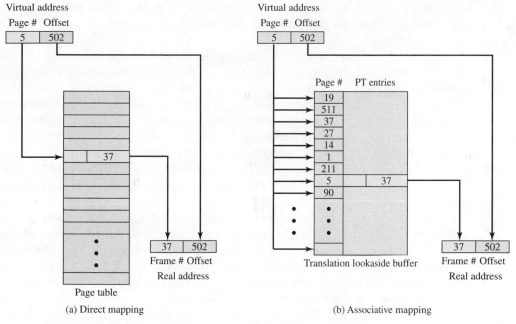

Figure 8.9   Direct versus Associative Lookup for Page Table Entries

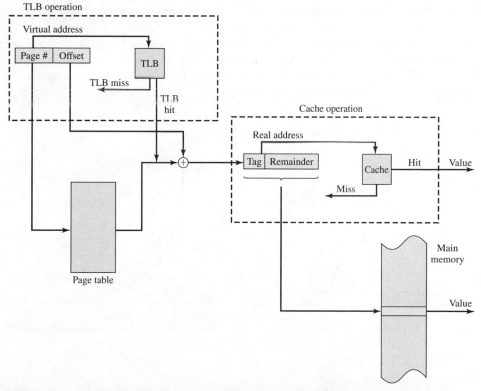

Figure 8.10   Translation Lookaside Buffer and Cache Operation

be loaded into main memory and its block loaded into the cache. In addition, the page table entry for that page must be updated.

PAGE SIZE   An important hardware design decision is the size of page to be used. There are several factors to consider. One is internal fragmentation. Clearly, the smaller the page size, the lesser is the amount of internal fragmentation. To optimize the use of main memory, we would like to reduce internal fragmentation. On the other hand, the smaller the page, the greater is the number of pages required per process. More pages per process means larger page tables. For large programs in a heavily multiprogrammed environment, this may mean that some portion of the page tables of active processes must be in virtual memory, not in main memory. Thus, there may be a double page fault for a single reference to memory: first to bring in the needed portion of the page table and second to bring in the process page. Another factor is that the physical characteristics of most secondary-memory devices, which are rotational, favor a larger page size for more efficient block transfer of data.

Complicating these matters is the effect of page size on the rate at which page faults occur. This behavior, in general terms, is depicted in Figure 8.11a and is based on the principle of locality. If the page size is very small, then ordinarily a relatively large number of pages will be available in main memory for a process. After a time, the pages in memory will all contain portions of the process near recent references. Thus, the page fault rate should be low. As the size of the page is increased, each individual page will contain locations further and further from any particular recent reference. Thus the effect of the principle of locality is weakened and the page fault rate begins to rise. Eventually, however, the page fault rate will begin to fall as the size of a page approaches the size of the entire process (point P in the diagram). When a single page encompasses the entire process, there will be no page faults.

A further complication is that the page fault rate is also determined by the number of frames allocated to a process. Figure 8.11b shows that, for a fixed page

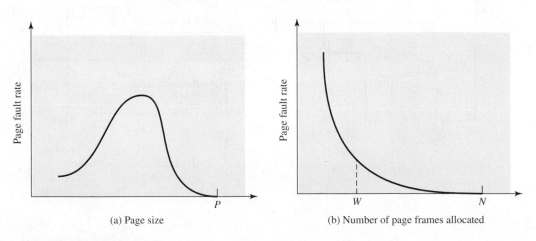

(a) Page size   (b) Number of page frames allocated

P = size of entire process
W = working set size
N = total number of pages in process

Figure 8.11   Typical Paging Behavior of a Program

Table 8.3 Example Page Sizes

Computer	Page Size
Atlas	512 48-bit words
Honeywell-Multics	1,024 36-bit words
IBM 370/XA and 370/ESA	4 Kbytes
VAX family	512 bytes
IBM AS/400	512 bytes
DEC Alpha	8 Kbytes
MIPS	4 Kbytes to 16 Mbytes
UltraSPARC	8 Kbytes to 4 Mbytes
Pentium	4 Kbytes or 4 Mbytes
Intel Itanium	4 Kbytes to 256 Mbytes
Intel core i7	4 Kbytes to 1 Gbyte

size, the fault rate drops as the number of pages maintained in main memory grows.[3] Thus, a software policy (the amount of memory to allocate to each process) interacts with a hardware design decision (page size).

Table 8.3 lists the page sizes used on some machines.

Finally, the design issue of page size is related to the size of physical main memory and program size. At the same time that main memory is getting larger, the address space used by applications is also growing. The trend is most obvious on personal computers and workstations, where applications are becoming increasingly complex. Furthermore, contemporary programming techniques used in large programs tend to decrease the locality of references within a process [HUCK93]. For example,

- Object-oriented techniques encourage the use of many small program and data modules with references scattered over a relatively large number of objects over a relatively short period of time.
- Multithreaded applications may result in abrupt changes in the instruction stream and in scattered memory references.

For a given size of TLB, as the memory size of processes grows and as locality decreases, the hit ratio on TLB accesses declines. Under these circumstances, the TLB can become a performance bottleneck (e.g., see [CHEN92]).

One way to improve TLB performance is to use a larger TLB with more entries. However, TLB size interacts with other aspects of the hardware design, such as the main memory cache and the number of memory accesses per instruction cycle [TALL92]. The upshot is that TLB size is unlikely to grow as rapidly as main memory size. An alternative is to use larger page sizes so that each page table entry in the TLB refers to a larger block of memory. But we have just seen that the use of large page sizes can lead to performance degradation.

---

[3]The parameter *W* represents working set size, a concept discussed in Section 8.2.

Accordingly, a number of designers have investigated the use of multiple page sizes [TALL92, KHAL93], and several microprocessor architectures support multiple pages sizes, including MIPS R4000, Alpha, UltraSPARC, Pentium, and IA-64. Multiple page sizes provide the flexibility needed to use a TLB effectively. For example, large contiguous regions in the address space of a process, such as program instructions, may be mapped using a small number of large pages rather than a large number of small pages, while thread stacks may be mapped using the small page size. However, most commercial operating systems still support only one page size, regardless of the capability of the underlying hardware. The reason for this is that page size affects many aspects of the OS; thus, a change to multiple page sizes is a complex undertaking (see [GANA98] for a discussion).

Segmentation

VIRTUAL MEMORY IMPLICATIONS   Segmentation allows the programmer to view memory as consisting of multiple address spaces or segments. Segments may be of unequal, indeed dynamic, size. Memory references consist of a (segment number, offset) form of address.

This organization has a number of advantages to the programmer over a non-segmented address space:

1. It simplifies the handling of growing data structures. If the programmer does not know ahead of time how large a particular data structure will become, it is necessary to guess unless dynamic segment sizes are allowed. With segmented virtual memory, the data structure can be assigned its own segment, and the OS will expand or shrink the segment as needed. If a segment that needs to be expanded is in main memory and there is insufficient room, the OS may move the segment to a larger area of main memory, if available, or swap it out. In the latter case, the enlarged segment would be swapped back in at the next opportunity.

2. It allows programs to be altered and recompiled independently, without requiring the entire set of programs to be relinked and reloaded. Again, this is accomplished using multiple segments.

3. It lends itself to sharing among processes. A programmer can place a utility program or a useful table of data in a segment that can be referenced by other processes.

4. It lends itself to protection. Because a segment can be constructed to contain a well-defined set of programs or data, the programmer or system administrator can assign access privileges in a convenient fashion.

ORGANIZATION   In the discussion of simple segmentation, we indicated that each process has its own segment table, and when all of its segments are loaded into main memory, the segment table for a process is created and loaded into main memory. Each segment table entry contains the starting address of the corresponding segment in main memory, as well as the length of the segment. The same device, a segment table, is needed when we consider a virtual memory scheme based on segmentation. Again, it is typical to associate a unique segment table with each process. In this case, however, the segment table entries become more complex (Figure 8.2b). Because only some of the segments of a process may be in main memory, a bit is needed in each segment table entry to indicate whether the corresponding segment is present in main memory or not. If the bit indicates that the segment is in memory, then the entry also includes the starting address and length of that segment.

Another control bit in the segmentation table entry is a modify bit, indicating whether the contents of the corresponding segment have been altered since the segment was last loaded into main memory. If there has been no change, then it is not necessary to write the segment out when it comes time to replace the segment in the frame that it currently occupies. Other control bits may also be present. For example, if protection or sharing is managed at the segment level, then bits for that purpose will be required.

The basic mechanism for reading a word from memory involves the translation of a virtual, or logical, address, consisting of segment number and offset, into a physical address, using a segment table. Because the segment table is of variable length, depending on the size of the process, we cannot expect to hold it in registers. Instead, it must be in main memory to be accessed. Figure 8.12 suggests a hardware implementation of this scheme (note similarity to Figure 8.3). When a particular process is running, a register holds the starting address of the segment table for that process. The segment number of a virtual address is used to index that table and look up the corresponding main memory address for the start of the segment. This is added to the offset portion of the virtual address to produce the desired real address.

Combined Paging and Segmentation

Both paging and segmentation have their strengths. Paging, which is transparent to the programmer, eliminates external fragmentation and thus provides efficient use of main memory. In addition, because the pieces that are moved in and out of

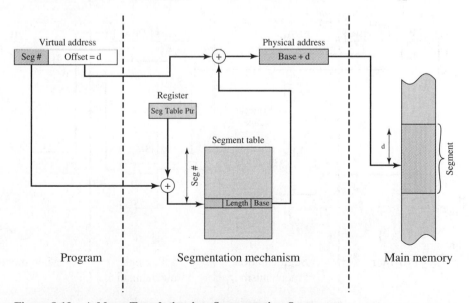

Figure 8.12   Address Translation in a Segmentation System

main memory are of fixed, equal size, it is possible to develop sophisticated memory management algorithms that exploit the behavior of programs, as we shall see. Segmentation, which is visible to the programmer, has the strengths listed earlier, including the ability to handle growing data structures, modularity, and support for sharing and protection. To combine the advantages of both, some systems are equipped with processor hardware and OS software to provide both.

In a combined paging/segmentation system, a user's address space is broken up into a number of segments, at the discretion of the programmer. Each segment is, in turn, broken up into a number of fixed-size pages, which are equal in length to a main memory frame. If a segment has length less than that of a page, the segment occupies just one page. From the programmer's point of view, a logical address still consists of a segment number and a segment offset. From the system's point of view, the segment offset is viewed as a page number and page offset for a page within the specified segment.

Figure 8.13 suggests a structure to support combined paging/segmentation (note similarity to Figure 8.5). Associated with each process is a segment table and a number of page tables, one per process segment. When a particular process is running, a register holds the starting address of the segment table for that process. Presented with a virtual address, the processor uses the segment number portion to index into the process segment table to find the page table for that segment. Then the page number portion of the virtual address is used to index the page table and look up the corresponding frame number. This is combined with the offset portion of the virtual address to produce the desired real address.

Figure 8.2c suggests the segment table entry and page table entry formats. As before, the segment table entry contains the length of the segment. It also contains

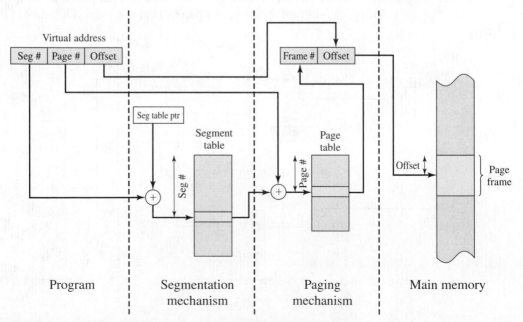

Figure 8.13   Address Translation in a Segmentation/Paging System

a base field, which now refers to a page table. The present and modified bits are not needed because these matters are handled at the page level. Other control bits may be used, for purposes of sharing and protection. The page table entry is essentially the same as is used in a pure paging system. Each page number is mapped into a corresponding frame number if the page is present in main memory. The modified bit indicates whether this page needs to be written back out when the frame is allocated to another page. There may be other control bits dealing with protection or other aspects of memory management.

Protection and Sharing

Segmentation lends itself to the implementation of protection and sharing policies. Because each segment table entry includes a length as well as a base address, a program cannot inadvertently access a main memory location beyond the limits of a segment. To achieve sharing, it is possible for a segment to be referenced in the segment tables of more than one process. The same mechanisms are, of course, available in a paging system. However, in this case the page structure of programs and data is not visible to the programmer, making the specification of protection and sharing requirements more awkward. Figure 8.14 illustrates the types of protection relationships that can be enforced in such a system.

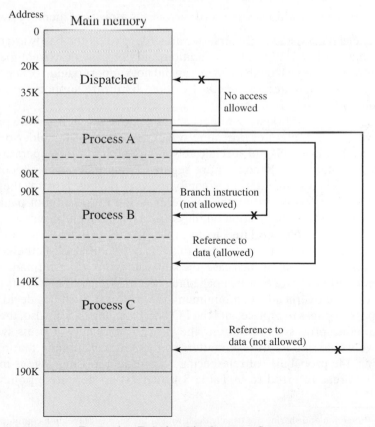

Figure 8.14   Protection Relationships between Segments

More sophisticated mechanisms can also be provided. A common scheme is to use a ring-protection structure, of the type we referred to in Chapter 3 (Figure 3.18). In this scheme, lower-numbered, or inner, rings enjoy greater privilege than higher-numbered, or outer, rings. Typically, ring 0 is reserved for kernel functions of the OS, with applications at a higher level. Some utilities or OS services may occupy an intermediate ring. Basic principles of the ring system are as follows:

1. A program may access only data that reside on the same ring or a less privileged ring.

2. A program may call services residing on the same or a more privileged ring.

8.2 OPERATING SYSTEM SOFTWARE

The design of the memory management portion of an OS depends on three fundamental areas of choice:

- Whether or not to use virtual memory techniques
- The use of paging or segmentation or both
- The algorithms employed for various aspects of memory management

The choices made in the first two areas depend on the hardware platform available. Thus, earlier UNIX implementations did not provide virtual memory because the processors on which the system ran did not support paging or segmentation. Neither of these techniques is practical without hardware support for address translation and other basic functions.

Two additional comments about the first two items in the preceding list: First, with the exception of operating systems for some of the older personal computers, such as MS-DOS, and specialized systems, all important operating systems provide virtual memory. Second, pure segmentation systems are becoming increasingly rare. When segmentation is combined with paging, most of the memory management issues confronting the OS designer are in the area of paging.[4] Thus, we can concentrate in this section on the issues associated with paging.

The choices related to the third item are the domain of operating system software and are the subject of this section. Table 8.4 lists the key design elements that we examine. In each case, the key issue is one of performance: We would like to minimize the rate at which page faults occur, because page faults cause considerable software overhead. At a minimum, the overhead includes deciding which resident page or pages to replace, and the I/O of exchanging pages. Also, the OS must schedule another process to run during the page I/O, causing a process switch. Accordingly, we would like to arrange matters so that, during the time that a process is executing, the probability of referencing a word on a missing page is minimized. In all of the areas referred to in Table 8.4, there is no definitive policy that works best.

---

[4]Protection and sharing are usually dealt with at the segment level in a combined segmentation/paging system. We will deal with these issues in later chapters.

Table 8.4 Operating System Policies for Virtual Memory

Fetch Policy	Resident Set Management
Demand paging	Resident set size
Prepaging	Fixed
	Variable
Placement Policy	Replacement Scope
	Global
Replacement Policy	Local
Basic Algorithms	
Optimal	**Cleaning Policy**
Least recently used (LRU)	Demand
First-in-first-out (FIFO)	Precleaning
Clock	
Page Buffering	**Load Control**
	Degree of multiprogramming

As we shall see, the task of memory management in a paging environment is fiend-ishly complex. Furthermore, the performance of any particular set of policies depends on main memory size, the relative speed of main and secondary memory, the size and number of processes competing for resources, and the execution behavior of indi-vidual programs. This latter characteristic depends on the nature of the application, the programming language and compiler employed, the style of the programmer who wrote it, and, for an interactive program, the dynamic behavior of the user. Thus, the reader must expect no final answers here or anywhere. For smaller systems, the OS designer should attempt to choose a set of policies that seems "good" over a wide range of conditions, based on the current state of knowledge. For larger systems, par-ticularly mainframes, the operating system should be equipped with monitoring and control tools that allow the site manager to tune the operating system to get "good" results based on site conditions.

Fetch Policy

The fetch policy determines when a page should be brought into main memory. The two common alternatives are demand paging and prepaging. With **demand paging**, a page is brought into main memory only when a reference is made to a location on that page. If the other elements of memory management policy are good, the following should happen. When a process is first started, there will be a flurry of page faults. As more and more pages are brought in, the principle of locality suggests that most future references will be to pages that have recently been brought in. Thus, after a time, matters should settle down and the number of page faults should drop to a very low level.

With **prepaging,** pages other than the one demanded by a page fault are brought in. Prepaging exploits the characteristics of most secondary memory devices, such as disks, which have seek times and rotational latency. If the pages of a process are stored contiguously in secondary memory, then it is more efficient to bring in a number of contiguous pages at one time rather than bringing them in one at a time over an extended period. Of course, this policy is ineffective if most of the extra pages that are brought in are not referenced.

The prepaging policy could be employed either when a process first starts up, in which case the programmer would somehow have to designate desired pages, or every time a page fault occurs. This latter course would seem preferable because it is invisible to the programmer. However, the utility of prepaging has not been established [MAEK87].

Prepaging should not be confused with swapping. When a process is swapped out of memory and put in a suspended state, all of its resident pages are moved out. When the process is resumed, all of the pages that were previously in main memory are returned to main memory.

Placement Policy

The placement policy determines where in real memory a process piece is to reside. In a pure segmentation system, the placement policy is an important design issue; policies such as best-fit, first-fit, and so on, which were discussed in Chapter 7, are possible alternatives. However, for a system that uses either pure paging or paging combined with segmentation, placement is usually irrelevant because the address translation hardware and the main memory access hardware can perform their functions for any page-frame combination with equal efficiency.

There is one area in which placement does become a concern, and this is a subject of research and development. On a so-called nonuniform memory access (NUMA) multiprocessor, the distributed, shared memory of the machine can be referenced by any processor on the machine, but the time for accessing a particular physical location varies with the distance between the processor and the memory module. Thus, performance depends heavily on the extent to which data reside close to the processors that use them [LARO92, BOLO89, COX89]. For NUMA systems, an automatic placement strategy is desirable to assign pages to the memory module that provides the best performance.

Replacement Policy

In most operating system texts, the treatment of memory management includes a section entitled "replacement policy," which deals with the selection of a page in main memory to be replaced when a new page must be brought in. This topic is sometimes difficult to explain because several interrelated concepts are involved:

- How many page frames are to be allocated to each active process
- Whether the set of pages to be considered for replacement should be limited to those of the process that caused the page fault or encompass all the page frames in main memory
- Among the set of pages considered, which particular page should be selected for replacement

We shall refer to the first two concepts as *resident set management*, which is dealt with in the next subsection, and reserve the term *replacement policy* for the third concept, which is discussed in this subsection.

The area of replacement policy is probably the most studied of any area of memory management. When all of the frames in main memory are occupied and it is necessary to bring in a new page to satisfy a page fault, the replacement policy determines which page currently in memory is to be replaced. All of the policies have as their objective that the page that is removed should be the page least likely to be referenced in the near future. Because of the principle of locality, there is often a high correlation between recent referencing history and near-future referencing patterns. Thus, most policies try to predict future behavior on the basis of past behavior. One trade-off that must be considered is that the more elaborate and sophisticated the replacement policy, the greater will be the hardware and software overhead to implement it.

FRAME LOCKING   One restriction on replacement policy needs to be mentioned before looking at various algorithms: Some of the frames in main memory may be locked. When a frame is locked, the page currently stored in that frame may not be replaced. Much of the kernel of the OS, as well as key control structures, are held in locked frames. In addition, I/O buffers and other time-critical areas may be locked into main memory frames. Locking is achieved by associating a lock bit with each frame. This bit may be kept in a frame table as well as being included in the current page table.

BASIC ALGORITHMS   Regardless of the resident set management strategy (discussed in the next subsection), there are certain basic algorithms that are used for the selection of a page to replace. Replacement algorithms that have been discussed in the literature include

- Optimal
- Least recently used (LRU)
- First-in-first-out (FIFO)
- Clock

The **optimal** policy selects for replacement that page for which the time to the next reference is the longest. It can be shown that this policy results in the fewest number of page faults [BELA66]. Clearly, this policy is impossible to implement, because it would require the OS to have perfect knowledge of future events. However, it does serve as a standard against which to judge real-world algorithms.

Figure 8.15 gives an example of the optimal policy. The example assumes a fixed frame allocation (fixed resident set size) for this process of three frames. The execution of the process requires reference to five distinct pages. The page address stream formed by executing the program is

$$2 \quad 3 \quad 2 \quad 1 \quad 5 \quad 2 \quad 4 \quad 5 \quad 3 \quad 2 \quad 5 \quad 2$$

which means that the first page referenced is 2, the second page referenced is 3, and so on. The optimal policy produces three page faults after the frame allocation has been filled.

The **least recently used (LRU)** policy replaces the page in memory that has not been referenced for the longest time. By the principle of locality, this should be the page least likely to be referenced in the near future. And, in fact, the LRU policy does nearly as well as the optimal policy. The problem with this approach is the difficulty in implementation. One approach would be to tag each page with the

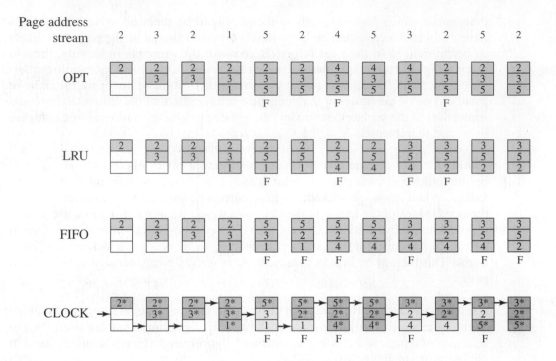

F = page fault occurring after the frame allocation is initially filled

Figure 8.15   Behavior of Four Page Replacement Algorithms

time of its last reference; this would have to be done at each memory reference, both instruction and data. Even if the hardware would support such a scheme, the overhead would be tremendous. Alternatively, one could maintain a stack of page references, again an expensive prospect.

Figure 8.15 shows an example of the behavior of LRU, using the same page address stream as for the optimal policy example. In this example, there are four page faults.

The **first-in-first-out (FIFO)** policy treats the page frames allocated to a process as a circular buffer, and pages are removed in round-robin style. All that is required is a pointer that circles through the page frames of the process. This is therefore one of the simplest page replacement policies to implement. The logic behind this choice, other than its simplicity, is that one is replacing the page that has been in memory the longest: A page fetched into memory a long time ago may have now fallen out of use. This reasoning will often be wrong, because there will often be regions of program or data that are heavily used throughout the life of a program. Those pages will be repeatedly paged in and out by the FIFO algorithm.

Continuing our example in Figure 8.15, the FIFO policy results in six page faults. Note that LRU recognizes that pages 2 and 5 are referenced more frequently than other pages, whereas FIFO does not.

Although the LRU policy does nearly as well as an optimal policy, it is difficult to implement and imposes significant overhead. On the other hand, the FIFO policy is very simple to implement but performs relatively poorly. Over the years, OS designers have tried a number of other algorithms to approximate the perform-ance of LRU while imposing little overhead. Many of these algorithms are variants of a scheme referred to as the **clock policy**.

The simplest form of clock policy requires the association of an additional bit with each frame, referred to as the use bit. When a page is first loaded into a frame in memory, the use bit for that frame is set to 1. Whenever the page is subsequently referenced (after the reference that generated the page fault), its use bit is set to 1. For the page replacement algorithm, the set of frames that are candidates for replacement (this process: local scope; all of main memory: global scope[5]) is considered to be a circular buffer, with which a pointer is associated. When a page is replaced, the pointer is set to indicate the next frame in the buffer after the one just updated. When it comes time to replace a page, the OS scans the buffer to find a frame with a use bit set to 0. Each time it encounters a frame with a use bit of 1, it resets that bit to 0 and continues on. If any of the frames in the buffer have a use bit of 0 at the beginning of this process, the first such frame encountered is chosen for replacement. If all of the frames have a use bit of 1, then the pointer will make one complete cycle through the buffer, setting all the use bits to 0, and stop at its original position, replacing the page in that frame. We can see that this policy is similar to FIFO, except that, in the clock policy, any frame with a use bit of 1 is passed over by the algorithm. The policy is referred to as a clock policy because we can visualize the page frames as laid out in a circle. A number of operating systems have employed some variation of this simple clock policy (e.g., Multics [CORB68]).

Figure 8.16 provides an example of the simple clock policy mechanism. A cir-cular buffer of n main memory frames is available for page replacement. Just prior to the replacement of a page from the buffer with incoming page 727, the next frame pointer points at frame 2, which contains page 45. The clock policy is now executed. Because the use bit for page 45 in frame 2 is equal to 1, this page is not replaced. Instead, the use bit is set to 0 and the pointer advances. Similarly, page 191 in frame 3 is not replaced; its use bit is set to 0 and the pointer advances. In the next frame, frame 4, the use bit is set to 0. Therefore, page 556 is replaced with page 727. The use bit is set to 1 for this frame and the pointer advances to frame 5, completing the page replacement procedure.

The behavior of the clock policy is illustrated in Figure 8.15. The presence of an asterisk indicates that the corresponding use bit is equal to 1, and the arrow indicates the current position of the pointer. Note that the clock policy is adept at protecting frames 2 and 5 from replacement.

Figure 8.17 shows the results of an experiment reported in [BAER80], which compares the four algorithms that we have been discussing; it is assumed that the number of page frames assigned to a process is fixed. The results are based on the execution of 0.25×10^6 references in a FORTRAN program, using a page size of 256 words. Baer ran the experiment with frame allocations of 6, 8, 10, 12, and 14 frames. The differences among the four policies are most striking at small allocations, with

---

[5]The concept of scope is discussed in the subsection "Replacement Scope," subsequently.

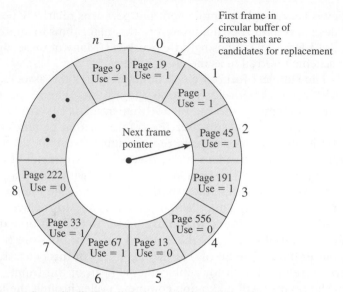

(a) State of buffer just prior to a page replacement

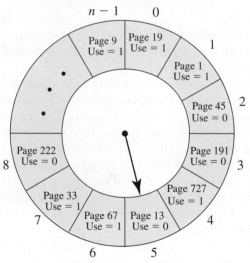

(b) State of buffer just after the next page replacement

Figure 8.16   Example of Clock Policy Operation

FIFO being over a factor of 2 worse than optimal. All four curves have the same shape as the idealized behavior shown in Figure 8.11b. In order to run efficiently, we would like to be to the right of the knee of the curve (with a small page fault rate) while keeping a small frame allocation (to the left of the knee of the curve). These two constraints indicate that a desirable mode of operation would be at the knee of the curve.

   Almost identical results have been reported in [FINK88], again showing a maximum spread of about a factor of 2. Finkel's approach was to simulate the effects of various policies on a synthesized page-reference string of 10,000 references selected

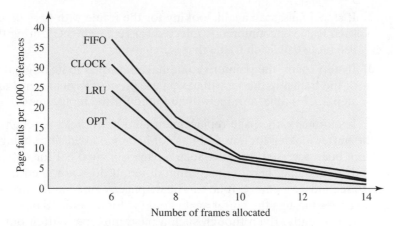

**Figure 8.17 Comparison of Fixed-Allocation, Local Page
Replacement Algorithms**

from a virtual space of 100 pages. To approximate the effects of the principle of
locality, an exponential distribution for the probability of referencing a particular
page was imposed. Finkel observes that some might be led to conclude that there
is little point in elaborate page replacement algorithms when only a factor of 2 is at
stake. But he notes that this difference will have a noticeable effect either on main
memory requirements (to avoid degrading operating system performance) or operating system performance (to avoid enlarging main memory).

The clock algorithm has also been compared to these other algorithms when
a variable allocation and either global or local replacement scope (see the following discussion of replacement policy) is used [CARR81, CARR84]. The clock algorithm was found to approximate closely the performance of LRU.

The clock algorithm can be made more powerful by increasing the number
of bits that it employs.[6] In all processors that support paging, a modify bit is associated with every page in main memory and hence with every frame of main memory.
This bit is needed so that, when a page has been modified, it is not replaced until it
has been written back into secondary memory. We can exploit this bit in the clock
algorithm in the following way. If we take the use and modify bits into account, each
frame falls into one of four categories:

- Not accessed recently, not modified ($u = 0; m = 0$)
- Accessed recently, not modified ($u = 1; m = 0$)
- Not accessed recently, modified ($u = 0; m = 1$)
- Accessed recently, modified ($u = 1; m = 1$)

With this classification, the clock algorithm performs as follows:

1. Beginning at the current position of the pointer, scan the frame buffer. During
   this scan, make no changes to the use bit. The first frame encountered with
   ($u = 0; m = 0$) is selected for replacement.

---

[6]On the other hand, if we reduce the number of bits employed to zero, the clock algorithm degenerates
to FIFO.

2. If step 1 fails, scan again, looking for the frame with ($u = 0$; $m = 1$). The first such frame encountered is selected for replacement. During this scan, set the use bit to 0 on each frame that is bypassed.

3. If step 2 fails, the pointer should have returned to its original position and all of the frames in the set will have a use bit of 0. Repeat step 1 and, if necessary, step 2. This time, a frame will be found for the replacement.

In summary, the page replacement algorithm cycles through all of the pages in the buffer looking for one that has not been modified since being brought in and has not been accessed recently. Such a page is a good bet for replacement and has the advantage that, because it is unmodified, it does not need to be written back out to secondary memory. If no candidate page is found in the first sweep, the algorithm cycles through the buffer again, looking for a modified page that has not been accessed recently. Even though such a page must be written out to be replaced, because of the principle of locality, it may not be needed again anytime soon. If this second pass fails, all of the frames in the buffer are marked as having not been accessed recently and a third sweep is performed.

This strategy was used on an earlier version of the Macintosh virtual memory scheme [GOLD89], illustrated in Figure 8.18. The advantage of this algorithm over

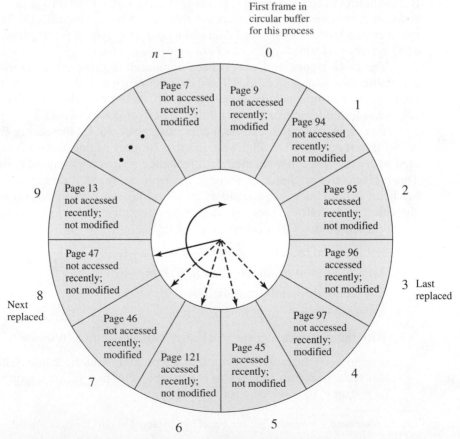

Figure 8.18   The Clock Page Replacement Algorithm [GOLD89]

the simple clock algorithm is that pages that are unchanged are given preference for replacement. Because a page that has been modified must be written out before being replaced, there is an immediate saving of time.

PAGE BUFFERING   Although LRU and the clock policies are superior to FIFO, they both involve complexity and overhead not suffered with FIFO. In addition, there is the related issue that the cost of replacing a page that has been modified is greater than for one that has not, because the former must be written back out to secondary memory.

An interesting strategy that can improve paging performance and allow the use of a simpler page replacement policy is page buffering. The VAX VMS approach is representative. The page replacement algorithm is simple FIFO. To improve performance, a replaced page is not lost but rather is assigned to one of two lists: the free page list if the page has not been modified, or the modified page list if it has. Note that the page is not physically moved about in main memory; instead, the entry in the page table for this page is removed and placed in either the free or modified page list.

The free page list is a list of page frames available for reading in pages. VMS tries to keep some small number of frames free at all times. When a page is to be read in, the page frame at the head of the list is used, destroying the page that was there. When an unmodified page is to be replaced, it remains in memory and its page frame is added to the tail of the free page list. Similarly, when a modified page is to be written out and replaced, its page frame is added to the tail of the modified page list.

The important aspect of these maneuvers is that the page to be replaced remains in memory. Thus if the process references that page, it is returned to the resident set of that process at little cost. In effect, the free and modified page lists act as a cache of pages. The modified page list serves another useful function: Modified pages are written out in clusters rather than one at a time. This significantly reduces the number of I/O operations and therefore the amount of disk access time.

A simpler version of page buffering is implemented in the Mach operating system [RASH88]. In this case, no distinction is made between modified and unmodified pages.

REPLACEMENT POLICY AND CACHE SIZE   As discussed earlier, main memory size is getting larger and the locality of applications is decreasing. In compensation, cache sizes have been increasing. Large cache sizes, even multimegabyte ones, are now feasible design alternatives [BORG90]. With a large cache, the replacement of virtual memory pages can have a performance impact. If the page frame selected for replacement is in the cache, then that cache block is lost as well as the page that it holds.

In systems that use some form of page buffering, it is possible to improve cache performance by supplementing the page replacement policy with a policy for page placement in the page buffer. Most operating systems place pages by selecting an arbitrary page frame from the page buffer; typically a first-in-first-out discipline is used. A study reported in [KESS92] shows that a careful page placement strategy can result in 10–20% fewer cache misses than naive placement.

Several page placement algorithms are examined in [KESS92]. The details are beyond the scope of this book, as they depend on the details of cache structure and policies. The essence of these strategies is to bring consecutive pages into main memory in such a way as to minimize the number of page frames that are mapped into the same cache slots.

Resident Set Management

RESIDENT SET SIZE   With paged virtual memory, it is not necessary and indeed may not be possible to bring all of the pages of a process into main memory to prepare it for execution. Thus, the OS must decide how many pages to bring in, that is, how much main memory to allocate to a particular process. Several factors come into play:

- The smaller the amount of memory allocated to a process, the more processes that can reside in main memory at any one time. This increases the probability that the OS will find at least one ready process at any given time and hence reduces the time lost due to swapping.
- If a relatively small number of pages of a process are in main memory, then, despite the principle of locality, the rate of page faults will be rather high (see Figure 8.11b).
- Beyond a certain size, additional allocation of main memory to a particular process will have no noticeable effect on the page fault rate for that process because of the principle of locality.

With these factors in mind, two sorts of policies are to be found in contemporary operating systems. A **fixed-allocation** policy gives a process a fixed number of frames in main memory within which to execute. That number is decided at initial load time (process creation time) and may be determined based on the type of process (interactive, batch, type of application) or may be based on guidance from the programmer or system manager. With a fixed-allocation policy, whenever a page fault occurs in the execution of a process, one of the pages of that process must be replaced by the needed page.

A **variable-allocation** policy allows the number of page frames allocated to a process to be varied over the lifetime of the process. Ideally, a process that is suffering persistently high levels of page faults, indicating that the principle of locality only holds in a weak form for that process, will be given additional page frames to reduce the page fault rate; whereas a process with an exceptionally low page fault rate, indicating that the process is quite well behaved from a locality point of view, will be given a reduced allocation, with the hope that this will not noticeably increase the page fault rate. The use of a variable-allocation policy relates to the concept of replacement scope, as explained in the next subsection.

The variable-allocation policy would appear to be the more powerful one. However, the difficulty with this approach is that it requires the OS to assess the behavior of active processes. This inevitably requires software overhead in the OS and is dependent on hardware mechanisms provided by the processor platform.

REPLACEMENT SCOPE   The scope of a replacement strategy can be categorized as global or local. Both types of policies are activated by a page fault when there are no free page frames. A **local replacement policy** chooses only among the resident pages of the process that generated the page fault in selecting a page to replace. A **global replacement policy** considers all unlocked pages in main memory as candidates for replacement, regardless of which process owns a particular page. While it happens that local policies are easier to analyze, there is no convincing evidence that they perform better than global policies, which are attractive because of their simplicity of implementation and minimal overhead [CARR84, MAEK87].

There is a correlation between replacement scope and resident set size (Table 8.5). A fixed resident set implies a local replacement policy: To hold the size of a resident set fixed, a page that is removed from main memory must be replaced by another page from the same process. A variable-allocation policy can clearly employ a global replacement policy: The replacement of a page from one process in main memory with that of another causes the allocation of one process to grow by one page and that of the other to shrink by one page. We shall also see that variable allocation and local replacement is a valid combination. We now examine these three combinations.

FIXED ALLOCATION, LOCAL SCOPE   For this case, we have a process that is running in main memory with a fixed number of frames. When a page fault occurs, the OS must choose which page from among the currently resident pages for this process is to be replaced. Replacement algorithms such as those discussed in the preceding subsection can be used.

With a fixed-allocation policy, it is necessary to decide ahead of time the amount of allocation to give to a process. This could be decided on the basis of the type of application and the amount requested by the program. The drawback to this approach is twofold: If allocations tend to be too small, then there will be a high page fault rate, causing the entire multiprogramming system to run slowly. If allocations tend to be unnecessarily large, then there will be too few programs in main memory and there will be either considerable processor idle time or considerable time spent in swapping.

Table 8.5   Resident Set Management

	Local Replacement	Global Replacement
Fixed Allocation	• Number of frames allocated to a process is fixed. • Page to be replaced is chosen from among the frames allocated to that process.	• Not possible.
Variable Allocation	• The number of frames allocated to a process may be changed from time to time to maintain the working set of the process. • Page to be replaced is chosen from among the frames allocated to that process.	• Page to be replaced is chosen from all available frames in main memory; this causes the size of the resident set of processes to vary.

VARIABLE ALLOCATION, GLOBAL SCOPE   This combination is perhaps the easiest to implement and has been adopted in a number of operating systems. At any given time, there are a number of processes in main memory, each with a certain number of frames allocated to it. Typically, the OS also maintains a list of free frames. When a page fault occurs, a free frame is added to the resident set of a process and the page is brought in. Thus, a process experiencing page faults will gradually grow in size, which should help reduce overall page faults in the system.

The difficulty with this approach is in the replacement choice. When there are no free frames available, the OS must choose a page currently in memory to replace. The selection is made from among all of the frames in memory, except for locked frames such as those of the kernel. Using any of the policies discussed in the preceding subsection, the page selected for replacement can belong to any of the resident processes; there is no discipline to determine which process should lose a page from its resident set. Therefore, the process that suffers the reduction in resident set size may not be optimum.

One way to counter the potential performance problems of a variable-allocation, global-scope policy is to use page buffering. In this way, the choice of which page to replace becomes less significant, because the page may be reclaimed if it is referenced before the next time that a block of pages are overwritten.

VARIABLE ALLOCATION, LOCAL SCOPE   The variable-allocation, local-scope strategy attempts to overcome the problems with a global-scope strategy. It can be summarized as follows:

1. When a new process is loaded into main memory, allocate to it a certain number of page frames as its resident set, based on application type, program request, or other criteria. Use either prepaging or demand paging to fill up the allocation.

2. When a page fault occurs, select the page to replace from among the resident set of the process that suffers the fault.

3. From time to time, reevaluate the allocation provided to the process, and increase or decrease it to improve overall performance.

With this strategy, the decision to increase or decrease a resident set size is a deliberate one and is based on an assessment of the likely future demands of active processes. Because of this evaluation, such a strategy is more complex than a simple global replacement policy. However, it may yield better performance.

The key elements of the variable-allocation, local-scope strategy are the criteria used to determine resident set size and the timing of changes. One specific strategy that has received much attention in the literature is known as the **working set strategy.** Although a true working set strategy would be difficult to implement, it is useful to examine it as a baseline for comparison.

The working set is a concept introduced and popularized by Denning [DENN68, DENN70, DENN80b]; it has had a profound impact on virtual memory management design. The working set with parameter Δ for a process at virtual time t, which we designate as $W(t, \Delta)$, is the set of pages of that process that have been referenced in the last Δ virtual time units.

Sequence of Page References W	Window Size, Δ			
	2	3	4	5
24	24	24	24	24
15	24 15	24 15	24 15	24 15
18	15 18	24 15 18	24 15 18	24 15 18
23	18 23	15 18 23	24 15 18 23	24 15 18 23
24	23 24	18 23 24	•	•
17	24 17	23 24 17	18 23 24 17	15 18 23 24 17
18	17 18	24 17 18	•	18 23 24 17
24	18 24	•	24 17 18	•
18	•	18 24	•	24 17 18
17	18 17	24 18 17	•	•
17	17	18 17	•	•
15	17 15	17 15	18 17 15	24 18 17 15
24	15 24	17 15 24	17 15 24	•
17	24 17	•	•	17 15 24
24	•	24 17	•	•
18	24 18	17 24 18	17 24 18	15 17 24 18

Figure 8.19   Working Set of Process as Defined by Window Size

Virtual time is defined as follows. Consider a sequence of memory references, $r(1)$, $r(2)$, ..., in which $r(i)$ is the page that contains the ith virtual address generated by a given process. Time is measured in memory references; thus $t = 1, 2, 3, \ldots$ measures the process's internal virtual time.

Let us consider each of the two variables of W. The variable Δ is a window of virtual time over which the process is observed. The working set size will be a nondecreasing function of the window size. The result is illustrated in Figure 8.19 (based on [BACH86]), which shows a sequence of page references for a process. The dots indicate time units in which the working set does not change. Note that the larger the window size, the larger is the working set. This can be expressed in the following relationship:

$$W(t,\Delta + 1) \supseteq W(t,\Delta)$$

The working set is also a function of time. If a process executes over Δ time units and uses only a single page, then $|W(t,\Delta)| = 1$. A working set can also grow as large as the number of pages N of the process if many different pages are rapidly addressed and if the window size allows. Thus,

$$1 \leq |W(t,\Delta)| \leq \min(\Delta,N)$$

Figure 8.20 indicates the way in which the working set size can vary over time for a fixed value of Δ. For many programs, periods of relatively stable working set

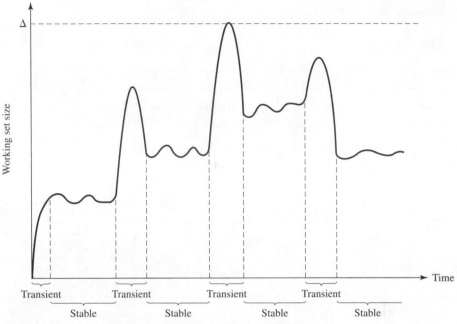

Figure 8.20   Typical Graph of Working Set Size [MAEK87]

sizes alternate with periods of rapid change. When a process first begins executing, it gradually builds up to a working set as it references new pages. Eventually, by the principle of locality, the process should stabilize on a certain set of pages. Subsequent transient periods reflect a shift of the program to a new locality. During the transition phase, some of the pages from the old locality remain within the window, Δ, causing a surge in the size of the working set as new pages are referenced. As the window slides past these page references, the working set size declines until it contains only those pages from the new locality.

This concept of a working set can be used to guide a strategy for resident set size:

1. Monitor the working set of each process.

2. Periodically remove from the resident set of a process those pages that are not in its working set. This is essentially an LRU policy.

3. A process may execute only if its working set is in main memory (i.e., if its resident set includes its working set).

This strategy is appealing because it takes an accepted principle, the principle of locality, and exploits it to achieve a memory management strategy that should minimize page faults. Unfortunately, there are a number of problems with the working set strategy:

1. The past does not always predict the future. Both the size and the membership of the working set will change over time (e.g., see Figure 8.20).

2. A true measurement of working set for each process is impractical. It would be necessary to time-stamp every page reference for every process using the

virtual time of that process and then maintain a time-ordered queue of pages for each process.

3. The optimal value of Δ is unknown and in any case would vary.

Nevertheless, the spirit of this strategy is valid, and a number of operating systems attempt to approximate a working set strategy. One way to do this is to focus not on the exact page references but on the page fault rate of a process. As Figure 8.11b illustrates, the page fault rate falls as we increase the resident set size of a process. The working set size should fall at a point on this curve such as indicated by W in the figure. Therefore, rather than monitor the working set size directly, we can achieve comparable results by monitoring the page fault rate. The line of reasoning is as follows: If the page fault rate for a process is below some minimum threshold, the system as a whole can benefit by assigning a smaller resident set size to this process (because more page frames are available for other processes) without harming the process (by causing it to incur increased page faults). If the page fault rate for a process is above some maximum threshold, the process can benefit from an increased resident set size (by incurring fewer faults) without degrading the system.

An algorithm that follows this strategy is the **page fault frequency (PFF)** algorithm [CHU72, GUPT78]. It requires a use bit to be associated with each page in memory. The bit is set to 1 when that page is accessed. When a page fault occurs, the OS notes the virtual time since the last page fault for that process; this could be done by maintaining a counter of page references. A threshold F is defined. If the amount of time since the last page fault is less than F, then a page is added to the resident set of the process. Otherwise, discard all pages with a use bit of 0, and shrink the resident set accordingly. At the same time, reset the use bit on the remaining pages of the process to 0. The strategy can be refined by using two thresholds: an upper threshold that is used to trigger a growth in the resident set size, and a lower threshold that is used to trigger a contraction in the resident set size.

The time between page faults is the reciprocal of the page fault rate. Although it would seem to be better to maintain a running average of the page fault rate, the use of a single time measurement is a reasonable compromise that allows decisions about resident set size to be based on the page fault rate. If such a strategy is supplemented with page buffering, the resulting performance should be quite good.

Nevertheless, there is a major flaw in the PFF approach, which is that it does not perform well during the transient periods when there is a shift to a new locality. With PFF, no page ever drops out of the resident set before F virtual time units have elapsed since it was last referenced. During interlocality transitions, the rapid succession of page faults causes the resident set of a process to swell before the pages of the old locality are expelled; the sudden peaks of memory demand may produce unnecessary process deactivations and reactivations, with the corresponding undesirable switching and swapping overheads.

An approach that attempts to deal with the phenomenon of interlocality transition with a similar relatively low overhead to that of PFF is the **variable-interval sampled working set (VSWS)** policy [FERR83]. The VSWS policy evaluates the working set of a process at sampling instances based on elapsed virtual time. At the beginning of a sampling interval, the use bits of all the resident pages for the process are reset; at the end, only the pages that have been referenced during the interval will have their use bit set; these pages are retained in the resident set of the process throughout the next interval, while the others are discarded. Thus the resident set size can only decrease at the end of an interval. During each interval, any faulted pages are added to the resident set; thus the resident set remains fixed or grows during the interval.

The VSWS policy is driven by three parameters:

M: The minimum duration of the sampling interval

L: The maximum duration of the sampling interval

Q: The number of page faults that are allowed to occur between sampling instances

The VSWS policy is as follows:

1. If the virtual time since the last sampling instance reaches L, then suspend the process and scan the use bits.

2. If, prior to an elapsed virtual time of L, Q page faults occur,
   a. If the virtual time since the last sampling instance is less than M, then wait until the elapsed virtual time reaches M to suspend the process and scan the use bits.
   b. If the virtual time since the last sampling instance is greater than or equal to M, suspend the process and scan the use bits.

The parameter values are to be selected so that the sampling will normally be triggered by the occurrence of the Qth page fault after the last scan (case 2b). The other two parameters (M and L) provide boundary protection for exceptional conditions. The VSWS policy tries to reduce the peak memory demands caused by abrupt interlocality transitions by increasing the sampling frequency, and hence the rate at which unused pages drop out of the resident set, when the page fault rate increases. Experience with this technique in the Bull mainframe operating system, GCOS 8, indicates that this approach is as simple to implement as PFF and more effective [PIZZ89].

Cleaning Policy

A cleaning policy is the opposite of a fetch policy; it is concerned with determining when a modified page should be written out to secondary memory. Two common alternatives are demand cleaning and precleaning. With **demand cleaning**, a page is written out to secondary memory only when it has been selected for replacement. A **precleaning** policy writes modified pages before their page frames are needed so that pages can be written out in batches.

There is a danger in following either policy to the full. With precleaning, a page is written out but remains in main memory until the page replacement algorithm dictates that it be removed. Precleaning allows the writing of pages in batches, but it makes little sense to write out hundreds or thousands of pages only to find that the majority of them have been modified again before they are replaced. The transfer capacity of secondary memory is limited and should not be wasted with unnecessary cleaning operations.

On the other hand, with demand cleaning, the writing of a dirty page is coupled to, and precedes, the reading in of a new page. This technique may minimize page writes, but it means that a process that suffers a page fault may have to wait for two page transfers before it can be unblocked. This may decrease processor utilization.

A better approach incorporates page buffering. This allows the adoption of the following policy: Clean only pages that are replaceable, but decouple the cleaning and replacement operations. With page buffering, replaced pages can be placed on two lists: modified and unmodified. The pages on the modified list can periodically be written out in batches and moved to the unmodified list. A page on the unmodified list is either reclaimed if it is referenced or lost when its frame is assigned to another page.

Load Control

Load control is concerned with determining the number of processes that will be resident in main memory, which has been referred to as the multiprogramming level. The load control policy is critical in effective memory management. If too few processes are resident at any one time, then there will be many occasions when all processes are blocked, and much time will be spent in swapping. On the other hand, if too many processes are resident, then, on average, the size of the resident set of each process will be inadequate and frequent faulting will occur. The result is thrashing.

MULTIPROGRAMMING LEVEL Thrashing is illustrated in Figure 8.21. As the multiprogramming level increases from a small value, one would expect to see processor utilization rise, because there is less chance that all resident processes are blocked. However, a point is reached at which the average resident set is inadequate. At this point, the number of page faults rises dramatically, and processor utilization collapses.

There are a number of ways to approach this problem. A working set or PFF algorithm implicitly incorporates load control. Only those processes whose resident set is sufficiently large are allowed to execute. In providing the required resident set

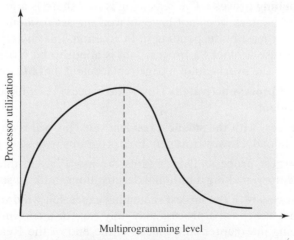

Figure 8.21   **Multiprogramming Effects**

size for each active process, the policy automatically and dynamically determines the number of active programs.

Another approach, suggested by Denning and his colleagues [DENN80b], is known as the *L = S criterion*, which adjusts the multiprogramming level so that the mean time between faults equals the mean time required to process a page fault. Performance studies indicate that this is the point at which processor utilization attained a maximum. A policy with a similar effect, proposed in [LERO76], is the *50% criterion*, which attempts to keep utilization of the paging device at approximately 50%. Again, performance studies indicate that this is a point of maximum processor utilization.

Another approach is to adapt the clock page replacement algorithm described earlier (Figure 8.16). [CARR84] describes a technique, using a global scope, that involves monitoring the rate at which the pointer scans the circular buffer of frames. If the rate is below a given lower threshold, this indicates one or both of two circumstances:

1. Few page faults are occurring, resulting in few requests to advance the pointer.
2. For each request, the average number of frames scanned by the pointer is small, indicating that there are many resident pages not being referenced and are readily replaceable.

In both cases, the multiprogramming level can safely be increased. On the other hand, if the pointer scan rate exceeds an upper threshold, this indicates either a high fault rate or difficulty in locating replaceable pages, which implies that the multiprogramming level is too high.

PROCESS SUSPENSION   If the degree of multiprogramming is to be reduced, one or more of the currently resident processes must be suspended (swapped out). [CARR84] lists six possibilities:

- **Lowest-priority process:** This implements a scheduling policy decision and is unrelated to performance issues.
- **Faulting process:** The reasoning is that there is a greater probability that the faulting task does not have its working set resident, and performance would suffer least by suspending it. In addition, this choice has an immediate payoff because it blocks a process that is about to be blocked anyway and it eliminates the overhead of a page replacement and I/O operation.
- **Last process activated:** This is the process least likely to have its working set resident.
- **Process with the smallest resident set:** This will require the least future effort to reload. However, it penalizes programs with strong locality.
- **Largest process:** This obtains the most free frames in an overcommitted memory, making additional deactivations unlikely soon.
- **Process with the largest remaining execution window:** In most process scheduling schemes, a process may only run for a certain quantum of time before being interrupted and placed at the end of the Ready queue. This approximates a shortest-processing-time-first scheduling discipline.

As in so many other areas of OS design, which policy to choose is a matter of judgment and depends on many other design factors in the OS as well as the characteristics of the programs being executed.

8.3   UNIX AND SOLARIS MEMORY MANAGEMENT

Because UNIX is intended to be machine independent, its memory management scheme will vary from one system to the next. Earlier versions of UNIX simply used variable partitioning with no virtual memory scheme. Current implementations of UNIX and Solaris make use of paged virtual memory.

In SVR4 and Solaris, there are actually two separate memory management schemes. The **paging system** provides a virtual memory capability that allocates page frames in main memory to processes and also allocates page frames to disk block buffers. Although this is an effective memory management scheme for user processes and disk I/O, a paged virtual memory scheme is less suited to managing the memory allocation for the kernel. For this latter purpose, a **kernel memory allocator** is used. We examine these two mechanisms in turn.

Paging System

DATA STRUCTURES   For paged virtual memory, UNIX makes use of a number of data structures that, with minor adjustment, are machine independent (Figure 8.22 and Table 8.6):

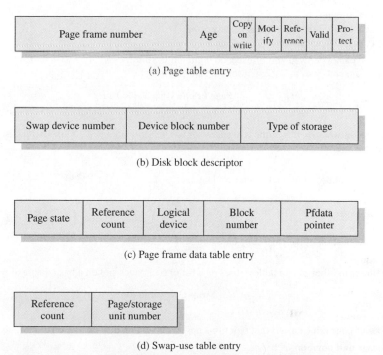

(a) Page table entry

(b) Disk block descriptor

(c) Page frame data table entry

(d) Swap-use table entry

Figure 8.22   UNIX SVR4 Memory Management Formats

Table 8.6   UNIX SVR4 Memory Management Parameters

Page Table Entry

Page frame number
Refers to frame in real memory.

Age
Indicates how long the page has been in memory without being referenced. The length and contents of this field are processor dependent.

Copy on write
Set when more than one process shares a page. If one of the processes writes into the page, a separate copy of the page must first be made for all other processes that share the page. This feature allows the copy operation to be deferred until necessary and avoided in cases where it turns out not to be necessary.

Modify
Indicates page has been modified.

Reference
Indicates page has been referenced. This bit is set to 0 when the page is first loaded and may be periodically reset by the page replacement algorithm.

Valid
Indicates page is in main memory.

Protect
Indicates whether write operation is allowed.

Disk Block Descriptor

Swap device number
Logical device number of the secondary device that holds the corresponding page. This allows more than one device to be used for swapping.

Device block number
Block location of page on swap device.

Type of storage
Storage may be swap unit or executable file. In the latter case, there is an indication as to whether the virtual memory to be allocated should be cleared first.

Page Frame Data Table Entry

Page state
Indicates whether this frame is available or has an associated page. In the latter case, the status of the page is specified: on swap device, in executable file, or DMA in progress.

Reference count
Number of processes that reference the page.

Logical device
Logical device that contains a copy of the page.

Block number
Block location of the page copy on the logical device.

Pfdata pointer
Pointer to other pfdata table entries on a list of free pages and on a hash queue of pages.

Swap-Use Table Entry

Reference count
Number of page table entries that point to a page on the swap device.

Page/storage unit number
Page identifier on storage unit.

- **Page table:** Typically, there will be one page table per process, with one entry for each page in virtual memory for that process.

- **Disk block descriptor:** Associated with each page of a process is an entry in this table that describes the disk copy of the virtual page.

- **Page frame data table:** Describes each frame of real memory and is indexed by frame number. This table is used by the replacement algorithm.

- **Swap-use table:** There is one swap-use table for each swap device, with one entry for each page on the device.

Most of the fields defined in Table 8.6 are self-explanatory. A few warrant further comment. The Age field in the page table entry is an indication of how long it has been since a program referenced this frame. However, the number of bits and the frequency of update of this field are implementation dependent. Therefore, there is no universal UNIX use of this field for page replacement policy.

The Type of Storage field in the disk block descriptor is needed for the following reason: When an executable file is first used to create a new process, only a portion of the program and data for that file may be loaded into real memory. Later, as page faults occur, new portions of the program and data are loaded. It is only at the time of first loading that virtual memory pages are created and assigned to locations on one of the devices to be used for swapping. At that time, the OS is told whether it needs to clear (set to 0) the locations in the page frame before the first loading of a block of the program or data.

PAGE REPLACEMENT   The page frame data table is used for page replacement. Several pointers are used to create lists within this table. All of the available frames are linked together in a list of free frames available for bringing in pages. When the number of available frames drops below a certain threshold, the kernel will steal a number of frames to compensate.

The page replacement algorithm used in SVR4 is a refinement of the clock policy algorithm (Figure 8.16) known as the two-handed clock algorithm (Figure 8.23). The algorithm uses the reference bit in the page table entry for each page in memory that is eligible (not locked) to be swapped out. This bit is set to 0 when the page is first brought in and set to 1 when the page is referenced for a read or write. One hand in the clock algorithm, the fronthand, sweeps through the pages on the list of eligible pages and sets the reference bit to 0 on each page. Sometime later, the backhand sweeps through the same list and checks the reference bit. If the bit is set to 1, then that page has been referenced since the fronthand swept by; these frames are ignored. If the bit is still set to 0, then the page has not been referenced in the time interval between the visit by fronthand and backhand; these pages are placed on a list to be paged out.

Two parameters determine the operation of the algorithm:

- **Scanrate:** The rate at which the two hands scan through the page list, in pages per second

- **Handspread:** The gap between fronthand and backhand

These two parameters have default values set at boot time based on the amount of physical memory. The scanrate parameter can be altered to meet changing

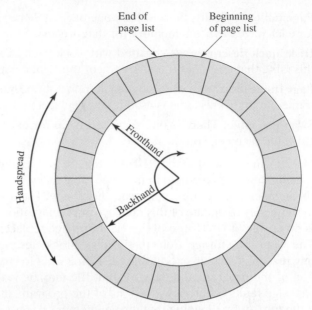

Figure 8.23   Two-Handed Clock Page Replacement Algorithm

conditions. The parameter varies linearly between the values slowscan and fastscan (set at configuration time) as the amount of free memory varies between the values *lotsfree* and *minfree*. In other words, as the amount of free memory shrinks, the clock hands move more rapidly to free up more pages. The handspread parameter determines the gap between the fronthand and the backhand and therefore, together with scanrate, determines the window of opportunity to use a page before it is swapped out due to lack of use.

Kernel Memory Allocator

The kernel generates and destroys small tables and buffers frequently during the course of execution, each of which requires dynamic memory allocation. [VAHA96] lists the following examples:

- The pathname translation routing may allocate a buffer to copy a pathname from user space.
- The `allocb()` routine allocates STREAMS buffers of arbitrary size.
- Many UNIX implementations allocate zombie structures to retain exit status and resource usage information about deceased processes.
- In SVR4 and Solaris, the kernel allocates many objects (such as proc structures, vnodes, and file descriptor blocks) dynamically when needed.

Most of these blocks are significantly smaller than the typical machine page size, and therefore the paging mechanism would be inefficient for dynamic kernel memory allocation. For SVR4, a modification of the buddy system, described in Section 7.2, is used.

In buddy systems, the cost to allocate and free a block of memory is low compared to that of best-fit or first-fit policies [KNUT97]. However, in the case of kernel memory management, the allocation and free operations must be made as fast as possible. The drawback of the buddy system is the time required to fragment and coalesce blocks.

Barkley and Lee at AT&T proposed a variation known as a lazy buddy system [BARK89], and this is the technique adopted for SVR4. The authors observed that UNIX often exhibits steady-state behavior in kernel memory demand; that is, the amount of demand for blocks of a particular size varies slowly in time. Therefore, if a block of size 2^i is released and is immediately coalesced with its buddy into a block of size 2^{i+1}, the kernel may next request a block of size 2^i, which may necessitate splitting the larger block again. To avoid this unnecessary coalescing and splitting, the lazy buddy system defers coalescing until it seems likely that it is needed, and then coalesces as many blocks as possible.

The lazy buddy system uses the following parameters:

N_i = current number of blocks of size 2^i.

A_i = current number of blocks of size 2^i that are allocated (occupied).

G_i = current number of blocks of size 2^i that are globally free; these are blocks that are eligible for coalescing; if the buddy of such a block becomes globally free, then the two blocks will be coalesced into a globally free block of size 2^{i+1}. All free blocks (holes) in the standard buddy system could be considered globally free.

L_i = current number of blocks of size 2^i that are locally free; these are blocks that are not eligible for coalescing. Even if the buddy of such a block becomes free, the two blocks are not coalesced. Rather, the locally free blocks are retained in anticipation of future demand for a block of that size.

The following relationship holds:

$$N_i = A_i + G_i + L_i$$

In general, the lazy buddy system tries to maintain a pool of locally free blocks and only invokes coalescing if the number of locally free blocks exceeds a threshold. If there are too many locally free blocks, then there is a chance that there will be a lack of free blocks at the next level to satisfy demand. Most of the time, when a block is freed, coalescing does not occur, so there is minimal bookkeeping and operational costs. When a block is to be allocated, no distinction is made between locally and globally free blocks; again, this minimizes bookkeeping.

The criterion used for coalescing is that the number of locally free blocks of a given size should not exceed the number of allocated blocks of that size (i.e., we must have $L_i \leq A_i$). This is a reasonable guideline for restricting the growth of locally free blocks, and experiments in [BARK89] confirm that this scheme results in noticeable savings.

To implement the scheme, the authors define a delay variable as follows:

$$D_i = A_i - L_i = N_i - 2L_i - G_i$$

Figure 8.24 shows the algorithm.

Initial value of D_i is 0
After an operation, the value of D_i is updated as follows

(I) if the next operation is a block allocate request:
    if there is any free block, select one to allocate
       if the selected block is locally free
          then $D_i := D_i + 2$
          else $D_i := D_i + 1$
    otherwise
       first get two blocks by splitting a larger one into two (recursive operation)
       allocate one and mark the other locally free
       D_i remains unchanged (but D may change for other block sizes because
            of the recursive call)

(II) if the next operation is a block free request
    Case $D_i \geqslant 2$
      mark it locally free and free it locally
      $D_i = 2$
    Case $D_i = 1$
      mark it globally free and free it globally; coalesce if possible
      $D_i = 0$
    Case $D_i = 0$
      mark it globally free and free it globally; coalesce if possible
      select one locally free block of size 2^i and free it globally; coalesce if possible
      $D_i := 0$

Figure 8.24 Lazy Buddy System Algorithm

8.4 LINUX MEMORY MANAGEMENT

Linux shares many of the characteristics of the memory management schemes of other UNIX implementations but has its own unique features. Overall, the Linux memory management scheme is quite complex [DUBE98]. In this section, we give a brief overview of the two main aspects of Linux memory management: process virtual memory and kernel memory allocation.

Linux Virtual Memory

VIRTUAL MEMORY ADDRESSING Linux makes use of a three-level page table structure, consisting of the following types of tables (each individual table is the size of one page):

- **Page directory:** An active process has a single page directory that is the size of one page. Each entry in the page directory points to one page of the page middle directory. The page directory must be in main memory for an active process.

- **Page middle directory:** The page middle directory may span multiple pages. Each entry in the page middle directory points to one page in the page table.
- **Page table:** The page table may also span multiple pages. Each page table entry refers to one virtual page of the process.

To use this three-level page table structure, a virtual address in Linux is viewed as consisting of four fields (Figure 8.25). The leftmost (most significant) field is used as an index into the page directory. The next field serves as an index into the page middle directory. The third field serves as an index into the page table. The fourth field gives the offset within the selected page of memory.

The Linux page table structure is platform independent and was designed to accommodate the 64-bit Alpha processor, which provides hardware support for three levels of paging. With 64-bit addresses, the use of only two levels of pages on the Alpha would result in very large page tables and directories. The 32-bit Pentium/x86 architecture has a two-level hardware paging mechanism. The Linux software accommodates the two-level scheme by defining the size of the page middle directory as one. Note that all references to an extra level of indirection are optimized away at compile time, not at run time. Therefore, there is no performance overhead for using generic three-level design on platforms which support only two levels in hardware.

PAGE ALLOCATION   To enhance the efficiency of reading in and writing out pages to and from main memory, Linux defines a mechanism for dealing with contiguous blocks of pages mapped into contiguous blocks of page frames. For this purpose, the buddy system is used. The kernel maintains a list of contiguous page frame groups of fixed size; a group may consist of 1, 2, 4, 8, 16, or 32 page frames. As pages

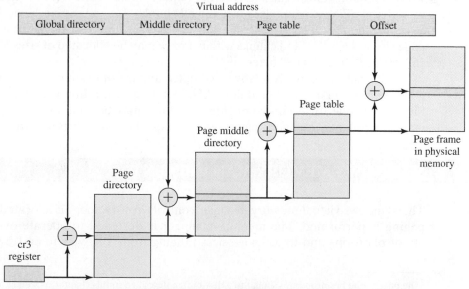

Figure 8.25   Address Translation in Linux Virtual Memory Scheme

are allocated and deallocated in main memory, the available groups are split and merged using the buddy algorithm.

PAGE REPLACEMENT ALGORITHM   The Linux page replacement algorithm is based on the clock algorithm described in Section 8.2 (see Figure 8.16). In the simple clock algorithm, a use bit and a modify bit are associated with each page in main memory. In the Linux scheme, the use bit is replaced with an 8-bit age variable. Each time that a page is accessed, the age variable is incremented. In the background, Linux periodically sweeps through the global page pool and decrements the age variable for each page as it rotates through all the pages in main memory. A page with an age of 0 is an "old" page that has not been referenced in some time and is the best candidate for replacement. The larger the value of age, the more frequently a page has been used in recent times and the less eligible it is for replacement. Thus, the Linux algorithm is a form of least frequently used policy.

Kernel Memory Allocation

The Linux kernel memory capability manages physical main memory page frames. Its primary function is to allocate and deallocate frames for particular uses. Possible owners of a frame include user-space processes (i.e., the frame is part of the virtual memory of a process that is currently resident in real memory), dynamically allocated kernel data, static kernel code, and the page cache.[7]

The foundation of kernel memory allocation for Linux is the page allocation mechanism used for user virtual memory management. As in the virtual memory scheme, a buddy algorithm is used so that memory for the kernel can be allocated and deallocated in units of one or more pages. Because the minimum amount of memory that can be allocated in this fashion is one page, the page allocator alone would be inefficient because the kernel requires small short-term memory chunks in odd sizes. To accommodate these small chunks, Linux uses a scheme known as *slab allocation* [BONW94] within an allocated page. On a Pentium/x86 machine, the page size is 4 Kbytes, and chunks within a page may be allocated of sizes 32, 64, 128, 252, 508, 2,040, and 4,080 bytes.

The slab allocator is relatively complex and is not examined in detail here; a good description can be found in [VAHA96]. In essence, Linux maintains a set of linked lists, one for each size of chunk. Chunks may be split and aggregated in a manner similar to the buddy algorithm and moved between lists accordingly.

8.5   WINDOWS MEMORY MANAGEMENT

The Windows virtual memory manager controls how memory is allocated and how paging is performed. The memory manager is designed to operate over a variety of platforms and to use page sizes ranging from 4 Kbytes to 64 Kbytes. Intel

---

[7]The page cache has properties similar to a disk buffer, described in this chapter, as well as a disk cache, described in Chapter 11. We defer a discussion of the Linux page cache to Chapter 11.

and AMD64 platforms have 4 Kbytes per page and Intel Itanium platforms have 8 Kbytes per page.

Windows Virtual Address Map

On 32-bit platforms, each Windows user process sees a separate 32-bit address space, allowing 4 Gbytes of virtual memory per process. By default, half of this memory is reserved for the OS, so each user actually has 2 Gbytes of available virtual address space and all processes share most of the upper 2 Gbytes of system space when running in kernel-mode. Large memory intensive applications, on both clients and servers, can run more effectively using 64-bit Windows. Other than netbooks, most modern PCs use the AMD64 processor architecture which is capable of running as either a 32-bit or 64-bit system.

Figure 8.26 shows the default virtual address space seen by a normal 32-bit user process. It consists of four regions:

- **0x00000000 to 0x0000FFFF**: Set aside to help programmers catch NULL-pointer assignments.
- **0x00010000 to 0x7FFEFFFF**: Available user address space. This space is divided into pages that may be loaded into main memory.

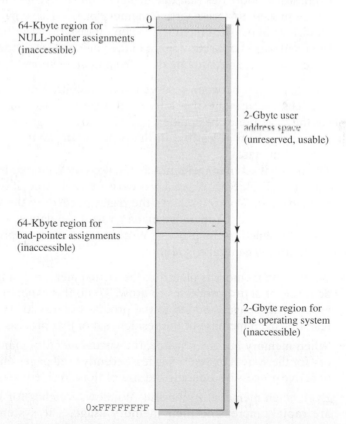

Figure 8.26   Windows Default 32-Bit Virtual Address Space

- **0x7FFF0000 to 0x7FFFFFFF**: A guard page inaccessible to the user. This page makes it easier for the OS to check on out-of-bounds pointer references.
- **0x80000000 to 0xFFFFFFFF**: System address space. This 2-Gbyte process is used for the Windows Executive, Kernel, HAL, and device drivers.
- On 64-bit platforms, 8 Tbytes of user address space is available in Windows 7.

Windows Paging

When a process is created, it can in principle make use of the entire user space of almost 2 Gbytes (or 8 Tbytes on 64-bit Windows). This space is divided into fixed-size pages, any of which can be brought into main memory, but the OS manages the addresses in contiguous regions allocated on 64-Kbyte boundaries. A region can be in one of three states:

- **Available:** addresses not currently used by this process.
- **Reserved:** addresses that the virtual memory manager has set aside for a process so they cannot be allocated to another use (e.g., saving contiguous space for a stack to grow).
- **Committed:** addresses that the virtual memory manager has initialized for use by the process to access virtual memory pages. These pages can reside either on disk or in physical memory. When on disk they can be either kept in files (mapped pages) or occupy space in the paging file (i.e., the disk file to which it writes pages when removing them from main memory).

The distinction between reserved and committed memory is useful because it (1) reduces the amount of total virtual memory space needed by the system, allowing the page file to be smaller; and (2) allows programs to reserve addresses without making them accessible to the program or having them charged against their resource quotas.

The resident set management scheme used by Windows is variable allocation, local scope (see Table 8.5). When a process is first activated, it is assigned data structures to manage its working set. As the pages needed by the process are brought into physical memory the memory manager uses the data structures to keep track of the pages assigned to the process. Working sets of active processes are adjusted using the following general conventions:

- When main memory is plentiful, the virtual memory manager allows the resident sets of active processes to grow. To do this, when a page fault occurs, a new physical page is added to the process but no older page is swapped out, resulting in an increase of the resident set of that process by one page.
- When memory becomes scarce, the virtual memory manager recovers memory for the system by removing less recently used pages out of the working sets of active processes, reducing the size of those resident sets.
- Even when memory is plentiful, Windows watches for large processes that are rapidly increasing their memory usage. The system begins to remove

pages that have not been recently used from the process. This policy makes the system more responsive because a new program will not suddenly cause a scarcity of memory and make the user wait while the system tries to reduce the resident sets of the processes that are already running.

8.6 SUMMARY

To use the processor and the I/O facilities efficiently, it is desirable to maintain as many processes in main memory as possible. In addition, it is desirable to free programmers from size restrictions in program development.

The way to address both of these concerns is virtual memory. With virtual memory, all address references are logical references that are translated at run time to real addresses. This allows a process to be located anywhere in main memory and for that location to change over time. Virtual memory also allows a process to be broken up into pieces. These pieces need not be contiguously located in main memory during execution and, indeed, it is not even necessary for all of the pieces of the process to be in main memory during execution.

Two basic approaches to providing virtual memory are paging and segmentation. With paging, each process is divided into relatively small, fixed-size pages. Segmentation provides for the use of pieces of varying size. It is also possible to combine segmentation and paging in a single memory management scheme.

A virtual memory management scheme requires both hardware and software support. The hardware support is provided by the processor. The support includes dynamic translation of virtual addresses to physical addresses and the generation of an interrupt when a referenced page or segment is not in main memory. Such an interrupt triggers the memory management software in the OS.

A number of design issues relate to OS support for memory management:

- **Fetch policy:** Process pages can be brought in on demand, or a prepaging policy can be used, which clusters the input activity by bringing in a number of pages at once.
- **Placement policy:** With a pure segmentation system, an incoming segment must be fit into an available space in memory.
- **Replacement policy:** When memory is full, a decision must be made as to which page or pages are to be replaced.
- **Resident set management:** The OS must decide how much main memory to allocate to a particular process when that process is swapped in. This can be a static allocation made at process creation time, or it can change dynamically.
- **Cleaning policy:** Modified process pages can be written out at the time of replacement, or a precleaning policy can be used, which clusters the output activity by writing out a number of pages at once.
- **Load control:** Load control is concerned with determining the number of processes that will be resident in main memory at any given time.

8.7 RECOMMENDED READING AND WEB SITES

As might be expected, virtual memory receives good coverage in most books on operating systems. [MILE92] provides a good summary of various research areas. [CARR84] provides an excellent in-depth examination of performance issues. The classic paper [DENN70] is still well worth a read. [DOWD93] provides an instructive performance analysis of various page replacement algorithms. [JACO98a] is a good survey of issues in virtual memory design; it includes a discussion of inverted page tables. [JACO98b] looks at virtual memory hardware organizations in various microprocessors.

It is a sobering experience to read [IBM86], which gives a detailed account of the tools and options available to a site manager in optimizing the virtual memory policies of MVS. The document illustrates the complexity of the problem.

[VAHA96] is one of the best treatments of the memory management schemes used in the various flavors of UNIX. [GORM04] is a thorough treatment of Linux memory management.

CARR84 Carr, R. *Virtual Memory Management.* Ann Arbor, MI: UMI Research Press, 1984.

DENN70 Denning, P. "Virtual Memory." *Computing Surveys*, September 1970.

DOWD93 Dowdy, L., and Lowery, C. *P.S. to Operating Systems.* Upper Saddle River, NJ: Prentice Hall, 1993.

GORM04 Gorman, M. *Understanding the Linux Virtual Memory Manager.* Upper Saddle River, NJ: Prentice Hall, 2004.

IBM86 IBM National Technical Support, Large Systems. *Multiple Virtual Storage (MVS) Virtual Storage Tuning Cookbook.* Dallas Systems Center Technical Bulletin G320-0597, June 1986.

JACO98a Jacob, B., and Mudge, T. "Virtual Memory: Issues of Implementation." *Computer*, June 1998.

JACO98b Jacob, B., and Mudge, T. "Virtual Memory in Contemporary Microprocessors." *IEEE Micro*, August 1998.

MILE92 Milenkovic, M. *Operating Systems: Concepts and Design.* New York: McGraw-Hill, 1992.

VAHA96 Vahalia, U. *UNIX Internals: The New Frontiers.* Upper Saddle River, NJ: Prentice Hall, 1996.

Recommended Web site:

- **The Memory Management Reference:** A good source of documents and links on all aspects of memory management.

8.8   KEY TERMS, REVIEW QUESTIONS, AND PROBLEMS

Key Terms

associative mapping	page	resident set management
demand paging	page fault	segment
external fragmentation	page placement policy	segment table
fetch policy	page replacement policy	segmentation
frame	page table	slab allocation
hash table	paging	thrashing
hashing	prepaging	translation lookaside buffer
internal fragmentation	real memory	virtual memory
locality	resident set	working set

Review Questions

8.1 What is the difference between simple paging and virtual memory paging?

8.2 Explain thrashing.

8.3 Why is the principle of locality crucial to the use of virtual memory?

8.4 What elements are typically found in a page table entry? Briefly define each element.

8.5 What is the purpose of a translation lookaside buffer?

8.6 Briefly define the alternative page fetch policies.

8.7 What is the difference between resident set management and page replacement policy?

8.8 What is the relationship between FIFO and clock page replacement algorithms?

8.9 What is accomplished by page buffering?

8.10 Why is it not possible to combine a global replacement policy and a fixed allocation policy?

8.11 What is the difference between a resident set and a working set?

8.12 What is the difference between demand cleaning and precleaning?

Problems

8.1 Suppose the page table for the process currently executing on the processor looks like the following. All numbers are decimal, everything is numbered starting from zero, and all addresses are memory byte addresses. The page size is 1,024 bytes.

Virtual page number	Valid bit	Reference bit	Modify bit	Page frame number
0	1	1	0	4
1	1	1	1	7
2	0	0	0	—
3	1	0	0	2
4	0	0	0	—
5	1	0	1	0

    a. Describe exactly how, in general, a virtual address generated by the CPU is translated into a physical main memory address.

    b. What physical address, if any, would each of the following virtual addresses correspond to? (Do not try to handle any page faults, if any.)

        (i) 1,052

        (ii) 2,221

        (iii) 5,499

8.2 Consider the following program.

```
#define Size 64
int A[Size; Size], B[Size; Size], C[Size; Size];
int register i, j;

for (j = 0; j< Size; j ++)
   for (i = 0; i< Size; i++)
C[i; j] = A[i; j] + B[i; j];
```

Assume that the program is running on a system using demand paging and the page size is 1 Kilobyte. Each integer is 4 bytes long. It is clear that each array requires a 16-page space. As an example, A[0, 0]-A[0, 63], A[1, 0]-A[1, 63], A[2, 0]-A[2, 63], and A[3, 0]-A[3, 63] will be stored in the first data page. A similar storage pattern can be derived for the rest of array A and for arrays B and C. Assume that the system allocates a 4-page working set for this process. One of the pages will be used by the program and three pages can be used for the data. Also, two index registers are assigned for i and j (so, no memory accesses are needed for references to these two variables).

    a. Discuss how frequently the page fault would occur (in terms of number of times C[i, j] = A[i, j] + B[i, j] are executed).

    b. Can you modify the program to minimize the page fault frequency?

    c. What will be the frequency of page faults after your modification?

8.3   **a.** How much memory space is needed for the user page table of Figure 8.4?

    b. Assume you want to implement a hashed inverted page table for the same addressing scheme as depicted in Figure 8.4, using a hash function that maps the 20-bit page number into a 6-bit hash value. The table entry contains the page number, the frame number, and a chain pointer. If the page table allocates space for up to 3 overflow entries per hashed entry, how much memory space does the hashed inverted page table take?

8.4 Consider the following string of page references 7, 0, 1, 2, 0, 3, 0, 4, 2, 3, 0, 3, 2. Complete a figure similar to Figure 8.15, showing the frame allocation for:

    a. FIFO (first-in-first-out)

    b. LRU (least recently used)

    c. Clock

    d. Optimal (assume the page reference string continues with 1, 2, 0, 1, 7, 0, 1)

    e. List the total number of page faults and the miss rate for each policy. Count page faults only after all frames have been initialized.

8.5 A process references five pages, A, B, C, D, and E, in the following order:

$$A; B; C; D; A; B; E; A; B; C; D; E$$

Assume that the replacement algorithm is first-in-first-out and find the number of page transfers during this sequence of references starting with an empty main memory with three page frames. Repeat for four page frames.

8.6 A process contains eight virtual pages on disk and is assigned a fixed allocation of four page frames in main memory. The following page trace occurs:

$$1, 0, 2, 2, 1, 7, 6, 7, 0, 1, 2, 0, 3, 0, 4, 5, 1, 5, 2, 4, 5, 6, 7, 6, 7, 2, 4, 2, 7, 3, 3, 2, 3$$

    a. Show the successive pages residing in the four frames using the LRU replacement policy. Compute the hit ratio in main memory. Assume that the frames are initially empty.

    b. Repeat part (a) for the FIFO replacement policy.

    c. Compare the two hit ratios and comment on the effectiveness of using FIFO to approximate LRU with respect to this particular trace.

8.7 In the VAX, user page tables are located at virtual addresses in the system space. What is the advantage of having user page tables in virtual rather than main memory? What is the disadvantage?

8.8 Suppose the program statement

```
for (i = 1; i <= n; i ++)
        a[i] = b[i] + c[i];
```

is executed in a memory with page size of 1,000 words. Let $n = 1,000$. Using a machine that has a full range of register-to-register instructions and employs index registers, write a hypothetical program to implement the foregoing statement. Then show the sequence of page references during execution.

8.9 The IBM System/370 architecture uses a two-level memory structure and refers to the two levels as segments and pages, although the segmentation approach lacks many of the features described earlier in this chapter. For the basic 370 architecture, the page size may be either 2 Kbytes or 4 Kbytes, and the segment size is fixed at either 64 Kbytes or 1 Mbyte. For the 370/XA and 370/ESA architectures, the page size is 4 Kbytes and the segment size is 1 Mbyte. Which advantages of segmentation does this scheme lack? What is the benefit of segmentation for the 370?

8.10 Assuming a page size of 4 Kbytes and that a page table entry takes 4 bytes, how many levels of page tables would be required to map a 64-bit address space, if the top level page table fits into a single page?

8.11 Consider a system with memory mapping done on a page basis and using a single-level page table. Assume that the necessary page table is always in memory.

    a. If a memory reference takes 200 ns, how long does a paged memory reference take?

    b. Now we add an MMU that imposes an overhead of 20 ns on a hit or a miss. If we assume that 85% of all memory references hit in the MMU TLB, what is the Effective Memory Access Time (EMAT)?

    c. Explain how the TLB hit rate affects the EMAT.

8.12 Consider a page reference string for a process with a working set of M frames, initially all empty. The page reference string is of length P with N distinct page numbers in it. For any page replacement algorithm,

    a. What is a lower bound on the number of page faults?

    b. What is an upper bound on the number of page faults?

8.13 In discussing a page replacement algorithm, one author makes an analogy with a snowplow moving around a circular track. Snow is falling uniformly on the track and a lone snowplow continually circles the track at constant speed. The snow that is plowed w the track disappears from the system.

    a. For which of the page replacement algorithms discussed in Section 8.2 is this a useful analogy?

    b. What does this analogy suggest about the behavior of the page replacement algorithm in question?

8.14 In the S/370 architecture, a storage key is a control field associated with each page-sized frame of real memory. Two bits of that key that are relevant for page replacement are the reference bit and the change bit. The reference bit is set to 1 when any address within the frame is accessed for read or write, and is set to 0 when a new page is loaded into the frame. The change bit is set to 1 when a write operation is performed on any location within the frame. Suggest an approach for determining which page frames are least-recently-used, making use of only the reference bit.

8.15 Consider the following sequence of page references (each element in the sequence represents a page number):

$$1\ 2\ 3\ 4\ 5\ 2\ 1\ 3\ 3\ 2\ 3\ 4\ 5\ 4\ 5\ 1\ 1\ 3\ 2\ 5$$

Define the *mean working set size* after the kth reference as $s_k(\Delta) = \dfrac{1}{k}\sum_{t=1}^{k}|W(t,\Delta)|$

and define the *missing page probability* after the kth reference as $m_k(\Delta) = \dfrac{1}{k}\sum_{t=1}^{k}F(t,\Delta)$

where $F(t, \Delta) = 1$ if a page fault occurs at virtual time t and 0 otherwise.

a. Draw a diagram similar to that of Figure 8.19 for the reference sequence just defined for the values $\Delta = 1, 2, 3, 4, 5, 6$.
b. Plot $s_{20}(\Delta)$ as a function of Δ.
c. Plot $m_{20}(\Delta)$ as a function of Δ.

8.16 A key to the performance of the VSWS resident set management policy is the value of Q. Experience has shown that, with a fixed value of Q for a process, there are considerable differences in page fault frequencies at various stages of execution. Furthermore, if a single value of Q is used for different processes, dramatically different frequencies of page faults occur. These differences strongly indicate that a mechanism that would dynamically adjust the value of Q during the lifetime of a process would improve the behavior of the algorithm. Suggest a simple mechanism for this purpose.

8.17 Assume that a task is divided into four equal-sized segments and that the system builds an eight-entry page descriptor table for each segment. Thus, the system has a combination of segmentation and paging. Assume also that the page size is 2 Kbytes.

a. What is the maximum size of each segment?
b. What is the maximum logical address space for the task?
c. Assume that an element in physical location 00021ABC is accessed by this task. What is the format of the logical address that the task generates for it? What is the maximum physical address space for the system?

8.18 Consider a paged logical address space (composed of 32 pages of 2 Kbytes each) mapped into a 1-Mbyte physical memory space.

a. What is the format of the processor's logical address?
b. What is the length and width of the page table (disregarding the "access rights" bits)?
c. What is the effect on the page table if the physical memory space is reduced by half?

8.19 The UNIX kernel will dynamically grow a process's stack in virtual memory as needed, but it will never try to shrink it. Consider the case in which a program calls a C subroutine that allocates a local array on the stack that consumes 10 K. The kernel will expand the stack segment to accommodate it. When the subroutine returns, the stack pointer is adjusted and this space could be released by the kernel, but it is not released. Explain why it would be possible to shrink the stack at this point and why the UNIX kernel does not shrink it.

PART 4 Scheduling

CHAPTER 9

UNIPROCESSOR SCHEDULING

9.1 Types of Processor Scheduling
Long-Term Scheduling
Medium-Term Scheduling
Short-Term Scheduling

9.2 Scheduling Algorithms
Short-Term Scheduling Criteria
The Use of Priorities
Alternative Scheduling Policies
Performance Comparison
Fair-Share Scheduling

9.3 Traditional UNIX Scheduling

9.4 Summary

9.5 Recommended Reading

9.6 Key Terms, Review Questions, and Problems

I take a two hour nap, from one o'clock to four.

— YOGI BERRA

LEARNING OBJECTIVES

After studying this chapter, you should be able to:

- Explain the differences among long-, medium-, and short-term scheduling.
- Assess the performance of different scheduling policies.
- Understand the scheduling technique used in traditional UNIX.

In a multiprogramming system, multiple processes exist concurrently in main memory. Each process alternates between using a processor and waiting for some event to occur, such as the completion of an I/O operation. The processor or processors are kept busy by executing one process while the others wait.

The key to multiprogramming is scheduling. In fact, four types of scheduling are typically involved (Table 9.1). One of these, I/O scheduling, is more conveniently addressed in Chapter 11, where I/O is discussed. The remaining three types of scheduling, which are types of processor scheduling, are addressed in this chapter and the next.

This chapter begins with an examination of the three types of processor scheduling, showing how they are related. We see that long-term scheduling and medium-term scheduling are driven primarily by performance concerns related to the degree of multiprogramming. These issues are dealt with to some extent in Chapter 3 and in more detail in Chapters 7 and 8. Thus, the remainder of this chapter concentrates on short-term scheduling and is limited to a consideration of scheduling on a uniprocessor system. Because the use of multiple processors adds additional complexity, it is best to focus on the uniprocessor case first, so that the differences among scheduling algorithms can be clearly seen.

Section 9.2 looks at the various algorithms that may be used to make short-term scheduling decisions. A set of animations that illustrate concepts in this chapter is available online. Click on the rotating globe at WilliamStallings.com/OS/OS7e.html for access.

Table 9.1 Types of Scheduling

Long-term scheduling	The decision to add to the pool of processes to be executed
Medium-term scheduling	The decision to add to the number of processes that are partially or fully in main memory
Short-term scheduling	The decision as to which available process will be executed by the processor
I/O scheduling	The decision as to which process's pending I/O request shall be handled by an available I/O device

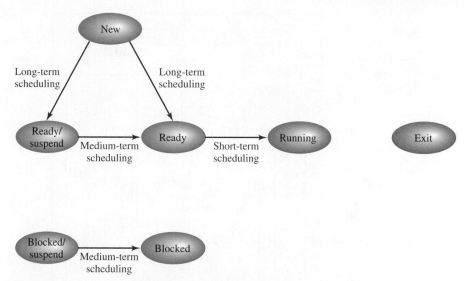

Figure 9.1   Scheduling and Process State Transitions

9.1   TYPES OF PROCESSOR SCHEDULING

The aim of processor scheduling is to assign processes to be executed by the processor or processors over time, in a way that meets system objectives, such as response time, throughput, and processor efficiency. In many systems, this scheduling activity is broken down into three separate functions: long-, medium-, and short-term scheduling. The names suggest the relative time scales with which these functions are performed.

Figure 9.1 relates the scheduling functions to the process state transition diagram (first shown in Figure 3.9b). Long-term scheduling is performed when a new process is created. This is a decision whether to add a new process to the set of processes that are currently active. Medium-term scheduling is a part of the swapping function. This is a decision whether to add a process to those that are at least partially in main memory and therefore available for execution. Short-term scheduling is the actual decision of which ready process to execute next. Figure 9.2 reorganizes the state transition diagram of Figure 3.9b to suggest the nesting of scheduling functions.

Scheduling affects the performance of the system because it determines which processes will wait and which will progress. This point of view is presented in Figure 9.3, which shows the queues involved in the state transitions of a process.[1] Fundamentally, scheduling is a matter of managing queues to minimize queueing delay and to optimize performance in a queueing environment.

Long-Term Scheduling

The long-term scheduler determines which programs are admitted to the system for processing. Thus, it controls the degree of multiprogramming. Once admitted, a job

---

[1]For simplicity, Figure 9.3 shows new processes going directly to the Ready state, whereas Figures 9.1 and 9.2 show the option of either the Ready state or the Ready/Suspend state.

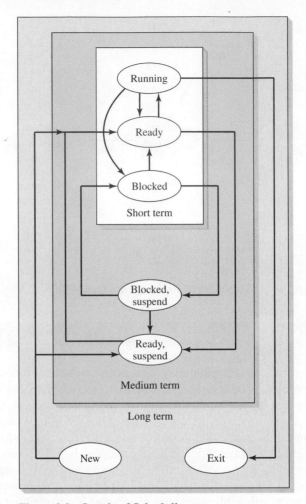

Figure 9.2   Levels of Scheduling

or user program becomes a process and is added to the queue for the short-term scheduler. In some systems, a newly created process begins in a swapped-out condition, in which case it is added to a queue for the medium-term scheduler.

In a batch system, or for the batch portion of an OS, newly submitted jobs are routed to disk and held in a batch queue. The long-term scheduler creates processes from the queue when it can. There are two decisions involved. The scheduler must decide when the OS can take on one or more additional processes. And the scheduler must decide which job or jobs to accept and turn into processes. We briefly consider these two decisions.

The decision as to when to create a new process is generally driven by the desired degree of multiprogramming. The more processes that are created, the smaller is the percentage of time that each process can be executed (i.e., more processes are competing for the same amount of processor time). Thus, the long-term scheduler may limit the degree of multiprogramming to provide satisfactory service

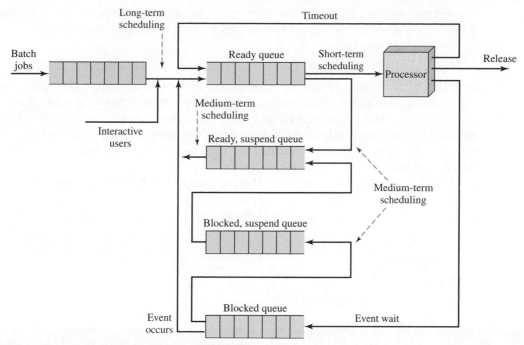

Figure 9.3   Queueing Diagram for Scheduling

to the current set of processes. Each time a job terminates, the scheduler may decide to add one or more new jobs. Additionally, if the fraction of time that the processor is idle exceeds a certain threshold, the long-term scheduler may be invoked.

The decision as to which job to admit next can be on a simple first-come-first-served (FCFS) basis, or it can be a tool to manage system performance. The criteria used may include priority, expected execution time, and I/O requirements. For example, if the information is available, the scheduler may attempt to keep a mix of processor-bound and I/O-bound processes.[2] Also, the decision can depend on which I/O resources are to be requested, in an attempt to balance I/O usage.

For interactive programs in a time-sharing system, a process creation request can be generated by the act of a user attempting to connect to the system. Time-sharing users are not simply queued up and kept waiting until the system can accept them. Rather, the OS will accept all authorized comers until the system is saturated, using some predefined measure of saturation. At that point, a connection request is met with a message indicating that the system is full and the user should try again later.

Medium–Term Scheduling

Medium-term scheduling is part of the swapping function. The issues involved are discussed in Chapters 3, 7, and 8. Typically, the swapping-in decision is based on the need to manage the degree of multiprogramming. On a system that does not

---

[2]A process is regarded as *processor bound* if it mainly performs computational work and occasionally uses I/O devices. A process is regarded as *I/O bound* if the time it takes to execute the process depends primarily on the time spent waiting for I/O operations.

use virtual memory, memory management is also an issue. Thus, the swapping-in decision will consider the memory requirements of the swapped-out processes.

Short-Term Scheduling

In terms of frequency of execution, the long-term scheduler executes relatively infrequently and makes the coarse-grained decision of whether or not to take on a new process and which one to take. The medium-term scheduler is executed somewhat more frequently to make a swapping decision. The short-term scheduler, also known as the dispatcher, executes most frequently and makes the fine-grained decision of which process to execute next.

The short-term scheduler is invoked whenever an event occurs that may lead to the blocking of the current process or that may provide an opportunity to preempt a currently running process in favor of another. Examples of such events include:

- Clock interrupts
- I/O interrupts
- Operating system calls
- Signals (e.g., semaphores)

9.2 SCHEDULING ALGORITHMS

Short-Term Scheduling Criteria

The main objective of short-term scheduling is to allocate processor time in such a way as to optimize one or more aspects of system behavior. Generally, a set of criteria is established against which various scheduling policies may be evaluated.

The commonly used criteria can be categorized along two dimensions. First, we can make a distinction between user-oriented and system-oriented criteria. User-oriented criteria relate to the behavior of the system as perceived by the individual user or process. An example is response time in an interactive system. Response time is the elapsed time between the submission of a request until the response begins to appear as output. This quantity is visible to the user and is naturally of interest to the user. We would like a scheduling policy that provides "good" service to various users. In the case of response time, a threshold may be defined, say two seconds. Then a goal of the scheduling mechanism should be to maximize the number of users who experience an average response time of two seconds or less.

Other criteria are system oriented. That is, the focus is on effective and efficient utilization of the processor. An example is throughput, which is the rate at which processes are completed. This is certainly a worthwhile measure of system performance and one that we would like to maximize. However, it focuses on system performance rather than service provided to the user. Thus, throughput is of concern to a system administrator but not to the user population.

Whereas user-oriented criteria are important on virtually all systems, system-oriented criteria are generally of minor importance on single-user systems. On a single-user system, it probably is not important to achieve high processor utilization or high throughput as long as the responsiveness of the system to user applications is acceptable.

Another dimension along which criteria can be classified is those that are performance related and those that are not directly performance related. Performance-related criteria are quantitative and generally can be readily measured. Examples include response time and throughput. Criteria that are not performance related are either qualitative in nature or do not lend themselves readily to measurement and analysis. An example of such a criterion is predictability. We would like for the service provided to users to exhibit the same characteristics over time, independent of other work being performed by the system. To some extent, this criterion can be measured by calculating variances as a function of workload. However, this is not nearly as straightforward as measuring throughput or response time as a function of workload.

Table 9.2 summarizes key scheduling criteria. These are interdependent, and it is impossible to optimize all of them simultaneously. For example, providing good

Table 9.2   Scheduling Criteria

User Oriented, Performance Related

Turnaround time   This is the interval of time between the submission of a process and its completion. Includes actual execution time plus time spent waiting for resources, including the processor. This is an appropriate measure for a batch job.

Response time   For an interactive process, this is the time from the submission of a request until the response begins to be received. Often a process can begin producing some output to the user while continuing to process the request. Thus, this is a better measure than turnaround time from the user's point of view. The scheduling discipline should attempt to achieve low response time and to maximize the number of interactive users receiving acceptable response time.

Deadlines   When process completion deadlines can be specified, the scheduling discipline should subordinate other goals to that of maximizing the percentage of deadlines met.

User Oriented, Other

Predictability   A given job should run in about the same amount of time and at about the same cost regardless of the load on the system. A wide variation in response time or turnaround time is distracting to users. It may signal a wide swing in system workloads or the need for system tuning to cure instabilities.

System Oriented, Performance Related

Throughput   The scheduling policy should attempt to maximize the number of processes completed per unit of time. This is a measure of how much work is being performed. This clearly depends on the average length of a process but is also influenced by the scheduling policy, which may affect utilization.

Processor utilization   This is the percentage of time that the processor is busy. For an expensive shared system, this is a significant criterion. In single-user systems and in some other systems, such as real-time systems, this criterion is less important than some of the others.

System Oriented, Other

Fairness   In the absence of guidance from the user or other system-supplied guidance, processes should be treated the same, and no process should suffer starvation.

Enforcing priorities   When processes are assigned priorities, the scheduling policy should favor higher-priority processes.

Balancing resources   The scheduling policy should keep the resources of the system busy. Processes that will underutilize stressed resources should be favored. This criterion also involves medium-term and long-term scheduling.

response time may require a scheduling algorithm that switches between processes frequently. This increases the overhead of the system, reducing throughput. Thus, the design of a scheduling policy involves compromising among competing requirements; the relative weights given the various requirements will depend on the nature and intended use of the system.

In most interactive operating systems, whether single user or time shared, adequate response time is the critical requirement. Because of the importance of this requirement, and because the definition of adequacy will vary from one application to another, the topic is explored further in Appendix G.

The Use of Priorities

In many systems, each process is assigned a priority and the scheduler will always choose a process of higher priority over one of lower priority. Figure 9.4 illustrates the use of priorities. For clarity, the queueing diagram is simplified, ignoring the existence of multiple blocked queues and of suspended states (compare Figure 3.8a). Instead of a single ready queue, we provide a set of queues, in descending order of priority: RQ0, RQ1, . . . , RQn, with priority[RQi] > priority[RQj] for $i > j$.[3] When a scheduling selection is to be made, the scheduler will start at the highest-priority ready queue (RQ0). If there are one or more processes in the queue, a process is selected using some scheduling policy. If RQ0 is empty, then RQ1 is examined, and so on.

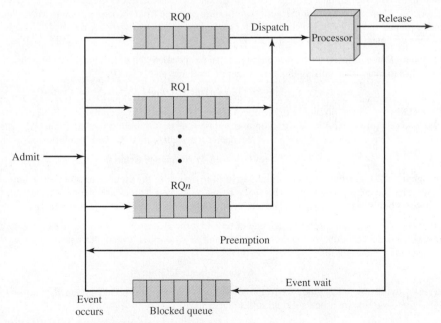

Figure 9.4   Priority Queueing

[3]In UNIX and many other systems, larger priority values represent lower priority processes; unless otherwise stated we follow that convention. Some systems, such as Windows, use the opposite convention: a higher number means a higher priority.

One problem with a pure priority scheduling scheme is that lower-priority processes may suffer starvation. This will happen if there is always a steady supply of higher-priority ready processes. If this behavior is not desirable, the priority of a process can change with its age or execution history. We will give one example of this subsequently.

Alternative Scheduling Policies

Table 9.3 presents some summary information about the various scheduling policies that are examined in this subsection. The **selection function** determines which process, among ready processes, is selected next for execution. The function may be based on priority, resource requirements, or the execution characteristics of the process. In the latter case, three quantities are significant:

w = time spent in system so far, waiting

e = time spent in execution so far

s = total service time required by the process, including e; generally, this quantity must be estimated or supplied by the user

For example, the selection function max[w] indicates an FCFS discipline.

Table 9.3 Characteristics of Various Scheduling Policies

	FCFS	Round Robin	SPN	SRT	HRRN	Feedback
Selection Function	max[w]	constant	min[s]	min[$s - e$]	$\max\left(\dfrac{w + s}{s}\right)$	(see text)
Decision Mode	Non-preemptive	Preemptive (at time quantum)	Non-preemptive	Preemptive (at arrival)	Non-preemptive	Preemptive (at time quantum)
Throughput	Not emphasized	May be low if quantum is too small	High	High	High	Not emphasized
Response Time	May be high, especially if there is a large variance in process execution times	Provides good response time for short processes	Provides good response time for short processes	Provides good response time	Provides good response time	Not emphasized
Overhead	Minimum	Minimum	Can be high	Can be high	Can be high	Can be high
Effect on Processes	Penalizes short processes; penalizes I/O bound processes	Fair treatment	Penalizes long processes	Penalizes long processes	Good balance	May favor I/O bound processes
Starvation	No	No	Possible	Possible	No	Possible

The **decision mode** specifies the instants in time at which the selection function is exercised. There are two general categories:

- **Nonpreemptive:** In this case, once a process is in the Running state, it continues to execute until (a) it terminates or (b) it blocks itself to wait for I/O or to request some OS service.

- **Preemptive:** The currently running process may be interrupted and moved to the Ready state by the OS. The decision to preempt may be performed when a new process arrives; when an interrupt occurs that places a blocked process in the Ready state; or periodically, based on a clock interrupt.

Preemptive policies incur greater overhead than nonpreemptive ones but may provide better service to the total population of processes, because they prevent any one process from monopolizing the processor for very long. In addition, the cost of preemption may be kept relatively low by using efficient process-switching mechanisms (as much help from hardware as possible) and by providing a large main memory to keep a high percentage of programs in main memory.

As we describe the various scheduling policies, we will use the set of processes in Table 9.4 as a running example. We can think of these as batch jobs, with the service time being the total execution time required. Alternatively, we can consider these to be ongoing processes that require alternate use of the processor and I/O in a repetitive fashion. In this latter case, the service times represent the processor time required in one cycle. In either case, in terms of a queueing model, this quantity corresponds to the service time.[4]

For the example of Table 9.4, Figure 9.5 shows the execution pattern for each policy for one cycle, and Table 9.5 summarizes some key results. First, the finish time of each process is determined. From this, we can determine the turnaround time. In terms of the queueing model, **turnaround time (TAT)** is the residence time T_r, or total time that the item spends in the system (waiting time plus service time). A more useful figure is the normalized turnaround time, which is the ratio of turnaround time to service time. This value indicates the relative

Table 9.4 Process Scheduling Example

Process	Arrival Time	Service Time
A	0	3
B	2	6
C	4	4
D	6	5
E	8	2

---

[4]See Appendix H for a summary of queueing model terminology, and Chapter 20 for a more detailed discussion of queueing analysis.

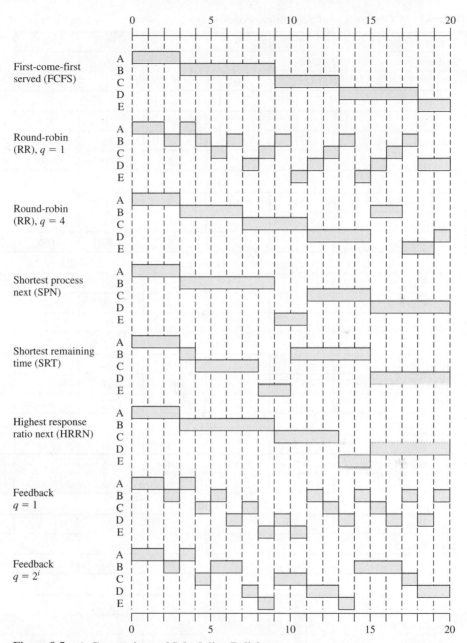

Figure 9.5   A Comparison of Scheduling Policies

delay experienced by a process. Typically, the longer the process execution time, the greater is the absolute amount of delay that can be tolerated. The minimum possible value for this ratio is 1.0; increasing values correspond to a decreasing level of service.

Table 9.5 A Comparison of Scheduling Policies

Process	A	B	C	D	E	
Arrival Time	0	2	4	6	8	
Service Time (T_s)	3	6	4	5	2	Mean
FCFS						
Finish Time	3	9	13	18	20	
Turnaround Time (T_r)	3	7	9	12	12	8.60
T_r/T_s	1.00	1.17	2.25	2.40	6.00	2.56
RR $q = 1$						
Finish Time	4	18	17	20	15	
Turnaround Time (T_r)	4	16	13	14	7	10.80
T_r/T_s	1.33	2.67	3.25	2.80	3.50	2.71
RR $q = 4$						
Finish Time	3	17	11	20	19	
Turnaround Time (T_r)	3	15	7	14	11	10.00
T_r/T_s	1.00	2.5	1.75	2.80	5.50	2.71
SPN						
Finish Time	3	9	15	20	11	
Turnaround Time (T_r)	3	7	11	14	3	7.60
T_r/T_s	1.00	1.17.	2.75	2.80	1.50	1.84
SRT						
Finish Time	3	15	8	20	10	
Turnaround Time (T_r)	3	13	4	14	2	7.20
T_r/T_s	1.00	2.17	1.00	2.80	1.00	1.59
HRRN						
Finish Time	3	9	13	20	15	
Turnaround Time (T_r)	3	7	9	14	7	8.00
T_r/T_s	1.00	1.17	2.25	2.80	3.5	2.14
FB $q = 1$						
Finish Time	4	20	16	19	11	
Turnaround Time (T_r)	4	18	12	13	3	10.00
T_r/T_s	1.33	3.00	3.00	2.60	1.5	2.29
FB $q = 2^i$						
Finish Time	4	17	18	20	14	
Turnaround Time (T_r)	4	15	14	14	6	10.60
T_r/T_s	1.33	2.50	3.50	2.80	3.00	2.63

FIRST-COME-FIRST-SERVED   The simplest scheduling policy is first-come-first-served (FCFS), also known as first-in-first-out (FIFO) or a strict queueing scheme. As each process becomes ready, it joins the ready queue. When the currently running process ceases to execute, the process that has been in the ready queue the longest is selected for running.

FCFS performs much better for long processes than short ones. Consider the following example, based on one in [FINK88]:

Process	Arrival Time	Service Time (T_s)	Start Time	Finish Time	Turnaround Time (T_r)	T_r/T_s
W	0	1	0	1	1	1
X	1	100	1	101	100	1
Y	2	1	101	102	100	100
Z	3	100	102	202	199	1.99
Mean					100	26

The normalized turnaround time for process Y is way out of line compared to the other processes: the total time that it is in the system is 100 times the required processing time. This will happen whenever a short process arrives just after a long process. On the other hand, even in this extreme example, long processes do not fare poorly. Process Z has a turnaround time that is almost double that of Y, but its normalized residence time is under 2.0.

Another difficulty with FCFS is that it tends to favor processor-bound processes over I/O-bound processes. Consider that there is a collection of processes, one of which mostly uses the processor (processor bound) and a number of which favor I/O (I/O bound). When a processor-bound process is running, all of the I/O bound processes must wait. Some of these may be in I/O queues (blocked state) but may move back to the ready queue while the processor-bound process is executing. At this point, most or all of the I/O devices may be idle, even though there is potentially work for them to do. When the currently running process leaves the Running state, the ready I/O-bound processes quickly move through the Running state and become blocked on I/O events. If the processor-bound process is also blocked, the processor becomes idle. Thus, FCFS may result in inefficient use of both the processor and the I/O devices.

FCFS is not an attractive alternative on its own for a uniprocessor system. However, it is often combined with a priority scheme to provide an effective scheduler. Thus, the scheduler may maintain a number of queues, one for each priority level, and dispatch within each queue on a first-come-first-served basis. We see one example of such a system later, in our discussion of feedback scheduling.

ROUND ROBIN   A straightforward way to reduce the penalty that short jobs suffer with FCFS is to use preemption based on a clock. The simplest such policy is round robin. A clock interrupt is generated at periodic intervals. When the interrupt occurs, the currently running process is placed in the ready queue, and the next ready job is selected on a FCFS basis. This technique is also known as **time slicing**, because each process is given a slice of time before being preempted.

With round robin, the principal design issue is the length of the time quantum, or slice, to be used. If the quantum is very short, then short processes will move through the system relatively quickly. On the other hand, there is processing overhead involved in handling the clock interrupt and performing the scheduling and dispatching function. Thus, very short time quanta should be avoided. One useful guide is that the time quantum should be slightly greater than the time required for a typical interaction or process function. If it is less, then most processes will require at least two time quanta. Figure 9.6 illustrates the effect this has on response time. Note that in the limiting case of a time quantum that is longer than the longest-running process, round robin degenerates to FCFS.

Figure 9.5 and Table 9.5 show the results for our example using time quanta q of 1 and 4 time units. Note that process E, which is the shortest job, enjoys significant improvement for a time quantum of 1.

Round robin is particularly effective in a general-purpose time-sharing system or transaction processing system. One drawback to round robin is its relative

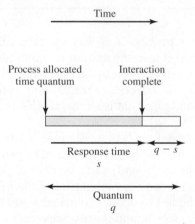

(a) Time quantum greater than typical interaction

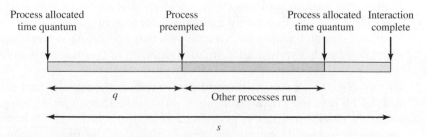

(b) Time quantum less than typical interaction

Figure 9.6   Effect of Size of Preemption Time Quantum

treatment of processor-bound and I/O-bound processes. Generally, an I/O-bound process has a shorter processor burst (amount of time spent executing between I/O operations) than a processor-bound process. If there is a mix of processor-bound and I/O-bound processes, then the following will happen: An I/O-bound process uses a processor for a short period and then is blocked for I/O; it waits for the I/O operation to complete and then joins the ready queue. On the other hand, a processor-bound process generally uses a complete time quantum while executing and immediately returns to the ready queue. Thus, processor-bound processes tend to receive an unfair portion of processor time, which results in poor performance for I/O-bound processes, inefficient use of I/O devices, and an increase in the variance of response time.

[HALD91] suggests a refinement to round robin that he refers to as a virtual round robin (VRR) and that avoids this unfairness. Figure 9.7 illustrates the scheme. New processes arrive and join the ready queue, which is managed on an FCFS basis. When a running process times out, it is returned to the ready queue. When a process is blocked for I/O, it joins an I/O queue. So far, this is as usual. The new feature is an FCFS auxiliary queue to which processes are moved after being released from an I/O block. When a dispatching decision is to be made, processes in the auxiliary queue get preference over those in the main ready queue. When a process is dispatched from the auxiliary queue, it runs no longer than a time equal to the basic time quantum minus the total time spent running since it was last selected from the

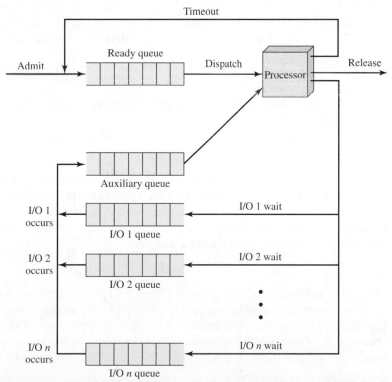

Figure 9.7   Queueing Diagram for Virtual Round-Robin Scheduler

main ready queue. Performance studies by the authors indicate that this approach is indeed superior to round robin in terms of fairness.

SHORTEST PROCESS NEXT Another approach to reducing the bias in favor of long processes inherent in FCFS is the shortest process next (SPN) policy. This is a nonpreemptive policy in which the process with the shortest expected processing time is selected next. Thus, a short process will jump to the head of the queue past longer jobs.

Figure 9.5 and Table 9.5 show the results for our example. Note that process E receives service much earlier than under FCFS. Overall performance is also significantly improved in terms of response time. However, the variability of response times is increased, especially for longer processes, and thus predictability is reduced.

One difficulty with the SPN policy is the need to know or at least estimate the required processing time of each process. For batch jobs, the system may require the programmer to estimate the value and supply it to the OS. If the programmer's estimate is substantially under the actual running time, the system may abort the job. In a production environment, the same jobs run frequently, and statistics may be gathered. For interactive processes, the OS may keep a running average of each "burst" for each process. The simplest calculation would be the following:

$$S_{n+1} = \frac{1}{n} \sum_{i=1}^{n} T_i \qquad (9.1)$$

where

T_i = processor execution time for the ith instance of this process (total execution time for batch job; processor burst time for interactive job)

S_i = predicted value for the ith instance

S_1 = predicted value for first instance; not calculated

To avoid recalculating the entire summation each time, we can rewrite Equation (9.1) as

$$S_{n+1} = \frac{1}{n} T_n + \frac{n-1}{n} S_n \qquad (9.2)$$

Note that each term in this summation is given equal weight; that is, each term is multiplied by the same constant $1/(n)$. Typically, we would like to give greater weight to more recent instances, because these are more likely to reflect future behavior. A common technique for predicting a future value on the basis of a time series of past values is **exponential averaging**:

$$S_{n+1} = \alpha T_n + (1 - \alpha)S_n \qquad (9.3)$$

where α is a constant weighting factor $(0 > \alpha > 1)$ that determines the relative weight given to more recent observations relative to older observations. Compare with Equation (9.2). By using a constant value of α, independent of the number of past observations, Equation (9.3) considers all past values, but the less recent ones have less weight. To see this more clearly, consider the following expansion of Equation (9.3):

$$S_{n+1} = \alpha T_n + (1 - \alpha)\alpha T_{n-1} + \ldots + (1 - \alpha)^i \alpha T_{n-i} + \ldots + (1 - \alpha)^n S_1 \qquad (9.4)$$

Because both α and $(1 - \alpha)$ are less than 1, each successive term in the preceding equation is smaller. For example, for $\alpha = 0.8$, Equation (9.4) becomes

$$S_{n+1} = 0.8T_n + 0.16T_{n-1} + 0.032T_{n-2} + 0.0064T_{n-3} + \ldots + (0.2)^n S_1$$

The older the observation, the less it is counted in to the average.

The size of the coefficient as a function of its position in the expansion is shown in Figure 9.8. The larger the value of , the greater is the weight given to the more recent observations. For $\alpha = 0.8$, virtually all of the weight is given to the four most recent observations, whereas for $\alpha = 0.2$, the averaging is effectively spread out over the eight or so most recent observations. The advantage of using a value of α close to 1 is that the average will quickly reflect a rapid change in the observed quantity. The disadvantage is that if there is a brief surge in the value of the observed quantity and it then settles back to some average value, the use of a large value of α will result in jerky changes in the average.

Figure 9.9 compares simple averaging with exponential averaging (for two different values of α). In Figure 9.9a, the observed value begins at 1, grows gradually to a value of 10, and then stays there. In Figure 9.9b, the observed value begins at 20, declines gradually to 10, and then stays there. In both cases, we start out with an estimate of $S_1 = 0$. This gives greater priority to new processes. Note that exponential averaging tracks changes in process behavior faster than does simple averaging and that the larger value of α results in a more rapid reaction to the change in the observed value.

A risk with SPN is the possibility of starvation for longer processes, as long as there is a steady supply of shorter processes. On the other hand, although SPN reduces the bias in favor of longer jobs, it still is not desirable for a time-sharing or transaction processing environment because of the lack of preemption. Looking back at our worst-case analysis described under FCFS, processes W, X, Y, and Z will still execute in the same order, heavily penalizing the short process Y.

SHORTEST REMAINING TIME The shortest remaining time (SRT) policy is a preemptive version of SPN. In this case, the scheduler always chooses the process

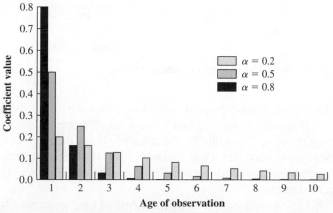

Figure 9.8   Exponential Smoothing Coefficients

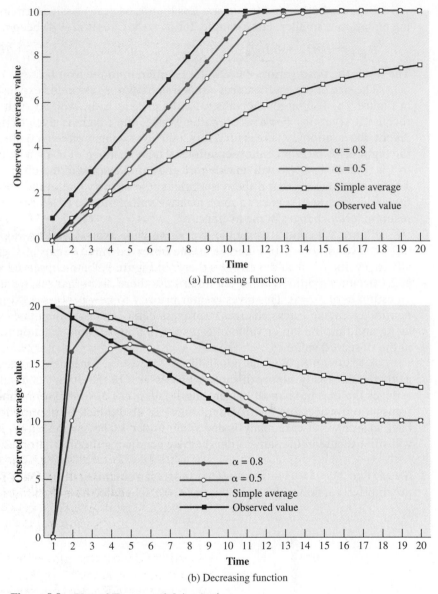

Figure 9.9   Use of Exponential Averaging

that has the shortest expected remaining processing time. When a new process joins the ready queue, it may in fact have a shorter remaining time than the currently running process. Accordingly, the scheduler may preempt the current process when a new process becomes ready. As with SPN, the scheduler must have an estimate of processing time to perform the selection function, and there is a risk of starvation of longer processes.

SRT does not have the bias in favor of long processes found in FCFS. Unlike round robin, no additional interrupts are generated, reducing overhead. On the other hand, elapsed service times must be recorded, contributing to overhead. SRT should also give superior turnaround time performance to SPN, because a short job is given immediate preference to a running longer job.

Note that in our example (Table 9.5), the three shortest processes all receive immediate service, yielding a normalized turnaround time for each of 1.0.

HIGHEST RESPONSE RATIO NEXT In Table 9.5, we have used the normalized turnaround time, which is the ratio of turnaround time to actual service time, as a figure of merit. For each individual process, we would like to minimize this ratio, and we would like to minimize the average value over all processes. In general, we cannot know ahead of time what the service time is going to be, but we can approximate it, either based on past history or some input from the user or a configuration manager. Consider the following ratio:

$$R = \frac{w + s}{s}$$

where

R = response ratio

w = time spent waiting for the processor

s = expected service time

If the process with this value is dispatched immediately, R is equal to the normalized turnaround time. Note that the minimum value of R is 1.0, which occurs when a process first enters the system.

Thus, our scheduling rule becomes the following: when the current process completes or is blocked, choose the ready process with the greatest value of R. This approach is attractive because it accounts for the age of the process. While shorter jobs are favored (a smaller denominator yields a larger ratio), aging without service increases the ratio so that a longer process will eventually get past competing shorter jobs.

As with SRT and SPN, the expected service time must be estimated to use highest response ratio next (HRRN).

FEEDBACK If we have no indication of the relative length of various processes, then none of SPN, SRT, and HRRN can be used. Another way of establishing a preference for shorter jobs is to penalize jobs that have been running longer. In other words, if we cannot focus on the time remaining to execute, let us focus on the time spent in execution so far.

The way to do this is as follows. Scheduling is done on a preemptive (at time quantum) basis, and a dynamic priority mechanism is used. When a process first enters the system, it is placed in RQ0 (see Figure 9.4). After its first preemption, when it returns to the Ready state, it is placed in RQ1. Each subsequent time that it is preempted, it is demoted to the next lower-priority queue. A short process will complete quickly, without migrating very far down the hierarchy of ready queues. A longer process will gradually drift downward. Thus, newer, shorter processes are favored over older, longer processes. Within each queue, except the lowest-priority queue, a simple FCFS mechanism is used. Once in the lowest-priority queue, a

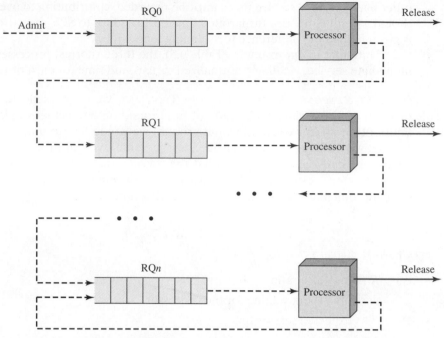

Figure 9.10   Feedback Scheduling

process cannot go lower, but is returned to this queue repeatedly until it completes execution. Thus, this queue is treated in round-robin fashion.

Figure 9.10 illustrates the feedback scheduling mechanism by showing the path that a process will follow through the various queues.[5] This approach is known as **multilevel feedback**, meaning that the OS allocates the processor to a process and, when the process blocks or is preempted, feeds it back into one of several priority queues.

There are a number of variations on this scheme. A simple version is to perform preemption in the same fashion as for round robin: at periodic intervals. Our example shows this (Figure 9.5 and Table 9.5) for a quantum of one time unit. Note that in this case, the behavior is similar to round robin with a time quantum of 1.

One problem with the simple scheme just outlined is that the turnaround time of longer processes can stretch out alarmingly. Indeed, it is possible for starvation to occur if new jobs are entering the system frequently. To compensate for this, we can vary the preemption times according to the queue: A process scheduled from RQ0 is allowed to execute for one time unit and then is preempted; a process scheduled from RQ1 is allowed to execute two time units, and so on. In general, a process scheduled from RQi is allowed to execute 2^i time units before preemption. This scheme is illustrated for our example in Figure 9.5 and Table 9.5.

---

[5]Dotted lines are used to emphasize that this is a time sequence diagram rather than a static depiction of possible transitions, such as Figure 9.4.

Even with the allowance for greater time allocation at lower priority, a longer process may still suffer starvation. A possible remedy is to promote a process to a higher-priority queue after it spends a certain amount of time waiting for service in its current queue.

Performance Comparison

Clearly, the performance of various scheduling policies is a critical factor in the choice of a scheduling policy. However, it is impossible to make definitive comparisons because relative performance will depend on a variety of factors, including the probability distribution of service times of the various processes, the efficiency of the scheduling and context switching mechanisms, and the nature of the I/O demand and the performance of the I/O subsystem. Nevertheless, we attempt in what follows to draw some general conclusions.

QUEUEING ANALYSIS   In this section, we make use of basic queueing formulas, with the common assumptions of Poisson arrivals and exponential service times.[6]
First, we make the observation that any such scheduling discipline that chooses the next item to be served independent of service time obeys the following relationship:

$$\frac{T_r}{T_s} = \frac{1}{1 - \rho}$$

where

T_r = turnaround time or residence time; total time in system, waiting plus execution

T_s = average service time; average time spent in Running state

ρ = processor utilization

In particular, a priority-based scheduler, in which the priority of each process is assigned independent of expected service time, provides the same average turnaround time and average normalized turnaround time as a simple FCFS discipline. Furthermore, the presence or absence of preemption makes no differences in these averages.

With the exception of round robin and FCFS, the various scheduling disciplines considered so far do make selections on the basis of expected service time. Unfortunately, it turns out to be quite difficult to develop closed analytic models of these disciplines. However, we can get an idea of the relative performance of such scheduling algorithms, compared to FCFS, by considering priority scheduling in which priority is based on service time.

If scheduling is done on the basis of priority and if processes are assigned to a priority class on the basis of service time, then differences do emerge. Table 9.6 shows the formulas that result when we assume two priority classes, with different service times for each class. In the table,   refers to the arrival rate. These results can

---

[6]The queueing terminology used in this chapter is summarized in Appendix H. Poisson arrivals essentially means random arrivals, as explained in Appendix H.

Table 9.6 Formulas for Single-Server Queues with Two Priority Categories

Assumptions:
1. Poisson arrival rate.
2. Priority 1 items are serviced before priority 2 items.
3. First-come-first-served dispatching for items of equal priority.
4. No item is interrupted while being served.
5. No items leave the queue (lost calls delayed).

(a) General formulas

$$\lambda = \lambda_1 + \lambda_2$$

$$\rho_1 = \lambda_1 T_{s1}; \; \rho_2 = \lambda_2 T_{s2}$$

$$\rho = \rho_1 + \rho_2$$

$$T_s = \frac{\lambda_1}{\lambda} T_{s1} + \frac{\lambda_2}{\lambda} T_{s2}$$

$$T_r = \frac{\lambda_1}{\lambda} T_{r1} + \frac{\lambda_2}{\lambda} T_{r2}$$

(b) No interrupts; exponential service times	**(c) Preemptive-resume queueing discipline; exponential service times**
$$T_{r1} = T_{s1} + \frac{\rho_1 T_{s1} + \rho_2 T_{s2}}{1 + \rho_1}$$	$$T_{r1} = T_{s1} + \frac{\rho_1 T_{s1}}{1 - \rho_1}$$
$$T_{r2} = T_{s2} + \frac{T_{r1} - T_{s1}}{1 - \rho}$$	$$T_{r2} = T_{s2} + \frac{1}{1 - \rho_1}\left(\rho_1 T_{s2} + \frac{\rho T_s}{1 - \rho}\right)$$

be generalized to any number of priority classes. Note that the formulas differ for nonpreemptive versus preemptive scheduling. In the latter case, it is assumed that a lower-priority process is immediately interrupted when a higher-priority process becomes ready.

As an example, let us consider the case of two priority classes, with an equal number of process arrivals in each class and with the average service time for the lower-priority class being five times that of the upper priority class. Thus, we wish to give preference to shorter processes. Figure 9.11 shows the overall result. By giving preference to shorter jobs, the average normalized turnaround time is improved at higher levels of utilization. As might be expected, the improvement is greatest with the use of preemption. Notice, however, that overall performance is not much affected.

However, significant differences emerge when we consider the two priority classes separately. Figure 9.12 shows the results for the higher-priority, shorter processes. For comparison, the upper line on the graph assumes that priorities are not used but that we are simply looking at the relative performance of that half of all processes that have the shorter processing time. The other two lines assume that these processes are assigned a higher priority. When the system is run using priority scheduling without preemption, the improvements are significant. They are even more significant when preemption is used.

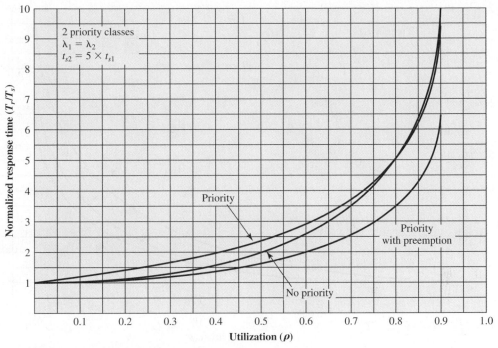

Figure 9.11   Overall Normalized Response Time

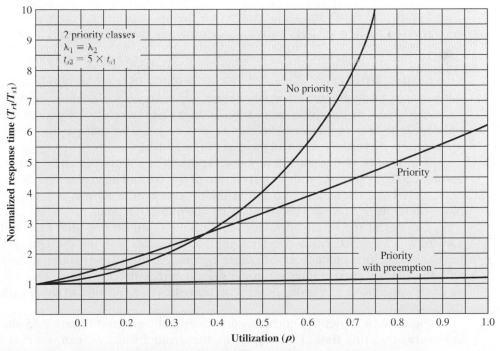

Figure 9.12   Normalized Response Time for Shorter Processes

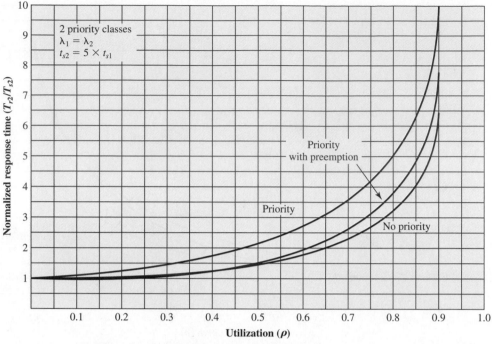

Figure 9.13   Normalized Response Time for Longer Processes

Figure 9.13 shows the same analysis for the lower-priority, longer processes. As expected, such processes suffer a performance degradation under priority scheduling.

SIMULATION MODELING   Some of the difficulties of analytic modeling are overcome by using discrete-event simulation, which allows a wide range of policies to be modeled. The disadvantage of simulation is that the results for a given "run" only apply to that particular collection of processes under that particular set of assumptions. Nevertheless, useful insights can be gained.

The results of one such study are reported in [FINK88]. The simulation involved 50,000 processes with an arrival rate of $\lambda = 0.8$ and an average service time of $T_s = 1$. Thus, the assumption is that the processor utilization is $\rho = \lambda T_s = 0.8$. Note, therefore, that we are only measuring one utilization point.

To present the results, processes are grouped into service-time percentiles, each of which has 500 processes. Thus, the 500 processes with the shortest service time are in the first percentile; with these eliminated, the 500 remaining processes with the shortest service time are in the second percentile; and so on. This allows us to view the effect of various policies on processes as a function of the length of the process.

Figure 9.14 shows the normalized turnaround time, and Figure 9.15 shows the average waiting time. Looking at the turnaround time, we can see that the performance of FCFS is very unfavorable, with one-third of the processes having

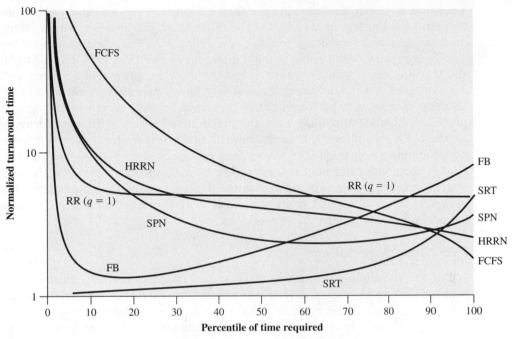

Figure 9.14   Simulation Result for Normalized Turnaround Time

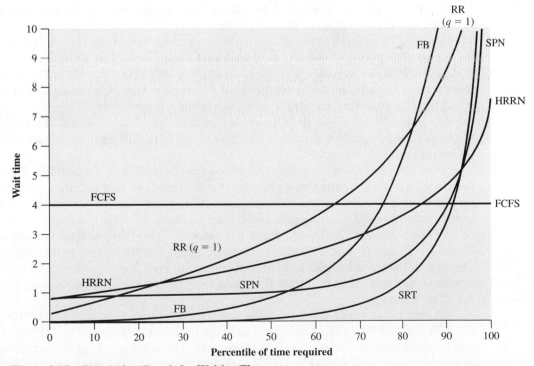

Figure 9.15   Simulation Result for Waiting Time

a normalized turnaround time greater than 10 times the service time; furthermore, these are the shortest processes. On the other hand, the absolute waiting time is uniform, as is to be expected because scheduling is independent of service time. The figures show round robin using a quantum of one time unit. Except for the shortest processes, which execute in less than one quantum, round robin yields a normalized turnaround time of about five for all processes, treating all fairly. Shortest process next performs better than round robin, except for the shortest processes. Shortest remaining time, the preemptive version of SPN, performs better than SPN except for the longest 7% of all processes. We have seen that, among nonpreemptive policies, FCFS favors long processes and SPN favors short ones. Highest response ratio next is intended to be a compromise between these two effects, and this is indeed confirmed in the figures. Finally, the figure shows feedback scheduling with fixed, uniform quanta in each priority queue. As expected, FB performs quite well for short processes.

Fair-Share Scheduling

All of the scheduling algorithms discussed so far treat the collection of ready processes as a single pool of processes from which to select the next running process. This pool may be broken down by priority but is otherwise homogeneous.

However, in a multiuser system, if individual user applications or jobs may be organized as multiple processes (or threads), then there is a structure to the collection of processes that is not recognized by a traditional scheduler. From the user's point of view, the concern is not how a particular process performs but rather how his or her set of processes, which constitute a single application, performs. Thus, it would be attractive to make scheduling decisions on the basis of these process sets. This approach is generally known as fair-share scheduling. Further, the concept can be extended to groups of users, even if each user is represented by a single process. For example, in a time-sharing system, we might wish to consider all of the users from a given department to be members of the same group. Scheduling decisions could then be made that attempt to give each group similar service. Thus, if a large number of people from one department log onto the system, we would like to see response time degradation primarily affect members of that department rather than users from other departments.

The term *fair share* indicates the philosophy behind such a scheduler. Each user is assigned a weighting of some sort that defines that user's share of system resources as a fraction of the total usage of those resources. In particular, each user is assigned a share of the processor. Such a scheme should operate in a more or less linear fashion, so that if user A has twice the weighting of user B, then in the long run, user A should be able to do twice as much work as user B. The objective of a fair-share scheduler is to monitor usage to give fewer resources to users who have had more than their fair share and more to those who have had less than their fair share.

A number of proposals have been made for fair-share schedulers [HENR84, KAY88, WOOD86]. In this section, we describe the scheme proposed in [HENR84] and implemented on a number of UNIX systems. The scheme is simply referred to as the fair-share scheduler (FSS). FSS considers the execution history of a related group of processes, along with the individual execution history of each process in making scheduling decisions. The system divides the user community into a set of fair-share groups and allocates a fraction of the processor resource to each group. Thus, there might be four groups, each with 25% of the processor usage. In effect, each fair-share group is provided with a virtual system that runs proportionally slower than a full system.

Scheduling is done on the basis of priority, which takes into account the underlying priority of the process, its recent processor usage, and the recent processor usage of the group to which the process belongs. The higher the numerical value of the priority, the lower is the priority. The following formulas apply for process j in group k:

$$CPU_j(i) = \frac{CPU_j(i-1)}{2}$$

$$GCPU_k(i) = \frac{GCPU_k(i-1)}{2}$$

$$P_j(i) = Base_j + \frac{CPU_j(i)}{2} + \frac{GCPU_k(i)}{4 \times W_k}$$

where

$CPU_j(i)$ = measure of processor utilization by process j through interval i

$GCPU_k(i)$ = measure of processor utilization of group k through interval i

$P_j(i)$ = priority of process j at beginning of interval i; lower values equal higher priorities

$Base_j$ = base priority of process j

W_k = weighting assigned to group k, with the constraint that $0 < W_k \leq 1$ and $\sum_k W_k = 1$

Each process is assigned a base priority. The priority of a process drops as the process uses the processor and as the group to which the process belongs uses the processor. In the case of the group utilization, the average is normalized by dividing by the weight of that group. The greater the weight assigned to the group, the less its utilization will affect its priority.

Figure 9.16 is an example in which process A is in one group and processes B and C are in a second group, with each group having a weighting of 0.5. Assume that all processes are processor bound and are usually ready to run. All processes have a base priority of 60. Processor utilization is measured as follows: The processor is interrupted 60 times per second; during each interrupt, the processor usage field of the currently running process is incremented, as is the corresponding group processor field. Once per second, priorities are recalculated.

In the figure, process A is scheduled first. At the end of one second, it is preempted. Processes B and C now have the higher priority, and process B is scheduled. At the end of the second time unit, process A has the highest priority. Note that the pattern repeats: the kernel schedules the processes in order: A, B, A, C, A, B, and so on. Thus, 50% of the processor is allocated to process A, which constitutes one group, and 50% to processes B and C, which constitute another group.

Time	Process A Priority	Process A Process CPU count	Process A Group CPU count	Process B Priority	Process B Process CPU count	Process B Group CPU count	Process C Priority	Process C Process CPU count	Process C Group CPU count
0	60	0 1 2 • • 60	0 1 2 • • 60	60	0	0	60	0	0
1	90	30	30	60	0 1 2 • • 60	0 1 2 • • 60	60	0	0 1 2 • • 60
2	74	15 16 17 • • 75	15 16 17 • • 75	90	30	30	75	0	30
3	96	37	37	74	15	15 16 17 • • 75	67	0 1 2 • • 60	15 16 17 • • 75
4	78	18 19 20 • • 78	18 19 20 • • 78	81	7	37	93	30	37
5	98	39	39	70	3	18	76	15	18

Group 1   Group 2

Colored rectangle represents executing process

Figure 9.16   Example of Fair-Share Scheduler—Three Processes, Two Groups

9.3 TRADITIONAL UNIX SCHEDULING

In this section we examine traditional UNIX scheduling, which is used in both SVR3 and 4.3 BSD UNIX. These systems are primarily targeted at the time-sharing interactive environment. The scheduling algorithm is designed to provide good response time for interactive users while ensuring that low-priority background jobs do not starve. Although this algorithm has been replaced in modern UNIX systems, it is worthwhile to examine the approach because it is representative of practical time-sharing scheduling algorithms. The scheduling scheme for SVR4 includes an accommodation for real-time requirements, and so its discussion is deferred to Chapter 10.

The traditional UNIX scheduler employs multilevel feedback using round robin within each of the priority queues. The system makes use of one-second preemption. That is, if a running process does not block or complete within one second, it is preempted. Priority is based on process type and execution history. The following formulas apply:

$$CPU_j(i) = \frac{CPU_j(i-1)}{2}$$

$$P_j(i) = Base_j + \frac{CPU_j(i)}{2} + nice_j$$

where

$CPU_j(i)$ = measure of processor utilization by process j through interval i

$P_j(i)$ = priority of process j at beginning of interval i; lower values equal higher priorities

$Base_j$ = base priority of process j

$nice_j$ = user-controllable adjustment factor

The priority of each process is recomputed once per second, at which time a new scheduling decision is made. The purpose of the base priority is to divide all processes into fixed bands of priority levels. The *CPU* and *nice* components are restricted to prevent a process from migrating out of its assigned band (assigned by the base priority level). These bands are used to optimize access to block devices (e.g., disk) and to allow the OS to respond quickly to system calls. In decreasing order of priority, the bands are:

- Swapper
- Block I/O device control
- File manipulation
- Character I/O device control
- User processes

This hierarchy should provide the most efficient use of the I/O devices. Within the user process band, the use of execution history tends to penalize proc- essor-bound processes at the expense of I/O-bound processes. Again, this should improve efficiency. Coupled with the round-robin preemption scheme, the sched- uling strategy is well equipped to satisfy the requirements for general-purpose time sharing.

An example of process scheduling is shown in Figure 9.17. Processes A, B, and C are created at the same time with base priorities of 60 (we will ignore the *nice* value). The clock interrupts the system 60 times per second and increments a counter for the running process. The example assumes that none of the proc- esses block themselves and that no other processes are ready to run. Compare this with Figure 9.16.

Time	Process A Priority	Process A CPU count	Process B Priority	Process B CPU count	Process C Priority	Process C CPU count
0	60	0 1 2 • • 60	60	0	60	0
1	75	30	60	0 1 2 • • 60	60	0
2	67	15	75	30	60	0 1 2 • • 60
3	63	7 8 9 • • 67	67	15	75	30
4	76	33	63	7 8 9 • • 67	67	15
5	68	16	76	33	63	7

Colored rectangle represents executing process

Figure 9.17 Example of a Traditional UNIX Process Scheduling

9.4 SUMMARY

The OS must make three types of scheduling decisions with respect to the execution of processes. Long-term scheduling determines when new processes are admitted to the system. Medium-term scheduling is part of the swapping function and determines when a program is brought partially or fully into main memory so that it may be executed. Short-term scheduling determines which ready process will be executed next by the processor. This chapter focuses on the issues relating to short-term scheduling.

A variety of criteria are used in designing the short-term scheduler. Some of these criteria relate to the behavior of the system as perceived by the individual user (user oriented), while others view the total effectiveness of the system in meeting the needs of all users (system oriented). Some of the criteria relate specifically to quantitative measures of performance, while others are more qualitative in nature. From a user's point of view, response time is generally the most important characteristic of a system, while from a system point of view, throughput or processor utilization is important.

A variety of algorithms have been developed for making the short-term scheduling decision among all ready processes:

- **First-come-first-served:** Select the process that has been waiting the longest for service.
- **Round robin:** Use time slicing to limit any running process to a short burst of processor time, and rotate among all ready processes.
- **Shortest process next:** Select the process with the shortest expected processing time, and do not preempt the process.
- **Shortest remaining time:** Select the process with the shortest expected remaining process time. A process may be preempted when another process becomes ready.
- **Highest response ratio next:** Base the scheduling decision on an estimate of normalized turnaround time.
- **Feedback:** Establish a set of scheduling queues and allocate processes to queues based on execution history and other criteria.

The choice of scheduling algorithm will depend on expected performance and on implementation complexity.

9.5   RECOMMENDED READING

Virtually every textbook on operating systems covers scheduling. Rigorous queueing analyses of various scheduling policies are presented in [KLEI04] and [CONW67]. [DOWD93] provides an instructive performance analysis of various scheduling algorithms.

CONW67   Conway, R., Maxwell, W., and Miller, L. *Theory of Scheduling.* Reading, MA: Addison-Wesley, 1967. Reprinted by Dover Publications, 2003.

DOWD93   Dowdy, L., and Lowery, C. *P.S. to Operating Systems.* Upper Saddle River, NJ: Prentice Hall, 1993.

KLEI04   Kleinrock, L. *Queuing Systems, Volume Three: Computer Applications.* New York: Wiley, 2004.

9.6   KEY TERMS, REVIEW QUESTIONS, AND PROBLEMS

Key Terms

arrival rate	medium-term scheduler	short-term scheduler
dispatcher	multilevel feedback	throughput
exponential averaging	predictability	time slicing
fair-share scheduling	residence time	turnaround time
fairness	response time	utilization
first-come-first-served	round robin	waiting time
first-in-first-out	scheduling priority	
long-term scheduler	service time	

Review Questions

9.1   Briefly describe the three types of processor scheduling.

9.2   What is usually the critical performance requirement in an interactive operating system?

9.3   What is the difference between turnaround time and response time?

9.4   For process scheduling, does a low-priority value represent a low priority or a high priority?

9.5   What is the difference between preemptive and nonpreemptive scheduling?

9.6   Briefly define FCFS scheduling.

9.7   Briefly define round-robin scheduling.

9.8   Briefly define shortest-process-next scheduling.

9.9   Briefly define shortest-remaining-time scheduling.

9.10   Briefly define highest-response-ratio-next scheduling.

9.11   Briefly define feedback scheduling.

Problems

9.1   Consider the following workload:

Process	Burst Time	Priority	Arrival Time
P1	50 ms	4	0 ms
P2	20 ms	1	20 ms
P3	100 ms	3	40 ms
P4	40 ms	2	60 ms

a.   Show the schedule using shortest remaining time, nonpreemptive priority (a smaller priority number implies higher priority) and round robin with quantum 30 ms. Use time scale diagram as shown below for the FCFS example to show the schedule for each requested scheduling policy.

Example for FCFS (1 unit = 10 ms):

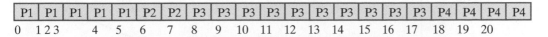

P1	P1	P1	P1	P1	P2	P2	P3	P3	P3	P3	P3	P3	P3	P3	P3	P3	P4	P4	P4	P4

0   1 2 3   4   5   6   7   8   9   10   11   12   13   14   15   16   17   18   19   20

        b. What is the average waiting time of the above scheduling policies?

9.2 Consider the following set of processes:

Process	Arrival Time	Processing Time
A	0	3
B	1	5
C	3	2
D	9	5
E	12	5

Perform the same analysis as depicted in Table 9.5 and Figure 9.5 for this set.

9.3 Prove that, among nonpreemptive scheduling algorithms, SPN provides the minimum average waiting time for a batch of jobs that arrive at the same time. Assume that the scheduler must always execute a task if one is available.

9.4 Assume the following burst-time pattern for a process: 6, 4, 6, 4, 13, 13, 13, and assume that the initial guess is 10. Produce a plot similar to those of Figure 9.9.

9.5 Consider the following pair of equations as an alternative to Equation (9.3):

$$S_{n+1} = \alpha T_n + (1 - \alpha)S_n$$
$$X_{n+1} = \min[Ubound, \max[Lbound, (\beta S_{n+1})]]$$

where *Ubound* and *Lbound* are prechosen upper and lower bounds on the estimated value of T. The value of X_{n+1} is used in the shortest-process-next algorithm, instead of the value of S_{n+1}. What functions do α and β perform, and what is the effect of higher and lower values on each?

9.6 In the bottom example in Figure 9.5, process A runs for two time units before control is passed to process B. Another plausible scenario would be that A runs for three time units before control is passed to process B. What policy differences in the feedback-scheduling algorithm would account for the two different scenarios?

9.7 In a nonpreemptive uniprocessor system, the ready queue contains three jobs at time t immediately after the completion of a job. These jobs arrived at times t_1, t_2, and t_3 with estimated execution times of r_1, r_2, and r_3, respectively. Figure 9.18 shows the linear increase of their response ratios over time. Use this example to find a variant of response ratio scheduling, known as minimax response ratio scheduling, that minimizes the maximum response ratio for a given batch of jobs ignoring further arrivals. (*Hint:* Decide, first, which job to schedule as the last one.)

9.8 Prove that the minimax response ratio algorithm of the preceding problem minimizes the maximum response ratio for a given batch of jobs. (*Hint*: Focus attention on the job that will achieve the highest response ratio and all jobs executed before it. Consider the same subset of jobs scheduled in any other order and observe the response ratio of the job that is executed as the last one among them. Notice that this subset may now be mixed with other jobs from the total set.)

9.9 Define residence time T_r as the average total time a process spends waiting and being served. Show that for FIFO, with mean service time T_s, we have $T_r = T_s/(1 - \rho)$, where ρ is utilization.

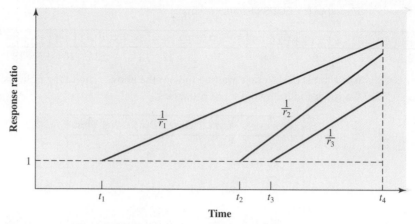

Figure 9.18   Response Ratio as a Function of Time

9.10   A processor is multiplexed at infinite speed among all processes present in a ready queue with no overhead. (This is an idealized model of round-robin scheduling among ready processes using time slices that are very small compared to the mean service time.) Show that for Poisson input from an infinite source with exponential service times, the mean response time R_x of a process with service time x is given by $R_x = x/(1 - \rho)$. (*Hint:* Review the basic queueing equations in Appendix H or Chapter 20. Then consider the number of items waiting, w, in the system upon arrival of the given process.)

9.11   Consider a variant of the RR scheduling algorithm where the entries in the ready queue are pointers to the PCBs.
   a.   What would be the effect of putting two pointers to the same process in the ready queue?
   b.   What would be the major advantage of this scheme?
   c.   How could you modify the basic RR algorithm to achieve the same effect without the duplicate pointers?

9.12   In a queueing system, new jobs must wait for a while before being served. While a job waits, its priority increases linearly with time from zero at a rate α. A job waits until its priority reaches the priority of the jobs in service; then, it begins to share the processor equally with other jobs in service using round robin while its priority continues to increase at a slower rate β. The algorithm is referred to as selfish round robin, because the jobs in service try (in vain) to monopolize the processor by increasing their priority continuously. Use Figure 9.19 to show that the mean response time R_x for a job of service time x is given by:

$$R_x = \frac{s}{1 - \rho} + \frac{x - s}{1 - \rho'}$$

where

$$\rho = \lambda s \quad \rho' = \rho\left(1 - \frac{\beta}{\alpha}\right) \quad 0 \le \beta < \alpha$$

assuming that arrival and service times are exponentially distributed with means $1/\lambda$ and s, respectively. (*Hint:* Consider the total system and the two subsystems separately.)

9.13   An interactive system using round-robin scheduling and swapping tries to give guaranteed response to trivial requests as follows: After completing a round-robin cycle among all ready processes, the system determines the time slice to allocate to each

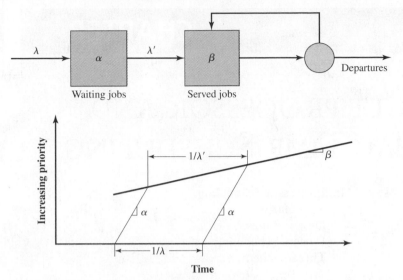

Figure 9.19 Selfish Round Robin

ready process for the next cycle by dividing a maximum response time by the number of processes requiring service. Is this a reasonable policy?

9.14 Which type of process is generally favored by a multilevel feedback queueing scheduler — a processor-bound process or an I/O-bound process? Briefly explain why.

9.15 In priority-based process scheduling, the scheduler only gives control to a particular process if no other process of higher priority is currently in the Ready state. Assume that no other information is used in making the process scheduling decision. Also assume that process priorities are established at process creation time and do not change. In a system operating with such assumptions, why would using Dekker's solution (see Section A.1) to the mutual exclusion problem be "dangerous"? Explain this by telling what undesired event could occur and how it could occur.

9.16 Five batch jobs, A through E, arrive at a computer center at essentially the same time. They have an estimated running time of 15, 9, 3, 6, and 12 minutes, respectively. Their (externally defined) priorities are 6, 3, 7, 9, and 4, respectively, with a lower value corresponding to a higher priority. For each of the following scheduling algorithms, determine the turnaround time for each process and the average turnaround for all jobs. Ignore process switching overhead. Explain how you arrived at your answers. In the last three cases, assume that only one job at a time runs until it finishes and that all jobs are completely processor bound.

a. round robin with a time quantum of 1 minute
b. priority scheduling
c. FCFS (run in order 15, 9, 3, 6, and 12)
d. shortest job first

CHAPTER 10

MULTIPROCESSOR AND REAL-TIME SCHEDULING

10.1 Multiprocessor Scheduling
Granularity
Design Issues
Process Scheduling
Thread Scheduling

10.2 Real-Time Scheduling
Background
Characteristics of Real-Time Operating Systems
Real-Time Scheduling
Deadline Scheduling
Rate Monotonic Scheduling
Priority Inversion

10.3 Linux Scheduling

10.4 UNIX SVR4 Scheduling

10.5 UNIX FreeBSD Scheduling

10.6 Windows Scheduling

10.7 Linux Virtual Machine Process Scheduling

10.8 Summary

10.9 Recommended Reading

10.10 Key Terms, Review Questions, and Problems

Bear in mind, Sir Henry, one of the phrases in that queer old legend which Dr. Mortimer has read to us, and avoid the moor in those hours of darkness when the powers of evil are exalted.

— *The Hound of the Baskervilles*, Arthur Conan Doyle

LEARNING OBJECTIVES

After studying this chapter, you should be able to:

- Understand the concept of thread granularity.
- Discuss the key design issues in multiprocessor thread scheduling and some of the key approaches to scheduling.
- Understand the requirements imposed by real-time scheduling.
- Explain the scheduling methods used in Linux, UNIX SVR4, and Windows 7.

This chapter continues our survey of process and thread scheduling. We begin with an examination of issues raised by the availability of more than one processor. A number of design issues are explored. This is followed by a look at the scheduling of processes on a multiprocessor system. Then the somewhat different design considerations for multiprocessor thread scheduling are examined. The second section of this chapter covers real-time scheduling. The section begins with a discussion of the characteristics of real-time processes and then looks at the nature of the scheduling process. Two approaches to real-time scheduling, deadline scheduling and rate monotonic scheduling, are examined.

10.1 MULTIPROCESSOR SCHEDULING

When a computer system contains more than a single processor, several new issues are introduced into the design of the scheduling function. We begin with a brief overview of multiprocessors and then look at the rather different considerations when scheduling is done at the process level and at the thread level.

We can classify multiprocessor systems as follows:

- **Loosely coupled or distributed multiprocessor, or cluster:** Consists of a collection of relatively autonomous systems, each processor having its own main memory and I/O channels. We address this type of configuration in Chapter 16.
- **Functionally specialized processors:** An example is an I/O processor. In this case, there is a master, general-purpose processor; specialized processors are controlled by the master processor and provide services to it. Issues relating to I/O processors are addressed in Chapter 11.
- **Tightly coupled multiprocessor:** Consists of a set of processors that share a common main memory and are under the integrated control of an operating system.

Table 10.1   Synchronization Granularity and Processes

Grain Size	Description	Synchronization Interval (Instructions)
Fine	Parallelism inherent in a single instruction stream	<20
Medium	Parallel processing or multitasking within a single application	20–200
Coarse	Multiprocessing of concurrent processes in a multiprogramming environment	200–2,000
Very Coarse	Distributed processing across network nodes to form a single computing environment	2,000–1M
Independent	Multiple unrelated processes	Not applicable

Our concern in this section is with the last category, and specifically with issues relating to scheduling.

Granularity

A good way of characterizing multiprocessors and placing them in context with other architectures is to consider the synchronization granularity, or frequency of synchronization, between processes in a system. We can distinguish five categories of parallelism that differ in the degree of granularity. These are summarized in Table 10.1, which is adapted from [GEHR87] and [WOOD89].

INDEPENDENT PARALLELISM   With independent parallelism, there is no explicit synchronization among processes. Each represents a separate, independent application or job. A typical use of this type of parallelism is in a time-sharing system. Each user is performing a particular application such as word processing or using a spreadsheet. The multiprocessor provides the same service as a multiprogrammed uniprocessor. Because more than one processor is available, average response time to the users will be less.

It is possible to achieve a similar performance gain by providing each user with a personal computer or workstation. If any files or information are to be shared, then the individual systems must be hooked together into a distributed system supported by a network. This approach is examined in Chapter 16. On the other hand, a single, multiprocessor shared system in many instances is more cost-effective than a distributed system, allowing economies of scale in disks and other peripherals.

COARSE AND VERY COARSE-GRAINED PARALLELISM   With coarse and very coarse-grained parallelism, there is synchronization among processes, but at a very gross level. This kind of situation is easily handled as a set of concurrent processes running on a multiprogrammed uniprocessor and can be supported on a multiprocessor with little or no change to user software.

A simple example of an application that can exploit the existence of a multiprocessor is given in [WOOD89]. The authors have developed a program that takes a specification of files needing recompilation to rebuild a piece of software and determines which of these compiles (usually all of them) can be run simultaneously.

The program then spawns one process for each parallel compile. The authors report that the speedup on a multiprocessor actually exceeds what would be expected by simply adding up the number of processors in use, due to synergies in the disk buffer caches (a topic explored in Chapter 11) and sharing of compiler code, which is loaded into memory only once.

In general, any collection of concurrent processes that need to communicate or synchronize can benefit from the use of a multiprocessor architecture. In the case of very infrequent interaction among processes, a distributed system can provide good support. However, if the interaction is somewhat more frequent, then the overhead of communication across the network may negate some of the potential speedup. In that case, the multiprocessor organization provides the most effective support.

MEDIUM-GRAINED PARALLELISM   We saw in Chapter 4 that a single application can be effectively implemented as a collection of threads within a single process. In this case, the programmer must explicitly specify the potential parallelism of an application. Typically, there will need to be rather a high degree of coordination and interaction among the threads of an application, leading to a medium-grain level of synchronization.

Whereas independent, very coarse, and coarse-grained parallelism can be supported on either a multiprogrammed uniprocessor or a multiprocessor with little or no impact on the scheduling function, we need to reexamine scheduling when dealing with the scheduling of threads. Because the various threads of an application interact so frequently, scheduling decisions concerning one thread may affect the performance of the entire application. We return to this issue later in this section.

FINE-GRAINED PARALLELISM   Fine-grained parallelism represents a much more complex use of parallelism than is found in the use of threads. Although much work has been done on highly parallel applications, this is so far a specialized and fragmented area, with many different approaches.

Chapter 4 provides an example of the use of granularity for the Valve game software.

Design Issues

Scheduling on a multiprocessor involves three interrelated issues:

- The assignment of processes to processors
- The use of multiprogramming on individual processors
- The actual dispatching of a process

In looking at these three issues, it is important to keep in mind that the approach taken will depend, in general, on the degree of granularity of the applications and on the number of processors available.

ASSIGNMENT OF PROCESSES TO PROCESSORS   If we assume that the architecture of the multiprocessor is uniform, in the sense that no processor has a particular physical advantage with respect to access to main memory or to I/O devices, then the simplest scheduling approach is to treat the processors as a pooled resource and assign processes to processors on demand. The question then arises as to whether the assignment should be static or dynamic.

If a process is permanently assigned to one processor from activation until its completion, then a dedicated short-term queue is maintained for each processor. An advantage of this approach is that there may be less overhead in the scheduling function, because the processor assignment is made once and for all. Also, the use of dedicated processors allows a strategy known as group or gang scheduling, as discussed later.

A disadvantage of static assignment is that one processor can be idle, with an empty queue, while another processor has a backlog. To prevent this situation, a common queue can be used. All processes go into one global queue and are scheduled to any available processor. Thus, over the life of a process, the process may be executed on different processors at different times. In a tightly coupled shared-memory architecture, the context information for all processes will be available to all processors, and therefore the cost of scheduling a process will be independent of the identity of the processor on which it is scheduled. Yet another option is dynamic load balancing, in which threads are moved for a queue for one processor to a queue for another processor; Linux uses this approach.

Regardless of whether processes are dedicated to processors, some means is needed to assign processes to processors. Two approaches have been used: master/slave and peer. With a master/slave architecture, key kernel functions of the operating system always run on a particular processor. The other processors may only execute user programs. The master is responsible for scheduling jobs. Once a process is active, if the slave needs service (e.g., an I/O call), it must send a request to the master and wait for the service to be performed. This approach is quite simple and requires little enhancement to a uniprocessor multiprogramming operating system. Conflict resolution is simplified because one processor has control of all memory and I/O resources. There are two disadvantages to this approach: (1) A failure of the master brings down the whole system, and (2) the master can become a performance bottleneck.

In a peer architecture, the kernel can execute on any processor, and each processor does self-scheduling from the pool of available processes. This approach complicates the operating system. The operating system must ensure that two processors do not choose the same process and that the processes are not somehow lost from the queue. Techniques must be employed to resolve and synchronize competing claims to resources.

There is, of course, a spectrum of approaches between these two extremes. One approach is to provide a subset of processors dedicated to kernel processing instead of just one. Another approach is simply to manage the difference between the needs of kernel processes and other processes on the basis of priority and execution history.

THE USE OF MULTIPROGRAMMING ON INDIVIDUAL PROCESSORS   When each process is statically assigned to a processor for the duration of its lifetime, a new question arises: Should that processor be multiprogrammed? The reader's first reaction may be to wonder why the question needs to be asked; it would appear particularly wasteful to tie up a processor with a single process when that process may frequently be blocked waiting for I/O or because of concurrency/synchronization considerations.

In the traditional multiprocessor, which is dealing with coarse-grained or independent synchronization granularity (see Table 10.1), it is clear that each individual processor should be able to switch among a number of processes to achieve high utilization and therefore better performance. However, for medium-grained applications running on a multiprocessor with many processors, the situation is less clear. When many processors are available, it is no longer paramount that every single processor be busy as much as possible. Rather, we are concerned to provide the best performance, on average, for the applications. An application that consists of a number of threads may run poorly unless all of its threads are available to run simultaneously.

PROCESS DISPATCHING   The final design issue related to multiprocessor scheduling is the actual selection of a process to run. We have seen that, on a multiprogrammed uniprocessor, the use of priorities or of sophisticated scheduling algorithms based on past usage may improve performance over a simple-minded first-come-first-served strategy. When we consider multiprocessors, these complexities may be unnecessary or even counterproductive, and a simpler approach may be more effective with less overhead. In the case of thread scheduling, new issues come into play that may be more important than priorities or execution histories. We address each of these topics in turn.

Process Scheduling

In most traditional multiprocessor systems, processes are not dedicated to processors. Rather there is a single queue for all processors, or if some sort of priority scheme is used, there are multiple queues based on priority, all feeding into the common pool of processors. In any case, we can view the system as being a multiserver queueing architecture.

Consider the case of a dual processor system in which each processor of the dual-processor system has half the processing rate of a processor in the single-processor system. [SAUE81] reports a queueing analysis that compares FCFS scheduling to round robin and to shortest remaining time. The study is concerned with process service time, which measures the amount of processor time a process needs, either for a total job or the amount of time needed each time the process is ready to use the processor. In the case of round robin, it is assumed that the time quantum is large compared to context-switching overhead and small compared to mean service time. The results depend on the variability that is seen in service times. A common measure of variability is the coefficient of variation, C_s.[1] A value of $C_s = 0$ corresponds to the case where there is no variability: the service times of all processes are equal. Increasing values of C_s correspond to increasing variability among the service times. That is, the larger the value of C_s, the more widely do the values of the service times vary. Values of C_s of 5 or more are not unusual for processor service time distributions.

Figure 10.1a compares round-robin throughput to FCFS throughput as a function of C_ss. Note that the difference in scheduling algorithms is much smaller in the dual-processor case. With two processors, a single process with long service time is

---

[1]The value of C_s is calculated as σ_s/T_s, where σ_s is the standard deviation of service time and T_s is the mean service time. For a further explanation of C_s, see the discussion in Chapter 20.

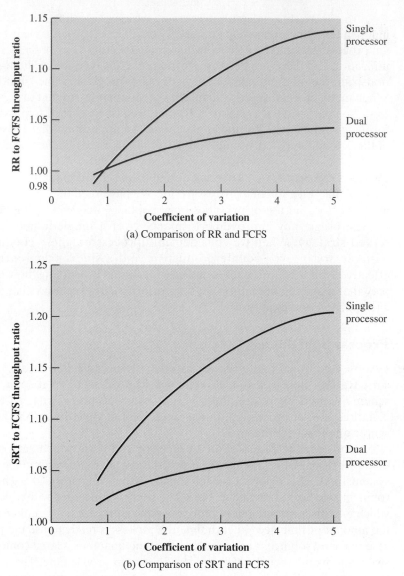

**Figure 10.1   Comparison of Scheduling Performance for One
and Two Processors**

much less disruptive in the FCFS case; other processes can use the other processor. Similar results are shown in Figure 10.1b.

The study in [SAUE81] repeated this analysis under a number of assumptions about degree of multiprogramming, mix of I/O-bound versus CPU-bound proc-esses, and the use of priorities. The general conclusion is that the specific scheduling discipline is much less important with two processors than with one. It should be evident that this conclusion is even stronger as the number of processors increases. Thus, a simple FCFS discipline or the use of FCFS within a static priority scheme may suffice for a multiple-processor system.

Thread Scheduling

As we have seen, with threads, the concept of execution is separated from the rest of the definition of a process. An application can be implemented as a set of threads that cooperate and execute concurrently in the same address space.

On a uniprocessor, threads can be used as a program structuring aid and to overlap I/O with processing. Because of the minimal penalty in doing a thread switch compared to a process switch, these benefits are realized with little cost. However, the full power of threads becomes evident in a multiprocessor system. In this environment, threads can be used to exploit true parallelism in an application. If the various threads of an application are simultaneously run on separate processors, dramatic gains in performance are possible. However, it can be shown that for applications that require significant interaction among threads (medium-grain parallelism), small differences in thread management and scheduling can have a significant performance impact [ANDE89].

Among the many proposals for multiprocessor thread scheduling and processor assignment, four general approaches stand out:

- **Load sharing:** Processes are not assigned to a particular processor. A global queue of ready threads is maintained, and each processor, when idle, selects a thread from the queue. The term **load sharing** is used to distinguish this strategy from load-balancing schemes in which work is allocated on a more permanent basis (e.g., see [FEIT90a]).[2]

- **Gang scheduling:** A set of related threads is scheduled to run on a set of processors at the same time, on a one-to-one basis.

- **Dedicated processor assignment:** This is the opposite of the load-sharing approach and provides implicit scheduling defined by the assignment of threads to processors. Each program, for the duration of its execution, is allocated a number of processors equal to the number of threads in the program. When the program terminates, the processors return to the general pool for possible allocation to another program.

- **Dynamic scheduling:** The number of threads in a process can be altered during the course of execution.

LOAD SHARING   Load sharing is perhaps the simplest approach and the one that carries over most directly from a uniprocessor environment. It has several advantages:

- The load is distributed evenly across the processors, assuring that no processor is idle while work is available to do.

- No centralized scheduler is required; when a processor is available, the scheduling routine of the operating system is run on that processor to select the next thread.

---

[2]Some of the literature on this topic refers to this approach as *self-scheduling*, because each processor schedules itself without regard to other processors. However, this term is also used in the literature to refer to programs written in a language that allows the programmer to specify the scheduling (e.g., see [FOST91]).

- The global queue can be organized and accessed using any of the schemes discussed in Chapter 9, including priority-based schemes and schemes that consider execution history or anticipated processing demands.

  [LEUT90] analyzes three different versions of load sharing:

- **First-come-first-served (FCFS):** When a job arrives, each of its threads is placed consecutively at the end of the shared queue. When a processor becomes idle, it picks the next ready thread, which it executes until completion or blocking.

- **Smallest number of threads first:** The shared ready queue is organized as a priority queue, with highest priority given to threads from jobs with the smallest number of unscheduled threads. Jobs of equal priority are ordered according to which job arrives first. As with FCFS, a scheduled thread is run to completion or blocking.

- **Preemptive smallest number of threads first:** Highest priority is given to jobs with the smallest number of unscheduled threads. An arriving job with a smaller number of threads than an executing job will preempt threads belonging to the scheduled job.

Using simulation models, the authors report that, over a wide range of job characteristics, FCFS is superior to the other two policies in the preceding list. Further, the authors find that some form of gang scheduling, discussed in the next subsection, is generally superior to load sharing.

There are several disadvantages of load sharing:

- The central queue occupies a region of memory that must be accessed in a manner that enforces mutual exclusion. Thus, it may become a bottleneck if many processors look for work at the same time. When there is only a small number of processors, this is unlikely to be a noticeable problem. However, when the multiprocessor consists of dozens or even hundreds of processors, the potential for bottleneck is real.

- Preempted threads are unlikely to resume execution on the same processor. If each processor is equipped with a local cache, caching becomes less efficient.

- If all threads are treated as a common pool of threads, it is unlikely that all of the threads of a program will gain access to processors at the same time. If a high degree of coordination is required between the threads of a program, the process switches involved may seriously compromise performance.

Despite the potential disadvantages, load sharing is one of the most commonly used schemes in current multiprocessors.

A refinement of the load-sharing technique is used in the Mach operating system [BLAC90, WEND89]. The operating system maintains a local run queue for each processor and a shared global run queue. The local run queue is used by threads that have been temporarily bound to a specific processor. A processor examines the local run queue first to give bound threads absolute preference over unbound threads. As an example of the use of bound threads, one or more processors could be dedicated to running processes that are part of the operating system.

Another example is that the threads of a particular application could be distributed among a number of processors; with the proper additional software, this provides support for gang scheduling, discussed next.

GANG SCHEDULING   The concept of scheduling a set of processes simultaneously on a set of processors predates the use of threads. [JONE80] refers to the concept as group scheduling and cites the following benefits:

- If closely related processes execute in parallel, synchronization blocking may be reduced, less process switching may be necessary, and performance will increase.
- Scheduling overhead may be reduced because a single decision affects a number of processors and processes at one time.

On the Cm* multiprocessor, the term *coscheduling* is used [GEHR87]. Coscheduling is based on the concept of scheduling a related set of tasks, called a task force. The individual elements of a task force tend to be quite small and are hence close to the idea of a thread.

The term *gang scheduling* has been applied to the simultaneous scheduling of the threads that make up a single process [FEIT90b]. Gang scheduling is useful for medium-grained to fine-grained parallel applications whose performance severely degrades when any part of the application is not running while other parts are ready to run. It is also beneficial for any parallel application, even one that is not quite so performance sensitive. The need for gang scheduling is widely recognized, and implementations exist on a variety of multiprocessor operating systems.

One obvious way in which gang scheduling improves the performance of a single application is that process switches are minimized. Suppose one thread of a process is executing and reaches a point at which it must synchronize with another thread of the same process. If that other thread is not running, but is in a ready queue, the first thread is hung up until a process switch can be done on some other processor to bring in the needed thread. In an application with tight coordination among threads, such switches will dramatically reduce performance. The simultaneous scheduling of cooperating threads can also save time in resource allocation. For example, multiple gang-scheduled threads can access a file without the additional overhead of locking during a seek, read/write operation.

The use of gang scheduling creates a requirement for processor allocation. One possibility is the following. Suppose that we have N processors and M applications, each of which has N or fewer threads. Then each application could be given $1/M$ of the available time on the N processors, using time slicing. [FEIT90a] notes that this strategy can be inefficient. Consider an example in which there are two applications, one with four threads and one with one thread. Using uniform time allocation wastes 37.5% of the processing resource, because when the single-thread application runs, three processors are left idle (see Figure 10.2). If there are several one-thread applications, these could all be fit together to increase processor utilization. If that option is not available, an alternative to uniform scheduling is scheduling that is weighted by the number of threads. Thus, the four-thread application could be given four-fifths of the time and the one-thread application given only one-fifth of the time, reducing the processor waste to 15%.

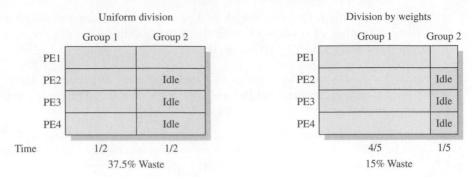

Figure 10.2   Example of Scheduling Groups with Four and One Threads [FEIT90b]

DEDICATED PROCESSOR ASSIGNMENT   An extreme form of gang scheduling, suggested in [TUCK89], is to dedicate a group of processors to an application for the duration of the application. That is, when an application is scheduled, each of its threads is assigned a processor that remains dedicated to that thread until the application runs to completion.

This approach would appear to be extremely wasteful of processor time. If a thread of an application is blocked waiting for I/O or for synchronization with another thread, then that thread's processor remains idle: there is no multiprogramming of processors. Two observations can be made in defense of this strategy:

1. In a highly parallel system, with tens or hundreds of processors, each of which represents a small fraction of the cost of the system, processor utilization is no longer so important as a metric for effectiveness or performance.

2. The total avoidance of process switching during the lifetime of a program should result in a substantial speedup of that program.

Both [TUCK89] and [ZAHO90] report analyses that support statement 2. Figure 10.3 shows the results of one experiment [TUCK89]. The authors ran two applications simultaneously (executing concurrently), a matrix multiplication and a fast Fourier transform (FFT) calculation, on a system with 16 processors. Each application breaks its problem into a number of tasks, which are mapped onto the threads executing that application. The programs are written in such a way as to allow the number of threads to be used to vary. In essence, a number of tasks are defined and queued by an application. Tasks are taken from the queue and mapped onto the available threads by the application. If there are fewer threads than tasks, then leftover tasks remain queued and are picked up by threads as they complete their assigned tasks. Clearly, not all applications can be structured in this way, but many numerical problems and some other applications can be dealt with in this fashion.

Figure 10.3 shows the speedup for the applications as the number of threads executing the tasks in each application is varied from 1 to 24. For example, we see that when both applications are started simultaneously with 24 threads each, the speedup obtained, compared to using a single thread for each application, is 2.8 for matrix multiplication and 2.4 for FFT. The figure shows that the performance of both applications worsens considerably when the number of threads in each application exceeds eight and thus the total number of processes in the system exceeds the number of processors. Furthermore, the larger the number of threads, the worse the

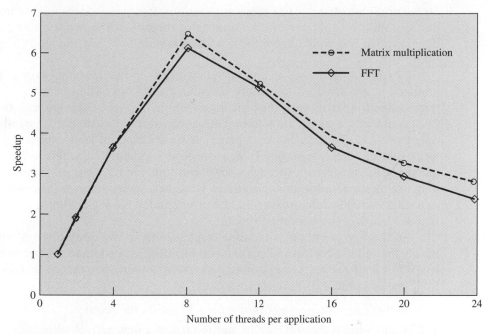

Figure 10.3   Application Speedup as a Function of Number of Threads [TUCK89]

performance gets, because there is a greater frequency of thread preemption and rescheduling. This excessive preemption results in inefficiency from many sources, including time spent waiting for a suspended thread to leave a critical section, time wasted in process switching, and inefficient cache behavior.

The authors conclude that an effective strategy is to limit the number of active threads to the number of processors in the system. If most of the applications are either single thread or can use the task-queue structure, this will provide an effective and reasonably efficient use of the processor resources.

Both dedicated processor assignment and gang scheduling attack the scheduling problem by addressing the issue of processor allocation. One can observe that the processor allocation problem on a multiprocessor more closely resembles the memory allocation problem on a uniprocessor than the scheduling problem on a uniprocessor. The issue is how many processors to assign to a program at any given time, which is analogous to how many page frames to assign to a given process at any time. [GEHR87] proposes the term *activity working set*, analogous to a virtual memory working set, as the minimum number of activities (threads) that must be scheduled simultaneously on processors for the application to make acceptable progress. As with memory management schemes, the failure to schedule all of the elements of an activity working set can lead to processor thrashing. This occurs when the scheduling of threads whose services are required induces the descheduling of other threads whose services will soon be needed. Similarly, processor fragmentation refers to a situation in which some processors are left over when others are allocated, and the leftover processors are either insufficient in number or unsuitably organized to support the requirements of waiting applications. Gang scheduling and dedicated processor allocation are meant to avoid these problems.

DYNAMIC SCHEDULING For some applications, it is possible to provide language and system tools that permit the number of threads in the process to be altered dynamically. This would allow the operating system to adjust the load to improve utilization.

[ZAHO90] proposes an approach in which both the operating system and the application are involved in making scheduling decisions. The operating system is responsible for partitioning the processors among the jobs. Each job uses the processors currently in its partition to execute some subset of its runnable tasks by mapping these tasks to threads. An appropriate decision about which subset to run, as well as which thread to suspend when a process is preempted, is left to the individual applications (perhaps through a set of run-time library routines). This approach may not be suitable for all applications. However, some applications could default to a single thread while others could be programmed to take advantage of this particular feature of the operating system.

In this approach, the scheduling responsibility of the operating system is primarily limited to processor allocation and proceeds according to the following policy. When a job requests one or more processors (either when the job arrives for the first time or because its requirements change),

1. If there are idle processors, use them to satisfy the request.

2. Otherwise, if the job making the request is a new arrival, allocate it a single processor by taking one away from any job currently allocated more than one processor.

3. If any portion of the request cannot be satisfied, it remains outstanding until either a processor becomes available for it or the job rescinds the request (e.g., if there is no longer a need for the extra processors).

Upon release of one or more processors (including job departure),

4. Scan the current queue of unsatisfied requests for processors. Assign a single processor to each job in the list that currently has no processors (i.e., to all waiting new arrivals). Then scan the list again, allocating the rest of the processors on an FCFS basis.

Analyses reported in [ZAHO90] and [MAJU88] suggest that for applications that can take advantage of dynamic scheduling, this approach is superior to gang scheduling or dedicated processor assignment. However, the overhead of this approach may negate this apparent performance advantage. Experience with actual systems is needed to prove the worth of dynamic scheduling.

10.2 REAL-TIME SCHEDULING

Background

Real-time computing is becoming an increasingly important discipline. The operating system, and in particular the scheduler, is perhaps the most important component of a real-time system. Examples of current applications of real-time systems include control of laboratory experiments, process control in industrial plants, robotics, air traffic control, telecommunications, and military command and control systems. Next-generation systems will include the autonomous land rover, controllers of robots with elastic joints, systems found in intelligent manufacturing, the space station, and undersea exploration.

Real-time computing may be defined as that type of computing in which the correctness of the system depends not only on the logical result of the computation but also on the time at which the results are produced. We can define a real-time system by defining what is meant by a real-time process, or task.[3] In general, in a real-time system, some of the tasks are real-time tasks, and these have a certain degree of urgency to them. Such tasks are attempting to control or react to events that take place in the outside world. Because these events occur in "real time," a real-time task must be able to keep up with the events with which it is concerned. Thus, it is usually possible to associate a deadline with a particular task, where the deadline specifies either a start time or a completion time. Such a task may be classified as hard or soft. A **hard real-time task** is one that must meet its deadline; otherwise it will cause unacceptable damage or a fatal error to the system. A **soft real-time task** has an associated deadline that is desirable but not mandatory; it still makes sense to schedule and complete the task even if it has passed its deadline.

Another characteristic of real-time tasks is whether they are periodic or aperiodic. An **aperiodic task** has a deadline by which it must finish or start, or it may have a constraint on both start and finish time. In the case of a **periodic task**, the requirement may be stated as "once per period T" or "exactly T units apart."

Characteristics of Real–Time Operating Systems

Real-time operating systems can be characterized as having unique requirements in five general areas [MORG92]:

- Determinism
- Responsiveness
- User control
- Reliability
- Fail-soft operation

An operating system is **deterministic** to the extent that it performs operations at fixed, predetermined times or within predetermined time intervals. When multiple processes are competing for resources and processor time, no system will be fully deterministic. In a real-time operating system, process requests for service are dictated by external events and timings. The extent to which an operating system can deterministically satisfy requests depends first on the speed with which it can

---

[3]As usual, terminology poses a problem, because various words are used in the literature with varying meanings. It is common for a particular process to operate under real-time constraints of a repetitive nature. That is, the process lasts for a long time and, during that time, performs some repetitive function in response to real-time events. Let us, for this section, refer to an individual function as a task. Thus, the process can be viewed as progressing through a sequence of tasks. At any given time, the process is engaged in a single task, and it is the process/task that must be scheduled.

respond to interrupts and, second, on whether the system has sufficient capacity to handle all requests within the required time.

One useful measure of the ability of an operating system to function deterministically is the maximum delay from the arrival of a high-priority device interrupt to when servicing begins. In non-real-time operating systems, this delay may be in the range of tens to hundreds of milliseconds, while in real-time operating systems that delay may have an upper bound of anywhere from a few microseconds to a millisecond.

A related but distinct characteristic is **responsiveness**. Determinism is concerned with how long an operating system delays before acknowledging an interrupt. Responsiveness is concerned with how long, after acknowledgment, it takes an operating system to service the interrupt. Aspects of responsiveness include the following:

1. The amount of time required to initially handle the interrupt and begin execution of the interrupt service routine (ISR). If execution of the ISR requires a process switch, then the delay will be longer than if the ISR can be executed within the context of the current process.

2. The amount of time required to perform the ISR. This generally is dependent on the hardware platform.

3. The effect of interrupt nesting. If an ISR can be interrupted by the arrival of another interrupt, then the service will be delayed.

Determinism and responsiveness together make up the response time to external events. Response time requirements are critical for real-time systems, because such systems must meet timing requirements imposed by individuals, devices, and data flows external to the system.

User control is generally much broader in a real-time operating system than in ordinary operating systems. In a typical non-real-time operating system, the user either has no control over the scheduling function of the operating system or can only provide broad guidance, such as grouping users into more than one priority class. In a real-time system, however, it is essential to allow the user fine-grained control over task priority. The user should be able to distinguish between hard and soft tasks and to specify relative priorities within each class. A real-time system may also allow the user to specify such characteristics as the use of paging or process swapping, what processes must always be resident in main memory, what disk transfer algorithms are to be used, what rights the processes in various priority bands have, and so on.

Reliability is typically far more important for real-time systems than non-real-time systems. A transient failure in a non-real-time system may be solved by simply rebooting the system. A processor failure in a multiprocessor non-real-time system may result in a reduced level of service until the failed processor is repaired or replaced. But a real-time system is responding to and controlling events in real time. Loss or degradation of performance may have catastrophic consequences, ranging from financial loss to major equipment damage and even loss of life.

As in other areas, the difference between a real-time and a non-real-time operating system is one of degree. Even a real-time system must be designed to respond to various failure modes. **Fail-soft operation** is a characteristic that refers to the ability of a system to fail in such a way as to preserve as much capability and data as possible. For example, a typical traditional UNIX system, when it detects a corruption of data within the kernel, issues a failure message on the system console, dumps the memory contents to disk for later failure analysis, and terminates execution of the system. In contrast, a real-time system will attempt either to correct the problem or minimize its effects while continuing to run. Typically, the system notifies a user or user process that it should attempt corrective action and then continues operation perhaps at a reduced level of service. In the event a shutdown is necessary, an attempt is made to maintain file and data consistency.

An important aspect of fail-soft operation is referred to as stability. A real-time system is stable if, in cases where it is impossible to meet all task deadlines, the system will meet the deadlines of its most critical, highest-priority tasks, even if some less critical task deadlines are not always met.

To meet the foregoing requirements, real-time operating systems typically include the following features [STAN89]:

- Fast process or thread switch
- Small size (with its associated minimal functionality)
- Ability to respond to external interrupts quickly
- Multitasking with interprocess communication tools such as semaphores, signals, and events
- Use of special sequential files that can accumulate data at a fast rate
- Preemptive scheduling based on priority
- Minimization of intervals during which interrupts are disabled
- Primitives to delay tasks for a fixed amount of time and to pause/resume tasks
- Special alarms and timeouts

The heart of a real time system is the short-term task scheduler. In designing such a scheduler, fairness and minimizing average response time are not paramount. What is important is that all hard real-time tasks complete (or start) by their deadline and that as many as possible soft real-time tasks also complete (or start) by their deadline.

Most contemporary real-time operating systems are unable to deal directly with deadlines. Instead, they are designed to be as responsive as possible to real-time tasks so that, when a deadline approaches, a task can be quickly scheduled. From this point of view, real-time applications typically require deterministic response times in the several-millisecond to submillisecond span under a broad set of conditions; leading-edge applications—in simulators for military aircraft, for example— often have constraints in the range of 10–100 μs [ATLA89].

Figure 10.4 illustrates a spectrum of possibilities. In a preemptive scheduler that uses simple round-robin scheduling, a real-time task would be added to the ready queue to await its next timeslice, as illustrated in Figure 10.4a. In this case, the scheduling time will generally be unacceptable for real-time applications. Alternatively, in a nonpreemptive scheduler, we could use a priority scheduling mechanism, giving real-time tasks higher priority. In this case, a real-time task that is ready would be scheduled as soon as the current process blocks or runs to completion (Figure 10.4b). This could lead to a delay of several seconds if a slow, low-priority task were

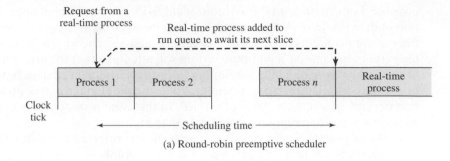

(a) Round-robin preemptive scheduler

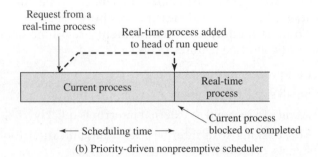

(b) Priority-driven nonpreemptive scheduler

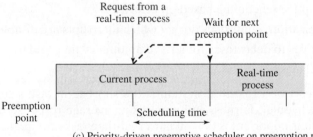

(c) Priority-driven preemptive scheduler on preemption points

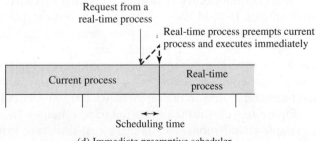

(d) Immediate preemptive scheduler

Figure 10.4   Scheduling of Real-Time Process

executing at a critical time. Again, this approach is not acceptable. A more promising approach is to combine priorities with clock-based interrupts. Preemption points occur at regular intervals. When a preemption point occurs, the currently running task is preempted if a higher-priority task is waiting. This would include the preemption of tasks that are part of the operating system kernel. Such a delay may be on the order of several milliseconds (Figure 10.4c). While this last approach may be adequate for some real-time applications, it will not suffice for more demanding applications. In those cases, the approach that has been taken is sometimes referred to as immediate preemption. In this case, the operating system responds to an interrupt almost immediately, unless the system is in a critical-code lockout section. Scheduling delays for a real-time task can then be reduced to 100 µs or less.

Real–Time Scheduling

Real-time scheduling is one of the most active areas of research in computer science. In this subsection, we provide an overview of the various approaches to real-time scheduling and look at two popular classes of scheduling algorithms.

In a survey of real-time scheduling algorithms, [RAMA94] observes that the various scheduling approaches depend on (1) whether a system performs schedulability analysis, (2) if it does, whether it is done statically or dynamically, and (3) whether the result of the analysis itself produces a schedule or plan according to which tasks are dispatched at run time. Based on these considerations, the authors identify the following classes of algorithms:

- **Static table-driven approaches:** These perform a static analysis of feasible schedules of dispatching. The result of the analysis is a schedule that determines, at run time, when a task must begin execution.
- **Static priority-driven preemptive approaches:** Again, a static analysis is performed, but no schedule is drawn up. Rather, the analysis is used to assign priorities to tasks, so that a traditional priority-driven preemptive scheduler can be used.
- **Dynamic planning-based approaches:** Feasibility is determined at run time (dynamically) rather than offline prior to the start of execution (statically). An arriving task is accepted for execution only if it is feasible to meet its time constraints. One of the results of the feasibility analysis is a schedule or plan that is used to decide when to dispatch this task.
- **Dynamic best effort approaches:** No feasibility analysis is performed. The system tries to meet all deadlines and aborts any started process whose deadline is missed.

Static table-driven scheduling is applicable to tasks that are periodic. Input to the analysis consists of the periodic arrival time, execution time, periodic ending deadline, and relative priority of each task. The scheduler attempts to develop a schedule that enables it to meet the requirements of all periodic tasks. This is a predictable approach but one that is inflexible, because any change to any task requirements requires that the schedule be redone. Earliest-deadline-first or other periodic deadline techniques (discussed subsequently) are typical of this category of scheduling algorithms.

Static priority-driven preemptive scheduling makes use of the priority-driven preemptive scheduling mechanism common to most non-real-time multiprogramming systems. In a non-real-time system, a variety of factors might be used to determine priority. For example, in a time-sharing system, the priority of a process changes depending on whether it is processor bound or I/O bound. In a real-time system, priority assignment is related to the time constraints associated with each task. One example of this approach is the rate monotonic algorithm (discussed subsequently), which assigns static priorities to tasks based on the length of their periods.

With **dynamic planning-based scheduling**, after a task arrives, but before its execution begins, an attempt is made to create a schedule that contains the previously scheduled tasks as well as the new arrival. If the new arrival can be scheduled in such a way that its deadlines are satisfied and that no currently scheduled task misses a deadline, then the schedule is revised to accommodate the new task.

Dynamic best effort scheduling is the approach used by many real-time systems that are currently commercially available. When a task arrives, the system assigns a priority based on the characteristics of the task. Some form of deadline scheduling, such as earliest-deadline scheduling, is typically used. Typically, the tasks are aperiodic and so no static scheduling analysis is possible. With this type of scheduling, until a deadline arrives or until the task completes, we do not know whether a timing constraint will be met. This is the major disadvantage of this form of scheduling. Its advantage is that it is easy to implement.

Deadline Scheduling

Most contemporary real-time operating systems are designed with the objective of starting real-time tasks as rapidly as possible, and hence emphasize rapid interrupt handling and task dispatching. In fact, this is not a particularly useful metric in evaluating real-time operating systems. Real-time applications are generally not concerned with sheer speed but rather with completing (or starting) tasks at the most valuable times, neither too early nor too late, despite dynamic resource demands and conflicts, processing overloads, and hardware or software faults. It follows that priorities provide a crude tool and do not capture the requirement of completion (or initiation) at the most valuable time.

There have been a number of proposals for more powerful and appropriate approaches to real-time task scheduling. All of these are based on having additional information about each task. In its most general form, the following information about each task might be used:

- **Ready time:** Time at which task becomes ready for execution. In the case of a repetitive or periodic task, this is actually a sequence of times that is known in advance. In the case of an aperiodic task, this time may be known in advance, or the operating system may only be aware when the task is actually ready.
- **Starting deadline:** Time by which a task must begin.
- **Completion deadline:** Time by which a task must be completed. The typical real-time application will either have starting deadlines or completion deadlines, but not both.

- **Processing time:** Time required to execute the task to completion. In some cases, this is supplied. In others, the operating system measures an exponential average (as defined in Chapter 9). For still other scheduling systems, this information is not used.
- **Resource requirements:** Set of resources (other than the processor) required by the task while it is executing.
- **Priority:** Measures relative importance of the task. Hard real-time tasks may have an "absolute" priority, with the system failing if a deadline is missed. If the system is to continue to run no matter what, then both hard and soft real-time tasks may be assigned relative priorities as a guide to the scheduler.
- **Subtask structure:** A task may be decomposed into a mandatory subtask and an optional subtask. Only the mandatory subtask possesses a hard deadline.

There are several dimensions to the real-time scheduling function when deadlines are taken into account: which task to schedule next, and what sort of preemption is allowed. It can be shown, for a given preemption strategy and using either starting or completion deadlines, that a policy of scheduling the task with the earliest deadline minimizes the fraction of tasks that miss their deadlines [BUTT99, HONG89, PANW88]. This conclusion holds for both single-processor and multi-processor configurations.

The other critical design issue is that of preemption. When starting deadlines are specified, then a nonpreemptive scheduler makes sense. In this case, it would be the responsibility of the real-time task to block itself after completing the mandatory or critical portion of its execution, allowing other real-time starting deadlines to be satisfied. This fits the pattern of Figure 10.4b. For a system with completion deadlines, a preemptive strategy (Figure 10.4c or 10.4d) is most appropriate. For example, if task X is running and task Y is ready, there may be circumstances in which the only way to allow both X and Y to meet their completion deadlines is to preempt X, execute Y to completion, and then resume X to completion.

As an example of scheduling periodic tasks with completion deadlines, consider a system that collects and processes data from two sensors, A and B. The deadline for collecting data from sensor A must be met every 20 ms, and that for B every 50 ms. It takes 10 ms, including operating system overhead, to process each sample of data from A and 25 ms to process each sample of data from B. Table 10.2 summarizes the execution profile of the two tasks. Figure 10.5 compares three scheduling techniques using the execution profile of Table 10.2. The first row of Figure 10.5 repeats the information in Table 10.2; the remaining three rows illustrate three scheduling techniques.

The computer is capable of making a scheduling decision every 10 ms.[4] Suppose that, under these circumstances, we attempted to use a priority scheduling scheme. The first two timing diagrams in Figure 10.5 show the result. If A has higher priority, the first instance of task B is given only 20 ms of processing time, in two 10-ms chunks, by the time its deadline is reached, and thus fails. If B is given higher priority, then A will miss its first deadline. The final timing diagram shows the use of earliest-deadline scheduling. At time $t = 0$, both A1 and B1 arrive. Because A1 has the

---

[4]This need not be on a 10-ms boundary if more than 10 ms has elapsed since the last scheduling decision.

Table 10.2   Execution Profile of Two Periodic Tasks

Process	Arrival Time	Execution Time	Ending Deadline
A(1)	0	10	20
A(2)	20	10	40
A(3)	40	10	60
A(4)	60	10	80
A(5)	80	10	100
•	•	•	•
•	•	•	•
•	•	•	•
B(1)	0	25	50
B(2)	50	25	100
•	•	•	•
•	•	•	•
•	•	•	•

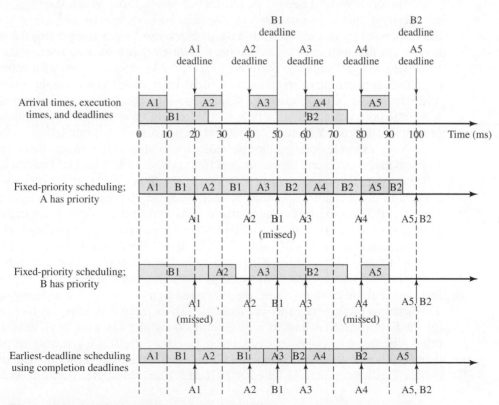

Figure 10.5   Scheduling of Periodic Real-Time Tasks with Completion Deadlines (Based on Table 10.2)

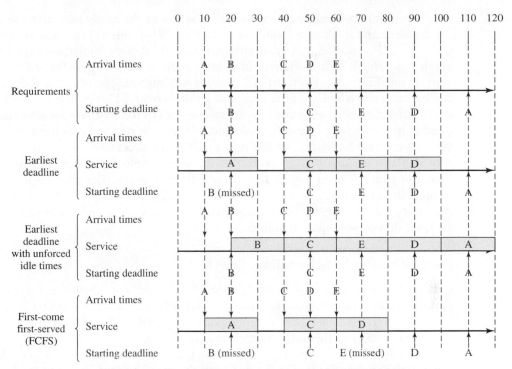

Figure 10.6 Scheduling of Aperiodic Real-Time Tasks with Starting Deadlines

earliest deadline, it is scheduled first. When A1 completes, B1 is given the processor. At $t = 20$, A2 arrives. Because A2 has an earlier deadline than B1, B1 is interrupted so that A2 can execute to completion. Then B1 is resumed at $t = 30$. At $t = 40$, A3 arrives. However, B1 has an earlier ending deadline and is allowed to execute to completion at $t = 45$. A3 is then given the processor and finishes at $t = 55$.

In this example, by scheduling to give priority at any preemption point to the task with the nearest deadline, all system requirements can be met. Because the tasks are periodic and predictable, a static table-driven scheduling approach is used.

Now consider a scheme for dealing with aperiodic tasks with starting deadlines. The top part of Figure 10.6 shows the arrival times and starting deadlines for an example consisting of five tasks each of which has an execution time of 20 ms. Table 10.3 summarizes the execution profile of the five tasks.

Table 10.3 Execution Profile of Five Aperiodic Tasks

Process	Arrival Time	Execution Time	Starting Deadline
A	10	20	110
B	20	20	20
C	40	20	50
D	50	20	90
E	60	20	70

A straightforward scheme is to always schedule the ready task with the earliest deadline and let that task run to completion. When this approach is used in the example of Figure 10.6, note that although task B requires immediate service, the service is denied. This is the risk in dealing with aperiodic tasks, especially with starting deadlines. A refinement of the policy will improve performance if deadlines can be known in advance of the time that a task is ready. This policy, referred to as earliest deadline with unforced idle times, operates as follows: Always schedule the eligible task with the earliest deadline and let that task run to completion. An eligible task may not be ready, and this may result in the processor remaining idle even though there are ready tasks. Note that in our example the system refrains from scheduling task A even though that is the only ready task. The result is that, even though the processor is not used to maximum efficiency, all scheduling requirements are met. Finally, for comparison, the FCFS policy is shown. In this case, tasks B and E do not meet their deadlines.

Rate Monotonic Scheduling

One of the more promising methods of resolving multitask scheduling conflicts for periodic tasks is rate monotonic scheduling (RMS). The scheme was first proposed in [LIU73] but has only recently gained popularity [BRIA99, SHA94]. RMS assigns priorities to tasks on the basis of their periods.

For RMS, the highest-priority task is the one with the shortest period, the second highest-priority task is the one with the second shortest period, and so on. When more than one task is available for execution, the one with the shortest period is serviced first. If we plot the priority of tasks as a function of their rate, the result is a monotonically increasing function (Figure 10.7); hence the name "rate monotonic scheduling."

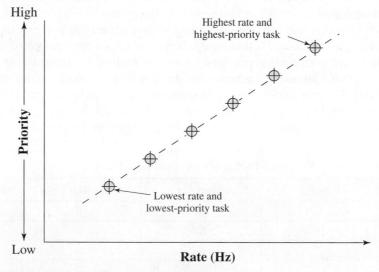

Figure 10.7   A Task Set with RMS [WARR91]

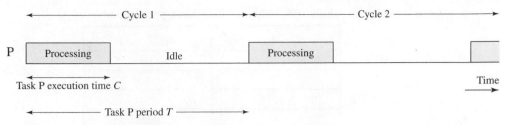

Figure 10.8   Periodic Task Timing Diagram

Figure 10.8 illustrates the relevant parameters for periodic tasks. The task's period, T, is the amount of time between the arrival of one instance of the task and the arrival of the next instance of the task. A task's rate (in hertz) is simply the inverse of its period (in seconds). For example, a task with a period of 50 ms occurs at a rate of 20 Hz. Typically, the end of a task's period is also the task's hard deadline, although some tasks may have earlier deadlines. The execution (or computation) time, C, is the amount of processing time required for each occurrence of the task. It should be clear that in a uniprocessor system, the execution time must be no greater than the period (must have $C \leq T$). If a periodic task is always run to completion, that is, if no instance of the task is ever denied service because of insufficient resources, then the utilization of the processor by this task is $U = C/T$. For example, if a task has a period of 80 ms and an execution time of 55 ms, its processor utilization is 55/80 = 0.6875.

One measure of the effectiveness of a periodic scheduling algorithm is whether or not it guarantees that all hard deadlines are met. Suppose that we have n tasks, each with a fixed period and execution time. Then for it to be possible to meet all deadlines, the following inequality must hold:

$$\frac{C_1}{T_1} + \frac{C_2}{T_2} + \cdots + \frac{C_n}{T_n} \leq 1 \qquad \textbf{(10.1)}$$

The sum of the processor utilizations of the individual tasks cannot exceed a value of 1, which corresponds to total utilization of the processor. Equation (10.1) provides a bound on the number of tasks that a perfect scheduling algorithm can successfully schedule. For any particular algorithm, the bound may be lower. For RMS, it can be shown that the following inequality holds:

$$\frac{C_1}{T_1} + \frac{C_2}{T_2} + \cdots + \frac{C_n}{T_n} \leq n(2^{1/n} - 1) \qquad \textbf{(10.2)}$$

Table 10.4 gives some values for this upper bound. As the number of tasks increases, the scheduling bound converges to $\ln 2 \approx 0.693$.

As an example, consider the case of three periodic tasks, where $U_i = C_i/T_i$:

- **Task P₁:** $C_1 = 20$; $T_1 = 100$; $U_1 = 0.2$
- **Task P₂:** $C_2 = 40$; $T_2 = 150$; $U_2 = 0.267$
- **Task P₃:** $C_3 = 100$; $T_3 = 350$; $U_3 = 0.286$

Table 10.4   Value of the RMS Upper Bound

n	$n(2^{1/n} - 1)$
1	1.0
2	0.828
3	0.779
4	0.756
5	0.743
6	0.734
•	•
•	•
•	•
∞	ln 2 ≈ 0.693

The total utilization of these three tasks is 0.2 + 0.267 + 0.286 = 0.753. The upper bound for the schedulability of these three tasks using RMS is

$$\frac{C_1}{T_1} + \frac{C_2}{T_2} + \frac{C_3}{T_3} \le n(2^{1/3} - 1) = 0.779$$

Because the total utilization required for the three tasks is less than the upper bound for RMS (0.753 < 0.779), we know that if RMS is used, all tasks will be successfully scheduled.

It can also be shown that the upper bound of Equation (10.1) holds for earliest deadline scheduling. Thus, it is possible to achieve greater overall processor utilization and therefore accommodate more periodic tasks with earliest deadline scheduling. Nevertheless, RMS has been widely adopted for use in industrial applications. [SHA91] offers the following explanation:

1. The performance difference is small in practice. The upper bound of Equation (10.2) is a conservative one and, in practice, utilization as high as 90% is often achieved.

2. Most hard real-time systems also have soft real-time components, such as certain noncritical displays and built-in self tests that can execute at lower priority levels to absorb the processor time that is not used with RMS scheduling of hard real-time tasks.

3. Stability is easier to achieve with RMS. When a system cannot meet all deadlines because of overload or transient errors, the deadlines of essential tasks need to be guaranteed provided that this subset of tasks is schedulable. In a static priority assignment approach, one only needs to ensure that essential tasks have relatively high priorities. This can be done in RMS by structuring essential tasks to have short periods or by modifying the RMS priorities to account for essential tasks. With earliest deadline scheduling, a periodic task's priority changes from one period to another. This makes it more difficult to ensure that essential tasks meet their deadlines.

Priority Inversion

Priority inversion is a phenomenon that can occur in any priority-based preemptive scheduling scheme but is particularly relevant in the context of real-time scheduling. The best-known instance of priority inversion involved the Mars Pathfinder mission. This rover robot landed on Mars on July 4, 1997 and began gathering and transmitting voluminous data back to Earth. But a few days into the mission, the lander software began experiencing total system resets, each resulting in losses of data. After much effort by the Jet Propulsion Laboratory (JPL) team that built the Pathfinder, the problem was traced to priority inversion [JONE97].

In any priority scheduling scheme, the system should always be executing the task with the highest priority. **Priority inversion** occurs when circumstances within the system force a higher-priority task to wait for a lower-priority task. A simple example of priority inversion occurs if a lower-priority task has locked a resource (such as a device or a binary semaphore) and a higher-priority task attempts to lock that same resource. The higher-priority task will be put in a blocked state until the resource is available. If the lower-priority task soon finishes with the resource and releases it, the higher-priority task may quickly resume and it is possible that no real-time constraints are violated.

A more serious condition is referred to as an **unbounded priority inversion**, in which the duration of a priority inversion depends not only on the time required to handle a shared resource but also on the unpredictable actions of other unrelated tasks. The priority inversion experienced in the Pathfinder software was unbounded and serves as a good example of the phenomenon. Our discussion follows that of [TIME02]. The Pathfinder software included the following three tasks, in decreasing order of priority:

T_1: Periodically checks the health of the spacecraft systems and software

T_2: Processes image data

T_3: Performs an occasional test on equipment status

After T_1 executes, it reinitializes a timer to its maximum value. If this timer ever expires, it is assumed that the integrity of the lander software has somehow been compromised. The processor is halted, all devices are reset, the software is completely reloaded, the spacecraft systems are tested, and the system starts over. This recovery sequence does not complete until the next day. T_1 and T_3 share a common data structure, protected by a binary semaphore s. Figure 10.9a shows the sequence that caused the priority inversion:

t_1: T_3 begins executing.

t_2: T_3 locks semaphore s and enters its critical section.

t_3: T_1, which has a higher priority than T_3, preempts T_3 and begins executing.

t_4: T_1 attempts to enter its critical section but is blocked because the semaphore is locked by T_3; T_3 resumes execution in its critical section.

t_5: T_2, which has a higher priority than T_3, preempts T_3 and begins executing.

t_6: T_2 is suspended for some reason unrelated to T_1 and T_3; T_3 resumes.

t_7: T_3 leaves its critical section and unlocks the semaphore. T_1 preempts T_3, locks the semaphore, and enters its critical section.

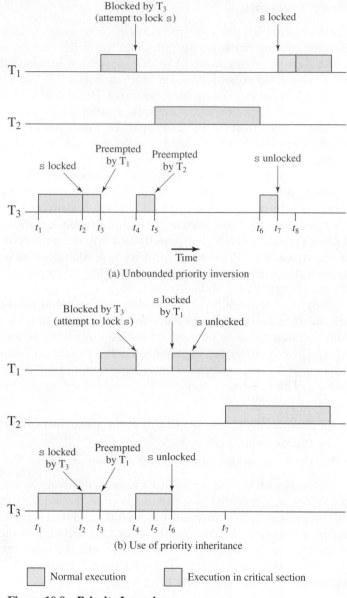

Figure 10.9   Priority Inversion

In this set of circumstances, T_1 must wait for both T_3 and T_2 to complete and fails to reset the timer before it expires.

In practical systems, two alternative approaches are used to avoid unbounded priority inversion: priority inheritance protocol and priority ceiling protocol.

The basic idea of **priority inheritance** is that a lower-priority task inherits the priority of any higher-priority task pending on a resource they share. This priority change takes place as soon as the higher-priority task blocks on the resource; it should end when the resource is released by the lower-priority task. Figure 10.9b shows that priority inheritance resolves the problem of unbounded priority inversion illustrated in Figure 10.9a. The relevant sequence of events is as follows:

t_1: T_3 begins executing.

t_2: T_3 locks semaphore s and enters its critical section.

t_3: T_1, which has a higher priority than T_3, preempts T_3 and begins executing.

t_4: T_1 attempts to enter its critical section but is blocked because the semaphore is locked by T_3. T_3 is immediately and temporarily assigned the same priority as T_1. T_3 resumes execution in its critical section.

t_5: T_2 is ready to execute but, because T_3 now has a higher priority, T_2 is unable to preempt T_3.

t_6: T_3 leaves its critical section and unlocks the semaphore: its priority level is downgraded to its previous default level. T_1 preempts T_3, locks the semaphore, and enters its critical section.

t_7: T_1 is suspended for some reason unrelated to T_2, and T_2 begins executing.

This was the approach taken to solving the Pathfinder problem.

In the **priority ceiling** approach, a priority is associated with each resource. The priority assigned to a resource is one level higher than the priority of its highest-priority user. The scheduler then dynamically assigns this priority to any task that accesses the resource. Once the task finishes with the resource, its priority returns to normal.

10.3 LINUX SCHEDULING

For Linux 2.4 and earlier, Linux provided a real-time scheduling capability coupled with a scheduler for non-real-time processes that made use of the traditional UNIX scheduling algorithm described in Section 9.3. Linux 2.6 includes essentially the same real-time scheduling capability as previous releases and a substantially revised scheduler for non-real-time processes. We examine these two areas in turn.

Real-Time Scheduling

The three Linux scheduling classes are

- **SCHED_FIFO:** First-in-first-out real-time threads
- **SCHED_RR:** Round-robin real-time threads
- **SCHED_OTHER:** Other, non-real-time threads

Within each class, multiple priorities may be used, with priorities in the real-time classes higher than the priorities for the SCHED_OTHER class. The default values are as follows: Real-time priority classes range from 0 to 99 inclusively, and SCHED_OTHER classes range from 100 to 139. A lower number equals a higher priority.

For FIFO threads, the following rules apply:

1. The system will not interrupt an executing FIFO thread except in the following cases:

    a. Another FIFO thread of higher priority becomes ready.

    b. The executing FIFO thread becomes blocked waiting for an event, such as I/O.

    c. The executing FIFO thread voluntarily gives up the processor following a call to the primitive `sched_yield`.

2. When an executing FIFO thread is interrupted, it is placed in the queue associated with its priority.

3. When a FIFO thread becomes ready and if that thread has a higher priority than the currently executing thread, then the currently executing thread is preempted and the highest-priority ready FIFO thread is executed. If more than one thread has that highest priority, the thread that has been waiting the longest is chosen.

The `SCHED_RR` policy is similar to the `SCHED_FIFO` policy, except for the addition of a timeslice associated with each thread. When a `SCHED_RR` thread has executed for its timeslice, it is suspended and a real-time thread of equal or higher priority is selected for running.

Figure 10.10 is an example that illustrates the distinction between FIFO and RR scheduling. Assume a process has four threads with three relative priorities assigned as shown in Figure 10.10a. Assume that all waiting threads are ready to execute when the current thread waits or terminates and that no higher-priority thread is awakened while a thread is executing. Figure 10.10b shows a flow in which all of the threads are in the `SCHED_FIFO` class. Thread D executes until it waits or terminates. Next, although threads B and C have the same priority, thread B starts because it has been waiting longer than thread C. Thread B executes until it waits or terminates, then thread C executes until it waits or terminates. Finally, thread A executes.

Figure 10.10c shows a sample flow if all of the threads are in the `SCHED_RR` class. Thread D executes until it waits or terminates. Next, threads B and C are time sliced, because they both have the same priority. Finally, thread A executes.

The final scheduling class is `SCHED_OTHER`. A thread in this class can only execute if there are no real-time threads ready to execute.

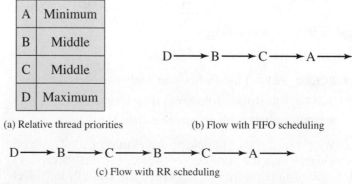

(a) Relative thread priorities   (b) Flow with FIFO scheduling

(c) Flow with RR scheduling

Figure 10.10   Example of Linux Real-Time Scheduling

Non-Real-Time Scheduling

The Linux 2.4 scheduler for the SCHED_OTHER class did not scale well with increasing number of processors and increasing number of processes. The drawbacks of this scheduler include the following:

- The Linux 2.4 scheduler uses a single runqueue for all processors in a symmetric multiprocessing system (SMP). This means a task can be scheduled on any processor, which can be good for load balancing but bad for memory caches. For example, suppose a task executed on CPU-1, and its data were in that processor's cache. If the task got rescheduled to CPU-2, its data would need to be invalidated in CPU-1 and brought into CPU-2.

- The Linux 2.4 scheduler uses a single runqueue lock. Thus, in an SMP system, the act of choosing a task to execute locks out any other processor from manipulating the runqueues. The result is idle processors awaiting release of the runqueue lock and decreased efficiency.

- Preemption is not possible in the Linux 2.4 scheduler; this means that a lower-priority task can execute while a higher-priority task waited for it to complete.

To correct these problems, Linux 2.6 uses a completely new priority scheduler known as the $O(1)$ scheduler.[5] The scheduler is designed so that the time to select the appropriate process and assign it to a processor is constant, regardless of the load on the system or the number of processors.

The kernel maintains two scheduling data structure for each processor in the system, of the following form (Figure 10.11):

```
struct prio_array {
int                 nr_active;              /* number of tasks in this array*/
unsigned long       bitmap[BITMAP_SIZE];  /* priority bitmap */
struct list_head queue[MAX_PRIO];          /* priority queues */
```

A separate queue is maintained for each priority level. The total number of queues in the structure is MAX_PRIO, which has a default value of 140. The structure also includes a bitmap array of sufficient size to provide one bit per priority level. Thus, with 140 priority levels and 32-bit words, BITMAP_SIZE has a value of 5. This creates a bitmap of 160 bits, of which 20 bits are ignored. The bitmap indicates which queues are not empty. Finally, nr_active indicates the total number of tasks present on all queues. Two structures are maintained: an active queues structure and an expired queues structure.

Initially, both bitmaps are set to all zeroes and all queues are empty. As a process becomes ready, it is assigned to the appropriate priority queue in the active queues structure and is assigned the appropriate timeslice. If a task is preempted before it completes its timeslice, it is returned to an active queue. When a task completes its timeslice, it goes into the appropriate queue in the expired queues structure and is assigned a new timeslice. All scheduling is done from among tasks in the active

---

[5]The term $O(1)$ is an example of the "big-O" notation, used for characterizing the time complexity of algorithms. Appendix I explains this notation.

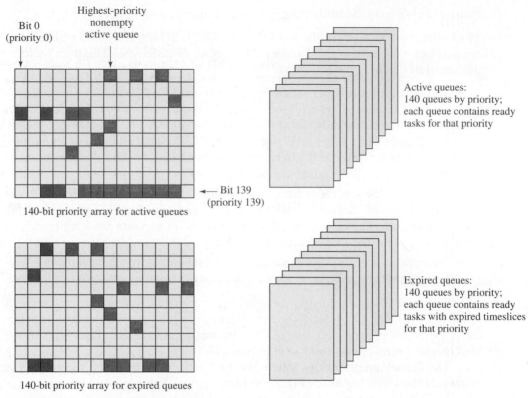

Figure 10.11   Linux Scheduling Data Structures for Each Processor

queues structure. When the active queues structure is empty, a simple pointer assignment results in a switch of the active and expired queues, and scheduling continues.

Scheduling is simple and efficient. On a given processor, the scheduler picks the highest-priority nonempty queue. If multiple tasks are in that queue, the tasks are scheduled in round-robin fashion.

Linux also includes a mechanism for moving tasks from the queue lists of one processor to that of another. Periodically, the scheduler checks to see if there is a substantial imbalance among the number of tasks assigned to each processor. To balance the load, the schedule can transfer some tasks. The highest-priority active tasks are selected for transfer, because it is more important to distribute high-priority tasks fairly.

CALCULATING PRIORITIES AND TIMESLICES   Each non-real-time task is assigned an initial priority in the range of 100–139, with a default of 120. This is the task's static priority and is specified by the user. As the task executes, a dynamic priority is calculated as a function of the task's static priority and its execution behavior. The Linux scheduler is designed to favor I/O-bound tasks over processor-bound tasks. This preference tends to provide good interactive response. The technique used by Linux to determine the dynamic priority is to keep a running tab on how much time a process sleeps (waiting for an event) versus how much time the process runs. In essence, a task that spends most of its time sleeping is given a higher priority.

Timeslices are assigned in the range of 10–200 ms. In general, higher-priority tasks are assigned larger timeslices.

RELATIONSHIP TO REAL-TIME TASKS Real-time tasks are handled in a different manner from non-real-time tasks in the priority queues. The following considerations apply:

1. All real-time tasks have only a static priority; no dynamic priority changes are made.

2. SCHED_FIFO tasks do not have assigned timeslices. Such tasks are scheduled in FIFO discipline. If a SHED_FIFO task is blocked, it returns to the same priority queue in the active queue list when it becomes unblocked.

3. Although SCHED_RR tasks do have assigned timeslices, they also are never moved to the expired queue list. When a SCHED_RR task exhausts its timeslice, it is returned to its priority queue with the same timeslice value. Timeslice values are never changed.

The effect of these rules is that the switch between the active queue list and the expired queue list only happens when there are no ready real-time tasks waiting to execute.

10.4 UNIX SVR4 SCHEDULING

The scheduling algorithm used in UNIX SVR4 is a complete overhaul of the scheduling algorithm used in earlier UNIX systems (described in Section 9.3). The new algorithm is designed to give highest preference to real-time processes, next-highest preference to kernel-mode processes, and lowest preference to other user-mode processes, referred to as time-shared processes.[6]

The two major modifications implemented in SVR4 are as follows:

1. The addition of a preemptable static priority scheduler and the introduction of a set of 160 priority levels divided into three priority classes.

2. The insertion of preemption points. Because the basic kernel is not preemptive, it can only be split into processing steps that must run to completion without interruption. In between the processing steps, safe places known as preemption points have been identified where the kernel can safely interrupt processing and schedule a new process. A safe place is defined as a region of code where all kernel data structures are either updated and consistent or locked via a semaphore.

Figure 10.12 illustrates the 160 priority levels defined in SVR4. Each process is defined to belong to one of three priority classes and is assigned a priority level within that class. The classes are as follows:

- **Real time (159-100):** Processes at these priority levels are guaranteed to be selected to run before any kernel or time-sharing process. In addition, real-time

---

[6]Time-shared processes are the processes that correspond to users in a traditional time-sharing system.

Priority class	Global value	Scheduling sequence
Real time	159 • • • • 100	First
Kernel	99 • • 60	
Time shared	59 • • • • 0	Last

Figure 10.12   SVR4 Priority Classses

processes can make use of preemption points to preempt kernel processes and user processes.

- **Kernel (99-60):** Processes at these priority levels are guaranteed to be selected to run before any time-sharing process but must defer to real-time processes.

- **Time-shared (59-0):** The lowest-priority processes, intended for user applications other than real-time applications.

Figure 10.13 indicates how scheduling is implemented in SVR4. A dispatch queue is associated with each priority level, and processes at a given priority level are executed in round-robin fashion. A bit-map vector, dqactmap, contains one bit for each priority level; the bit is set to one for any priority level with a nonempty queue. Whenever a running process leaves the Running state, due to a block, times-lice expiration, or preemption, the dispatcher checks dqactmap and dispatches a ready process from the highest-priority nonempty queue. In addition, whenever a defined preemption point is reached, the kernel checks a flag called kprunrun. If set, this indicates that at least one real-time process is in the Ready state, and the kernel preempts the current process if it is of lower priority than the highest-priority real-time ready process.

Within the time-sharing class, the priority of a process is variable. The scheduler reduces the priority of a process each time it uses up a time quantum, and it raises its

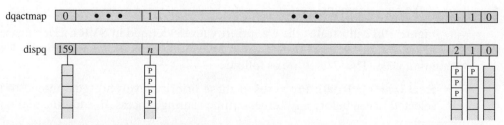

Figure 10.13   SVR4 Dispatch Queues

priority if it blocks on an event or resource. The time quantum allocated to a time-sharing process depends on its priority, ranging from 100 ms for priority 0 to 10 ms for priority 59. Each real-time process has a fixed priority and a fixed time quantum.

10.5 UNIX FREEBSD SCHEDULING

The UNIX FreeBSD scheduler is designed to provide a more efficient operation than previous UNIX schedulers under heavy load and when used on a multiprocessor or multicore platform. The scheduler is quite complex and here we present an overview of the most significant design features; for more detail, see [MCKU05] and [ROBE03].

Priority Classes

The underlying priority mechanism in the FreeBSD 5.1 scheduler is similar to that of UNIX SVR4. For FreeBSD, five priority classes are defined (Table 10.5); the first two classes are for kernel-mode thread and the remaining classes for user-mode threads. Kernel threads execute code that is complied into the kernel's load image and operate with the kernel's privileged execution code.

The highest-priority threads are referred to as *bottom-half kernel*. Threads in this class run in the kernel are scheduled based on interrupt priorities. These priorities are set when the corresponding devices are configured and do not change. *Top-half kernel* threads also run in the kernel and execute various kernel functions. These priorities are set based on predefined priorities and never change.

The next lower priority class is referred to as *real-time user*. A thread with a real-time priority is not subject to priority degradation. That is, a real-time thread maintains the priority it began with and does not drop to a lower priority as a result of using resources. Next comes the *time-sharing user* priority class. For threads in this class, priority is periodically recalculated based on a number of parameters, including the amount of processor time used, the amount of memory resources held, and other resource consumption parameters. The lowest range of priorities is referred to as the *idle user* class. This class is intended for applications that will only consume processor time when no other threads are ready to execute.

Table 10.5 FreeBSD Thread Scheduling Classes

Priority Class	Thread Type	Description
0–63	Bottom-half kernel	Scheduled by interrupts. Can block to await a resource.
64–127	Top-half kernel	Runs until blocked or done. Can block to await a resource.
128–159	Real-time user	Allowed to run until blocked or until a higher-priority thread becomes available. Preemptive scheduling.
160–223	Time-sharing user	Adjusts priorities based on processor usage.
224–255	Idle user	Only run when there are no time sharing or real-time threads to run.
Note: Lower number corresponds to higher priority.		

SMP and Multicore Support

The latest version of the FreeBSD scheduler, introduced with FreeBSD 5.0, was designed to provide effective scheduling for a SMP or multicore system. The new scheduler meets three design goals:

- Address the need for processor affinity in SMP and multicore systems. The term *processor affinity* refers to a scheduler that only migrates a thread (moves thread from one processor to another) when necessary to avoid having an idle processor.
- Provide better support for multithreading on multicore systems.
- Improve the performance of the scheduling algorithm, so that it is no longer a function of the number of threads in the system.

In this subsection, we look at three key features of the new scheduler: queue structure, interactivity scoring, and thread migration.

QUEUE STRUCTURE   The previous version of the FreeBSD schedule used a single global scheduling queue for all processors that it traverses once per second to recalculate their priorities. The use of a single list for all threads means that the performance of the scheduler is dependent on the number of tasks in the system, and as the number of tasks grows, more processor time must be spent in the scheduler maintaining the list.

The new scheduler performs scheduling independently for each processor. For each processor, three queues are maintained. Each of the queues has the structure shown in Figure 10.14 for SVR4. Two runqueues implement the kernel, real-time, and time-sharing scheduling classes (priorities 0 through 223). The third queue is only for the idle class (priorities 224 through 255).

The two runqueues are designated *current* and *next*. Every thread that is granted a timeslice (place in the Ready state) is placed in either the current queue or the next queue, as explained subsequently, at the appropriate priority for that thread. The scheduler for a processor selects threads from the current queue in priority order until the current queue is empty. When the current queue is empty, the scheduler swaps the current and next queue and begins to schedule threads from the new current queue. The use of two runqueues guarantees that each thread will be granted processor time at least once every two queue switches regardless of priority, avoiding starvation.

Several rules determine the assignment of a thread to either the current queue or the next queue:

1. Kernel and real-time threads are always inserted onto the current queue.
2. A time-sharing thread is assigned to the current queue if it is interactive (explained in the next subsection) or to the next queue otherwise. Inserting interactive threads onto the current queue results in a low interactive response time for such threads, compared to other time-sharing threads that do not exhibit a high degree of interactivity.

INTERACTIVITY SCORING   A thread is considered to be **interactive** if the ratio of its voluntary sleep time versus its run time is below a certain threshold. Interactive threads typically have high sleep times as they wait for user input. These sleep intervals are followed by bursts of processor activity as the thread processes the user's request.

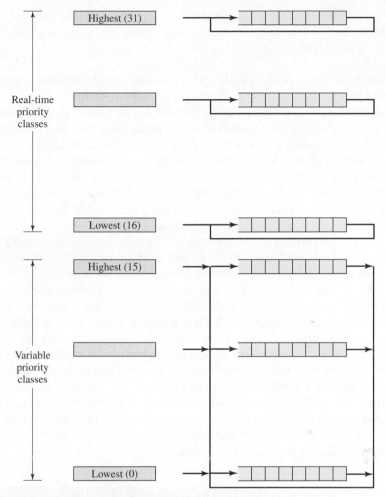

Figure 10.14   Windows Thread Dispatching Priorities

The interactivity threshold is defined in the scheduler code and is not configurable. The scheduler uses two equations to compute the interactivity score of a thread. First, we define a scaling factor:

$$\text{Scaling factor} = \frac{\text{Maximum interactivity score}}{2}$$

For threads whose sleep time exceeds their run time, the following equation is used:

$$\text{Interactivity score} = \text{Scaling factor}\left(\frac{\text{run}}{\text{sleep}}\right)$$

When a thread's run time exceeds its sleep time, the following equation is used instead:

$$\text{Interactivity score} = \text{Scaling factor}\left(1 + \frac{\text{sleep}}{\text{run}}\right)$$

The result is that threads whose sleep time exceeds their run time score in the lower half of the range of interactivity scores, and threads whose run time exceeds their sleep time score in the upper half of the range.

THREAD MIGRATION   In general, it is desirable to schedule a Ready thread onto the last processor that it ran on; this is called **processor affinity**. The alternative is to allow a thread to migrate to another processor for its next execution time slice. Processor affinity is significant because of local caches dedicated to a single processor. When a thread is run, it may still have data in the cache of its last processor. Changing to another processor means that the necessary data must be loaded into caches in the new processor and cache lines from the preceding processor must be invalidated. On the other hand, processor migration may allow a better load balancing and may prevent idle periods on some processors while other processor have more work than they can handle in a timely fashion.

The FreeBSD scheduler supports two mechanisms for thread migration to balance load: pull and push. With the **pull mechanism**, and idle processor steals a thread from a nonidle processor. When a processor has no work to do, it sets a bit in a global bit-mask indicating that it is idle. When an active processor is about to add work to its own run queue, it first checks for such idle bits and if a set idle bit is found, passes the thread to the idle processor. It is primarily useful when there is a light or sporadic load, or in situations where processes are starting and exiting very frequently.

The pull mechanism is effective in preventing the waste of a processor due to idleness. But it is not effective, or indeed relevant, in a situation in which every processor has work to do but the load has developed in an uneven fashion. With the **push mechanism**, a periodic scheduler task evaluates the current load situation and evens it out. Twice per second, this task picks the most-loaded and least-loaded processors in the system and equalizes their run queues. Push migration ensures fairness among the runnable threads.

10.6 WINDOWS SCHEDULING

Windows is designed to be as responsive as possible to the needs of a single user in a highly interactive environment or in the role of a server. Windows implements a preemptive scheduler with a flexible system of priority levels that includes round-robin scheduling within each level and, for some levels, dynamic priority variation on the basis of their current thread activity. Threads are the unit of scheduling in Windows rather than processes.

Process and Thread Priorities

Priorities in Windows are organized into two bands, or classes: real time and variable. Each of these bands consists of 16 priority levels. Threads requiring immediate attention are in the real-time class, which includes functions such as communications and real-time tasks.

Overall, because Windows makes use of a priority-driven preemptive scheduler, threads with real-time priorities have precedence over other threads. When a thread becomes ready whose priority is higher than the currently executing thread, the lower-priority thread is preempted and the processor given to the higher-priority thread.

Priorities are handled somewhat differently in the two classes (Figure 10.14). In **the real-time priority class**, all threads have a fixed priority that never changes. All of the active threads at a given priority level are in a round-robin queue. In the **variable priority class**, a thread's priority begins an initial priority value and then may be temporarily boosted (raised) during the thread's lifetime. There is a FIFO queue at each priority level; a thread will change queues among the variable priority classes as its own priority changes. However, a thread at priority level 15 or below is never boosted to level 16 or any other level in the real-time class.

The initial priority of a thread in the variable priority class is determined by two quantities: process base priority and thread base priority. The process base priority is an attribute of the process object, and can take on any value from 1 through 15 (priority 0 is reserved for the Executive's per-processor idle threads). Each thread object associated with a process object has a thread base priority attribute that indicates the thread's base priority relative to that of the process. The thread's base priority can be equal to that of its process or within two levels above or below that of the process. So, for example, if a process has a base priority of 4 and one of its threads has a base priority of −1, then the initial priority of that thread is 3.

Once a thread in the variable priority class has been created, its actual priority, referred to as the thread's current priority, may fluctuate within given boundaries. The current priority may never fall below the thread's base priority and it may never exceed 15. Figure 10.15 gives an example. The process object has a base priority attribute of 4. Each thread object associated with this process object must have an initial priority of between 2 and 6. Suppose the base priority for thread is 4. Then the current priority for that thread may fluctuate in the range from 4 through 15 depending on what boosts it has been given. If a thread is interrupted to wait on an I/O event, the kernel boosts its priority. If a boosted thread is interrupted because

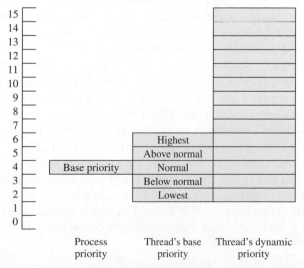

Figure 10.15   Example of Windows Priority Relationship

it has used up its current time quantum, the kernel lowers its priority. Thus, processor-bound threads tend toward lower priorities and I/O-bound threads tend toward higher priorities. In the case of I/O-bound threads, the kernel boosts the priority more for interactive waits (e.g., wait on keyboard or mouse) than for other types of I/O (e.g., disk I/O). Thus, interactive threads tend to have the highest priorities within the variable priority class.

Multiprocessor Scheduling

When Windows is run on a single processor, the highest-priority thread is always active unless it is waiting on an event. If there is more than one thread that has the same highest priority, then the processor is shared, round robin, among all the threads at that priority level. In a multiprocessor system with N processors, the kernel tries to give the N processors to the N highest-priority threads that are ready to run. The remaining, lower priority, threads must wait until the other threads block or have their priority decay. Lower-priority threads may also have their priority boosted to 15 for a very short time if they are being starved, solely to correct instances of priority inversion.

The foregoing scheduling discipline is affected by the processor affinity attribute of a thread. If a thread is ready to execute but the only available processors are not in its processor affinity set, then that thread is forced to wait, and the kernel schedules the next available thread.

10.7 LINUX VIRTUAL MACHINE PROCESS SCHEDULING

The Linux VServer virtual machine facility, introduced in Chapter 2, provides a way of controlling VM use of processor time. VServer overlays a token bucket filter (TBF) on top of the standard Linux schedule. The purpose of the TBF is to determine how much of the processor execution time (single processor, multiprocessor, or multicore) is allocated to each VM. If only the underlying Linux scheduler is used to globally schedule processes across all VMs, then resource hunger processes in one VM crowd out processes in other VMs.

Figure 10.16 illustrates the TBF concept. For each VM, a bucket is defined with a capacity of S tokens. Tokens are added to the bucket at a rate of R tokens during every time interval of length T. When the bucket is full, additional incoming tokens are simply discarded. When a process is executing on this VM, it consumes one token for each timer clock tick. If the bucket empties, the process is put on hold and cannot be restarted until the bucket is refilled to a minimum threshold value of M tokens. At that point, the process is rescheduled. A significant consequence of the TBF approach is that a VM may accumulate tokens during a period of quiescence, and then later use the tokens in a burst when required.

Adjusting the values of R and T allows for regulating the percentage of capacity that a VM can claim. For a single processor, we can define capacity allocation as follows:

$$\frac{R}{T} = \text{Fraction of processor allocation}$$

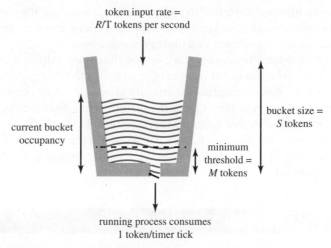

token input rate =
R/T tokens per second

current bucket
occupancy

bucket size =
S tokens

minimum
threshold =
M tokens

running process consumes
1 token/timer tick

Figure 10.16   Linux VServer Token Bucket Scheme

This equation denotes the fraction of a single processor in a system. Thus, for example, if a system is multicore with four cores and we wish to provide one VM on an average of one dedicated processor, then we set $R = 1$ and $T = 4$. The overall system is limited as follows. If there are N VMs, then:

$$\sum_{i=1}^{N} \frac{R_i}{T_i} \leq 1$$

The parameters S and M are set so as to penalize a VM after a certain amount of burst time. The following parameters must be configured or allocated for a VM: following a burst time of B, the VM suffers a hold time of H. With these parameters, it is possible to calculate the desired values of S and M as follows:

$$M = W \times H \times \frac{R}{T}$$

$$S = W \times B \times \left(1 - \frac{R}{T}\right)$$

where W is the rate at which the schedule runs (makes decisions). For example, consider a VM with a limit of 1/2 of processor time, and we wish to say that after using the processor for 30 seconds, there will be a hold time of 5 seconds. The scheduler runs at 1,000 Hz. This requirement is met with the following values: $M = 1,000 \times 5 \times 0.5 = 2,500$ tokens; $S = 1,000 \times 30 \times (1 - 0.5) = 15,000$ tokens.

10.8 SUMMARY

With a tightly coupled multiprocessor, multiple processors have access to the same main memory. In this configuration, the scheduling structure is somewhat more complex. For example, a given process may be assigned to the same processor for its entire life or dispatched to any processor each time it enters the Running state. Performance studies suggest that the differences among various scheduling algorithms are less significant in a multiprocessor system.

A real-time process or task is one that is executed in connection with some process or function or set of events external to the computer system and that must meet one or more deadlines to interact effectively and correctly with the external environment. A real-time operating system is one that is capable of managing real-time processes. In this context, the traditional criteria for a scheduling algorithm do not apply. Rather, the key factor is the meeting of deadlines. Algorithms that rely heavily on preemption and on reacting to relative deadlines are appropriate in this context.

10.9 RECOMMENDED READING

[WEND89] is an interesting discussion of approaches to multiprocessor scheduling. A good treatment of real-time scheduling is contained in [LIU00]. The following collections of papers all contain important articles on real-time operating systems and scheduling: [KRIS94], [STAN93], [LEE93], and [TILB91]. [SHA90] provides a good explanation of priority inversion, priority inheritance, and priority ceiling. [ZEAD97] analyzes the performance of the SVR4 real-time scheduler. [LIND04] provides an overview of the Linux 2.6 scheduler; [LOVE10] contains a more detailed discussion.

KRIS94 Krishna, C., and Lee, Y., eds. "Special Issue on Real-Time Systems." *Proceedings of the IEEE*, January 1994.

LEE93 Lee, Y., and Krishna, C., eds. *Readings in Real-Time Systems.* Los Alamitos, CA: IEEE Computer Society Press, 1993.

LIND04 Lindsley, R. "What's New in the 2.6 Scheduler." *Linux Journal*, March 2004.

LIU00 Liu, J. *Real-Time Systems.* Upper Saddle River, NJ: Prentice Hall, 2000.

LOVE10 Love, R. *Linux Kernel Development.* Upper Saddle River, NJ: Addison-Wesley, 2010.

SHA90 Sha, L., Rajkumar, R., and Lehoczky, J. "Priority Inheritance Protocols: An Approach to Real-Time Synchronization." *IEEE Transactions on Computers*, September 1990.

STAN93 Stankovic, J., and Ramamritham, K., eds. *Advances in Real-Time Systems.* Los Alamitos, CA: IEEE Computer Society Press, 1993.

TILB91 Tilborg, A., and Koob, G., eds. *Foundations of Real-Time Computing: Scheduling and Resource Management.* Boston: Kluwer Academic Publishers, 1991.

WEND89 Wendorf, J., Wendorf, R., and Tokuda, H. "Scheduling Operating System Processing on Small-Scale Microprocessors." *Proceedings, 22nd Annual Hawaii International Conference on System Science*, January 1989.

ZEAD97 Zeadally, S. "An Evaluation of the Real-Time Performance of SVR4.0 and SVR4.2." *Operating Systems Review*, January 1977.

10.10 KEY TERMS, REVIEW QUESTIONS, AND PROBLEMS

Key Terms

aperiodic task	hard real-time task	real-time scheduling
deadline scheduling	load sharing	responsiveness
deterministic operating system	periodic task	soft real-time task
fail-soft operation	priority inversion	thread scheduling
gang scheduling	rate monotonic scheduling	unbounded priority
granularity	real-time operating system	inversion

Review Questions

10.1 List and briefly define five different categories of synchronization granularity.

10.2 List and briefly define four techniques for thread scheduling.

10.3 List and briefly define three versions of load sharing.

10.4 What is the difference between hard and soft real-time tasks?

10.5 What is the difference between periodic and aperiodic real-time tasks?

10.6 List and briefly define five general areas of requirements for a real-time operating system.

10.7 List and briefly define four classes of real-time scheduling algorithms.

10.8 What items of information about a task might be useful in real-time scheduling?

Problems

10.1 Consider a set of three periodic tasks with the execution profiles of Table 10.6. Develop scheduling diagrams similar to those of Figure 10.5 for this set of tasks.

Table 10.6 Execution Profile for Problem 10.1

Process	Arrival Time	Execution Time	Ending Deadline
A(1)	0	10	20
A(2)	20	10	40
•	•	•	•
•	•	•	•
•	•	•	•
B(1)	0	10	50
B(2)	50	10	100
•	•	•	•
•	•	•	•
•	•	•	•
C(1)	0	15	50
C(2)	50	15	100
•	•	•	•
•	•	•	•
•	•	•	•

Table 10.7   Execution Profile for Problem 10.2

Process	Arrival Time	Execution Time	Starting Deadline
A	10	20	100
B	20	20	30
C	40	20	60
D	50	20	80
E	60	20	70

10.2   Consider a set of five aperiodic tasks with the execution profiles of Table 10.7. Develop scheduling diagrams similar to those of Figure 10.6 for this set of tasks.

10.3   Least laxity first (LLF) is a real-time scheduling algorithm for periodic tasks. Slack time, or laxity, is the amount of time between when a task would complete if it started now and its next deadline. This is the size of the available scheduling window. Laxity can be expressed as

$$\text{Laxity} = (\text{deadline time}) - (\text{current time}) - (\text{processor time needed})$$

LLF selects the task with the minimum laxity to execute next. If two or more tasks have the same minimum laxity value, they are serviced on a FCFS basis.

a. Suppose a task currently has a laxity of t. By how long may the scheduler delay starting this task and still meet its deadline?

b. Suppose a task currently has a laxity of 0. What does this mean?

c. What does it mean if a task has negative laxity?

d. Consider a set of three periodic tasks with the execution profiles of Table 10.8a. Develop scheduling diagrams similar to those of Figure 10.4 for this set of tasks that compare rate monotonic, earliest deadline first, and LLF. Assume preemption may occur at 5-ms intervals. Comment on the results.

10.4   Repeat Problem 10.3d for the execution profiles of Table 10.8b. Comment on the results.

10.5   Maximum urgency first (MUF) is a real-time scheduling algorithm for periodic tasks. Each task is assigned an urgency that is defined as a combination of two fixed priorities and one dynamic priority. One of the fixed priorities, the criticality, has precedence over the dynamic priority. Meanwhile, the dynamic priority has precedence over the other fixed priority, called the user priority. The dynamic priority is inversely

Table 10.8   Execution Profiles for Problems 10.3 through 10.6

(a) Light load		
Task	**Period**	**Execution Time**
A	6	2
B	8	2
C	12	3

(b) Heavy load		
Task	**Period**	**Execution Time**
A	6	2
B	8	5
C	12	3

proportional to the laxity of a task. MUF can be explained as follows. First, tasks are ordered from shortest to longest period. Define the critical task set as the first N tasks such that worst-case processor utilization does not exceed 100%. Among critical set tasks that are ready, the scheduler selects the task with the least laxity. If no critical set tasks are ready, the schedule chooses among the noncritical tasks the one with the least laxity. Ties are broken through an optional user priority and then by FCFS. Repeat Problem 10.3d, adding MUF to the diagrams. Assume that user-defined priorities are A highest, B next, C lowest. Comment on the results.

10.6. Repeat Problem 10.4, adding MUF to the diagrams. Comment on the results.

10.7 This problem demonstrates that although Equation (10.2) for rate monotonic scheduling is a sufficient condition for successful scheduling, it is not a necessary condition (i.e., sometimes successful scheduling is possible even if Equation (10.2) is not satisfied).

a. Consider a task set with the following independent periodic tasks:
   - **Task P_1:** $C_1 = 20; T_1 = 100$
   - **Task P_2:** $C_2 = 30; T_2 = 145$

   Can these tasks be successfully scheduled using rate monotonic scheduling?

b. Now add the following task to the set:
   - **Task P_3:** $C_3 = 68; T_3 = 150$

   Is Equation (10.2) satisfied?

c. Suppose that the first instance of the preceding three tasks arrives at time $t = 0$. Assume that the first deadline for each task is the following:

$$D_1 = 100; \quad D_2 = 145; \quad D_3 = 150$$

Using rate monotonic scheduling, will all three deadlines be met? What about deadlines for future repetitions of each task?

10.8 Draw a diagram similar to that of Figure 10.9b that shows the sequence events for this same example using priority ceiling.

PART 5 Input/Output and Files

CHAPTER 11

I/O MANAGEMENT AND DISK SCHEDULING

11.1 **I/O Devices**

11.2 **Organization of the I/O Function**
    The Evolution of the I/O Function
    Direct Memory Access

11.3 **Operating System Design Issues**
    Design Objectives
    Logical Structure of the I/O Function

11.4 **I/O Buffering**
    Single Buffer
    Double Buffer
    Circular Buffer
    The Utility of Buffering

11.5 **Disk Scheduling**
    Disk Performance Parameters
    Disk Scheduling Policies

11.6 **RAID**

11.7 **Disk Cache**
    Design Considerations
    Performance Considerations

11.8 **UNIX SVR4 I/O**

11.9 **Linux I/O**

11.10 **Windows I/O**

11.11 **Summary**

11.12 **Recommended Reading**

11.13 **Key Terms, Review Questions, and Problems**

An artifact can be thought of as a meeting point—an "interface" in today's terms between an "inner" environment, the substance and organization of the artifact itself, and an "outer" environment, the surroundings in which it operates. If the inner environment is appropriate to the outer environment, or vice versa, the artifact will serve its intended purpose.

— THE SCIENCES OF THE ARTIFICIAL, HERBERT SIMON

LEARNING OBJECTIVES

After studying this chapter, you should be able to:

- Summarize key categories of I/O devices on computers.
- Discuss the organization of the I/O function.
- Explain some of the key issues in the design of OS support for I/O.
- Analyze the performance implications of various I/O buffering alternatives.
- Understand the performance issues involved in magnetic disk access.
- Explain the concept of RAID and describe the various levels.
- Understand the performance implications of disk cache.
- Describe the I/O mechanisms in UNIX, Linux, and Windows 7.

Perhaps the messiest aspect of operating system design is input/output. Because there is such a wide variety of devices and applications of those devices, it is difficult to develop a general, consistent solution.

We begin with a brief discussion of I/O devices and the organization of the I/O function. These topics, which generally come within the scope of computer architecture, set the stage for an examination of I/O from the point of view of the OS.

The next section examines operating system design issues, including design objectives, and the way in which the I/O function can be structured. Then I/O buffering is examined; one of the basic I/O services provided by the operating system is a buffering function, which improves overall performance.

The next sections of the chapter are devoted to magnetic disk I/O. In contemporary systems, this form of I/O is the most important and is key to the performance as perceived by the user. We begin by developing a model of disk I/O performance and then examine several techniques that can be used to enhance performance.

Appendix J summarizes characteristics of secondary storage devices, including magnetic disk and optical memory. A set of animations that illustrate concepts in this chapter is available online. Click on the rotating globe at WilliamStallings.com/OS/OS7e.html for access.

11.1 I/O DEVICES

As was mentioned in Chapter 1, external devices that engage in I/O with computer systems can be roughly grouped into three categories:

- **Human readable:** Suitable for communicating with the computer user. Examples include printers and terminals, the latter consisting of video display, keyboard, and perhaps other devices such as a mouse.

- **Machine readable:** Suitable for communicating with electronic equipment. Examples are disk drives, USB keys, sensors, controllers, and actuators.
- **Communication:** Suitable for communicating with remote devices. Examples are digital line drivers and modems.

There are great differences across classes and even substantial differences within each class. Among the key differences are the following:

- **Data rate:** There may be differences of several orders of magnitude between the data transfer rates. Figure 11.1 gives some examples.
- **Application:** The use to which a device is put has an influence on the software and policies in the OS and supporting utilities. For example, a disk used for files requires the support of file management software. A disk used as a backing store for pages in a virtual memory scheme depends on the use of virtual memory hardware and software. Furthermore, these applications have an impact on disk scheduling algorithms (discussed later in this chapter). As another example, a terminal may be used by an ordinary user or a system administrator. These uses imply different privilege levels and perhaps different priorities in the OS.
- **Complexity of control:** A printer requires a relatively simple control interface. A disk is much more complex. The effect of these differences on the OS is filtered to some extent by the complexity of the I/O module that controls the device, as discussed in the next section.

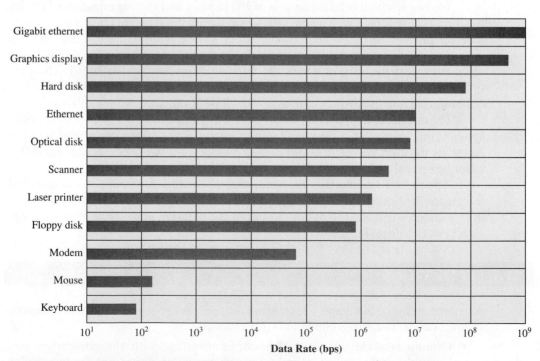

Figure 11.1   Typical I/O Device Data Rates

- **Unit of transfer:** Data may be transferred as a stream of bytes or characters (e.g., terminal I/O) or in larger blocks (e.g., disk I/O).
- **Data representation:** Different data encoding schemes are used by different devices, including differences in character code and parity conventions.
- **Error conditions:** The nature of errors, the way in which they are reported, their consequences, and the available range of responses differ widely from one device to another.

This diversity makes a uniform and consistent approach to I/O, both from the point of view of the operating system and from the point of view of user processes, difficult to achieve.

11.2 ORGANIZATION OF THE I/O FUNCTION

Appendix C summarizes three techniques for performing I/O:

- **Programmed I/O:** The processor issues an I/O command, on behalf of a process, to an I/O module; that process then busy waits for the operation to be completed before proceeding.
- **Interrupt-driven I/O:** The processor issues an I/O command on behalf of a process. There are then two possibilities. If the I/O instruction from the process is nonblocking, then the processor continues to execute instructions from the process that issued the I/O command. If the I/O instruction is blocking, then the next instruction that the processor executes is from the OS, which will put the current process in a blocked state and schedule another process.
- **Direct memory access (DMA):** A DMA module controls the exchange of data between main memory and an I/O module. The processor sends a request for the transfer of a block of data to the DMA module and is interrupted only after the entire block has been transferred.

Table 11.1 indicates the relationship among these three techniques. In most computer systems, DMA is the dominant form of transfer that must be supported by the operating system.

The Evolution of the I/O Function

As computer systems have evolved, there has been a pattern of increasing complexity and sophistication of individual components. Nowhere is this more

Table 11.1   I/O Techniques

	No Interrupts	**Use of Interrupts**
I/O-to-Memory Transfer through Processor	Programmed I/O	Interrupt-driven I/O
Direct I/O-to-Memory Transfer		Direct memory access (DMA)

evident than in the I/O function. The evolutionary steps can be summarized as follows:

1. The processor directly controls a peripheral device. This is seen in simple microprocessor-controlled devices.

2. A controller or I/O module is added. The processor uses programmed I/O without interrupts. With this step, the processor becomes somewhat divorced from the specific details of external device interfaces.

3. The same configuration as step 2 is used, but now interrupts are employed. The processor need not spend time waiting for an I/O operation to be performed, thus increasing efficiency.

4. The I/O module is given direct control of memory via DMA. It can now move a block of data to or from memory without involving the processor, except at the beginning and end of the transfer.

5. The I/O module is enhanced to become a separate processor, with a specialized instruction set tailored for I/O. The central processing unit (CPU) directs the I/O processor to execute an I/O program in main memory. The I/O processor fetches and executes these instructions without processor intervention. This allows the processor to specify a sequence of I/O activities and to be interrupted only when the entire sequence has been performed.

6. The I/O module has a local memory of its own and is, in fact, a computer in its own right. With this architecture, a large set of I/O devices can be controlled, with minimal processor involvement. A common use for such an architecture has been to control communications with interactive terminals. The I/O processor takes care of most of the tasks involved in controlling the terminals.

As one proceeds along this evolutionary path, more and more of the I/O function is performed without processor involvement. The central processor is increasingly relieved of I/O-related tasks, improving performance. With the last two steps (5 and 6), a major change occurs with the introduction of the concept of an I/O module capable of executing a program.

A note about terminology: For all of the modules described in steps 4 through 6, the term *direct memory access* is appropriate, because all of these types involve direct control of main memory by the I/O module. Also, the I/O module in step 5 is often referred to as an **I/O channel**, and that in step 6 as an **I/O processor**; however, each term is, on occasion, applied to both situations. In the latter part of this section, we will use the term *I/O channel* to refer to both types of I/O modules.

Direct Memory Access

Figure 11.2 indicates, in general terms, the DMA logic. The DMA unit is capable of mimicking the processor and, indeed, of taking over control of the system bus just like a processor. It needs to do this to transfer data to and from memory over the system bus.

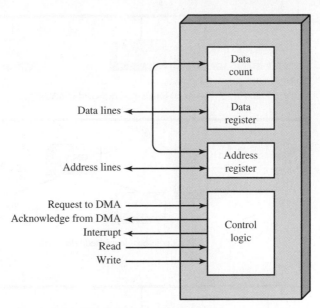

Figure 11.2   Typical DMA Block Diagram

The DMA technique works as follows. When the processor wishes to read or write a block of data, it issues a command to the DMA module by sending to the DMA module the following information:

- Whether a read or write is requested, using the read or write control line between the processor and the DMA module
- The address of the I/O device involved, communicated on the data lines
- The starting location in memory to read from or write to, communicated on the data lines and stored by the DMA module in its address register
- The number of words to be read or written, again communicated via the data lines and stored in the data count register

The processor then continues with other work. It has delegated this I/O operation to the DMA module. The DMA module transfers the entire block of data, one word at a time, directly to or from memory, without going through the processor. When the transfer is complete, the DMA module sends an interrupt signal to the processor. Thus, the processor is involved only at the beginning and end of the transfer (Figure C.4c).

The DMA mechanism can be configured in a variety of ways. Some possibilities are shown in Figure 11.3. In the first example, all modules share the same system bus. The DMA module, acting as a surrogate processor, uses programmed I/O to exchange data between memory and an I/O module through the DMA module. This configuration, while it may be inexpensive, is clearly inefficient: As with processor-controlled programmed I/O, each transfer of a word consumes two bus cycles (transfer request followed by transfer).

The number of required bus cycles can be cut substantially by integrating the DMA and I/O functions. As Figure 11.3b indicates, this means that there is a path between the DMA module and one or more I/O modules that does not include the

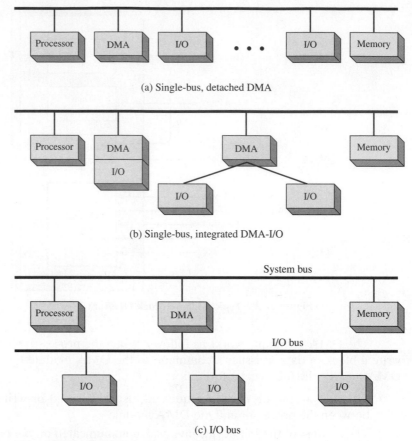

(a) Single-bus, detached DMA

(b) Single-bus, integrated DMA-I/O

(c) I/O bus

Figure 11.3   **Alternative DMA Configurations**

system bus. The DMA logic may actually be a part of an I/O module, or it may be a separate module that controls one or more I/O modules. This concept can be taken one step further by connecting I/O modules to the DMA module using an I/O bus (Figure 11.3c). This reduces the number of I/O interfaces in the DMA module to one and provides for an easily expandable configuration. In all of these cases (Figure 11.3b and 11.3c), the system bus that the DMA module shares with the processor and main memory is used by the DMA module only to exchange data with memory and to exchange control signals with the processor. The exchange of data between the DMA and I/O modules takes place off the system bus.

11.3 OPERATING SYSTEM DESIGN ISSUES

Design Objectives

Two objectives are paramount in designing the I/O facility: efficiency and generality. **Efficiency** is important because I/O operations often form a bottleneck in a computing system. Looking again at Figure 11.1, we see that most I/O devices are extremely slow compared with main memory and the processor. One way to tackle this problem is multiprogramming, which, as we have seen, allows some processes to be waiting on I/O operations while another process is executing. However, even with the vast size of main memory in today's machines, it will still often be the case that I/O is not keeping up with the activities of the processor. Swapping is used to bring in additional ready processes to keep the processor busy, but this in itself is an I/O operation. Thus, a major effort in I/O design has been schemes for improving the efficiency of the I/O. The area that has received the most attention, because of its importance, is disk I/O, and much of this chapter will be devoted to a study of disk I/O efficiency.

The other major objective is **generality**. In the interests of simplicity and freedom from error, it is desirable to handle all devices in a uniform manner. This applies both to the way in which processes view I/O devices and to the way in which the OS manages I/O devices and operations. Because of the diversity of device characteristics, it is difficult in practice to achieve true generality. What can be done is to use a hierarchical, modular approach to the design of the I/O function. This approach hides most of the details of device I/O in lower-level routines so that user processes and upper levels of the OS see devices in terms of general functions, such as read, write, open, close, lock, and unlock. We turn now to a discussion of this approach.

Logical Structure of the I/O Function

In Chapter 2, in the discussion of system structure, we emphasized the hierarchical nature of modern operating systems. The hierarchical philosophy is that the functions of the OS should be separated according to their complexity, their characteristic time scale, and their level of abstraction. Following this approach leads to an organization of the OS into a series of layers. Each layer performs a related subset of the functions required of the OS. It relies on the next lower layer to perform more primitive functions and to conceal the details of those functions. It provides services to the next higher layer. Ideally, the layers should be defined so that changes in one layer do not require changes in other layers. Thus, we have decomposed one problem into a number of more manageable subproblems.

In general, lower layers deal with a far shorter time scale. Some parts of the OS must interact directly with the computer hardware, where events can have a time scale as brief as a few billionths of a second. At the other end of the spectrum, parts of the OS communicate with the user, who issues commands at a much more leisurely pace, perhaps one every few seconds. The use of a set of layers conforms nicely to this environment.

Applying this philosophy specifically to the I/O facility leads to the type of organization suggested by Figure 11.4. The details of the organization will depend on the type of device and the application. The three most important logical structures are presented in the figure. Of course, a particular operating system may not conform exactly to these structures. However, the general principles are valid, and most operating systems approach I/O in approximately this way.

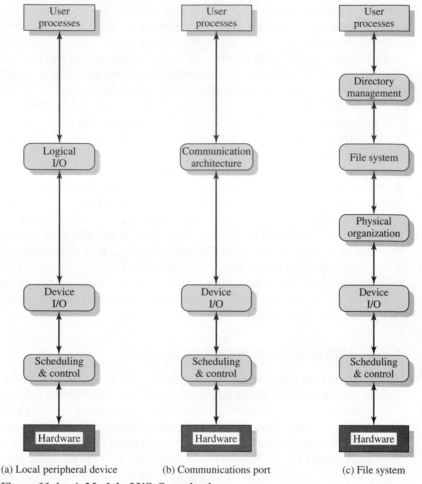

Figure 11.4 A Model of I/O Organization

Let us consider the simplest case first, that of a local peripheral device that communicates in a simple fashion, such as a stream of bytes or records (Figure 11.4a). The following layers are involved:

- **Logical I/O:** The logical I/O module deals with the device as a logical resource and is not concerned with the details of actually controlling the device. The logical I/O module is concerned with managing general I/O functions on behalf of user processes, allowing them to deal with the device in terms of a device identifier and simple commands such as open, close, read, and write.

- **Device I/O:** The requested operations and data (buffered characters, records, etc.) are converted into appropriate sequences of I/O instructions, channel commands, and controller orders. Buffering techniques may be used to improve utilization.

- **Scheduling and control:** The actual queueing and scheduling of I/O operations occurs at this layer, as well as the control of the operations. Thus, interrupts are handled at this layer and I/O status is collected and reported. This is the layer of software that actually interacts with the I/O module and hence the device hardware.

For a communications device, the I/O structure (Figure 11.4b) looks much the same as that just described. The principal difference is that the logical I/O module is replaced by a communications architecture, which may itself consist of a number of layers. An example is TCP/IP, which is discussed in Chapter 17.

Figure 11.4c shows a representative structure for managing I/O on a secondary storage device that supports a file system. The three layers not previously discussed are as follows:

- **Directory management:** At this layer, symbolic file names are converted to identifiers that either reference the file directly or indirectly through a file descriptor or index table. This layer is also concerned with user operations that affect the directory of files, such as add, delete, and reorganize.

- **File system:** This layer deals with the logical structure of files and with the operations that can be specified by users, such as open, close, read, and write. Access rights are also managed at this layer.

- **Physical organization:** Just as virtual memory addresses must be converted into physical main memory addresses, taking into account the segmentation and paging structure, logical references to files and records must be converted to physical secondary storage addresses, taking into account the physical track and sector structure of the secondary storage device. Allocation of secondary storage space and main storage buffers is generally treated at this layer as well.

Because of the importance of the file system, we will spend some time, in this chapter and the next, looking at its various components. The discussion in this chapter focuses on the lower three layers, while the upper two layers are examined in Chapter 12.

11.4 I/O BUFFERING

Suppose that a user process wishes to read blocks of data from a disk one at a time, with each block having a length of 512 bytes. The data are to be read into a data area within the address space of the user process at virtual location 1000 to 1511. The simplest way would be to execute an I/O command (something like `Read_Block[1000, disk]`) to the disk unit and then wait for the data to become available. The waiting could either be busy waiting (continuously test the device status) or, more practically, process suspension on an interrupt.

There are two problems with this approach. First, the program is hung up waiting for the relatively slow I/O to complete. The second problem is that this approach to I/O interferes with swapping decisions by the OS. Virtual locations 1000 to 1511 must remain in main memory during the course of the block transfer. Otherwise, some of the data may be lost. If paging is being used, at least the page containing the target locations must be locked into main memory. Thus, although portions of the process may be paged out to disk, it is impossible to swap the process out completely, even if this is desired by the operating system. Notice also that there is a risk of single-process deadlock. If a process issues an I/O command, is suspended awaiting the result, and then is swapped out prior to the beginning of the operation, the process is blocked waiting on the I/O event, and the I/O operation is blocked waiting for the process to be swapped in. To avoid this deadlock, the user memory involved in the I/O operation must be locked in main memory immediately before the I/O request is issued, even though the I/O operation is queued and may not be executed for some time.

The same considerations apply to an output operation. If a block is being transferred from a user process area directly to an I/O module, then the process is blocked during the transfer and the process may not be swapped out.

To avoid these overheads and inefficiencies, it is sometimes convenient to perform input transfers in advance of requests being made and to perform output transfers some time after the request is made. This technique is known as buffering. In this section, we look at some of the buffering schemes that are supported by operating systems to improve the performance of the system.

In discussing the various approaches to buffering, it is sometimes important to make a distinction between two types of I/O devices: block oriented and stream oriented. A **block-oriented device** stores information in blocks that are usually of fixed size, and transfers are made one block at a time. Generally, it is possible to reference data by its block number. Disks and USB keys are examples of block-oriented devices. A **stream-oriented device** transfers data in and out as a stream of bytes, with no block structure. Terminals, printers, communications ports, mouse and other pointing devices, and most other devices that are not secondary storage are stream oriented.

Single Buffer

The simplest type of support that the OS can provide is single buffering (Figure 11.5b). When a user process issues an I/O request, the OS assigns a buffer in the system portion of main memory to the operation.

For block-oriented devices, the single buffering scheme can be described as follows: Input transfers are made to the system buffer. When the transfer is complete, the process moves the block into user space and immediately requests another block. This is called reading ahead, or anticipated input; it is done in the expectation that the block will eventually be needed. For many types of computation, this is a reasonable assumption most of the time because data are usually accessed sequentially. Only at the end of a sequence of processing will a block be read in unnecessarily.

This approach will generally provide a speedup compared to the lack of system buffering. The user process can be processing one block of data while the next block is being read in. The OS is able to swap the process out because the input operation is taking place in system memory rather than user process memory. This technique does, however, complicate the logic in the operating system. The OS must keep track of the assignment of system buffers to user processes. The swapping logic is also affected: If the I/O operation involves the same disk that is used for swapping,

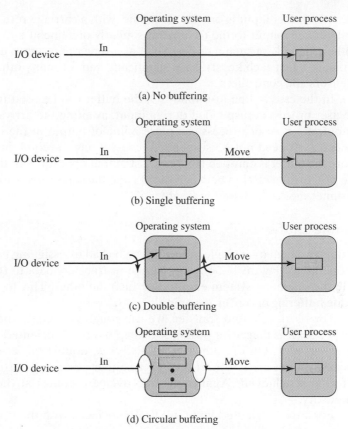

(a) No buffering

(b) Single buffering

(c) Double buffering

(d) Circular buffering

Figure 11.5   I/O Buffering Schemes (Input)

it hardly makes sense to queue disk writes to the same device for swapping the process out. This attempt to swap the process and release main memory will itself not begin until after the I/O operation finishes, at which time swapping the process to disk may no longer be appropriate.

Similar considerations apply to block-oriented output. When data are being transmitted to a device, they are first copied from the user space into the system buffer, from which they will ultimately be written. The requesting process is now free to continue or to be swapped as necessary.

[KNUT97] suggests a crude but informative performance comparison between single buffering and no buffering. Suppose that T is the time required to input one block and that C is the computation time that intervenes between input requests. Without buffering, the execution time per block is essentially $T + C$. With a single buffer, the time is max $[C, T] + M$, where M is the time required to move the data from the system buffer to user memory. In most cases, execution time per block is substantially less with a single buffer compared to no buffer.

For stream-oriented I/O, the single buffering scheme can be used in a line-at-a-time fashion or a byte-at-a-time fashion. Line-at-a-time operation is appropriate for scroll-mode terminals (sometimes called dumb terminals). With this form of terminal, user input is one line at a time, with a carriage return signaling the end of a line, and output to the terminal is similarly one line at a time. A line printer is another example of such a device. Byte-at-a-time operation is used on forms-mode terminals, when each keystroke is significant, and for many other peripherals, such as sensors and controllers.

In the case of line-at-a-time I/O, the buffer can be used to hold a single line. The user process is suspended during input, awaiting the arrival of the entire line. For output, the user process can place a line of output in the buffer and continue processing. It need not be suspended unless it has a second line of output to send before the buffer is emptied from the first output operation. In the case of byte-at-a-time I/O, the interaction between the OS and the user process follows the producer/consumer model discussed in Chapter 5.

Double Buffer

An improvement over single buffering can be had by assigning two system buffers to the operation (Figure 11.5c). A process now transfers data to (or from) one buffer while the operating system empties (or fills) the other. This technique is known as **double buffering** or **buffer swapping**.

For block-oriented transfer, we can roughly estimate the execution time as max $[C, T]$. It is therefore possible to keep the block-oriented device going at full speed if $C \leq T$. On the other hand, if $C > T$, double buffering ensures that the process will not have to wait on I/O. In either case, an improvement over single buffering is achieved. Again, this improvement comes at the cost of increased complexity.

For stream-oriented input, we again are faced with the two alternative modes of operation. For line-at-a-time I/O, the user process need not be suspended for input or output, unless the process runs ahead of the double buffers. For byte-at-a-time operation, the double buffer offers no particular advantage over a single buffer of twice the length. In both cases, the producer/consumer model is followed.

Circular Buffer

A double-buffer scheme should smooth out the flow of data between an I/O device and a process. If the performance of a particular process is the focus of our concern, then we would like for the I/O operation to be able to keep up with the process. Double buffering may be inadequate if the process performs rapid bursts of I/O. In this case, the problem can often be alleviated by using more than two buffers.

When more than two buffers are used, the collection of buffers is itself referred to as a circular buffer (Figure 11.5d), with each individual buffer being one unit in the circular buffer. This is simply the bounded-buffer producer/consumer model studied in Chapter 5.

The Utility of Buffering

Buffering is a technique that smoothes out peaks in I/O demand. However, no amount of buffering will allow an I/O device to keep pace with a process indefinitely when the average demand of the process is greater than the I/O device can service. Even with multiple buffers, all of the buffers will eventually fill up and the process will have to wait after processing each chunk of data. However, in a multi-programming environment, when there is a variety of I/O activity and a variety of process activity to service, buffering is one tool that can increase the efficiency of the OS and the performance of individual processes.

11.5 DISK SCHEDULING

Over the last 40 years, the increase in the speed of processors and main memory has far outstripped that for disk access, with processor and main memory speeds increasing by about two orders of magnitude compared to one order of magnitude for disk. The result is that disks are currently at least four orders of magnitude slower than main memory. This gap is expected to continue into the foreseeable future. Thus, the performance of disk storage subsystem is of vital concern, and much research has gone into schemes for improving that performance. In this section, we highlight some of the key issues and look at the most important approaches. Because the performance of the disk system is tied closely to file system design issues, the discussion continues in Chapter 12.

Disk Performance Parameters

The actual details of disk I/O operation depend on the computer system, the operating system, and the nature of the I/O channel and disk controller hardware. A general timing diagram of disk I/O transfer is shown in Figure 11.6.

When the disk drive is operating, the disk is rotating at constant speed. To read or write, the head must be positioned at the desired track and at the beginning of the desired sector on that track.[1] Track selection involves moving the head in a movable-head system or electronically selecting one head on a fixed-head system. On a movable-head system, the time it takes to position the head at the track is known as **seek time**. In either case, once the track is selected, the disk controller waits until the appropriate sector rotates to line up with the head. The time it takes for the beginning of the sector to reach the head is known as **rotational delay**, or rotational latency. The sum of the seek time, if any, and the rotational delay equals the **access time**, which is the time it takes to get into position to read or write. Once the head is in position, the read or write operation is then performed as the sector moves under the head; this is the data transfer portion of the operation; the time required for the transfer is the **transfer time**.

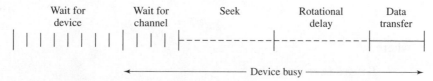

Figure 11.6   Timing of a Disk I/O Transfer

---

[1]See Appendix J for a discussion of disk organization and formatting.

In addition to the access time and transfer time, there are several queueing delays normally associated with a disk I/O operation. When a process issues an I/O request, it must first wait in a queue for the device to be available. At that time, the device is assigned to the process. If the device shares a single I/O channel or a set of I/O channels with other disk drives, then there may be an additional wait for the channel to be available. At that point, the seek is performed to begin disk access.

In some high-end systems for servers, a technique known as rotational positional sensing (RPS) is used. This works as follows: When the seek command has been issued, the channel is released to handle other I/O operations. When the seek is completed, the device determines when the data will rotate under the head. As that sector approaches the head, the device tries to reestablish the communication path back to the host. If either the control unit or the channel is busy with another I/O, then the reconnection attempt fails and the device must rotate one whole revolution before it can attempt to reconnect, which is called an RPS miss. This is an extra delay element that must be added to the time line of Figure 11.6.

SEEK TIME Seek time is the time required to move the disk arm to the required track. It turns out that this is a difficult quantity to pin down. The seek time consists of two key components: the initial startup time and the time taken to traverse the tracks that have to be crossed once the access arm is up to speed. Unfortunately, the traversal time is not a linear function of the number of tracks but includes a settling time (time after positioning the head over the target track until track identification is confirmed).

Much improvement comes from smaller and lighter disk components. Some years ago, a typical disk was 14 inches (36 cm) in diameter, whereas the most common size today is 3.5 inches (8.9 cm), reducing the distance that the arm has to travel. A typical average seek time on contemporary hard disks is under 10 ms.

ROTATIONAL DELAY Rotational delay is the time required for the addressed area of the disk to rotate into a position where it is accessible by the read/write head. Disks rotate at speeds ranging from 3,600 rpm (for handheld devices such as digital cameras) up to, as of this writing, 15,000 rpm; at this latter speed, there is one revolution per 4 ms. Thus, on the average, the rotational delay will be 2 ms.

TRANSFER TIME The transfer time to or from the disk depends on the rotation speed of the disk in the following fashion:

$$T = \frac{b}{rN}$$

where

T = transfer time
b = number of bytes to be transferred
N = number of bytes on a track
r = rotation speed, in revolutions per second

Thus, the total average access time can be expressed as

$$T_a = T_s + \frac{1}{2r} + \frac{b}{rN}$$

where T_s is the average seek time.

A *TIMING COMPARISON*   With the foregoing parameters defined, let us look at two different I/O operations that illustrate the danger of relying on average values. Consider a disk with an advertised average seek time of 4 ms, rotation speed of 7,500 rpm, and 512-byte sectors with 500 sectors per track. Suppose that we wish to read a file consisting of 2,500 sectors for a total of 1.28 Mbytes. We would like to estimate the total time for the transfer.

First, let us assume that the file is stored as compactly as possible on the disk. That is, the file occupies all of the sectors on 5 adjacent tracks (5 tracks × 500 sectors/track = 2,500 sectors). This is known as *sequential organization*. The time to read the first track is as follows:

Average seek	4 ms
Rotational delay	4 ms
Read 500 sectors	8 ms
	16 ms

Suppose that the remaining tracks can now be read with essentially no seek time. That is, the I/O operation can keep up with the flow from the disk. Then, at most, we need to deal with rotational delay for each succeeding track. Thus, each successive track is read in $4 + 8 = 12 \, rmms$. To read the entire file,

Total time $= 16 + (4 \times 12) = 64 \, ms = 0.064 \, seconds$

Now let us calculate the time required to read the same data using random access rather than sequential access; that is, accesses to the sectors are distributed randomly over the disk. For each sector, we have:

Average seek	4	ms
Rotational delay	4	ms
Read 1 sector	0.016	ms
	8.016	ms

Total time $= 2,500 \times 8.016 = 20,040 \, ms = 20.04 \, seconds$

It is clear that the order in which sectors are read from the disk has a tremendous effect on I/O performance. In the case of file access in which multiple sectors are read or written, we have some control over the way in which sectors of data are deployed, and we shall have something to say on this subject in the next chapter. However, even in the case of a file access, in a multiprogramming environment, there will be I/O requests competing for the same disk. Thus, it is worthwhile to examine ways in which the performance of disk I/O can be improved over that achieved with purely random access to the disk.

Disk Scheduling Policies

In the example just described, the reason for the difference in performance can be traced to seek time. If sector access requests involve selection of tracks at random, then the performance of the disk I/O system will be as poor as possible. To improve matters, we need to reduce the average time spent on seeks.

Consider the typical situation in a multiprogramming environment, in which the OS maintains a queue of requests for each I/O device. So, for a single disk, there will be a number of I/O requests (reads and writes) from various processes in the queue. If we selected items from the queue in random order, then we can expect that the tracks to be visited will occur randomly, giving poor performance. This **random scheduling** is useful as a benchmark against which to evaluate other techniques.

Figure 11.7 compares the performance of various scheduling algorithms for an example sequence of I/O requests. The vertical axis corresponds to the tracks on the disk. The horizontal axis corresponds to time or, equivalently, the number of tracks traversed. For this figure, we assume that the disk head is initially located at track 100. In this example, we assume a disk with 200 tracks and that the disk request queue has random requests in it. The requested tracks, in the order received by the disk scheduler, are 55, 58, 39, 18, 90, 160, 150, 38, 184. Table 11.2a tabulates the results.

FIRST IN FIRST OUT   The simplest form of scheduling is first-in-first-out (FIFO) scheduling, which processes items from the queue in sequential order. This strategy has the advantage of being fair, because every request is honored and the requests are honored in the order received. Figure 11.7a illustrates the disk arm movement with FIFO. This graph is generated directly from the data in Table 11.2a. As can be seen, the disk accesses are in the same order as the requests were originally received.

With FIFO, if there are only a few processes that require access and if many of the requests are to clustered file sectors, then we can hope for good performance. However, this technique will often approximate random scheduling in performance, if there are many processes competing for the disk. Thus, it may be profitable to consider a more sophisticated scheduling policy. A number of these are listed in Table 11.3 and will now be considered.

PRIORITY   With a system based on priority (PRI), the control of the scheduling is outside the control of disk management software. Such an approach is not intended to optimize disk utilization but to meet other objectives within the OS. Often short batch jobs and interactive jobs are given higher priority than longer jobs that require longer computation. This allows a lot of short jobs to be flushed through the system quickly and may provide good interactive response time. However, longer jobs may have to wait excessively long times. Furthermore, such a policy could lead to countermeasures on the part of users, who split their jobs into smaller pieces to beat the system. This type of policy tends to be poor for database systems.

SHORTEST SERVICE TIME FIRST   The shortest-service-time-first (SSTF) policy is to select the disk I/O request that requires the least movement of the disk arm from its current position. Thus, we always choose to incur the minimum seek time. Of course, always choosing the minimum seek time does not guarantee that the

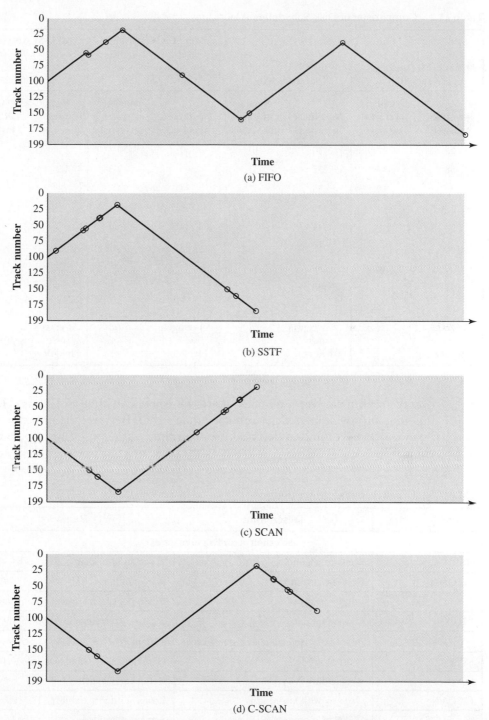

Figure 11.7   Comparison of Disk Scheduling Algorithms (see Table 11.2)

Table 11.2 Comparison of Disk Scheduling Algorithms

(a) FIFO (starting at track 100)		(b) SSTF (starting at track 100)		(c) SCAN (starting at track 100, in the direction of increasing track number)		(d) C-SCAN (starting at track 100, in the direction of increasing track number)	
Next track accessed	Number of tracks traversed	Next track accessed	Number of tracks traversed	Next track accessed	Number of tracks traversed	Next track accessed	Number of tracks traversed
55	45	90	10	150	50	150	50
58	3	58	32	160	10	160	10
39	19	55	3	184	24	184	24
18	21	39	16	90	94	18	166
90	72	38	1	58	32	38	20
160	70	18	20	55	3	39	1
150	10	150	132	39	16	55	16
38	112	160	10	38	1	58	3
184	146	184	24	18	20	90	32
Average seek length	55.3	**Average seek length**	27.5	**Average seek length**	27.8	**Average seek length**	35.8

average seek time over a number of arm movements will be minimum. However, this should provide better performance than FIFO. Because the arm can move in two directions, a random tie-breaking algorithm may be used to resolve cases of equal distances.

Table 11.3 Disk Scheduling Algorithms

Name	Description	Remarks
Selection according to requestor		
RSS	Random scheduling	For analysis and simulation
FIFO	First-in-first-out	Fairest of them all
PRI	Priority by process	Control outside of disk queue management
LIFO	Last in first out	Maximize locality and resource utilization
Selection according to requested item		
SSTF	Shortest-service-time first	High utilization, small queues
SCAN	Back and forth over disk	Better service distribution
C-SCAN	One way with fast return	Lower service variability
N-step-SCAN	SCAN of *N* records at a time	Service guarantee
FSCAN	*N*-step-SCAN with *N* = queue size at beginning of SCAN cycle	Load sensitive

Figure 11.7b and Table 11.2b show the performance of SSTF on the same example as was used for FIFO. The first track accessed is 90, because this is the closest requested track to the starting position. The next track accessed is 58 because this is the closest of the remaining requested tracks to the current position of 90. Subsequent tracks are selected accordingly.

SCAN With the exception of FIFO, all of the policies described so far can leave some request unfulfilled until the entire queue is emptied. That is, there may always be new requests arriving that will be chosen before an existing request. A simple alternative that prevents this sort of starvation is the SCAN algorithm, also known as the elevator algorithm because it operates much the way an elevator does.

With SCAN, the arm is required to move in one direction only, satisfying all outstanding requests en route, until it reaches the last track in that direction or until there are no more requests in that direction. This latter refinement is sometimes referred to as the LOOK policy. The service direction is then reversed and the scan proceeds in the opposite direction, again picking up all requests in order.

Figure 11.7c and Table 11.2c illustrate the SCAN policy. Assuming that the initial direction is of increasing track number, then the first track selected is 150, since this is the closest track to the starting track of 100 in the increasing direction.

As can be seen, the SCAN policy behaves almost identically with the SSTF policy. Indeed, if we had assumed that the arm was moving in the direction of lower track numbers at the beginning of the example, then the scheduling pattern would have been identical for SSTF and SCAN. However, this is a static example in which no new items are added to the queue. Even when the queue is dynamically changing, SCAN will be similar to SSTF unless the request pattern is unusual.

Note that the SCAN policy is biased against the area most recently traversed. Thus it does not exploit locality as well as SSTF.

It is not difficult to see that the SCAN policy favors jobs whose requests are for tracks nearest to both innermost and outermost tracks and favors the latest-arriving jobs. The first problem can be avoided via the C-SCAN policy, while the second problem is addressed by the N-step-SCAN policy.

C-SCAN The C-SCAN (circular SCAN) policy restricts scanning to one direction only. Thus, when the last track has been visited in one direction, the arm is returned to the opposite end of the disk and the scan begins again. This reduces the maximum delay experienced by new requests. With SCAN, if the expected time for a scan from inner track to outer track is t, then the expected service interval for sectors at the periphery is $2t$. With C-SCAN, the interval is on the order of $t + s_{max}$, where s_{max} is the maximum seek time.

Figure 11.7d and Table 11.2d illustrate C-SCAN behavior. In this case the first three requested tracks encountered are 150, 160, and 184. Then the scan begins starting at the lowest track number, and the next requested track encountered is 18.

N-STEP-SCAN AND FSCAN With SSTF, SCAN, and C-SCAN, it is possible that the arm may not move for a considerable period of time. For example, if one or a few processes have high access rates to one track, they can monopolize the entire device by repeated requests to that track. High-density multisurface disks are more likely to be affected by this characteristic than lower-density disks and/or disks with only one or two surfaces. To avoid this "arm stickiness," the disk request queue can be segmented, with one segment at a time being processed completely. Two examples of this approach are N-step-SCAN and FSCAN.

The N-step-SCAN policy segments the disk request queue into subqueues of length N. Subqueues are processed one at a time, using SCAN. While a queue is being processed, new requests must be added to some other queue. If fewer than N requests are available at the end of a scan, then all of them are processed with the next scan. With large values of N, the performance of N-step-SCAN approaches that of SCAN; with a value of $N = 1$, the FIFO policy is adopted.

FSCAN is a policy that uses two subqueues. When a scan begins, all of the requests are in one of the queues, with the other empty. During the scan, all new requests are put into the other queue. Thus, service of new requests is deferred until all of the old requests have been processed.

11.6 RAID

As discussed earlier, the rate in improvement in secondary storage performance has been considerably less than the rate for processors and main memory. This mismatch has made the disk storage system perhaps the main focus of concern in improving overall computer system performance.

As in other areas of computer performance, disk storage designers recognize that if one component can only be pushed so far, additional gains in performance are to be had by using multiple parallel components. In the case of disk storage, this leads to the development of arrays of disks that operate independently and in parallel. With multiple disks, separate I/O requests can be handled in parallel, as long as the data required reside on separate disks. Further, a single I/O request can be executed in parallel if the block of data to be accessed is distributed across multiple disks.

With the use of multiple disks, there is a wide variety of ways in which the data can be organized and in which redundancy can be added to improve reliability. This could make it difficult to develop database schemes that are usable on a number of platforms and operating systems. Fortunately, industry has agreed on a standardized scheme for multiple-disk database design, known as RAID (redundant array of independent disks). The RAID scheme consists of seven levels,[2] zero through six. These levels do not imply a hierarchical relationship but designate different design architectures that share three common characteristics:

1. RAID is a set of physical disk drives viewed by the OS as a single logical drive.
2. Data are distributed across the physical drives of an array in a scheme known as striping, described subsequently.
3. Redundant disk capacity is used to store parity information, which guarantees data recoverability in case of a disk failure.

---

[2]Additional levels have been defined by some researchers and some companies, but the seven levels described in this section are the ones universally agreed on.

The details of the second and third characteristics differ for the different RAID levels. RAID 0 and RAID 1 do not support the third characteristic.

The term *RAID* was originally coined in a paper by a group of researchers at the University of California at Berkeley [PATT88].[3] The paper outlined various RAID configurations and applications and introduced the definitions of the RAID levels that are still used. The RAID strategy employs multiple disk drives and distributes data in such a way as to enable simultaneous access to data from multiple drives, thereby improving I/O performance and allowing easier incremental increases in capacity.

The unique contribution of the RAID proposal is to address effectively the need for redundancy. Although allowing multiple heads and actuators to operate simultaneously achieves higher I/O and transfer rates, the use of multiple devices increases the probability of failure. To compensate for this decreased reliability, RAID makes use of stored parity information that enables the recovery of data lost due to a disk failure.

We now examine each of the RAID levels. Table 11.4 provides a rough guide to the seven levels. In the table, I/O performance is shown both in terms of data transfer capacity, or ability to move data, and I/O request rate, or ability to satisfy I/O requests, since these RAID levels inherently perform differently relative to these two metrics. Each RAID level's strong point is highlighted in color. Figure 11.8 is an example that illustrates the use of the seven RAID schemes to support a data capacity requiring four disks with no redundancy. The figure highlights the layout of user data and redundant data and indicates the relative storage requirements of the various levels. We refer to this figure throughout the following discussion.

Of the seven RAID levels described, only four are commonly used: RAID levels 0, 1, 5, and 6.

RAID Level 0

RAID level 0 is not a true member of the RAID family, because it does not include redundancy to improve performance or provide data protection. However, there are a few applications, such as some on supercomputers in which performance and capacity are primary concerns and low cost is more important than improved reliability.

For RAID 0, the user and system data are distributed across all of the disks in the array. This has a notable advantage over the use of a single large disk: If two different I/O requests are pending for two different blocks of data, then there is a good chance that the requested blocks are on different disks. Thus, the two requests can be issued in parallel, reducing the I/O queueing time.

But RAID 0, as with all of the RAID levels, goes further than simply distributing the data across a disk array: The data are *striped* across the available disks.

---

[3]In that paper, the acronym RAID stood for Redundant Array of Inexpensive Disks. The term *inexpensive* was used to contrast the small relatively inexpensive disks in the RAID array to the alternative, a single large expensive disk (SLED). The SLED is essentially a thing of the past, with similar disk technology being used for both RAID and non-RAID configurations. Accordingly, the industry has adopted the term *independent* to emphasize that the RAID array creates significant performance and reliability gains.

Table 11.4 RAID Levels

Category	Level	Description	Disks Required	Data Availability	Large I/O Data Transfer Capacity	Small I/O Request Rate
Striping	0	Nonredundant	N	Lower than single disk	Very high	Very high for both read and write
Mirroring	1	Mirrored	$2N$	Higher than RAID 2, 3, 4, or 5; lower than RAID 6	Higher than single disk for read; similar to single disk for write	Up to twice that of a single disk for read; similar to single disk for write
Parallel access	2	Redundant via Hamming code	$N+m$	Much higher than single disk; comparable to RAID 3, 4, or 5	Highest of all listed alternatives	Approximately twice that of a single disk
	3	Bit-interleaved parity	$N+1$	Much higher than single disk; comparable to RAID 2, 4, or 5	Highest of all listed alternatives	Approximately twice that of a single disk
Independent access	4	Block-interleaved parity	$N+1$	Much higher than single disk; comparable to RAID 2, 3, or 5	Similar to RAID 0 for read; significantly lower than single disk for write	Similar to RAID 0 for read; significantly lower than single disk for write
	5	Block-interleaved distributed parity	$N+1$	Much higher than single disk; comparable to RAID 2, 3, or 4	Similar to RAID 0 for read; lower than single disk for write	Similar to RAID 0 for read; generally lower than single disk for write
	6	Block-interleaved dual distributed parity	$N+2$	Highest of all listed alternatives	Similar to RAID 0 for read; lower than RAID 5 for write	Similar to RAID 0 for read; significantly lower than RAID 5 for write

Note: N, number of data disks; m, proportional to log N.

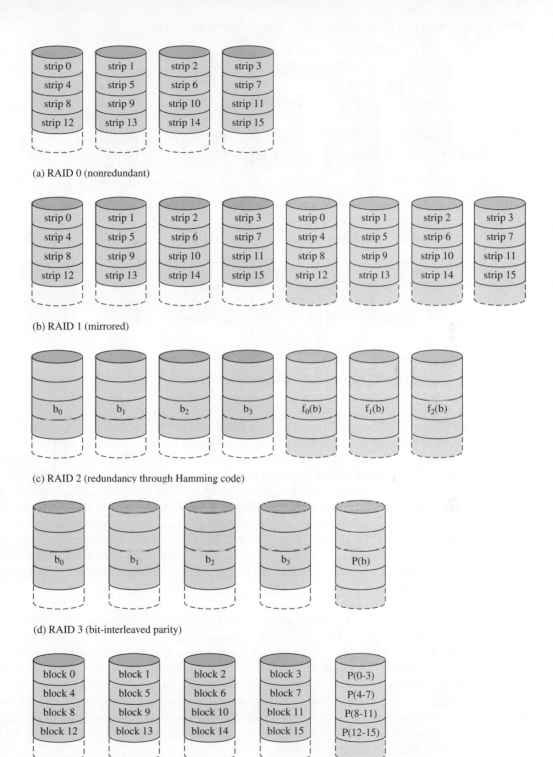

(a) RAID 0 (nonredundant)

(b) RAID 1 (mirrored)

(c) RAID 2 (redundancy through Hamming code)

(d) RAID 3 (bit-interleaved parity)

(e) RAID 4 (block-level parity)

Figure 11.8   RAID Levels

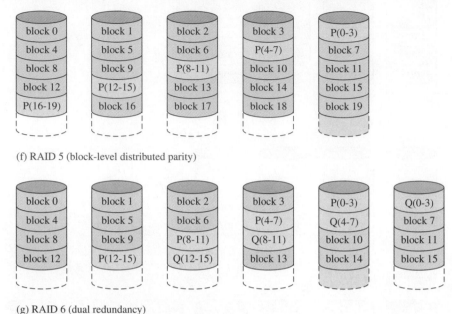

(f) RAID 5 (block-level distributed parity)

(g) RAID 6 (dual redundancy)

Figure 11.8   RAID Levels (Continued)

This is best understood by considering Figure 11.8. All user and system data are viewed as being stored on a logical disk. The logical disk is divided into strips; these strips may be physical blocks, sectors, or some other unit. The strips are mapped round robin to consecutive physical disks in the RAID array. A set of logically consecutive strips that maps exactly one strip to each array member is referred to as a **stripe**. In an n-disk array, the first n logical strips are physically stored as the first strip on each of the n disks, forming the first stripe; the second n strips are distributed as the second strips on each disk; and so on. The advantage of this layout is that if a single I/O request consists of multiple logically contiguous strips, then up to n strips for that request can be handled in parallel, greatly reducing the I/O transfer time.

RAID 0 FOR HIGH DATA TRANSFER CAPACITY   The performance of any of the RAID levels depends critically on the request patterns of the host system and on the layout of the data. These issues can be most clearly addressed in RAID 0, where the impact of redundancy does not interfere with the analysis. First, let us consider the use of RAID 0 to achieve a high data transfer rate. For applications to experience a high transfer rate, two requirements must be met. First, a high transfer capacity must exist along the entire path between host memory and the individual disk drives. This includes internal controller buses, host system I/O buses, I/O adapters, and host memory buses.

The second requirement is that the application must make I/O requests that drive the disk array efficiently. This requirement is met if the typical request is for large amounts of logically contiguous data, compared to the size of a strip. In this case, a single I/O request involves the parallel transfer of data from multiple disks, increasing the effective transfer rate compared to a single-disk transfer.

RAID 0 FOR HIGH I/O REQUEST RATE In a transaction-oriented environment, the user is typically more concerned with response time than with transfer rate. For an individual I/O request for a small amount of data, the I/O time is dominated by the motion of the disk heads (seek time) and the movement of the disk (rotational latency).

In a transaction environment, there may be hundreds of I/O requests per second. A disk array can provide high I/O execution rates by balancing the I/O load across multiple disks. Effective load balancing is achieved only if there are typically multiple I/O requests outstanding. This, in turn, implies that there are multiple independent applications or a single transaction-oriented application that is capable of multiple asynchronous I/O requests. The performance will also be influenced by the strip size. If the strip size is relatively large, so that a single I/O request only involves a single disk access, then multiple waiting I/O requests can be handled in parallel, reducing the queueing time for each request.

RAID Level 1

RAID 1 differs from RAID levels 2 through 6 in the way in which redundancy is achieved. In these other RAID schemes, some form of parity calculation is used to introduce redundancy, whereas in RAID 1, redundancy is achieved by the simple expedient of duplicating all the data. Figure 11.8b shows data striping being used, as in RAID 0. But in this case, each logical strip is mapped to two separate physical disks so that every disk in the array has a mirror disk that contains the same data. RAID 1 can also be implemented without data striping, though this is less common.

There are a number of positive aspects to the RAID 1 organization:

1. A read request can be serviced by either of the two disks that contains the requested data, whichever one involves the minimum seek time plus rotational latency.
2. A write request requires that both corresponding strips be updated, but this can be done in parallel. Thus, the write performance is dictated by the slower of the two writes (i.e., the one that involves the larger seek time plus rotational latency). However, there is no "write penalty" with RAID 1. RAID levels 2 through 6 involve the use of parity bits. Therefore, when a single strip is updated, the array management software must first compute and update the parity bits as well as updating the actual strip in question.
3. Recovery from a failure is simple. When a drive fails, the data may still be accessed from the second drive.

The principal disadvantage of RAID 1 is the cost; it requires twice the disk space of the logical disk that it supports. Because of that, a RAID 1 configuration is likely to be limited to drives that store system software and data and other highly critical files. In these cases, RAID 1 provides real-time backup of all data so that in the event of a disk failure, all of the critical data is still immediately available.

In a transaction-oriented environment, RAID 1 can achieve high I/O request rates if the bulk of the requests are reads. In this situation, the performance of RAID 1 can approach double of that of RAID 0. However, if a substantial fraction of the I/O requests are write requests, then there may be no significant performance gain over RAID 0. RAID 1 may also provide improved performance over RAID 0 for data transfer-intensive applications with a high percentage of reads. Improvement occurs if the application can split each read request so that both disk members participate.

RAID Level 2

RAID levels 2 and 3 make use of a parallel access technique. In a parallel access array, all member disks participate in the execution of every I/O request. Typically, the spindles of the individual drives are synchronized so that each disk head is in the same position on each disk at any given time.

As in the other RAID schemes, data striping is used. In the case of RAID 2 and 3, the strips are very small, often as small as a single byte or word. With RAID 2, an error-correcting code is calculated across corresponding bits on each data disk, and the bits of the code are stored in the corresponding bit positions on multiple parity disks. Typically, a Hamming code is used, which is able to correct single-bit errors and detect double-bit errors.

Although RAID 2 requires fewer disks than RAID 1, it is still rather costly. The number of redundant disks is proportional to the log of the number of data disks. On a single read, all disks are simultaneously accessed. The requested data and the associated error-correcting code are delivered to the array controller. If there is a single-bit error, the controller can recognize and correct the error instantly, so that the read access time is not slowed. On a single write, all data disks and parity disks must be accessed for the write operation.

RAID 2 would only be an effective choice in an environment in which many disk errors occur. Given the high reliability of individual disks and disk drives, RAID 2 is overkill and is not implemented.

RAID Level 3

RAID 3 is organized in a similar fashion to RAID 2. The difference is that RAID 3 requires only a single redundant disk, no matter how large the disk array. RAID 3 employs parallel access, with data distributed in small strips. Instead of an error-correcting code, a simple parity bit is computed for the set of individual bits in the same position on all of the data disks.

REDUNDANCY   In the event of a drive failure, the parity drive is accessed and data is reconstructed from the remaining devices. Once the failed drive is replaced, the missing data can be restored on the new drive and operation resumed.

Data reconstruction is simple. Consider an array of five drives in which X0 through X3 contain data and X4 is the parity disk. The parity for the ith bit is calculated as follows:

$$X4(i) = X3(i) \oplus X2(i) \oplus X1(i) \oplus X0(i)$$

where $\oplus$ is exclusive-OR function.

Suppose that drive X1 has failed. If we add $X4(i) \oplus X1(i)$ to both sides of the preceding equation, we get

$$X1(i) = X4(i) \oplus X3(i) \oplus X2(i) \oplus X0(i)$$

Thus, the contents of each strip of data on X1 can be regenerated from the contents of the corresponding strips on the remaining disks in the array. This principle is true for RAID levels 3 through 6.

In the event of a disk failure, all of the data are still available in what is referred to as reduced mode. In this mode, for reads, the missing data are regenerated on the fly using the exclusive-OR calculation. When data are written to a reduced RAID 3 array, consistency of the parity must be maintained for later regeneration. Return to full operation requires that the failed disk be replaced and the entire contents of the failed disk be regenerated on the new disk.

PERFORMANCE   Because data are striped in very small strips, RAID 3 can achieve very high data transfer rates. Any I/O request will involve the parallel transfer of data from all of the data disks. For large transfers, the performance improvement is especially noticeable. On the other hand, only one I/O request can be executed at a time. Thus, in a transaction-oriented environment, performance suffers.

RAID Level 4

RAID levels 4 through 6 make use of an independent access technique. In an independent access array, each member disk operates independently, so that separate I/O requests can be satisfied in parallel. Because of this, independent access arrays are more suitable for applications that require high I/O request rates and are relatively less suited for applications that require high data transfer rates.

As in the other RAID schemes, data striping is used. In the case of RAID 4 through 6, the strips are relatively large. With RAID 4, a bit-by-bit parity strip is calculated across corresponding strips on each data disk, and the parity bits are stored in the corresponding strip on the parity disk.

RAID 4 involves a write penalty when an I/O write request of small size is performed. Each time that a write occurs, the array management software must update not only the user data but also the corresponding parity bits. Consider an array of five drives in which X0 through X3 contain data and X4 is the parity disk. Suppose that a write is performed that only involves a strip on disk X1. Initially, for each bit i, we have the following relationship:

$$X4(i) = X3(i) \oplus X2(i) \oplus X1(i) \oplus X0(i) \tag{11.1}$$

After the update, with potentially altered bits indicated by a prime symbol:

$$
\begin{aligned}
X4'(i) &= X3(i) \oplus X2(i) \oplus X1'(i) \oplus X0(i) \\
&= X3(i) \oplus X2(i) \oplus X1'(i) \oplus X0(i) \oplus X1(i) \oplus X1(i) \\
&= X3(i) \oplus X2(i) \oplus X1(i) \oplus X0(i) \oplus X1(i) \oplus X1'(i) \\
&= X4(i) \oplus X1(i) \oplus X1'(i)
\end{aligned}
$$

The preceding set of equations is derived as follows. The first line shows that a change in X1 will also affect the parity disk X4. In the second line, we add the terms $[\oplus\, X1(i) \oplus X1(i)]$. Because the exclusive-OR of any quantity with itself is 0, this does not affect the equation. However, it is a convenience that is used to create the third line, by reordering. Finally, Equation (11.1) is used to replace the first four terms by $X4(i)$.

To calculate the new parity, the array management software must read the old user strip and the old parity strip. Then it can update these two strips with the new data and the newly calculated parity. Thus, each strip write involves two reads and two writes.

In the case of a larger size I/O write that involves strips on all disk drives, parity is easily computed by calculation using only the new data bits. Thus, the parity drive can be updated in parallel with the data drives and there are no extra reads or writes.

In any case, every write operation must involve the parity disk, which therefore can become a bottleneck.

RAID Level 5

RAID 5 is organized in a similar fashion to RAID 4. The difference is that RAID 5 distributes the parity strips across all disks. A typical allocation is a round-robin scheme, as illustrated in Figure 11.8f. For an n-disk array, the parity strip is on a different disk for the first n stripes, and the pattern then repeats.

The distribution of parity strips across all drives avoids the potential I/O bottleneck of the single parity disk found in RAID 4. Further, RAID 5 has the characteristic that the loss of any one disk does not result in data loss.

RAID Level 6

RAID 6 was introduced in a subsequent paper by the Berkeley researchers [KATZ89]. In the RAID 6 scheme, two different parity calculations are carried out and stored in separate blocks on different disks. Thus, a RAID 6 array whose user data require N disks consists of $N + 2$ disks.

Figure 11.8g illustrates the scheme. P and Q are two different data check algorithms. One of the two is the exclusive-OR calculation used in RAID 4 and 5. But the other is an independent data check algorithm. This makes it possible to regenerate data even if two disks containing user data fail.

The advantage of RAID 6 is that it provides extremely high data availability. Three disks would have to fail within the MTTR (mean time to repair) interval to cause data to be lost. On the other hand, RAID 6 incurs a substantial write penalty, because each write affects two parity blocks. Performance benchmarks [EISC07] show that a RAID 6 controller can suffer more than a 30% drop in overall write performance compared with a RAID 5 implementation. RAID 5 and RAID 6 read performance is comparable.

11.7 DISK CACHE

In Section 1.6 and Appendix 1A, we summarized the principles of cache memory. The term *cache memory* is usually used to apply to a memory that is smaller and faster than main memory and that is interposed between main memory and the processor. Such a cache memory reduces average memory access time by exploiting the principle of locality.

The same principle can be applied to disk memory. Specifically, a disk cache is a buffer in main memory for disk sectors. The cache contains a copy of some of the sectors on the disk. When an I/O request is made for a particular sector, a check is made to determine if the sector is in the disk cache. If so, the request is satisfied via the cache. If not, the requested sector is read into the disk cache from the disk. Because of the phenomenon of locality of reference, when a block of data is fetched into the cache to satisfy a single I/O request, it is likely that there will be future references to that same block.

Design Considerations

Several design issues are of interest. First, when an I/O request is satisfied from the disk cache, the data in the disk cache must be delivered to the requesting process. This can be done either by transferring the block of data within main memory from the disk cache to memory assigned to the user process, or simply by using a shared memory capability and passing a pointer to the appropriate slot in the disk cache. The latter approach saves the time of a memory-to-memory transfer and also allows shared access by other processes using the readers/writers model described in Chapter 5.

A second design issue has to do with the replacement strategy. When a new sector is brought into the disk cache, one of the existing blocks must be replaced. This is the identical problem presented in Chapter 8; there the requirement was for a page replacement algorithm. A number of algorithms have been tried. The most commonly used algorithm is least recently used (LRU): Replace that block that has been in the cache longest with no reference to it. Logically, the cache consists of a stack of blocks, with the most recently referenced block on the top of the stack. When a block in the cache is referenced, it is moved from its existing position on the stack to the top of the stack. When a block is brought in from secondary memory, remove the block that is on the bottom of the stack and push the incoming block onto the top of the stack. Naturally, it is not necessary actually to move these blocks around in main memory; a stack of pointers can be associated with the cache.

Another possibility is **least frequently used (LFU)**: Replace that block in the set that has experienced the fewest references. LFU could be implemented by associating a counter with each block. When a block is brought in, it is assigned a count of 1; with each reference to the block, its count is incremented by 1. When replacement is required, the block with the smallest count is selected. Intuitively, it might seem that LFU is more appropriate than LRU because LFU makes use of more pertinent information about each block in the selection process.

A simple LFU algorithm has the following problem. It may be that certain blocks are referenced relatively infrequently overall, but when they are referenced, there are short intervals of repeated references due to locality, thus building up high reference counts. After such an interval is over, the reference count may be misleading and not reflect the probability that the block will soon be referenced again. Thus, the effect of locality may actually cause the LFU algorithm to make poor replacement choices.

To overcome this difficulty with LFU, a technique known as frequency-based replacement is proposed in [ROBI90]. For clarity, let us first consider a simplified version, illustrated in Figure 11.9a. The blocks are logically organized in a stack, as with the LRU algorithm. A certain portion of the top part of the stack is designated the new section. When there is a cache hit, the referenced block is moved to the top of the stack. If the block was already in the new section, its reference count is not incremented; otherwise it is incremented by 1. Given a sufficiently large new section, this results in the reference counts for blocks that are repeatedly re-referenced within a short interval remaining unchanged. On a miss, the block with the smallest reference count that is not in the new section is chosen for replacement; the least recently used such block is chosen in the event of a tie.

The authors report that this strategy achieved only slight improvement over LRU. The problem is the following:

1. On a cache miss, a new block is brought into the new section, with a count of 1.

2. The count remains at 1 as long as the block remains in the new section.

3. Eventually the block ages out of the new section, with its count still at 1.

4. If the block is not now re-referenced fairly quickly, it is very likely to be replaced because it necessarily has the smallest reference count of those blocks that are not in the new section. In other words, there does not seem to be a sufficiently long interval for blocks aging out of the new section to build up their reference counts even if they were relatively frequently referenced.

A further refinement addresses this problem: Divide the stack into three sections: new, middle, and old (Figure 11.9b). As before, reference counts are not incremented on blocks in the new section. However, only blocks in the old section are eligible for replacement. Assuming a sufficiently large middle section, this allows

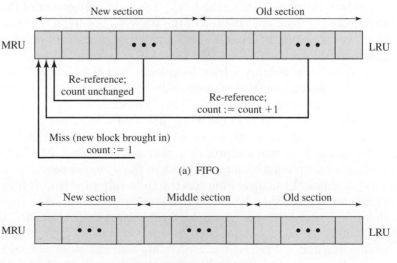

(a) FIFO

(b) Use of three sections

Figure 11.9 Frequency-Based Replacement

relatively frequently referenced blocks a chance to build up their reference counts before becoming eligible for replacement. Simulation studies by the authors indicate that this refined policy is significantly better than simple LRU or LFU.

Regardless of the particular replacement strategy, the replacement can take place on demand or preplanned. In the former case, a sector is replaced only when the slot is needed. In the latter case, a number of slots are released at a time. The reason for this latter approach is related to the need to write back sectors. If a sector is brought into the cache and only read, then when it is replaced, it is not necessary to write it back out to the disk. However, if the sector has been updated, then it is necessary to write it back out before replacing it. In this latter case, it makes sense to cluster the writing and to order the writing to minimize seek time.

Performance Considerations

The same performance considerations discussed in Appendix 1A apply here. The issue of cache performance reduces itself to a question of whether a given miss ratio can be achieved. This will depend on the locality behavior of the disk references, the replacement algorithm, and other design factors. Principally, however, the miss ratio is a function of the size of the disk cache. Figure 11.10 summarizes results from several studies using LRU, one for a UNIX system running on a VAX [OUST85] and one for IBM mainframe operating systems [SMIT85]. Figure 11.11 shows results for simulation studies of the frequency-based replacement algorithm. A comparison of the two figures points out one of the risks of this sort of performance assessment.

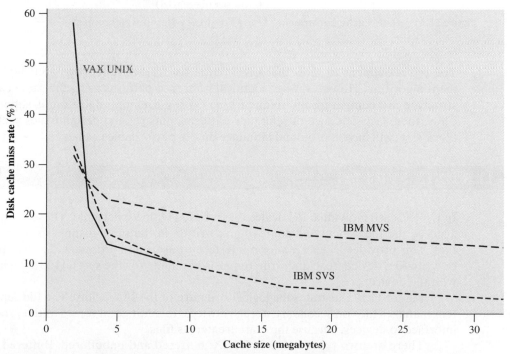

Figure 11.10   Some Disk Cache Performance Results Using LRU

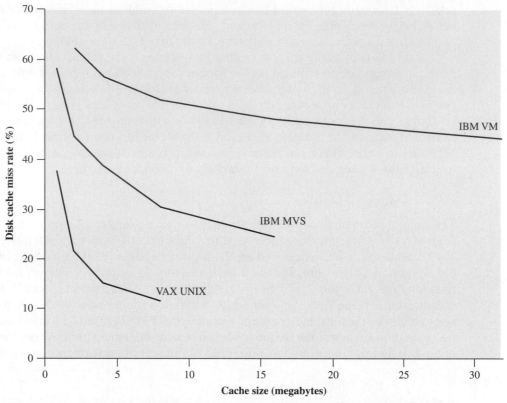

Figure 11.11   Disk Cache Performance Using Frequency-Based Replacement

The figures appear to show that LRU outperforms the frequency-based replacement algorithm. However, when identical reference patterns using the same cache structure are compared, the frequency-based replacement algorithm is superior. Thus, the exact sequence of reference patterns, plus related design issues such as block size, will have a profound influence on the performance achieved.

11.8 UNIX SVR4 I/O

In UNIX, each individual I/O device is associated with a special file. These are managed by the file system and are read and written in the same manner as user data files. This provides a clean, uniform interface to users and processes. To read from or write to a device, read and write requests are made for the special file associated with the device.

Figure 11.12 illustrates the logical structure of the I/O facility. The file subsystem manages files on secondary storage devices. In addition, it serves as the process interface to devices, because these are treated as files.

There are two types of I/O in UNIX: buffered and unbuffered. Buffered I/O passes through system buffers, whereas unbuffered I/O typically involves the DMA

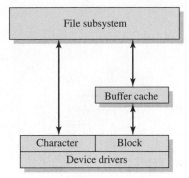

Figure 11.12   UNIX I/O Structure

facility, with the transfer taking place directly between the I/O module and the process I/O area. For buffered I/O, two types of buffers are used: system buffer caches and character queues.

Buffer Cache

The buffer cache in UNIX is essentially a disk cache. I/O operations with disk are handled through the buffer cache. The data transfer between the buffer cache and the user process space always occurs using DMA. Because both the buffer cache and the process I/O area are in main memory, the DMA facility is used in this case to perform a memory-to-memory copy. This does not use up any processor cycles, but it does consume bus cycles.

To manage the buffer cache, three lists are maintained:

- **Free list:** List of all slots in the cache (a slot is referred to as a buffer in UNIX; each slot holds one disk sector) that are available for allocation
- **Device list:** List of all buffers currently associated with each disk
- **Driver I/O queue:** List of buffers that are actually undergoing or waiting for I/O on a particular device

All buffers should be on the free list or on the driver I/O queue list. A buffer, once associated with a device, remains associated with the device even if it is on the free list, until is actually reused and becomes associated with another device. These lists are maintained as pointers associated with each buffer rather than physically separate lists.

When a reference is made to a physical block number on a particular device, the OS first checks to see if the block is in the buffer cache. To minimize the search time, the device list is organized as a hash table, using a technique similar to the overflow with chaining technique discussed in Appendix F (Figure F.1b). Figure 11.13 depicts the general organization of the buffer cache. There is a hash table of fixed length that contains pointers into the buffer cache. Each reference to a (device#, block#) maps into a particular entry in the hash table. The pointer in that entry points to the first buffer in the chain. A hash pointer associated with each buffer points to the next buffer in the chain for that hash table entry. Thus, for all (device#, block#)

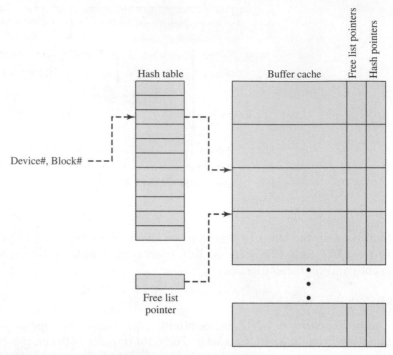

Figure 11.13   UNIX Buffer Cache Organization

references that map into the same hash table entry, if the corresponding block is in the buffer cache, then that buffer will be in the chain for that hash table entry. Thus, the length of the search of the buffer cache is reduced by a factor on the order of N, where N is the length of the hash table.

For block replacement, a least-recently-used algorithm is used: After a buffer has been allocated to a disk block, it cannot be used for another block until all other buffers have been used more recently. The free list preserves this least-recently-used order.

Character Queue

Block-oriented devices, such as disk and USB keys, can be effectively served by the buffer cache. A different form of buffering is appropriate for character-oriented devices, such as terminals and printers. A character queue is either written by the I/O device and read by the process or written by the process and read by the device. In both cases, the producer/consumer model introduced in Chapter 5 is used. Thus, character queues may only be read once; as each character is read, it is effectively destroyed. This is in contrast to the buffer cache, which may be read multiple times and hence follows the readers/writers model (also discussed in Chapter 5).

Unbuffered I/O

Unbuffered I/O, which is simply DMA between device and process space, is always the fastest method for a process to perform I/O. A process that is

Table 11.5 Device I/O in UNIX

	Unbuffered I/O	Buffer Cache	Character Queue
Disk Drive	X	X	
Tape Drive	X	X	
Terminals			X
Communication Lines			X
Printers	X		X

performing unbuffered I/O is locked in main memory and cannot be swapped out. This reduces the opportunities for swapping by tying up part of main memory, thus reducing the overall system performance. Also, the I/O device is tied up with the process for the duration of the transfer, making it unavailable for other processes.

UNIX Devices

Among the categories of devices recognized by UNIX are the following:

- Disk drives
- Tape drives
- Terminals
- Communication lines
- Printers

Table 11.5 shows the types of I/O suited to each type of device. Disk drives are heavily used in UNIX, are block oriented, and have the potential for reasonable high throughput. Thus, I/O for these devices tends to be unbuffered or via buffer cache. Tape drives are functionally similar to disk drives and use similar I/O schemes.

Because terminals involve relatively slow exchange of characters, terminal I/O typically makes use of the character queue. Similarly, communication lines require serial processing of bytes of data for input or output and are best handled by character queues. Finally, the type of I/O used for a printer will generally depend on its speed. Slow printers will normally use the character queue, while a fast printer might employ unbuffered I/O. A buffer cache could be used for a fast printer. However, because data going to a printer are never reused, the overhead of the buffer cache is unnecessary.

11.9 LINUX I/O

In general terms, the Linux I/O kernel facility is very similar to that of other UNIX implementation, such as SVR4. The Linux kernel associates a special file with each I/O device driver. Block, character, and network devices are recognized. In this section, we look at several features of the Linux I/O facility.

Disk Scheduling

The default disk scheduler in Linux 2.4 is known as the Linux Elevator, which is a variation on the LOOK algorithm discussed in Section 11.5. For Linux 2.6, the Elevator algorithm has been augmented by two additional algorithms: the deadline I/O scheduler and the anticipatory I/O scheduler [LOVE04]. We examine each of these in turn.

THE ELEVATOR SCHEDULER   The elevator scheduler maintains a single queue for disk read and write requests and performs both sorting and merging functions on the queue. In general terms, the elevator scheduler keeps the list of requests sorted by block number. Thus, as the disk requests are handled, the drive moves in a single direction, satisfying each request as it is encountered. This general strategy is refined in the following manner. When a new request is added to the queue, four operations are considered in order:

1. If the request is to the same on-disk sector or an immediately adjacent sector to a pending request in the queue, then the existing request and the new request are merged into one request.

2. If a request in the queue is sufficiently old, the new request is inserted at the tail of the queue.

3. If there is a suitable location, the new request is inserted in sorted order.

4. If there is no suitable location, the new request is placed at the tail of the queue.

DEADLINE SCHEDULER   Operation 2 in the preceding list is intended to prevent starvation of a request, but is not very effective [LOVE04]. It does not attempt to service requests in a given time frame but merely stops insertion-sorting requests after a suitable delay. Two problems manifest themselves with the elevator scheme. The first problem is that a distant block request can be delayed for a substantial time because the queue is dynamically updated. For example, consider the following stream of requests for disk blocks: 20, 30, 700, 25. The elevator scheduler reorders these so that the requests are placed in the queue as 20, 25, 30, 700, with 20 being the head of the queue. If a continuous sequence of low-numbered block requests arrive, then the request for 700 continues to be delayed.

An even more serious problem concerns the distinction between read and write requests. Typically, a write request is issued asynchronously. That is, once a process issues the write request, it need not wait for the request to actually be satisfied. When an application issues a write, the kernel copies the data into an appropriate buffer, to be written out as time permits. Once the data are captured in the kernel's buffer, the application can proceed. However, for many read operations, the process must wait until the requested data are delivered to the application before proceeding. Thus, a stream of write requests (e.g., to place a large file on the disk) can block a read request for a considerable time and thus block a process.

To overcome these problems, the deadline I/O scheduler makes use of three queues (Figure 11.14). Each incoming request is placed in the sorted

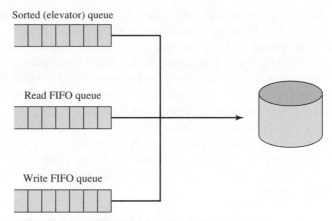

Sorted (elevator) queue

Read FIFO queue

Write FIFO queue

Figure 11.14   The Linux Deadline I/O Scheduler

elevator queue, as before. In addition, the same request is placed at the tail of a read FIFO queue for a read request or a write FIFO queue for a write request. Thus, the read and write queues maintain a list of requests in the sequence in which the requests were made. Associated with each request is an expiration time, with a default value of 0.5 seconds for a read request and 5 seconds for a write request. Ordinarily, the scheduler dispatches from the sorted queue. When a request is satisfied, it is removed from the head of the sorted queue and also from the appropriate FIFO queue. However, when the item at the head of one of the FIFO queues becomes older than its expiration time, then the scheduler next dispatches from that FIFO queue, taking the expired request, plus the next few requests from the queue. As each request is dispatched, it is also removed from the sorted queue.

The deadline I/O scheduler scheme overcomes the starvation problem and also the read versus write problem.

ANTICIPATORY I/O SCHEDULER   The original elevator scheduler and the deadline scheduler both are designed to dispatch a new request as soon as the existing request is satisfied, thus keeping the disk as busy as possible. This same policy applies to all of the scheduling algorithms discussed in Section 11.5. However, such a policy can be counterproductive if there are numerous synchronous read requests. Typically, an application will wait until a read request is satisfied and the data available before issuing the next request. The small delay between receiving the data for the last read and issuing the next read enables the scheduler to turn elsewhere for a pending request and dispatch that request.

Because of the principle of locality, it is likely that successive reads from the same process will be to disk blocks that are near one another. If the scheduler were to delay a short period of time after satisfying a read request, to see if a new nearby read request is made, the overall performance of the system could be enhanced. This is the philosophy behind the anticipatory scheduler, proposed in [IYER01], and implemented in Linux 2.6.

In Linux, the anticipatory scheduler is superimposed on the deadline scheduler. When a read request is dispatched, the anticipatory scheduler causes the scheduling system to delay for up to 6 ms, depending on the configuration. During this small delay, there is a good chance that the application that issued the last read request will issue another read request to the same region of the disk. If so, that request will be serviced immediately. If no such read request occurs, the scheduler resumes using the deadline scheduling algorithm.

[LOVE04] reports on two tests of the Linux scheduling algorithms. The first test involved the reading of a 200-MB file while doing a long streaming write in the background. The second test involved doing a read of a large file in the background while reading every file in the kernel source tree. The results are listed in the following table:

I/O Scheduler and Kernel	Test 1	Test 2
Linux elevator on 2.4	45 seconds	30 minutes, 28 seconds
Deadline I/O scheduler on 2.6	40 seconds	3 minutes, 30 seconds
Anticipatory I/O scheduler on 2.6	4.6 seconds	15 seconds

As can be seen, the performance improvement depends on the nature of the workload. But in both cases, the anticipatory scheduler provides a dramatic improvement.

Linux Page Cache

In Linux 2.2 and earlier releases, the kernel maintained a page cache for reads and writes from regular file system files and for virtual memory pages, and a separate buffer cache for block I/O. For Linux 2.4 and later, there is a single unified page cache that is involved in all traffic between disk and main memory.

The page cache confers two benefits. First, when it is time to write back dirty pages to disk, a collection of them can be ordered properly and written out efficiently. Second, because of the principle of temporal locality, pages in the page cache are likely to be referenced again before they are flushed from the cache, thus saving a disk I/O operation.

Dirty pages are written back to disk in two situations:

- When free memory falls below a specified threshold, the kernel reduces the size of the page cache to release memory to be added to the free memory pool.
- When dirty pages grow older than a specified threshold, a number of dirty pages are written back to disk.

11.10 WINDOWS I/O

Figure 11.15 shows the key kernel-mode components related to the Windows I/O manager. The I/O manager is responsible for all I/O for the operating system and provides a uniform interface that all types of drivers can call.

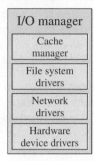

Figure 11.15   Windows I/O Manager

Basic I/O Facilities

The I/O manager works closely with four types of kernel components:

- **Cache manager:** The cache manager handles file caching for all file systems. It can dynamically increase and decrease the size of the cache devoted to a particular file as the amount of available physical memory varies. The system records updates in the cache only and not on disk. A kernel thread, the lazy writer, periodically batches the updates together to write to disk. Writing the updates in batches allows the I/O to be more efficient. The cache manager works by mapping regions of files into kernel virtual memory and then relying on the virtual memory manager to do most of the work to copy pages to and from the files on disk.

- **File system drivers:** The I/O manager treats a file system driver as just another device driver and routes I/O requests for file system volumes to the appropriate software driver for that volume. The file system, in turn, sends I/O requests to the software drivers that manage the hardware device adapter.

- **Network drivers:** Windows includes integrated networking capabilities and support for remote file systems. The facilities are implemented as software drivers rather than part of the Windows Executive.

- **Hardware device drivers:** These software drivers access the hardware registers of the peripheral devices using entry points in the Hardware Abstraction Layer. A set of these routines exists for every platform that Windows supports; because the routine names are the same for all platforms, the source code of Windows device drivers is portable across different processor types.

Asynchronous and Synchronous I/O

Windows offers two modes of I/O operation: asynchronous and synchronous. The asynchronous mode is used whenever possible to optimize application performance. With asynchronous I/O, an application initiates an I/O operation and then can continue processing while the I/O request is fulfilled. With synchronous I/O, the application is blocked until the I/O operation completes.

Asynchronous I/O is more efficient, from the point of view of the calling thread, because it allows the thread to continue execution while the I/O operation is queued by the I/O manager and subsequently performed. However, the application that invoked the asynchronous I/O operation needs some way to determine when the operation is complete. Windows provides five different techniques for signaling I/O completion:

- **Signaling the file object:** With this approach, the event associated with a file object is set when an operation on that object is complete. The thread that invoked the I/O operation can continue to execute until it reaches a point where it must stop until the I/O operation is complete. At that point, the thread can wait until the operation is complete and then continue. This technique is simple and easy to use but is not appropriate for handling multiple I/O requests. For example, if a thread needs to perform multiple simultaneous actions on a single file, such as reading from one portion and writing to another portion of the file, with this technique the thread could not distinguish between the completion of the read and the completion of the write. It would simply know that one of the requested I/O operations on this file had finished.

- **Signaling an event object:** This technique allows multiple simultaneous I/O requests against a single device or file. The thread creates an event for each request. Later, the thread can wait on a single one of these requests or on an entire collection of requests.

- **Asynchronous procedure call:** This technique makes use of a queue associated with a thread, known as the asynchronous procedure call (APC) queue. In this case, the thread makes I/O requests, specifying a user-mode routine to call when the I/O completes. The I/O manager places the results of each request in the calling thread's APC queue. The next time the thread blocks in the kernel, the APCs will be delivered, each causing the thread to return to user mode and execute the specified routine.

- **I/O completion ports:** This technique is used on a Windows server to optimize the use of threads. The application creates a pool of threads for handling the completion of I/O requests. Each thread waits on the completion port, and the Kernel wakes threads to handle each I/O completion. One of the advantages of this approach is that the application can specify a limit for how many of these threads will run at the same time.

- **Polling:** Asynchronous I/O requests write a status and transfer count into the process' user virtual memory when the operation completes. A thread can just check these values to see if the operation has completed.

Software RAID

Windows supports two sorts of RAID configurations, defined in [MS96] as follows:

- **Hardware RAID:** Separate physical disks combined into one or more logical disks by the disk controller or disk storage cabinet hardware.

- **Software RAID:** Noncontiguous disk space combined into one or more logical partitions by the fault-tolerant software disk driver, FTDISK.

In hardware RAID, the controller interface handles the creation and regeneration of redundant information. The software RAID, available on Windows Server, implements the RAID functionality as part of the operating system and can be used with any set of multiple disks. The software RAID facility implements RAID 1 and RAID 5. In the case of RAID 1 (disk mirroring), the two disks containing the primary and mirrored partitions may be on the same disk controller or different disk controllers. The latter configuration is referred to as *disk duplexing*.

Volume Shadow Copies

Shadow copies are an efficient way of making consistent snapshots of volumes so that they can be backed up. They are also useful for archiving files on a per-volume basis. If a user deletes a file he or she can retrieve an earlier copy from any available shadow copy made by the system administrator. Shadow copies are implemented by a software driver that makes copies of data on the volume before it is overwritten.

Volume Encryption

Windows supports the encryption of entire volumes, using a feature called BitLocker. This is more secure than encrypting individual files, as the entire system works to be sure that the data is safe. Up to three different methods of supplying the cryptographic key can be provided, allowing multiple interlocking layers of security.

11.11 SUMMARY

The computer system's interface to the outside world is its I/O architecture. This architecture is designed to provide a systematic means of controlling interaction with the outside world and to provide the operating system with the information it needs to manage I/O activity effectively.

The I/O function is generally broken up into a number of layers, with lower layers dealing with details that are closer to the physical functions to be performed and higher layers dealing with I/O in a logical and generic fashion. The result is that changes in hardware parameters need not affect most of the I/O software.

A key aspect of I/O is the use of buffers that are controlled by I/O utilities rather than by application processes. Buffering smoothes out the differences between the internal speeds of the computer system and the speeds of I/O devices. The use of buffers also decouples the actual I/O transfer from the address space of the application process. This allows the operating system more flexibility in performing its memory-management function.

The aspect of I/O that has the greatest impact on overall system performance is disk I/O. Accordingly, there has been greater research and design effort in this area than in any other kind of I/O. Two of the most widely used approaches to improve disk I/O performance are disk scheduling and the disk cache.

At any time, there may be a queue of requests for I/O on the same disk. It is the object of disk scheduling to satisfy these requests in a way that minimizes the mechanical seek time of the disk and hence improves performance. The physical layout of pending requests plus considerations of locality come into play.

A disk cache is a buffer, usually kept in main memory, that functions as a cache of disk blocks between disk memory and the rest of main memory. Because of the principle of locality, the use of a disk cache should substantially reduce the number of block I/O transfers between main memory and disk.

11.12 RECOMMENDED READING

General discussions of computer I/O can be found in most books on computer architecture, such as [STAL10]. [MEE96a] provides a good survey of the underlying recording technology of disk and tape systems. [MEE96b] focuses on the data storage techniques for disk and tape systems. [WIED87] contains an excellent discussion of disk performance issues, including those relating to disk scheduling. [NG98] looks at disk hardware performance issues. [CAO96] analyzes disk caching and disk scheduling. Good surveys of disk scheduling algorithms, with a performance analysis, are [WORT94] and [SELT90].

[PAI00] is an instructive description of an integrated operating-system scheme for I/O buffering and caching.

[DELL00] provides a detailed discussion of Windows NT device drivers plus a good overview of the entire Windows I/O architecture.

An excellent survey of RAID technology, written by the inventors of the RAID concept, is [CHEN94]. [CHEN96] analyzes RAID performance. Another good paper is [FRIE96]. [DALT96] describes the Windows NT software RAID facility in detail. [LEVE10] examines the need to move beyond RAID 6 to a triple-parity configuration. [STAI10] is a good survey of the standard RAID levels plus a number of common RAID enhancements.

CAO96 Cao, P., Felten, E., Karlin, A., and Li, K. "Implementation and Performance of Integrated Application-Controlled File Caching, Prefetching, and Disk Scheduling." *ACM Transactions on Computer Systems*, November 1996.

CHEN94 Chen, P., Lee, E., Gibson, G., Katz, R., and Patterson, D. "RAID: High-Performance, Reliable Secondary Storage." *ACM Computing Surveys*, June 1994.

CHEN96 Chen, S., and Towsley, D. "A Performance Evaluation of RAID Architectures." *IEEE Transactions on Computers*, October 1996.

DALT96 Dalton, W., et al. *Windows NT Server 4: Security, Troubleshooting, and Optimization.* Indianapolis, IN: New Riders Publishing, 1996.

DELL00 Dekker, E., and Newcomer, J. *Developing Windows NT Device Drivers: A Programmer's Handbook.* Reading, MA: Addison Wesley, 2000.

FRIE96 Friedman, M. "RAID Keeps Going and Going and..." *IEEE Spectrum*, April 1996.

LEVE10 Leventhal, A. "Triple-Parity RAID and Beyond." *Communications of the ACM*, January 2010.

MEE96a Mee, C., and Daniel, E. eds. *Magnetic Recording Technology.* New York: McGraw Hill, 1996.

MEE96b Mee, C., and Daniel, E. eds. *Magnetic Storage Handbook*. New York: McGraw Hill, 1996.

NG98 Ng, S. "Advances in Disk Technology: Performance Issues." *Computer*, May 1989.

PAI00 Pai, V., Druschel, P., and Zwaenepoel, W. "IO-Lite: A Unified I/O Buffering and Caching System." *ACM Transactions on Computer Systems*, February 2000.

SELT90 Seltzer, M., Chen, P., and Ousterhout, J. "Disk Scheduling Revisited." *Proceedings, USENIX Winter Technical Conference*, January 1990.

STAI10 Staimer, M. "Alternatives to RAID." *Storage Magazine*, May 2010.

STAL10 Stallings, W. *Computer Organization and Architecture*, 8th ed. Upper Saddle River, NJ: Prentice Hall, 2010.

WIED87 Wiederhold, G. *File Organization for Database Design*. New York: McGraw-Hill, 1987.

WORT94 Worthington, B., Ganger, G., and Patt, Y. "Scheduling Algorithms for Modern Disk Drives." *ACM SiGMETRICS*, May 1994.

11.13 KEY TERMS, REVIEW QUESTIONS, AND PROBLEMS

Key Terms

block	input/output (I/O)	redundant array of independent disks
block-oriented device	I/O buffer	removable disk
circular buffer	I/O channel	rotational delay
device I/O	I/O processor	sector
direct memory access	logical I/O	seek time
disk access time	magnetic disk	stream-oriented device
disk cache	nonremovable disk	track
gap	programmed I/O	transfer time
hard disk	read/write head	
interrupt-driven I/O		

Review Questions

11.1 List and briefly define three techniques for performing I/O.

11.2 What is the difference between logical I/O and device I/O?

11.3 What is the difference between block-oriented devices and stream-oriented devices? Give a few examples of each.

11.4 Why would you expect improved performance using a double buffer rather than a single buffer for I/O?

11.5 What delay elements are involved in a disk read or write?

11.6 Briefly define the disk scheduling policies illustrated in Figure 11.7.

11.7 Briefly define the seven RAID levels.

11.8 What is the typical disk sector size?

Problems

11.1 Consider a program that accesses a single I/O device and compare unbuffered I/O to the use of a buffer. Show that the use of the buffer can reduce the running time by at most a factor of two.

11.2 Generalize the result of Problem 11.1 to the case in which a program refers to n devices.

11.3 **a.** Perform the same type of analysis as that of Table 11.2 for the following sequence of disk track requests: 27, 129, 110, 186, 147, 41, 10, 64, 120. Assume that the disk head is initially positioned over track 100 and is moving in the direction of decreasing track number.
    b. Do the same analysis, but now assume that the disk head is moving in the direction of increasing track number.

11.4 Consider a disk with N tracks numbered from 0 to $(N - 1)$ and assume that requested sectors are distributed randomly and evenly over the disk. We want to calculate the average number of tracks traversed by a seek.
    a. Calculate the probability of a seek of length j when the head is currently positioned over track t. (*Hint:* This is a matter of determining the total number of combinations, recognizing that all track positions for the destination of the seek are equally likely.)
    b. Calculate the probability of a seek of length K, for an arbitrary current position of the head. (*Hint:* This involves the summing over all possible combinations of movements of K tracks.)
    c. Calculate the average number of tracks traversed by a seek, using the formula for expected value

$$E[x] = \sum_{i=0}^{N-1} i \times \Pr[x = i]$$

Hint: Use the equalities $\sum_{i=1}^{n} = \dfrac{n(n + 1)}{2}$; $\sum_{i=1}^{n} i^2 = \dfrac{n(n + 1)(2n + 1)}{6}$.

    d. Show that for large values of N, the average number of tracks traversed by a seek approaches $N/3$.

11.5 The following equation was suggested both for cache memory and disk cache memory:

$$T_S = T_C + M \times T_D$$

Generalize this equation to a memory hierarchy with N levels instead of just 2.

11.6 For the frequency-based replacement algorithm (Figure 11.9), define F_{new}, F_{middle}, and F_{old} as the fraction of the cache that comprises the new, middle, and old sections, respectively. Clearly, $F_{new} + F_{middle} + F_{old} = 1$. Characterize the policy when
    a. $F_{old} = 1 - F_{new}$
    b. $F_{old} = 1/(\text{cache size})$

11.7 Calculate how much disk space (in sectors, tracks, and surfaces) will be required to store 300,000 120-byte logical records if the disk is fixed sector with 512 bytes/sector, with 96 sectors/track, 110 tracks per surface, and 8 usable surfaces. Ignore any file header record(s) and track indexes, and assume that records cannot span two sectors.

11.8 Consider the disk system described in Problem 11.7, and assume that the disk rotates at 360 rpm. A processor reads one sector from the disk using interrupt-driven I/O, with one interrupt per byte. If it takes 2.5 μs to process each interrupt, what percentage of the time will the processor spend handling I/O (disregard seek time)?

11.9 Repeat the preceding problem using DMA, and assume one interrupt per sector.

11.10 A 32-bit computer has two selector channels and one multiplexor channel. Each selector channel supports two magnetic disk and two magnetic tape units. The multiplexor channel has two line printers, two card readers, and ten VDT terminals connected to it. Assume the following transfer rates:

Disk drive	800 Kbytes/s
Magnetic tape drive	200 Kbytes/s
Line printer	6.6 Kbytes/s
Card reader	1.2 Kbytes/s
VDT	1 Kbyte/s

Estimate the maximum aggregate I/O transfer rate in this system.

11.11 It should be clear that disk striping can improve the data transfer rate when the strip size is small compared to the I/O request size. It should also be clear that RAID 0 provides improved performance relative to a single large disk, because multiple I/O requests can be handled in parallel. However, in this latter case, is disk striping necessary? That is, does disk striping improve I/O request rate performance compared to a comparable disk array without striping?

11.12 Consider a 4-drive, 200 GB-per-drive RAID array. What is the available data storage capacity for each of the RAID levels, 0, 1, 3, 4, 5, and 6?

CHAPTER 12

FILE MANAGEMENT

12.1 Overview
Files and File Systems
File Structure
File Management Systems

12.2 File Organization and Access
The Pile
The Sequential File
The Indexed Sequential File
The Indexed File
The Direct or Hashed File

12.3 B-Trees

12.4 File Directories
Contents
Structure
Naming

12.5 File Sharing
Access Rights
Simultaneous Access

12.6 Record Blocking

12.7 Secondary Storage Management
File Allocation
Free Space Management
Volumes
Reliability

12.8 File System Security

12.9 UNIX File Management

12.10 Linux Virtual File System

12.11 Windows File System

12.12 Summary

12.13 Recommended Reading

12.14 Key Terms, Review Questions, and Problems

If there is one singular characteristic that makes squirrels unique among small mammals it is their natural instinct to hoard food. Squirrels have developed sophisticated capabilities in their hoarding. Different types of food are stored in different ways to maintain quality. Mushrooms, for instance, are usually dried before storing. This is done by impaling them on branches or leaving them in the forks of trees for later retrieval. Pine cones, on the other hand, are often harvested while green and cached in damp conditions that keep seeds from ripening. Gray squirrels usually strip outer husks from walnuts before storing.

—SQUIRRELS: A WILDLIFE HANDBOOK, KIM LONG

LEARNING OBJECTIVES

After studying this chapter, you should be able to:

- Describe the basic concepts of files and file systems.
- Understand the principal techniques for file organization and access.
- Define B-trees.
- Explain file directories.
- Understand the requirements for file sharing.
- Understand the concept of record blocking.
- Describe the principal design issues for secondary storage management.
- Understand the design issues for file system security.
- Explain the OS file systems used in Linux, UNIX, and Windows 7.

In most applications, the file is the central element. With the exception of real-time applications and some other specialized applications, the input to the application is by means of a file; and in virtually all applications, output is saved in a file for long-term storage and for later access by the user and by other programs.

Files have a life outside of any individual application that uses them for input and/or output. Users wish to be able to access files, save them, and maintain the integrity of their contents. To aid in these objectives, virtually all operating systems provide file management systems. Typically, a file management system consists of system utility programs that run as privileged applications. However, at the very least, a file management system needs special services from the operating system; at the most, the entire file management system is considered part of the operating system. Thus, it is appropriate to consider the basic elements of file management in this book.

We begin with an overview, followed by a look at various file organization schemes. Although file organization is generally beyond the scope of the operating system, it is essential to have a general understanding of the common alternatives to appreciate some of the design trade-offs involved in file management. The remainder of this chapter looks at other topics in file management.

Files and File Systems

From the user's point of view, one of the most important parts of an operating system is the file system. The file system provides the resource abstractions typically associated with secondary storage. The file system permits users to create data collections, called files, with desirable properties, such as:

- **Long-term existence:** Files are stored on disk or other secondary storage and do not disappear when a user logs off.
- **Sharable between processes:** Files have names and can have associated access permissions that permit controlled sharing.
- **Structure:** Depending on the file system, a file can have an internal structure that is convenient for particular applications. In addition, files can be organized into hierarchical or more complex structure to reflect the relationships among files.

Any file system provides not only a means to store data organized as files, but a collection of functions that can be performed on files. Typical operations include the following:

- **Create:** A new file is defined and positioned within the structure of files.
- **Delete:** A file is removed from the file structure and destroyed.
- **Open:** An existing file is declared to be "opened" by a process, allowing the process to perform functions on the file.
- **Close:** The file is closed with respect to a process, so that the process no longer may perform functions on the file, until the process opens the file again.
- **Read:** A process reads all or a portion of the data in a file.
- **Write:** A process updates a file, either by adding new data that expands the size of the file or by changing the values of existing data items in the file.

Typically, a file system maintains a set of attributes associated with the file. These include owner, creation time, time last modified, access privileges, and so on.

File Structure

Four terms are in common use when discussing files:

- Field
- Record
- File
- Database

A **field** is the basic element of data. An individual field contains a single value, such as an employee's last name, a date, or the value of a sensor reading. It is characterized by its length and data type (e.g., ASCII string, decimal). Depending on the file design, fields may be fixed length or variable length. In the latter case, the field often consists of two or three subfields: the actual value to be stored, the name of the field, and, in some cases, the length of the field. In other cases of variable-length fields, the length of the field is indicated by the use of special demarcation symbols between fields.

A **record** is a collection of related fields that can be treated as a unit by some application program. For example, an employee record would contain such fields as name, social security number, job classification, date of hire, and so on. Again, depending on design, records may be of fixed length or variable length. A record will be of variable length if some of its fields are of variable length or if the number of fields may vary. In the latter case, each field is usually accompanied by a field name. In either case, the entire record usually includes a length field.

A **file** is a collection of similar records. The file is treated as a single entity by users and applications and may be referenced by name. Files have file names and may be created and deleted. Access control restrictions usually apply at the file level. That is, in a shared system, users and programs are granted or denied access to entire files. In some more sophisticated systems, such controls are enforced at the record or even the field level.

Some file systems are structured only in terms of fields, not records. In that case, a file is a collection of fields.

A **database** is a collection of related data. The essential aspects of a database are that the relationships that exist among elements of data are explicit and that the database is designed for use by a number of different applications. A database may contain all of the information related to an organization or project, such as a business or a scientific study. The database itself consists of one or more types of files. Usually, there is a separate database management system that is independent of the operating system, although that system may make use of some file management programs.

Users and applications wish to make use of files. Typical operations that must be supported include the following:

- Retrieve_All: Retrieve all the records of a file. This will be required for an application that must process all of the information in the file at one time. For example, an application that produces a summary of the information in the file would need to retrieve all records. This operation is often equated with the term *sequential processing*, because all of the records are accessed in sequence.

- Retrieve_One: This requires the retrieval of just a single record. Interactive, transaction-oriented applications need this operation.

- Retrieve_Next: This requires the retrieval of the record that is "next" in some logical sequence to the most recently retrieved record. Some interactive applications, such as filling in forms, may require such an operation. A program that is performing a search may also use this operation.

- Retrieve_Previous: Similar to Retrieve_Next, but in this case the record that is "previous" to the currently accessed record is retrieved.

- Insert_One: Insert a new record into the file. It may be necessary that the new record fit into a particular position to preserve a sequencing of the file.

- `Delete_One`: Delete an existing record. Certain linkages or other data structures may need to be updated to preserve the sequencing of the file.
- `Update_One`: Retrieve a record, update one or more of its fields, and rewrite the updated record back into the file. Again, it may be necessary to preserve sequencing with this operation. If the length of the record has changed, the update operation is generally more difficult than if the length is preserved.
- `Retrieve_Few`: Retrieve a number of records. For example, an application or user may wish to retrieve all records that satisfy a certain set of criteria.

The nature of the operations that are most commonly performed on a file will influence the way the file is organized, as discussed in Section 12.2.

It should be noted that not all file systems exhibit the sort of structure discussed in this subsection. On UNIX and UNIX-like systems, the basic file structure is just a stream of bytes. For example, a C program is stored as a file but does not have physical fields, records, and so on.

File Management Systems

A file management system is that set of system software that provides services to users and applications in the use of files. Typically, the only way that a user or application may access files is through the file management system. This relieves the user or programmer of the necessity of developing special-purpose software for each application and provides the system with a consistent, well-defined means of controlling its most important asset. [GROS86] suggests the following objectives for a file management system:

- To meet the data management needs and requirements of the user, which include storage of data and the ability to perform the aforementioned operations
- To guarantee, to the extent possible, that the data in the file are valid
- To optimize performance, both from the system point of view in terms of overall throughput and from the user's point of view in terms of response time
- To provide I/O support for a variety of storage device types
- To minimize or eliminate the potential for lost or destroyed data
- To provide a standardized set of I/O interface routines to user processes
- To provide I/O support for multiple users, in the case of multiple-user systems

With respect to the first point, meeting user requirements, the extent of such requirements depends on the variety of applications and the environment in which the computer system will be used. For an interactive, general-purpose system, the following constitute a minimal set of requirements:

1. Each user should be able to create, delete, read, write, and modify files.
2. Each user may have controlled access to other users' files.
3. Each user may control what types of accesses are allowed to the user's files.
4. Each user should be able to restructure the user's files in a form appropriate to the problem.

5. Each user should be able to move data between files.

6. Each user should be able to back up and recover the user's files in case of damage.

7. Each user should be able to access his or her files by name rather than by numeric identifier.

These objectives and requirements should be kept in mind throughout our discussion of file management systems.

FILE SYSTEM ARCHITECTURE   One way of getting a feel for the scope of file management is to look at a depiction of a typical software organization, as suggested in Figure 12.1. Of course, different systems will be organized differently, but this organization is reasonably representative. At the lowest level, **device drivers** communicate directly with peripheral devices or their controllers or channels. A device driver is responsible for starting I/O operations on a device and processing the completion of an I/O request. For file operations, the typical devices controlled are disk and tape drives. Device drivers are usually considered to be part of the operating system.

The next level is referred to as the **basic file system**, or the **physical I/O** level. This is the primary interface with the environment outside of the computer system. It deals with blocks of data that are exchanged with disk or tape systems. Thus, it is concerned with the placement of those blocks on the secondary storage device and on the buffering of those blocks in main memory. It does not understand the content of the data or the structure of the files involved. The basic file system is often considered part of the operating system.

The **basic I/O supervisor** is responsible for all file I/O initiation and termination. At this level, control structures are maintained that deal with device I/O, scheduling, and file status. The basic I/O supervisor selects the device on which file I/O is to be performed, based on the particular file selected. It is also concerned with scheduling disk and tape accesses to optimize performance. I/O buffers are

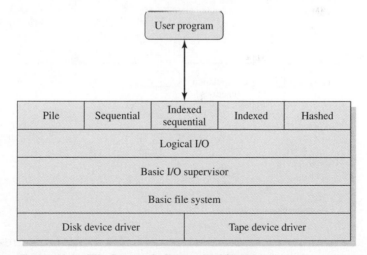

Figure 12.1   File System Software Architecture

assigned and secondary memory is allocated at this level. The basic I/O supervisor is part of the operating system.

Logical I/O enables users and applications to access records. Thus, whereas the basic file system deals with blocks of data, the logical I/O module deals with file records. Logical I/O provides a general-purpose record I/O capability and maintains basic data about files.

The level of the file system closest to the user is often termed the **access method.** It provides a standard interface between applications and the file systems and devices that hold the data. Different access methods reflect different file structures and different ways of accessing and processing the data. Some of the most common access methods are shown in Figure 12.1, and these are briefly described in Section 12.2.

FILE MANAGEMENT FUNCTIONS Another way of viewing the functions of a file system is shown in Figure 12.2. Let us follow this diagram from left to right. Users and application programs interact with the file system by means of commands for creating and deleting files and for performing operations on files. Before performing any operation, the file system must identify and locate the selected file. This requires the use of some sort of directory that serves to describe the location of all files, plus their attributes. In addition, most shared systems enforce user access control: Only authorized users are allowed to access particular files in particular ways. The basic operations that a user or application may perform on a file are performed at the record level. The user or application views the file as having some structure that organizes the records, such as a sequential structure (e.g., personnel records are stored alphabetically by last name). Thus, to translate user commands into specific

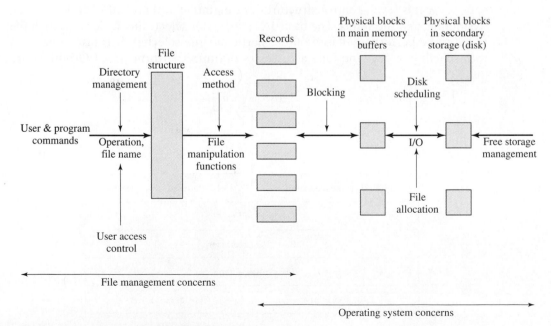

Figure 12.2   Elements of File Management

file manipulation commands, the access method appropriate to this file structure must be employed.

Whereas users and applications are concerned with records or fields, I/O is done on a block basis. Thus, the records or fields of a file must be organized as a sequence of blocks for output and unblocked after input. To support block I/O of files, several functions are needed. The secondary storage must be managed. This involves allocating files to free blocks on secondary storage and managing free storage so as to know what blocks are available for new files and growth in existing files. In addition, individual block I/O requests must be scheduled; this issue was dealt with in Chapter 11. Both disk scheduling and file allocation are concerned with optimizing performance. As might be expected, these functions therefore need to be considered together. Furthermore, the optimization will depend on the structure of the files and the access patterns. Accordingly, developing an optimum file management system from the point of view of performance is an exceedingly complicated task.

Figure 12.2 suggests a division between what might be considered the concerns of the file management system as a separate system utility and the concerns of the operating system, with the point of intersection being record processing. This division is arbitrary; various approaches are taken in various systems.

In the remainder of this chapter, we look at some of the design issues suggested in Figure 12.2. We begin with a discussion of file organizations and access methods. Although this topic is beyond the scope of what is usually considered the concerns of the operating system, it is impossible to assess the other file-related design issues without an appreciation of file organization and access. Next, we look at the concept of file directories. These are often managed by the operating system on behalf of the file management system. The remaining topics deal with the physical I/O aspects of file management and are properly treated as aspects of OS design. One such issue is the way in which logical records are organized into physical blocks. Finally, there are the related issues of file allocation on secondary storage and the management of free secondary storage.

12.2 FILE ORGANIZATION AND ACCESS

In this section, we use the term *file organization* to refer to the logical structuring of the records as determined by the way in which they are accessed. The physical organization of the file on secondary storage depends on the blocking strategy and the file allocation strategy, issues dealt with later in this chapter.

In choosing a file organization, several criteria are important:

- Short access time
- Ease of update
- Economy of storage
- Simple maintenance
- Reliability

The relative priority of these criteria will depend on the applications that will use the file. For example, if a file is only to be processed in batch mode, with all of the records accessed every time, then rapid access for retrieval of a single record is of minimal concern. A file stored on CD-ROM will never be updated, and so ease of update is not an issue.

These criteria may conflict. For example, for economy of storage, there should be minimum redundancy in the data. On the other hand, redundancy is a primary means of increasing the speed of access to data. An example of this is the use of indexes.

The number of alternative file organizations that have been implemented or just proposed is unmanageably large, even for a book devoted to file systems. In this brief survey, we will outline five fundamental organizations. Most structures used in actual systems either fall into one of these categories or can be implemented with a combination of these organizations. The five organizations, the first four of which are depicted in Figure 12.3, are as follows:

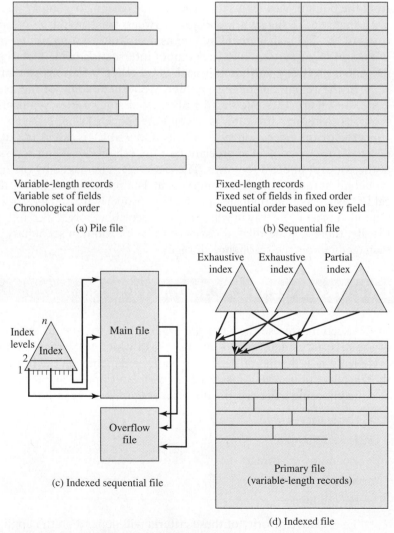

Variable-length records
Variable set of fields
Chronological order

(a) Pile file

Fixed-length records
Fixed set of fields in fixed order
Sequential order based on key field

(b) Sequential file

(c) Indexed sequential file

(d) Indexed file

Figure 12.3   Common File Organizations

- The pile
- The sequential file
- The indexed sequential file
- The indexed file
- The direct, or hashed, file

Table 12.1 summarizes relative performance aspects of these five organizations.[1]

The Pile

The least-complicated form of file organization may be termed the *pile*. Data are collected in the order in which they arrive. Each record consists of one burst of data. The purpose of the pile is simply to accumulate the mass of data and save it. Records may have different fields, or similar fields in different orders. Thus, each field should be self-describing, including a field name as well as a value. The length of each field must be implicitly indicated by delimiters, explicitly included as a sub-field, or known as default for that field type.

Because there is no structure to the pile file, record access is by exhaustive search. That is, if we wish to find a record that contains a particular field with a particular value, it is necessary to examine each record in the pile until the desired

Table 12.1   Grades of Performance for Five Basic File Organizations [WIED87]

File Method	Space Attributes		Update Record Size		Retrieval		
	Variable	Fixed	Equal	Greater	Single record	Subset	Exhaustive
Pile	A	B	A	F	E	D	B
Sequential	F	A	D	F	F	D	A
Indexed sequential	F	B	B	D	B	D	B
Indexed	B	C	C	C	A	B	D
Hashed	F	B	B	F	B	F	E

A = Excellent, well suited to this purpose $\approx O(r)$
B = Good $\approx O(o \times r)$
C = Adequate $\approx O(r \log n)$
D = Requires some extra effort $\approx O(n)$
E = Possible with extreme effort $\approx O(r \times n)$
F = Not reasonable for this purpose $\approx O(n > 1)$

where
   r = size of the result
   o = number of records that overflow
   n = number of records in file

---

[1]The table employs the "big-O" notation, used for characterizing the time complexity of algorithms. Appendix I explains this notation.

record is found or the entire file has been searched. If we wish to find all records that contain a particular field or contain that field with a particular value, then the entire file must be searched.

Pile files are encountered when data are collected and stored prior to processing or when data are not easy to organize. This type of file uses space well when the stored data vary in size and structure, is perfectly adequate for exhaustive searches, and is easy to update. However, beyond these limited uses, this type of file is unsuitable for most applications.

The Sequential File

The most common form of file structure is the sequential file. In this type of file, a fixed format is used for records. All records are of the same length, consisting of the same number of fixed-length fields in a particular order. Because the length and position of each field are known, only the values of fields need to be stored; the field name and length for each field are attributes of the file structure.

One particular field, usually the first field in each record, is referred to as the **key field**. The key field uniquely identifies the record; thus key values for different records are always different. Further, the records are stored in key sequence: alphabetical order for a text key, and numerical order for a numerical key.

Sequential files are typically used in batch applications and are generally optimum for such applications if they involve the processing of all the records (e.g., a billing or payroll application). The sequential file organization is the only one that is easily stored on tape as well as disk.

For interactive applications that involve queries and/or updates of individual records, the sequential file provides poor performance. Access requires the sequential search of the file for a key match. If the entire file, or a large portion of the file, can be brought into main memory at one time, more efficient search techniques are possible. Nevertheless, considerable processing and delay are encountered to access a record in a large sequential file. Additions to the file also present problems. Typically, a sequential file is stored in simple sequential ordering of the records within blocks. That is, the physical organization of the file on tape or disk directly matches the logical organization of the file. In this case, the usual procedure is to place new records in a separate pile file, called a log file or transaction file. Periodically, a batch update is performed that merges the log file with the master file to produce a new file in correct key sequence.

An alternative is to organize the sequential file physically as a linked list. One or more records are stored in each physical block. Each block on disk contains a pointer to the next block. The insertion of new records involves pointer manipulation but does not require that the new records occupy a particular physical block position. Thus, some added convenience is obtained at the cost of additional processing and overhead.

The Indexed Sequential File

A popular approach to overcoming the disadvantages of the sequential file is the indexed sequential file. The indexed sequential file maintains the key characteristic of the sequential file: Records are organized in sequence based on a key field. Two features are added: an index to the file to support random access, and an overflow file. The index provides a lookup capability to reach quickly the vicinity of a desired record. The overflow file is similar to the log file used with a sequential file but is integrated so that a record in the overflow file is located by following a pointer from its predecessor record.

In the simplest indexed sequential structure, a single level of indexing is used. The index in this case is a simple sequential file. Each record in the index file consists of two fields: a key field, which is the same as the key field in the main file, and a pointer into the main file. To find a specific field, the index is searched to find the highest key value that is equal to or precedes the desired key value. The search continues in the main file at the location indicated by the pointer.

To see the effectiveness of this approach, consider a sequential file with 1 million records. To search for a particular key value will require on average one-half million record accesses. Now suppose that an index containing 1,000 entries is constructed, with the keys in the index more or less evenly distributed over the main file. Now it will take on average 500 accesses to the index file followed by 500 accesses to the main file to find the record. The average search length is reduced from 500,000 to 1,000.

Additions to the file are handled in the following manner: Each record in the main file contains an additional field not visible to the application, which is a pointer to the overflow file. When a new record is to be inserted into the file, it is added to the overflow file. The record in the main file that immediately precedes the new record in logical sequence is updated to contain a pointer to the new record in the overflow file. If the immediately preceding record is itself in the overflow file, then the pointer in that record is updated. As with the sequential file, the indexed sequential file is occasionally merged with the overflow file in batch mode.

The indexed sequential file greatly reduces the time required to access a single record, without sacrificing the sequential nature of the file. To process the entire file sequentially, the records of the main file are processed in sequence until a pointer to the overflow file is found, then accessing continues in the overflow file until a null pointer is encountered, at which time accessing of the main file is resumed where it left off.

To provide even greater efficiency in access, multiple levels of indexing can be used. Thus the lowest level of index file is treated as a sequential file and a higher-level index file is created for that file. Consider again a file with 1 million records. A lower-level index with 10,000 entries is constructed. A higher-level index into the lower-level index of 100 entries can then be constructed. The search begins at the higher-level index (average length = 50 accesses) to find an entry point into the lower-level index. This index is then searched (average length = 50) to find an entry point into the main file, which is then searched (average length = 50). Thus the average length of search has been reduced from 500,000 to 1,000 to 150.

The Indexed File

The indexed sequential file retains one limitation of the sequential file: Effective processing is limited to that which is based on a single field of the file. For example, when it is necessary to search for a record on the basis of some other attribute than the key field, both forms of sequential file are inadequate. In some applications, the flexibility of efficiently searching by various attributes is desirable.

To achieve this flexibility, a structure is needed that employs multiple indexes, one for each type of field that may be the subject of a search. In the general indexed file, the concept of sequentiality and a single key are abandoned. Records are accessed only through their indexes. The result is that there is now no restriction on the placement of records as long as a pointer in at least one index refers to that record. Furthermore, variable-length records can be employed.

Two types of indexes are used. An exhaustive index contains one entry for every record in the main file. The index itself is organized as a sequential file for ease of searching. A partial index contains entries to records where the field of interest exists. With variable-length records, some records will not contain all fields. When a new record is added to the main file, all of the index files must be updated.

Indexed files are used mostly in applications where timeliness of information is critical and where data are rarely processed exhaustively. Examples are airline reservation systems and inventory control systems.

The Direct or Hashed File

The direct, or hashed, file exploits the capability found on disks to access directly any block of a known address. As with sequential and indexed sequential files, a key field is required in each record. However, there is no concept of sequential ordering here.

The direct file makes use of hashing on the key value. This function is explained in Appendix F. Figure F.1b shows the type of hashing organization with an overflow file that is typically used in a hash file.

Direct files are often used where very rapid access is required, where fixed-length records are used, and where records are always accessed one at a time. Examples are directories, pricing tables, schedules, and name lists.

12.3 B-TREES

The preceding section referred to the use of an index file to access individual records in a file or database. For a large file or database, a single sequential file of indexes on the primary key does not provide for rapid access. To provide more efficient access, a structured index file is typically used. The simplest such structure is a two-level organization in which the original file is broken into sections and the upper level consists of a sequenced set of pointers to the lower-level sections. This structure can then be extended to more than two levels, resulting in a tree structure. Unless some discipline is imposed on the construction of the tree index, it is likely to end up with an uneven structure, with some short branches and some long branches, so that the time to search the index is uneven. Therefore, a balanced tree structure, with all branches of equal length, would appear to give the best average performance. Such a structure is the B-tree, which has become the standard method of organizing indexes for databases and is commonly used in OS file systems, including those supported by Mac OS X, Windows, and several Linux file systems. The B-tree structure provides for efficient searching, adding, and deleting of items.

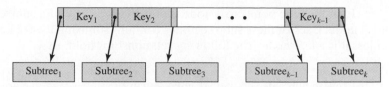

Figure 12.4 A B-tree Node with k Children

Before illustrating the concept of B-tree, let us define a B-tree and its characteristics more precisely. A B-tree is a tree structure (no closed loops) with the following characteristics (Figure 12.4).

1. The tree consists of a number of nodes and leaves.
2. Each node contains at least one key which uniquely identifies a file record, and more than one pointer to child nodes or leaves. The number of keys and pointers contained in a node may vary, within limits explained below.
3. Each node is limited to the same number of maximum keys.
4. The keys in a node are stored in nondecreasing order. Each key has an associated child that is the root of a subtree containing all nodes with keys less than or equal to the key but greater than the preceding key. A node also has an additional rightmost child that is the root for a subtree containing all keys greater than any keys in the node. Thus, each node has one more pointer than keys.

A B-tree is characterized by its minimum degree d and satisfies the following properties:

1. Every node has at most $2d - 1$ keys and $2d$ children or, equivalently, $2d$ pointers.[2]
2. Every node, except for the root, has at least $d - 1$ keys and d pointers. As a result, each internal node, except the root, is at least half full and has at least d children.
3. The root has at least 1 key and 2 children.
4. All leaves appear on the same level and contain no information. This is a logical construct to terminate the tree; the actual implementation may differ. For example, each bottom-level node may contain keys alternating with null pointers.
5. A nonleaf node with k pointers contains $k - 1$ keys.

Typically, a B-tree has a relatively large branching factor (large number of children) resulting in a tree of low height.

Figure 12.4 illustrates two levels of a B-tree. The upper level has $(k - 1)$ keys and k pointers and satisfies the following relationship:

$$\text{Key}_1 < \text{Key}_3 < \ldots < \text{Key}_{k-1}$$

---

[2]Some treatments require, as stated here, that the maximum number of keys in a node is odd (e.g., [CORM09]); others specify even [COME79]; still others allow odd or even [KNUT98]. The choice does not fundamentally affect the performance of B-trees.

Each pointer points to a node that is the top level of a subtree of this upper-level node. Each of these subtree nodes contains some number of keys and pointers, unless it is a leaf node. The following relationships hold:

All the keys in Subtree$_1$		are less than Key$_1$
All the keys in Subtree$_2$	are greater than Key$_1$	and are less than Key$_2$
All the keys in Subtree$_3$	are greater than Key$_2$	and are less than Key$_3$
•	•	•
•	•	•
•	•	•
All the keys in Subtree$_{k-1}$	are greater than Key$_{k-2}$	and are less than Key$_{k-1}$
All the keys in Subtree$_k$	are greater than Key$_{k-1}$	

To search for a key, you start at the root node. If the key you want is in the node, you're done. If not, you go down one level. There are three cases:

1. The key you want is less then the smallest key in this node. Take the leftmost pointer down to the next level.

2. The key you want is greater than the largest key in this node. Take the rightmost pointer down to the next level.

3. The value of the key is between the values of two adjacent keys in this node. Take the pointer between these keys down to the next level.

For example, consider the tree in Figure 12.5d and the desired key is 84. At the root level, 84 > 51, so you take the rightmost branch down to the next level. Here, we have 61 < 84 < 71, so you take the pointer between 61 and 71 down to the next level, where the key 84 is found. Associated with this key is a pointer to the desired record. An advantage of this tree structure over other tree structures is that it is broad and shallow, so that the search terminates quickly. Furthermore, because it is balanced (all branches from root to leaf are of equal length), there are no long searches compared to other searches.

The rules for inserting a new key into the B-tree must maintain a balanced tree. This is done as follows:

1. Search the tree for the key. If the key is not in the tree, then you have reached a node at the lowest level.

2. If this node has fewer than $2d - 1$ keys, then insert the key into this node in the proper sequence.

3. If the node is full (having $2d - 1$ keys), then split this node around its median key into two new nodes with $d - 1$ keys each and promote the median key to the next higher level, as described in step 4. If the new key has a value less than the median key, insert it into the left–hand new node; otherwise insert it into the right–hand new node. The result is that the original node has been split into two nodes, one with $d - 1$ keys and one with d keys.

4. The promoted node is inserted into the parent node following the rules of step 3. Therefore, if the parent node is already full, it must be split and its median key promoted to the next highest layer.

5. If the process of promotion reaches the root node and the root node is already full, then insertion again follows the rules of step 3. However, in this case the median key becomes a new root node and the height of the tree increases by 1.

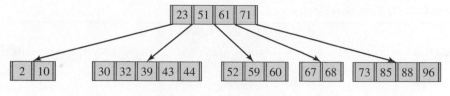

(a) B-tree of minimum degree $d = 3$.

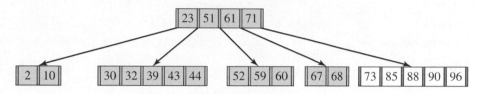

(b) Key = 90 inserted. This is a simple insertion into a node.

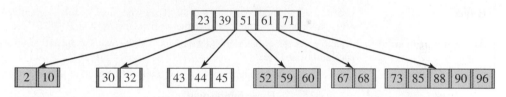

(c) Key = 45 inserted. This requires splitting a node into two parts and promoting one key to the root node.

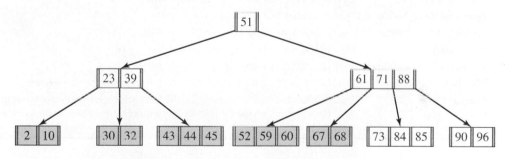

(d) Key = 84 inserted. This requires splitting a node into two parts and promoting one key to the root node. This then requires the root node to be split and a new root created.

Figure 12.5   Inserting Nodes into a B-tree

Figure 12.5 illustrates the insertion process on a B-tree of degree $d = 3$. In each part of the figure, the nodes affected by the insertion process are unshaded.

12.4 FILE DIRECTORIES

Contents

Associated with any file management system and collection of files is a file directory. The directory contains information about the files, including attributes, location, and ownership. Much of this information, especially that concerned with storage,

Table 12.2 Information Elements of a File Directory

Basic Information	
File Name	Name as chosen by creator (user or program). Must be unique within a specific directory
File Type	For example: text, binary, load module, etc.
File Organization	For systems that support different organizations
Address Information	
Volume	Indicates device on which file is stored
Starting Address	Starting physical address on secondary storage (e.g., cylinder, track, and block number on disk)
Size Used	Current size of the file in bytes, words, or blocks
Size Allocated	The maximum size of the file
Access Control Information	
Owner	User who is assigned control of this file. The owner may be able to grant/deny access to other users and to change these privileges.
Access Information	A simple version of this element would include the user's name and password for each authorized user.
Permitted Actions	Controls reading, writing, executing, and transmitting over a network
Usage Information	
Date Created	When file was first placed in directory
Identity of Creator	Usually but not necessarily the current owner
Date Last Read Access	Date of the last time a record was read
Identity of Last Reader	User who did the reading
Date Last Modified	Date of the last update, insertion, or deletion
Identity of Last Modifier	User who did the modifying
Date of Last Backup	Date of the last time the file was backed up on another storage medium
Current Usage	Information about current activity on the file, such as process or processes that have the file open, whether it is locked by a process, and whether the file has been updated in main memory but not yet on disk

is managed by the operating system. The directory is itself a file, accessible by various file management routines. Although some of the information in directories is available to users and applications, this is generally provided indirectly by system routines.

Table 12.2 suggests the information typically stored in the directory for each file in the system. From the user's point of view, the directory provides a mapping between file names, known to users and applications, and the files themselves. Thus, each file entry includes the name of the file. Virtually all systems deal with different types of files and different file organizations, and this information is also provided. An important category of information about each file concerns its storage, including its location and size. In shared systems, it is also important to provide information that is used to control access to the file. Typically, one user is the owner of the file and may grant certain access privileges to other users. Finally, usage information is needed to manage the current use of the file and to record the history of its usage.

Structure

The way in which the information of Table 12.2 is stored differs widely among various systems. Some of the information may be stored in a header record associated with the file; this reduces the amount of storage required for the directory, making it easier to keep all or much of the directory in main memory to improve speed.

The simplest form of structure for a directory is that of a list of entries, one for each file. This structure could be represented by a simple sequential file, with the name of the file serving as the key. In some earlier single-user systems, this technique has been used. However, it is inadequate when multiple users share a system and even for single users with many files.

To understand the requirements for a file structure, it is helpful to consider the types of operations that may be performed on the directory:

- **Search:** When a user or application references a file, the directory must be searched to find the entry corresponding to that file.
- **Create file:** When a new file is created, an entry must be added to the directory.
- **Delete file:** When a file is deleted, an entry must be removed from the directory.
- **List directory:** All or a portion of the directory may be requested. Generally, this request is made by a user and results in a listing of all files owned by that user, plus some of the attributes of each file (e.g., type, access control information, usage information).
- **Update directory:** Because some file attributes are stored in the directory, a change in one of these attributes requires a change in the corresponding directory entry.

The simple list is not suited to supporting these operations. Consider the needs of a single user. The user may have many types of files, including word-processing text files, graphic files, spreadsheets, and so on. The user may like to have these organized by project, by type, or in some other convenient way. If the directory is a simple sequential list, it provides no help in organizing the files and forces the user to be careful not to use the same name for two different types of files. The problem is much worse in a shared system. Unique naming becomes a serious problem. Furthermore, it is difficult to conceal portions of the overall directory from users when there is no inherent structure in the directory.

A start in solving these problems would be to go to a two-level scheme. In this case, there is one directory for each user, and a master directory. The master directory has an entry for each user directory, providing address and access control information. Each user directory is a simple list of the files of that user. This arrangement means that names must be unique only within the collection of files of a single user and that the file system can easily enforce access restriction on directories. However, it still provides users with no help in structuring collections of files.

A more powerful and flexible approach, and one that is almost universally adopted, is the hierarchical, or tree-structure, approach (Figure 12.6). As before, there is a master directory, which has under it a number of user directories. Each of

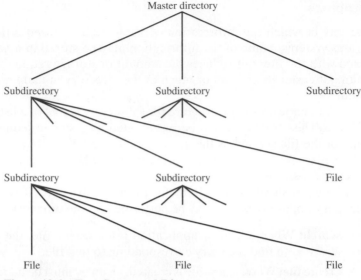

Figure 12.6   Tree-Structured Directory

these user directories, in turn, may have subdirectories and files as entries. This is true at any level: That is, at any level, a directory may consist of entries for subdirectories and/or entries for files.

It remains to say how each directory and subdirectory is organized. The simplest approach, of course, is to store each directory as a sequential file. When directories may contain a very large number of entries, such an organization may lead to unnecessarily long search times. In that case, a hashed structure is to be preferred.

Naming

Users need to be able to refer to a file by a symbolic name. Clearly, each file in the system must have a unique name in order that file references be unambiguous. On the other hand, it is an unacceptable burden on users to require that they provide unique names, especially in a shared system.

The use of a tree-structured directory minimizes the difficulty in assigning unique names. Any file in the system can be located by following a path from the root or master directory down various branches until the file is reached. The series of directory names, culminating in the file name itself, constitutes a **pathname** for the file. As an example, the file in the lower left-hand corner of Figure 12.7 has the pathname User_B/Word/Unit_A/ABC. The slash is used to delimit names in the sequence. The name of the master directory is implicit, because all paths start at that directory. Note that it is perfectly acceptable to have several files with the same file name, as long as they have unique pathnames, which is equivalent to saying that the same file name may be used in different directories. In our example, there is another file in the system with the file name ABC, but that has the pathname /User_B/Draw/ABC.

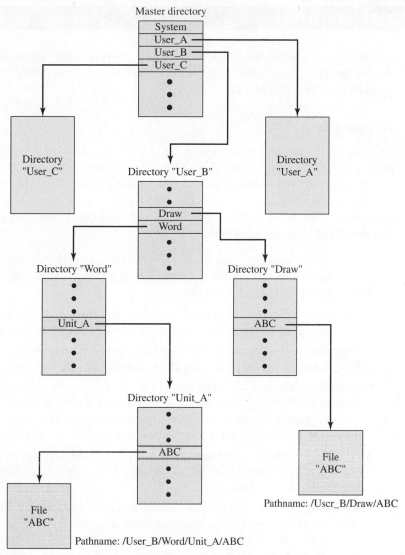

Figure 12.7 Example of Tree-Structured Directory

Although the pathname facilitates the selection of file names, it would be awkward for a user to have to spell out the entire pathname every time a reference is made to a file. Typically, an interactive user or a process has associated with it a current directory, often referred to as the **working directory**. Files are then referenced relative to the working directory. For example, if the working directory for user B is "Word," then the pathname Unit_A/ABC is sufficient to identify the file in the lower left-hand corner of Figure 12.7. When an interactive user logs on, or when a process is created, the default for the working directory is the user home directory. During execution, the user can navigate up or down in the tree to change to a different working directory.

12.5 FILE SHARING

In a multiuser system, there is almost always a requirement for allowing files to be shared among a number of users. Two issues arise: access rights and the management of simultaneous access.

Access Rights

The file system should provide a flexible tool for allowing extensive file sharing among users. The file system should provide a number of options so that the way in which a particular file is accessed can be controlled. Typically, users or groups of users are granted certain access rights to a file. A wide range of access rights has been used. The following list is representative of access rights that can be assigned to a particular user for a particular file:

- **None:** The user may not even learn of the existence of the file, much less access it. To enforce this restriction, the user would not be allowed to read the user directory that includes this file.

- **Knowledge:** The user can determine that the file exists and who its owner is. The user is then able to petition the owner for additional access rights.

- **Execution:** The user can load and execute a program but cannot copy it. Proprietary programs are often made accessible with this restriction.

- **Reading:** The user can read the file for any purpose, including copying and execution. Some systems are able to enforce a distinction between viewing and copying. In the former case, the contents of the file can be displayed to the user, but the user has no means for making a copy.

- **Appending:** The user can add data to the file, often only at the end, but cannot modify or delete any of the file's contents. This right is useful in collecting data from a number of sources.

- **Updating:** The user can modify, delete, and add to the file's data. This normally includes writing the file initially, rewriting it completely or in part, and removing all or a portion of the data. Some systems distinguish among different degrees of updating.

- **Changing protection:** The user can change the access rights granted to other users. Typically, this right is held only by the owner of the file. In some systems, the owner can extend this right to others. To prevent abuse of this mechanism, the file owner will typically be able to specify which rights can be changed by the holder of this right.

- **Deletion:** The user can delete the file from the file system.

These rights can be considered to constitute a hierarchy, with each right implying those that precede it. Thus, if a particular user is granted the updating right for a particular file, then that user is also granted the following rights: knowledge, execution, reading, and appending.

One user is designated as owner of a given file, usually the person who initially created a file. The owner has all of the access rights listed previously and may grant rights to others. Access can be provided to different classes of users:

- **Specific user:** Individual users who are designated by user ID
- **User groups:** A set of users who are not individually defined. The system must have some way of keeping track of the membership of user groups.
- **All:** All users who have access to this system. These are public files.

Simultaneous Access

When access is granted to append or update a file to more than one user, the operating system or file management system must enforce discipline. A brute-force approach is to allow a user to lock the entire file when it is to be updated. A finer grain of control is to lock individual records during update. Essentially, this is the readers/writers problem discussed in Chapter 5. Issues of mutual exclusion and deadlock must be addressed in designing the shared access capability.

12.6 RECORD BLOCKING

As indicated in Figure 12.2, records are the logical unit of access of a structured file,[3] whereas blocks are the unit of I/O with secondary storage. For I/O to be performed, records must be organized as blocks.

There are several issues to consider. First, should blocks be of fixed or variable length? On most systems, blocks are of fixed length. This simplifies I/O, buffer allocation in main memory, and the organization of blocks on secondary storage. Second, what should the relative size of a block be compared to the average record size? The trade-off is this: The larger the block, the more records that are passed in one I/O operation. If a file is being processed or searched sequentially, this is an advantage, because the number of I/O operations is reduced by using larger blocks, thus speeding up processing. On the other hand, if records are being accessed randomly and no particular locality of reference is observed, then larger blocks result in the unnecessary transfer of unused records. However, combining the frequency of sequential operations with the potential for locality of reference, we can say that the I/O transfer time is reduced by using larger blocks. The competing concern is that larger blocks require larger I/O buffers, making buffer management more difficult.

Given the size of a block, there are three methods of blocking that can be used:

- **Fixed blocking:** Fixed-length records are used, and an integral number of records are stored in a block. There may be unused space at the end of each block. This is referred to as internal fragmentation.
- **Variable-length spanned blocking:** Variable-length records are used and are packed into blocks with no unused space. Thus, some records must span two blocks, with the continuation indicated by a pointer to the successor block.

---

[3]As opposed to a file that is treated only as a stream of bytes, such as in the UNIX file system.

- **Variable-length unspanned blocking:** Variable-length records are used, but spanning is not employed. There is wasted space in most blocks because of the inability to use the remainder of a block if the next record is larger than the remaining unused space.

Figure 12.8 illustrates these methods assuming that a file is stored in sequential blocks on a disk. The figure assumes that the file is large enough to span two tracks.[4] The effect would not be changed if some other file allocation scheme were used (see Section 12.6).

Fixed blocking is the common mode for sequential files with fixed-length records. Variable-length spanned blocking is efficient of storage and does not limit

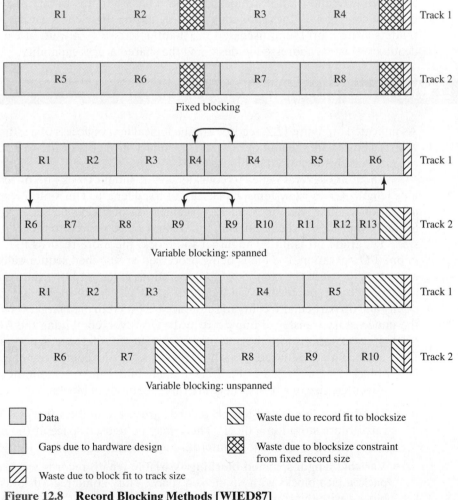

Figure 12.8   Record Blocking Methods [WIED87]

---

[4]Recall from Appendix J that the organization of data on a disk is in a concentric set of rings, called *tracks*. Each track is the same width as the read/write head.

the size of records. However, this technique is difficult to implement. Records that span two blocks require two I/O operations, and files are difficult to update, regardless of the organization. Variable-length unspanned blocking results in wasted space and limits record size to the size of a block.

The record-blocking technique may interact with the virtual memory hardware, if such is employed. In a virtual memory environment, it is desirable to make the page the basic unit of transfer. Pages are generally quite small, so that it is impractical to treat a page as a block for unspanned blocking. Accordingly, some systems combine multiple pages to create a larger block for file I/O purposes. This approach is used for VSAM files on IBM mainframes.

12.7 SECONDARY STORAGE MANAGEMENT

On secondary storage, a file consists of a collection of blocks. The operating system or file management system is responsible for allocating blocks to files. This raises two management issues. First, space on secondary storage must be allocated to files, and second, it is necessary to keep track of the space available for allocation. We will see that these two tasks are related; that is, the approach taken for file allocation may influence the approach taken for free space management. Further, we will see that there is an interaction between file structure and allocation policy.

We begin this section by looking at alternatives for file allocation on a single disk. Then we look at the issue of free space management, and finally we discuss reliability.

File Allocation

Several issues are involved in file allocation:

1. When a new file is created, is the maximum space required for the file allocated at once?
2. Space is allocated to a file as one or more contiguous units, which we shall refer to as portions. That is, a **portion** is a contiguous set of allocated blocks. The size of a portion can range from a single block to the entire file. What size of portion should be used for file allocation?
3. What sort of data structure or table is used to keep track of the portions assigned to a file? An example of such a structure is a **file allocation table (FAT),** found on DOS and some other systems.

Let us examine these issues in turn.

PREALLOCATION VERSUS DYNAMIC ALLOCATION   A preallocation policy requires that the maximum size of a file be declared at the time of the file creation request. In a number of cases, such as program compilations, the production of summary data files, or the transfer of a file from another system over a communications network, this value can be reliably estimated. However, for many applications, it is difficult if not impossible to estimate reliably the maximum potential size of the file. In those cases, users and application programmers would tend to overestimate file size so as not to run out of space. This clearly is wasteful from the point of view of secondary storage allocation. Thus, there are advantages to the use of dynamic allocation, which allocates space to a file in portions as needed.

PORTION SIZE   The second issue listed is that of the size of the portion allocated to a file. At one extreme, a portion large enough to hold the entire file is allocated. At the other extreme, space on the disk is allocated one block at a time. In choosing a portion size, there is a trade-off between efficiency from the point of view of a single file versus overall system efficiency. [WIED87] lists four items to be considered in the trade-off:

1. Contiguity of space increases performance, especially for `Retrieve_Next` operations, and greatly for transactions running in a transaction-oriented operating system.
2. Having a large number of small portions increases the size of tables needed to manage the allocation information.
3. Having fixed-size portions (e.g., blocks) simplifies the reallocation of space.
4. Having variable-size or small fixed-size portions minimizes waste of unused storage due to overallocation.

Of course, these items interact and must be considered together. The result is that there are two major alternatives:

- **Variable, large contiguous portions:** This will provide better performance. The variable size avoids waste, and the file allocation tables are small. However, space is hard to reuse.
- **Blocks:** Small fixed portions provide greater flexibility. They may require large tables or complex structures for their allocation. Contiguity has been abandoned as a primary goal; blocks are allocated as needed.

Either option is compatible with preallocation or dynamic allocation. In the case of variable, large contiguous portions, a file is preallocated one contiguous group of blocks. This eliminates the need for a file allocation table; all that is required is a pointer to the first block and the number of blocks allocated. In the case of blocks, all of the portions required are allocated at one time. This means that the file allocation table for the file will remain of fixed size, because the number of blocks allocated is fixed.

With variable-size portions, we need to be concerned with the fragmentation of free space. This issue was faced when we considered partitioned main memory in Chapter 7. The following are possible alternative strategies:

- **First fit:** Choose the first unused contiguous group of blocks of sufficient size from a free block list.
- **Best fit:** Choose the smallest unused group that is of sufficient size.
- **Nearest fit:** Choose the unused group of sufficient size that is closest to the previous allocation for the file to increase locality.

It is not clear which strategy is best. The difficulty in modeling alternative strategies is that so many factors interact, including types of files, pattern of file

Table 12.3 File Allocation Methods

	Contiguous	**Chained**	**Indexed**	
Preallocation?	Necessary	Possible	Possible	
Fixed or Variable Size Portions?	Variable	Fixed blocks	Fixed blocks	Variable
Portion Size	Large	Small	Small	Medium
Allocation Frequency	Once	Low to high	High	Low
Time to Allocate	Medium	Long	Short	Medium
File Allocation Table Size	One entry	One entry	Large	Medium

access, degree of multiprogramming, other performance factors in the system, disk caching, disk scheduling, and so on.

FILE ALLOCATION METHODS   Having looked at the issues of preallocation versus dynamic allocation and portion size, we are in a position to consider specific file allocation methods. Three methods are in common use: contiguous, chained, and indexed. summarizes some of the characteristics of each method.

With **contiguous allocation**, a single contiguous set of blocks is allocated to a file at the time of file creation (Figure 12.9). Thus, this is a preallocation strategy, using variable-size portions. The file allocation table needs just a single entry for each file, showing the starting block and the length of the file. Contiguous allocation is the best from the point of view of the individual sequential file. Multiple blocks can be read in at a time to improve I/O performance for sequential processing. It is also easy to retrieve a single block. For example, if a file starts at block b, and the ith block of the file is wanted, its location on secondary storage is simply $b + i - 1$. Contiguous allocation presents some problems. External fragmentation will occur, making it difficult to find contiguous blocks of space of sufficient length. From time

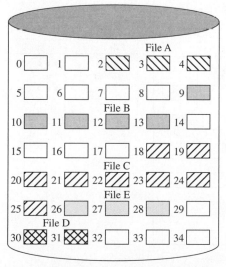

Figure 12.9   Contiguous File Allocation

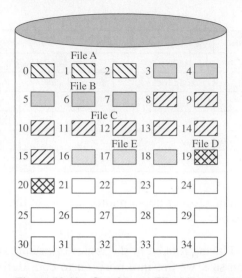

Figure 12.10   Contiguous File Allocation (After Compaction)

to time, it will be necessary to perform a compaction algorithm to free up additional space on the disk (Figure 12.10). Also, with preallocation, it is necessary to declare the size of the file at the time of creation, with the problems mentioned earlier.

At the opposite extreme from contiguous allocation is **chained allocation** (Figure 12.11). Typically, allocation is on an individual block basis. Each block contains a pointer to the next block in the chain. Again, the file allocation table needs just a single entry for each file, showing the starting block and the length of the file. Although preallocation is possible, it is more common simply to allocate blocks as needed. The selection of blocks is now a simple matter: Any free block can be added to a chain. There is no external fragmentation to worry about because only

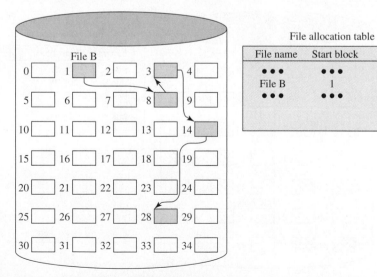

Figure 12.11   Chained Allocation

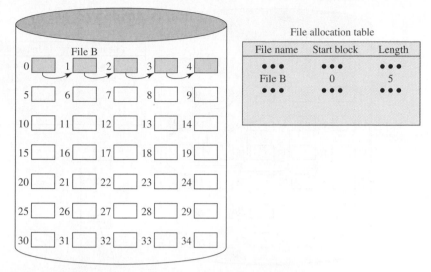

Figure 12.12   Chained Allocation (After Consolidation)

one block at a time is needed. This type of physical organization is best suited to sequential files that are to be processed sequentially. To select an individual block of a file requires tracing through the chain to the desired block.

One consequence of chaining, as described so far, is that there is no accommodation of the principle of locality. Thus, if it is necessary to bring in several blocks of a file at a time, as in sequential processing, then a series of accesses to different parts of the disk are required. This is perhaps a more significant effect on a single-user system but may also be of concern on a shared system. To overcome this problem, some systems periodically consolidate files (Figure 12.12).

Indexed allocation addresses many of the problems of contiguous and chained allocation. In this case, the file allocation table contains a separate one-level index for each file; the index has one entry for each portion allocated to the file. Typically, the file indexes are not physically stored as part of the file allocation table. Rather, the file index for a file is kept in a separate block, and the entry for the file in the file allocation table points to that block. Allocation may be on the basis of either fixed-size blocks (Figure 12.13) or variable-size portions (Figure 12.14). Allocation by blocks eliminates external fragmentation, whereas allocation by variable-size portions improves locality. In either case, file consolidation may be done from time to time. File consolidation reduces the size of the index in the case of variable-size portions, but not in the case of block allocation. Indexed allocation supports both sequential and direct access to the file and thus is the most popular form of file allocation.

Free Space Management

Just as the space that is allocated to files must be managed, so the space that is not currently allocated to any file must be managed. To perform any of the file allocation techniques described previously, it is necessary to know what blocks on the disk are available. Thus we need a **disk allocation table** in addition to a file allocation table. We discuss here a number of techniques that have been implemented.

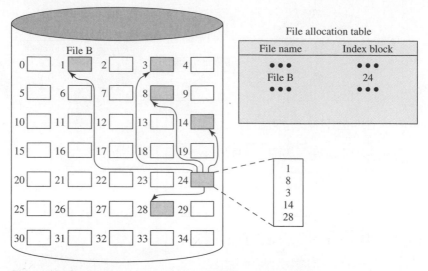

Figure 12.13   Indexed Allocation with Block Portions

BIT TABLES   This method uses a vector containing one bit for each block on the disk. Each entry of a 0 corresponds to a free block, and each 1 corresponds to a block in use. For example, for the disk layout of Figure 12.9, a vector of length 35 is needed and would have the following value:

$$00111000011111000011111111111011000$$

A bit table has the advantage that it is relatively easy to find one or a contiguous group of free blocks. Thus, a bit table works well with any of the file allocation methods outlined. Another advantage is that it is as small as possible.

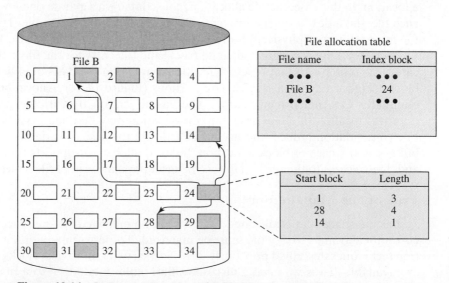

Figure 12.14   Indexed Allocation with Variable-Length Portions

However, it can still be sizable. The amount of memory (in bytes) required for a block bitmap is

$$\frac{\text{disk size in bytes}}{8 \times \text{file system block size}}$$

Thus, for a 16-Gbyte disk with 512-byte blocks, the bit table occupies about 4 Mbytes. Can we spare 4 Mbytes of main memory for the bit table? If so, then the bit table can be searched without the need for disk access. But even with today's memory sizes, 4 Mbytes is a hefty chunk of main memory to devote to a single function. The alternative is to put the bit table on disk. But a 4-Mbyte bit table would require about 8,000 disk blocks. We can't afford to search that amount of disk space every time a block is needed, so a bit table resident in memory is indicated.

Even when the bit table is in main memory, an exhaustive search of the table can slow file system performance to an unacceptable degree. This is especially true when the disk is nearly full and there are few free blocks remaining. Accordingly, most file systems that use bit tables maintain auxiliary data structures that summarize the contents of subranges of the bit table. For example, the table could be divided logically into a number of equal-size subranges. A summary table could include, for each subrange, the number of free blocks and the maximum-sized contiguous number of free blocks. When the file system needs a number of contiguous blocks, it can scan the summary table to find an appropriate subrange and then search that subrange.

CHAINED FREE PORTIONS The free portions may be chained together by using a pointer and length value in each free portion. This method has negligible space overhead because there is no need for a disk allocation table, merely for a pointer to the beginning of the chain and the length of the first portion. This method is suited to all of the file allocation methods. If allocation is a block at a time, simply choose the free block at the head of the chain and adjust the first pointer or length value. If allocation is by variable-length portion, a first-fit algorithm may be used: The headers from the portions are fetched one at a time to determine the next suitable free portion in the chain. Again, pointer and length values are adjusted.

This method has its own problems. After some use, the disk will become quite fragmented and many portions will be a single block long. Also note that every time you allocate a block, you need to read the block first to recover the pointer to the new first free block before writing data to that block. If many individual blocks need to be allocated at one time for a file operation, this greatly slows file creation. Similarly, deleting highly fragmented files is very time consuming.

INDEXING The indexing approach treats free space as a file and uses an index table as described under file allocation. For efficiency, the index should be on the basis of variable-size portions rather than blocks. Thus, there is one entry in the table for every free portion on the disk. This approach provides efficient support for all of the file allocation methods.

FREE BLOCK LIST In this method, each block is assigned a number sequentially and the list of the numbers of all free blocks is maintained in a reserved portion of the disk. Depending on the size of the disk, either 24 or 32 bits will be needed to store a single block number, so the size of the free block list is 24 or 32 times the size of the corresponding bit table and thus must be stored on disk rather than in main memory. However, this is a satisfactory method. Consider the following points:

1. The space on disk devoted to the free block list is less than 1% of the total disk space. If a 32-bit block number is used, then the space penalty is 4 bytes for every 512-byte block.

2. Although the free block list is too large to store in main memory, there are two effective techniques for storing a small part of the list in main memory.

   a. The list can be treated as a push-down stack (Appendix P) with the first few thousand elements of the stack kept in main memory. When a new block is allocated, it is popped from the top of the stack, which is in main memory. Similarly, when a block is deallocated, it is pushed onto the stack. There only has to be a transfer between disk and main memory when the in-memory portion of the stack becomes either full or empty. Thus, this technique gives almost zero-time access most of the time.

   b. The list can be treated as a FIFO queue, with a few thousand entries from both the head and the tail of the queue in main memory. A block is allocated by taking the first entry from the head of the queue and deallocated by adding it to the end of the tail of the queue. There only has to be a transfer between disk and main memory when either the in-memory portion of the head of the queue becomes empty or the in-memory portion of the tail of the queue becomes full.

In either of the strategies listed in the preceding point (stack or FIFO queue), a background thread can slowly sort the in-memory list or lists to facilitate contiguous allocation.

Volumes

The term *volume* is used somewhat differently by different operating systems and file management systems, but in essence a volume is a logical disk. [CARR05] defines a volume as follows:

> **Volume:** A collection of addressable sectors in secondary memory that an OS or application can use for data storage. The sectors in a volume need not be consecutive on a physical storage device; instead, they need only appear that way to the OS or application. A volume may be the result of assembling and merging smaller volumes.

In the simplest case, a single disk equals one volume. Frequently, a disk is divided into partitions, with each partition functioning as a separate volume. It is also common to treat multiple disks as a single volume or partitions on multiple disks as a single volume.

Reliability

Consider the following scenario:

1. User A requests a file allocation to add to an existing file.
2. The request is granted and the disk and file allocation tables are updated in main memory but not yet on disk.
3. The system crashes and subsequently restarts.
4. User B requests a file allocation and is allocated space on disk that overlaps the last allocation to user A.
5. User A accesses the overlapped portion via a reference that is stored inside A's file.

This difficulty arose because the system maintained a copy of the disk allocation table and file allocation table in main memory for efficiency. To prevent this type of error, the following steps could be performed when a file allocation is requested:

1. Lock the disk allocation table on disk. This prevents another user from causing alterations to the table until this allocation is completed.
2. Search the disk allocation table for available space. This assumes that a copy of the disk allocation table is always kept in main memory. If not, it must first be read in.
3. Allocate space, update the disk allocation table, and update the disk. Updating the disk involves writing the disk allocation table back onto disk. For chained disk allocation, it also involves updating some pointers on disk.
4. Update the file allocation table and update the disk.
5. Unlock the disk allocation table.

This technique will prevent errors. However, when small portions are allocated frequently, the impact on performance will be substantial. To reduce this overhead, a batch storage allocation scheme could be used. In this case, a batch of free portions on the disk is obtained for allocation. The corresponding portions on disk are marked "in use." Allocation using this batch may proceed in main memory. When the batch is exhausted, the disk allocation table is updated on disk and a new batch may be acquired. If a system crash occurs, portions on the disk marked "in use" must be cleaned up in some fashion before they can be reallocated. The technique for cleanup will depend on the file system's particular characteristics.

12.8 FILE SYSTEM SECURITY

Following successful log-on, the user has been granted access to one or a set of hosts and applications. This is generally not sufficient for a system that includes sensitive data in its database. Through the user–access control procedure, a user can be identified to the system. Associated with each user, there can be a profile that specifies permissible operations and file accesses. The operating system can then enforce rules based on the user profile. The database management system, however, must control access to specific records or even portions of records. For example, it may be permissible for anyone in administration to obtain a list of company personnel, but only selected individuals may have access to salary information. The issue is more than just a matter of level of detail. Whereas the operating system may grant a user permission to access a file or use an application, following which there are no further security checks, the database management system must make a decision on each individual access attempt. That decision will depend not only on the user's identity but also on the specific parts of the data being accessed and even on the information already divulged to the user.

A general model of access control as exercised by a file or database management system is that of an **access matrix** (Figure 12.15a, based on a figure in [SAND94]). The basic elements of the model are as follows:

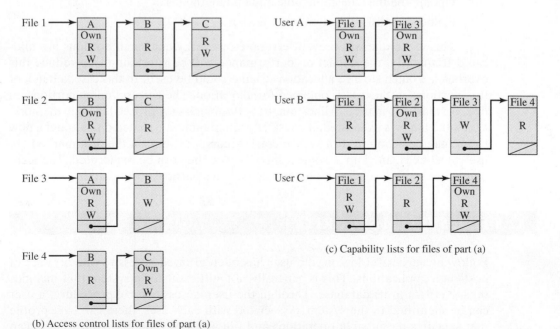

	File 1	File 2	File 3	File 4	Account 1	Account 2
User A	Own R W		Own R W		Inquiry credit	
User B	R	Own R W	W	R	Inquiry debit	Inquiry credit
User C	R W	R		Own R W		Inquiry debit

(a) Access matrix

(b) Access control lists for files of part (a)

(c) Capability lists for files of part (a)

Figure 12.15   Example of Access Control Structures

- **Subject:** An entity capable of accessing objects. Generally, the concept of subject equates with that of process. Any user or application actually gains access to an object by means of a process that represents that user or application.
- **Object:** Anything to which access is controlled. Examples include files, portions of files, programs, segments of memory, and software objects (e.g., Java objects).
- **Access right:** The way in which an object is accessed by a subject. Examples are read, write, execute, and functions in software objects.

One dimension of the matrix consists of identified subjects that may attempt data access. Typically, this list will consist of individual users or user groups, although access could be controlled for terminals, hosts, or applications instead of or in addition to users. The other dimension lists the objects that may be accessed. At the greatest level of detail, objects may be individual data fields. More aggregate groupings, such as records, files, or even the entire database, may also be objects in the matrix. Each entry in the matrix indicates the access rights of that subject for that object.

In practice, an access matrix is usually sparse and is implemented by decomposition in one of two ways. The matrix may be decomposed by columns, yielding **access control lists** (Figure 12.15b). Thus for each object, an access control list lists users and their permitted access rights. The access control list may contain a default, or public, entry. This allows users that are not explicitly listed as having special rights to have a default set of rights. Elements of the list may include individual users as well as groups of users.

Decomposition by rows yields **capability tickets** (Figure 12.15c). A capability ticket specifies authorized objects and operations for a user. Each user has a number of tickets and may be authorized to loan or give them to others. Because tickets may be dispersed around the system, they present a greater security problem than access control lists. In particular, the ticket must be unforgeable. One way to accomplish this is to have the operating system hold all tickets on behalf of users. These tickets would have to be held in a region of memory inaccessible to users.

Network considerations for data–oriented access control parallel those for user–oriented access control. If only certain users are permitted to access certain items of data, then encryption may be needed to protect those items during transmission to authorized users. Typically, data access control is decentralized, that is, controlled by host–based database management systems. If a network database server exists on a network, then data access control becomes a network function.

12.9 UNIX FILE MANAGEMENT

In the UNIX file system, six types of files are distinguished:

- **Regular, or ordinary:** Contains arbitrary data in zero or more data blocks. Regular files contain information entered in them by a user, an application program, or a system utility program. The file system does not impose any internal structure to a regular file but treats it as a stream of bytes.
- **Directory:** Contains a list of file names plus pointers to associated inodes (index nodes), described later. Directories are hierarchically organized (Figure 12.6).

Directory files are actually ordinary files with special write protection privileges so that only the file system can write into them, while read access is available to user programs.

- **Special:** Contains no data but provides a mechanism to map physical devices to file names. The file names are used to access peripheral devices, such as terminals and printers. Each I/O device is associated with a special file, as discussed in Section 11.8.
- **Named pipes:** As discussed in Section 6.7, a pipe is an interprocess communications facility. A pipe file buffers data received in its input so that a process that reads from the pipe's output receives the data on a first-in-first-out basis.
- **Links:** In essence, a link is an alternative file name for an existing file.
- **Symbolic links:** This is a data file that contains the name of the file it is linked to.

In this section, we are concerned with the handling of ordinary files, which correspond to what most systems treat as files.

Inodes

Modern UNIX operating systems support multiple file systems but map all of these into a uniform underlying system for supporting file systems and allocating disk space to files. All types of UNIX files are administered by the OS by means of inodes. An inode (index node) is a control structure that contains the key information needed by the operating system for a particular file. Several file names may be associated with a single inode, but an active inode is associated with exactly one file, and each file is controlled by exactly one inode.

The attributes of the file as well as its permissions and other control information are stored in the inode. The exact inode structure varies from one UNIX implementation to another. The FreeBSD inode structure, shown in Figure 12.16, includes the following data elements:

- The type and access mode of the file
- The file's owner and group-access identifiers
- The time that the file was created, when it was most recently read and written, and when its inode was most recently updated by the system
- The size of the file in bytes
- A sequence of block pointers, explained in the next subsection
- The number of physical blocks used by the file, including blocks used to hold indirect pointers and attributes
- The number of directory entries that reference the file
- The kernel and user-settable flags that describe the characteristics of the file
- The generation number of the file (a randomly selected number assigned to the inode each time that the latter is allocated to a new file; the generation number is used to detect references to deleted files)
- The blocksize of the data blocks referenced by the inode (typically the same as, but sometimes larger than, the file system blocksize)

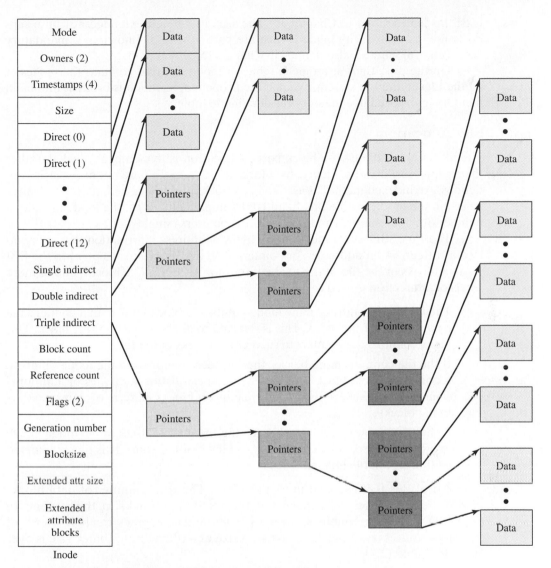

Figure 12.16   Structure of FreeBSD Inode and File

- The size of the extended attribute information
- Zero or more extended attribute entries

The blocksize value is typically the same as, but sometimes larger than, the file system blocksize. On traditional UNIX systems, a fixed blocksize of 512 bytes was used. FreeBSD has a minimum blocksize of 4,096 bytes (4 Kbytes); the blocksize can be any power of 2 greater than or equal to 4,096. For typical file systems, the blocksize is 8 Kbytes or 16 Kbytes. The default FreeBSD blocksize is 16 Kbytes.

Extended attribute entries are variable-length entries used to store auxiliary data that are separate from the contents of the file. The first two extended attributes defined for FreeBSD deal with security. The first of these support access control lists; this is described in Chapter 15. The second defined extended attribute supports the use of security labels, which are part of what is known as a mandatory access control scheme, also defined in Chapter 15.

On the disk, there is an inode table, or inode list, that contains the inodes of all the files in the file system. When a file is opened, its inode is brought into main memory and stored in a memory-resident inode table.

File Allocation

File allocation is done on a block basis. Allocation is dynamic, as needed, rather than using preallocation. Hence, the blocks of a file on disk are not necessarily contiguous. An indexed method is used to keep track of each file, with part of the index stored in the inode for the file. In all UNIX implementations, the inode includes a number of direct pointers and three indirect pointers (single, double, triple).

The FreeBSD inode includes 120 bytes of address information that is organized as fifteen 64-bit addresses, or pointers. The first 12 addresses point to the first 12 data blocks of the file. If the file requires more than 12 data blocks, one or more levels of indirection is used as follows:

- The thirteenth address in the inode points to a block on disk that contains the next portion of the index. This is referred to as the single indirect block. This block contains the pointers to succeeding blocks in the file.
- If the file contains more blocks, the fourteenth address in the inode points to a double indirect block. This block contains a list of addresses of additional single indirect blocks. Each of single indirect blocks, in turn, contains pointers to file blocks.
- If the file contains still more blocks, the fifteenth address in the inode points to a triple indirect block that is a third level of indexing. This block points to additional double indirect blocks.

All of this is illustrated in Figure 12.16. The total number of data blocks in a file depends on the capacity of the fixed-size blocks in the system. In FreeBSD, the minimum block size is 4 Kbytes, and each block can hold a total of 512 block addresses. Thus, the maximum size of a file with this block size is over 500 GB (Table 12.4).

This scheme has several advantages:

1. The inode is of fixed size and relatively small and hence may be kept in main memory for long periods.

Table 12.4   Capacity of a FreeBSD File with 4-Kbyte Block Size

Level	Number of Blocks	Number of Bytes
Direct	12	48K
Single Indirect	512	2M
Double Indirect	$512 \times 512 = 256K$	1G
Triple Indirect	$512 \times 256K = 128M$	512G

2. Smaller files may be accessed with little or no indirection, reducing processing and disk access time.

3. The theoretical maximum size of a file is large enough to satisfy virtually all applications.

Directories

Directories are structured in a hierarchical tree. Each directory can contain files and/or other directories. A directory that is inside another directory is referred to as a subdirectory. As was mentioned, a directory is simply a file that contains a list of file names plus pointers to associated inodes. Figure 12.17 shows the overall structure. Each directory entry (dentry) contains a name for the associated file or subdirectory plus an integer called the i-number (index number). When the file or directory is accessed, its i-number is used as an index into the inode table.

Volume Structure

A UNIX file system resides on a single logical disk or disk partition and is laid out with the following elements:

- **Boot block:** Contains code required to boot the operating system
- **Superblock:** Contains attributes and information about the file system, such as partition size, and inode table size
- **Inode table:** The collection of inodes for each file
- **Data blocks:** Storage space available for data files and subdirectories

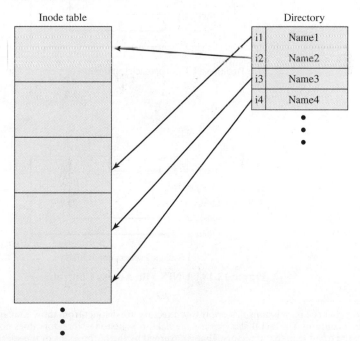

Figure 12.17   UNIX Directories and Inodes

Traditional UNIX File Access Control

Most UNIX systems depend on, or at least are based on, the file access control scheme introduced with the early versions of UNIX. Each UNIX user is assigned a unique user identification number (user ID). A user is also a member of a primary group, and possibly a number of other groups, each identified by a group ID. When a file is created, it is designated as owned by a particular user and marked with that user's ID. It also belongs to a specific group, which initially is either its creator's primary group, or the group of its parent directory if that directory has SetGID permission set. Associated with each file is a set of 12 protection bits. The owner ID, group ID, and protection bits are part of the file's inode.

Nine of the protection bits specify read, write, and execute permission for the owner of the file, other members of the group to which this file belongs, and all other users. These form a hierarchy of owner, group, and all others, with the highest relevant set of permissions being used. Figure 12.18a shows an example in which the file owner has read and write access; all other members of the file's group have read access, and users outside the group have no access rights to the file. When applied to a directory, the read and write bits grant the right to list and to create/rename/delete files in the directory.[5] The execute bit grants the right to search the directory for a component of a filename.

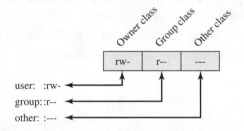

(a) Traditional UNIX approach (minimal access control list)

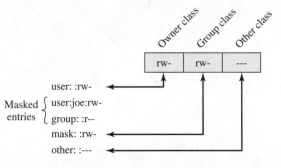

(b) Extended access control list

Figure 12.18   UNIX File Access Control

---

[5]Note that the permissions that apply to a directory are distinct from those that apply to any file or directory it contains. The fact that a user has the right to write to the directory does not give the user the right to write to a file in that directory. That is governed by the permissions of the specific file. The user would, however, have the right to rename the file.

The remaining three bits define special additional behavior for files or directories. Two of these are the "set user ID" (SetUID) and "set group ID" (SetGID) permissions. If these are set on an executable file, the operating system functions as follows. When a user (with execute privileges for this file) executes the file, the system temporarily allocates the rights of the user's ID of the file creator, or the file's group, respectively, to those of the user executing the file. These are known as the "effective user ID" and "effective group ID" and are used in addition to the "real user ID" and "real group ID" of the executing user when making access control decisions for this program. This change is only effective while the program is being executed. This feature enables the creation and use of privileged programs that may use files normally inaccessible to other users. It enables users to access certain files in a controlled fashion. Alternatively, when applied to a directory, the SetGID permission indicates that newly created files will inherit the group of this directory. The SetUID permission is ignored.

The final permission bit is the "Sticky" bit. When set on a file, this originally indicated that the system should retain the file contents in memory following execution. This is no longer used. When applied to a directory, though, it specifies that only the owner of any file in the directory can rename, move, or delete that file. This is useful for managing files in shared temporary directories.

One particular user ID is designated as "superuser." The superuser is exempt from the usual file access control constraints and has systemwide access. Any program that is owned by, and SetUID to, the "superuser" potentially grants unrestricted access to the system to any user executing that program. Hence, great care is needed when writing such programs.

This access scheme is adequate when file access requirements align with users and a modest number of groups of users. For example, suppose a user wants to give read access for file X to users A and B and read access for file Y to users B and C. We would need at least two user groups, and user B would need to belong to both groups in order to access the two files. However, if there are a large number of different groupings of users requiring a range of access rights to different files, then a very large number of groups may be needed to provide this. This rapidly becomes unwieldy and difficult to manage, even if possible at all.[6] One way to overcome this problem is to use access control lists, which are provided in most modern UNIX systems.

A final point to note is that the traditional UNIX file access control scheme implements a simple protection domain structure. A domain is associated with the user, and switching the domain corresponds to changing the user ID temporarily.

Access Control Lists in UNIX

Many modern UNIX and UNIX-based operating systems support access control lists, including FreeBSD, OpenBSD, Linux, and Solaris. In this section, we describe the FreeBSD approach, but other implementations have essentially the same features and interface. The feature is referred to as extended access control list, while the traditional UNIX approach is referred to as minimal access control list.

---

[6]Most UNIX systems impose a limit on the maximum number of groups any user may belong to, as well as to the total number of groups possible on the system.

FreeBSD allows the administrator to assign a list of UNIX user IDs and groups to a file by using the `setfacl` command. Any number of users and groups can be associated with a file, each with three protection bits (read, write, execute), offering a flexible mechanism for assigning access rights. A file need not have an ACL but may be protected solely by the traditional UNIX file access mechanism. FreeBSD files include an additional protection bit that indicates whether the file has an extended ACL.

FreeBSD and most UNIX implementations that support extended ACLs use the following strategy (e.g., Figure 12.18b):

1. The owner class and other class entries in the nine-bit permission field have the same meaning as in the minimal ACL case.

2. The group class entry specifies the permissions for the owner group for this file. These permissions represent the maximum permissions that can be assigned to named users or named groups, other than the owning user. In this latter role, the group class entry functions as a mask.

3. Additional named users and named groups may be associated with the file, each with a three-bit permission field. The permissions listed for a named user or named group are compared to the mask field. Any permission for the named user or named group that is not present in the mask field is disallowed.

When a process requests access to a file system object, two steps are performed. Step 1 selects the ACL entry that most closely matches the requesting process. The ACL entries are looked at in the following order: owner, named users, (owning or named) groups, and others. Only a single entry determines access. Step 2 checks if the matching entry contains sufficient permissions. A process can be a member in more than one group; so more than one group entry can match. If any of these matching group entries contain the requested permissions, one that contains the requested permissions is picked (the result is the same no matter which entry is picked). If none of the matching group entries contains the requested permissions, access will be denied no matter which entry is picked.

12.10 LINUX VIRTUAL FILE SYSTEM

Linux includes a versatile and powerful file-handling facility, designed to support a wide variety of file management systems and file structures. The approach taken in Linux is to make use of a **virtual file system (VFS)**, which presents a single, uniform file system interface to user processes. The VFS defines a common file model that is capable of representing any conceivable file system's general feature and behavior. The VFS assumes that files are objects in a computer's mass storage memory that share basic properties regardless of the target file system or the underlying processor hardware. Files have symbolic names that allow them to be uniquely identified within a specific directory within the file system. A file has an owner, protection against unauthorized access or modification, and a variety of other properties. A file may be created, read from, written to, or deleted. For any specific file system, a

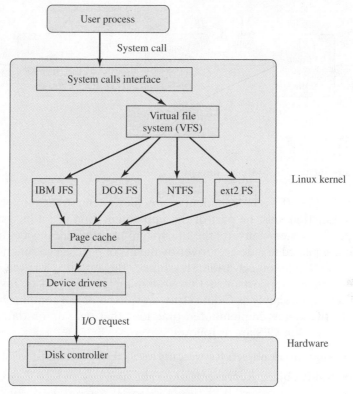

Figure 12.19 Linux Virtual File System Context

mapping module is needed to transform the characteristics of the real file system to the characteristics expected by the virtual file system.

Figure 12.19 indicates the key ingredients of the Linux file system strategy. A user process issues a file system call (e.g., read) using the VFS file scheme. The VFS converts this into an internal (to the kernel) file system call that is passed to a mapping function for a specific file system [e.g., IBM's Journaling File System (JFS)]. In most cases, the mapping function is simply a mapping of file system functional calls from one scheme to another. In some cases, the mapping function is more complex. For example, some file systems use a file allocation table (FAT), which stores the position of each file in the directory tree. In these file systems, directories are not files. For such file systems, the mapping function must be able to construct dynamically, and when needed, the files corresponding to the directories. In any case, the original user file system call is translated into a call that is native to the target file system. The target file system software is then invoked to perform the requested function on a file or directory under its control and secondary storage. The results of the operation are then communicated back to the user in a similar fashion.

Figure 12.20 indicates the role that VFS plays within the Linux kernel. When a process initiates a file-oriented system call (e.g., read), the kernel calls a function in the VFS. This function handles the file-system-independent manipulations and initiates a call to a function in the target file system code. This call passes through a mapping function that converts the call from the VFS into a call to the target file

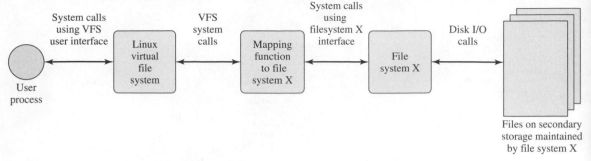

Figure 12.20   Linux Virtual File System Concept

system. The VFS is independent of any file system, so the implementation of a mapping function must be part of the implementation of a file system on Linux. The target file system converts the file system request into device-oriented instructions that are passed to a device driver by means of page cache functions.

VFS is an object-oriented scheme. Because it is written in C, rather than a language that supports object programming (such as C++ or Java), VFS objects are implemented simply as C data structures. Each object contains both data and pointers to file-system-implemented functions that operate on data. The four primary object types in VFS are as follows:

- **Superblock object:** Represents a specific mounted file system
- **Inode object:** Represents a specific file
- **Dentry object:** Represents a specific directory entry
- **File object:** Represents an open file associated with a process

This scheme is based on the concepts used in UNIX file systems, as described in Section 12.7. The key concepts of UNIX file system to remember are the following. A file system consists of a hierarchal organization of directories. A directory is the same as what is known as a folder on many non-UNIX platforms and may contain files and/or other directories. Because a directory may contain other directories, a tree structure is formed. A path through the tree structure from the root consists of a sequence of directory entries, ending in either a directory entry (dentry) or a file name. In UNIX, a directory is implemented as a file that lists the files and directories contained within it. Thus, file operations can be performed on either files or directories.

The Superblock Object

The superblock object stores information describing a specific file system. Typically, the superblock corresponds to the file system superblock or file system control block, which is stored in a special sector on disk.

The superblock object consists of a number of data items. Examples include the following:

- The device that this file system is mounted on
- The basic block size of the file system

- Dirty flag, to indicate that the superblock has been changed but not written back to disk
- File system type
- Flags, such as a read-only flag
- Pointer to the root of the file system directory
- List of open files
- Semaphore for controlling access to the file system
- List of superblock operations

The last item on the preceding list refers to an operations object contained within the superblock object. The operations object defines the object methods (functions) that the kernel can invoke against the superblock object. The methods defined for the superblock object include the following:

- `read_inode`: Read a specified inode from a mounted file system.
- `write_inode`: Write given inode to disk.
- `put_inode`: Release inode.
- `delete_inode`: Delete inode from disk.
- `notify_change`: Called when inode attributes are changed.
- `put_super`: Called by the VFS on unmount to release the given superblock.
- `write_super`: Called when the VFS decides that the superblock needs to be written to disk.
- `statfs`: Obtain file system statistics.
- `remount_fs`: Called by the VFS when the file system is remounted with new mount options
- `clear_inode`: Release inode and clear any pages containing related data.

The Inode Object

An inode is associated with each file. The inode object holds all the information about a named file except its name and the actual data contents of the file. Items contained in an inode object include owner, group, permissions, access times for a file, size of data it holds, and number of links.

The inode object also includes an inode operations object that describes the file system's implemented functions that the VFS can invoke on an inode. The methods defined for the inode object include the following:

- `create`: Creates a new inode for a regular file associated with a dentry object in some directory
- `lookup`: Searches a directory for an inode corresponding to a file name
- `mkdir`: Creates a new inode for a directory associated with a dentry object in some directory

The Dentry Object

A dentry (directory entry) is a specific component in a path. The component may be either a directory name or a file name. Dentry objects facilitate access to files and directories and are used in a dentry cache for that purpose. The dentry object includes a pointer to the inode and superblock. It also includes a pointer to the parent dentry and pointers to any subordinate dentrys.

The File Object

The file object is used to represent a file opened by a process. The object is created in response to the open() system call and destroyed in response to the close() system call. The file object consists of a number of items, including the following:

- Dentry object associated with the file
- File system containing the file
- File objects usage counter
- User's user ID
- User's group ID
- File pointer, which is the current position in the file from which the next operation will take place

The file object also includes an inode operations object that describes the file system's implemented functions that the VFS can invoke on a file object. The methods defined for the file object include read, write, open, release, and lock.

12.11 WINDOWS FILE SYSTEM

The developers of Windows NT designed a new file system, the New Technology File System (NTFS), which is intended to meet high-end requirements for workstations and servers. Examples of high-end applications include the following:

- Client/server applications such as file servers, compute servers, and database servers
- Resource-intensive engineering and scientific applications
- Network applications for large corporate systems

This section provides an overview of NTFS.

Key Features of NTFS

NTFS is a flexible and powerful file system built, as we shall see, on an elegantly simple file system model. The most noteworthy features of NTFS include the following:

- **Recoverability:** High on the list of requirements for the new Windows file system was the ability to recover from system crashes and disk failures. In the event of such failures, NTFS is able to reconstruct disk volumes and return them to a consistent state. It does this by using a transaction-processing model for changes to the file system; each significant change is treated as an atomic action that is either entirely performed or not performed at all. Each transaction that was in process at the time of a failure is subsequently backed out or brought to completion. In addition, NTFS uses redundant storage for critical file system data, so that failure of a disk sector does not cause the loss of data describing the structure and status of the file system.

- **Security:** NTFS uses the Windows object model to enforce security. An open file is implemented as a file object with a security descriptor that defines its security attributes. The security descriptor is persisted as an attribute of each file on disk.
- **Large disks and large files:** NTFS supports very large disks and very large files more efficiently than other file systems, such as FAT.
- **Multiple data streams:** The actual contents of a file are treated as a stream of bytes. In NTFS, it is possible to define multiple data streams for a single file. An example of the utility of this feature is that it allows Windows to be used by remote Macintosh systems to store and retrieve files. On Macintosh, each file has two components: the file data and a resource fork that contains information about the file. NTFS treats these two components as two data streams within a single file.
- **Journaling:** NTFS keeps a log of all changes made to files on the volumes. Programs, such as desktop search, can read the journal to identify what files have changed.
- **Compression and encryption:** Entire directories and individual files can be transparently compressed and/or encrypted.
- **Hard and symbolic links:** In order to support POSIX, Windows has always supported "hard links," which allow a single file to be accessible by multiple path names on the same volume. Starting with Windows Vista, "symbolic links" are supported which allow a file or directory to be accessible by multiple path names, even if the names are on different volumes. Windows also supports "mount points" which allow volumes to appear at junction points on other volumes, rather than be named by driver letters, such as "D:".

NTFS Volume and File Structure

NTFS makes use of the following disk storage concepts:

- **Sector:** The smallest physical storage unit on the disk. The data size in bytes is a power of 2 and is almost always 512 bytes.
- **Cluster:** One or more contiguous (next to each other on the disk) sectors. The cluster size in sectors is a power of 2.
- **Volume:** A logical partition on a disk, consisting of one or more clusters and used by a file system to allocate space. At any time, a volume consists of file system information, a collection of files, and any additional unallocated space remaining on the volume that can be allocated to files. A volume can be all or a portion of a single disk or it can extend across multiple disks. If hardware or

Table 12.5   Windows NTFS Partition and Cluster Sizes

Volume Size	Sectors per Cluster	Cluster Size
≤512 Mbyte	1	512 bytes
512 Mbyte–1 Gbyte	2	1K
1 Gbyte–2 Gbyte	4	2K
2 Gbyte–4 Gbyte	8	4K
4 Gbyte–8 Gbyte	16	8K
8 Gbyte–16 Gbyte	32	16K
16 Gbyte–32 Gbyte	64	32K
>32 Gbyte	128	64K

software RAID 5 is employed, a volume consists of stripes spanning multiple disks. The maximum volume size for NTFS is 264 bytes.

The cluster is the fundamental unit of allocation in NTFS, which does not recognize sectors. For example, suppose each sector is 512 bytes and the system is configured with two sectors per cluster (one cluster = 1K bytes). If a user creates a file of 1,600 bytes, two clusters are allocated to the file. Later, if the user updates the file to 3,200 bytes, another two clusters are allocated. The clusters allocated to a file need not be contiguous; it is permissible to fragment a file on the disk. Currently, the maximum file size supported by NTFS is 2^{32} clusters, which is equivalent to a maximum of 2^{48} bytes. A cluster can have at most 2^{16} bytes.

The use of clusters for allocation makes NTFS independent of physical sector size. This enables NTFS to support easily nonstandard disks that do not have a 512-byte sector size and to support efficiently very large disks and very large files by using a larger cluster size. The efficiency comes from the fact that the file system must keep track of each cluster allocated to each file; with larger clusters, there are fewer items to manage.

Table 12.5 shows the default cluster sizes for NTFS. The defaults depend on the size of the volume. The cluster size that is used for a particular volume is established by NTFS when the user requests that a volume be formatted.

NTFS VOLUME LAYOUT   NTFS uses a remarkably simple but powerful approach to organizing information on a disk volume. Every element on a volume is a file, and every file consists of a collection of attributes. Even the data contents of a file is treated as an attribute. With this simple structure, a few general-purpose functions suffice to organize and manage a file system.

Figure 12.21 shows the layout of an NTFS volume, which consists of four regions. The first few sectors on any volume are occupied by the **partition boot**

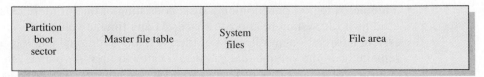

Figure 12.21   NTFS Volume Layout

sector (although it is called a sector, it can be up to 16 sectors long), which contains information about the volume layout and the file system structures as well as boot startup information and code. This is followed by the **master file table (MFT)**, which contains information about all of the files and folders (directories) on this NTFS volume. In essence, the MFT is a list of all files and their attributes on this NTFS volume, organized as a set of rows in a table structure.

Following the MFT is a region containing **system files**. Among the files in this region are the following:

- **MFT2:** A mirror of the first few rows of the MFT, used to guarantee access to the volume in the case of a single-sector failure in the sectors storing the MFT.

- **Log file:** A list of transaction steps used for NTFS recoverability.

- **Cluster bit map:** A representation of the space on the volume, showing which clusters are in use.

- **Attribute definition table:** Defines the attribute types supported on this volume and indicates whether they can be indexed and whether they can be recovered during a system recovery operation.

MASTER FILE TABLE   The heart of the Windows file system is the MFT. The MFT is organized as a table of 1,024-byte rows, called records. Each row describes a file on this volume, including the MFT itself, which is treated as a file. If the contents of a file are small enough, then the entire file is located in a row of the MFT. Otherwise, the row for that file contains partial information and the remainder of the file spills over into other available clusters on the volume, with pointers to those clusters in the MFT row of that file.

Each record in the MFT consists of a set of attributes that serve to define the file (or folder) characteristics and the file contents. Table 12.6 lists the attributes that may be found in a row, with the required attributes indicated by shading.

Table 12.6   Windows NTFS File and Directory Attribute Types

Attribute Type	Description
Standard information	Includes access attributes (read-only, read/write, etc.); time stamps, including when the file was created or last modified; and how many directories point to the file (link count)
Attribute list	A list of attributes that make up the file and the file reference of the MFT file record in which each attribute is located. Used when all attributes do not fit into a single MFT file record
File name	A file or directory must have one or more names.
Security descriptor	Specifies who owns the file and who can access it
Data	The contents of the file. A file has one default unnamed data attribute and may have one or more named data attributes.
Index root	Used to implement folders
Index allocation	Used to implement folders
Volume information	Includes volume-related information, such as the version and name of the volume
Bitmap	Provides a map representing records in use on the MFT or folder

Note: Green-colored rows refer to required file attributes; the other attributes are optional.

Recoverability

NTFS makes it possible to recover the file system to a consistent state following a system crash or disk failure. The key elements that support recoverability are as follows (Figure 12.22):

- **I/O manager:** Includes the NTFS driver, which handles the basic open, close, read, and write functions of NTFS. In addition, the software RAID module FTDISK can be configured for use.
- **Log file service:** Maintains a log of file system metadata changes on disk. The log file is used to recover an NTFS-formatted volume in the case of a system failure (i.e., without having to run the file system check utility).
- **Cache manager:** Responsible for caching file reads and writes to enhance performance. The cache manager optimizes disk I/O.
- **Virtual memory manager:** The NTFS accesses cached files by mapping file references to virtual memory references and reading and writing virtual memory.

It is important to note that the recovery procedures used by NTFS are designed to recover file system metadata, not file contents. Thus, the user should never lose a volume or the directory/file structure of an application because of a crash. However, user data are not guaranteed by the file system. Providing full recoverability, including user data, would make for a much more elaborate and resource-consuming recovery facility.

The essence of the NTFS recovery capability is logging. Each operation that alters a file system is treated as a transaction. Each suboperation of a transaction

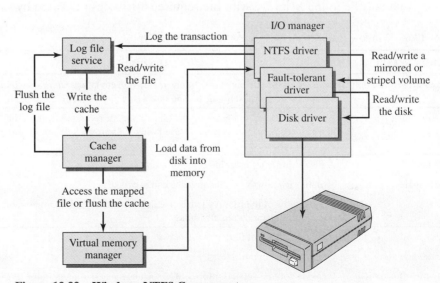

Figure 12.22   Windows NTFS Components

that alters important file system data structures is recorded in a log file before being recorded on the disk volume. Using the log, a partially completed transaction at the time of a crash can later be redone or undone when the system recovers.

In general terms, these are the steps taken to ensure recoverability, as described in [RUSS11]:

1. NTFS first calls the log file system to record in the log file (in the cache) any transactions that will modify the volume structure.
2. NTFS modifies the volume (in the cache).
3. The cache manager calls the log file system to prompt it to flush the log file to disk.
4. Once the log file updates are safely on disk, the cache manager flushes the volume changes to disk.

12.12 SUMMARY

A file management system is a set of system software that provides services to users and applications in the use of files, including file access, directory maintenance, and access control. The file management system is typically viewed as a system service that itself is served by the operating system, rather than being part of the operating system itself. However, in any system, at least part of the file management function is performed by the operating system.

A file consists of a collection of records. The way in which these records may be accessed determines its logical organization, and to some extent its physical organization on disk. If a file is primarily to be processed as a whole, then a sequential file organization is the simplest and most appropriate. If sequential access is needed but random access to individual file is also desired, then an indexed sequential file may give the best performance. If access to the file is principally at random, then an indexed file or hashed file may be the most appropriate.

Whatever file structure is chosen, a directory service is also needed. This allows files to be organized in a hierarchical fashion. This organization is useful to the user in keeping track of files and is useful to the file management system in providing access control and other services to users.

File records, even when of fixed size, generally do not conform to the size of a physical disk block. Accordingly, some sort of blocking strategy is needed. A trade-off among complexity, performance, and space utilization determines the blocking strategy to be used.

A key function of any file management scheme is the management of disk space. Part of this function is the strategy for allocating disk blocks to a file. A variety of methods have been employed, and a variety of data structures have been used to keep track of the allocation for each file. In addition, the space on disk that has not been allocated must be managed. This latter function primarily consists of maintaining a disk allocation table indicating which blocks are free.

12.13 RECOMMENDED READING

There are a number of good books on file structures and file management. The following all focus on file management systems but also address related OS issues. Perhaps the most useful is [WIED87], which takes a quantitative approach to file management and deals with all of the issues raised in Figure 12.2, from disk scheduling to file structure. [VENU09] presents an object-oriented design approach toward file structure implementation. [LIVA90] emphasizes file structures, providing a good and lengthy survey with comparative performance analyses. [GROS86] provides a balanced look at issues relating to both file I/O and file access methods. It also contains general descriptions of all of the control structures needed by a file system. These provide a useful checklist in assessing a file system design. [FOLK98] emphasizes the processing of files, addressing such issues as maintenance, searching and sorting, and sharing.

[COME79] provides a thorough discussion of B-trees. [CORM09] and [KNUT98] also include good treatments.

The Linux file system is examined in detail in [LOVE10] and [BOVE06]. A good overview is [RUBI97].

[CUST94] provides a good overview of the NT file system. [NAGA97] covers the material in more detail.

BOVE06   Bovet, D., and Cesati, M. *Understanding the Linux Kernel.* Sebastopol, CA: O'Reilly, 2006.

COME79   Comer, D. "The Ubiquitous B-Tree." *Computing Surveys,* June 1979.

CORM09   Cormen, T., et al. *Introduction to Algorithms.* Cambridge, MA: MIT Press, 2009.

CUST94   Custer, H. *Inside the Windows NT File System.* Redmond, WA: Microsoft Press, 1994.

FOLK98   Folk, M., and Zoellick, B. *File Structures: An Object-Oriented Approach with C++.* Reading, MA: Addison-Wesley, 1998.

GROS86   Grosshans, D. *File Systems: Design and Implementation.* Englewood Cliffs, NJ: Prentice Hall, 1986.

KNUT98   Knuth, D. *The Art of Computer Programming, Volume 3: Sorting and Searching.* Reading, MA: Addison-Wesley, 1998.

LIVA90   Livadas, P. *File Structures: Theory and Practice.* Englewood Cliffs, NJ: Prentice Hall, 1990.

LOVE10   Love, R. *Linux Kernel Development.* Upper Saddle River, NJ: Addison-Wesley, 2010.

NAGA97   Nagar, R. *Windows NT File System Internals.* Sebastopol, CA: O'Reilly, 1997.

RUBI97   Rubini, A. "The Virtual File System in Linux." *Linux Journal,* May 1997.

VENU09   Venugopal, K. *Files Structures Using C++.* New York: McGraw-Hill, 2009.

WIED87   Wiederhold, G. *File Organization for Database Design.* New York: McGraw-Hill, 1987.

12.14 KEY TERMS, REVIEW QUESTIONS, AND PROBLEMS

Key Terms

access method	file allocation	inode
bit table	file allocation table	key field
block	file directory	pathname
chained file allocation	file management system	pile
contiguous file allocation	file name	record
database	hashed file	sequential file
disk allocation table	indexed file	working directory
field	indexed file allocation	
file	indexed sequential file	

Review Questions

12.1 What is the difference between a field and a record?

12.2 What is the difference between a file and a database?

12.3 What is a file management system?

12.4 What criteria are important in choosing a file organization?

12.5 List and briefly define five file organizations.

12.6 Why is the average search time to find a record in a file less for an indexed sequential file than for a sequential file?

12.7 What are typical operations that may be performed on a directory?

12.8 What is the relationship between a pathname and a working directory?

12.9 What are typical access rights that may be granted or denied to a particular user for a particular file?

12.10 List and briefly define three blocking methods.

12.11 List and briefly define three file allocation methods.

Problems

12.1 Define:
   B = block size
   R = record size
   P = size of block pointer
   F = blocking factor; expected number of records within a block

   Give a formula for F for the three blocking methods depicted in Figure 12.8.

12.2 One scheme to avoid the problem of preallocation versus waste or lack of contiguity is to allocate portions of increasing size as the file grows. For example, begin with a portion size of one block, and double the portion size for each allocation. Consider a file of n records with a blocking factor of F, and suppose that a simple one-level index is used as a file allocation table.
   a. Give an upper limit on the number of entries in the file allocation table as a function of F and n.
   b. What is the maximum amount of the allocated file space that is unused at any time?

12.3 What file organization would you choose to maximize efficiency in terms of speed of access, use of storage space, and ease of updating (adding/deleting/modifying) when the data are
    a. updated infrequently and accessed frequently in random order?
    b. updated frequently and accessed in its entirety relatively frequently?
    c. updated frequently and accessed frequently in random order?

12.4 For the B-tree in Figure 12.4c, show the result of inserting the key 97.

12.5 An alternative algorithm for insertion into a B-tree is the following: As the insertion algorithm travels down the tree, each full node that is encountered is immediately split, even though it may turn out that the split was unnecessary.
    a. What is the advantage of this technique?
    b. What are the disadvantages?

12.6 Both the search and the insertion time for a B-tree are a function of the height of the tree. We would like to develop a measure of the worst-case search or insertion time. Consider a B-tree of degree d that contains a total of n keys. Develop an inequality that shows an upper bound on the height h of the tree as a function of d and n.

12.7 Ignoring overhead for directories and file descriptors, consider a file system in which files are stored in blocks of 16K bytes. For each of the following file sizes, calculate the percentage of wasted file space due to incomplete filling of the last block: 41,600 bytes; 640,000 bytes; 4.064,000 bytes.

12.8 What are the advantages of using directories?

12.9 Directories can be implemented either as "special files" that can only be accessed in limited ways or as ordinary data files. What are the advantages and disadvantages of each approach?

12.10 Some operating systems have a tree–structured file system but limit the depth of the tree to some small number of levels. What effect does this limit have on users? How does this simplify file system design (if it does)?

12.11 Consider a hierarchical file system in which free disk space is kept in a free space list.
    a. Suppose the pointer to free space is lost. Can the system reconstruct the free space list?
    b. Suggest a scheme to ensure that the pointer is never lost as a result of a single memory failure.

12.12 In UNIX System V, the length of a block is 1 Kbyte, and each block can hold a total of 256 block addresses. Using the inode scheme, what is the maximum size of a file?

12.13 Consider the organization of a UNIX file as represented by the inode (Figure 12.16). Assume that there are 12 direct block pointers, and a singly, doubly, and triply indirect pointer in each inode. Further, assume that the system block size and the disk sector size are both 8K. If the disk block pointer is 32 bits, with 8 bits to identify the physical disk and 24 bits to identify the physical block, then
    a. What is the maximum file size supported by this system?
    b. What is the maximum file system partition supported by this system?
    c. Assuming no information other than that the file inode is already in main memory, how many disk accesses are required to access the byte in position 13,423,956?

PART 6 Embedded Systems

CHAPTER 13

EMBEDDED OPERATING SYSTEMS

13.1 Embedded Systems

13.2 Characteristics of Embedded Operating Systems
 Adapting an Existing Commercial Operating System
 Purpose-Built Embedded Operating System

13.3 eCos
 Configurability
 eCos Components
 eCos Scheduler
 eCos Thread Synchronization

13.4 TinyOS
 Wireless Sensor Networks
 TinyOS Goals
 TinyOS Components
 TinyOS Scheduler
 Example Configuration
 TinyOS Resource Interface

13.5 Recommended Reading and Web Sites

13.6 Key Terms, Review Questions, and Problems

In brief, the conventional arguments that bird brains are too small or do not have particular structures needed for intelligence are based on ignorance of brains in general and bird brains in particular. It is unwarranted to argue that the small brains and small bodies of birds render them less capable of behaving with intelligent awareness than animals with large brains and large bodies.

—*THE HUMAN NATURE OF BIRDS*, THEODORE BARBER

LEARNING OBJECTIVES

After studying this chapter, you should be able to:

- Explain the concept of embedded system.
- Understand the characteristics of embedded operating systems.
- Describe the architecture and key features of eCos.
- Describe the architecture and key features of TinyOS.

In this chapter, we examine one of the most important and widely used categories of operating systems: embedded operating systems. The embedded system environment places unique and demanding requirements on the OS and calls for design strategies quite different than that found in ordinary operating systems.

We begin with an overview of the concept of embedded systems and then turn to an examination of the principles of embedded operating systems. Finally, this chapter surveys two very different approaches to embedded OS design.

13.1 EMBEDDED SYSTEMS

The term *embedded system* refers to the use of electronics and software within a product, as opposed to a general-purpose computer, such as a laptop or desktop system. The following is a good general definition:[1]

Embedded system: A combination of computer hardware and software, and perhaps additional mechanical or other parts, designed to perform a dedicated function. In many cases, embedded systems are part of a larger system or product, as in the case of an antilock braking system in a car.

Embedded systems far outnumber general-purpose computer systems, encompassing a broad range of applications (Table 13.1). These systems have widely varying requirements and constraints, such as the following [GRIM05]:

- Small to large systems, implying very different cost constraints, thus different needs for optimization and reuse

---

[1]Michael Barr, *Embedded Systems Glossary*. Netrino Technical Library. http://www.netrino.com/Embedded-Systems/Glossary

Table 13.1   Examples of Embedded Systems and Their Markets [NOER05]

Market	Embedded Device
Automotive	Ignition system Engine control Brake system
Consumer electronics	Cell phones mp3 players ebook readers Digital and analog televisions Set-top boxes (DVDs, VCRs, Cable boxes) Kitchen appliances (refrigerators, toasters, microwave ovens) Automobiles Toys/games Telephones/cell phones/pagers Cameras Global positioning systems
Industrial control	Robotics and controls systems for manufacturing Sensors
Medical	Infusion pumps Dialysis machines Prosthetic devices Cardiac monitors
Office automation	Fax machine Photocopier Printers Monitors Scanners

- Relaxed to very strict requirements and combinations of different quality requirements, for example, with respect to safety, reliability, real-time, flexibility, and legislation
- Short to long lifetimes
- Different environmental conditions in terms of, for example, radiation, vibrations, and humidity
- Different application characteristics resulting in static versus dynamic loads, slow to fast speed, compute versus interface intensive tasks, and/or combinations thereof
- Different models of computation ranging from discrete-event systems to those involving continuous time dynamics (usually referred to as hybrid systems)

Often, embedded systems are tightly coupled to their environment. This can give rise to real-time constraints imposed by the need to interact with the environment. Constraints, such as required speeds of motion, required precision of measurement, and required time durations, dictate the timing of software operations. If multiple activities must be managed simultaneously, this imposes more complex real-time constraints.

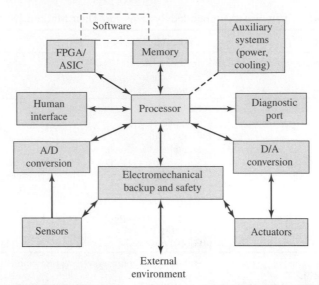

Figure 13.1   Possible Organization of an Embedded System

Figure 13.1, based on [KOOP96], shows in general terms an embedded system organization. In addition to the processor and memory, there are a number of elements that differ from the typical desktop or laptop computer:

- There may be a variety of interfaces that enable the system to measure, manipulate, and otherwise interact with the external environment.
- The human interface may be as simple as a flashing light or as complicated as real-time robotic vision.
- The diagnostic port may be used for diagnosing the system that is being controlled—not just for diagnosing the embedded computer.
- Special-purpose field programmable (FPGA), application specific (ASIC), or even nondigital hardware may be used to increase performance or safety.
- Software often has a fixed function and is specific to the application.

13.2 CHARACTERISTICS OF EMBEDDED OPERATING SYSTEMS

A simple embedded system, with simple functionality, may be controlled by a special-purpose program or set of programs with no other software. Typically, more complex embedded systems include an OS. Although it is possible in principle to use a general-purpose OS, such as Linux, for an embedded system, constraints of memory space, power consumption, and real-time requirements typically dictate the use of a special-purpose OS designed for the embedded system environment.

The following are some of the unique characteristics and design requirements for embedded operating systems:

- **Real-time operation:** In many embedded systems, the correctness of a computation depends, in part, on the time at which it is delivered. Often, real-time constraints are dictated by external I/O and control stability requirements.

- **Reactive operation:** Embedded software may execute in response to external events. If these events do not occur periodically or at predictable intervals, the embedded software may need to take into account worst-case conditions and set priorities for execution of routines.

- **Configurability:** Because of the large variety of embedded systems, there is a large variation in the requirements, both qualitative and quantitative, for embedded OS functionality. Thus, an embedded OS intended for use on a variety of embedded systems must lend itself to flexible configuration so that only the functionality needed for a specific application and hardware suite is provided. [MARW06] gives the following examples. The linking and loading functions can be used to select only the necessary OS modules to load. Conditional compilation can be used. If an object-oriented structure is used, proper subclasses can be defined. However, verification is a potential problem for designs with a large number of derived tailored operating systems. Takada cites this as a potential problem for eCos [TAKA01].

- **I/O device flexibility:** There is virtually no device that needs to be supported by all versions of the OS, and the range of I/O devices is large. [MARW06] suggests that it makes sense to handle relatively slow devices such as disks and network interfaces by using special tasks instead of integrating their drives into the OS kernel.

- **Streamlined protection mechanisms:** Embedded systems are typically designed for a limited, well-defined functionality. Untested programs are rarely added to the software. After the software has been configured and tested, it can be assumed to be reliable. Thus, apart from security measures, embedded systems have limited protection mechanisms. For example, I/O instructions need not be privileged instructions that trap to the OS; tasks can directly perform their own I/O. Similarly, memory protection mechanisms can be minimized. [MARW06] provides the following example. Let `switch` correspond to the memory-mapped I/O address of a value that needs to be checked as part of an I/O operation. We can allow the I/O program to use an instruction such as `load register, switch` to determine the current value. This approach is preferable to the use of an OS service call, which would generate overhead for saving and restoring the task context.

- **Direct use of interrupts:** General-purpose operating systems typically do not permit any user process to use interrupts directly. [MARW06] lists three reasons why it is possible to let interrupts directly start or stop tasks (e.g., by storing the task's start address in the interrupt vector address table) rather than going through OS interrupt service routines: (1) Embedded systems can be considered to be thoroughly tested, with infrequent modifications to the OS or application code; (2) protection is not necessary, as discussed in the preceding bullet item; and (3) efficient control over a variety of devices is required.

There are two general approaches to developing an embedded OS. The first approach is to take an existing OS and adapt it for the embedded application. The other approach is to design and implement an OS intended solely for embedded use.[2]

Adapting an Existing Commercial Operating System

An existing commercial OS can be used for an embedded system by adding real-time capability, streamlining operation, and adding necessary functionality. This approach typically makes use of Linux, but FreeBSD, Windows, and other general-purpose operating systems have also been used. Such operating systems are typically slower and less predictable than a special-purpose embedded OS. An advantage of this approach is that the embedded OS derived from a commercial general-purpose OS is based on a set of familiar interfaces, which facilitates portability.

The disadvantage of using a general-purpose OS is that it is not optimized for real-time and embedded applications. Thus, considerable modification may be required to achieve adequate performance. In particular, a typical OS optimizes for the average case rather than the worst case for scheduling, usually assigns resources on demand, and ignores most if not all semantic information about an application.

Purpose–Built Embedded Operating System

A significant number of operating systems have been designed from the ground up for embedded applications. Two prominent examples of this latter approach are eCos and TinyOS, both of which are discussed in this chapter.

Typical characteristics of a specialized embedded OS include the following:

- Has a fast and lightweight process or thread switch
- Scheduling policy is real time and dispatcher module is part of scheduler instead of separate component.
- Has a small size
- Responds to external interrupts quickly; typical requirement is response time of less than 10 μs
- Minimizes intervals during which interrupts are disabled
- Provides fixed or variable-sized partitions for memory management as well as the ability to lock code and data in memory
- Provides special sequential files that can accumulate data at a fast rate

  To deal with timing constraints, the kernel

- Provides bounded execution time for most primitives
- Maintains a real-time clock

---

[2]Much of the discussion in the remainder of Section 13.2 is based on course notes on embedded systems from Prof. Rajesh Gupta, University of California at San Diego.

- Provides for special alarms and time-outs
- Supports real-time queuing disciplines such as earliest deadline first and primitives for jamming a message into the front of a queue
- Provides primitives to delay processing by a fixed amount of time and to suspend/resume execution

The characteristics just listed are common in embedded operating systems with real-time requirements. However, for complex embedded systems, the requirement may emphasize predictable operation over fast operation, necessitating different design decisions, particularly in the area of task scheduling.

13.3 ECOS

The Embedded Configurable Operating System (eCos) is an open source, royalty-free, real-time OS intended for embedded applications. The system is targeted at high-performance small embedded systems. For such systems, an embedded form of Linux or other commercial OS would not provide the streamlined software required. The eCos software has been implemented on a wide variety of processor platforms, including Intel IA32, PowerPC, SPARC, ARM, CalmRISC, MIPS, and NEC V8xx. It is one of the most widely used embedded operating systems. It is implemented in C/C++.

Configurability

An embedded OS that is flexible enough to be used in a wide variety of embedded applications and on a wide variety of embedded platforms must provide more functionality than will be needed for any particular application and platform. For example, many real-time operating systems support task switching, concurrency controls, and a variety of priority scheduling mechanisms. A relatively simple embedded system would not need all these features.

The challenge is to provide an efficient, user-friendly mechanism for configuring selected components and for enabling and disabling particular features within components. The eCos configuration tool, which runs on Windows or Linux, is used to configure an eCos package to run on a target embedded system. The complete eCos package is structured hierarchically, making it easy, using the configuration tool, to assemble a target configuration. At a top level, eCos consists of a number of components, and the configuration user may select only those components needed for the target application. For example, a system might have a particular serial I/O device. The configuration user would select serial I/O for this configuration, then select one or more specific I/O devices to be supported. The configuration tool would include the minimum necessary software for that support. The configuration user can also select specific parameters, such as default data rate and the size of I/O buffers to be used.

This configuration process can be extended down to finer levels of detail, even to the level of individual lines of code. For example, the configuration tool provides the option of including or omitting a priority inheritance protocol.

Figure 13.2 shows the top level of the eCos configuration tool as seen by the tool user. Each of the items on the list in the left-hand window can be selected or deselected. When an item is highlighted, the lower right-hand window provides a description and the upper right-hand window provides a link to further documentation plus additional information about the highlighted item. Items on the list can be expanded to provide a finer-grained menu of options. Figure 13.3 illustrates an expansion of the eCos kernel option. In this figure, note that exception handling has been selected for inclusion, but SMP (symmetric multiprocessing) has been omitted. In general, components and individual options can be selected or omitted. In some cases, individual values can be set; for example, a minimum acceptable stack size is an integer value that can be set or left to a default value.

Figure 13.4 shows a typical example of the overall process of creating the binary image to execute in the embedded system. This process is run on a source system, such as a Windows or Linux platform, and the executable image is destined to execute on a target embedded system, such as a sensor in an industrial environment. At the highest software level is the application source code for the particular embedded application. This code is independent of eCos but makes use of application programming interfaces (API) to sit on top of the eCos software. There may be only one version of the application source code, or there may be variations for different versions of the target embedded platform. In this example, the GNU make utility is used to selectively determine which pieces of a program

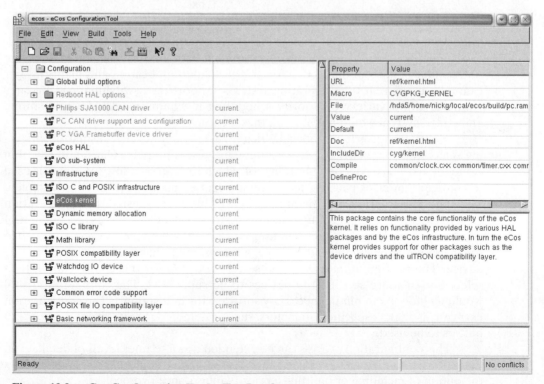

Figure 13.2   eCos Configuration Tool—Top Level

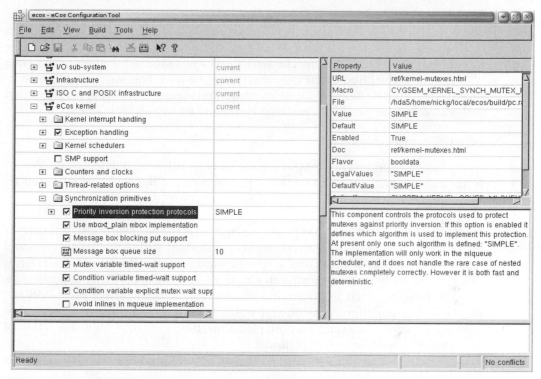

Figure 13.3   eCos Configuration Tool — Kernel Details

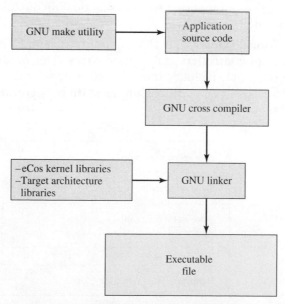

Figure 13.4   Loading an eCos Configuration

need to be compiled or recompiled (in the case of a modified version of the source code) and issues the commands to recompile them. The GNU cross compiler, executing on the source platform, then generates the binary executable code for the target embedded platform. The GNU linker links the application object code with the code generated by the eCos configuration tool. This latter set of software includes selected portions of the eCos kernel plus selected software for the target embedded system. The result can then be loaded into the target system.

eCos Components

A key design requirement for eCos is portability to different architectures and platforms with minimal effort. To meet this requirement, eCos consists of a layered set of components (Figure 13.5).

HARDWARE ABSTRACTION LAYER   At the bottom is the hardware abstraction layer (HAL). The HAL is software that presents a consistent API to the upper layers and maps upper-layer operations onto a specific hardware platform. Thus, the HAL is different for each hardware platform. Figure 13.6 is an example that demonstrates how the HAL abstracts hardware-specific implementations for the same API call on two different platforms. As this example shows, the call from an upper layer to enable interrupts is the same on both platforms, but the C code implementation of the function is specific to each platform.

The HAL is implemented as three separate modules:

- **Architecture:** Defines the processor family type. This module contains the code necessary for processor startup, interrupt delivery, context switching, and other functionality specific to the instruction set architecture of that processor family.
- **Variant:** Supports the features of the specific processor in the family. An example of a supported feature is an on-chip module such as a memory management unit (MMU).
- **Platform:** Extends the HAL support to tightly coupled peripherals like interrupt controllers and timer devices. This module defines the platform or board that includes the selected processor architecture and variant. It includes code for startup, chip selection configuration, interrupt controllers, and timer devices.

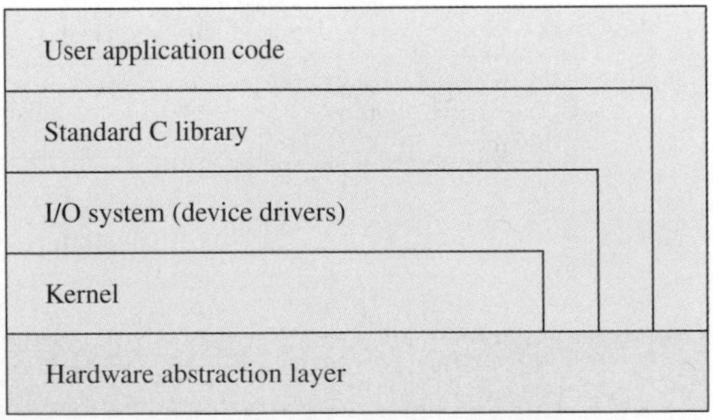

Figure 13.5   eCos Layered Structure

```
1 #define HAL_ENABLE_INTERRUPTS()                          \
2   asm volatile (                                         \
3     "mrs r3, cpsr;"                                      \
4     "bic r3, r3, #0xC0;"                                 \
5     "mrs cpsr, r3;"                                      \
6     :                                                    \
7     :                                                    \
8     : "r3"                                               \
9     );                                                   \
```

(a) ARM architecture

```
 1 #define HAL_ENABLE_INTERRUPTS()                         \
 2   CYG_MACRO_START                                       \
 3   cyg_uint32 tmp1, tmp2                                 \
 4   asm volatile (                                        \
 5     "mfmsr %0;"                                         \
 6     "ori %1,%1,0x800;"                                  \
 7     "rlwimi %0,%1,0,16,16;"                             \
 8     "mtmsr %0;"                                         \
 9     : "=r" (tmp1), "=r" (tmp2));                        \
10   CYG_MACRO_END                                         \
```

(b) PowerPC architecture

Figure 13.6 Two Implementations of `Hal_Enable_Interrupts()` **Macro**

Note that the HAL interface can be directly used by any of the upper layers, promoting efficient code.

eCos Kernel   The eCos kernel was designed to satisfy four main objectives:

- **Low interrupt latency:** The time it takes to respond to an interrupt and begin executing an ISR.
- **Low task switching latency:** The time it takes from when a thread becomes available to when actual execution begins.
- **Small memory footprint:** Memory resources for both program and data are kept to a minimum by allowing all components to configure memory as needed.
- **Deterministic behavior:** Throughout all aspect of execution, the kernels performance must be predictable and bounded to meet real-time application requirements.

The eCos kernel provides the core functionality needed for developing multi-threaded applications:

1. The ability to create new threads in the system, either during startup or when the system is already running
2. Control over the various threads in the system: for example, manipulating their priorities
3. A choice of schedulers, determining which thread should currently be running

4. A range of synchronization primitives, allowing threads to interact and share data safely

5. Integration with the system's support for interrupts and exceptions

Some functionality that is typically included in the kernel of an OS is not included in the eCos kernel. For example, memory allocation is handled by a separate package. Similarly, each device driver is a separate package. Various packages are combined and configured using the eCos configuration technology to meet the requirements of the application. This makes for a lean kernel. Further, the minimal nature of the kernel means that for some embedded platforms, the eCos kernel is not used at all. Simple single-threaded applications can be run directly on HAL. Such configurations can incorporate needed C library functions and device drivers but avoid the space and time overhead of the kernel.

There are two different techniques for utilizing kernel functions in eCos. One way to employ kernel functionality is by using the C API of kernel. Examples of such functions are cyg_thread_create and cyg_mutex_lock. These functions can be invoked directly from application code. On the other hand, kernel functions can also be invoked by using compatibility packages for existing API's, for example POSIX threads or µITRON. The compatibility packages allow application code to call standard functions like pthread_create, and those functions are implemented using the basic functions provided by the eCos kernel. Code sharing and reusability of already developed code is easily achieved by use of compatibility packages.

I/O SYSTEM The eCos I/O system is a framework for supporting device drivers. A variety of drivers for a variety of platforms are provided in the eCos configuration package. These include drivers for serial devices, Ethernet, flash memory interfaces, and various I/O interconnects such as PCI (Peripheral Component Interconnect) and USB (Universal Serial Bus). In addition, users can develop their own device drivers.

The principal objective for the I/O system is efficiency, with no unnecessary software layering or extraneous functionality. Device drivers provide the necessary functions for input, output, buffering, and device control.

As mentioned, device drivers and other higher-layer software may be implemented directly on the HAL if this is appropriate. If specialized kernel-type functions are needed, then the device driver is implemented using kernel APIs. The kernel provides a three-level interrupt model [ECOS07]:

- **Interrupt service routines (ISRs):** Invoked in response to a hardware interrupt. Hardware interrupts are delivered with minimal intervention to an ISR. The HAL decodes the hardware source of the interrupt and calls the ISR of the attached interrupt object. This ISR may manipulate the hardware but is only allowed to make a restricted set of calls on the driver API. When it returns, an ISR may request that its DSR should be scheduled to run.

- **Deferred service routines (DSRs):** Invoked in response to a request by an ISR. A DSR will be run when it is safe to do so without interfering with the scheduler. Most of the time the DSR will run immediately after the ISR, but if the current thread is in the scheduler, it will be delayed until the thread is finished.

A DSR is allowed to make a larger set of driver API calls, including, in particular, being able to call `cyg_drv_cond_signal()` to wake up waiting threads.

- **Threads:** The clients of the driver. Threads are able to make all API calls and in particular are allowed to wait on mutexes and condition variables.

Tables 13.2 and 13.3 show the device driver interface to the kernel. These tables give a good feel for the type of functionality available in the kernel to support

Table 13.2 Device Driver Interface to the eCos Kernel: Concurrency

`cyg_drv_spinlock_init`   Initialize a spinlock in a locked or unlocked state.
`cyg_drv_spinlock_destroy`   Destroy a spinlock that is no longer of use.
`cyg_drv_spinlock_spin`   Claim a spinlock, waiting in a busy loop until it is available.
`cyg_drv_spinlock_clear`   Clear a spinlock. This clears the spinlock and allows another CPU to claim it. If there is more than one CPU waiting in `cyg_drv_spinlock_spin`, then just one of them will be allowed to proceed.
`cyg_drv_spinlock_test`   Inspect the state of the spinlock. If the spinlock is not locked, then the result is TRUE. If it is locked, then the result will be FALSE.
`cyg_drv_spinlock_spin_intsave`   This function behaves like `cyg_drv_spinlock_spin` except that it also disables interrupts before attempting to claim the lock. The current interrupt enable state is saved in *istate. Interrupts remain disabled once the spinlock has been claimed and must be restored by calling `cyg_drv_spinlock_clear_intsave`. Device drivers should use this function to claim and release spinlocks rather than the non-_intsave() variants, to ensure proper exclusion with code running on both other CPUs and this CPU.
`cyg_drv_mutex_init`   Initialize a mutex.
`cyg_drv_mutex_destroy`   Destroy a mutex. The mutex should be unlocked and there should be no threads waiting to lock it when this call in made.
`cyg_drv_mutex_lock`   Attempt to lock the mutex pointed to by the mutex argument. If the mutex is already locked by another thread, then this thread will wait until that thread is finished. If the result from this function is FALSE, then the thread was broken out of its wait by some other thread. In this case, the mutex will not have been locked.
`cyg_drv_mutex_trylock`   Attempt to lock the mutex pointed to by the mutex argument without waiting. If the mutex is already locked by some other thread then this function returns FALSE. If the function can lock the mutex without waiting, then TRUE is returned.
`cyg_drv_mutex_unlock`   Unlock the mutex pointed to by the mutex argument. If there are any threads waiting to claim the lock, one of them is woken up to try and claim it.
`cyg_drv_mutex_release`   Release all threads waiting on the mutex.
`cyg_drv_cond_init`   Initialize a condition variable associated with a mutex with. A thread may only wait on this condition variable when it has already locked the associated mutex. Waiting will cause the mutex to be unlocked, and when the thread is reawakened, it will automatically claim the mutex before continuing.
`cyg_drv_cond_destroy`   Destroy the condition variable.
`cyg_drv_cond_wait`   Wait for a signal on a condition variable.
`cyg_drv_cond_signal`   Signal a condition variable. If there are any threads waiting on this variable, at least one of them will all be awakened.
`cyg_drv_cond_broadcast`   Signal a condition variable. If there are any threads waiting on this variable, they will all be awakened.

Table 13.3   Device Driver Interface to the eCos Kernel: Interrupts

`cyg_drv_isr_lock`   Disable delivery of interrupts, preventing all ISRs running. This function maintains a counter of the number of times it is called.
`cyg_drv_isr_unlock`   Reenable delivery of interrupts, allowing ISRs to run. This function decrements the counter maintained by `cyg_drv_isr_lock`, and only reallows interrupts when it goes to zero.
`cyg_ISR_t` Define ISR.
`cyg_drv_dsr_lock`   Disable scheduling of DSRs. This function maintains a counter of the number of times it has been called.
`cyg_drv_dsr_unlock`   Reenable scheduling of DSRs. This function decrements the counter incremented by `cyg_drv_dsr_lock`.   DSRs are only allowed to be delivered when the counter goes to zero.
`cyg_DSR_t` Define DSR prototype.
`cyg_drv_interrupt_create`   Create an interrupt object and returns a handle to it.
`cyg_drv_interrupt_delete`   Detach the interrupt from the vector and free the memory for reuse.
`cyg_drv_interrupt_attach`   Attach an interrupt to a vector so that interrupts will be delivered to the ISR when the interrupt occurs.
`cyg_drv_interrupt_detach`   Detach the interrupt from the vector so that interrupts will no longer be delivered to the ISR.
`cyg_drv_interrupt_mask`   Program the interrupt controller to stop delivery of interrupts on the given vector.
`cyg_drv_interrupt_mask_intunsafe`   Program the interrupt controller to stop delivery of interrupts on the given vector. This version differs from `cyg_drv_interrupt_mask` in not being interrupt safe. So in situations where, for example, interrupts are already known to be disabled, this may be called to avoid the extra overhead.
`cyg_drv_interrupt_unmask`, `cyg_drv_interrupt_unmask_intunsafe`   Program the interrupt controller to reallow delivery of interrupts on the given vector.
`cyg_drv_interrupt_acknowledge`   Perform any processing required at the interrupt controller and in the CPU to cancel the current interrupt request.
`cyg_drv_interrupt_configure`   Program the interrupt controller with the characteristics of the interrupt source.
`cyg_drv_interrupt_level`   Program the interrupt controller to deliver the given interrupt at the supplied priority level.
`cyg_drv_interrupt_set_cpu`   On multiprocessor systems, this function causes all interrupts on the given vector to be routed to the specified CPU. Subsequently, all such interrupts will be handled by that CPU.
`cyg_drv_interrupt_get_cpu`   On multiprocessor systems, this function returns the ID of the CPU to which interrupts on the given vector are currently being delivered.

device drivers. Note that the device driver interface can be configured for one or more of the following concurrency mechanisms: spinlocks, condition variables, and mutexes. These are described in a subsequent portion of this discussion.

Standard C Libraries   A complete Standard C run-time library is provided. Also included is a complete math run time library for high-level mathematics functions, including a complete IEEE-754 floating-point library for those platforms without hardware floating points.

eCos Scheduler

The eCos kernel can be configured to provide one of two scheduler designs: the bitmap scheduler and a multilevel queue scheduler. The configuration user selects the appropriate scheduler for the environment and the application. The bitmap scheduler provides efficient scheduling for a system with a small number of threads that may be active at any point in time. The multiqueue scheduler is appropriate if the number of threads is dynamic or if it is desirable to have multiple threads at the same priority level. The multilevel scheduler is also needed if time slicing is desired.

BITMAP SCHEDULER   A bitmap scheduler supports multiple priority levels, but only one thread can exist at each priority level at any given time. Scheduling decisions are quite simple with this scheduler (Figure 13.7a). When a blocked thread becomes ready to run, it may preempt a thread of lower priority. When a running thread suspends, the ready thread with the highest priority is dispatched. A thread can be suspended because it is blocked on a synchronization primitive, because it is interrupted, or because it relinquishes control. Because there is only one thread, at most, at each priority level, the scheduler does not have to make a decision as to which thread at a given priority level should be dispatched next.

The bitmap scheduler is configured with 8, 16, or 32 priority levels. A simple bitmap is kept of the threads that are ready to execute. The scheduler need only determine the position of the most significant one bit in the bitmap to make a scheduling decision.

MULTILEVEL QUEUE SCHEDULER   As with the bitmap scheduler, the multilevel queue scheduler supports up to 32 priority levels. The multilevel queue scheduler allows for multiple active threads at each priority level, limited only by system resources.

Figure 13.7b illustrates the nature of the multilevel queue scheduler. A data structure represents the number of ready threads at each priority level. When a blocked thread becomes ready to run, it may preempt a thread of lower priority. As with the bitmap scheduler, a running thread may be blocked on a synchronization primitive, because it is interrupted, or because it relinquishes control. When a thread is blocked, the scheduler must first determine if one or more threads at the same priority level as the blocked thread is ready. If so, the scheduler chooses the one at the front of the queue. Otherwise, the scheduler looks for the next highest priority level with one or more ready threads and dispatches one of these threads.

In addition, the multilevel queue scheduler can be configured for time slicing. Thus, if a thread is running and there is one or more ready threads at the same priority level, the scheduler will suspend the running thread after one time slice and choose the next thread in the queue at that priority level. This is a round-robin policy within one priority level. Not all applications require time slicing. For example, an application may contain only threads that block regularly for some other reason. For these applications, the user can disable time slicing, which reduces the overhead associated with timer interrupts.

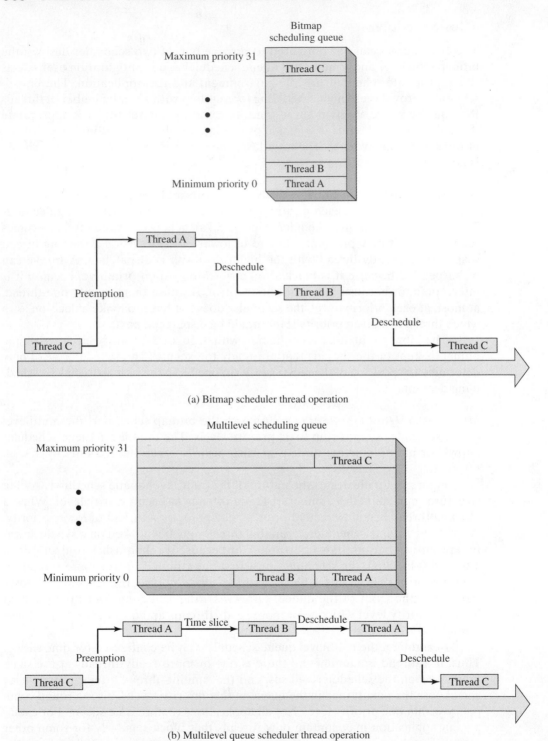

(a) Bitmap scheduler thread operation

(b) Multilevel queue scheduler thread operation

Figure 13.7   eCos Scheduler Options

eCos Thread Synchronization

The eCos kernel can be configured to include one or more of six different thread synchronization mechanisms. These include the classic synchronization mechanisms: mutexes, semaphores, and condition variables. In addition, eCos supports two synchronization/communication mechanisms that are common in real-time systems, namely event flags and mailboxes. Finally, the eCos kernel supports spin-locks, which are useful in SMP (symmetric multiprocessing) systems.

MUTEXES   The mutex (mutual exclusion lock) was introduced in Chapter 6. Recall that a mutex is used to enforce mutually exclusive access to a resource, allowing only one thread at a time to gain access. The mutex has only two states: locked and unlocked. This is similar to a binary semaphore: When a mutex is locked by one thread, any other thread attempting to lock the mutex is blocked; when the mutex is unlocked, then one of the threads blocked on this mutex is unblocked and allowed to lock the mutex and gain access to the resource.

The mutex differs from a binary semaphore in two respects. First, the thread that locks the mutex must be the one to unlock it. In contrast, it is possible for one thread to lock a binary semaphore and for another to unlock it. The other difference is that a mutex provides protection against priority inversion, whereas a semaphore does not.

The eCos kernel can be configured to support either a priority inheritance protocol or a priority ceiling protocol. These are described in Chapter 10.

SEMAPHORES   The eCos kernel provides support for a counting semaphore. Recall from Chapter 5 that a counting semaphore is an integer value used for signaling among threads. The cyg_semaphore_init is used to initialize a semaphore. The cyg_semaphore_post command increments the semaphore count when an event occurs. If the new count is less than or equal to zero, then a thread is waiting on this semaphore and is awakened. The cyg_semaphore_wait function checks the value of a semaphore count. If the count is zero, the thread calling this function will wait for the semaphore. If the count is nonzero, the count is decremented and the thread continues.

Counting semaphores are suited to enabling threads to wait until an event has occurred. The event may be generated by a producer thread, or by a DSR in response to a hardware interrupt. Associated with each semaphore is an integer counter that keeps track of the number of events that have not yet been processed. If this counter is zero, an attempt by a consumer thread to wait on the semaphore will block until some other thread or a DSR posts a new event to the semaphore. If the counter is greater than zero, then an attempt to wait on the semaphore will consume one event, in other words decrement the counter, and return immediately. Posting to a semaphore will wake up the first thread that is currently waiting, which will then resume inside the semaphore wait operation and decrement the counter again.

Another use of semaphores is for certain forms of resource management. The counter would correspond to how many of a certain type of resource are currently available, with threads waiting on the semaphore to claim a resource and posting to release the resource again. In practice, condition variables are usually much better suited for operations like this.

CONDITION VARIABLES   A condition variable is used to block a thread until a particular condition is true. Condition variables are used with mutexes to allow multiple threads to access shared data. They can be used to implement monitors of the type discussed in Chapter 6 (e.g., Figure 6.14). The basic commands are as follows:

`cyg_cond_wait`	Causes the current threat to wait on the specified condition variable and simultaneously unlocks the mutex attached to the condition variable
`cyg_cond_signal`	Wakes up one of the threads waiting on this condition variable, causing that thread to become the owner of the mutex
`cyg_cond_broadcast`	Wakes up all the threads waiting on this condition variable. Each thread that was waiting on the condition variable becomes the owner of the mutex when it runs.

In eCos, condition variables are typically used in conjunction with mutexes to implement long-term waits for some condition to become true. We use an example from [ECOS07] to illustrate. Figure 13.8 defines a set of functions to control access to a pool of resources using mutexes. The mutex is used to make the allocation and freeing of resources from a pool atomic. The function `res_t res_allocate` checks to see if one or more units of a resource are available and, if so, takes one unit. This operation is protected by a mutex so that no other thread can check or alter the resource pool while this thread has control of the mutex. The function `res_free(res_t res)` enables a thread to release one unit of a resource that it had previously acquired. Again, this operation is made atomic by a mutex.

In this example, if a thread attempts to access a resource and none are available, the function returns RES_NONE. Suppose, however, that we want the thread to be blocked and wait for a resource to become available, rather than returning RES_NONE. Figure 13.9 accomplishes this with the use of a condition variable associated with the mutex. When `res_allocate` detects that there are no resources, it calls `cyg_cond_wait`. This latter function unlocks the mutex and puts the calling thread to sleep on the condition variable. When `res_free` is eventually called, it puts a resource back into the pool and calls `cyg_cond_signal` to wake up any thread waiting on the condition variable. When the waiting thread eventually gets to run again, it will relock the mutex before returning from `cyg_cond_wait`.

[ECOS07] points out two significant features of this example, and of the use of condition variables in general. First, the mutex unlock and wait in `cyg_cond_wait` are atomic: No other thread can run between the unlock and the wait. If this were not the case, then a call to `res_free` by some other thread would release the resource, but the call to `cyg_cond_signal` would be lost, and the first thread would end up waiting when there were resources available.

```
cyg_mutex_t res_lock;
res_t res_pool[RES_MAX];
int res_count = RES_MAX;
void res_init(void)
{
    cyg_mutex_init(&res_lock);
    <fill pool with resources>
}
res_t res_allocate(void)
{
    res_t res;

    cyg_mutex_lock(&res_lock);                          // lock the mutex

    if( res_count == 0 )                                // check for free resource
        res = RES_NONE;                                 // return RES_NONE if none
    else
    {
        res_count--;                                    // allocate a resources
        res = res_pool[res_count];
    }

    cyg_mutex_unlock(&res_lock);                        // unlock the mutex

    return res;
}

void res_free(res_t res)
{
    cyg_mutex_lock(&res_lock);                          // lock the mutex

    res_pool[res_count] = res;                          // free the resource
    res_count++;

    cyg_mutex_unlock(&res_lock);                        // unlock the mutex
}
```

Figure 13.8   Controlling Access to a Pool of Resources Using Mutexes

The second feature is that the call to cyg_cond_wait is in a while loop and not a simple if statement. This is because of the need to relock the mutex in cyg_cond_wait when the signaled thread reawakens. If there are other threads already queued to claim the lock, then this thread must wait. Depending on the scheduler and the queue order, many other threads may have entered the critical section before this one gets to run. So the condition that it was waiting for may have been rendered false. Using a loop around all condition variable wait operations is the only way to guarantee that the condition being waited for is still true after waiting.

EVENT FLAGS   An event flag is a 32-bit word used as a synchronization mechanism. Application code may associate a different event with each bit in a flag. A thread can wait for either a single event or a combination of events by checking one or multiple bits in the corresponding flag. The thread is blocked until all of the required bits are set (AND) or until at least one of the bits is set (OR). A signaling thread can set or reset bits based on specific conditions or events so that the appropriate

```
cyg_mutex_t res_lock;
cyg_cond_t res_wait;
res_t res_pool[RES_MAX];
int res_count = RES_MAX;

void res_init(void)
{
    cyg_mutex_init(&res_lock);
    cyg_cond_init(&res_wait, &res_lock);
    <fill pool with resources>
}

res_t res_allocate(void)
{
    res_t res;

    cyg_mutex_lock(&res_lock);                    //  lock the mutex

    while( res_count == 0 )                        //  wait for a resources
            cyg_cond_wait(&res_wait);

    res_count--;                                    //  allocate a resource
    res = res_pool[res_count];

    cyg_mutex_unlock(&res_lock);                   //  unlock the mutex

    return res;
}

void res_free(res_t res)
{
    cyg_mutex_lock(&res_lock);                     //  lock the mutex

    res_pool[res_count] = res;                     //  free the resource
    res_count++;

    cyg_cond_signal(&res_wait);                    //  wake up any waiting allocators

    cyg_mutex_unlock(&res_lock);                   //  unlock the mutex
}
```

Figure 13.9   Controlling Access to a Pool of Resources Using Mutexes and Condition Variables

thread is unblocked. For example, bit 0 could represent completion of a specific I/O operation, making data available, and bit 1 could indicate that the user has pressed a start button. A producer thread or DSR could set these two bits, and a consumer thread waiting on these two events will be woken up.

A thread can wait on one or more events using the cyg_flag_wait command, which takes three arguments: a particular event flag, a combination of bit positions in the flag, and a mode parameter. The mode parameter specifies whether the thread will block until all the bits are set (AND) or until at least one of the bits is set (OR). The mode parameter may also specify that when the wait succeeds, the entire event flag is cleared (set to all zeros).

MAILBOXES   Mailboxes, also called message boxes, are an eCos synchronization mechanism that provides a means for two threads to exchange information.

Section 5.5 provides a general discussion of message-passing synchronization. Here, we look at the specifics of the eCos version.

The eCos mailbox mechanism can be configured for blocking or nonblocking on both the send and receive side. The maximum size of the message queue associated with a given mailbox can also be configured.

The send message primitive, called put, includes two arguments: a handle to the mailbox and a pointer for the message itself. There are three variants to this primitive:

cyg_mbox_put	If there is a spare slot in the mailbox, then the new message is placed there; if there is a waiting thread, it will be woken up so that it can receive the message. If the mailbox is currently full, cyg_mbox_put blocks until there has been a corresponding get operation and a slot ids available.
cyg_mbox_timed_put	Same as cyg_mbox_put if there is a spare slot. Otherwise, the function will wait a specified time limit and place the message if a slot becomes available. If the time limit expires, the operation returns false. Thus, cyg_mbox_timed_ put is blocking only for less than or equal to a specified time interval.
cyg_mbox_tryput	This is a nonblocking version, which returns true if the message is sent successfully and false if the mailbox is full.

Similarly, there are three variants to the get primitive.

cyg_mbox_get	If there is a pending message in the specified mailbox, cyg_mbox_get returns with the message that was put into the mailbox. Otherwise this function blocks until there is a put operation.
cyg_mbox_timed_get	Immediately returns a message if one is available. Otherwise, the function will wait until either a message is available or until a number of clock ticks have occurred. If the time limit expires, the operation returns a null pointer. Thus, cyg_box_ timed_get is blocking only for less than or equal to a specified time interval.
cyg_mbox_tryget	This is a nonblocking version, which returns a message if one is available and a null pointer if the mailbox is empty.

SPINLOCKS   A spinlock is a flag that a thread can check before executing a particular piece of code. Recall from our discussion of Linux spinlocks in Chapter 6 the basic operation of the spinlock: Only one thread at a time can acquire a spinlock. Any other thread attempting to acquire the same lock will keep trying (spinning) until it can acquire the lock. In essence, a spinlock is built on an integer location in memory that is checked by each thread before it enters its critical section. If the value is 0, the thread sets the value to 1 and enters its critical section. If the value is nonzero, the thread continually checks the value until it is zero.

A spinlock should not be used on a single-processor system, which is why it is compiled away on Linux. As an example of the danger, consider a uniprocessor system with preemptive scheduling, in which a higher-priority thread attempts to acquire a spinlock already held by a lower priority thread. The lower-priority thread cannot execute so as to finish its work and release the spinlock, because the higher-priority thread preempts it. The higher-priority thread can execute but is stuck checking the spinlock. As a result, the higher-priority thread will just loop forever and the lower-priority thread will never get another chance to run and release the spinlock. On an SMP system, the current owner of a spinlock can continue running on a different processor.

13.4 TINYOS

The eCos system provides a more streamlined approach for an embedded OS than one based on a commercial general-purpose OS, such as an embedded version of Linux. Thus, eCos and similar systems are better suited for small embedded systems with tight requirements on memory, processing time, real-time response, power consumption, and so on. TinyOS takes the process of streamlining to a much further point, resulting in a very minimal OS for embedded systems. The core OS requires 400 bytes of code and data memory, combined.

TinyOS represents a significant departure from other embedded operating systems. One striking difference is that TinyOS is not a real-time OS. The reason for this is the expected workload, which is in the context of a wireless sensor network, as described in the next subsection. Because of power consumption, these devices are off most of the time. Applications tend to be simple, with processor contention not much of an issue.

Additionally, in TinyOS there is no kernel, as there is no memory protection and it is a component-based OS; there are no processes; the OS itself does not have a memory allocation system (although some rarely used components do introduce one); interrupt and exception handling is dependent on the peripheral; and it is completely nonblocking, so there are few explicit synchronization primitives.

TinyOS has become a popular approach to implementing wireless sensor network software. Currently, over 500 organizations are developing and contributing to an open source standard for Tiny OS.

Wireless Sensor Networks

TinyOS was developed primarily for use with networks of small wireless sensors. A number of trends have enabled the development of extremely compact, low-power sensors. The well-known Moore's law continues to drive down the size of memory and processing logic elements. Smaller size in turn reduces power consumption. Low power and small size trends are also evident in wireless communications hardware, micro-electromechanical sensors (MEMS), and transducers. As a result, it is possible to develop an entire sensor complete with logic in a cubic millimeter. The application and system software must be compact enough that sensing, communication, and computation capabilities can be incorporated into a complete, but tiny, architecture.

Low–cost, small–size, low-power-consuming wireless sensors can be used in a host of applications [ROME04]. Figure 13.10 shows a typical configuration. A base

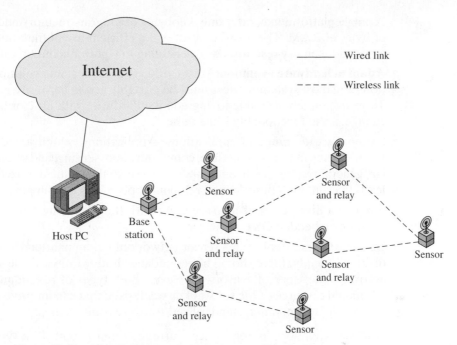

Figure 13.10   Typical Wireless Sensor Network Topology

station connects the sensor network to a host PC and passes on sensor data from the network to the host PC, which can do data analysis and/or transmit the data over a corporate network or Internet to an analysis server. Individual sensors collect data and transmit these to the base station, either directly or through sensors that act as data relays. Routing functionality is needed to determine how to relay the data through the sensor network to the base station. [BUON01] points out that, in many applications, the user will want to be able to quickly deploy a large number of low-cost devices without having to configure or manage them. This means that they must be capable of assembling themselves into an ad hoc network. The mobility of individual sensors and the presence of RF interference means that the network will have to be capable of reconfiguring itself in a matter of seconds.

TinyOS Goals

With the tiny, distributed sensor application in mind, a group of researchers from UC Berkeley [HILL00] set the following goals for TinyOS:

- **Allow high concurrency:** In a typical wireless sensor network application, the devices are concurrency intensive. Several different flows of data must be kept moving simultaneously. While sensor data are input in a steady stream, processed results must be transmitted in a steady stream. In addition, external controls from remote sensors or base stations must be managed.
- **Operate with limited resources:** The target platform for TinyOS will have limited memory and computational resources and run on batteries or solar power.

A single platform may offer only kilobytes of program memory and hundreds of bytes of RAM. The software must make efficient use of the available processor and memory resources while enabling low-power communication.

- **Adapt to hardware evolution:** Most hardware is in constant evolution; applications and most system services must be portable across hardware generations. Thus, it should be possible to upgrade the hardware with little or no software change, if the functionality is the same.

- **Support a wide range of applications:** Applications exhibit a wide range of requirements in terms of lifetime, communication, sensing, and so on. A modular, general-purpose embedded OS is desired so that a standardized approach leads to economies of scale in developing applications and support software.

- **Support a diverse set of platforms:** As with the preceding point, a general-purpose embedded OS is desirable.

- **Be robust:** Once deployed, a sensor network must run unattended for months or years. Ideally, there should be redundancy both within a single system and across the network of sensors. However, both types of redundancy require additional resources. One software characteristic that can improve robustness is to use highly modular, standardized software components.

It is worth elaborating on the concurrency requirement. In a typical application, there will be dozens, hundreds, or even thousands of sensors networked together. Usually, little buffering is done, because of latency issues. For example, if you are sampling every 5 minutes and want to buffer four samples before sending, the average latency is 10 minutes. Thus, information is typically captured, processed, and streamed onto the network in a continuous flow. Further, if the sensor sampling produces a significant amount of data, the limited memory space available limits the number of samples that could be buffered. Even so, in some applications, each of the flows may involve a large number of low-level events interleaved with higher-level processing. Some of the high-level processing will extend over multiple real-time events. Further, sensors in a network, because of the low power of transmission available, typically operate over a short physical range. Thus data from outlying sensors must be relayed to one or more base stations by intermediate nodes.

TinyOS Components

An embedded software system built using TinyOS consists of a set of small modules, called components, each of which performs a simple task or set of tasks and which interface with each other and with hardware in limited and well-defined ways. The only other software module is the scheduler, discussed subsequently. In fact, because there is no kernel, there is no actual OS. But we can take the following view. The application area of interest is the wireless sensor network (WSN). To meet the demanding software requirements of this application, a rigid, simplified software architecture is dictated, consisting of components. The TinyOS development community has implemented a number of open-source components that provide the basic functions needed for the WSN application. Examples of such standardized components include single-hop networking, ad-hoc routing, power management, timers, and nonvolatile storage control. For specific configurations and applications, users build additional special-purpose components and link and load all of the components needed for the user's application. TinyOS, then, consists of a suite of standardized components. Some but not all of these components are used, together with application-specific user-written components, for any given implementation. The OS for that implementation is simply the set of standardized components from the TinyOS suite.

All components in a TinyOS configuration have the same structure, an example of which is shown in Figure 13.11a. The shaded box in the diagram indicates the component, which is treated as an object that can only be accessed by defined interfaces, indicated by white boxes. A component may be hardware or software. Software components are implemented in nesC, which is an extension of C with two distinguishing features: a programming model where components interact via interfaces, and an event-based concurrency model with run-to-completion task and interrupt handlers, explained subsequently.

The architecture consists of a layered arrangement of components. Each component can link to only two other components, one below it in the hierarchy and one above it. A component issues commands to its lower-level component and receives event signals from it. Similarly, the component accepts commands from its upper-level

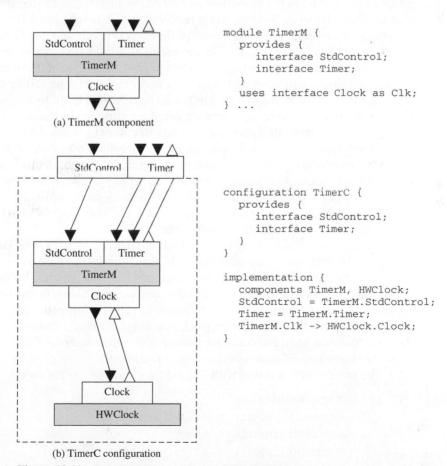

```
module TimerM {
    provides {
        interface StdControl;
        interface Timer;
    }
    uses interface Clock as Clk;
} ...
```

(a) TimerM component

```
configuration TimerC {
    provides {
        interface StdControl;
        interface Timer;
    }
}

implementation {
    components TimerM, HWClock;
    StdControl = TimerM.StdControl;
    Timer = TimerM.Timer;
    TimerM.Clk -> HWClock.Clock;
}
```

(b) TimerC configuration

Figure 13.11 Example Component and Configuration

component and issues event signals to it. At the bottom of the hierarchy are hardware components and at the top of the hierarchy are application components, which may not be part of the standardized TinyOS suite but which must conform to the TinyOS component structure.

A software component implements one or more tasks. Each **task** in a component is similar to a thread in an ordinary OS, with certain limitations. Within a component, tasks are atomic: Once a task has started, it runs to completion. It cannot be preempted by another task in the same component, and there is no time slicing. However, a task can be preempted by an event. A task cannot block or spin wait. These limitations greatly simplify the scheduling and management of tasks within a component. There is only a single stack, assigned to the currently running task. Tasks can perform computations, call lower-level components (commands) and signal higher-level events, and schedule other tasks.

Commands are nonblocking requests. That is, a task that issues a command does not block or spin wait for a reply from the lower-level component. A command is typically a request for the lower-level component to perform some service, such as initiating a sensor reading. The effect on the component that receives the command is specific to the command given and the task required to satisfy the command. Generally, when a command is received, a task is scheduled for later execution, because a command cannot preempt the currently running task. The command returns immediately to the calling component; at a later time, an event will signal completion to the calling component. Thus, a command does not cause a preemption in the called component and does not cause blocking in the calling component.

Events in TinyOS may be tied either directly or indirectly to hardware events. The lowest–level software components interface directly to hardware interrupts, which may be external interrupts, timer events, or counter events. An event handler in a lowest-level component may handle the interrupt itself or may propagate event messages up through the component hierarchy. A command can post a task that will signal an event in the future. In this case, there is no tie of any kind to a hardware event.

A task can be viewed as having three phases. A caller posts a command to a module. The module then runs the requested task. The module then notifies the caller, via an event, that the task is complete.

The component depicted in Figure 13.11a, TimerM, is part of the TinyOS timer service. This component **provides** the StdControl and Timer interface and **uses** a Clock interface. Providers implement commands (i.e., the logic in this component). Users implement events (i.e., external to the component). Many TinyOS components use the StdControl interface to be initialized, started, or stopped. TimerM provides the logic that maps from a hardware clock into TinyOS's timer abstraction. The timer abstraction can be used for counting down a given time interval. Figure 13.11a also shows the formal specification of the TimerM interfaces.

The interfaces associated with TimerM are specified as follows:

```
interface StdControl {
    command result_t init();
    command result_t start();
    command result_t stop();
}
```

```
interface Timer {
    command result_t start(char type, uint32_t interval);
    command result_t stop();
    event result_t fired();
}
interface Clock {
    command result_t setRate(char interval, char scale);
    event result_t fire();
}
```

Components are organized into configurations by "wiring" them together at their interfaces and equating the interfaces of the configuration with some of the interfaces of the components. A simple example is shown in Figure 13.11b. The uppercase C stands for Component. It is used to distinguish between an interface (e.g., Timer) and a component that provides the interface (e.g., TimerC).The uppercase M stands for Module. This naming convention is used when a single logical component has both a configuration and a module. The TimerC component, providing the Timer interface, is a configuration that links its implementation (TimerM) to Clock and LED providers. Otherwise, any user of TimerC would have to explicitly wire its subcomponents.

TinyOS Scheduler

The TinyOS scheduler operates across all components. Virtually all embedded systems using TinyOS will be uniprocessor systems, so that only one task among all the tasks in all the components may execute at a time. The scheduler is a separate component. It is the one portion of TinyOS that must be present in any system.

The default scheduler in TinyOS is a simple FIFO (first-in-first-out) queue. A task is posted to the scheduler (place in the queue) either as a result of an event, which triggers the posting, or as a result of a specific request by a running task to schedule another task. The scheduler is power aware. This means that the scheduler puts the processor to sleep when there are no tasks in the queue. The peripherals remain operating, so that one of them can wake up the system by means of a hardware event signaled to a lowest-level component. Once the queue is empty, another task can be scheduled only as a result of a direct hardware event. This behavior enables efficient battery usage.

The scheduler has gone through two generations. In TinyOS 1.x, there is a shared task queue for all tasks, and a component can post a task to the scheduler multiple times. If the task queue is full, the post operation fails. Experience with networking stacks showed this to be problematic, as the task might signal completion of a split-phase operation: If the post fails, the component above might block forever, waiting for the completion event. In TinyOS 2.x, every task has its own reserved slot in the task queue, and a task can only be posted once. A post fails if and only if the task has already been posted. If a component needs to post a task multiple times, it can set an internal state variable so that when the task executes, it reposts itself. This slight change in semantics greatly simplifies a lot of component code. Rather than test to see if a task is posted already before posting it, a component can just post the task. Components do not have to try to recover from failed posts and retry. The cost is one byte of state per task.

A user can replace the default scheduler with one that uses a different dispatching scheme, such as a priority-based scheme or a deadline scheme. However, preemption and time slicing should not be used because of the overhead such systems generate. More importantly, they violate the TinyOS concurrency model, which assumes tasks do not preempt each other.

Example Configuration

Figure 13.12 shows a configuration assembled from software and hardware components. This simplified example, called Surge and described in [GAY03], performs

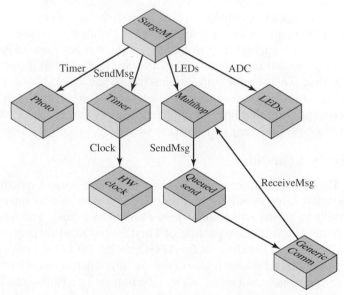

(a) Simplified view of the Surge Application

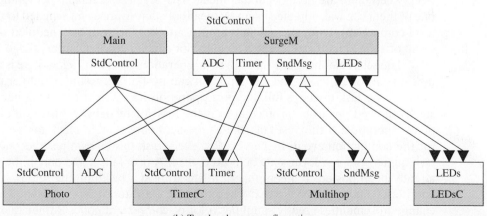

(b) Top-level surge configuration

LED = light-emitting diode
ADC = analog-to-digital converter

Figure 13.12   Examples TinyOS Application

periodic sensor sampling and uses ad-hoc multihop routing over the wireless network to deliver samples to the base station. The upper part of the figure shows the components of Surge (represented by boxes) and the interfaces by which they are wired (represented by arrowed lines). The SurgeM component is the application-level component that orchestrates the operation of the configuration.

Figure 13.12b shows a portion of the configuration for the Surge application. The following is a simplified excerpt from the SurgeM specification.

```
module SurgeM {
    provides interface StdControl;
    uses interface ADC;
    uses interface Timer;
    uses interface SendMsg;
    uses interface LEDs;
}
implementation {
    uint16_t sensorReading;
    command result_t StdControl.init() {
    return call Timer.start(TIMER_REPEAT, 1000);
    }
    event result_t Timer.fired() {
    call ADC.getData();
    return SUCCESS;
    }
    event result_t ADC.dataReady(uint16_t data) {
    sensorReading = data;
    ...send message with data in it...
    return SUCCESS;
    }
    ...
}
```

This example illustrates the strength of the TinyOS approach. The software is organized as an interconnected set of simple modules, each of which defines one or a few tasks. Components have simple, standardized interfaces to other components, be they hardware or software. Thus, components can easily be replaced. Components can be hardware or software, with a boundary change not visible to the application programmer.

TinyOS Resource Interface

TinyOS provides a simple but powerful set of conventions for dealing with resources. Three abstractions for resources are used in TinyOS:

- **Dedicated:** A resource that a subsystem needs exclusive access to at all times. In this class of resources, no sharing policy is needed since only a single component ever requires use of the resource. Examples of dedicated abstractions include interrupts and counters.

- **Virtualized:** Every client of a virtualized resource interacts with it as if it were a dedicated resource, with all virtualized instances being multiplexed on top of a single underlying resource. The virtualized abstraction may be used when the underlying resource need not be protected by mutual exclusion. An example is a clock or timer.

- **Shared:** The shared resource abstraction provides access to a dedicated resource through an arbiter component. The arbiter enforces mutual exclusion, allowing only one user (called a client) at a time to have access to a resource and enabling the client to lock the resource.

In the remainder of this subsection, we briefly define the shared resource facility of TinyOS. The arbiter determines which client has access to the resource at which time. While a client holds a resource, it has complete and unfettered control. Arbiters assume that clients are cooperative, only acquiring the resource when needed and holding on to it no longer than necessary. Clients explicitly release resources: There is no way for an arbiter to forcibly reclaim it.

Figure 13.13 shows a simplified view of the shared resource configuration used to provide access to an underlying resource. Associated with each resource to be shared is an arbiter component. The arbiter enforces a policy that enables a client to lock

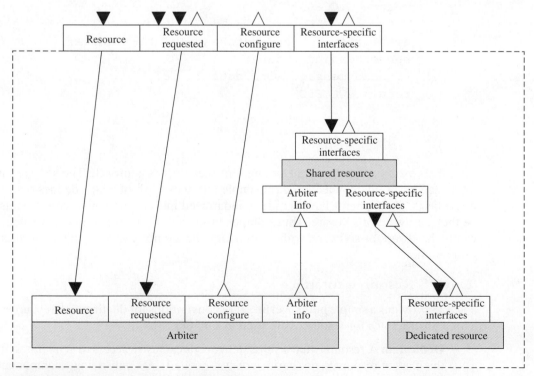

Figure 13.13   Shared Resource Configuration

the resource, use it, and then release the resource. The shared resource configuration provides the following interfaces to a client:

- **Resource:** The client issues a request at this interface, requesting access to the resource. If the resource is currently locked, the arbiter places the request in a queue. When a client is finished with the resource, it issues a release command at this interface.

- **Resource requested:** This is similar to the Resource interface. In this case, the client is able to hold on to a resource until the client is notified that someone else needs the resource.

- **Resource configure:** This interface allows a resource to be automatically configured just before a client is granted access to it. Components providing the ResourceConfigure interface use the interfaces provided by an underlying dedicated resource to configure it into one of its desired modes of operation.

- **Resource-specific interfaces:** Once a client has access to a resource, it uses resource-specific interfaces to exchange data and control information with the resource.

In addition to the dedicated resource, the shared resource configuration consists of two components. The Arbiter accepts requests for access and configuration from a client and enforces the lock on the underlying resource. The shared resource component mediates data exchange between the client and the underlying resource. Arbiter information passed from the arbiter to the shared resource component controls the access of the client to the underlying resource.

13.5 RECOMMENDED READING AND WEB SITES

[KOOP96] provides a systematic discussion of the requirements for embedded systems. [STAN96] is a useful overview of real-time and embedded systems.

[MASS03] and [ECOS07] both provide a detailed description of eCos internals. [THOM01] provides a brief overview with some code examples from the kernel. [LARM05] gives a more detailed description of the eCos configuration process.

[HILL00] gives an overview and design rationale for TinyOS. [GAY05] is an interesting discussion of software design strategies using TinyOS. [BUON01] provides a good example of the use of TinyOS in building a network or wireless sensors. Two excellent references for the current version of TinyOS are [GAY03] and [LEVI05].

BUON01   Buonadonna, P. Hill, J. and Culler, D. "Active Message Communication for Tiny Networked Sensors." *Proceedings, IEEE INFOCOM 2001*, April 2001

ECOS07   eCosCentric Limited, and Red Hat, Inc. *eCos Reference Manual*, 2007. http://www.ecoscentric.com/ecospro/doc/html/ref/ecos-ref.html

GAY03   Gay, D., et al. "The nesC Language: A Holistic Approach to Networked Embedded Systems." *Proceedings of the ACM SIGPLAN 2003 Conference on Programming Language Design and Implementation*, 2003.

GAY05 Gay, D., Levis, P., and Culler, D. "Software Design Patterns for TinyOS." *Proceedings, Conference on Languages, Compilers, and Tools for Embedded Systems*, 2005.

HILL00 Hill, J., et al. "System Architecture Directions for Networked Sensors." *Proceedings, Architectural Support for Programming Languages and Operating Systems*, 2000.

KOOP96 Koopman, P. "Embedded System Design Issues (the Rest of the Story)." *Proceedings, 1996 International Conference on Computer Design*, 1996.

LARM05 Larmour, J. "How eCos Can Be Shrunk to Fit." *Embedded Systems Europe*, May 2005. www.embedded.com/europe/esemay05.htm

LEVI05 Levis, P., et al. "T2: A Second Generation OS for Embedded Sensor Networks." Technical Report TKN-05-007, Telecommunication Networks Group, Technische Universitat Berlin, 2005. http://csl.stanford.edu/~pal/pubs.html

MASS03 Massa, A. *Embedded Software Development with eCos.* Upper Saddle River, NJ: Prentice Hall, 2003.

STAN96 Stankovic, J., et al. "Strategic Directions in Real-Time and Embedded Systems." *ACM Computing Surveys*, December 1996.

THOM01 Thomas, G. "eCos: An Operating System for Embedded Systems." *Dr. Dobb's Journal*, January 2001.

Recommended Web sites:

- **Embedded.com:** Wide variety of information on embedded systems
- **eCos:** Downloadable software, information, and links on eCos
- **TinyOS Community Forum:** Downloadable software, information, and links on TinyOS

13.6 KEY TERMS, REVIEW QUESTIONS, AND PROBLEMS

Key Terms

eCos	embedded system
embedded operating system	TinyOS

Review Questions

13.1 What is an embedded system?

13.2 What are some typical requirements or constraints on embedded systems?

13.3 What is an embedded OS?

13.4 What are some of the key characteristics of an embedded OS?

13.5 Explain the relative advantages and disadvantages of an embedded OS based on an existing commercial OS compared to a purpose-built embedded OS.

13.6 What are the principal objectives that guided the design of the eCos kernel?

13.7 In eCos, what is the difference between an interrupt service routine and a deferred service routine?

13.8 What concurrency mechanisms are available in eCos?

13.9 What is the target application for TinyOS?

13.10 What are the design goals for TinyOS?

13.11 What is a TinyOS component?

13.12 What software comprises the TinyOS operating system?

13.13 What is the default scheduling discipline for TinyOS?

Problems

13.1 With reference to the device driver interface to the eCos kernel (Table 13.2), it is recommended that device drivers should use the `_intsave()` variants to claim and release spinlocks rather than the non-`_intsave()` variants. Explain why.

13.2 Also in Table 13.2, it is recommended that `cyg_drv_spinlock_spin` should be used sparingly, and in situations where deadlocks/livelocks cannot occur. Explain why.

13.3 In Table 13.2, what should be the limitations on the use of `cyg_drv_spinlock_destroy`? Explain.

13.4 In Table 13.2, what limitations should be placed in the use of `cyg_drv_mutex_destroy`?

13.5 Why does the eCos bitmap scheduler not support time slicing?

13.6 The implementation of mutexes within the eCos kernel does not support recursive locks. If a thread has locked a mutex and then attempts to lock the mutex again, typically as a result of some recursive call in a complicated call graph, then either an assertion failure will be reported or the thread will deadlock. Suggest a reason for this policy.

13.7 Figure 13.14 is a listing of code intended for use on the eCos kernel.
  a. Explain the operation of the code. Assume thread B begins execution first and thread A begins to execute after some event occurs.
  b. What would happen if the mutex unlock and wait code execution in the call to cyg_cond_wait, on line 30, were not atomic?
  c. Why is the while loop on line 26 needed?

13.8 The discussion of eCos spinlocks included an example showing why spinlocks should not be used on a uniprocessor system if two threads of different priorities can compete for the same spinlock. Explain why the problem still exists even if only threads of the same priority can claim the same spinlock.

13.9 TinyOS's scheduler serves tasks in FIFO order. Many other schedulers for TinyOS have been proposed, but none have caught on. What characteristics of the sensornet domain might cause a lack of need for more complex scheduling?

13.10 a. The TinyOS Resource interface does not allow a component that already has a request in the queue for a resource to make a second request. Suggest a reason.

b. However, the TinyOS Resource interface allows a component holding the resource lock to re-request the lock. This request is enqueued for a later grant. Suggest a reason for this policy. *Hint:* What might cause there to be latency between one component releasing a lock and the next requester being granted it?

```
1    unsigned char buffer_empty = true;
2    cyg_mutex_t mut_cond_var;
3    cyg_cond-t cond_var;
4
5    void thread_a( cyg_addrword_t index )
6    {
7      while ( 1 ) // run this thread forever
8      {
9          // acquire data into the buffer…
10
11         // there is data in the buffer now
12         buffer_empty = false;
13
14         cyg_mutex_lock( &mut_cond_var );
15
16         cyg_cond_signal( &cond_var );
17
18         cyg_mutex_unlock( &mut_cond_var );
19     }
20   }
21
22   void thread_b( cyg_addrword_t index )
23   {
24     while ( 1 ) // run this thread forever
25     {
26         cyg_mutex_lock( &mut_cond_var );
27
28         while ( buffer_empty == true )
29         {
30         cyg_cond_wait( &cond_var );
31         }
32
33
34         // get the buffer data…
35
36         // set flag to indicate the data in the buffer has been processed
37         buffer_empty = true;
38
39         cyg_mutex_unlock( &mut_cond_var );
40
41         // process the data in the buffer
42     }
43   {
```

Figure 13.14   Condition Variable Example Code

PART 7 Computer Security

CHAPTER 14

COMPUTER SECURITY THREATS

14.1 Computer Security Concepts

14.2 Threats, Attacks, and Assets
Threats and Attacks
Threats and Assets

14.3 Intruders
Intruder Behavior Patterns
Intrusion Techniques

14.4 Malicious Software Overview
Backdoor
Logic Bomb
Trojan Horse
Mobile Code
Multiple-Threat Malware

14.5 Viruses, Worms, and Bots
Viruses
Worms
Bots

14.6 Rootkits
Rootkit Installation
System-Level Call Attacks

14.6 Recommended Reading and Web Sites

14.7 Key Terms, Review Questions, and Problems

The art of war teaches us to rely not on the likelihood of the enemy's not coming, but on our own readiness to receive him; not on the chance of his not attacking, but rather on the fact that we have made our position unassailable.

— *THE ART OF WAR*, SUN TZU

LEARNING OBJECTIVES

After studying this chapter, you should be able to:

- List and explain the key concepts that comprise computer security.
- Understand the spectrum of computer security attacks.
- Distinguish among various types of intruder behavior patterns and understand the types of intrusion techniques used to breach computer security.
- Summarize the principal types of malicious software.
- Present an overview of viruses, including typical virus structure and typical virus behavior.
- Understand the security threat posed by worms.
- Understand the security threat posed by bots.
- Explain key aspects of rootkits.

This chapter provides an overview of security threats. We begin with a discussion of what we mean by computer security. In essence, computer security deals with computer-related assets that are subject to a variety of threats and for which various measures are taken to protect those assets. The remainder of the chapter looks at the two broad categories of computer and network security threats: intruders and malicious software.

Cryptographic algorithms, such as encryption and hash functions, play a role both in computer security threats and computer security techniques. Appendix K provides an overview of these algorithms.

14.1 COMPUTER SECURITY CONCEPTS

The NIST *Computer Security Handbook* [NIST95] defines the term *computer security* as follows:

Computer security: The protection afforded to an automated information system in order to attain the applicable objectives of preserving the integrity, availability, and confidentiality of information system resources (includes hardware, software, firmware, information/data, and telecommunications).

This definition introduces three key objectives that are at the heart of computer security:

- **Confidentiality:** This term covers two related concepts:
  - **Data**[1] **confidentiality:** Assures that private or confidential information is not made available or disclosed to unauthorized individuals
  - **Privacy:** Assures that individuals control or influence what information related to them may be collected and stored and by whom and to whom that information may be disclosed

- **Integrity:** This term covers two related concepts:
  - **Data integrity:** Assures that information and programs are changed only in a specified and authorized manner
  - **System integrity:** Assures that a system performs its intended function in an unimpaired manner, free from deliberate or inadvertent unauthorized manipulation of the system

- **Availability:** Assures that systems work promptly and service is not denied to authorized users

These three concepts form what is often referred to as the **CIA triad** (Figure 14.1). The three concepts embody the fundamental security objectives for both data and for information and computing services. For example, the NIST standard FIPS 199 (*Standards for Security Categorization of Federal Information and Information Systems*) lists confidentiality, integrity, and availability as the three security objectives for information and for information systems. FIPS PUB 199 provides a useful characterization

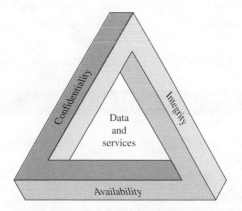

Figure 14.1   The Security Requirements Triad

---

[1]RFC 2828 (*Internet Security Glossary*) defines *information* as "facts and ideas, which can be represented (encoded) as various forms of data," and *data* as "information in a specific physical representation, usually a sequence of symbols that have meaning; especially a representation of information that can be processed or produced by a computer." Security literature typically does not make much of a distinction; nor does this chapter.

of these three objectives in terms of requirements and the definition of a loss of security in each category:

- **Confidentiality:** Preserving authorized restrictions on information access and disclosure, including means for protecting personal privacy and proprietary information. A loss of confidentiality is the unauthorized disclosure of information.
- **Integrity:** Guarding against improper information modification or destruction, including ensuring information nonrepudiation and authenticity. A loss of integrity is the unauthorized modification or destruction of information.
- **Availability:** Ensuring timely and reliable access to and use of information. A loss of availability is the disruption of access to or use of information or an information system.

Although the use of the CIA triad to define security objectives is well established, some in the security field feel that additional concepts are needed to present a complete picture. Two of the most commonly mentioned are as follows:

- **Authenticity:** The property of being genuine and being able to be verified and trusted; confidence in the validity of a transmission, a message, or message originator. This means verifying that users are who they say they are and that each input arriving at the system came from a trusted source.
- **Accountability:** The security goal that generates the requirement for actions of an entity to be traced uniquely to that entity. This supports nonrepudiation, deterrence, fault isolation, intrusion detection and prevention, and after-action recovery and legal action. Because truly secure systems aren't yet an achievable goal, we must be able to trace a security breach to a responsible party. Systems must keep records of their activities to permit later forensic analysis to trace security breaches or to aid in transaction disputes.

Note that FIPS PUB 199 includes authenticity under integrity.

14.2 THREATS, ATTACKS, AND ASSETS

We turn now to a look at threats, attacks, and assets as related to computer security.

Threats and Attacks

Table 14.1, based on RFC 2828, describes four kinds of threat consequences and lists the kinds of attacks that result in each consequence.

Unauthorized disclosure is a threat to confidentiality. The following types of attacks can result in this threat consequence:

- **Exposure:** This can be deliberate, as when an insider intentionally releases sensitive information, such as credit card numbers, to an outsider. It can also be the result of a human, hardware, or software error, which results in an entity gaining unauthorized knowledge of sensitive data. There have been numerous instances

Table 14.1   Threat Consequences, and the Types of Threat Actions that Cause Each Consequence (Based on RFC 2828)

Threat Consequence	Threat Action (Attack)
Unauthorized Disclosure A circumstance or event whereby an entity gains access to data for which the entity is not authorized.	**Exposure:** Sensitive data are directly released to an unauthorized entity. **Interception:** An unauthorized entity directly accesses sensitive data, traveling between authorized sources and destinations. **Inference:** A threat action whereby an unauthorized entity indirectly accesses sensitive data (but not necessarily the data contained in the communication) by reasoning from characteristics or by-products of communications. **Intrusion:** An unauthorized entity gains access to sensitive data by circumventing a system's security protections.
Deception A circumstance or event that may result in an authorized entity receiving false data and believing it to be true.	**Masquerade:** An unauthorized entity gains access to a system or performs a malicious act by posing as an authorized entity. **Falsification:** False data deceive an authorized entity. **Repudiation:** An entity deceives another by falsely denying responsibility for an act.
Disruption A circumstance or event that interrupts or prevents the correct operation of system services and functions.	**Incapacitation:** Prevents or interrupts system operation by disabling a system component. **Corruption:** Undesirably alters system operation by adversely modifying system functions or data. **Obstruction:** A threat action that interrupts delivery of system services by hindering system operation.
Usurpation A circumstance or event that results in control of system services or functions by an unauthorized entity.	**Misappropriation:** An entity assumes unauthorized logical or physical control of a system resource. **Misuse:** Causes a system component to perform a function or service that is detrimental to system security.

of this, such as universities accidentally posting student confidential information on the Web.

- **Interception:** Interception is a common attack in the context of communications. On a shared local area network (LAN), such as a wireless LAN or a broadcast Ethernet, any device attached to the LAN can receive a copy of packets intended for another device. On the Internet, a determined hacker can gain access to e-mail traffic and other data transfers. All of these situations create the potential for unauthorized access to data.

- **Inference:** An example of inference is known as traffic analysis, in which an adversary is able to gain information from observing the pattern of traffic on a network, such as the amount of traffic between particular pairs of hosts on the network. Another example is the inference of detailed information from a database by a user who has only limited access; this is accomplished by repeated queries whose combined results enable inference.

- **Intrusion:** An example of intrusion is an adversary gaining unauthorized access to sensitive data by overcoming the system's access control protections.

Deception is a threat to either system integrity or data integrity. The following types of attacks can result in this threat consequence:

- **Masquerade:** One example of masquerade is an attempt by an unauthorized user to gain access to a system by posing as an authorized user; this could happen if the unauthorized user has learned another user's logon ID and password. Another example is malicious logic, such as a Trojan horse, that appears to perform a useful or desirable function but actually gains unauthorized access to system resources or tricks a user into executing other malicious logic.

- **Falsification:** This refers to the altering or replacing of valid data or the introduction of false data into a file or database. For example, a student may alter his or her grades on a school database.

- **Repudiation:** In this case, a user either denies sending data or a user denies receiving or possessing the data.

Disruption is a threat to availability or system integrity. The following types of attacks can result in this threat consequence:

- **Incapacitation:** This is an attack on system availability. This could occur as a result of physical destruction of or damage to system hardware. More typically, malicious software, such as Trojan horses, viruses, or worms, could operate in such a way as to disable a system or some of its services.

- **Corruption:** This is an attack on system integrity. Malicious software in this context could operate in such a way that system resources or services function in an unintended manner. Or a user could gain unauthorized access to a system and modify some of its functions. An example of the latter is a user placing backdoor logic in the system to provide subsequent access to a system and its resources by other than the usual procedure.

- **Obstruction:** One way to obstruct system operation is to interfere with communications by disabling communication links or altering communication control information. Another way is to overload the system by placing excess burden on communication traffic or processing resources.

Usurpation is a threat to system integrity. The following types of attacks can result in this threat consequence:

- **Misappropriation:** This can include theft of service. An example is a distributed denial of service attack, when malicious software is installed on a number of hosts to be used as platforms to launch traffic at a target host. In this case, the malicious software makes unauthorized use of processor and operating system resources.

- **Misuse:** Misuse can occur either by means of malicious logic or a hacker that has gained unauthorized access to a system. In either case, security functions can be disabled or thwarted.

Threats and Assets

The assets of a computer system can be categorized as hardware, software, data, and communication lines and networks. In this subsection, we briefly describe these four categories and relate these to the concepts of integrity, confidentiality, and availability introduced in Section 14.1 (see Figure 14.2 and Table 14.2).

HARDWARE   A major threat to computer system hardware is the threat to availability. Hardware is the most vulnerable to attack and the least susceptible to automated controls. Threats include accidental and deliberate damage to equipment as well as theft. The proliferation of personal computers and workstations and the widespread use of LANs increase the potential for losses in this area. Theft of CD-ROMs and DVDs can lead to loss of confidentiality. Physical and administrative security measures are needed to deal with these threats.

SOFTWARE   Software includes the operating system, utilities, and application programs. A key threat to software is an attack on availability. Software, especially application software, is often easy to delete. Software can also be altered or damaged to render it useless. Careful software configuration management, which includes making backups of the most recent version of software, can maintain high availability. A more difficult problem to deal with is software modification that results in a program that still functions but that behaves differently than before, which is a threat to integrity/authenticity. Computer viruses and related attacks fall into this category. A final problem is protection against software piracy. Although

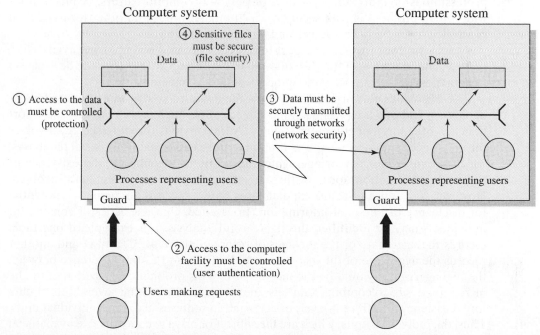

Figure 14.2   Scope of System Security

Table 14.2 Computer and Network Assets, with Examples of Threats

	Availability	Confidentiality	Integrity
Hardware	Equipment is stolen or disabled, thus denying service.		
Software	Programs are deleted, denying access to users.	An unauthorized copy of software is made.	A working program is modified, either to cause it to fail during execution or to cause it to do some unintended task.
Data	Files are deleted, denying access to users.	An unauthorized read of data is performed. An analysis of statistical data reveals underlying data.	Existing files are modified or new files are fabricated.
Communication Lines	Messages are destroyed or deleted. Communication lines or networks are rendered unavailable.	Messages are read. The traffic pattern of messages is observed.	Messages are modified, delayed, reordered, or duplicated. False messages are fabricated.

certain countermeasures are available, by and large the problem of unauthorized copying of software has not been solved.

DATA   Hardware and software security are typically concerns of computing center professionals or individual concerns of personal computer users. A much more widespread problem is data security, which involves files and other forms of data controlled by individuals, groups, and business organizations.

Security concerns with respect to data are broad, encompassing availability, secrecy, and integrity. In the case of availability, the concern is with the destruction of data files, which can occur either accidentally or maliciously.

The obvious concern with secrecy is the unauthorized reading of data files or databases, and this area has been the subject of perhaps more research and effort than any other area of computer security. A less obvious threat to secrecy involves the analysis of data and manifests itself in the use of so-called statistical databases, which provide summary or aggregate information. Presumably, the existence of aggregate information does not threaten the privacy of the individuals involved. However, as the use of statistical databases grows, there is an increasing potential for disclosure of personal information. In essence, characteristics of constituent individuals may be identified through careful analysis. For example, if one table records the aggregate of the incomes of respondents A, B, C, and D and another records the aggregate of the incomes of A, B, C, D, and E, the difference between the two aggregates would be the income of E. This problem is exacerbated by the increasing desire to combine data sets. In many cases, matching several sets of data for consistency at different levels of aggregation requires access to individual units. Thus, the individual units, which are the subject of privacy concerns, are available at various stages in the processing of data sets.

Finally, data integrity is a major concern in most installations. Modifications to data files can have consequences ranging from minor to disastrous.

COMMUNICATION LINES AND NETWORKS Network security attacks can be classified as *passive attacks* and *active attacks*. A passive attack attempts to learn or make use of information from the system but does not affect system resources. An active attack attempts to alter system resources or affect their operation.

Passive attacks are in the nature of eavesdropping on, or monitoring of, transmissions. The goal of the attacker is to obtain information that is being transmitted. Two types of passive attacks are release of message contents and traffic analysis.

The concept of **release of message contents** is easily understood. A telephone conversation, an electronic mail message, and a transferred file may contain sensitive or confidential information. We would like to prevent an opponent from learning the contents of these transmissions.

Traffic analysis is a more subtle form of passive attack. Suppose that we had a way of masking the contents of messages or other information traffic so that opponents, even if they captured the message, could not extract the information from the message. The common technique for masking contents is encryption. If we had encryption protection in place, an opponent might still be able to observe the pattern of these messages. The opponent could determine the location and identity of communicating hosts and could observe the frequency and length of messages being exchanged. This information might be useful in guessing the nature of the communication that was taking place.

Passive attacks are very difficult to detect because they do not involve any alteration of the data. Typically, the message traffic is sent and received in an apparently normal fashion, and neither the sender nor the receiver is aware that a third party has read the messages or observed the traffic pattern. However, it is feasible to prevent the success of these attacks, usually by means of encryption. Thus, the emphasis in dealing with passive attacks is on prevention rather than detection.

Active attacks involve some modification of the data stream or the creation of a false stream and can be subdivided into four categories: replay, masquerade, modification of messages, and denial of service.

Replay involves the passive capture of a data unit and its subsequent retransmission to produce an unauthorized effect.

A **masquerade** takes place when one entity pretends to be a different entity. A masquerade attack usually includes one of the other forms of active attack. For example, authentication sequences can be captured and replayed after a valid authentication sequence has taken place, thus enabling an authorized entity with few privileges to obtain extra privileges by impersonating an entity that has those privileges.

Modification of messages simply means that some portion of a legitimate message is altered, or that messages are delayed or reordered, to produce an unauthorized effect. For example, a message stating, "Allow John Smith to read confidential file `accounts`" is modified to say, "Allow Fred Brown to read confidential file `accounts`."

The **denial of service** prevents or inhibits the normal use or management of communications facilities. This attack may have a specific target; for example, an entity may suppress all messages directed to a particular destination (e.g., the security audit service). Another form of service denial is the disruption of an entire network, either by disabling the network or by overloading it with messages so as to degrade performance.

Active attacks present the opposite characteristics of passive attacks. Whereas passive attacks are difficult to detect, measures are available to prevent their success. On the other hand, it is quite difficult to prevent active attacks absolutely, because to do so would require physical protection of all communications facilities and paths at all times. Instead, the goal is to detect them and to recover from any disruption or delays caused by them. Because the detection has a deterrent effect, it may also contribute to prevention.

14.3 INTRUDERS

The concept of intruder was introduced in Section 3.6. [GRAN04] lists the following examples of intrusion:

- Performing a remote root compromise of an e-mail server
- Defacing a Web server
- Guessing and cracking passwords
- Copying a database containing credit card numbers
- Viewing sensitive data, including payroll records and medical information, without authorization
- Running a packet sniffer on a workstation to capture usernames and passwords
- Using a permission error on an anonymous FTP server to distribute pirated software and music files
- Dialing into an unsecured modem and gaining internal network access
- Posing as an executive, calling the help desk, resetting the executive's e-mail password, and learning the new password
- Using an unattended, logged-in workstation without permission

Intruder Behavior Patterns

The techniques and behavior patterns of intruders are constantly shifting, to exploit newly discovered weaknesses and to evade detection and countermeasures. Even so, intruders typically follow one of a number of recognizable behavior patterns, and these patterns typically differ from those of ordinary users. In the following, we look at three broad examples of intruder behavior patterns to give the reader some feel for the challenge facing the security administrator. Table 14.3, based on [RADC04], summarizes the behavior.

HACKERS Traditionally, those who hack into computers do so for the thrill of it or for status. The hacking community is a strong meritocracy in which status is determined by level of competence. Thus, attackers often look for targets of opportunity and then share the information with others. A typical example is a

Table 14.3 Some Examples of Intruder Patterns of Behavior

(a) Hacker

1. Select the target using IP lookup tools such as NSLookup, Dig, and others.
2. Map network for accessible services using tools such as NMAP.
3. Identify potentially vulnerable services (in this case, pcAnywhere).
4. Brute force (guess) pcAnywhere password.
5. Install remote administration tool called DameWare.
6. Wait for administrator to log on and capture his or her password.
7. Use that password to access remainder of network.

(b) Criminal Enterprise

1. Act quickly and precisely to make their activities harder to detect.
2. Exploit perimeter through vulnerable ports.
3. Use Trojan horses (hidden software) to leave backdoors for reentry.
4. Use sniffers to capture passwords.
5. Do not stick around until noticed.
6. Make few or no mistakes.

(c) Internal Threat

1. Create network accounts for themselves and their friends.
2. Access accounts and applications they wouldn't normally use for their daily jobs.
3. E-mail former and prospective employers.
4. Conduct furtive instant-messaging chats.
5. Visit Web sites that cater to disgruntled employees, such as f'dcompany.com.
6. Perform large downloads and file copying.
7. Access the network during off hours.

break-in at a large financial institution reported in [RADC04]. The intruder took advantage of the fact that the corporate network was running unprotected services, some of which were not even needed. In this case, the key to the break-in was the pcAnywhere application. The manufacturer, Symantec, advertises this program as a remote control solution that enables secure connection to remote devices. But the attacker had an easy time gaining access to pcAnywhere; the administrator used the same three-letter username and password for the program. In this case, there was no intrusion detection system on the 700-node corporate network. The intruder was only discovered when a vice president walked into her office and saw the cursor moving files around on her Windows workstation.

Benign intruders might be tolerable, although they do consume resources and may slow performance for legitimate users. However, there is no way in advance to know whether an intruder will be benign or malign. Consequently, even for systems with no particularly sensitive resources, there is a motivation to control this problem.

Intrusion detection systems (IDSs) and intrusion prevention systems (IPSs), of the type described in this Chapter 15, are designed to counter this type of hacker threat. In addition to using such systems, organizations can consider restricting remote logons to specific IP addresses and/or use virtual private network technology.

One of the results of the growing awareness of the intruder problem has been the establishment of a number of computer emergency response teams (CERTs). These cooperative ventures collect information about system vulnerabilities and disseminate it to systems managers. Hackers also routinely read CERT reports. Thus, it is important for system administrators to quickly insert all software patches to discovered vulnerabilities. Unfortunately, given the complexity of many IT systems and the rate at which patches are released, this is increasingly difficult to achieve without automated updating. Even then, there are problems caused by incompatibilities resulting from the updated software (hence the need for multiple layers of defense in managing security threats to IT systems).

CRIMINALS   Organized groups of hackers have become a widespread and common threat to Internet-based systems. These groups can be in the employ of a corporation or government but often are loosely affiliated gangs of hackers. Typically, these gangs are young, often Eastern European, Russian, or southeast Asian hackers who do business on the Web [ANTE06]. They meet in underground forums with names like DarkMarket.org and theftservices.com to trade tips and data and coordinate attacks. A common target is a credit card file at an e-commerce server. Attackers attempt to gain root access. The card numbers are used by organized crime gangs to purchase expensive items and are then posted to carder sites, where others can access and use the account numbers; this obscures usage patterns and complicates investigation.

Whereas traditional hackers look for targets of opportunity, criminal hackers usually have specific targets, or at least classes of targets in mind. Once a site is penetrated, the attacker acts quickly, scooping up as much valuable information as possible and exiting.

IDSs and IPSs can also be used for these types of attackers but may be less effective because of the quick in-and-out nature of the attack. For e-commerce sites, database encryption should be used for sensitive customer information, especially credit cards. For hosted e-commerce sites (provided by an outsider service), the e-commerce organization should make use of a dedicated server (not used to support multiple customers) and closely monitor the provider's security services.

INSIDER ATTACKS   Insider attacks are among the most difficult to detect and prevent. Employees already have access to and knowledge of the structure and content of corporate databases. Insider attacks can be motivated by revenge or simply a feeling of entitlement. An example of the former is the case of Kenneth Patterson, fired from his position as data communications manager for American Eagle Outfitters. Patterson disabled the company's ability to process credit card purchases during 5 days of the holiday season of 2002. As for a sense of entitlement, there have always been many employees who felt entitled to take extra office supplies for home use, but this now extends to corporate data. An example is that of a vice president of sales for a stock analysis firm who quit and went to a competitor. Before she left, she copied the customer database to take with her. The offender reported feeling no animus toward her former employee; she simply wanted the data because it would be useful to her.

Although IDS and IPS facilities can be useful in countering insider attacks, other more direct approaches are of higher priority. Examples include the following:

- Enforce least privilege, only allowing access to the resources employees need to do their job.
- Set logs to see what users access and what commands they are entering.
- Protect sensitive resources with strong authentication.
- Upon termination, delete employee's computer and network access.
- Upon termination, make a mirror image of employee's hard drive before reissuing it. That evidence might be needed if your company information turns up at a competitor.

Intrusion Techniques

The objective of the intruder is to gain access to a system or to increase the range of privileges accessible on a system. Most initial attacks use system or software vulnerabilities that allow a user to execute code that opens a back door into the system. Intruders can get access to a system by exploiting attacks such as buffer overflows on a program that runs with certain privileges.

Alternatively, the intruder attempts to acquire information that should have been protected. In some cases, this information is in the form of a user password. With knowledge of some other user's password, an intruder can log in to a system and exercise all the privileges accorded to the legitimate user. Password guessing and password acquisition techniques are discussed in Chapter 15.

14.4 MALICIOUS SOFTWARE OVERVIEW

The concept of malicious software, or malware, was introduced in Section 3.6. Malware is software designed to cause damage to or use up the resources of a target computer. It is frequently concealed within or masquerades as legitimate software. In some cases, it spreads itself to other computers via e-mail or infected discs. The terminology in this area presents problems because of a lack of universal agreement on all of the terms and because some of the categories overlap. Table 14.4 is a useful guide.

In this section, we briefly survey some of the key categories of malicious software, deferring discussion on the key topics of viruses, worms, bots, and rootkits until the following sections.

Backdoor

A **backdoor**, also known as a **trapdoor**, is a secret entry point into a program that allows someone who is aware of the backdoor to gain access without going through the usual security access procedures. Programmers have used backdoors legitimately for many years to debug and test programs; such a backdoor is called a **maintenance hook**. This usually is done when the programmer is developing an application that has an authentication procedure, or a long setup, requiring the user to enter many different values to run the application. To debug the program, the

Table 14.4   Terminology of Malicious Programs

Name	Description
Virus	Malware that, when executed, tries to replicate itself into other executable code; when it succeeds the code is said to be infected. When the infected code is executed, the virus also executes.
Worm	A computer program that can run independently and can propagate a complete working version of itself onto other hosts on a network.
Logic bomb	A program inserted into software by an intruder. A logic bomb lies dormant until a predefined condition is met; the program then triggers an unauthorized act.
Trojan horse	A computer program that appears to have a useful function but also has a hidden and potentially malicious function that evades security mechanisms, sometimes by exploiting legitimate authorizations of a system entity that invokes the Trojan horse program.
Backdoor (trapdoor)	Any mechanism that bypasses a normal security check; it may allow unauthorized access to functionality.
Mobile code	Software (e.g., script, macro, or other portable instruction) that can be shipped unchanged to a heterogeneous collection of platforms and execute with identical semantics.
Exploits	Code specific to a single vulnerability or set of vulnerabilities.
Downloaders	Program that installs other items on a machine that is under attack. Usually, a downloader is sent in an e-mail.
Auto-rooter	Malicious hacker tools used to break into new machines remotely.
Kit (virus generator)	Set of tools for generating new viruses automatically.
Spammer programs	Used to send large volumes of unwanted e-mail.
Flooders	Used to attack networked computer systems with a large volume of traffic to carry out a denial-of-service (DoS) attack.
Keyloggers	Captures keystrokes on a compromised system.
Rootkit	Set of hacker tools used after attacker has broken into a computer system and gained root-level access.
Zombie, bot	Program activated on an infected machine that is activated to launch attacks on other machines.
Spyware	Software that collects information from a computer and transmits it to another system.
Adware	Advertising that is integrated into software. It can result in pop-up ads or redirection of a browser to a commercial site.

developer may wish to gain special privileges or to avoid all the necessary setup and authentication. The programmer may also want to ensure that there is a method of activating the program should something be wrong with the authentication procedure that is being built into the application. The backdoor is code that recognizes some special sequence of input or is triggered by being run from a certain user ID or by an unlikely sequence of events.

Backdoors become threats when unscrupulous programmers use them to gain unauthorized access. The backdoor was the basic idea for the vulnerability portrayed in the movie *War Games*. Another example is that during the development of Multics, penetration tests were conducted by an Air Force "tiger team" (simulating adversaries). One tactic employed was to send a bogus operating system update to a site running Multics. The update contained a Trojan horse (described later) that could be activated by a backdoor and that allowed the tiger team to gain access. The threat was so well implemented that the Multics developers could not find it, even after they were informed of its presence [ENGE80].

It is difficult to implement operating system controls for backdoors. Security measures must focus on the program development and software update activities.

Logic Bomb

One of the oldest types of program threat, predating viruses and worms, is the logic bomb. The logic bomb is code embedded in some legitimate program that is set to "explode" when certain conditions are met. Examples of conditions that can be used as triggers for a logic bomb are the presence or absence of certain files, a particular day of the week or date, or a particular user running the application. Once triggered, a bomb may alter or delete data or entire files, cause a machine halt, or do some other damage. A striking example of how logic bombs can be employed was the case of Tim Lloyd, who was convicted of setting a logic bomb that cost his employer, Omega Engineering, more than $10 million, derailed its corporate growth strategy, and eventually led to the layoff of 80 workers [GAUD00]. Ultimately, Lloyd was sentenced to 41 months in prison and ordered to pay $2 million in restitution.

Trojan Horse

A Trojan horse is a useful, or apparently useful, program or command procedure containing hidden code that, when invoked, performs some unwanted or harmful function.

Trojan horse programs can be used to accomplish functions indirectly that an unauthorized user could not accomplish directly. For example, to gain access to the files of another user on a shared system, a user could create a Trojan horse program that, when executed, changes the invoking user's file permissions so that the files are readable by any user. The author could then induce users to run the program by placing it in a common directory and naming it such that it appears to be a useful utility program or application. An example is a program that ostensibly produces a listing of the user's files in a desirable format. After another user has run the program, the author of the program can then access the information in the user's files. An example of a Trojan horse program that would be difficult to detect is a compiler that has been modified to insert additional code into certain programs as they are compiled, such as a system login program [THOM84]. The code creates a backdoor in the login program that permits the author to log on to the system using a special password. This Trojan horse can never be discovered by reading the source code of the login program.

Another common motivation for the Trojan horse is data destruction. The program appears to be performing a useful function (e.g., a calculator program), but it may also be quietly deleting the user's files. For example, a CBS executive was victimized by a Trojan horse that destroyed all information contained in his computer's memory [TIME90]. The Trojan horse was implanted in a graphics routine offered on an electronic bulletin board system.

Trojan horses fit into one of three models:

- Continuing to perform the function of the original program and additionally performing a separate malicious activity
- Continuing to perform the function of the original program but modifying the function to perform malicious activity (e.g., a Trojan horse version of a login program that collects passwords) or to disguise other malicious activity (e.g., a Trojan horse version of a process listing program that does not display certain processes that are malicious)
- Performing a malicious function that completely replaces the function of the original program

Mobile Code

Mobile code refers to programs (e.g., script, macro, or other portable instruction) that can be shipped unchanged to a heterogeneous collection of platforms and execute with identical semantics [JANS01]. The term also applies to situations involving a large homogeneous collection of platforms (e.g., Microsoft Windows).

Mobile code is transmitted from a remote system to a local system and then executed on the local system without the user's explicit instruction. Mobile code often acts as a mechanism for a virus, worm, or Trojan horse to be transmitted to the user's workstation. In other cases, mobile code takes advantage of vulnerabilities to perform its own exploits, such as unauthorized data access or root compromise. Popular vehicles for mobile code include Java applets, ActiveX, JavaScript, and VBScript. The most common ways of using mobile code for malicious operations on local system are cross-site scripting, interactive and dynamic Web sites, e-mail attachments, and downloads from untrusted sites or of untrusted software.

Multiple–Threat Malware

Viruses and other malware may operate in multiple ways. The terminology is far from uniform; this subsection gives a brief introduction to several related concepts that could be considered multiple-threat malware.

A **multipartite** virus infects in multiple ways. Typically, the multipartite virus is capable of infecting multiple types of files, so that virus eradication must deal with all of the possible sites of infection.

A **blended attack** uses multiple methods of infection or transmission, to maximize the speed of contagion and the severity of the attack. Some writers characterize a blended attack as a package that includes multiple types of malware. An example of a blended attack is the Nimda attack, erroneously referred to as simply a worm. Nimda uses four distribution methods:

- **E-mail:** A user on a vulnerable host opens an infected e-mail attachment; Nimda looks for e-mail addresses on the host and then sends copies of itself to those addresses.

- **Windows shares:** Nimda scans hosts for unsecured Windows file shares; it can then use NetBIOS86 as a transport mechanism to infect files on that host in the hopes that a user will run an infected file, which will activate Nimda on that host.

- **Web servers:** Nimda scans Web servers, looking for known vulnerabilities in Microsoft IIS. If it finds a vulnerable server, it attempts to transfer a copy of itself to the server and infect it and its files.

- **Web clients:** If a vulnerable Web client visits a Web server that has been infected by Nimda, the client's workstation will become infected.

Thus, Nimda has worm, virus, and mobile code characteristics. Blended attacks may also spread through other services, such as instant messaging and peer-to-peer file sharing.

14.5 VIRUSES, WORMS, AND BOTS

Viruses

A computer virus is a piece of software that can "infect" other programs by modifying them; the modification includes injecting the original program with a routine to make copies of the virus program, which can then go on to infect other programs.

Biological viruses are tiny scraps of genetic code—DNA or RNA—that can take over the machinery of a living cell and trick it into making thousands of flawless replicas of the original virus. Like its biological counterpart, a computer virus carries in its instructional code the recipe for making perfect copies of itself. The typical virus becomes embedded in a program on a computer. Then, whenever the infected computer comes into contact with an uninfected piece of software, a fresh copy of the virus passes into the new program. Thus, the infection can be spread from computer to computer by unsuspecting users who either swap disks or send programs to one another over a network. In a network environment, the ability to access applications and system services on other computers provides a perfect culture for the spread of a virus.

THE NATURE OF VIRUSES   A virus can do anything that other programs do. The only difference is that it attaches itself to another program and executes secretly when the host program is run. Once a virus is executing, it can perform any function that is allowed by the privileges of the current user, such as erasing files and programs.

A computer virus has three parts [AYCO06]:

- **Infection mechanism**: The means by which a virus spreads, enabling it to replicate. The mechanism is also referred to as the **infection vector**.

- **Trigger:** The event or condition that determines when the payload is activated or delivered.

- **Payload:** What the virus does, besides spreading. The payload may involve damage or may involve benign but noticeable activity.

During its lifetime, a typical virus goes through the following four phases:

- **Dormant phase:** The virus is idle. The virus will eventually be activated by some event, such as a date, the presence of another program or file, or the capacity of the disk exceeding some limit. Not all viruses have this stage.

- **Propagation phase:** The virus places an identical copy of itself into other programs or into certain system areas on the disk. Each infected program will now contain a clone of the virus, which will itself enter a propagation phase.

- **Triggering phase:** The virus is activated to perform the function for which it was intended. As with the dormant phase, the triggering phase can be caused by a variety of system events, including a count of the number of times that this copy of the virus has made copies of itself.

- **Execution phase:** The function is performed. The function may be harmless, such as a message on the screen, or damaging, such as the destruction of programs and data files.

Most viruses carry out their work in a manner that is specific to a particular operating system and, in some cases, specific to a particular hardware platform. Thus, they are designed to take advantage of the details and weaknesses of particular systems.

VIRUS STRUCTURE   A virus can be prepended or postpended to an executable program, or it can be embedded in some other fashion. The key to its operation is that the infected program, when invoked, will first execute the virus code and then execute the original code of the program.

A very general depiction of virus structure is shown in Figure 14.3 (based on [COHE94]). In this case, the virus code, V, is prepended to infected programs, and it is assumed that the entry point to the program, when invoked, is the first line of the program.

The infected program begins with the virus code and works as follows. The first line of code is a jump to the main virus program. The second line is a special marker that is used by the virus to determine whether or not a potential victim program has already been infected with this virus. When the program is invoked, control is immediately transferred to the main virus program. The virus program may first seek out uninfected executable files and infect them. Next, the virus may perform some action, usually detrimental to the system. This action could be performed every time the program is invoked, or it could be a logic bomb that triggers only under certain conditions. Finally, the virus transfers control to the original program. If the infection phase of the program is reasonably rapid, a user is unlikely to notice any difference between the execution of an infected and an uninfected program.

A virus such as the one just described is easily detected because an infected version of a program is longer than the corresponding uninfected one. A way to thwart such a simple means of detecting a virus is to compress the executable file so that both the infected and uninfected versions are of identical length. Figure 14.4 [COHE94] shows in general terms the logic required. The important lines in this virus are numbered. We assume that program P_1 is infected with the virus CV. When

```
    program V :=

{goto main;
    1234567;

    subroutine infect-executable :=
        {loop:
        file := get-random-executable-file;
        if (first-line-of-file = 1234567)
            then goto loop
            else prepend V to file; }

    subroutine do-damage :=
        {whatever damage is to be done}

    subroutine trigger-pulled :=
        {return true if some condition holds}

main:   main-program :=
        {infect-executable;
        if trigger-pulled then do-damage;
        goto next;}

next:

}
```

Figure 14.3   A Simple Virus

this program is invoked, control passes to its virus, which performs the following steps:

1. For each uninfected file P_2 that is found, the virus first compresses that file to produce P'_2, which is shorter than the original program by the size of the virus.

2. A copy of the virus is prepended to the compressed program.

```
program CV :=

{goto main;
    01234567;

    subroutine infect-executable :=
        {loop:
                file := get-random-executable-file;
            if (first-line-of-file = 01234567) then goto loop;
        (1)     compress file;
        (2)     prepend CV to file;
        }

main:   main-program :=
            {if ask-permission then infect-executable;
        (3)     uncompress rest-of-file;
        (4)     run uncompressed file;}
        }
```

Figure 14.4   Logic for a Compression Virus

3. The compressed version of the original infected program, P'_1, is uncompressed.

4. The uncompressed original program is executed.

In this example, the virus does nothing other than propagate. As previously mentioned, the virus may include a logic bomb.

INITIAL INFECTION   Once a virus has gained entry to a system by infecting a single program, it is in a position to potentially infect some or all other executable files on that system when the infected program executes. Thus, viral infection can be completely prevented by preventing the virus from gaining entry in the first place. Unfortunately, prevention is extraordinarily difficult because a virus can be part of any program outside a system. Thus, unless one is content to take an absolutely bare piece of iron and write all one's own system and application programs, one is vulnerable. Many forms of infection can also be blocked by denying normal users the right to modify programs on the system.

The lack of access controls on early PCs is a key reason that traditional machine code based viruses spread rapidly on these systems. In contrast, while it is easy enough to write a machine code virus for UNIX systems, they were almost never seen in practice, because the existence of access controls on these systems prevented effective propagation of the virus. Traditional machine code based viruses are now less prevalent, because modern PC operating systems have more effective access controls. However, virus creators have found other avenues, such as macro and e-mail viruses, as discussed subsequently.

VIRUSES CLASSIFICATION   There has been a continuous arms race between virus writers and writers of antivirus software since viruses first appeared. As effective countermeasures are developed for existing types of viruses, newer types are developed. There is no simple or universally agreed-upon classification scheme for viruses. In this section, we follow [AYCO06] and classify viruses along two orthogonal axes: the type of target the virus tries to infect, and the method the virus uses to conceal itself from detection by users and antivirus software.

A virus **classification by target** includes the following categories:

- **Boot sector infector:** Infects a master boot record or boot record and spreads when a system is booted from the disk containing the virus

- **File infector:** Infects files that the operating system or shell considers to be executable

- **Macro virus:** Infects files with macro code that is interpreted by an application

A virus classification by concealment strategy includes the following categories:

- **Encrypted virus:** A typical approach is as follows. A portion of the virus creates a random encryption key and encrypts the remainder of the virus. The key is stored with the virus. When an infected program is invoked, the virus uses the stored random key to decrypt the virus. When the virus replicates, a different random key is selected. Because the bulk of the virus is encrypted with a different key for each instance, there is no constant bit pattern to observe.

- **Stealth virus:** A form of virus explicitly designed to hide itself from detection by antivirus software. Thus, the entire virus, not just a payload is hidden.
- **Polymorphic virus:** A virus that mutates with every infection, making detection by the "signature" of the virus impossible.
- **Metamorphic virus:** As with a polymorphic virus, a metamorphic virus mutates with every infection. The difference is that a metamorphic virus rewrites itself completely at each iteration, increasing the difficulty of detection. Metamorphic viruses may change their behavior as well as their appearance.

One example of a **stealth virus** was discussed earlier: A virus that uses compression so that the infected program is exactly the same length as an uninfected version. Far more sophisticated techniques are possible. For example, a virus can place intercept logic in disk I/O routines, so that when there is an attempt to read suspected portions of the disk using these routines, the virus will present back the original, uninfected program. Thus, *stealth* is not a term that applies to a virus as such but, rather, refers to a technique used by a virus to evade detection.

A **polymorphic virus** creates copies during replication that are functionally equivalent but have distinctly different bit patterns. As with a stealth virus, the purpose is to defeat programs that scan for viruses. In this case, the "signature" of the virus will vary with each copy. To achieve this variation, the virus may randomly insert superfluous instructions or interchange the order of independent instructions. A more effective approach is to use encryption. The strategy of the encryption virus is followed. The portion of the virus that is responsible for generating keys and performing encryption/decryption is referred to as the *mutation engine*. The mutation engine itself is altered with each use.

VIRUS KITS Another weapon in the virus writers' armory is the virus-creation toolkit. Such a toolkit enables a relative novice to quickly create a number of different viruses. Although viruses created with toolkits tend to be less sophisticated than viruses designed from scratch, the sheer number of new viruses that can be generated using a toolkit creates a problem for antivirus schemes.

MACRO VIRUSES In the mid-1990s, macro viruses became by far the most prevalent type of virus. Macro viruses are particularly threatening for a number of reasons:

1. A macro virus is platform independent. Many macro viruses infect Microsoft Word documents or other Microsoft Office documents. Any hardware platform and operating system that supports these applications can be infected.
2. Macro viruses infect documents, not executable portions of code. Most of the information introduced onto a computer system is in the form of a document rather than a program.
3. Macro viruses are easily spread. A very common method is by electronic mail.
4. Because macro viruses infect user documents rather than system programs, traditional file system access controls are of limited use in preventing their spread.

Macro viruses take advantage of a feature found in Word and other Office applications such as Microsoft Excel—namely, the macro. In essence, a macro is an executable program embedded in a word processing document or other type of file.

Typically, users employ macros to automate repetitive tasks and thereby save keystrokes. The macro language is usually some form of the Basic programming language. A user might define a sequence of keystrokes in a macro and set it up so that the macro is invoked when a function key or special short combination of keys is input.

Successive releases of MS Office products provide increased protection against macro viruses. For example, Microsoft offers an optional Macro Virus Protection tool that detects suspicious Word files and alerts the customer to the potential risk of opening a file with macros. Various antivirus product vendors have also developed tools to detect and correct macro viruses. As in other types of viruses, the arms race continues in the field of macro viruses, but they no longer are the predominant virus threat.

E-MAIL VIRUSES A more recent development in malicious software is the e-mail virus. The first rapidly spreading e-mail viruses, such as Melissa, made use of a Microsoft Word macro embedded in an attachment. If the recipient opens the e-mail attachment, the Word macro is activated. Then

1. The e-mail virus sends itself to everyone on the mailing list in the user's e-mail package.
2. The virus does local damage on the user's system.

In 1999, a more powerful version of the e-mail virus appeared. This newer version can be activated merely by opening an e-mail that contains the virus rather than opening an attachment. The virus uses the Visual Basic scripting language supported by the e-mail package.

Thus we see a new generation of malware that arrives via e-mail and uses e-mail software features to replicate itself across the Internet. The virus propagates itself as soon as it is activated (either by opening an e-mail attachment or by opening the e-mail) to all of the e-mail addresses known to the infected host. As a result, whereas viruses used to take months or years to propagate, they now do so in hours. This makes it very difficult for antivirus software to respond before much damage is done. Ultimately, a greater degree of security must be built into Internet utility and application software on PCs to counter the growing threat.

Worms

A worm is a program that can replicate itself and send copies from computer to computer across network connections. Upon arrival, the worm may be activated to replicate and propagate again. In addition to propagation, the worm usually performs some unwanted function. An e-mail virus has some of the characteristics of a worm because it propagates itself from system to system. However, we can still classify it as a virus because it uses a document modified to contain viral macro content and requires human action. A worm actively seeks out more machines to infect, and each machine that is infected serves as an automated launching pad for attacks on other machines.

Network worm programs use network connections to spread from system to system. Once active within a system, a network worm can behave as a computer virus or bacteria, or it could implant Trojan horse programs or perform any number of disruptive or destructive actions.

To replicate itself, a network worm uses some sort of network vehicle. Examples include the following:

- **Electronic mail facility:** A worm mails a copy of itself to other systems, so that its code is run when the e-mail or an attachment is received or viewed.
- **Remote execution capability:** A worm executes a copy of itself on another system, either using an explicit remote execution facility or by exploiting a program flaw in a network service to subvert its operations (such as buffer overflow, described in Chapter 7).
- **Remote login capability:** A worm logs on to a remote system as a user and then uses commands to copy itself from one system to the other, where it then executes.

The new copy of the worm program is then run on the remote system where, in addition to any functions that it performs at that system, it continues to spread in the same fashion.

A network worm exhibits the same characteristics as a computer virus: a dormant phase, a propagation phase, a triggering phase, and an execution phase. The propagation phase generally performs the following functions:

1. Search for other systems to infect by examining host tables or similar repositories of remote system addresses.
2. Establish a connection with a remote system.
3. Copy itself to the remote system and cause the copy to be run.

The network worm may also attempt to determine whether a system has previously been infected before copying itself to the system. In a multiprogramming system, it may also disguise its presence by naming itself as a system process or using some other name that may not be noticed by a system operator.

As with viruses, network worms are difficult to counter.

WORM PROPAGATION MODEL   [ZOU05] describes a model for worm propagation based on an analysis of recent worm attacks. The speed of propagation and the total number of hosts infected depend on a number of factors, including the mode of propagation, the vulnerability or vulnerabilities exploited, and the degree of similarity to preceding attacks. For the latter factor, an attack that is a variation of a recent previous attack may be countered more effectively than a more novel attack. Figure 14.5 shows the dynamics for one typical set of parameters. Propagation proceeds through three phases. In the initial phase, the number of hosts increases exponentially. To see that this is so, consider a simplified case in which a worm is launched from a single host and infects two nearby hosts. Each of these hosts infects two more hosts, and so on. This results in exponential growth. After a time, infecting hosts waste some time attacking already infected hosts, which reduces the rate of infection. During this middle phase, growth is approximately linear, but the rate of infection is rapid. When most vulnerable computers have been infected, the attack enters a slow finish phase as the worm seeks out those remaining hosts that are difficult to identify.

Clearly, the objective in countering a worm is to catch the worm in its slow start phase, at a time when few hosts have been infected.

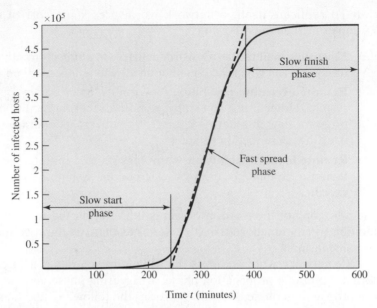

Figure 14.5   Worm Propagation Model

STATE OF WORM TECHNOLOGY   The state of the art in worm technology includes the following:

- **Multiplatform:** Newer worms are not limited to Windows machines but can attack a variety of platforms, especially the popular varieties of UNIX.

- **Multiexploit:** New worms penetrate systems in a variety of ways, using exploits against Web servers, browsers, e-mail, file sharing, and other network-based applications.

- **Ultrafast spreading:** One technique to accelerate the spread of a worm is to conduct a prior Internet scan to accumulate Internet addresses of vulnerable machines.

- **Polymorphic:** To evade detection, skip past filters, and foil real-time analysis, worms adopt the virus polymorphic technique. Each copy of the worm has new code generated on the fly using functionally equivalent instructions and encryption techniques.

- **Metamorphic:** In addition to changing their appearance, metamorphic worms have a repertoire of behavior patterns that are unleashed at different stages of propagation.

- **Transport vehicles:** Because worms can rapidly compromise a large number of systems, they are ideal for spreading other distributed attack tools, such as distributed denial of service bots.

- **Zero-day exploit:** To achieve maximum surprise and distribution, a worm should exploit an unknown vulnerability that is only discovered by the general network community when the worm is launched.

Bots

A bot (robot), also known as a zombie or drone, is a program that secretly takes over another Internet-attached computer and then uses that computer to launch attacks that are difficult to trace to the bot's creator. The bot is typically planted on hundreds or thousands of computers belonging to unsuspecting third parties. The collection of bots often is capable of acting in a coordinated manner; such a collection is referred to as a **botnet**.

A botnet exhibits three characteristics: the bot functionality, a remote control facility, and a spreading mechanism to propagate the bots and construct the botnet. We examine each of these characteristics in turn.

USES OF BOTS [HONE05] lists the following uses of bots:

- **Distributed denial-of-service (DDoS) attacks:** A DDoS attack is an attack on a computer system or network that causes a loss of service to users.

- **Spamming:** With the help of a botnet and thousands of bots, an attacker is able to send massive amounts of bulk e-mail (spam).

- **Sniffing traffic:** Bots can also use a packet sniffer to watch for interesting clear-text data passing by a compromised machine. The sniffers are mostly used to retrieve sensitive information like usernames and passwords.

- **Keylogging:** If the compromised machine uses encrypted communication channels (e.g., IITTPS or POP3S), then just sniffing the network packets on the victim's computer is useless because the appropriate key to decrypt the packets is missing. But by using a keylogger, which captures keystrokes on the infected machine, an attacker can retrieve sensitive information. An implemented filtering mechanism (e.g., "I am only interested in key sequences near the keyword 'paypal.com' ") further helps in stealing secret data.

- **Spreading new malware:** Botnets are used to spread new bots. This is very easy since all bots implement mechanisms to download and execute a file via HTTP or FTP. A botnet with 10,000 hosts that acts as the start base for a worm or mail virus allows very fast spreading and thus causes more harm.

- **Installing advertisement add-ons and browser helper objects (BHOs):** Botnets can also be used to gain financial advantages. This works by setting up a fake Web site with some advertisements: The operator of this Web site negotiates a deal with some hosting companies that pay for clicks on ads. With the help of a botnet, these clicks can be "automated" so that instantly a few thousand bots click on the pop-ups. This process can be further enhanced if the bot hijacks the start page of a compromised machine so that the "clicks" are executed each time the victim uses the browser.

- **Attacking IRC chat networks:** Botnets are also used for attacks against Internet Relay Chat (IRC) networks. Popular among attackers is especially the so-called clone attack: In this kind of attack, the controller orders each bot to connect a large number of clones to the victim IRC network. The victim is flooded by service requests from thousands of bots or thousands of channel-joins by these cloned bots. In this way, the victim IRC network is brought down, similar to a DDoS attack.

- **Manipulating online polls/games:** Online polls/games are getting more and more attention, and it is rather easy to manipulate them with botnets. Since every bot has a distinct IP address, every vote will have the same credibility as a vote cast by a real person. Online games can be manipulated in a similar way.

REMOTE CONTROL FACILITY   The remote control facility is what distinguishes a bot from a worm. A worm propagates itself and activates itself, whereas a bot is controlled from some central facility, at least initially.

A typical means of implementing the remote control facility is on an IRC server. All bots join a specific channel on this server and treat incoming messages as commands. More recent botnets tend to avoid IRC mechanisms and use covert communication channels via protocols such as HTTP. Distributed control mechanisms are also used, to avoid a single point of failure.

Once a communications path is established between a control module and the bots, the control module can activate the bots. In its simplest form, the control module simply issues command to the bot that causes the bot to execute routines that are already implemented in the bot. For greater flexibility, the control module can issue update commands that instruct the bots to download a file from some Internet location and execute it. The bot in this latter case becomes a more general-purpose tool that can be used for multiple attacks.

CONSTRUCTING THE ATTACK NETWORK   The first step in a botnet attack is for the attacker to infect a number of machines with bot software that will ultimately be used to carry out the attack. The essential ingredients in this phase of the attack are the following:

1. Software that can carry out the attack. The software must be able to run on a large number of machines, must be able to conceal its existence, must be able to communicate with the attacker or have some sort of time-triggered mechanism, and must be able to launch the intended attack toward the target.

2. A vulnerability in a large number of systems. The attacker must become aware of a vulnerability that many system administrators and individual users have failed to patch and that enables the attacker to install the bot software.

3. A strategy for locating and identifying vulnerable machines, a process known as **scanning** or **fingerprinting**.

In the scanning process, the attacker first seeks out a number of vulnerable machines and infects them. Then, typically, the bot software that is installed in the infected machines repeats the same scanning process, until a large distributed network of infected machines is created. [MIRK04] lists the following types of scanning strategies:

- **Random:** Each compromised host probes random addresses in the IP address space, using a different seed. This technique produces a high volume of Internet traffic, which may cause generalized disruption even before the actual attack is launched.

- **Hit list:** The attacker first compiles a long list of potential vulnerable machines. This can be a slow process done over a long period to avoid detection that an attack is underway. Once the list is compiled, the attacker begins infecting machines on the list. Each infected machine is provided with a portion of the list to scan. This strategy results in a very short scanning period, which may make it difficult to detect that infection is taking place.

- **Topological:** This method uses information contained on an infected victim machine to find more hosts to scan.

- **Local subnet:** If a host can be infected behind a firewall, that host then looks for targets in its own local network. The host uses the subnet address structure to find other hosts that would otherwise be protected by the firewall.

14.6 ROOTKITS

A rootkit is a set of programs installed on a system to maintain administrator (or root) access to that system. Root access provides access to all the functions and services of the operating system. The rootkit alters the host's standard functionality in a malicious and stealthy way. With root access, an attacker has complete control of the system and can add or change programs and files, monitor processes, send and receive network traffic, and get backdoor access on demand.

A rootkit can make many changes to a system to hide its existence, making it difficult for the user to determine that the rootkit is present and to identify what changes have been made. In essence, a rootkit hides by subverting the mechanisms that monitor and report on the processes, files, and registries on a computer.

Rootkits can be classified based on whether they can survive a reboot and execution mode. A rootkit may be

- **Persistent:** Activates each time the system boots. The rootkit must store code in a persistent store, such as the registry or file system, and configure a method by which the code executes without user intervention.

- **Memory based:** Has no persistent code and therefore cannot survive a reboot

- **User mode:** Intercepts calls to APIs (Application Program Interfaces) and modifies returned results. For example, when an application performs a directory listing, the return results don't include entries identifying the files associated with the rootkit.

- **Kernel mode:** Can intercept calls to native APIs in kernel mode. The rootkit can also hide the presence of a malware process by removing it from the kernel's list of active processes.

Rootkit Installation

Unlike worms or bots, rootkits do not directly rely on vulnerabilities or exploits to get on a computer. One method of rootkit installation is via a Trojan horse program. The user is induced to load the Trojan horse, which then installs the rootkit.

Another means of rootkit installation is by hacker activity. The following sequence is representative of a hacker attack to install a rootkit [GEER06].

1. The attacker uses a utility to identify open ports or other vulnerabilities.
2. The attacker uses password cracking, malware, or a system vulnerability to gain initial access and, eventually, root access.
3. The attacker uploads the rootkit to the victim's machine.
4. The attacker can add a virus, denial of service, or other type of attack to the rootkit's payload.
5. The attacker then runs the rootkit's installation script.
6. The rootkit replaces binaries, files, commands, or system utilities to hide its presence.
7. The rootkit listens at a port in the target server, installs sniffers or keyloggers, activates a malicious payload, or takes other steps to compromise the victim.

System-Level Call Attacks

Programs operating at the user level interact with the kernel through system calls. Thus, system calls are a primary target of kernel-level rootkits to achieve concealment. As an example of how rootkits operate, we look at the implementation of system calls in Linux. In Linux, each system call is assigned a unique *syscall number*. When a user-mode process executes a system call, the process refers to the system call by this number. The kernel maintains a system call table with one entry per system call routine; each entry contains a pointer to the corresponding routine. The syscall number serves as an index into the system call table.

[LEVI06] lists three techniques that can be used to change system calls:

- **Modify the system call table:** The attacker modifies selected syscall addresses stored in the system call table. This enables the rootkit to direct a system call away from the legitimate routine to the rootkit's replacement. Figure 14.6 shows how the knark rootkit achieves this.

- **Modify system call table targets:** The attacker overwrites selected legitimate system call routines with malicious code. The system call table is not changed.

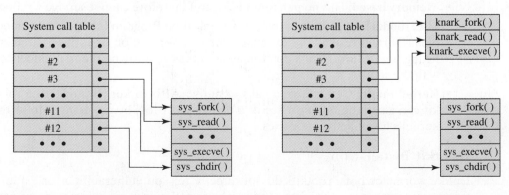

(a) Normal kernel memory layout   (b) After knark install

Figure 14.6 System Call Table Modification by Rootkit

- **Redirect the system call table:** The attacker redirects references to the entire system call table to a new table in a new kernel memory location.

14.6 RECOMMENDED READING AND WEB SITES

The topics in this chapter are covered in more detail in [STAL08]. It is useful to read some of the classic tutorial papers on computer security; these provide a historical perspective from which to appreciate current work and thinking. The papers to read are [WARE79], [BROW72], [SALT75], [SHAN77], and [SUMM84]. Two more recent short treatments of computer security are [ANDR04] and [LAMP04]. [NIST95] is an exhaustive (290 pages) treatment of the subject. Another good treatment is [NRC91]. Also useful is [FRAS97].

ANDR04   Andrews, M., and Whittaker, J. "Computer Security." *IEEE Security and Privacy*, September/October 2004.

BROW72   Browne, P. "Computer Security—A Survey." *ACM SIGMIS Database*, Fall 1972.

FRAS97   Fraser, B. *Site Security Handbook*. RFC 2196, September 1997.

LAMP04   Lampson, B. "Computer Security in the Real World." *Computer*, June 2004.

NIST95   National Institute of Standards and Technology. *An Introduction to Computer Security: The NIST Handbook*. Special Publication 800-12. October 1995.

NRC91   National Research Council. *Computers at Risk: Safe Computing in the Information Age.* Washington, DC: National Academy Press, 1991.

SALT75   Saltzer, J., and Schroeder, M. "The Protection of Information in Computer Systems." *Proceedings of the IEEE*, September 1975.

SHAN77   Shanker, K. "The Total Computer Security Problem: An Overview." *Computer*, June 1977.

STAL08   Stallings, W., and Brown L. *Computer Security. Principles and Practice.* Upper Saddle River, NJ: Prentice Hall, 2008.

SUMM84   Summers, R. "An Overview of Computer Security." *IBM Systems Journal*, Vol. 23, No. 4, 1984.

WARE79   Ware, W., ed. *Security Controls for Computer Systems*. RAND Report 609-1, October 1979. http://www.rand.org/pubs/reports/R609-1/index2.html

Recommended Web sites:

- **Computer Security Resource Center:** Maintained by the National Institute on Standards and Technology (NIST). Contains a broad range of information on security threats, technology, and standards.

- **CERT Coordination Center:** The organization that grew from the computer emergency response team formed by the Defense Advanced Research Projects Agency. Site provides good information on Internet security threats, vulnerabilities, and attack statistics.

- **Vmyths:** Dedicated to exposing virus hoaxes and dispelling misconceptions about real viruses.

14.7 KEY TERMS, REVIEW QUESTIONS, AND PROBLEMS

Key Terms

accountability	e-mail virus	passive attack
active attack	falsification	privacy
asset	hacker	replay
attack	insider attack	repudiation
authenticity	integrity	system integrity
availability	interception	threat
backdoor	intruder	traffic analysis
confidentiality	intrusion	trapdoor
data integrity	logic bomb	Trojan horse
deception	macro virus	usurpation
denial of service	malicious software	virus
disruption	malware	virus kit
exposure	masquerade	worm

Review Questions

14.1 Define *computer security*.

14.2 What are the fundamental requirements addressed by computer security?

14.3 What is the difference between passive and active security threats?

14.4 List and briefly define three classes of intruders.

14.5 List and briefly define three intruder behavior patterns.

14.6 What is the role of compression in the operation of a virus?

14.7 What is the role of encryption in the operation of a virus?

14.8 What are typical phases of operation of a virus or worm?

14.9 In general terms, how does a worm propagate?

14.10 What is the difference between a bot and a rootkit?

Problems

14.1 Consider an automated teller machine (ATM) in which users provide a personal identification number (PIN) and a card for account access. Give examples of confidentiality, integrity, and availability requirements associated with the system and, in each case, indicate the degree of importance of the requirement.

14.2 Repeat the preceding problem for a telephone switching system that routes calls through a switching network based on the telephone number requested by the caller.

14.3 Consider a desktop publishing system used to produce documents for various organizations.

    a. Give an example of a type of publication for which confidentiality of the stored data is the most important requirement.

    b. Give an example of a type of publication in which data integrity is the most important requirement.

    c. Give an example in which system availability is the most important requirement.

14.4 For each of the following assets, assign a low, moderate, or high impact level for the loss of confidentiality, availability, and integrity, respectively. Justify your answers.

    a. An organization managing public information on its Web server.

    b. A law enforcement organization managing extremely sensitive investigative information.

    c. A financial organization managing routine administrative information (not privacy-related information).

    d. An information system used for large acquisitions in a contracting organization contains both sensitive, pre-solicitation phase contract information and routine administrative information. Assess the impact for the two data sets separately and the information system as a whole.

    e. A power plant contains a SCADA (supervisory control and data acquisition) system controlling the distribution of electric power for a large military installation. The SCADA system contains both real-time sensor data and routine administrative information. Assess the impact for the two data sets separately and the information system as a whole.

14.5 Assume that passwords are selected from four-character combinations of 26 alphabetic characters. Assume that an adversary is able to attempt passwords at a rate of one per second.

    a. Assuming no feedback to the adversary until each attempt has been completed, what is the expected time to discover the correct password?

    b. Assuming feedback to the adversary flagging an error as each incorrect character is entered, what is the expected time to discover the correct password?

14.6 There is a flaw in the virus program of Figure 14.1. What is it?

14.7 The question arises as to whether it is possible to develop a program that can analyze a piece of software to determine if it is a virus. Consider that we have a program D that is supposed to be able to do that. That is, for any program P, if we run D(P), the result returned is TRUE (P is a virus) or FALSE (P is not a virus). Now consider the following program:

```
Program CV :=
   { ...
   main-program :=
           {if D(CV) then goto next:
                  else infect-executable;
           }
   next:
   }
```

In the preceding program, infect-executable is a module that scans memory for executable programs and replicates itself in those programs. Determine if D can correctly decide whether CV is a virus.

14.8 The point of this problem is to demonstrate the type of puzzles that must be solved in the design of malicious code and therefore, the type of mind-set that one wishing to counter such attacks must adopt.

    a. Consider the following C program:

```
begin
      print (*begin print (); end.*);
end
```

What do you think the program was intended to do? Does it work?

b. Answer the same questions for the following program:

```
char [] = {'0', ' ', '}', ';', 'm', 'a', 'i', 'n', '(', ')', '{',
and so on... 't', ')', '0'};
    main ()
    {
        int I;
        printf(*char t[] = (*);
        for (i=0; t[i]!=0; i=i+1)
                printf("%d, ", t[i]);
        printf("%s", t);
    }
```

c. What is the specific relevance of this problem to this chapter?

14.9 Consider the following fragment:

```
legitimate code
if data is Friday the 13th;
    crash_computer();
legitimate code
```

What type of malicious software is this?

14.10 Consider the following fragment in an authentication program:

```
username = read_username();
password = read_password();
if username is "133t h4ck0r"
    return ALLOW_LOGIN;
if username and password are valid
    return ALLOW_LOGIN;
else return DENY_LOGIN
```

What type of malicious software is this?

14.11 The following code fragments show a sequence of virus instructions and a polymorphic version of the virus. Describe the effect produced by the metamorphic code.

Original Code	Metamorphic Code
mov eax, 5	mov eax, 5
add eax, ebx	push ecx
call [eax]	pop ecx
	add eax, ebx
	swap eax, ebx
	swap ebx, eax
	call [eax]
	nop

CHAPTER 15

COMPUTER SECURITY TECHNIQUES

15.1 Authentication
> Password-Based Authentication
> Token-Based Authentication
> Biometric Authentication

15.2 Access Control
> Discretionary Access Control
> Role-Based Access Control

15.3 Intrusion Detection
> Basic Principles
> Host-Based Intrusion Detection Techniques
> Audit Records

15.4 Malware Defense
> Antivirus Approaches
> Worm Countermeasures
> Bot Countermeasures
> Rootkit Countermeasures

15.5 Dealing with Buffer Overflow Attacks
> Compile-Time Defenses
> Run-Time Defenses

15.6 Windows 7 Security
> Access Control Scheme
> Access Token
> Security Descriptors

15.7 Recommended Reading and Web Sites

15.8 Key Terms, Review Questions, and Problems

To guard against the baneful influence exerted by strangers is therefore an elementary dictate of savage prudence. Hence before strangers are allowed to enter a district, or at least before they are permitted to mingle freely with the inhabitants, certain ceremonies are often performed by the natives of the country for the purpose of disarming the strangers of their magical powers, or of disinfecting, so to speak, the tainted atmosphere by which they are supposed to be surrounded.

—*THE GOLDEN BOUGH*, SIR JAMES GEORGE FRAZER

LEARNING OBJECTIVES

After studying this chapter, you should be able to:

- Define and compare three methods of user authentication.
- Compare and contrast two methods of access control.
- Explain the basic principles and techniques of intrusion detection.
- Explain the basic principles and techniques of malware defense.
- Understand how to defend against buffer overflow attacks.
- Explain the file system used in Windows 7.

This chapter introduces common measures used to counter the security threats discussed in Chapter 14.

15.1 AUTHENTICATION

User authentication was introduced in Section 3.6. Note that user authentication is distinct from message authentication. Message authentication is a procedure that allows communicating parties to verify that the contents of a received message have not been altered and that the source is authentic. This chapter is concerned solely with user authentication.

Password–Based Authentication

A widely used line of defense against intruders is the password system. Virtually all multiuser systems, network-based servers, Web-based e-commerce sites, and other similar services require that a user provide not only a name or identifier (ID) but also a password. The system compares the password to a previously stored password for that user ID, maintained in a system password file. The password serves to authenticate the ID of the individual logging on to the system. In turn, the ID provides security in the following ways:

- The ID determines whether the user is authorized to gain access to a system. In some systems, only those who already have an ID filed on the system are allowed to gain access.

- The ID determines the privileges accorded to the user. A few users may have supervisory or "superuser" status that enables them to read files and perform functions that are especially protected by the operating system. Some systems have guest or anonymous accounts, and users of these accounts have more limited privileges than others.

- The ID is used in what is referred to as discretionary access control. For example, by listing the IDs of the other users, a user may grant permission to them to read files owned by that user.

THE USE OF HASHED PASSWORDS A widely used password security technique is the use of hashed passwords and a salt value. This scheme is found on virtually all UNIX variants as well as on a number of other operating systems. The following procedure is employed (Figure 15.1a). To load a new password into the system, the user selects or is assigned a password. This password is combined with a fixed-length **salt value** [MORR79]. In older implementations, this value is related to the time at which the password is assigned to the user. Newer implementations use a pseudorandom or random number. The password and salt serve as inputs to a hashing algorithm to produce a fixed-length hash code. The hash algorithm is designed to be slow to execute to thwart attacks. The hashed password is then stored, together with a plaintext copy of the salt, in the password file for the corresponding user ID. The hashed-password method has been shown to be secure against a variety of cryptanalytic attacks [WAGN00].

When a user attempts to log on to a UNIX system, the user provides an ID and a password (Figure 15.1b). The operating system uses the ID to index into the password file and retrieve the plaintext salt and the encrypted password. The salt and user-supplied password are used as input to the encryption routine. If the result matches the stored value, the password is accepted.

The salt serves three purposes:

- It prevents duplicate passwords from being visible in the password file. Even if two users choose the same password, those passwords will be assigned different salt values. Hence, the hashed passwords of the two users will differ.

- It greatly increases the difficulty of offline dictionary attacks. For a salt of length b bits, the number of possible passwords is increased by a factor of 2^b, increasing the difficulty of guessing a password in a dictionary attack.

- It becomes nearly impossible to find out whether a person with passwords on two or more systems has used the same password on all of them.

To see the second point, consider the way that an offline dictionary attack would work. The attacker obtains a copy of the password file. Suppose first that the salt is not used. The attacker's goal is to guess a single password. To that end, the attacker submits a large number of likely passwords to the hashing function. If any of the guesses matches one of the hashes in the file, then the attacker has found a password that is in the file. But faced with the UNIX scheme, the attacker must take each guess and submit it to the hash function once for each salt value in the dictionary file, multiplying the number of guesses that must be checked.

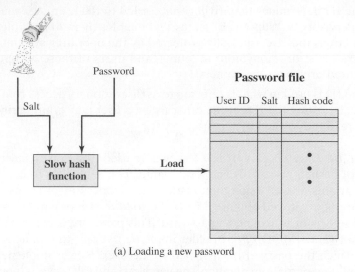

(a) Loading a new password

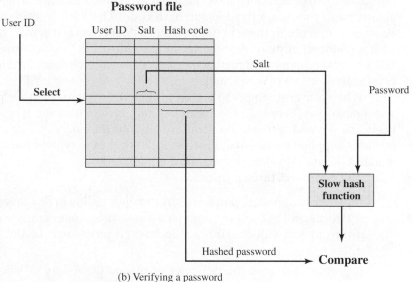

(b) Verifying a password

Figure 15.1   UNIX Password Scheme

There are two threats to the UNIX password scheme. First, a user can gain access on a machine using a guest account or by some other means and then run a password guessing program, called a password cracker, on that machine. The attacker should be able to check many thousands of possible passwords with little resource consumption. Second, if an opponent is able to obtain a copy of the password file, then a cracker program can be run on another machine at leisure. This enables the opponent to run through millions of possible passwords in a reasonable period.

UNIX IMPLEMENTATIONS   Since the original development of UNIX, most implementations have relied on the following password scheme. Each user selects a password of up to eight printable characters in length. This is converted into a 56-bit value (using 7-bit ASCII) that serves as the key input to an encryption routine. The hash routine, known as crypt(3), is based on DES. A 12-bit salt value is used. The modified DES algorithm is executed with a data input consisting of a 64-bit block of zeros. The output of the algorithm then serves as input for a second encryption. This process is repeated for a total of 25 encryptions. The resulting 64-bit output is then translated into an 11-character sequence. The modification of the DES algorithm converts it into a one-way hash function. The crypt(3) routine is designed to discourage guessing attacks. Software implementations of DES are slow compared to hardware versions, and the use of 25 iterations multiplies the time required by 25.

This particular implementation is now considered woefully inadequate. For example, [PERR03] reports the results of a dictionary attack using a supercomputer. The attack was able to process over 50 million password guesses in about 80 minutes. Further, the results showed that for about $10,000 anyone should be able to do the same in a few months using one uniprocessor machine. Despite its known weaknesses, this UNIX scheme is still often required for compatibility with existing account management software or in multivendor environments.

There are other, much stronger, hash/salt schemes available for UNIX. The recommended hash function for many UNIX systems, including Linux, Solaris, and FreeBSD, is based on the MD5 secure hash algorithm (which is similar to, but not as secure as, SHA-1).[1] The MD5 crypt routine uses a salt of up to 48 bits and effectively has no limitations on password length. It produces a 128-bit hash value. It is also far slower than crypt(3). To achieve the slowdown, MD5 crypt uses an inner loop with 1,000 iterations.

Probably the most secure version of the UNIX hash/salt scheme was developed for OpenBSD, another widely used open source UNIX. This scheme, reported in [PROV99], uses a hash function based on the Blowfish symmetric block cipher. The hash function, called Bcrypt, is quite slow to execute. Bcrypt allows passwords of up to 55 characters in length and requires a random salt value of 128 bits, to produce a 192-bit hash value. Bcrypt also includes a cost variable; an increase in the cost variable causes a corresponding increase in the time required to perform a Bcyrpt hash. The cost assigned to a new password is configurable, so that administrators can assign a higher cost to privileged users.

Token–Based Authentication

Objects that a user possesses for the purpose of user authentication are called tokens. In this subsection, we examine two types of tokens that are widely used; these are cards that have the appearance and size of bank cards.

MEMORY CARDS Memory cards can store but not process data. The most common such card is the bank card with a magnetic stripe on the back. A magnetic stripe can store only a simple security code, which can be read (and unfortunately reprogrammed) by an inexpensive card reader. There are also memory cards that include an internal electronic memory.

---

[1]See Appendix K for a discussion of secure hash algorithms.

Memory cards can be used alone for physical access, such as a hotel room. For computer user authentication, such cards are typically used with some form of password or personal identification number (PIN). A typical application is an automatic teller machine (ATM).

The memory card, when combined with a PIN or password, provides significantly greater security than a password alone. An adversary must gain physical possession of the card (or be able to duplicate it) plus must gain knowledge of the PIN. Among the potential drawbacks are the following [NIST95]:

- **Requires special reader:** This increases the cost of using the token and creates the requirement to maintain the security of the reader's hardware and software.

- **Token loss:** A lost token temporarily prevents its owner from gaining system access. Thus, there is an administrative cost in replacing the lost token. In addition, if the token is found, stolen, or forged, then an adversary now need only determine the PIN to gain unauthorized access.

- **User dissatisfaction:** Although users may have no difficulty in accepting the use of a memory card for ATM access, its use for computer access may be deemed inconvenient.

SMART CARDS   A wide variety of devices qualify as smart tokens. These can be categorized along three dimensions that are not mutually exclusive:

- **Physical characteristics:** Smart tokens include an embedded microprocessor. A smart token that looks like a bank card is called a smart card. Other smart tokens can look like calculators, keys, or other small portable objects.

- **Interface:** Manual interfaces include a keypad and display for human/token interaction. Smart tokens with an electronic interface communicate with a compatible reader/writer.

- **Authentication protocol:** The purpose of a smart token is to provide a means for user authentication. We can classify the authentication protocols used with smart tokens into three categories:

  — **Static:** With a static protocol, the user authenticates himself or herself to the token and then the token authenticates the user to the computer. The latter half of this protocol is similar to the operation of a memory token.

  — **Dynamic password generator:** In this case, the token generates a unique password periodically (e.g., every minute). This password is then entered into the computer system for authentication, either manually by the user or electronically via the token. The token and the computer system must be initialized and kept synchronized so that the computer knows the password that is current for this token.

  — **Challenge-response:** In this case, the computer system generates a challenge, such as a random string of numbers. The smart token generates a response based on the challenge. For example, public-key cryptography could be used and the token could encrypt the challenge string with the token's private key.

For user authentication to computer, the most important category of smart token is the smart card, which has the appearance of a credit card, has an electronic interface, and may use any of the type of protocols just described. The remainder of this section discusses smart cards.

A smart card contains within it an entire microprocessor, including processor, memory, and I/O ports. Some versions incorporate a special coprocessing circuit for cryptographic operation to speed the task of encoding and decoding messages or generating digital signatures to validate the information transferred. In some cards, the I/O ports are directly accessible by a compatible reader by means of exposed electrical contacts. Other cards rely instead on an embedded antenna for wireless communication with the reader.

Biometric Authentication

A biometric authentication system attempts to authenticate an individual based on his or her unique physical characteristics. These include static characteristics, such as fingerprints, hand geometry, facial characteristics, and retinal and iris patterns; and dynamic characteristics, such as voiceprint and signature. In essence, biometrics is based on pattern recognition. Compared to passwords and tokens, biometric authentication is both technically complex and expensive. While it is used in a number of specific applications, biometrics has yet to mature as a standard tool for user authentication to computer systems.

A number of different types of physical characteristics are either in use or under study for user authentication. The most common are the following:

- **Facial characteristics:** Facial characteristics are the most common means of human-to-human identification; thus it is natural to consider them for identification by computer. The most common approach is to define characteristics based on relative location and shape of key facial features, such as eyes, eyebrows, nose, lips, and chin shape. An alternative approach is to use an infrared camera to produce a face thermogram that correlates with the underlying vascular system in the human face.

- **Fingerprints:** Fingerprints have been used as a means of identification for centuries, and the process has been systematized and automated particularly for law enforcement purposes. A fingerprint is the pattern of ridges and furrows on the surface of the fingertip. Fingerprints are believed to be unique across the entire human population. In practice, automated fingerprint recognition and matching system extract a number of features from the fingerprint for storage as a numerical surrogate for the full fingerprint pattern.

- **Hand geometry:** Hand geometry systems identify features of the hand, including shape, and lengths and widths of fingers.

- **Retinal pattern:** The pattern formed by veins beneath the retinal surface is unique and therefore suitable for identification. A retinal biometric system obtains a digital image of the retinal pattern by projecting a low-intensity beam of visual or infrared light into the eye.

- **Iris:** Another unique physical characteristic is the detailed structure of the iris.

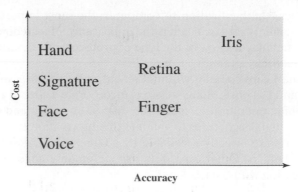

Figure 15.2   Cost versus Accuracy of Various Biometric Characteristics in User Authentication Schemes

- **Signature:** Each individual has a unique style of handwriting, and this is reflected especially in the signature, which is typically a frequently written sequence. However, multiple signature samples from a single individual will not be identical. This complicates the task of developing a computer representation of the signature that can be matched to future samples.

- **Voice:** Whereas the signature style of an individual reflects not only the unique physical attributes of the writer but also the writing habit that has developed, voice patterns are more closely tied to the physical and anatomical characteristics of the speaker. Nevertheless, there is still a variation from sample to sample over time from the same speaker, complicating the biometric recognition task.

Figure 15.2 gives a rough indication of the relative cost and accuracy of these biometric measures. The concept of accuracy does not apply to user authentication schemes using smart cards or passwords. For example, if a user enters a password, it either matches exactly the password expected for that user or not. In the case of biometric parameters, the system instead must determine how closely a presented biometric characteristic matches a stored characteristic. Before elaborating on the concept of biometric accuracy, we need to have a general idea of how biometric systems work.

15.2 ACCESS CONTROL

An access control policy dictates what types of access are permitted, under what circumstances, and by whom. Access control policies are generally grouped into the following categories:

- **Discretionary access control (DAC):** Controls access based on the identity of the requestor and on access rules (authorizations) stating what requestors are (or are not) allowed to do. This policy is termed *discretionary* because an entity might have access rights that permit the entity, by its own volition, to enable another entity to access some resource.

- **Mandatory access control (MAC):** Controls access based on comparing security labels (which indicate how sensitive or critical system resources are) with security clearances (which indicate system entities are eligible to access certain resources). This policy is termed *mandatory* because an entity that has clearance to access a resource may not, just by its own volition, enable another entity to access that resource.

- **Role-based access control (RBAC):** Controls access based on the roles that users have within the system and on rules stating what accesses are allowed to users in given roles.

DAC is the traditional method of implementing access control. This method was introduced in Chapter 12; we provide more detail in this section. MAC is a concept that evolved out of requirements for military information security and is beyond the scope of this book. RBAC has become increasingly popular and is introduced later in this section.

These three policies are not mutually exclusive (Figure 15.3). An access control mechanism can employ two or even all three of these policies to cover different classes of system resources.

Discretionary Access Control[2]

This section introduces a general model for DAC developed by Lampson, Graham, and Denning [LAMP71, GRAH72, DENN71]. The model assumes a set of subjects, a set of objects, and a set of rules that govern the access of subjects to objects. Let us define the protection state of a system to be the set of information, at a given point in time, that specifies the access rights for each subject with respect to each object. We can identify three requirements: representing the protection state, enforcing access rights, and allowing subjects to alter the protection state in certain ways. The model addresses all three requirements, giving a general, logical description of a DAC system.

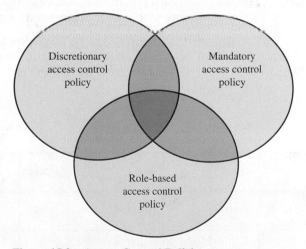

Figure 15.3   Access Control Policies

---

[2]Before continuing, the reader should review Section 12.8 and the discussion of UNIX file access control in Section 12.9.

To represent the protection state, we extend the universe of objects in the access control matrix to include the following:

- **Processes:** Access rights include the ability to delete a process, stop (block), and wake up a process.
- **Devices:** Access rights include the ability to read/write the device, to control its operation (e.g., a disk seek), and to block/unblock the device for use.
- **Memory locations or regions:** Access rights include the ability to read/write certain locations of regions of memory that are protected so that the default is that access is not allowed.
- **Subjects:** Access rights with respect to a subject have to do with the ability to grant or delete access rights of that subject to other objects, as explained subsequently.

Figure 15.4 is an example (compare Figure 12.13a). For an access control matrix A, each entry $A[S, X]$ contains strings, called access attributes, that specify the access rights of subject S to object X. For example, in Figure 15.4, S_1 may read file F_2, because *read* appears in $A[S_1, F_1]$.

From a logical or functional point of view, a separate access control module is associated with each type of object (Figure 15.5). The module evaluates each request by a subject to access an object to determine if the access right exists. An access attempt triggers the following steps:

1. A subject S_0 issues a request of type α for object X.
2. The request causes the system (the operating system or an access control interface module of some sort) to generate a message of the form (S_0, α, X) to the controller for X.
3. The controller interrogates the access matrix A to determine if α is in $A[S_0, X]$. If so, the access is allowed; if not, the access is denied and a protection violation occurs. The violation should trigger a warning and an appropriate action.

Figure 15.5 suggests that every access by a subject to an object is mediated by the controller for that object, and that the controller's decision is based on the

| | | Objects | | | | | | | |
| | Subjects | | | Files | | Processes | | Disk drives | |
	S_1	S_2	S_3	F_1	F_2	P_1	P_2	D_1	D_2
S_1	control	owner	owner control	read *	read owner	wakeup	wakeup	seek	owner
S_2		control		write *	execute			owner	seek *
S_3			control		write	stop			

Subjects label at left applies to rows S_1, S_2, S_3.

* = copy flag set

Figure 15.4 Extended Access Control Matrix

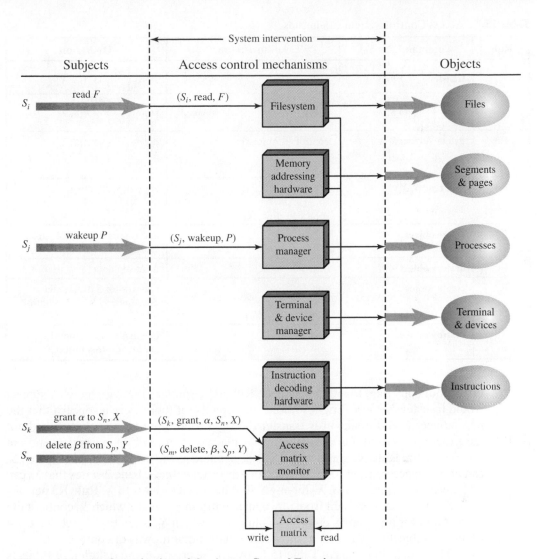

Figure 15.5   An Organization of the Access Control Function

current contents of the matrix. In addition, certain subjects have the authority to make specific changes to the access matrix. A request to modify the access matrix is treated as an access to the matrix, with the individual entries in the matrix treated as objects. Such accesses are mediated by an access matrix controller, which controls updates to the matrix.

The model also includes a set of rules that govern modifications to the access matrix, shown in Table 15.1. For this purpose, we introduce the access rights *owner* and *control* and the concept of a copy flag, explained in the subsequent paragraphs.

The first three rules deal with transferring, granting, and deleting access rights. Suppose that the entry α exists in $A[S_0, X]$. This means that S_0 has access right α to subject X and, because of the presence of the copy flag, can transfer this right, with

Table 15.1 Access Control System Commands

Rule	Command (by S_0)	Authorization	Operation
R1	**transfer** $\left\{ \begin{matrix} \alpha* \\ \alpha \end{matrix} \right\}$ **to** S, X	' *' in $A[So, X]$	store $\left\{ \begin{matrix} \alpha* \\ \alpha \end{matrix} \right\}$ in $A[S, X]$
R2	**grant** $\left\{ \begin{matrix} \alpha* \\ \alpha \end{matrix} \right\}$ **to** S, X	'owner' in $A[So, X]$	store $\left\{ \begin{matrix} \alpha* \\ \alpha \end{matrix} \right\}$ in $A[S, X]$
R3	**delete** α **from** S, X	'control' in $A[So, S]$ or 'owner' in $A[So, X]$	delete α from $A[S, X]$
R4	w α **read** S, X	'control' in $A[So, S]$ or 'owner' in $A[So, X]$	copy $A[S, X]$ into w
R5	**create object** X	None	add column for X to A; store 'owner' in $A[So, X]$
R6	**destroy object** X	'owner' in $A[So, X]$	delete column for X from A
R7	**create subject** S	None	add row for S to A; execute **create object** S; store 'control' in $A[S, S]$
R8	**destroy subject** S	'owner' in $A[So, S]$	delete row for S from A; execute **destroy object** S

or without copy flag, to another subject. Rule R1 expresses this capability. A subject would transfer the access right without the copy flag if there were a concern that the new subject would maliciously transfer the right to another subject that should not have that access right. For example, S_1 may place *read* or *read** in any matrix entry in the F_1 column. Rule R2 states that if S_0 is designated as the owner of object X, then S_0 can grant an access right to that object for any other subject. Rule 2 states that S_0 can add any access right to $A[S, X]$ for any S, if S_0 has *owner* access to X. Rule R3 permits S_0 to delete any access right from any matrix entry in a row for which S_0 controls the subject and for any matrix entry in a column for which S_0 owns the object. Rule R4 permits a subject to read that portion of the matrix that it owns or controls.

The remaining rules in Table 15.1 govern the creation and deletion of subjects and objects. Rule R5 states that any subject can create a new object, which it owns, and can then grant and delete access to the object. Under rule R6, the owner of an object can destroy the object, resulting in the deletion of the corresponding column of the access matrix. Rule R7 enables any subject to create a new subject; the creator owns the new subject and the new subject has control access to itself. Rule R8 permits the owner of a subject to delete the row and column (if there are subject columns) of the access matrix designated by that subject.

The set of rules in Table 15.1 is an example of the rule set that could be defined for an access control system. The following are examples of additional or alternative rules that could be included. A transfer-only right could be defined, which results in the transferred right being added to the target subject and deleted from the transferring subject. The number of owners of an object or a subject could be limited to one by not allowing the copy flag to accompany the owner right.

The ability of one subject to create another subject and to have *owner* access right to that subject can be used to define a hierarchy of subjects. For example, in Figure 15.4, S_1 owns S_2 and S_3, so that S_2 and S_3 are subordinate to S_1. By the rules of Table 15.1, S_1 can grant and delete to S_2 access rights that S_1 already has. Thus, a subject can create another subject with a subset of its own access rights. This might be useful, for example, if a subject is invoking an application that is not fully trusted, and does not want that application to be able to transfer access rights to other subjects.

Role-Based Access Control

Traditional DAC systems define the access rights of individual users and groups of users. In contrast, RBAC is based on the roles that users assume in a system rather than the user's identity. Typically, RBAC models define a role as a job function within an organization. RBAC systems assign access rights to roles instead of individual users. In turn, users are assigned to different roles, either statically or dynamically, according to their responsibilities.

RBAC now enjoys widespread commercial use and remains an area of active research. The National Institute of Standards and Technology (NIST) has issued a standard, *Security Requirements for Cryptographic Modules* (FIPS PUB 140-2, May 25, 2001), that requires support for access control and administration through roles.

The relationship of users to roles is many to many, as is the relationship of roles to resources, or system objects (Figure 15.6). The set of users changes, in some

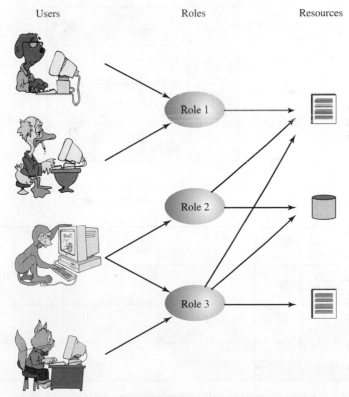

Figure 15.6   Users, Roles, and Resources

environments frequently, and the assignment of a user to one or more roles may also be dynamic. The set of roles in the system in most environments is likely to be static, with only occasional additions or deletions. Each role will have specific access rights to one or more resources. The set of resources and the specific access rights associated with a particular role are also likely to change infrequently.

We can use the access matrix representation to depict the key elements of an RBAC system in simple terms, as shown in Figure 15.7. The upper matrix relates individual users to roles. Typically there are many more users than roles. Each matrix entry is either blank or marked, the latter indicating that this user is assigned

	R_1	R_2	• • •	R_n
U_1	✕			
U_2	✕			
U_3		✕		✕
U_4				✕
U_5				✕
U_6				✕
• • •				
U_m	✕			

	Objects								
Roles	R_1	R_2	R_n	F_1	F_1	P_1	P_2	D_1	D_2
R_1	control	owner	owner control	read *	read owner	wakeup	wakeup	seek	owner
R_2		control		write *	execute			owner	seek *
• • •									
R_n			control		write	stop			

Figure 15.7 Access Control Matrix Representation of RBAC

to this role. Note that a single user may be assigned multiple roles (more than one mark in a row) and that multiple users may be assigned to a single role (more than one mark in a column). The lower matrix has the same structure as the DAC matrix, with roles as subjects. Typically, there are few roles and many objects, or resources. In this matrix the entries are the specific access rights enjoyed by the roles. Note that a role can be treated as an object, allowing the definition of role hierarchies.

RBAC lends itself to an effective implementation of the principle of least privilege. That is, each role should contain the minimum set of access rights needed for that role. A user is assigned to a role that enables him or her to perform only what is required for that role. Multiple users assigned to the same role enjoy the same minimal set of access rights.

15.3 INTRUSION DETECTION

Intrusion detection systems were introduced in Section 3.6.

Basic Principles

Authentication facilities, access control facilities, and firewalls all play a role in countering intrusions. Another line of defense is intrusion detection, and this has been the focus of much research in recent years. This interest is motivated by a number of considerations, including the following:

1. If an intrusion is detected quickly enough, the intruder can be identified and ejected from the system before any damage is done or any data are compromised. Even if the detection is not sufficiently timely to preempt the intruder, the sooner that the intrusion is detected, the less the amount of damage and the more quickly that recovery can be achieved.
2. An effective IDS can serve as a deterrent, thus acting to prevent intrusions.
3. Intrusion detection enables the collection of information about intrusion techniques that can be used to strengthen intrusion prevention measures.

Intrusion detection is based on the assumption that the behavior of the intruder differs from that of a legitimate user in ways that can be quantified. Of course, we cannot expect that there will be a crisp, exact distinction between an attack by an intruder and the normal use of resources by an authorized user. Rather, we must expect that there will be some overlap.

Figure 15.8 suggests, in abstract terms, the nature of the task confronting the designer of an IDS. Although the typical behavior of an intruder differs from the typical behavior of an authorized user, there is an overlap in these behaviors. Thus, a loose interpretation of intruder behavior, which will catch more intruders, will also lead to a number of **false positives**, or authorized users identified as intruders. On the other hand, an attempt to limit false positives by a tight interpretation of intruder behavior will lead to an increase in **false negatives**, or intruders not identified as intruders. Thus, there is an element of compromise and art in the practice of intrusion detection.

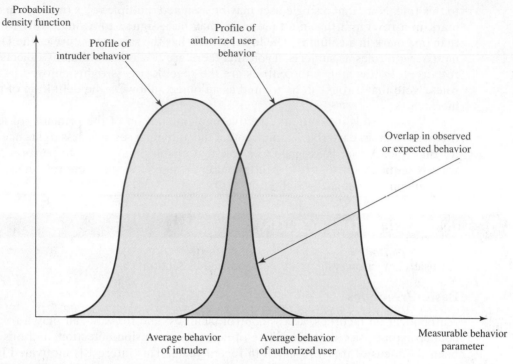

Figure 15.8   Profiles of Behavior of Intruders and Authorized Users

In Anderson's study [ANDE80], it was postulated that one could, with reasonable confidence, distinguish between a masquerader and a legitimate user. Patterns of legitimate user behavior can be established by observing past history, and significant deviation from such patterns can be detected. Anderson suggests that the task of detecting a misfeasor (legitimate user performing in an unauthorized fashion) is more difficult, in that the distinction between abnormal and normal behavior may be small. Anderson concluded that such violations would be undetectable solely through the search for anomalous behavior. However, misfeasor behavior might nevertheless be detectable by intelligent definition of the class of conditions that suggest unauthorized use. Finally, the detection of the clandestine user was felt to be beyond the scope of purely automated techniques. These observations, which were made in 1980, remain true today.

For the remainder of this section, we concentrate on host-based intrusion detection.

Host–Based Intrusion Detection Techniques

Host-based IDSs add a specialized layer of security software to vulnerable or sensitive systems; examples include database servers and administrative systems. The host-based IDS monitors activity on the system in a variety of ways to detect suspicious behavior. In some cases, an IDS can halt an attack before any damage is done, but its primary purpose is to detect intrusions, log suspicious events, and send alerts.

The primary benefit of a host-based IDS is that it can detect both external and internal intrusions, something that is not possible either with network-based IDSs or firewalls.

Host-based IDSs follow one of two general approaches to intrusion detection:

1. **Anomaly detection:** Involves the collection of data relating to the behavior of legitimate users over a period of time. Then statistical tests are applied to observed behavior to determine with a high level of confidence whether that behavior is not legitimate user behavior. The following are two approaches to statistical anomaly detection:

   a. *Threshold detection:* This approach involves defining thresholds, independent of user, for the frequency of occurrence of various events.

   b. *Profile based:* A profile of the activity of each user is developed and used to detect changes in the behavior of individual accounts.

2. **Signature detection:** Involves an attempt to define a set of rules or attack patterns that can be used to decide that a given behavior is that of an intruder.

In essence, anomaly approaches attempt to define normal, or expected, behavior, whereas signature-based approaches attempt to define proper behavior.

In terms of the types of attackers listed earlier, anomaly detection is effective against masqueraders, who are unlikely to mimic the behavior patterns of the accounts they appropriate. On the other hand, such techniques may be unable to deal with misfeasors. For such attacks, signature-based approaches may be able to recognize events and sequences that, in context, reveal penetration. In practice, a system may employ a combination of both approaches to be effective against a broad range of attacks.

Audit Records

A fundamental tool for intrusion detection is the audit record. Some record of ongoing activity by users must be maintained as input to an IDS. Basically, two plans are used:

- **Native audit records:** Virtually all multiuser operating systems include accounting software that collects information on user activity. The advantage of using this information is that no additional collection software is needed. The disadvantage is that the native audit records may not contain the needed information or may not contain it in a convenient form.

- **Detection-specific audit records:** A collection facility can be implemented that generates audit records containing only that information required by the IDS. One advantage of such an approach is that it could be made vendor independent and ported to a variety of systems. The disadvantage is the extra overhead involved in having, in effect, two accounting packages running on a machine.

A good example of detection-specific audit records is one developed by Dorothy Denning [DENN87]. Each audit record contains the following fields:

- **Subject:** Initiators of actions. A subject is typically a terminal user but might also be a process acting on behalf of users or groups of users. All activity arises through commands issued by subjects. Subjects may be grouped into different access classes, and these classes may overlap.

- **Action:** Operation performed by the subject on or with an object; for example, login, read, perform I/O, and execute.
- **Object:** Receptors of actions. Examples include files, programs, messages, records, terminals, printers, and user- or program-created structures. When a subject is the recipient of an action, such as electronic mail, then that subject is considered an object. Objects may be grouped by type. Object granularity may vary by object type and by environment. For example, database actions may be audited for the database as a whole or at the record level.
- **Exception-condition:** Denotes which, if any, exception condition is raised on return.
- **Resource-usage:** A list of quantitative elements in which each element gives the amount used of some resource (e.g., number of lines printed or displayed, number of records read or written, processor time, I/O units used, session elapsed time).
- **Time-stamp:** Unique time-and-date stamp identifying when the action took place.

Most user operations are made up of a number of elementary actions. For example, a file copy involves the execution of the user command, which includes doing access validation and setting up the copy, plus the read from one file, plus the write to another file. Consider the command

COPY GAME.EXE TO <Library> GAME.EXE

issued by Smith to copy an executable file GAME from the current directory to the <Library> directory. The following audit records may be generated:

| Smith | execute | <Library>COPY.EXE | 0 | CPU = 00002 | 11058721678 |

| Smith | Read | <Smith>GAME.EXE | 0 | RECORDS = 0 | 11058721679 |

| Smith | execute | <Library>COPY.EXE | write-viol | RECORDS = 0 | 11058721680 |

In this case, the copy is aborted because Smith does not have write permission to <Library>.

The decomposition of a user operation into elementary actions has three advantages:

1. Because objects are the protectable entities in a system, the use of elementary actions enables an audit of all behavior affecting an object. Thus, the system can detect attempted subversions of access controls (by noting an abnormality in the number of exception conditions returned) and can detect successful subversions (by noting an abnormality in the set of objects accessible to the subject).

2. Single-object, single-action audit records simplify the model and the implementation.

3. Because of the simple, uniform structure of the detection-specific audit records, it may be relatively easy to obtain this information or at least part of it by a straightforward mapping from existing native audit records to the detection-specific audit records.

15.4 MALWARE DEFENSE

Antivirus Approaches

The ideal solution to the threat of viruses is prevention: Do not allow a virus to get into the system in the first place. This goal is, in general, impossible to achieve, although prevention can reduce the number of successful viral attacks. The next best approach is to be able to do the following:

- **Detection:** Once the infection has occurred, determine that it has occurred and locate the virus.
- **Identification:** Once detection has been achieved, identify the specific virus that has infected a program.
- **Removal:** Once the specific virus has been identified, remove all traces of the virus from the infected program and restore it to its original state. Remove the virus from all infected systems so that the disease cannot spread further.

If detection succeeds but either identification or removal is not possible, then the alternative is to discard the infected program and reload a clean backup version.

Advances in virus and antivirus technology go hand in hand. Early viruses were relatively simple code fragments and could be identified and purged with relatively simple antivirus software packages. As the virus arms race has evolved, both viruses and, necessarily, antivirus software have grown more complex and sophisticated. Increasingly sophisticated antivirus approaches and products continue to appear. In this subsection, we highlight two of the most important.

GENERIC DECRYPTION Generic decryption (GD) technology enables the antivirus program to easily detect even the most complex polymorphic viruses while maintaining fast scanning speeds [NACH97]. Recall that when a file containing a polymorphic virus is executed, the virus must decrypt itself to activate. In order to detect such a structure, executable files are run through a GD scanner, which contains the following elements:

- **CPU emulator:** A software-based virtual computer. Instructions in an executable file are interpreted by the emulator rather than executed on the underlying processor. The emulator includes software versions of all registers and other processor hardware, so that the underlying processor is unaffected by programs interpreted on the emulator.
- **Virus signature scanner:** A module that scans the target code looking for known virus signatures.
- **Emulation control module:** Controls the execution of the target code.

At the start of each simulation, the emulator begins interpreting instructions in the target code, one at a time. Thus, if the code includes a decryption routine that decrypts and hence exposes the virus, that code is interpreted. In effect, the virus does the work for the antivirus program by exposing the virus. Periodically, the control module interrupts interpretation to scan the target code for virus signatures.

During interpretation, the target code can cause no damage to the actual personal computer environment, because it is being interpreted in a completely controlled environment.

The most difficult design issue with a GD scanner is to determine how long to run each interpretation. Typically, virus elements are activated soon after a program begins executing, but this need not be the case. The longer the scanner emulates a particular program, the more likely it is to catch any hidden viruses. However, the antivirus program can take up only a limited amount of time and resources before users complain of degraded system performance.

DIGITAL IMMUNE SYSTEM The digital immune system is a comprehensive approach to virus protection developed by IBM [KEPH97a, KEPH97b, WHIT99] and subsequently refined by Symantec [SYMA01]. The motivation for this development has been the rising threat of Internet-based virus propagation. We first say a few words about this threat and then summarize IBM's approach.

Traditionally, the virus threat was characterized by the relatively slow spread of new viruses and new mutations. Antivirus software was typically updated on a monthly basis, and this was sufficient to control the problem. Also traditionally, the Internet played a comparatively small role in the spread of viruses. But as [CHES97] points out, two major trends in Internet technology have had an increasing impact on the rate of virus propagation in recent years:

- **Integrated mail systems:** Systems such as Lotus Notes and Microsoft Outlook make it very simple to send anything to anyone and to work with objects that are received.
- **Mobile-program systems:** Capabilities such as Java and ActiveX allow programs to move on their own from one system to another.

In response to the threat posed by these Internet-based capabilities, IBM has developed a prototype digital immune system. This system expands on the use of program emulation discussed in the preceding subsection and provides a general-purpose emulation and virus-detection system. The objective of this system is to provide rapid response time so that viruses can be stamped out almost as soon as they are introduced. When a new virus enters an organization, the immune system automatically captures it, analyzes it, adds detection and shielding for it, removes it, and passes information about that virus to systems running IBM AntiVirus so that it can be detected before it is allowed to run elsewhere.

Figure 15.9 illustrates the typical steps in digital immune system operation:

1. A monitoring program on each PC uses a variety of heuristics based on system behavior, suspicious changes to programs, or family signature to infer that a virus may be present. The monitoring program forwards a copy of any program thought to be infected to an administrative machine within the organization.

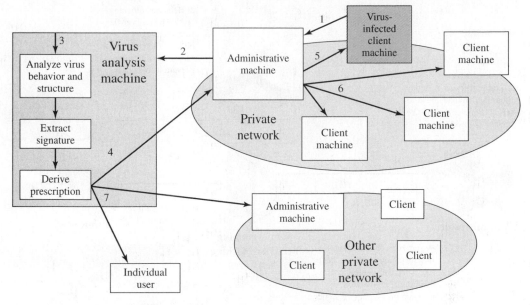

Figure 15.9   Digital Immune System

2. The administrative machine encrypts the sample and sends it to a central virus analysis machine.

3. This machine creates an environment in which the infected program can be safely run for analysis. Techniques used for this purpose include emulation, or the creation of a protected environment within which the suspect program can be executed and monitored. The virus analysis machine then produces a prescription for identifying and removing the virus.

4. The resulting prescription is sent back to the administrative machine.

5. The administrative machine forwards the prescription to the infected client.

6. The prescription is also forwarded to other clients in the organization.

7. Subscribers around the world receive regular antivirus updates that protect them from the new virus.

The success of the digital immune system depends on the ability of the virus analysis machine to detect new and innovative virus strains. By constantly analyzing and monitoring the viruses found in the wild, it should be possible to continually update the digital immune software to keep up with the threat.

BEHAVIOR-BLOCKING SOFTWARE   Unlike heuristics or fingerprint-based scanners, behavior blocking software integrates with the operating system of a host computer and monitors program behavior in real time for malicious actions [CONR02, NACH02]. The behavior blocking software then blocks potentially malicious actions before they have a chance to affect the system. Monitored behaviors can include

- Attempts to open, view, delete, and/or modify files;
- Attempts to format disk drives and other unrecoverable disk operations;

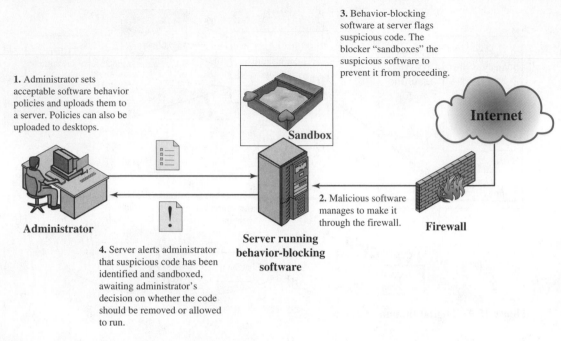

1. Administrator sets acceptable software behavior policies and uploads them to a server. Policies can also be uploaded to desktops.

3. Behavior-blocking software at server flags suspicious code. The blocker "sandboxes" the suspicious software to prevent it from proceeding.

Sandbox

Internet

2. Malicious software manages to make it through the firewall.

Firewall

Administrator

Server running behavior-blocking software

4. Server alerts administrator that suspicious code has been identified and sandboxed, awaiting administrator's decision on whether the code should be removed or allowed to run.

Figure 15.10   Behavior-Blocking Software Operation

- Modifications to the logic of executable files or macros;
- Modification of critical system settings, such as start-up settings;
- Scripting of e-mail and instant messaging clients to send executable content; and
- Initiation of network communications.

Figure 15.10 illustrates the operation of a behavior blocker. Behavior-blocking software runs on server and desktop computers and is instructed through policies set by the network administrator to let benign actions take place but to intercede when unauthorized or suspicious actions occur. The module blocks any suspicious software from executing. A blocker isolates the code in a sandbox, which restricts the code's access to various OS resources and applications. The blocker then sends an alert.

Because a behavior blocker can block suspicious software in real time, it has an advantage over such established antivirus detection techniques as fingerprinting or heuristics. While there are literally trillions of different ways to obfuscate and rearrange the instructions of a virus or worm, many of which will evade detection by a fingerprint scanner or heuristic, eventually malicious code must make a well-defined request to the operating system. Given that the behavior blocker can intercept all such requests, it can identify and block malicious actions regardless of how obfuscated the program logic appears to be.

Behavior blocking alone has limitations. Because the malicious code must run on the target machine before all its behaviors can be identified, it can cause harm before it has been detected and blocked. For example, a new virus might shuffle a number of seemingly unimportant files around the hard drive before infecting a single file and being blocked. Even though the actual infection was blocked, the user may be unable to locate his or her files, causing a loss to productivity or possibly worse.

Worm Countermeasures

There is considerable overlap in techniques for dealing with viruses and worms. Once a worm is resident on a machine, antivirus software can be used to detect it. In addition, because worm propagation generates considerable network activity, network activity and usage monitoring can form the basis of a worm defense.

To begin, let us consider the requirements for an effective worm countermeasure scheme:

- **Generality:** The approach taken should be able to handle a wide variety of worm attacks, including polymorphic worms.

- **Timeliness:** The approach should respond quickly so as to limit the number infected systems and the number of generated transmissions from infected systems.

- **Resiliency:** The approach should be resistant to evasion techniques employed by attackers to evade worm countermeasures.

- **Minimal denial-of-service costs:** The approach should result in minimal reduction in capacity or service due to the actions of the countermeasure software. That is, in an attempt to contain worm propagation, the countermeasure should not significantly disrupt normal operation.

- **Transparency:** The countermeasure software and devices should not require modification to existing (legacy) OSs, application software, and hardware.

- **Global and local coverage:** The approach should be able to deal with attack sources both from outside and inside the enterprise network.

No existing worm countermeasure scheme appears to satisfy all these requirements. Thus, administrators typically need to use multiple approaches in defending against worm attacks.

Following [JHI07], we list six classes of worm defense:

A. **Signature-based worm scan filtering:** This type of approach generates a worm signature, which is then used to prevent worm scans from entering/leaving a network/host. Typically, this approach involves identifying suspicious flows and generating a worm signature. This approach is vulnerable to the use of polymorphic worms: Either the detection software misses the worm or, if it is sufficiently sophisticated to deal with polymorphic worms, the scheme may take a long time to react. [NEWS05] is an example of this approach.

B. **Filter-based worm containment:** This approach is similar to class A but focuses on worm content rather than a scan signature. The filter checks a message to determine if it contains worm code. An example is Vigilante [COST05], which relies on collaborative worm detection at end hosts. This approach can be quite effective but requires efficient detection algorithms and rapid alert dissemination.

C. **Payload-classification-based worm containment:** These network-based techniques examine packets to see if they contain a worm. Various anomaly detection techniques can be used, but care is needed to avoid high levels of false positives or negatives. An example of this approach is reported in [CHIN05], which looks for exploit code in network flows. This approach does not generate signatures based on byte patterns but rather looks for control and data flow structures that suggest an exploit.

D. **Threshold random walk (TRW) scan detection:** TRW exploits randomness in picking destinations to connect to as a way of detecting if a scanner is in operation [JUNG04]. TRW is suitable for deployment in high-speed, low-cost network devices. It is effective against the common behavior seen in worm scans.

E. **Rate limiting:** This class limits the rate of scanlike traffic from an infected host. Various strategies can be used, including limiting the number of new machines a host can connect to in a window of time, detecting a high connection failure rate, and limiting the number of unique IP addresses a host can scan in a window of time. [CHEN04] is an example. This class of countermeasures may introduce longer delays for normal traffic. This class is also not suited for slow, stealthy worms that spread slowly to avoid detection based on activity level.

F. **Rate halting:** This approach immediately blocks outgoing traffic when a threshold is exceeded either in outgoing connection rate or diversity of connection attempts [JHI07]. The approach must include measures to quickly unblock mistakenly blocked hosts in a transparent way. Rate halting can integrate with a signature- or filter-based approach so that once a signature or filter is generated, every blocked host can be unblocked. Rate halting appears to offer a very effective countermeasure. As with rate limiting, rate halting techniques are not suitable for slow, stealthy worms.

Bot Countermeasures

A number of the countermeasures discussed in this chapter make sense against bots, including IDSs and digital immune systems. Once bots are activated and an attack is underway, these countermeasures can be used to detect the attack. But the primary objective is to try to detect and disable the botnet during its construction phase.

Rootkit Countermeasures

Rootkits can be extraordinarily difficult to detect and neutralize, particularly so for kernel-level rootkits. Many of the administrative tools that could be used to detect a rootkit or its traces can be compromised by the rootkit precisely so that it is undetectable.

Countering rootkits requires a variety of network- and computer-level security tools. Both network-based and host-based intrusion detection systems can look for the code signatures of known rootkit attacks in incoming traffic. Host-based antivirus software can also be used to recognize the known signatures.

Of course, there are always new rootkits and modified versions of existing rootkits that display novel signatures. For these cases, a system needs to look for behaviors that could indicate the presence of a rootkit, such as the interception of system calls or a keylogger interacting with a keyboard driver. Such behavior detection is far from straightforward. For example, antivirus software typically intercepts system calls.

Another approach is to do some sort of file integrity check. An example of this is RootkitRevealer, a freeware package from SysInternals. The package compares the results of a system scan using APIs with the actual view of storage using instructions that do not go through an API. Because a rootkit conceals itself by modifying the view of storage seen by administrator calls, RootkitRevealer catches the discrepancy.

If a kernel-level rootkit is detected, by any means, the only secure and reliable way to recover is to do an entire new OS install on the infected machine.

15.5 DEALING WITH BUFFER OVERFLOW ATTACKS[3]

Finding and exploiting a stack buffer overflow is not difficult. The large number of exploits over the previous couple of decades clearly illustrates this. There is consequently a need to defend systems against such attacks by either preventing them, or at least detecting and aborting such attacks. This section discusses possible approaches to implementing such protections. These can be broadly classified into two categories:

- Compile-time defenses, which aim to harden programs to resist attacks in new programs
- Run-time defenses, which aim to detect and abort attacks in existing programs

While suitable defenses have been known for a couple of decades, the very large existing base of vulnerable software and systems hinders their deployment; hence the interest in run-time defenses, which can be deployed in operating systems and updates and can provide some protection for existing vulnerable programs. Most of these techniques are mentioned in [LHEE03].

Compile-Time Defenses

Compile-time defenses aim to prevent or detect buffer overflows by instrumenting programs when they are compiled. The possibilities for doing this range from choosing a high-level language that does not permit buffer overflows to encouraging safe coding standards, using safe standard libraries, or including additional code to detect corruption of the stack frame.

CHOICE OF PROGRAMMING LANGUAGE One possibility is to write the program using a modern high-level programming language, one that has a strong notion of variable type and what constitutes permissible operations on them. Such languages are not vulnerable to buffer overflow attacks, because their compilers include additional code to enforce range checks automatically, removing the need for the programmer to explicitly code them. The flexibility and safety provided by these languages

---

[3]The material in this section was developed by Lawrie Brown of the Australian Defence Force Academy.

does come at a cost in resource use, both at compile time and also in additional code that must execute at run-time to impose checks such as that on buffer limits. These disadvantages are much less significant than they used to be, due to the rapid increase in processor performance. Increasingly programs are being written in these languages and hence should be immune to buffer overflows in their code (though if they use existing system libraries or run-time execution environments written in less safe languages, they may still be vulnerable). The distance from the underlying machine language and architecture also means that access to some instructions and hardware resources is lost. This limits their usefulness in writing code, such as device drivers, that must interact with such resources. For these reasons, there is still likely to be at least some code written in less safe languages such as C.

SAFE CODING TECHNIQUES   If languages such as C are being used, programmers need to be aware that their ability to manipulate pointer addresses and access memory directly comes at a cost. C was designed as a systems programming language, running on systems that were vastly smaller and more constrained than we now use. This meant that C's designers placed much more emphasis on space efficiency and performance considerations than on type safety. They assumed that programmers would exercise due care in writing code using these languages and take responsibility for ensuring the safe use of all data structures and variables.

Unfortunately, as several decades of experience has shown, this has not been the case. This may be seen in large legacy body of potentially unsafe code in the UNIX and Linux operating systems and applications, some of which are potentially vulnerable to buffer overflows.15.6 azx.

In order to harden these systems, the programmer needs to inspect the code and rewrite any unsafe coding constructs in a safe manner. Given the rapid uptake of buffer overflow exploits, this process has begun in some cases. A good example is the OpenBSD project, which produces a free, multiplatform 4.4BSD-based UNIX-like operating system. Among other technology changes, programmers have undertaken an extensive audit of the existing code base, including the operating system, standard libraries, and common utilities. This has resulted in what is widely regarded as one of the safest operating systems in widespread use. The OpenBSD project claims as of mid-2006 that there has only been one remote hole discovered in the default install in more than 8 years. This is a clearly enviable record. Microsoft have also undertaken a major project in reviewing their code base, partly in response to continuing bad publicity over the number of vulnerabilities, including many buffer overflow issues, that have been found in their operating systems and applications code. This has clearly been a difficult process, though they claim that their new Vista operating system will benefit greatly from this process.

LANGUAGE EXTENSIONS AND USE OF SAFE LIBRARIES   Given the problems that can occur in C with unsafe array and pointer references, there have been a number of proposals to augment compilers to automatically insert range checks on such references. While this is fairly easy for statically allocated arrays, handling dynamically allocated memory is more problematic, because the size information is not available at compile-time. Handling this requires an extension to the semantics of a pointer to include bounds information and the use of library routines to ensure that these values are set correctly. Several such approaches are listed in [LHEE03]. However, there is generally a performance penalty with the use of such techniques that may or may not be acceptable. These techniques also require all programs and libraries that require these safety features to be recompiled with the modified compiler. While this can be feasible for a new release of an operating system and its associated utilities, there will still likely be problems with third-party applications.

A common concern with C comes from the use of unsafe standard library routines, especially some of the string manipulation routines. One approach to improving the safety of systems has been to replace these with safer variants. This can include the provision of new functions, such as `strlcpy()` in the BSD family of systems, including OpenBSD. Using these requires rewriting the source to conform to the new safer semantics. Alternatively, it involves replacement of the standard string library with a safer variant. Libsafe is a well-known example of this. It implements the standard semantics but includes additional checks to ensure that the copy operations do not extend beyond the local variable space in the stack frame. So, while it cannot prevent corruption of adjacent local variables, it can prevent any modification of the old stack frame and return address values, and thus prevent the classic stack buffer overflow types of attack we examined previously. This library is implemented as a dynamic library, arranged to load before the existing standard libraries, and can thus provide protection for existing programs without requiring them to be recompiled, provided they dynamically access the standard library routines (as most programs do). The modified library code has been found to typically be at least as efficient as the standard libraries, and thus its use is an easy way of protecting existing programs against some forms of buffer overflow attacks.

STACK PROTECTION MECHANISMS   An effective method for protecting programs against classic stack overflow attacks is to instrument the function entry and exit code to setup and then check its stack frame for any evidence of corruption. If any modification is found, the program is aborted rather than allowing the attack to proceed. There are several approaches to providing this protection, which we discuss next.

Stackguard is one of the best known protection mechanisms. It is a GCC (GNU Compiler Collection) compiler extension that inserts additional function entry and exit code. The added function entry code writes a **canary**[4] value below the old frame pointer address, before the allocation of space for local variables. The added function exit code checks that the canary value has not changed before continuing with the usual function exit operations of restoring the old frame pointer and transferring control back to the return address. Any attempt at a classic stack buffer overflow would have to alter this value in order to change the old frame pointer and return addresses, and would thus be detected, resulting in the program being aborted. For this defense to function successfully, it is critical that the canary

---

[4]Named after the miner's canary used to detect poisonous air in a mine and thus warn the miners in time for them to escape.

value be unpredictable and should be different on different systems. If this were not the case, the attacker would simply ensure the shellcode included the correct canary value in the required location. Typically, a random value is chosen as the canary value on process creation and saved as part of the processes state. The code added to the function entry and exit then uses this value.

There are some issues with using this approach. First, it requires that all programs needing protection be recompiled. Second, because the structure of the stack frame has changed, it can cause problems with programs, such as debuggers, which analyze stack frames. However, the canary technique has been used to recompile an entire Linux distribution and provide it with a high level of resistance to stack overflow attacks. Similar functionality is available for Windows programs by compiling them using Microsoft's /GS Visual C++ compiler option.

Run-Time Defenses

As has been noted, most of the compile-time approaches require recompilation of existing programs. Hence, there is interest in run-time defenses that can be deployed as operating systems updates to provide some protection for existing vulnerable programs. These defenses involve changes to the memory management of the virtual address space of processes. These changes act either to alter the properties of regions of memory or to make predicting the location of targeted buffers sufficiently difficult to thwart many types of attacks.

EXECUTABLE ADDRESS SPACE PROTECTION   Many of the buffer overflow attacks involve copying machine code into the targeted buffer and then transferring execution to it. A possible defense is to block the execution of code on the stack, on the assumption that executable code should only be found elsewhere in the processes address space.

To support this feature efficiently requires support from the processor's memory management unit (MMU) to tag pages of virtual memory as being nonexecutable. Some processors, such as the SPARC used by Solaris, have had support for this for some time. Enabling its use in Solaris requires a simple kernel parameter change. Other processors, such as the x86 family, have not had this support until recently, with the relatively recent addition of the **no-execute** bit in its MMU. Extensions have been made available to Linux, BSD, and other UNIX-style systems to support the use of this feature. Some indeed are also capable of protecting the heap as well as the stack, which also is the target of attacks. Support for enabling no-execute protection is also included in recent Windows systems.

Making the stack (and heap) nonexecutable provides a high degree of protection against many types of buffer overflow attacks for existing programs; hence the inclusion of this practice is standard in a number of recent operating systems releases. However, one issue is support for programs that do need to place executable code on the stack. This can occur, for example, in just-in-time compilers, such as is used in the Java Run-time system. Executable code on the stack is also used to implement nested functions in C (a GCC extension) and also Linux signal handlers. Special provisions are needed to support these requirements. Nonetheless, this is regarded as one of the best methods for protecting existing programs and hardening systems against some attacks.

ADDRESS SPACE RANDOMIZATION   Another run-time technique that can be used to thwart attacks involves manipulation of the location of key data structures in a processes address space. In particular, recall that in order to implement the classic stack overflow attack, the attacker needs to be able to predict the approximate location of the targeted buffer. The attacker uses this predicted address to determine a suitable return address to use in the attack to transfer control to the shellcode. One technique to greatly increase the difficulty of this prediction is to change the address at which the stack is located in a random manner for each process. The range of addresses available on modern processors is large (32 bits), and most programs only need a small fraction of that. Therefore, moving the stack memory region around by a megabyte or so has minimal impact on most programs but makes predicting the targeted buffer's address almost impossible.

Another target of attack is the location of standard library routines. In an attempt to bypass protections such as nonexecutable stacks, some buffer overflow variants exploit existing code in standard libraries. These are typically loaded at the same address by the same program. To counter this form of attack, we can use a security extension that randomizes the order of loading standard libraries by a program and their virtual memory address locations. This makes the address of any specific function sufficiently unpredictable as to render the chance of a given attack correctly predicting its address very low.

The OpenBSD system includes versions of these extensions in its technological support for a secure system.

GUARD PAGES   A final run-time technique that can be used places **guard pages** between critical regions of memory in a processes address space. Again, this exploits the fact that a process has much more virtual memory available than it typically needs. Gaps are placed between the ranges of addresses used for each of the components of the address space. These gaps, or guard pages, are flagged in the MMU as illegal addresses, and any attempt to access them results in the process being aborted. This can prevent buffer overflow attacks, typically of global data, which attempt to overwrite adjacent regions in the processes address space.

A further extension places guard pages between stack frames or between different allocations on the heap. This can provide further protection against stack and heap overflow attacks, but at cost in execution time supporting the large number of page mappings necessary.

15.6 WINDOWS 7 SECURITY

A good example of the access control concepts we have been discussing is the Windows access control facility, which exploits object-oriented concepts to provide a powerful and flexible access control capability.

Windows provides a uniform access control facility that applies to processes, threads, files, semaphores, windows, and other objects. Access control is governed by two entities: an access token associated with each process and a security descriptor associated with each object for which interprocess access is possible.

Access Control Scheme

When a user logs on to a Windows system, Windows uses a name/password scheme to authenticate the user. If the logon is accepted, a process is created for the user and an access token is associated with that process object. The access token, whose details are described later, include a security ID (SID), which is the identifier by which this user is known to the system for purposes of security. The token also contains SIDs for the security groups to which the user belongs. If the initial user process spawns a new process, the new process object inherits the same access token.

The access token serves two purposes:

1. It keeps all necessary security information together to speed access validation. When any process associated with a user attempts access, the security subsystem can make use of the token associated with that process to determine the user's access privileges.

2. It allows each process to modify its security characteristics in limited ways without affecting other processes running on behalf of the user.

The chief significance of the second point has to do with privileges that may be associated with a user. The access token indicates which privileges a user may have. Generally, the token is initialized with each of these privileges in a disabled state. Subsequently, if one of the user's processes needs to perform a privileged operation, the process may enable the appropriate privilege and attempt access. It would be undesirable to share the same token among all of the user's processes, because in that case enabling a privilege for one process enables it for all of them.

Associated with each object for which interprocess access is possible is a security descriptor. The chief component of the security descriptor is an access control list that specifies access rights for various users and user groups for this object. When a process attempts to access this object, the SIDs in the process token are matched against the access control list of the object to determine if access will be allowed or denied.

When an application opens a reference to a securable object, Windows verifies that the object's security descriptor grants the process the requested access. If the check succeeds, Windows caches the resulting granted access rights.

An important aspect of Windows security is the concept of impersonation, which simplifies the use of security in a client/server environment. If client and server talk through a RPC connection, the server can temporarily assume the identity of the client so that it can evaluate a request for access relative to that client's rights. After the access, the server reverts to its own identity.

Access Token

Figure 15.11a shows the general structure of an access token, which includes the following parameters:

- **Security ID:** Identifies a user uniquely across all of the machines on the network. This generally corresponds to a user's logon name. Special user SIDs were added in Windows 7 for use by processes and services. These specially managed SIDs are designed for secure management; they do not use the ordinary password polices human accounts do.

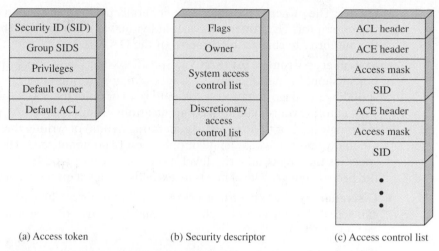

Security ID (SID)	Flags	ACL header
Group SIDS	Owner	ACE header
Privileges	System access	Access mask
Default owner	control list	SID
Default ACL	Discretionary	ACE header
	access	Access mask
	control list	SID

(a) Access token   (b) Security descriptor   (c) Access control list

Figure 15.11   Windows Security Structures

- **Group SIDs:** A list of the groups to which this user belongs. A group is simply a set of user IDs that are identified as a group for purposes of access control. Each group has a unique group SID. Access to an object can be defined on the basis of group SIDs, individual SIDs, or a combination. There is also a SID which reflects the process integrity level (low, medium, high, or system).

- **Privileges:** A list of security-sensitive system services that this user may call, for example CreateToken. Another example is the SeBackupPrivilege; users with this privilege are allowed to use a backup tool to back up files that they normally would not be able to read.

- **Default owner:** If this process creates another object, this field specifies the owner of the new object. Generally, the owner of a new object is the same as the owner of the spawning process. However, a user may specify that the default owner of any processes spawned by this process is a group SID to which this user belongs.

- **Default ACL:** This is an initial list of protections applied to the objects that the user creates. The user may subsequently alter the ACL for any object that it owns or that one of its groups owns.

Security Descriptors

Figure 15.11b shows the general structure of a security descriptor, which includes the following parameters:

- **Flags:** Define the type and contents of a security descriptor. The flags indicate whether or not the SACL and DACL are present, whether or not they were placed on the object by a defaulting mechanism, and whether the pointers in the descriptor use absolute or relative addressing. Relative descriptors are required for objects that are transmitted over a network, such as information transmitted in a RPC.

- **Owner:** The owner of the object can generally perform any action on the security descriptor. The owner can be an individual or a group SID. The owner has the authority to change the contents of the DACL.

- **System access control list (SACL):** Specifies what kinds of operations on the object should generate audit messages. An application must have the corresponding privilege in its access token to read or write the SACL of any object. This is to prevent unauthorized applications from reading SACLs (thereby learning what not to do to avoid generating audits) or writing them (to generate many audits to cause an illicit operation to go unnoticed). The SACL also specifies the object integrity level. Processes cannot modify an object unless the process integrity level meets or exceeds the level on the object.

- **Discretionary access control list (DACL):** Determines which users and groups can access this object for which operations. It consists of a list of access control entries (ACEs).

When an object is created, the creating process can assign as owner its own SID or any group SID in its access token. The creating process cannot assign an owner that is not in the current access token. Subsequently, any process that has been granted the right to change the owner of an object may do so, but again with the same restriction. The reason for the restriction is to prevent a user from covering his or her tracks after attempting some unauthorized action.

Let us look in more detail at the structure of access control lists, because these are at the heart of the Windows access control facility (Figure 15.11c). Each list consists of an overall header and a variable number of access control entries. Each entry specifies an individual or group SID and an access mask that defines the rights to be granted to this SID. When a process attempts to access an object, the object manager in the Windows Executive reads the SID and group SIDs from the access token along with the integrity level SID. If the access requested includes modifying the object, the integrity level is checked against the object integrity level in the SACL. If that test passes, the object manager then scans down the object's DACL. If a match is found—that is, if an ACE is found with a SID that matches one of the SIDs from the access token—then the process can have the access rights specified by the access mask in that ACE. This also may include denying access, in which case the access request fails. The first matching ACE determines the result of the access check.

Figure 15.12 shows the contents of the access mask. The least significant 16 bits specify access rights that apply to a particular type of object. For example, bit 0 for a file object is FILE_READ_DATA access and bit 0 for an event object is EVENT_QUERY_STATE access.

The most significant 16 bits of the mask contains bits that apply to all types of objects. Five of these are referred to as standard access types:

- **Synchronize:** Gives permission to synchronize execution with some event associated with this object. In particular, this object can be used in a wait function.

- **Write_owner:** Allows a program to modify the owner of the object. This is useful because the owner of an object can always change the protection on the object. (The owner may not be denied Write DAC access.)

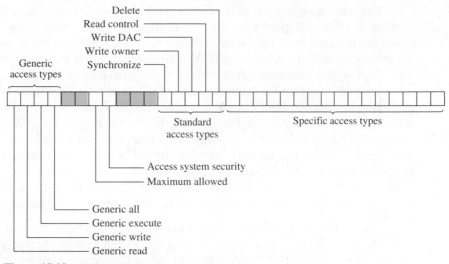

Figure 15.12   Access Mask

- **Write_DAC:** Allows the application to modify the DACL and hence the protection on this object.

- **Read_control:** Allows the application to query the owner and DACL fields of the security descriptor of this object.

- **Delete:** Allows the application to delete this object.

The high-order half of the access mask also contains the four generic access types. These bits provide a convenient way to set specific access types in a number of different object types. For example, suppose an application wishes to create several types of objects and ensure that users have read access to the objects, even though read has a somewhat different meaning for each object type. To protect each object of each type without the generic access bits, the application would have to construct a different ACE for each type of object and be careful to pass the correct ACE when creating each object. It is more convenient to create a single ACE that expresses the generic concept "allow read," and simply apply this ACE to each object that is created, and have the right thing happen. That is the purpose of the generic access bits, which are

- **Generic_all**: Allow all access

- **Generic_execute**: Allow execution if executable

- **Generic_write**: Allow write access

- **Generic_read**: Allow read-only access

The generic bits also affect the standard access types. For example, for a file object, the Generic_Read bit maps to the standard bits Read_Control and Synchronize and to the object-specific bits File_Read_Data, File_Read_Attributes, and File_Read_EA. Placing an ACE on a file object that grants some SID Generic_ Read grants those five access rights as if they had been specified individually in the access mask.

The remaining two bits in the access mask have special meanings. The Access_System_Security bit allows modifying audit and alarm control for this object. However, not only must this bit be set in the ACE for a SID but the access token for the process with that SID must have the corresponding privilege enabled.

Finally, the Maximum_Allowed bit is not really an access bit, but a bit that modifies the algorithm for scanning the DACL for this SID. Normally, Windows will scan through the DACL until it reaches an ACE that specifically grants (bit set) or denies (bit not set) the access requested by the requesting process or until it reaches the end of the DACL, in which latter case access is denied. The Maximum_Allowed bit allows the object's owner to define a set of access rights that is the maximum that will be allowed to a given user. With this in mind, suppose that an application does not know all of the operations that it is going to be asked to perform on an object during a session. There are three options for requesting access:

1. Attempt to open the object for all possible accesses. The disadvantage of this approach is that the access may be denied even though the application may have all of the access rights actually required for this session.

2. Only open the object when a specific access is requested, and open a new handle to the object for each different type of request. This is generally the preferred method because it will not unnecessarily deny access, nor will it allow more access than necessary. In many cases the object itself does not need to be referenced a second time, but the DuplicateHandle function can be used to make a copy of the handle with a lower level of access.

3. Attempt to open the object for as much access as the object will allow this SID. The advantage is that the user will not be artificially denied access, but the application may have more access than it needs. This latter situation may mask bugs in the application.

An important feature of Windows security is that applications can make use of the Windows security framework for user-defined objects. For example, a database server might create its own security descriptors and attach them to portions of a database. In addition to normal read/write access constraints, the server could secure database-specific operations, such as scrolling within a result set or performing a join. It would be the server's responsibility to define the meaning of special rights and perform access checks. But the checks would occur in a standard context, using systemwide user/group accounts and audit logs. The extensible security model should also prove useful to implementers of non-Microsoft file systems.

15.7 RECOMMENDED READING AND WEB SITES

The topics in this chapter are covered in more detail in [STAL08].

[OGOR03] is the paper to read for an authoritative survey of user authentication. [BURR04] is also a worthwhile survey. [SAND94] is an excellent overview of access control. [SAND96] is a comprehensive overview of RBAC. [SAUN01] compares RBAC and DAC. [SCAR07] is a detailed and worthwhile treatment of intrusion detection. Two short but useful survey articles on the subject are [KENT00] and [MCHU00]. [NING04] surveys recent advances in intrusion detection techniques. Good overview articles on antivirus approaches and malware defense generally are [CASS01], [FORR97], [KEPH97a], and [NACH97]. [LHEE03] surveys a range of alternative buffer overflow techniques, including a number not mentioned in this chapter, along with possible defensive techniques. The original published description of buffer overflow attacks is given in [LEVY96]. [KUPE05] is a good overview.

BURR04 Burr, W., Dodson, D., and Polk, W. *Electronic Authentication Guideline.* Gaithersburg, MD: National Institute of Standards and Technology, Special Publication 800-63, September 2004.

CASS01 Cass, S. "Anatomy of Malice." *IEEE Spectrum*, November 2001.

FORR97 Forrest, S., Hofmeyr, S., and Somayaji, A. "Computer Immunology." *Communications of the ACM*, October 1997.

KENT00 Kent, S. "On the Trail of Intrusions into Information Systems." *IEEE Spectrum*, December 2000.

KEPH97a Kephart, J., Sorkin, G., Chess, D., and White, S. "Fighting Computer Viruses." *Scientific American*, November 1997.

KUPE05 Kuperman, B., et al. "Detection and Prevention of Stack Buffer Overflow Attacks." *Communications of the ACM*, November 2005.

LEVY96 Levy, E., "Smashing the Stack for Fun and Profit." *Phrack Magazine*, File 14, Issue 49, November 1996.

LHEE03 Lhee, K., and Chapin, S., "Buffer Overflow and Format String Overflow Vulnerabilities." *Software—Practice and Experience*, Vol. 33, 2003.

MCHU00 McHugh, J., Christie, A., and Allen, J. "The Role of Intrusion Detection Systems." *IEEE Software*, September/October 2000.

NACH97 Nachenberg, C. "Computer Virus-Antivirus Coevolution." *Communications of the ACM*, January 1997.

NING04 Ning, P., et al. "Techniques and Tools for Analyzing Intrusion Alerts." *ACM Transactions on Information and System Security*, May 2004.

OGOR03 O'Gorman, L. "Comparing Passwords, Tokens and Biometrics for User Authentication." *Proceedings of the IEEE*, December 2003.

SAND94 Sandhu, R., and Samarati, P. "Access Control: Principles and Practice." *IEEE Communications Magazine*, February 1996.

SAND96 Sandhu, R., et al. "Role-Based Access Control Models." *Computer*, September 1994.

SAUN01 Saunders, G., Hitchens, M., and Varadharajan, V. "Role-Based Access Control and the Access Control Matrix." *Operating Systems Review*, October 2001.

SCAR07 Scarfone, K., and Mell, P. *Guide to Intrusion Detection and Prevention Systems.* NIST Special Publication SP 800-94, February 2007.

STAL08 Stallings, W., and Brown L. *Computer Security: Principles and Practice.* Upper Saddle River, NJ: Prentice Hall, 2008.

Recommended Web sites:

- **Password usage and generation:** NIST documents on this topic
- **Biometrics Consortium:** Government-sponsored site for the research, testing, and evaluation of biometric technology
- **NIST RBAC site:** Includes numerous documents, standards, and software on RBAC
- **STAT Project:** A research and open source project that focuses on signature-based intrusion detection tools for hosts, applications, and networks
- **Snort:** Web site for Snort, an open source network intrusion prevention and detection system
- **AntiVirus Online:** IBM's site on virus information
- **VirusList:** Site maintained by commercial antivirus software provider. Good collection of useful information

15.8 KEY TERMS, REVIEW QUESTIONS, AND PROBLEMS

Key Terms

access control	discretionary access control (DAC)	malware
antivirus		memory cards
audit records	hashed passwords	role-based access control (RBAC)
authentication	host-based IDS	
bot	intrusion detection	rootkit
buffer overflow	intrusion detections system (IDS)	smart cards
digital immune system		worm

Review Questions

15.1 In general terms, what are four means of authenticating a user's identity?

15.2 Explain the purpose of the salt in Figure 15.1.

15.3 Explain the difference between a simple memory card and a smart card.

15.4 List and briefly describe the principal physical characteristics used for biometric identification.

15.5 Briefly describe the difference between DAC and RBAC.

15.6 Explain the difference between anomaly intrusion detection and signature intrusion detection.

15.7 What is a digital immune system?

15.8 How does behavior-blocking software work?

15.9 Describe some worm countermeasures.

15.10 What types of programming languages are vulnerable to buffer overflows?

15.11 What are the two broad categories of defenses against buffer overflows?

15.12 List and briefly describe some of the defenses against buffer overflows that can be used when compiling new programs.

15.13 List and briefly describe some of the defenses against buffer overflows that can be implemented when running existing, vulnerable programs.

Problems

15.1 Explain the suitability or unsuitability of the following passwords:

a. YK 334	**e.** Aristotle
b. mfmitm (for "my favorite movie is tender mercies")	**f.** tv9stove
	g. 12345678
c. Natalie1	**h.** dribgib
d. Washington	

15.2 An early attempt to force users to use less predictable passwords involved computer-supplied passwords. The passwords were eight characters long and were taken from the character set consisting of lowercase letters and digits. They were generated by a pseudorandom number generator with 2^{15} possible starting values. Using the technology of the time, the time required to search through all character strings of length 8 from a 36-character alphabet was 112 years. Unfortunately, this is not a true reflection of the actual security of the system. Explain the problem.

15.3 Assume that passwords are selected from four-character combinations of 26 alphabetic characters. Assume that an adversary is able to attempt passwords at a rate of one per second.
   a. Assuming no feedback to the adversary until each attempt has been completed, what is the expected time to discover the correct password?
   b. Assuming feedback to the adversary flagging an error as each incorrect character is entered, what is the expected time to discover the correct password?

15.4 Assume that source elements of length k are mapped in some uniform fashion into a target elements of length p. If each digit can take on one of r values, then the number of source elements is r^k and the number of target elements is the smaller number r^p. A particular source element xi is mapped to a particular target element y_j.
   a. What is the probability that the correct source element can be selected by an adversary on one try?
   b. What is the probability that a different source element x_k ($x_i \neq x_k$) that results in the same target element, y_j, could be produced by an adversary?
   c. What is the probability that the correct target element can be produced by an adversary on one try?

15.5 Assume that passwords are limited to the use of the 95 printable ASCII characters and that all passwords are 10 characters in length. Assume a password cracker with an encryption rate of 6.4 million encryptions per second. How long will it take to test exhaustively all possible passwords on a UNIX system?

15.6 Because of the known risks of the UNIX password system, the SunOS-4.0 documentation recommends that the password file be removed and replaced with a publicly readable file called /etc/publickey. An entry in the file for user A consists of a user's identifier ID_A, the user's public key, PU_a, and the corresponding private key, PR_a. This private key is encrypted using DES with a key derived from the user's login password P_a. When A logs in, the system decrypts $E(P_a, PR_a)$ to obtain PR_a.
   a. The system then verifies that P_a was correctly supplied. How?
   b. How can an opponent attack this system?

15.7 It was stated that the inclusion of the salt in the UNIX password scheme increases the difficulty of guessing by a factor of 4096. But the salt is stored in plaintext in the same entry as the corresponding ciphertext password. Therefore, those two characters are known to the attacker and need not be guessed. Why is it asserted that the salt increases security?

15.8 Assuming that you have successfully answered the preceding problem and understand the significance of the salt, here is another question. Wouldn't it be possible to thwart completely all password crackers by dramatically increasing the salt size to, say, 24 or 48 bits?

15.9 For the DAC model discussed in Section 15.2, an alternative representation of the protection state is a directed graph. Each subject and each object in the protection state is represented by a node (a single node is used for an entity that is both subject and object). A directed line from a subject to an object indicates an access right, and the label on the link defines the access right.

    a. Draw a directed graph that corresponds to the access matrix of Figure 12.15a.

    b. Draw a directed graph that corresponds to the access matrix of Figure 15.4.

    c. Is there a one-to-one correspondence between the directed graph representation and the access matrix representation? Explain.

15.10 UNIX treats file directories in the same fashion as files; that is, both are defined by the same type of data structure, called an inode. As with files, directories include a 9-bit protection string. If care is not taken, this can create access control problems. For example, consider a file with protection mode 644 (octal) contained in a directory with protection mode 730. How might the file be compromised in this case?

15.11 In the traditional UNIX file access model, UNIX systems provide a default setting for newly created files and directories, which the owner may later change. The default is typically full access for the owner combined with one of the following: no access for group and other, read/execute access for group and none for other, or read/execute access for both group and other. Briefly discuss the advantages and disadvantages of each of these cases, including an example of a type of organization where each would be appropriate.

15.12 Consider user accounts on a system with a Web server configured to provide access to user Web areas. In general, this scheme uses a standard directory name, such as `public_html`, in a user's home directory. This acts as the user's Web area if it exists. However, to allow the Web server to access the pages in this directory, it must have at least search (execute) access to the user's home directory, read/execute access to the Web directory, and read access to any Web pages in it. Consider the interaction of this requirement with the cases you discussed for the preceding problem. What consequences does this requirement have? Note that a Web server typically executes as a special user, and in a group that is not shared with most users on the system. Are there some circumstances when running such a Web service is simply not appropriate? Explain.

15.13 Assume a system with N job positions. For job position i, the number of individual users in that position is U_i and the number of permissions required for the job position is P_i.

    a. For a traditional DAC scheme, how many relationships between users and permissions must be defined?

    b. For a RBAC scheme, how many relationships between users and permissions must be defined?

15.14 In the context of an IDS, we define a false positive to be an alarm generated by an IDS in which the IDS alerts to a condition that is actually benign. A false negative occurs when an IDS fails to generate an alarm when an alert-worthy condition is in effect. Using the following diagram, depict two curves that roughly indicate false positives and false negatives, respectively.

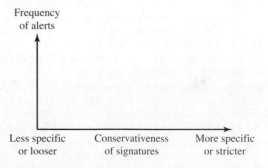

15.15 Rewrite the function shown in Figure 7.13a so that it is no longer vulnerable to a stack buffer overflow.

PART 8 Distributed Systems

CHAPTER **16**

DISTRIBUTED PROCESSING, CLIENT/SERVER, AND CLUSTERS

16.1 Client/Server Computing
What Is Client/Server Computing?
Client/Server Applications
Middleware

16.2 Service-Oriented Architecture

16.3 Distributed Message Passing
Reliability versus Unreliability
Blocking versus Nonblocking

16.4 Remote Procedure Calls
Parameter Passing
Parameter Representation
Client/Server Binding
Synchronous versus Asynchronous
Object-Oriented Mechanisms

16.5 Clusters
Cluster Configurations
Operating System Design Issues
Cluster Computer Architecture
Clusters Compared to SMP

16.6 Windows Cluster Server

16.7 Beowulf and Linux Clusters
Beowulf Features
Beowulf Software

16.8 Summary

16.9 Recommended Reading and Web Sites

16.10 Key Terms, Review Questions, and Problems

The reader who has persevered thus far in this account will realize the difficulties that were coped with, the hazards that were encountered, the mistakes that were made, and the work that was done.

— *THE WORLD CRISIS*, WINSTON CHURCHILL

LEARNING OBJECTIVES

After studying this chapter, you should be able to:

- Present a summary of the key aspects of client/server computing.
- Define service-oriented architecture.
- Understand the principle design issues for distributed message passing.
- Understand the principle design issues for remote procedure calls.
- Understand the principle design issues for clusters.
- Describe the cluster mechanisms in Windows 7 and Beowulf.

In this chapter, we begin with an examination of some of the key concepts in distributed software, including client/server architecture, message passing, and remote procedure calls. Then we examine the increasingly important cluster architecture.

Chapters 17 and 18 complete our discussion of distributed systems.

16.1 CLIENT/SERVER COMPUTING

The concept of client/server computing, and related concepts, has become increasingly important in information technology systems. This section begins with a description of the general nature of client/server computing. This is followed by a discussion of alternative ways of organizing the client/server functions. The issue of file cache consistency, raised by the use of file servers, is then examined. Finally, this section introduces the concept of middleware.

What Is Client/Server Computing?

As with other new waves in the computer field, client/server computing comes with its own set of jargon words. Table 16.1 lists some of the terms that are commonly found in descriptions of client/server products and applications.

Figure 16.1 attempts to capture the essence of the client/server concept. As the term suggests, a *client/server environment* is populated by clients and servers. The **client** machines are generally single-user PCs or workstations that provide a highly user-friendly interface to the end user. The client-based station generally presents the type of graphical interface that is most comfortable to users, including the use of windows and a mouse. Microsoft Windows and Macintosh OS provide examples of such interfaces. Client-based applications are tailored for ease of use and include such familiar tools as the spreadsheet.

Each **server** in the client/server environment provides a set of shared services to the clients. The most common type of server currently is the database server,

Table 16.1 Client/Server Terminology

Applications Programming Interface (API)

A set of function and call programs that allow clients and servers to intercommunicate

Client

A networked information requester, usually a PC or workstation, that can query database and/or other information from a server

Middleware

A set of drivers, APIs, or other software that improves connectivity between a client application and a server

Relational Database

A database in which information access is limited to the selection of rows that satisfy all search criteria

Server

A computer, usually a high-powered workstation, a minicomputer, or a mainframe, that houses information for manipulation by networked clients

Structured Query Language (SQL)

A language developed by IBM and standardized by ANSI for addressing, creating, updating, or querying relational databases

usually controlling a relational database. The server enables many clients to share access to the same database and enables the use of a high-performance computer system to manage the database.

In addition to clients and servers, the third essential ingredient of the client/server environment is the **network**. Client/server computing is typically distributed computing. Users, applications, and resources are distributed in response to business requirements and linked by a single LAN or WAN or by an internet of networks.

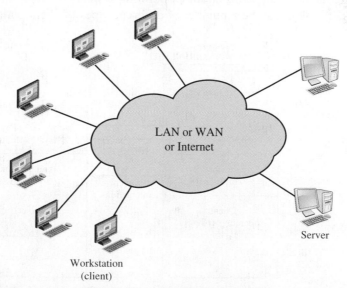

Workstation
(client)

Server

Figure 16.1   Generic Client/Server Environment

How does a client/server configuration differ from any other distributed processing solution? There are a number of characteristics that stand out and that, together, make client/server distinct from other types of distributed processing:

- There is a heavy reliance on bringing user-friendly applications to the user on his or her own system. This gives the user a great deal of control over the timing and style of computer usage and gives department-level managers the ability to be responsive to their local needs.

- Although applications are dispersed, there is an emphasis on centralizing corporate databases and many network management and utility functions. This enables corporate management to maintain overall control of the total capital investment in computing and information systems and to provide interoperability so that systems are tied together. At the same time it relieves individual departments and divisions of much of the overhead of maintaining sophisticated computer-based facilities but enables them to choose just about any type of machine and interface they need to access data and information.

- There is a commitment, both by user organizations and vendors, to open and modular systems. This means that the user has more choice in selecting products and in mixing equipment from a number of vendors.

- Networking is fundamental to the operation. Thus, network management and network security have a high priority in organizing and operating information systems.

Client/Server Applications

The key feature of a client/server architecture is the allocation of application-level tasks between clients and servers. Figure 16.2 illustrates the general case. In both client and server, of course, the basic software is an operating system running on the hardware platform. The platforms and the operating systems of client and server may differ. Indeed, there may be a number of different types of client platforms and operating

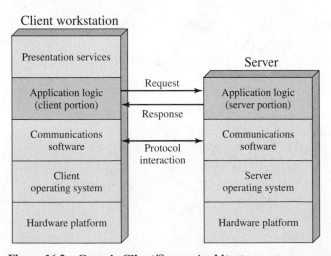

Figure 16.2   Generic Client/Server Architecture

systems and a number of different types of server platforms in a single environment. As long as a particular client and server share the same communications protocols and support the same applications, these lower-level differences are irrelevant.

It is the communications software that enables client and server to interoperate. The principal example of such software is TCP/IP. Of course, the point of all of this support software (communications and operating system) is to provide a base for distributed applications. Ideally, the actual functions performed by the application can be split up between client and server in a way that optimizes the use of resources. In some cases, depending on the application needs, the bulk of the applications software executes at the server, while in other cases, most of the application logic is located at the client.

An essential factor in the success of a client/server environment is the way in which the user interacts with the system as a whole. Thus, the design of the user interface on the client machine is critical. In most client/server systems, there is heavy emphasis on providing a **graphical user interface (GUI)** that is easy to use, easy to learn, yet powerful and flexible. Thus, we can think of a presentation services module in the client workstation that is responsible for providing a user-friendly interface to the distributed applications available in the environment.

DATABASE APPLICATIONS   As an example that illustrates the concept of splitting application logic between client and server, let us consider one of the most common families of client/server applications: those that use relational databases. In this environment, the server is essentially a database server. Interaction between client and server is in the form of transactions in which the client makes a database request and receives a database response.

Figure 16.3 illustrates, in general terms, the architecture of such a system. The server is responsible for maintaining the database, for which purpose a complex

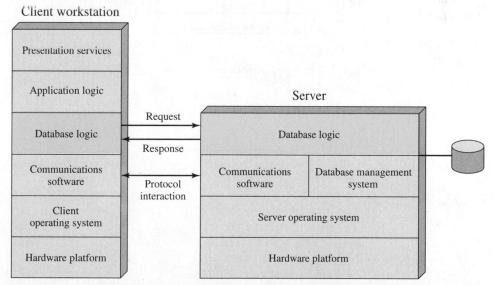

Figure 16.3   Client/Server Architecture for Database Applications

database management system software module is required. A variety of different applications that make use of the database can be housed on client machines. The "glue" that ties client and server together is software that enables the client to make requests for access to the server's database. A popular example of such logic is the structured query language (SQL).

Figure 16.3 suggests that all of the application logic—the software for "number crunching" or other types of data analysis—is on the client side, while the server is only concerned with managing the database. Whether such a configuration is appropriate depends on the style and intent of the application. For example, suppose that the primary purpose is to provide online access for record lookup. Figure 16.4a suggests how this might work. Suppose that the server is maintaining a database of 1 million records (called rows in relational database terminology), and the user wants to perform a lookup that should result in zero, one, or at most a few records. The user could search for these records using a number of search criteria (e.g., records older than 1992, records referring to individuals in Ohio, records referring to a specific event or characteristic, etc.). An initial client query may yield a server response that there are 100,000 records that satisfy the search criteria. The user then adds additional qualifiers and issues a new query. This time, a response indicating that there are 1,000 possible records is returned. Finally, the client issues a third request with additional qualifiers. The resulting search criteria yield a single match, and the record is returned to the client.

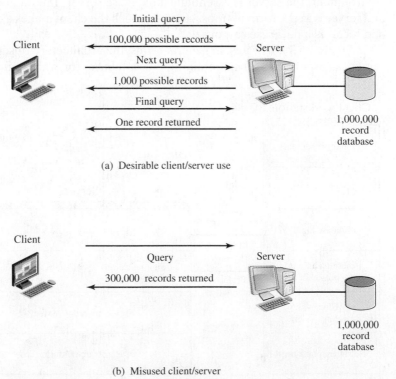

(a) Desirable client/server use

(b) Misused client/server

Figure 16.4   Client/Server Database Usage

The preceding application is well suited to a client/server architecture for two reasons:

1. There is a massive job of sorting and searching the database. This requires a large disk or bank of disks, a high-speed CPU, and a high-speed I/O architecture. Such capacity and power is not needed and is too expensive for a single-user workstation or PC.

2. It would place too great a traffic burden on the network to move the entire 1-million record file to the client for searching. Therefore, it is not enough for the server just to be able to retrieve records on behalf of a client; the server needs to have database logic that enables it to perform searches on behalf of a client.

Now consider the scenario of Figure 16.4b, which has the same 1-million-record database. In this case, a single query results in the transmission of 300,000 records over the network. This might happen if, for example, the user wishes to find the grand total or mean value of some field across many records or even the entire database.

Clearly, this latter scenario is unacceptable. One solution to this problem, which maintains the client/server architecture with all of its benefits, is to move part of the application logic over to the server. That is, the server can be equipped with application logic for performing data analysis as well as data retrieval and data searching.

CLASSES OF CLIENT/SERVER APPLICATIONS Within the general framework of client/server, there is a spectrum of implementations that divide the work between client and server differently. Figure 16.5 illustrates in general terms some of the major options for database applications. Other splits are possible, and the options may have a different characterization for other types of applications. In any case, it is useful to examine this figure to get a feel for the kind of trade-offs possible.

Figure 16.5 depicts four classes:

- **Host-based processing:** *Host-based processing* is not true client/server computing as the term is generally used. Rather, host-based processing refers to the traditional mainframe environment in which all or virtually all of the processing is done on a central host. Often the user interface is via a dumb terminal. Even if the user is employing a microcomputer, the user's station is generally limited to the role of a terminal emulator.

- **Server-based processing:** The most basic class of client/server configuration is one in which the client is principally responsible for providing a graphical user interface, while virtually all of the processing is done on the server. This configuration is typical of early client/server efforts, especially departmental-level systems. The rationale behind such configurations is that the user workstation is best suited to providing a user-friendly interface and that databases and applications can easily be maintained on central systems. Although the user gains the advantage of a better interface, this type of configuration does not generally lend itself to any significant gains in productivity or to any fundamental changes in the actual business functions that the system supports.

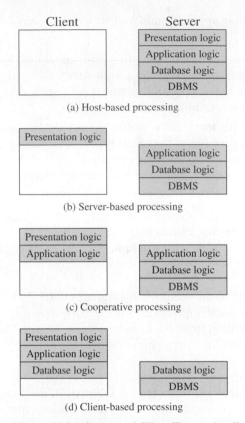

Figure 16.5   Classes of Client/Server Applications

- **Client-based processing:** At the other extreme, virtually all application processing may be done at the client, with the exception of data validation routines and other database logic functions that are best performed at the server. Generally, some of the more sophisticated database logic functions are housed on the client side. This architecture is perhaps the most common client/server approach in current use. It enables the user to employ applications tailored to local needs.

- **Cooperative processing:** In a cooperative processing configuration, the application processing is performed in an optimized fashion, taking advantage of the strengths of both client and server machines and of the distribution of data. Such a configuration is more complex to set up and maintain but, in the long run, this type of configuration may offer greater user productivity gains and greater network efficiency than other client/server approaches.

Figures 16.5c and 16.5d correspond to configurations in which a considerable fraction of the load is on the client. This so-called **fat client** model has been popularized by application development tools such as Sybase Inc.'s PowerBuilder and Gupta Corp.'s SQL Windows. Applications developed with these tools are typically departmental in scope, supporting between 25 and 150 users [ECKE95]. The main benefit of the fat client model is that it takes advantage of desktop power, offloading application processing from servers and making them more efficient and less likely to be bottlenecks.

There are, however, several disadvantages to the fat client strategy. The addition of more functions rapidly overloads the capacity of desktop machines, forcing companies to upgrade. If the model extends beyond the department to incorporate many users, the company must install high-capacity LANs to support the large volumes of transmission between the thin servers and the fat clients. Finally, it is difficult to maintain, upgrade, or replace applications distributed across tens or hundreds of desktops.

Figure 16.5b is representative of a **thin client** approach. This approach more nearly mimics the traditional host-centered approach and is often the migration path for evolving corporate-wide applications from the mainframe to a distributed environment.

THREE-TIER CLIENT/SERVER ARCHITECTURE The traditional client/server architecture involves two levels, or tiers: a client tier and a server tier. A three-tier architecture is also common (Figure 16.6). In this architecture, the application software is distributed among three types of machines: a user machine, a middle-tier server, and a backend server. The user machine is the client machine we have been discussing and, in the three-tier model, is typically a thin client. The middle-tier machines are essentially gateways between the thin user clients and a variety of

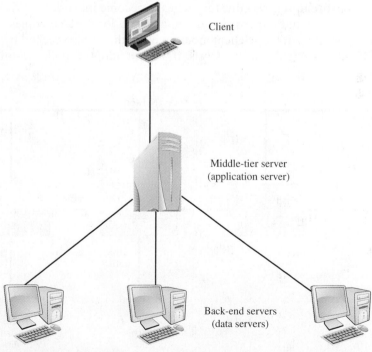

Client

Middle-tier server
(application server)

Back-end servers
(data servers)

Figure 16.6   Three-Tier Client/Server Architecture

backend database servers. The middle-tier machines can convert protocols and map from one type of database query to another. In addition, the middle-tier machine can merge/integrate results from different data sources. Finally, the middle-tier machine can serve as a gateway between the desktop applications and the backend legacy applications by mediating between the two worlds.

The interaction between the middle-tier server and the backend server also follows the client/server model. Thus, the middle-tier system acts as both a client and a server.

FILE CACHE CONSISTENCY When a file server is used, performance of file I/O can be noticeably degraded relative to local file access because of the delays imposed by the network. To reduce this performance penalty, individual systems can use file caches to hold recently accessed file records. Because of the principle of locality, use of a local file cache should reduce the number of remote server accesses that must be made.

Figure 16.7 illustrates a typical distributed mechanism for caching files among a networked collection of workstations. When a process makes a file access, the request is presented first to the cache of the process's workstation ("file traffic"). If not satisfied there, the request is passed either to the local disk, if the file is stored there ("disk traffic"), or to a file server, where the file is stored ("server traffic"). At the server, the server's cache is first interrogated and, if there is a miss, then the server's disk is accessed. The dual caching approach is used to reduce communications traffic (client cache) and disk I/O (server cache).

When caches always contain exact copies of remote data, we say that the caches are **consistent**. It is possible for caches to become inconsistent when the remote data are changed and the corresponding obsolete local cache copies are not discarded. This can happen if one client modifies a file that is also cached by other clients. The difficulty is actually at two levels. If a client adopts a policy of immediately writing

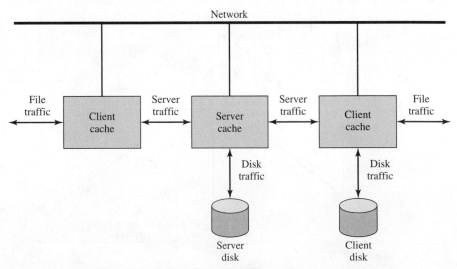

Figure 16.7   Distributed File Cacheing in Sprite

any changes to a file back to the server, then any other client that has a cache copy of the relevant portion of the file will have obsolete data. The problem is made even worse if the client delays writing back changes to the server. In that case, the server itself has an obsolete version of the file, and new file read requests to the server might obtain obsolete data. The problem of keeping local cache copies up to date to changes in remote data is known as the **cache consistency** problem.

The simplest approach to cache consistency is to use file-locking techniques to prevent simultaneous access to a file by more than one client. This guarantees consistency at the expense of performance and flexibility. A more powerful approach is provided with the facility in Sprite [NELS88, OUST88]. Any number of remote processes may open a file for read and create their own client cache. But when an open file request to a server requests write access and other processes have the file open for read access, the server takes two actions. First, it notifies the writing process that, although it may maintain a cache, it must write back all altered blocks immediately upon update. There can be at most one such client. Second, the server notifies all reading processes that have the file open that the file is no longer cacheable.

Middleware

The development and deployment of client/server products has far outstripped efforts to standardize all aspects of distributed computing, from the physical layer up to the application layer. This lack of standards makes it difficult to implement an integrated, multivendor, enterprise-wide client/server configuration. Because much of the benefit of the client/server approach is tied up with its modularity and the ability to mix and match platforms and applications to provide a business solution, this interoperability problem must be solved.

To achieve the true benefits of the client/server approach, developers must have a set of tools that provide a uniform means and style of access to system resources across all platforms. This will enable programmers to build applications that not only look and feel the same on various PCs and workstations but that use the same method to access data regardless of the location of that data.

The most common way to meet this requirement is by the use of standard programming interfaces and protocols that sit between the application above and communications software and operating system below. Such standardized interfaces and protocols have come to be referred to as middleware. With standard programming interfaces, it is easy to implement the same application on a variety of server types and workstation types. This obviously benefits the customer, but vendors are also motivated to provide such interfaces. The reason is that customers buy applications, not servers; customers will only choose among those server products that run the applications they want. The standardized protocols are needed to link these various server interfaces back to the clients that need access to them.

There is a variety of middleware packages ranging from the very simple to the very complex. What they all have in common is the capability to hide the complexities and disparities of different network protocols and operating systems. Client and server vendors generally provide a number of the more popular middleware packages as options. Thus, a user can settle on a particular middleware strategy and then assemble equipment from various vendors that support that strategy.

MIDDLEWARE ARCHITECTURE Figure 16.8 suggests the role of middleware in a client/server architecture. The exact role of the middleware component will depend on the style of client/server computing being used. Referring back to Figure 16.5, recall that there are a number of different client/server approaches, depending on the way in which application functions are split up. In any case, Figure 16.8 gives a good general idea of the architecture involved.

Note that there is both a client and server component of middleware. The basic purpose of middleware is to enable an application or user at a client to access a variety of services on servers without being concerned about differences among servers. To look at one specific application area, the structured query language (SQL) is supposed to provide a standardized means for access to a relational database by either a local or remote user or application. However, many relational database vendors, although they support SQL, have added their own proprietary extensions to SQL. This enables vendors to differentiate their products but also creates potential incompatibilities.

As an example, consider a distributed system used to support, among other things, the personnel department. The basic employee data, such as employee name and address, might be stored on a Gupta database, whereas salary information might be contained on an Oracle database. When a user in the personnel department requires access to particular records, that user does not want to be concerned with which vendor's database contains the records needed. Middleware provides a layer of software that enables uniform access to these differing systems.

It is instructive to look at the role of middleware from a logical, rather than an implementation, point of view. This viewpoint is illustrated in Figure 16.9. Middleware enables the realization of the promise of distributed client/server computing. The entire distributed system can be viewed as a set of applications and resources available to users. Users need not be concerned with the location of data

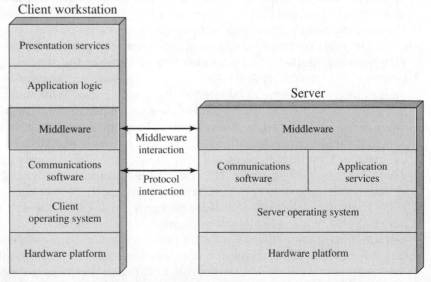

Figure 16.8   The Role of Middleware in Client/Server Architecture

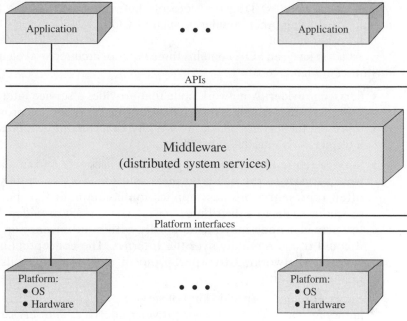

Figure 16.9   Logical View of Middleware

or indeed the location of applications. All applications operate over a uniform applications programming interface (API). The middleware, which cuts across all client and server platforms, is responsible for routing client requests to the appropriate server.

Although there is a wide variety of middleware products, these products are typically based on one of two underlying mechanisms: message passing or remote procedure calls. These two methods are examined in the next two sections.

16.2 SERVICE-ORIENTED ARCHITECTURE

The service-oriented architecture (SOA) is a form of client/server architecture that now enjoys widespread use in enterprise systems. An SOA organizes business functions into a modular structure rather than as monolithic applications for each department. As a result, common functions can be used by different departments internally and by external business partners as well. The more fine-grained the modules, the more they can be reused. In general, an SOA consists of a set of services and a set of client applications that use these services. A client request may involve a single service or may involve two or more services to coordinating some activity, requiring communication of services with each other. The services are available through published and discoverable interfaces.

Standardized interfaces are used to enable service modules to communicate with one another and to enable client applications to communicate with service modules. The most popular interface is the use of XML (Extensible Markup Language) over HTTP (Hypertext Transfer Protocol), known as *Web services*. SOAs are also implemented using other standards, such as CORBA (Common Object Request Broker Architecture).

At a top level, an SOA contains three types of architectural elements [BIH06], illustrated in Figure 16.10:

- **Service provider:** A network node that provides a service interface for a software asset that manages a specific set of tasks. A service provider node can represent the services of a business entity, or it can simply represent the service interface for a reusable subsystem.

- **Service requestor:** A network node that discovers and invokes other software services to provide a business solution. Service requestor nodes will often represent a business application component that performs remote procedure calls to a distributed object, the service provider. In some cases, the provider node may reside locally within an intranet or in other cases it could reside remotely over the Internet. The conceptual nature of SOA leaves the networking, transport protocol, and security details to the specific implementation.

- **Service broker:** A specific kind of service provider that acts as a registry and allows for the lookup of service provider interfaces and service locations. The service broker can pass on service requests to one or more additional service providers.

[BROW03] lists the following as key characteristics for effective use of services:

- **Coarse-grained:** Operations on services are frequently implemented to encompass more functionality and operate on larger data sets, compared with component-interface design.

- **Interface-based design:** Services implement separately defined interfaces. The benefit of this is that multiple services can implement a common interface and a service can implement multiple interfaces.

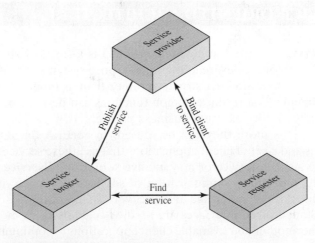

Figure 16.10   SOA Model

- **Discoverable:** Services need to be found at both design time and run time, not only by unique identity but also by interface identity and by service kind.
- **Single instance:** Unlike component-based development, which instantiates components as needed, each service is a single, always running instance that a number of clients communicate with.
- **Loosely coupled:** Services are connected to other services and clients using standard, dependency-reducing, decoupled message-based methods such as XML document exchanges.
- **Asynchronous:** In general, services use an asynchronous message-passing approach; however, this is not required. In fact, many services will use synchronous message passing at times.

To give the reader some feel for the use of SOA, we look at an example. Figure 16.11a shows a common approach to building applications targeted at specific user categories. For each specific application, a single self-contained application module is built. What ties together the various applications in the enterprise is an application-independent database management system that supports a number of databases. Multiple applications may have access to a single database. For example, in this configuration all three applications require access to a customer information database. The advantages of this arrangement are clear. By separating the data from the applications and providing a uniform database interface, multiple applications can be developed and revised independently from one another.

This typical approach, of a variety of applications using a common set of databases, has some drawbacks. The addition of a new feature or user service, such as ATM, generally requires building a new application independent of existing applications. This is despite the fact that much of the necessary logic has already been implemented in related applications.

We can achieve greater efficiency and flexibility by migrating to an SOA, as shown in Figure 16.11b. Here, the strategy is to isolate services that may be of common use to multiple applications and implement these as separate service modules. In this particular example of the SOA, there are some core applications that deal with the functionality of individual databases. These applications are accessible by application programming interfaces by service modules that implement common services. Finally, the specific applications visible to users deal primarily with presentation issues and with specific business logic.

16.3 DISTRIBUTED MESSAGE PASSING

It is usually the case in a distributed processing systems that the computers do not share main memory; each is an isolated computer system. Thus, interprocessor communication techniques that rely on shared memory, such as semaphores, cannot be used. Instead, techniques that rely on message passing are used. In this section and the next, we look at the two most common approaches. The first is the straightforward application of messages as they are used in a single system. The second is a separate technique that relies on message passing as a basic function: the remote procedure call.

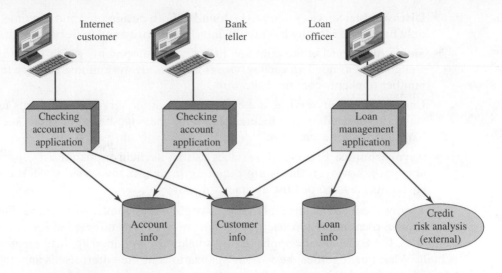

(a) Typical application structure

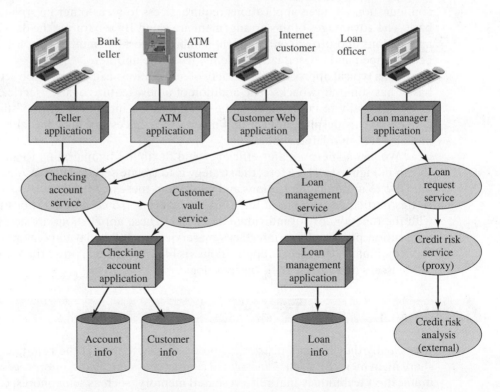

(b) An architecture reflecting SOA principles

Figure 16.11   Example Use of SOA

Figure 16.12a shows the use of message passing to implement client/server functionality. A client process requires some service (e.g., read a file, print) and sends a message containing a request for service to a server process. The server process honors the request and sends a message containing a reply. In its simplest form, only two functions are needed: Send and Receive. The Send function specifies a destination and includes the message content. The Receive function tells from whom a message is desired (including "all") and provides a buffer where the incoming message is to be stored.

Figure 16.13 suggests an implementation for message passing. Processes make use of the services of a message-passing module. Service requests can be expressed in terms of primitives and parameters. A primitive specifies the function to be performed, and the parameters are used to pass data and control information. The actual form of a primitive depends on the message-passing software. It may be a procedure call, or it may itself be a message to a process that is part of the operating system.

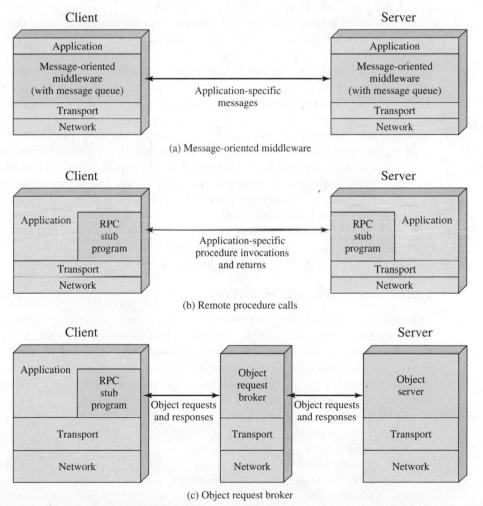

Client   Server

(a) Message-oriented middleware

(b) Remote procedure calls

(c) Object request broker

Figure 16.12   Middleware Mechanisms

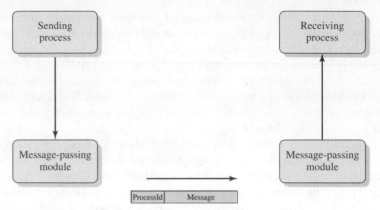

Figure 16.13   Basic Message-Passing Primitives

The Send primitive is used by the process that desires to send the message. Its parameters are the identifier of the destination process and the contents of the message. The message-passing module constructs a data unit that includes these two elements. This data unit is sent to the machine that hosts the destination process, using some sort of communications facility, such as TCP/IP. When the data unit is received in the target system, it is routed by the communications facility to the message-passing module. This module examines the process ID field and stores the message in the buffer for that process.

In this scenario, the receiving process must announce its willingness to receive messages by designating a buffer area and informing the message-passing module by a Receive primitive. An alternative approach does not require such an announcement. Instead, when the message-passing module receives a message, it signals the destination process with some sort of Receive signal and then makes the received message available in a shared buffer.

Several design issues are associated with distributed message passing, and these are addressed in the remainder of this section.

Reliability versus Unreliability

A reliable message-passing facility is one that guarantees delivery if possible. Such a facility makes use of a reliable transport protocol or similar logic and performs error checking, acknowledgment, retransmission, and reordering of misordered messages. Because delivery is guaranteed, it is not necessary to let the sending process know that the message was delivered. However, it might be useful to provide an acknowledgment back to the sending process so that it knows that delivery has already taken place. In either case, if the facility fails to achieve delivery (e.g., persistent network failure, crash of destination system), the sending process is notified of the failure.

At the other extreme, the message-passing facility may simply send the message out into the communications network but will report neither success nor failure. This alternative greatly reduces the complexity and processing and communications overhead of the message-passing facility. For those applications that require confirmation that a message has been delivered, the applications them-selves may use request and reply messages to satisfy the requirement.

Blocking versus Nonblocking

With nonblocking, or asynchronous, primitives, a process is not suspended as a result of issuing a Send or Receive. Thus, when a process issues a Send primi-tive, the operating system returns control to the process as soon as the message has been queued for transmission or a copy has been made. If no copy is made, any changes made to the message by the sending process before or even while it is being transmitted are made at the risk of the process. When the message has been transmitted or copied to a safe place for subsequent transmission, the send-ing process is interrupted to be informed that the message buffer may be reused. Similarly, a nonblocking Receive is issued by a process that then proceeds to run. When a message arrives, the process is informed by interrupt, or it can poll for status periodically.

Nonblocking primitives provide for efficient, flexible use of the message-passing facility by processes. The disadvantage of this approach is that it is difficult to test and debug programs that use these primitives. Irreproducible, timing-dependent sequences can create subtle and difficult problems.

The alternative is to use blocking, or synchronous, primitives. A blocking Send does not return control to the sending process until the message has been transmitted (unreliable service) or until the message has been sent and an acknowl-edgment received (reliable service). A blocking Receive does not return control until a message has been placed in the allocated buffer.

16.4 REMOTE PROCEDURE CALLS

A variation on the basic message-passing model is the remote procedure call. This is now a widely accepted and common method for encapsulating communica-tion in a distributed system. The essence of the technique is to allow programs on different machines to interact using simple procedure call/return semantics, just as if the two programs were on the same machine. That is, the procedure call is used for access to remote services. The popularity of this approach is due to the following advantages.

1. The procedure call is a widely accepted, used, and understood abstraction.
2. The use of remote procedure calls enables remote interfaces to be specified as a set of named operations with designated types. Thus, the interface can be clearly documented and distributed programs can be statically checked for type errors.
3. Because a standardized and precisely defined interface is specified, the communication code for an application can be generated automatically.
4. Because a standardized and precisely defined interface is specified, develop-ers can write client and server modules that can be moved among computers and operating systems with little modification and recoding.

The remote procedure call mechanism can be viewed as a refinement of reliable, blocking message passing. Figure 16.12b illustrates the general architecture, and Figure 16.14 provides a more detailed look. The calling program makes a normal procedure call with parameters on its machine. For example,

$$\text{CALL } P(X,Y)$$

where

P = procedure name

X = passed arguments

Y = returned values

It may or may not be transparent to the user that the intention is to invoke a remote procedure on some other machine. A dummy or stub procedure P must be included in the caller's address space or be dynamically linked to it at call time. This procedure creates a message that identifies the procedure being called and includes the parameters. It then sends this message to a remote system and waits for a reply. When a reply is received, the stub procedure returns to the calling program, providing the returned values.

At the remote machine, another stub program is associated with the called procedure. When a message comes in, it is examined and a local CALL $P(X, Y)$ is generated. This remote procedure is thus called locally, so its normal assumptions about where to find parameters, the state of the stack, and so on are identical to the case of a purely local procedure call.

Several design issues are associated with remote procedure calls, and these are addressed in the remainder of this section.

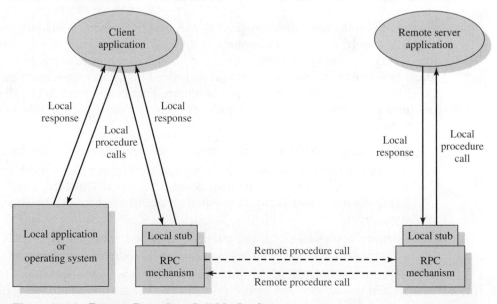

Figure 16.14   Remote Procedure Call Mechanism

Parameter Passing

Most programming languages allow parameters to be passed as values (call by value) or as pointers to a location that contains the value (call by reference). Call by value is simple for a remote procedure call: The parameters are simply copied into the message and sent to the remote system. It is more difficult to implement call by reference. A unique, systemwide pointer is needed for each object. The overhead for this capability may not be worth the effort.

Parameter Representation

Another issue is how to represent parameters and results in messages. If the called and calling programs are in identical programming languages on the same type of machines with the same operating system, then the representation requirement may present no problems. If there are differences in these areas, then there will probably be differences in the ways in which numbers and even text are represented. If a full-blown communications architecture is used, then this issue is handled by the presentation layer. However, the overhead of such an architecture has led to the design of remote procedure call facilities that bypass most of the communications architecture and provide their own basic communications facility. In that case, the conversion responsibility falls on the remote procedure call facility (e.g., see [GIBB87]).

The best approach to this problem is to provide a standardized format for common objects, such as integers, floating-point numbers, characters, and character strings. Then the native parameters on any machine can be converted to and from the standardized representation.

Client/Server Binding

Binding specifies how the relationship between a remote procedure and the calling program will be established. A binding is formed when two applications have made a logical connection and are prepared to exchange commands and data.

Nonpersistent binding means that a logical connection is established between the two processes at the time of the remote procedure call and that as soon as the values are returned, the connection is dismantled. Because a connection requires the maintenance of state information on both ends, it consumes resources. The nonpersistent style is used to conserve those resources. On the other hand, the overhead involved in establishing connections makes nonpersistent binding inappropriate for remote procedures that are called frequently by the same caller.

With **persistent binding**, a connection that is set up for a remote procedure call is sustained after the procedure return. The connection can then be used for future remote procedure calls. If a specified period of time passes with no activity on the connection, then the connection is terminated. For applications that make many repeated calls to remote procedures, persistent binding maintains the logical connection and allows a sequence of calls and returns to use the same connection.

Synchronous versus Asynchronous

The concepts of synchronous and asynchronous remote procedure calls are analogous to the concepts of blocking and nonblocking messages. The traditional remote procedure call is synchronous, which requires that the calling process wait until the called process returns a value. Thus, the **synchronous RPC** behaves much like a subroutine call.

The synchronous RPC is easy to understand and program because its behavior is predictable. However, it fails to exploit fully the parallelism inherent in distributed applications. This limits the kind of interaction the distributed application can have, resulting in lower performance.

To provide greater flexibility, various **asynchronous RPC** facilities have been implemented to achieve a greater degree of parallelism while retaining the familiarity and simplicity of the RPC [ANAN92]. Asynchronous RPCs do not block the caller; the replies can be received as and when they are needed, thus allowing client execution to proceed locally in parallel with the server invocation.

A typical asynchronous RPC use is to enable a client to invoke a server repeatedly so that the client has a number of requests in the pipeline at one time, each with its own set of data. Synchronization of client and server can be achieved in one of two ways:

1. A higher-layer application in the client and server can initiate the exchange and then check at the end that all requested actions have been performed.

2. A client can issue a string of asynchronous RPCs followed by a final synchronous RPC. The server will respond to the synchronous RPC only after completing all of the work requested in the preceding asynchronous RPCs.

In some schemes, asynchronous RPCs require no reply from the server and the server cannot send a reply message. Other schemes either require or allow a reply, but the caller does not wait for the reply.

Object–Oriented Mechanisms

As object-oriented technology becomes more prevalent in operating system design, client/server designers have begun to embrace this approach. In this approach, clients and servers ship messages back and forth between objects. Object communications may rely on an underlying message or RPC structure or be developed directly on top of object-oriented capabilities in the operating system.

A client that needs a service sends a request to an object request broker, which acts as a directory of all the remote service available on the network (Figure 16.12c). The broker calls the appropriate object and passes along any relevant data. Then the remote object services the request and replies to the broker, which returns the response to the client.

The success of the object-oriented approach depends on standardization of the object mechanism. Unfortunately, there are several competing designs in this area. One is Microsoft's Component Object Model (COM), the basis for Object Linking and Embedding (OLE). A competing approach, developed by the Object Management Group, is the Common Object Request Broker Architecture (CORBA), which has wide industry support. IBM, Apple, Sun, and many other vendors support the CORBA approach.

16.5 CLUSTERS

Clustering is an alternative to symmetric multiprocessing (SMP) as an approach to providing high performance and high availability and is particularly attractive for server applications. We can define a cluster as a group of interconnected, whole computers working together as a unified computing resource that can create the illusion of being one machine. The term *whole computer* means a system that can run on its own, apart from the cluster; in the literature, each computer in a cluster is typically referred to as a *node*.

[BREW97] lists four benefits that can be achieved with clustering. These can also be thought of as objectives or design requirements:

- **Absolute scalability:** It is possible to create large clusters that far surpass the power of even the largest stand-alone machines. A cluster can have dozens or even hundreds of machines, each of which is a multiprocessor.
- **Incremental scalability:** A cluster is configured in such a way that it is possible to add new systems to the cluster in small increments. Thus, a user can start out with a modest system and expand it as needs grow, without having to go through a major upgrade in which an existing small system is replaced with a larger system.
- **High availability:** Because each node in a cluster is a stand-alone computer, the failure of one node does not mean loss of service. In many products, fault tolerance is handled automatically in software.
- **Superior price/performance:** By using commodity building blocks, it is possible to put together a cluster with equal or greater computing power than a single large machine, at much lower cost.

Cluster Configurations

In the literature, clusters are classified in a number of different ways. Perhaps the simplest classification is based on whether the computers in a cluster share access to the same disks. Figure 16.15a shows a two-node cluster in which the only interconnection is by means of a high-speed link that can be used for message exchange to coordinate cluster activity. The link can be a LAN that is shared with other computers that are not part of the cluster, or the link can be a dedicated interconnection facility. In the latter case, one or more of the computers in the cluster will have a link to a LAN or WAN so that there is a connection between the server cluster and remote client systems. Note that in the figure, each computer is depicted as being a multiprocessor. This is not necessary but does enhance both performance and availability.

In the simple classification depicted in Figure 16.15, the other alternative is a shared-disk cluster. In this case, there generally is still a message link between nodes. In addition, there is a disk subsystem that is directly linked to multiple computers within the cluster. In Figure 16.15b, the common disk subsystem is a RAID system. The use of RAID or some similar redundant disk technology is common in clusters so that the high availability achieved by the presence of multiple computers is not compromised by a shared disk that is a single point of failure.

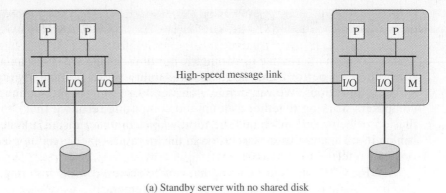

(a) Standby server with no shared disk

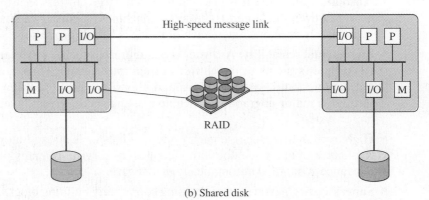

RAID

(b) Shared disk

Figure 16.15   Cluster Configurations

A clearer picture of the range of clustering approaches can be gained by look-ing at functional alternatives. A white paper from Hewlett Packard [HP96] provides a useful classification along functional lines (Table 16.2), which we now discuss.

A common, older method, known as **passive standby**, is simply to have one computer handle all of the processing load while the other computer remains inac-tive, standing by to take over in the event of a failure of the primary. To coordi-nate the machines, the active, or primary, system periodically sends a "heartbeat" message to the standby machine. Should these messages stop arriving, the standby assumes that the primary server has failed and puts itself into operation. This approach increases availability but does not improve performance. Further, if the only information that is exchanged between the two systems is a heartbeat message, and if the two systems do not share common disks, then the standby provides a functional backup but has no access to the databases managed by the primary.

The passive standby is generally not referred to as a cluster. The term *cluster* is reserved for multiple interconnected computers that are all actively doing processing while maintaining the image of a single system to the outside world. The term **active secondary** is often used in referring to this configuration. Three classifications of clustering can be identified: separate servers, shared nothing, and shared memory.

Table 16.2 Clustering Methods: Benefits and Limitations

Clustering Method	Description	Benefits	Limitations
Passive Standby	A secondary server takes over in case of primary server failure.	Easy to implement	High cost because the secondary server is unavailable for other processing tasks
Active Secondary	The secondary server is also used for processing tasks.	Reduced cost because secondary servers can be used for processing	Increased complexity
Separate Servers	Separate servers have their own disks. Data are continuously copied from primary to secondary server.	High availability	High network and server overhead due to copying operations
Servers Connected to Disks	Servers are cabled to the same disks, but each server owns its disks. If one server fails, its disks are taken over by the other server.	Reduced network and server overhead due to elimination of copying operations	Usually requires disk mirroring or RAID technology to compensate for risk of disk failure
Servers Share Disks	Multiple servers simultaneously share access to disks.	Low network and server overhead. Reduced risk of downtime caused by disk failure	Requires lock manager software. Usually used with disk mirroring or RAID technology

In one approach to clustering, each computer is a **separate server** with its own disks and there are no disks shared between systems (Figure 16.15a). This arrangement provides high performance as well as high availability. In this case, some type of management or scheduling software is needed to assign incoming client requests to servers so that the load is balanced and high utilization is achieved. It is desirable to have a failover capability, which means that if a computer fails while executing an application, another computer in the cluster can pick up and complete the application. For this to happen, data must constantly be copied among systems so that each system has access to the current data of the other systems. The overhead of this data exchange ensures high availability at the cost of a performance penalty.

To reduce the communications overhead, most clusters now consist of servers connected to common disks (Figure 16.15b). In one variation of this approach, called **shared nothing**, the common disks are partitioned into volumes, and each volume is owned by a single computer. If that computer fails, the cluster must be reconfigured so that some other computer has ownership of the volumes of the failed computer.

It is also possible to have multiple computers share the same disks at the same time (called the **shared disk** approach), so that each computer has access to all of the volumes on all of the disks. This approach requires the use of some type of locking facility to ensure that data can only be accessed by one computer at a time.

Operating System Design Issues

Full exploitation of a cluster hardware configuration requires some enhancements to a single-system operating system.

FAILURE MANAGEMENT   How failures are managed by a cluster depends on the clustering method used (Table 16.2). In general, two approaches can be taken to dealing with failures: highly available clusters and fault-tolerant clusters. A highly available cluster offers a high probability that all resources will be in service. If a failure occurs, such as a node goes down or a disk volume is lost, then the queries in progress are lost. Any lost query, if retried, will be serviced by a different computer in the cluster. However, the cluster operating system makes no guarantee about the state of partially executed transactions. This would need to be handled at the application level.

A fault-tolerant cluster ensures that all resources are always available. This is achieved by the use of redundant shared disks and mechanisms for backing out uncommitted transactions and committing completed transactions.

The function of switching an application and data resources over from a failed system to an alternative system in the cluster is referred to as **failover**. A related function is the restoration of applications and data resources to the original system once it has been fixed; this is referred to as **failback**. Failback can be automated, but this is desirable only if the problem is truly fixed and unlikely to recur. If not, automatic failback can cause subsequently failed resources to bounce back and forth between computers, resulting in performance and recovery problems.

LOAD BALANCING   A cluster requires an effective capability for balancing the load among available computers. This includes the requirement that the cluster be incrementally scalable. When a new computer is added to the cluster, the load-balancing facility should automatically include this computer in scheduling applications. Middleware mechanisms need to recognize that services can appear on different members of the cluster and may migrate from one member to another.

PARALLELIZING COMPUTATION   In some cases, effective use of a cluster requires executing software from a single application in parallel. [KAPP00] lists three general approaches to the problem:

- **Parallelizing compiler:** A parallelizing compiler determines, at compile time, which parts of an application can be executed in parallel. These are then split off to be assigned to different computers in the cluster. Performance depends on the nature of the problem and how well the compiler is designed.

- **Parallelized application:** In this approach, the programmer writes the application from the outset to run on a cluster and uses message passing to move data, as required, between cluster nodes. This places a high burden on the programmer but may be the best approach for exploiting clusters for some applications.

- **Parametric computing:** This approach can be used if the essence of the application is an algorithm or program that must be executed a large number of times, each time with a different set of starting conditions or parameters. A good example is a simulation model, which will run a large number of different scenarios and then develop statistical summaries of the results. For this approach to be effective, parametric processing tools are needed to organize, run, and manage the jobs in an orderly manner.

Cluster Computer Architecture

Figure 16.16 shows a typical cluster architecture. The individual computers are connected by some high-speed LAN or switch hardware. Each computer is capable of operating independently. In addition, a middleware layer of software is installed in each computer to enable cluster operation. The cluster middleware provides a unified system image to the user, known as a **single-system image**. The middleware may also be responsible for providing high availability, by means of load balancing and responding to failures in individual components. [HWAN99] lists the following as desirable cluster middleware services and functions:

- **Single entry point:** A user logs on to the cluster rather than to an individual computer.
- **Single file hierarchy:** The user sees a single hierarchy of file directories under the same root directory.
- **Single control point:** There is a default node used for cluster management and control.
- **Single virtual networking:** Any node can access any other point in the cluster, even though the actual cluster configuration may consist of multiple interconnected networks. There is a single virtual network operation.
- **Single memory space:** Distributed shared memory enables programs to share variables.

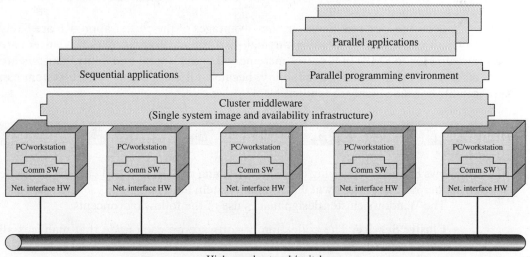

Figure 16.16   Cluster Computer Architecture

- **Single job-management system:** Under a cluster job scheduler, a user can submit a job without specifying the host computer to execute the job.
- **Single user interface:** A common graphic interface supports all users, regardless of the workstation from which they enter the cluster.
- **Single I/O space:** Any node can remotely access any I/O peripheral or disk device without knowledge of its physical location.
- **Single process space:** A uniform process-identification scheme is used. A process on any node can create or communicate with any other process on a remote node.
- **Checkpointing:** This function periodically saves the process state and intermediate computing results, to allow rollback recovery after a failure.
- **Process migration:** This function enables load balancing.

The last four items on the preceding list enhance the availability of the cluster. The remaining items are concerned with providing a single system image.

Returning to Figure 16.16, a cluster will also include software tools for enabling the efficient execution of programs that are capable of parallel execution.

Clusters Compared to SMP

Both clusters and symmetric multiprocessors provide a configuration with multiple processors to support high-demand applications. Both solutions are commercially available, although SMP has been around far longer.

The main strength of the SMP approach is that an SMP is easier to manage and configure than a cluster. The SMP is much closer to the original single-processor model for which nearly all applications are written. The principal change required in going from a uniprocessor to an SMP is to the scheduler function. Another benefit of the SMP is that it usually takes up less physical space and draws less power than a comparable cluster. A final important benefit is that the SMP products are well established and stable.

Over the long run, however, the advantages of the cluster approach are likely to result in clusters dominating the high-performance server market. Clusters are far superior to SMPs in terms of incremental and absolute scalability. Clusters are also superior in terms of availability, because all components of the system can readily be made highly redundant.

16.6 WINDOWS CLUSTER SERVER

Windows Failover Clustering is a shared-nothing cluster, in which each disk volume and other resources are owned by a single system at a time.

The Windows cluster design makes use of the following concepts:

- **Cluster Service:** The collection of software on each node that manages all cluster-specific activity.
- **Resource:** An item managed by the cluster service. All resources are objects representing actual resources in the system, including hardware devices such

as disk drives and network cards and logical items such as logical disk volumes, TCP/IP addresses, entire applications, and databases.

- **Online:** A resource is said to be online at a node when it is providing service on that specific node.
- **Group:** A collection of resources managed as a single unit. Usually, a group contains all of the elements needed to run a specific application and for client systems to connect to the service provided by that application.

The concept of *group* is of particular importance. A group combines resources into larger units that are easily managed, both for failover and load balancing. Operations performed on a group, such as transferring the group to another node, automatically affect all of the resources in that group. Resources are implemented as dynamically linked libraries (DLLs) and managed by a resource monitor. The resource monitor interacts with the cluster service via remote procedure calls and responds to cluster service commands to configure and move resource groups.

Figure 16.17 depicts the Windows clustering components and their relationships in a single system of a cluster. The **node manager** is responsible for maintaining this node's membership in the cluster. Periodically, it sends heartbeat messages to the node managers on other nodes in the cluster. In the event that one node manager detects a loss of heartbeat messages from another cluster node, it broadcasts a

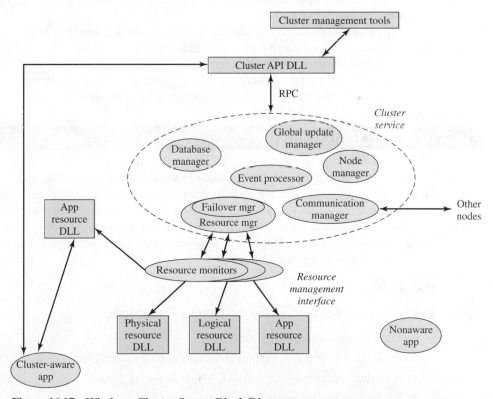

Figure 16.17   Windows Cluster Server Block Diagram

message to the entire cluster, causing all members to exchange messages to verify their view of current cluster membership. If a node manager does not respond, it is removed from the cluster and its active groups are transferred to one or more other active nodes in the cluster.

The **configuration database manager** maintains the cluster configuration database. The database contains information about resources and groups and node ownership of groups. The database managers on each of the cluster nodes cooperate to maintain a consistent picture of configuration information. Fault-tolerant transaction software is used to assure that changes in the overall cluster configuration are performed consistently and correctly.

The **resource manager/failover manager** makes all decisions regarding resource groups and initiates appropriate actions such as startup, reset, and failover. When failover is required, the failover managers on the active node cooperate to negotiate a distribution of resource groups from the failed system to the remaining active systems. When a system restarts after a failure, the failover manager can decide to move some groups back to this system. In particular, any group may be configured with a preferred owner. If that owner fails and then restarts, the group is moved back to the node in a rollback operation.

The **event processor** connects all of the components of the cluster service, handles common operations, and controls cluster service initialization. The communications manager manages message exchange with all other nodes of the cluster. The global update manager provides a service used by other components within the cluster service.

Microsoft is continuing to ship their cluster product, but they have also developed virtualization solutions based on efficient live migration of virtual machines between hypervisors running on different computer systems as part of Windows Server 2008 R2. For new applications, live migration offers many benefits over the cluster approach, such as simpler management, and improved flexibility.

16.7 BEOWULF AND LINUX CLUSTERS

In 1994, the Beowulf project was initiated under the sponsorship of the NASA High Performance Computing and Communications (HPCC) project. Its goal was to investigate the potential of clustered PCs for performing important computation tasks beyond the capabilities of contemporary workstations at minimum cost. Today, the Beowulf approach is widely implemented and is perhaps the most important cluster technology available.

Beowulf Features

Key features of Beowulf include the following [RIDG97]:

- Mass market commodity components
- Dedicated processors (rather than scavenging cycles from idle workstations)
- A dedicated, private network (LAN or WAN or internetted combination)
- No custom components

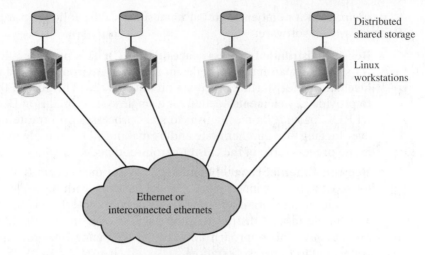

Figure 16.18   Generic Beowulf Configuration

- Easy replication from multiple vendors
- Scalable I/O
- A freely available software base
- Use of freely available distribution computing tools with minimal changes
- Return of the design and improvements to the community

Although elements of Beowulf software have been implemented on a number of different platforms, the most obvious choice for a base is Linux, and most Beowulf implementations use a cluster of Linux workstations and/or PCs. Figure 16.18 depicts a representative configuration. The cluster consists of a number of workstations, perhaps of differing hardware platforms, all running the Linux operating system. Secondary storage at each workstation may be made available for distributed access (for distributed file sharing, distributed virtual memory, or other uses). The cluster nodes (the Linux systems) are interconnected with a commodity networking approach, typically Ethernet. The Ethernet support may be in the form of a single Ethernet switch or an interconnected set of switches. Commodity Ethernet products at the standard data rates (10 Mbps, 100 Mbps, 1 Gbps) are used.

Beowulf Software

The Beowulf software environment is implemented as an add-on to commercially available, royalty-free base Linux distributions. The principal source of open-source Beowulf software is the Beowulf site at *www.beowulf.org*, but numerous other organizations also offer free Beowulf tools and utilities.

Each node in the Beowulf cluster runs its own copy of the Linux kernel and can function as an autonomous Linux system. To support the Beowulf cluster concept, extensions are made to the Linux kernel to allow the individual nodes to participate in a number of global namespaces. The following are examples of Beowulf system software:

- **Beowulf distributed process space (BPROC):** This package allows a process ID space to span multiple nodes in a cluster environment and also provides mechanisms for starting processes on other nodes. The goal of this package is to provide key elements needed for a single system image on Beowulf cluster. BPROC provides a mechanism to start processes on remote nodes without ever logging into another node and by making all the remote processes visible in the process table of the cluster's front-end node.

- **Beowulf Ethernet channel bonding:** This is a mechanism that joins multiple low-cost networks into a single logical network with higher bandwidth. The only additional work over using single network interface is the computationally simple task of distributing the packets over the available device transmit queues. This approach allows load balancing over multiple Ethernets connected to Linux workstations.

- **Pvmsync:** This is a programming environment that provides synchronization mechanisms and shared data objects for processes in a Beowulf cluster.

- **EnFuzion:** EnFuzion consists of a set of tools for doing parametric computing, as described in Section 16.4. Parametric computing involves the execution of a program as a large number of jobs, each with different parameters or starting conditions. EnFusion emulates a set of robot users on a single root node machine, each of which will log into one of the many clients that form a cluster. Each job is set up to run with a unique, programmed scenario, with an appropriate set of starting conditions [KAPP00].

16.8 SUMMARY

Client/server computing is the key to realizing the potential of information systems and networks to improve productivity significantly in organizations. With client/server computing, applications are distributed to users on single-user workstations and personal computers. At the same time, resources that can and should be shared are maintained on server systems that are available to all clients. Thus, the client/server architecture is a blend of decentralized and centralized computing.

Typically, the client system provides a graphical user interface (GUI) that enables a user to exploit a variety of applications with minimal training and relative ease. Servers support shared utilities, such as database management systems. The actual application is divided between client and server in a way intended to optimize ease of use and performance.

The key mechanism required in any distributed system is interprocess communication. Two techniques are in common use. A message-passing facility generalizes the use of messages within a single system. The same sorts of conventions and synchronization rules apply. Another approach is the use of the remote procedure call. This is a technique by which two programs on different machines interact using procedure call/return syntax and semantics. Both the called and calling program behave as if the partner program were running on the same machine.

A cluster is a group of interconnected, whole computers working together as a unified computing resource that can create the illusion of being one machine. The term *whole computer* means a system that can run on its own, apart from the cluster.

16.9 RECOMMENDED READING AND WEB SITES

[BERS96] provides a good technical discussion of the design issues involved in allocating applications to client and server and in middleware approaches; the book also discusses products and standardization efforts. [REAG00a] and [REAG00b] cover client/server computing and network design approaches for supporting client/server computing.

A good overview of middleware technology and products is [BRIT04]. [MENA05] provides a performance comparison of remote procedure calls and distributed message passing.

Two worthwhile surveys of SOA are [BROW03] and [BIH06]. [CHER05] and [BIEB05] analyze the impact of migrating to a SOA. [HUTC08] discusses strategies for migrating to an SOA. [CARE08] looks at the role of data services in an SOA.

[TANE85] is a survey of distributed operating systems that covers both distributed process communication and distributed process management. [CHAN90] provides an overview of distributed message passing operating systems. [TAY90] is a survey of the approach taken by various operating systems in implementing remote procedure calls.

A thorough treatment of clusters can be found in [BUYY99a] and [BUYY99b]. The former has a good treatment of Beowulf, which is also nicely covered in [RIDG97]. A more detailed treatment of Beowulf is [STER99].Windows Cluster Server is described in [SHOR97]; [RAJA00] provides a more detailed treatment. [LAI06] provides a close examination of thin client architecture.

BERS96   Berson, A. *Client/Server Architecture.* New York: McGraw-Hill, 1996.

BIEB05   Bieberstein, N., et al. "Impact of Service-Oriented Architecture on Enterprise Systems, Organizational Structures, and Individuals." *IBM Systems Journal*, Vol. 44, No. 4, 2005.

BIH06   Bih, J. "Service Oriented Architecture (SOA): A New Paradigm to Implement Dynamic E-Business Solutions." *ACM Ubiquity*, August 2006; acm.org/ubiquity/views/v7i30_soa.html

BRIT04   Britton, C. *IT Architectures and Middleware.* Reading, MA: Addison-Wesley, 2004.

BROW03   Brown, A., Johnston, S., and Kelly, K. *Using Service-Oriented Architecture and Component-Based Development to Build Web Service Applications.* IBM Rational Software Technical Report, 2003. ibm.com/developerworks/rational/library/510.html

BUYY99a   Buyya, R. *High Performance Cluster Computing: Architectures and Systems.* Upper Saddle River, NJ: Prentice Hall, 1999.

BUYY99b   Buyya, R. *High Performance Cluster Computing: Programming and Applications.* Upper Saddle River, NJ: Prentice Hall, 1999.

CARE08 Carey, M. "SOA What?" *IEEE Computer*, March 2008.

CHAN90 Chandras, R. "Distributed Message Passing Operating Systems." *Operating Systems Review*, January 1990.

CHER05 Cherbacko, L., et al. "Impact of Service Orientation at the Business Level." *IBM Systems Journal*, Vol 44., No. 4, 2005.

HUTC08 Hutchinson, J., et al. "Migrating to SOAs by Way of Hybrid Systems." *IT Pro*, January/February 2008.

LAI06 Lai, A., and Nieh, J. "On the Performance of Wide-Area Thin-Client Computing." *ACM Transactions on Computer Systems*, May 2006.

MENA05 Menasce, D. "MOM vs. RPC: Communication Models for Distributed Applications." *IEEE Internet Computing*, March/April 2005.

RAJA00 Rajagopal, R. *Introduction to Microsoft Windows NT Cluster Server.* Boca Raton, FL: CRC Press, 2000.

REAG00a Reagan, P. *Client/Server Computing.* Upper Saddle River, NJ: Prentice Hall, 2000.

REAG00b Reagan, P. *Client/Server Network: Design, Operation, and Management.* Upper Saddle River, NJ: Prentice Hall, 2000.

RIDG97 Ridge, D., et al. "Beowulf: Harnessing the Power of Parallelism in a Pile-of-PCs." *Proceedings, IEEE Aerospace Conference*, 1997.

SHOR97 Short, R., Gamache, R., Vert, J., and Massa, M. "Windows NT Clusters for Availability and Scalability." *Proceedings, COMPCON Spring 97*, February 1997.

STER99 Sterling, T., et al. *How to Build a Beowulf.* Cambridge, MA: MIT Press, 1999.

TANE85 Tanenbaum, A., and Renesse, R. "Distributed Operating Systems." *Computing Surveys*, December 1985.

TAY90 Tay, B., and Ananda, A. "A Survey of Remote Procedure Calls." *Operating Systems Review*, July 1990.

Recommended Web sites:

- **SQL Standards:** A central source of information about the SQL standards process and its current documents
- **IEEE Computer Society Task Force on Cluster Computing:** An international forum to promote cluster computing research and education
- **Beowulf:** An international forum to promote cluster computing research and education

16.10 KEY TERMS, REVIEW QUESTIONS, AND PROBLEMS

Key Terms

applications programming interface	Client	distributed message passing
Beowulf	client/server	failback
	cluster	failover

fat client	message	server
file cache consistency	middleware	thin client
graphical user interface	remote procedure call (RPC)	

Review Questions

16.1 What is client/server computing?

16.2 What distinguishes client/server computing from any other form of distributed data processing?

16.3 What is the role of a communications architecture such as TCP/IP in a client/server environment?

16.4 Discuss the rationale for locating applications on the client, the server, or split between client and server.

16.5 What are fat clients and thin clients, and what are the differences in philosophy of the two approaches?

16.6 Suggest pros and cons for fat client and thin client strategies.

16.7 Explain the rationale behind the three-tier client/server architecture.

16.8 What is middleware?

16.9 Because we have standards such as TCP/IP, why is middleware needed?

16.10 List some benefits and disadvantages of blocking and nonblocking primitives for message passing.

16.11 List some benefits and disadvantages of nonpersistent and persistent binding for RPCs.

16.12 List some benefits and disadvantages of synchronous and asynchronous RPCs.

16.13 List and briefly define four different clustering methods.

Problems

16.1 Let α be the percentage of program code that can be executed simultaneously by n computers in a cluster, each computer using a different set of parameters or initial conditions. Assume that the remaining code must be executed sequentially by a single processor. Each processor has an execution rate of x MIPS.

  a. Derive an expression for the effective MIPS rate when using the system for exclusive execution of this program, in terms of n, α, and x.

  b. If $n = 16$ and $x = 4$ MIPS, determine the value of that will yield a system performance of 40 MIPS.

16.2 An application program is executed on a nine-computer cluster. A benchmark program takes time T on this cluster. Further, 25% of T is time in which the application is running simultaneously on all nine computers. The remaining time, the application has to run on a single computer.

  a. Calculate the effective speedup under the aforementioned condition as compared to executing the program on a single computer. Also calculate, the percentage of code that has been parallelized (programmed or compiled so as to use the cluster mode) in the preceding program.

  b. Suppose that we are able to effectively use 18 computers rather than 9 computers on the parallelized portion of the code. Calculate the effective speedup that is achieved.

16.3 The following FORTRAN program is to be executed on a computer, and a parallel version is to be executed on a 32-computer cluster.

L1:   **DO** 10 I = 1, 1024
L2:   SUM(I) = 0
L3:   **DO** 20 J = 1, I
L4: 20 SUM(I) = SUM(I) + I
L5: 10 **CONTINUE**

Suppose lines 2 and 4 each take two machine cycle times, including all processor and memory-access activities. Ignore the overhead caused by the software loop control statements (lines 1, 3, 5) and all other system overhead and resource conflicts.

a. What is the total execution time (in machine cycle times) of the program on a single computer?

b. Divide the I-loop iterations among the 32 computers as follows: Computer 1 executes the first 32 iterations (I = 1 to 32), processor 2 executes the next 32 iterations, and so on. What are the execution time and speedup factor compared with part (a)? (Note that the computational workload, dictated by the J-loop, is unbalanced among the computers.)

c. Explain how to modify the parallelizing to facilitate a balanced parallel execution of all the computational workload over 32 computers. A balanced load means an equal number of additions assigned to each computer with respect to both loops.

d. What is the minimum execution time resulting from the parallel execution on 32 computers? What is the resulting speedup over a single computer?

APPENDIX A

TOPICS IN CONCURRENCY

A.1 Mutual Exclusion: Software Approaches
Dekker's Algorithm
Peterson's Algorithm

A.2 Race Conditions and Semaphores
Problem Statement
First Attempt
Second Attempt
Third Attempt
Fourth Attempt
A Good Attempt

A.3 A Barbership Problem
An Unfair Barbershop
A Fair Barbershop

A.4 Problems

It was impossible to get a conversation going; everybody was talking too much.

— YOGI BERRA

A.1 MUTUAL EXCLUSION: SOFTWARE APPROACHES

Software approaches can be implemented for concurrent processes that execute on a single processor or a multiprocessor machine with shared main memory. These approaches usually assume elementary mutual exclusion at the memory access level ([LAMP91], but see Problem A.3). That is, simultaneous accesses (reading and/or writing) to the same location in main memory are serialized by some sort of memory arbiter, although the order of access granting is not specified ahead of time. Beyond this, no support in the hardware, operating system, or programming language is assumed.

Dekker's Algorithm

Dijkstra [DIJK65] reported an algorithm for mutual exclusion for two processes, designed by the Dutch mathematician Dekker. Following Dijkstra, we develop the solution in stages. This approach has the advantage of illustrating many of the common bugs encountered in developing concurrent programs.

FIRST ATTEMPT   As mentioned earlier, any attempt at mutual exclusion must rely on some fundamental exclusion mechanism in the hardware. The most common of these is the constraint that only one access to a memory location can be made at a time. Using this constraint, we reserve a global memory location labeled turn. A process (P0 or P1) wishing to execute its critical section first examines the contents of turn. If the value of turn is equal to the number of the process, then the process may proceed to its critical section. Otherwise, it is forced to wait. Our waiting process repeatedly reads the value of turn until it is allowed to enter its critical section. This procedure is known as **busy waiting**, or **spin waiting**, because the thwarted process can do nothing productive until it gets permission to enter its critical section. Instead, it must linger and periodically check the variable; thus it consumes processor time (busy) while waiting for its chance.

After a process has gained access to its critical section and after it has completed that section, it must update the value of turn to that of the other process.

In formal terms, there is a shared global variable:

```
int turn = 0;
```

Figure A.1a shows the program for the two processes. This solution guarantees the mutual exclusion property but has two drawbacks. First, processes must strictly alternate in their use of their critical section; therefore, the pace of execution is dictated by the slower of the two processes. If P0 uses its critical section only once per hour but P1 would like to use its critical section at a rate of 1,000 times per hour, P1 is forced to adopt the pace of P0. A much more serious problem is that if one process fails, the other process is permanently blocked. This is true whether a process fails in its critical section or outside of it.

```
/* PROCESS 0 /*                    /* PROCESS 1 */
    .                                  .
    .                                  .
while (turn != 0)                  while (turn != 1)
    /* do nothing */ ;                 /* do nothing */;
/* critical section*/;             /* critical section*/;
turn = 1;                          turn = 0;
    .                                  .
```

(a) First attempt

```
/* PROCESS 0 */                    /* PROCESS 1 */
    .                                  .
    .                                  .
while (flag[1])                    while (flag[0])
    /* do nothing */;                  /* do nothing */;
flag[0] = true;                    flag[1] = true;
/*critical section*/;              /* critical section*/;
flag[0] = false;                   flag[1] = false;
    .                                  .
```

(b) Second attempt

```
/* PROCESS 0 */                    /* PROCESS 1 */
    .                                  .
    .                                  .
flag[0] = true;                    flag[1] = true;
while (flag[1])                    while (flag[0])
    /* do nothing */;                  /* do nothing */;
/* critical section*/;             /* critical section*/;
flag[0] = false;                   flag[1] = false;
```

(c) Third attempt

```
/* PROCESS 0 */                    /* PROCESS 1 */
    .                                  .
    .                                  .
flag[0] = true;                    flag[1] = true;
while (flag[1]) {                  while (flag[0]) {
  flag[0] = false;                   flag[1] = false;
  /*delay */;                        /*delay */;
  flag[0] = true;                    flag[1] = true;
}                                  }
/*critical section*/;              /* critical section*/;
flag[0] = false;                   flag[1] = false;
    .
```

(d) Fourth attempt

Figure A.1   Mutual Exclusion Attempts

The foregoing construction is that of a **coroutine**. Coroutines are designed to be able to pass execution control back and forth between themselves (see Problem 5.2). While this is a useful structuring technique for a single process, it is inadequate to support concurrent processing.

SECOND ATTEMPT   The flaw in the first attempt is that it stores the name of the process that may enter its critical section, when in fact we need state information about both processes. In effect, each process should have its own key to the critical section so that if one fails, the other can still access its critical section. To meet this requirement a Boolean vector flag is defined, with flag[0] corresponding to P0 and flag[1] corresponding to P1. Each process may examine the other's flag but may not alter it. When a process wishes to enter its critical section, it periodically checks the other's flag until that flag has the value false, indicating that the other process is not in its critical section. The checking process immediately sets its own flag to true and proceeds to its critical section. When it leaves its critical section, it sets its flag to false.

The shared global variable[1] now is

```
enum        boolean (false = 0; true = 1);
boolean     flag[2] = {0, 0}
```

Figure A.1b shows the algorithm. If one process fails outside the critical section, including the flag-setting code, then the other process is not blocked. In fact, the other process can enter its critical section as often as it likes, because the flag of the other process is always false. However, if a process fails inside its critical section or after setting its flag to true just before entering its critical section, then the other process is permanently blocked.

This solution is, if anything, worse than the first attempt because it does not even guarantee mutual exclusion. Consider the following sequence:

P0 executes the **while** statement and finds flag[1] set to false

P1 executes the **while** statement and finds flag[0] set to false

P0 sets flag[0] to true and enters its critical section

P1 sets flag[1] to true and enters its critical section

Because both processes are now in their critical sections, the program is incorrect. The problem is that the proposed solution is not independent of relative process execution speeds.

THIRD ATTEMPT   Because a process can change its state after the other process has checked it but before the other process can enter its critical section, the second attempt failed. Perhaps we can fix this problem with a simple interchange of two statements, as shown in Figure A.1c.

As before, if one process fails inside its critical section, including the flag-setting code controlling the critical section, then the other process is blocked, and if a process fails outside its critical section, then the other process is not blocked.

---

[1]The **enum** declaration is used here to declare a data type (boolean) and to assign its values.

Next, let us check that mutual exclusion is guaranteed, using the point of view of process P0. Once P0 has set `flag[0]` to `true`, P1 cannot enter its critical section until after P0 has entered and left its critical section. It could be that P1 is already in its critical section when P0 sets its flag. In that case, P0 will be blocked by the **while** statement until P1 has left its critical section. The same reasoning applies from the point of view of P1.

This guarantees mutual exclusion but creates yet another problem. If both processes set their flags to `true` before either has executed the **while** statement, then each will think that the other has entered its critical section, causing deadlock.

FOURTH ATTEMPT   In the third attempt, a process sets its state without knowing the state of the other process. Deadlock occurs because each process can insist on its right to enter its critical section; there is no opportunity to back off from this position. We can try to fix this in a way that makes each process more deferential: Each process sets its flag to indicate its desire to enter its critical section but is prepared to reset the flag to defer to the other process, as shown in Figure A.1d.

This is close to a correct solution but is still flawed. Mutual exclusion is still guaranteed, using similar reasoning to that followed in the discussion of the third attempt. However, consider the following sequence of events:

P0 sets `flag[0]` to `true`.

P1 sets `flag[1]` to `true`.

P0 checks `flag[1]`.

P1 checks `flag[0]`.

P0 sets `flag[0]` to `false`.

P1 sets `flag[1]` to `false`.

P0 sets `flag[0]` to `true`.

P1 sets `flag[1]` to `true`.

This sequence could be extended indefinitely, and neither process could enter its critical section. Strictly speaking, this is not deadlock, because any alteration in the relative speed of the two processes will break this cycle and allow one to enter the critical section. This condition is referred to as **livelock**. Recall that deadlock occurs when a set of processes wishes to enter their critical sections but no process can succeed. With livelock, there are possible sequences of executions that succeed, but it is also possible to describe one or more execution sequences in which no process ever enters its critical section.

Although the scenario just described is not likely to be sustained for very long, it is nevertheless a possible scenario. Thus we reject the fourth attempt.

A CORRECT SOLUTION   We need to be able to observe the state of both processes, which is provided by the array variable `flag`. But, as the fourth attempt shows, this is not enough. We must impose an order on the activities of the two processes to avoid the problem of "mutual courtesy" that we have just observed. The variable `turn` from the first attempt can be used for this purpose; in this case the variable indicates which process has the right to insist on entering its critical region.

We can describe this solution, referred to as Dekker's algorithm, as follows. When P0 wants to enter its critical section, it sets its flag to `true`. It then checks the flag of P1. If that is `false`, P0 may immediately enter its critical section. Otherwise, P0 consults `turn`. If it finds that `turn` = 0, then it knows that it is its turn to insist and periodically checks P1's flag. P1 will at some point note that it is its turn to defer and set its to flag `false`, allowing P0 to proceed. After P0 has used its critical section, it sets its flag to `false` to free the critical section and sets `turn` to 1 to transfer the right to insist to P1.

```
boolean flag [2];
int turn;
void P0()
{
    while (true) {
        flag [0] = true;
        while (flag [1]) {
            if (turn == 1) {
                flag [0] = false;
                while (turn == 1) /* do nothing */;
                flag [0] = true;
            }
        }
        /* critical section */;
        turn = 1;
        flag [0] = false;
        /* remainder */;
    }
}
void P1( )
{
    while (true) {
        flag [1] = true;
        while (flag [0]) {
            if (turn == 0) {
                flag [1] = false;
                while (turn == 0) /* do nothing */;
                flag [1] = true;
            }
        }
        /* critical section */;
        turn = 0;
        flag [1] = false;
        /* remainder */;
    }
}
void main ()
{
    flag [0] = false;
    flag [1] = false;
    turn = 1;
    parbegin (P0, P1);
}
```

Figure A.2   Dekker's Algorithm

Figure A.2 provides a specification of Dekker's algorithm. The construct **parbegin** (P1, P2, . . . , P*n*) means the following: suspend the execution of the main program; initiate concurrent execution of procedures P1, P2, . . . , P*n*; when all of P1, P2, . . . , P*n* have terminated, resume the main program. A verification of Dekker's algorithm is left as an exercise (see Problem A.1).

Peterson's Algorithm

Dekker's algorithm solves the mutual exclusion problem but with a rather complex program that is difficult to follow and whose correctness is tricky to prove. Peterson [PETE81] has provided a simple, elegant solution. As before, the global array variable `flag` indicates the position of each process with respect to mutual exclusion, and the global variable `turn` resolves simultaneity conflicts. The algorithm is presented in Figure A.3.

That mutual exclusion is preserved is easily shown. Consider process P0. Once it has set `flag[0]` to `true`, P1 cannot enter its critical section. If P1 already is in its critical section, then `flag[1] = true` and P0 is blocked from entering its critical section. On the other hand, mutual blocking is prevented. Suppose that P0 is blocked in its **while** loop. This means that `flag[1]` is `true` and `turn = 1`. P0 can

```
boolean flag [2];
int turn;
void P0()
{
      while (true) {
              flag [0] = true;
              turn = 1;
              while (flag [1] && turn == 1) /* do nothing */;
              /* critical section */;
              flag [0] = false;
              /* remainder */;
      }
}
void P1()
{
      while (true) {
              flag [1] = true;
              turn = 0;
              while (flag [0] && turn == 0) /* do nothing */;
              /* critical section */;
              flag [1] = false;
              /* remainder */
      }
}
void main()
{
      flag [0] = false;
      flag [1] = false;
      parbegin (P0, P1);
}
```

Figure A.3   Peterson's Algorithm for Two Processes

enter its critical section when either `flag[1]` becomes `false` or `turn` becomes 0. Now consider three exhaustive cases:

1. P1 has no interest in its critical section. This case is impossible, because it implies `flag[1]` = `false`.

2. P1 is waiting for its critical section. This case is also impossible, because if `turn` = 1, P1 is able to enter its critical section.

3. P1 is using its critical section repeatedly and therefore monopolizing access to it. This cannot happen, because P1 is obliged to give P0 an opportunity by setting `turn` to 0 before each attempt to enter its critical section.

Thus we have a simple solution to the mutual exclusion problem for two processes. Furthermore, Peterson's algorithm is easily generalized to the case of n processes [HOFR90].

A.2 RACE CONDITIONS AND SEMAPHORES

Although the definition of a race condition, provided in Section 5.1, seems straightforward, experience has shown that students usually have difficulty pinpointing race conditions in their programs. The purpose of this section, which is based on [CARR01],[2] is to step through a series of examples using semaphores that should help clarify the topic of race conditions.

Problem Statement

Assume that there are two processes, **A** and **B**, each of which consists of a number of concurrent threads. Each thread includes an infinite loop in which a message is exchanged with a thread in the other process. Each message consists of an integer placed in a shared global buffer. There are two requirements:

1. After a thread A1 of process **A** makes a message available to some thread B1 in **B**, A1 can only proceed after it receives a message from B1. Similarly, after B1 makes a message available to A1, it can only proceed after it receives a message from A1.

2. Once a thread A1 makes a message available, it must make sure that no other thread in **A** overwrites the global buffer before the message is retrieved by a thread in **B**.

In the remainder of this section, we show four attempts to implement this scheme using semaphores, each of which can result in a race condition. Finally, we show a correct solution.

---

[2]I am grateful to Professor Ching-Kuang Shene of Michigan Technological University for permission to use this example.

First Attempt

Consider this approach:

```
semaphore a = 0, b = 0;
int buf_a, buf_b;
```

```
thread_A(...)                       thread_B(...)
{                                   {
    int var_a;                          int var_b;
    ...                                 ...
    while (true) {                      while (true) {
        ...                                 ...
        var_a =...;                         var_b =...;
        semSignal(b);                       semSignal(a);
        semWait(a);                         semWait(b);
        buf_a = var_a;                      buf_b = var_b;
        var_a = buf_b;                      var_b = buf_a;
        ...;                                ...;
    }                                   }
}                                   }
```

This is a simple handshaking protocol. When a thread A1 in **A** is ready to exchange messages, it sends a signal to a thread in **B** and then waits for a thread B1 in **B** to be ready. Once a signal comes back from B1, which A perceives by performing semWait(a), then A1 assumes that B1 is ready and performs the exchange. B1 behaves similarly, and the exchange happens regardless of which thread is ready first.

This attempt can lead to race conditions. For example, consider the following sequence, with time going vertically down the table:

Thread A1	Thread B1
semSignal(b)	
semWait(a)	
	semSignal(a)
	semWait(b)
buf_a = var_a	
var_a = buf_b	
	buf_b = var_b

In the preceding sequence, A1 reaches semWait(a) and is blocked. B1 reaches semWait(b) and is not blocked, but is switched out before it can update its buf_b. Meanwhile, A1 executes and reads from buf_b before it has the intended value. At this point, buf_b may have a value provided previously by another thread or provided by B1 in a previous exchange. This is a race condition.

A subtler race condition can be seen if two threads in **A** and **B** are active. Consider the following sequence:

Thread A1	Thread A2	Thread B1	Thread B2
semSignal(b)			
semWait(a)			
		semSignal(a)	
		semWait(b)	
	semSignal(b)		
	semWait(a)		
		buf_b = var_b1	
			semSignal(a)
buf_a = var_a1			
	buf_a = var_a2		

In this sequence, threads A1 and B1 attempt to exchange messages and go through the proper semaphore signaling instructions. However, immediately after the two semWait signals occur (in threads A1 and B1), thread A2 runs and executes semSignal(b) and semWait(a), which causes thread B2 to execute semSignal(a) to release A2 from semWait(a). At this point, either A1 or A2 could update buf_a next, and we have a race condition. By changing the sequence of execution among the threads, we can readily find other race conditions.

Lesson Learned: When a variable is shared by multiple threads, race conditions are likely to occur unless proper mutual exclusion protection is used.

Second Attempt

For this attempt, we use a semaphore to protect the shared variable. The purpose is to ensure that access to buf_a and buf_b are mutually exclusive. The program is as follows:

```
semaphore a = 0, b = 0; mutex = 1;
int buf_a, buf_b;

thread_A(...)                        thread_B(...)
{                                    {
   int var_a;                           int var_b;
   . . .                                . . .
   while (true) {                       while (true) {
      . . .                                . . .
      var_a =...;                          var_b =...;
      semSignal(b);                        semSignal(a);
      semWait(a);                          semWait(b);
         semWait(mutex);                      semWait(mutex);
            buf_a = var_a;                       buf_b = var_b;
         semSignal(mutex);                    semSignal(mutex);
      semSignal(b);                        semSignal(a);
      semWait(a);                          semWait(b);
         semWait(mutex);                      semWait(mutex);
            var_a = buf_b;                       var_b = buf_a;
         semSignal(mutex);                    semSignal(mutex);
      . . .;                               . . .;
   }                                    }
}                                    }
```

Before a thread can exchange a message, it follows the same handshaking protocol as in the first attempt. The semaphore `mutex` protects `buf_a` and `buf_b` in an attempt to assure that update precedes reading. But the protection is not adequate. Once both threads complete the first handshaking stage, the values of semaphores a and b are both 1. There are three possibilities that could occur:

1. Two threads, say A1 and B1, complete the first handshaking and continue with the second stage of the exchange.

2. Another pair of threads starts the first stage.

3. One of the current pair will continue and exchange a message with a newcomer in the other pair.

All of these possibilities can lead to race conditions. As an example of a race condition based on the third possibility, consider the following sequence:

Thread A1	Thread A2	Thread B1
semSignal(b)		
semWait(a)		
		semSignal(a)
		semWait(b)
buf_a = var_a1		
		buf_b = var_b1
	semSignal(b)	
	semWait(a)	
		semSignal(a)
		semWait(b)
	buf_a = var_a2	

In this example, after A1 and B1 go through the first handshake, they both update the corresponding global buffers. Then A2 initiates the first handshaking stage. Following this, B1 initiates the second handshaking stage. At this point, A2 updates `buf_a` before B1 can retrieve the value placed in `buf_a` by A1. This is a race condition.

Lesson Learned: Protecting a single variable may be insufficient if the use of that variable is part of a long execution sequence. Protect the whole execution sequence.

Third Attempt

For this attempt, we want to expand the critical section to include the entire message exchange (two threads each update one of two buffers and read from the other buffer). A single semaphore is insufficient because this could lead to deadlock, with each side waiting on the other. The program is as follows:

```
semaphore aready = 1, adone = 0, bready = 1 bdone = 0;
int buf_a, buf_b;
```

thread_A(...)	thread_B(...)
| ```
{
    int var_a;
    ...
    while (true) {
        . . .
        var_a =...;
        semWait(aready);
            buf_a = var_a;
            semSignal(adone);
            semWait(bdone);
            var_a = buf_b;
        semSignal(aready);
        . . .;
    }
}
``` | ```
{
    int var_b;
    ...
    while (true) {
        . . .
        var_b =...;
        semWait(bready);
            buf_b = var_b;
            semSignal(bdone);
            semWait(adone);
            var_b = buf_a;
        semSignal(bready);
        . . .;
    }
}
``` |

The semaphore aready is intended to insure that no other thread in A can update buf_a while one thread from **A** enters its critical section. The semaphore adone is intended to insure that no thread from **B** will attempt to read buf_a until buf_a has been updated. The same considerations apply to bready and bdone. However, this scheme does not prevent race conditions. Consider the following sequence:

Thread A1	Thread B1
buf_a = var_a	
semSignal(adone)	
semWait(bdone)	
	buf_b = var_b
	semSignal(bdone)
	semWait(adone)
var_a = buf_b;	
semSignal(aready)	
...loop back...	
semWait(aready)	
buf_a = var_a	
	var_b = buf_a

In this sequence, both A1 and B1 enter their critical sections, deposit their messages, and reach the second wait. Then A1 copies the message from B1 and leaves its critical section. At this point, A1 could loop back in its program, generate a new message, and deposit it in buf_a, as shown in the preceding execution sequence. Another possibility is that at this same point another thread of **A** could generate a message and put it in buf_a. In either case, a message is lost and a race condition occurs.

Lesson Learned: If we have a number of cooperating thread groups, mutual exclusion guaranteed for one group may not prevent interference from threads in other groups. Further, if a critical section is repeatedly entered by one thread, then the timing of the cooperation between threads must be managed properly.

Fourth Attempt

The third attempt fails to force a thread to remain in its critical section until the other thread retrieves the message. Here is an attempt to achieve this objective:

```
semaphore aready = 1, adone = 0, bready = 1 bdone = 0;
int buf_a, buf_b;
```

thread_A(...)	thread_B(...)
{	{
int var_a;	int var_b;
...	...
while (true) {	while (true) {
...	...
var_a =...;	var_b =...;
semWait(bready);	semWait(aready);
buf_a = var_a;	buf_b = var_b;
semSignal(adone);	semSignal(bdone);
semWait(bdone);	semWait(adone);
var_a = buf_b;	var_b = buf_a;
semSignal(aready);	semSignal(bready);
...;	...;
}	}
}	}

In this case, the first thread in **A** to enter its critical section decrements bready to 0. No subsequent thread from **A** can attempt a message exchange until a thread from **B** completes the message exchange and increments bready to 1. This approach too can lead to race conditions, such as in the following sequence:

Thread A1	Thread A2	Thread B1
semWait(bready)		
buf_a = var_a1		
semSignal(adone)		
		semWait(aready)
		buf_b = var_b1
		semSignal(bdone)
		semWait(adone)
		var_b = buf_a
		semSignal(bready)
	semWait(bready)	
	...	
	semWait(bdone)	
	var_a2 = buf_b	

In this sequence, threads A1 and B1 enter corresponding critical sections in order to exchange messages. Thread B1 retrieves its message and signals `bready`. This enables another thread from **A**, A2, to enter its critical section. If A2 is faster than A1, then A2 may retrieve the message that was intended for A1.

Lesson Learned: If the semaphore for mutual exclusion is not released by its owner, race conditions can occur. In this fourth attempt, a semaphore is locked by a thread in **A** and then unlocked by a thread in **B**. This is risky programming practice.

A Good Attempt

The reader may notice that the problem in this section is a variation of the bounded-buffer problem and can be approached in a manner similar to the discussion in Section 5.4. The most straightforward approach is to use two buffers, one for B-to-A messages and one for A-to-B messages. The size of each buffer needs to be one. To see the reason for this, consider that there is no ordering assumption for releasing threads from a synchronization primitive. If a buffer has more than one slot, then we cannot guarantee that the messages will be properly matched. For example, B1 could receive a message from A1 and then send a message to A1. But if the buffer has multiple slots, another thread in **A** may retrieve the message from the slot intended for A1.

Using the same basic approach as was used in Section 5.4, we can develop the following program:

```
semaphore notFull_A = 1, notFull_B = 1;
semaphore notEmpty_A = 0, notEmpty_B = 0;
int buf_a, buf_b;
```

```
thread_A(...)                          thread_B(...)
{                                      {
    int var_a;                             int var_b;
    ...                                    ...
    while (true) {                         while (true) {
        ...                                    ...
        var_a =...;                            var_b =...;
        semWait(notFull_A);                    semWait(notFull_B);
            buf_a = var_a;                         buf_b = var_b;
            semSignal(notEmpty_A);                 semSignal(notEmpty_B);
        semWait(notEmpty_B);                   semWait(notEmpty_A);
            var_a = buf_b;                         var_b = buf_a;
            semSignal(notFull_B);                  semSignal(notFull_A);
        ...;                                   ...;
    }                                      }
}                                      }
```

To verify that this solution works, we need to address three issues:

1. The message exchange section is mutually exclusive within the thread group. Because the initial value of `notFull_A` is 1, only one thread in **A** can pass through `semWait(notFull_A)` until the exchange is complete as signaled

by a thread in **B** that executes `semSignal(notFull_A)`. A similar reasoning applies to threads in **B**. Thus, this condition is satisfied.

2. Once two threads enter their critical sections, they exchange messages without interference from any other threads. No other thread in **A** can enter its critical section until the thread in **B** is completely done with the exchange, and no other thread in **B** can enter its critical section until the thread in **A** is completely done with the exchange. Thus, this condition is satisfied.

3. After one thread exits its critical section, no thread in the same group can rush in and ruin the existing message. This condition is satisfied because a one-slot buffer is used in each direction. Once a thread in **A** has executed `semWait(notFull_A)` and entered its critical section, no other thread in **A** can update `buf_a` until the corresponding thread in **B** has retrieved the value in `buf_a` and issued a `semSignal(notFull_A)`.

Lesson Learned: It is well to review the solutions to well-known problems, because a correct solution to the problem at hand may be a variation of a solution to a known problem.

A.3 A BARBERSHIP PROBLEM

As another example of the use of semaphores to implement concurrency, we consider a simple barbershop problem.[3] This example is instructive because the problems encountered when attempting to provide tailored access to barbershop resources are similar to those encountered in a real operating system.

Our barbershop has three chairs, three barbers, and a waiting area that can accommodate four customers on a sofa and that has standing room for additional customers (Figure A.4). Fire codes limit the total number of customers in the shop

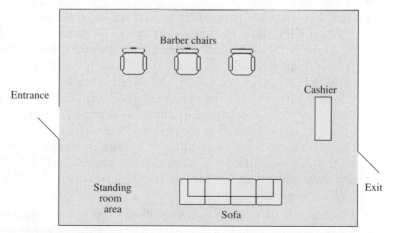

Figure A.4 The Barbershop

---

[3]I am indebted to Professor Ralph Hilzer of California State University at Chico for supplying this treatment of the problem.

to 20. In this example, we assume that the barbershop will eventually process 50 customers.

A customer will not enter the shop if it is filled to capacity with other customers. Once inside, the customer takes a seat on the sofa or stands if the sofa is filled. When a barber is free, the customer that has been on the sofa the longest is served and, if there are any standing customers, the one that has been in the shop the longest takes a seat on the sofa. When a customer's haircut is finished, any barber can accept payment, but because there is only one cash register, payment is accepted for one customer at a time. The barbers divide their time among cutting hair, accepting payment, and sleeping in their chair waiting for a customer.

An Unfair Barbershop

Figure A.5 shows an implementation using semaphores; the three procedures are listed side-by-side to conserve space. We assume that all semaphore queues are handled with a first-in-first-out policy.

The main body of the program activates 50 customers, 3 barbers, and the cashier process. We now consider the purpose and positioning of the various synchronization operators:

- **Shop and sofa capacity:** The capacity of the shop and the capacity of the sofa are governed by the semaphores max_capacity and sofa, respectively. Every time a customer attempts to enter the shop, the max_capacity semaphore is decremented by 1; every time a customer leaves, the semaphore is incremented. If a customer finds the shop full, then that customer's process is blocked on max_capacity by the semWait function. Similarly, the semWait and semSignal operations surround the actions of sitting on and getting up from the sofa.

- **Barber chair capacity:** There are three barber chairs, and care must be taken that they are used properly. The semaphore barber_chair assures that no more than three customers attempt to obtain service at a time, trying to avoid the undignified occurrence of one customer sitting on the lap of another. A customer will not get up from the sofa until at least one chair is free [semWait(barber_chair)], and each barber signals when a customer has left that barber's chair [semSignal(barber_chair)]. Fair access to the barber chairs is guaranteed by the semaphore queue organization: The first customer to be blocked is the first one allowed into an available chair. Note that, in the customer procedure, if semWait(barber_chair) occurred after semSignal(sofa), each customer would only briefly sit on the sofa and then stand in line at the barber chairs, creating congestion and leaving the barbers with little elbow room.

- **Ensuring customers are in barber chair:** The semaphore cust_ready provides a wakeup signal for a sleeping barber, indicating that a customer has just taken a chair. Without this semaphore, a barber would never sleep but would begin cutting hair as soon as a customer left the chair; if no new customer had grabbed the seat, the barber would be cutting air.

```
/* program barbershop1 */
semaphore max_capacity = 20;
semaphore sofa = 4;
semaphore barber_chair = 3;
semaphore coord = 3;
semaphore cust_ready = 0, finished = 0, leave_b_chair = 0, payment = 0, receipt = 0;

void customer()
{
    semWait(max_capacity);
    enter_shop();
    semWait(sofa);
    sit_on_sofa();
    semWait(barber_chair);
    get_up_from_sofa();
    semSignal(sofa);
    sit_in_barber_chair();
    semSignal(cust_ready);
    semWait(finished);
    leave_barber_chair();
    semSignal(leave_b_chair);
    pay();
    semSignal(payment);
    semWait(receipt);
    exit_shop();
    semSignal(max_capacity)
}

void barber()
{
    while (true)
    {
        semWait(cust_ready);
        semWait(coord);
        cut_hair();
        semSignal(coord);
        semSignal(finished);
        semWait(leave_b_chair);
        semSignal(barber_chair);
    }
}

void cashier()
{
    while (true)
    {
        semWait(payment);
        semWait(coord);
        accept_pay();
        semSignal(coord);
        semSignal(receipt);
    }
}

void main()
{
    parbegin (customer,...50 times,...customer, barber, barber, barber, cashier);
}
```

Figure A.5   An Unfair Barbershop

A-17

- **Holding customers in barber chair:** Once seated, a customer remains in the chair until the barber gives the signal that the haircut is complete, using the semaphore `finished`.

- **Limiting one customer to a barber chair:** The semaphore `barber_chair` is intended to limit the number of customers in barber chairs to three. However, by itself, `barber_chair` does not succeed in doing this. A customer that fails to get the processor immediately after his barber executes `semSignal(finished)` (i.e., one who falls into a trance or stops to chat with a neighbor) may still be in the chair when the next customer is given the go ahead to be seated. The semaphore `leave_b_chair` is intended to correct this problem by restraining the barber from inviting a new customer into the chair until the lingering one has announced his departure from it. In the problems at the end of this chapter, we will find that even this precaution fails to stop the mettlesome customer lap sittings.

- **Paying and receiving:** Naturally, we want to be careful when dealing with money. The cashier wants to be assured that each customer pays before leaving the shop, and the customer wants verification that payment was received (a receipt). This is accomplished, in effect, by a face-to-face transfer of the money. Each customer, upon arising from a barber chair, pays, then alerts the cashier that money has been passed over [`semSignal(payment)`], and then waits for a receipt [`semWait(receipt)`]. The cashier process repeatedly takes payments: It waits for a payment to be signaled, accepts the money, and then signals acceptance of the money. Several programming errors need to be avoided here. If `semSignal(payment)` occurred just before the action pay, then a customer could be interrupted after signaling; this would leave the cashier free to accept payment even though none had been offered. An even more serious error would be to reverse the positions of the `semSignal(payment)` and `semWait(receipt)` lines. This would lead to deadlock because that would cause all customers and the cashier to block at their respective `semWait` operators.

- **Coordinating barber and cashier functions:** To save money, this barbershop does not employ a separate cashier. Each barber is required to perform that task when not cutting hair. The semaphore `coord` ensures that barbers perform only one task at a time.

Table A.1 summarizes the use of each of the semaphores in the program.

The cashier process could be eliminated by merging the payment function into the barber procedure. Each barber would sequentially cut hair and then accept pay. However, with a single cash register, it is necessary to limit access to the accept pay function to one barber at a time. This could be done by treating that function as a critical section and guarding it with a semaphore.

A Fair Barbershop

Figure A.5 is a good effort, but some difficulties remain. One problem is solved in the remainder of this section; others are left as exercises for the reader (see Problem A.6).

Table A.1   Purpose of Semaphores in Figure A.5

Semaphore	Wait Operation	Signal Operation
max_capacity	Customer waits for space to enter shop.	Exiting customer signals customer waiting to enter.
sofa	Customer waits for seat on sofa.	Customer leaving sofa signals customer waiting for sofa.
barber_chair	Customer waits for empty barber chair.	Barber signals when that barber's chair is empty.
cust_ready	Barber waits until a customer is in the chair.	Customer signals barber that customer is in the chair.
finished	Customer waits until his haircut is complete.	Barber signals when cutting hair of this customer is done.
leave_b_chair	Barber waits until customer gets up from the chair.	Customer signals barber when customer gets up from chair.
payment	Cashier waits for a customer to pay.	Customer signals cashier that he has paid.
receipt	Customer waits for a receipt for payment.	Cashier signals that payment has been accepted.
coord	Wait for a barber resource to be free to perform either the hair cutting or cashiering function.	Signal that a barber resource is free.

There is a timing problem in Figure A.5 that could lead to unfair treatment of customers. Suppose that three customers are currently seated in the three barber chairs. In that case, the customers would most likely be blocked on semWait(finished), and due to the queue organization they would be released in the order they entered the barber chair. However, what if one of the barbers is very fast or one of the customers is quite bald? Releasing the first customer to enter the chair could result in a situation where one customer is summarily ejected from his seat and forced to pay full price for a partial haircut while another is restrained from leaving his chair even though his haircut is complete.

The problem is solved with more semaphores, as shown in . We assign a unique customer number to each customer; this is equivalent to having each customer take a number upon entering the shop. The semaphore mutex1 protects access to the global variable count so that each customer receives a unique number. The semaphore finished is redefined to be an array of 50 semaphores. Once a customer is seated in a barber chair, he executes semWait(finished[custnr]) to wait on his own unique semaphore; when the barber is finished with that customer, the barber executes semSignal(finished[b_cust]) to release the correct customer.

It remains to say how a customer's number is known to the barber. A customer places his number on the queue enqueue1 just prior to signaling the barber with the semaphore cust_ready. When a barber is ready to cut hair, dequeue1(b_cust) removes the top customer number from queue1 and places it in the barber's local variable b_cust.

```
/* program barbershop2 */
semaphore max_capacity = 20;
semaphore sofa = 4;
semaphore barber_chair = 3, coord = 3;
semaphore mutex1 = 1, mutex2 = 1;
semaphore cust_ready = 0, leave_b_chair = 0, payment= 0, receipt = 0;
semaphore finished [50] = {0};
int count;

void customer ()
{
    int custnr;
    semWait(max_capacity);
    enter_shop();
    semWait(mutex1);
    custnr = count;
    count++;
    semSignal(mutex1);
    semWait(sofa);
    sit_on_sofa();
    semWait(barber_chair);
    get_up_from_sofa();
    semSignal(sofa);
    sit_in_barber_chair();
    semWait(mutex2);
    enqueue1(custnr);
    semSignal(cust_ready);
    semSignal(mutex2);
    semWait(finished[custnr]);
    leave_barber_chair();
    semSignal(leave_b_chair);
    pay();
    semSignal(payment);
    semWait(receipt);
    exit_shop();
        semSignal(max_capacity)
}

void barber()
{
    int b_cust;
    while (true)
    {
        semWait(cust_ready);
        semWait(mutex2);
        dequeue1(b_cust);
        semSignal(mutex2);
        semWait(coord);
        cut_hair();
        semSignal(coord);
        semSignal(finished[b_cust]);
        semWait(leave_b_chair);
        semSignal(barber_chair);
    }
}

void cashier()
{
    while (true)
    {
        semWait(payment);
        semWait(coord);
        accept_pay();
        semSignal(coord);
        semSignal(receipt);
    }
}

void main()
{
    count := 0;
    parbegin (customer,...50 times,...customer, barber, barber, barber, barber, cashier);
}
```

Figure A.6   A Fair Barbershop

A.4 PROBLEMS

A.1 Demonstrate the correctness of Dekker's algorithm.
   a. Show that mutual exclusion is enforced. *Hint:* Show that when Pi enters its critical section, the following expression is true:

```
flag[i] and ( not flag[1 - i] )
```

   b. Show that a process requiring access to its critical section will not be delayed indefinitely. *Hint:* Consider the following cases: (1) A single process is attempting to enter the critical section; (2) both processes are attempting to enter the critical section, and (2a) `turn = 0` and `flag[0] = false`, and (2b) `turn = 0` and `flag[0] = true`.

A.2 Consider Dekker's algorithm, written for an arbitrary number of processes by changing the statement executed when leaving the critical section from

$$\text{turn} = 1 - i \quad /* \text{ i.e. P0 sets turn to 1 and P1 sets turn to 0 } */$$

to

$$\text{turn} = (\text{turn} + 1) \; \% \; n \quad /* \; n = \text{number of processes } */$$

Evaluate the algorithm when the number of concurrently executing processes is greater than two.

A.3 Demonstrate that the following software approaches to mutual exclusion do not depend on elementary mutual exclusion at the memory access level:
   a. the bakery algorithm
   b. Peterson's algorithm

A.4 Answer the following questions relating to the fair barbershop (Figure A.6):
   a. Does the code require that the barber who finishes a customer's haircut collect that customer's payment?
   b. Do barbers always use the same barber chair?

A.5 A number of problems remain with the fair barbershop of Figure A.6. Modify the program to correct the following problems.
   a. The cashier may accept pay from one customer and release another if two or more are waiting to pay. Fortunately, once a customer presents payment, there is no way for him to un-present it, so in the end, the right amount of money ends up in the cash register. Nevertheless, it is desirable to release the right customer as soon as his payment is taken.
   b. The semaphore `leave_b_chair` supposedly prevents multiple access to a single barber chair. Unfortunately, this semaphore does not succeed in all cases. For example, suppose that all three barbers have finished cutting hair and are blocked at `semWait(leave_b_chair)`. Two of the customers are in an interrupted state just prior to `leave barber chair`. The third customer leaves his chair and executes `semSignal(leave_b_chair)`. Which barber is released? Because the `leave_b_chair` queue is first in first out, the first barber that was blocked is released. Is that the barber that was cutting the signaling customer's hair? Maybe, but maybe not. If not, then a new customer will come along and sit on the lap of a customer that was just about to get up.
   c. The program requires a customer first sits on the sofa even if a barber chair is empty. Granted, this is a rather minor problem, and fixing it makes code that is already a bit messy even messier. Nevertheless, give it a try.

APPENDIX B

PROGRAMMING AND OPERATING SYSTEM PROJECTS

B.1   **OS/161**

B.2   **Simulations**

B.3   **Programming Projects**
        Textbook-Defined Projects
        Additional Major Programming Projects
        Small Programming Projects

B.4   **Research Projects**

B.5   **Reading/Report Assignments**

B.6   **Writing Assignments**

B.7   **Discussion Topics**

B.8   **BACI**

Analysis and observation, theory and experience must never disdain
or exclude each other; on the contrary, they support each other.

— On War, Carl Von Clausewitz

Many instructors believe that implementation or research projects are crucial to the clear understanding of operating system concepts. Without projects, it may be difficult for students to grasp some of the basic OS abstractions and interactions among components; a good example of a concept that many students find difficult to master is that of semaphores. Projects reinforce the concepts introduced in this book, give the student a greater appreciation of how the different pieces of an OS fit together, and can motivate students and give them confidence that they are capable of not only understanding but also implementing the details of an OS.

In this text, I have tried to present the concepts of OS internals as clearly as possible and have provided numerous homework problems to reinforce those concepts. Many instructors will wish to supplement this material with projects. This appendix provides some guidance in that regard and describes support material available at the instructor's Web site. The support material covers eight types of projects and other student exercises:

- OS/161 projects
- Simulation projects
- Programming projects
- Research projects
- Reading/report assignments
- Writing assignments
- Discussion topics
- BACI

B.1 OS/161

The **Instructor's Resource Center (IRC)** for this book provides support for using OS/161 as an active learning component.

OS/161 is an educational operating system developed at Harvard University [HOLL02]. It aims to strike a balance between giving students experience in working on a real operating system, and potentially overwhelming students with the complexity that exists in a fully-fledged operating system, such as Linux. Compared to most deployed operating systems, OS/161 is quite small (approximately 20,000 lines of code and comments), and therefore it is much easier to develop an understanding of the entire code base.

The source code distribution contains a full operating system source tree, including the kernel, libraries, various utilities (ls, cat,...), and some test programs. OS/161 boots on the simulated machine in the same manner as a real system might boot on real hardware.

System/161 simulates a "real" machine to run OS/161 on. The machine features a MIPS R2000/R3000 CPU including an MMU, but no floating-point unit or cache. It also features simplified hardware devices hooked up to the system bus. These devices are much simpler than real hardware, and thus make it feasible for students to get their hands dirty without having to deal with the typical level of complexity of physical hardware. Using a simulator has several advantages: Unlike other software students write, buggy OS software may result in completely locking up the machine, making it difficult to debug and requiring a reboot. A simulator enables debuggers to access the machine below the software architecture level as if debugging was built into the CPU. In some senses, the simulator is similar to an in-circuit emulator (ICE) that you might find in industry, only it is implemented in software. The other major advantage is the speed of reboots. Rebooting real hardware takes minutes, and hence the development cycle can be frustratingly slow on real hardware. System/161 boots OS/161 in mere seconds.

The OS/161 and System/161 simulators can be hosted on a variety of platforms, including Unix, Linux, Mac OS X, and Cygwin (the free Unix environment for Windows).

The IRC includes the following:

- **Package for instructor's Web server:** A set of html and pdf files that can be easily uploaded to the instructor's site for the OS course, which provide all the online resources for OS/161 and S/161 access, user's guides for students, assignments, and other useful material.

- **Getting started for instructors:** This guide lists all of the files that make up the Web site for the course and instructions on how to set up the Web site.

- **Getting started for students:** This guide explains to students step-by-step how to download and install OS/161 and S/161 on their PC.

- **Background material for students:** This consists of two documents that provide an overview of the architecture of S/161 and the internals of OS/161. These overviews are intended to be sufficient so that the student is not overwhelmed with figuring out what these systems are.

- **Student exercises:** A set of exercises that cover some of the key aspects of OS internals, including support for system calls, threading, synchronization, locks and condition variables, scheduling, virtual memory, files systems, and security

The IRC OS/161 package was prepared by Andrew Peterson and other colleagues and students at the University of Toronto.

B.2 SIMULATIONS

The IRC provides support for assigning projects based on a set of simulations developed at the University of Texas, San Antonio. Table B.1 lists the simulations by chapter. The simulators are all written in Java and can be run either locally as a Java application or online through a browser.

Table B.1   OS Simulations by Chapter

Chapter 5 – Concurrency: Mutual Exclusion and Synchronization	
Producer-consumer	Allows the user to experiment with a bounded buffer synchronization problem in the context of a single producer and a single consumer
UNIX Fork-pipe	Simulates a program consisting of `pipe`, `dup2`, `close`, `fork`, `read`, `write`, and `print` instructions
Chapter 6 – Concurrency: Deadlock and Starvation	
Starving philosophers	Simulates the dining philosophers problem
Chapter 8 – Virtual Memory	
Address translation	Used for exploring aspects of address translation. It supports 1- and 2-level page tables and a translation lookaside buffer
Chapter 9 – Uniprocessor Scheduling	
Process scheduling	Allows users to experiment with various process scheduling algorithms on a collection of processes and to compare such statistics as throughput and waiting time
Chapter 11 – I/O Management and Disk Scheduling	
Disk head scheduling	Supports the standard scheduling algorithms such as FCFS, SSTF, SCAN, LOOK, C-SCAN, and C-LOOK as well as double buffered versions of these
Chapter 12 – File Management	
Concurrent I/O	Simulates a program consisting of `open`, `close`, `read`, `write`, `fork`, `wait`, `pthread_create`, `pthread_detach`, and `pthread_join` instructions

The IRC includes the following:

1. A brief overview of the simulations available.
2. How to port them to the local environment.
3. Specific assignments to give to students, telling them specifically what they are to do and what results are expected. For each simulation, this section provides one or two original assignments that the instructor can assign to students.

These simulation assignments were developed by Adam Critchley (University of Texas at San Antonio).

B.3   PROGRAMMING PROJECTS

Three sets of programming projects are provided.

Textbook-Defined Projects

Two major programming projects, one to build a shell, or command line interpreter, and one to build a process dispatcher are described in the online portion of the textbook. The projects can be assigned after Chapter 3 and after Chapter 9, respectively. The IRC provides further information and step-by-step exercises for developing the programs.

These projects were developed by Ian G. Graham of Griffith University, Australia.

Additional Major Programming Projects

A set of programming assignments, called machine problems (MPs), are available that are based on the Posix Programming Interface. The first of these assignments is a crash course in C, to enable the student to develop sufficient proficiency in C to be able to do the remaining assignments. The set consists of nine machine problems with different difficulty degrees. It may be advisable to assign each project to a team of two students.

Each MP includes not only a statement of the problem but a number of C files that are used in each assignment, step-by-step instructions, and a set of questions for each assignment that the student must answer that indicate a full understanding of each project. The scope of the assignments includes:

1. Create a program to run in a shell environment using basic I/O and string manipulation functions.
2. Explore and extend a simple Unix shell interpreter.
3. Modify faulty code that utilizes threads.
4. Implement a multithreaded application using thread synchronization primitives.
5. Write a user–mode thread scheduler
6. Simulate a time-sharing system by using signals and timers
7. A six-week project aimed at creating a simple yet functional networked file system. Covers I/O and file system concepts, memory management, and networking primitives.

The IRC provides specific instructions for setting up the appropriate support files on the instructor's Web site of local server.

These project assignments were developed at the University of Illinois at Urbana-Champaign, Department of Computer Science and adapted by Matt Sparks (University of Illinois at Urbana-Champagne) for use with this textbook.

Small Programming Projects

The instructor can also assign a number of small programming projects described in the IRC. The projects can be programmed by the students on any available computer and in any appropriate language: They are platform and language independent.

These small projects have certain advantages over the larger projects. Larger projects usually give students more of a sense of achievement, but students with less ability or fewer organizational skills can be left behind. Larger projects usually elicit more overall effort from the best students. Smaller projects can have a higher concepts-to-code ratio, and because more of them can be assigned, the opportunity exists to address a variety of different areas. Accordingly, the instructor's IRC contains a series of small projects, each intended to be completed in a week or so, which can be very satisfying to both student and teacher. These projects were developed at Worcester Polytechnic Institute by Stephen Taylor, who has used and refined the projects in the course of teaching operating systems a dozen times.

B.4 RESEARCH PROJECTS

An effective way of reinforcing basic concepts from the course and for teaching students research skills is to assign a research project. Such a project could involve a literature search as well as a Web search of vendor products, research lab activities, and standardization efforts. Projects could be assigned to teams or, for smaller projects, to individuals. In any case, it is best to require some sort of project proposal early in the term, giving the instructor time to evaluate the proposal for appropriate topic and appropriate level of effort. Student handouts for research projects should include

- A format for the proposal
- A format for the final report
- A schedule with intermediate and final deadlines
- A list of possible project topics

The students can select one of the listed topics or devise their own comparable project. The IRC includes a suggested format for the proposal and final report as well as a list of possible research topics developed by Professor Tan N. Nguyen of George Mason University.

B.5 READING/REPORT ASSIGNMENTS

Another excellent way to reinforce concepts from the course and to give students research experience is to assign papers from the literature to be read and analyzed. The IRC includes a suggested list of papers to be assigned, organized by chapter. The Premium Content Web site provides a copy of each of the papers. The IRC also includes a suggested assignment wording.

B.6 WRITING ASSIGNMENTS

Writing assignments can have a powerful multiplier effect in the learning process in a technical discipline such as OS internals. Adherents of the Writing Across the Curriculum (WAC) movement (http://wac.colostate.edu/) report substantial benefits of writing assignments in facilitating learning. Writing assignments lead to more detailed and complete thinking about a particular topic. In addition, writing assignments help to overcome the tendency of students to pursue a subject with a minimum of personal engagement, just learning facts and problem-solving techniques without obtaining a deep understanding of the subject matter.

The IRC contains a number of suggested writing assignments, organized by chapter. Instructors may ultimately find that this is an important part of their approach to teaching the material. I would greatly appreciate any feedback on this area and any suggestions for additional writing assignments.

B.7 DISCUSSION TOPICS

One way to provide a collaborative experience is discussion topics, a number of which are included in the IRC. Each topic relates to material in the book. The instructor can set it up so that students can discuss a topic either in a class setting, an online chat room, or a message board. Again, I would greatly appreciate any feedback on this area and any suggestions for additional discussion topics.

B.8 BACI

In addition to all of the support provided at the IRC, the Ben-Ari Concurrent Interpreter (BACI) is a publicly available package that instructors may wish to use. BACI simulates concurrent process execution and supports binary and counting semaphores and monitors. BACI is accompanied by a number of project assignments to be used to reinforce concurrency concepts.

Appendix O provides a more detailed introduction to BACI, with information about how to obtain the system and the assignments.

GLOSSARY

In studying the Imperium, Arrakis, and the whole culture which produced Maud'Dib, many unfamiliar terms occur. To increase understanding is a laudable goal, hence the definitions and explanations given below

—DUNE, FRANK HERBERT

access method The method that is used to find a file, a record, or a set of records.

address space The range of addresses available to a computer program.

address translator A functional unit that transforms virtual addresses to real addresses.

application programming interface (API) A standardized library of programming tools used by software developers to write applications that are compatible with a specific operating system or graphic user interface.

asynchronous operation An operation that occurs without a regular or predictable time relationship to a specified event, for example, the calling of an error diagnostic routine that may receive control at any time during the execution of a computer program.

base address An address that is used as the origin in the calculation of addresses in the execution of a computer program.

batch processing Pertaining to the technique of executing a set of computer programs such that each is completed before the next program of the set is started.

Beowulf Defines a class of clustered computing that focuses on minimizing the price-to-performance ratio of the overall system without compromising its ability to perform the computation work for which it is being built. Most Beowulf systems are implemented on Linux computers.

binary semaphore A semaphore that takes on only the values 0 and 1. A binary semaphore allows only one process or thread to have access to a shared critical resource at a time.

block (1) A collection of contiguous records that are recorded as a unit; the units are separated by interblock gaps. (2) A group of bits that are transmitted as a unit.

B-tree A technique for organizing indexes. In order to keep access time to a minimum, it stores the data keys in a balanced hierarchy that continually realigns itself as items are inserted and deleted. Thus, all nodes always have a similar number of keys.

busy waiting The repeated execution of a loop of code while waiting for an event to occur.

cache memory A memory that is smaller and faster than main memory and that is interposed between the processor and main memory. The cache acts as a buffer for recently used memory locations.

central processing unit (CPU) That portion of a computer that fetches and executes instructions. It consists of an Arithmetic and Logic Unit (ALU), a control unit, and registers. Often simply referred to as a *processor.*

chained list A list in which data items may be dispersed but in which each item contains an identifier for locating the next item.

client A process that requests services by sending messages to server processes.

cluster A group of interconnected, whole computers working together as a unified computing resource that can create the illusion of being one machine. The term *whole computer* means a system that can run on its own, apart from the cluster.

communications architecture The hardware and software structure that implements the communications function.

compaction A technique used when memory is divided into variable-size partitions. From time to time, the operating system shifts the partitions so that they are contiguous and so that all of the free memory is together in one block. See *external fragmentation*.

concurrent Pertaining to processes or threads that take place within a common interval of time during which they may have to alternately share common resources.

consumable resource A resource that can be created (produced) and destroyed (consumed). When a resource is acquired by a process, the resource ceases to exist. Examples of consumable resources are interrupts, signals, messages, and information in I/O buffers.

critical section In an asynchronous procedure of a computer program, a part that cannot be executed simultaneously with an associated critical section of another asynchronous procedure. See *mutual exclusion*.

database A collection of interrelated data, often with controlled redundancy, organized according to a schema to serve one or more applications; the data are stored so that they can be used by different programs without concern for the data structure or organization. A common approach is used to add new data and to modify and retrieve existing data.

deadlock (1) An impasse that occurs when multiple processes are waiting for the availability of a resource that will not become available because it is being held by another process that is in a similar wait state. (2) An impasse that occurs when multiple processes are waiting for an action by or a response from another process that is in a similar wait state.

deadlock avoidance A dynamic technique that examines each new resource request for deadlock. If the new request could lead to a deadlock, then the request is denied.

deadlock detection A technique in which requested resources are always granted when available. Periodically, the operating system tests for deadlock.

deadlock prevention A technique that guarantees that a deadlock will not occur. Prevention is achieved by assuring that one of the necessary conditions for deadlock is not met.

demand paging The transfer of a page from secondary memory to main memory storage at the moment of need. Compare *prepaging*.

device driver An operating system module (usually in the kernel) that deals directly with a device or I/O module.

direct access The capability to obtain data from a storage device or to enter data into a storage device in a sequence independent of their relative position, by means of addresses that indicate the physical location of the data.

direct memory access (DMA) A form of I/O in which a special module, called a DMA module, controls the exchange of data between main memory and an I/O device. The processor sends a request for the transfer of a block of data to the DMA module and is interrupted only after the entire block has been transferred.

disabled interrupt A condition, usually created by the operating system, during which the processor will ignore interrupt request signals of a specified class.

disk allocation table A table that indicates which blocks on secondary storage are free and available for allocation to files.

disk cache A buffer, usually kept in main memory, that functions as a cache of disk blocks between disk memory and the rest of main memory.

dispatch To allocate time on a processor to jobs or tasks that are ready for execution.

distributed operating system A common operating system shared by a network of computers. The distributed operating system provides support for interprocess communication, process migration, mutual exclusion, and the prevention or detection of deadlock.

dynamic relocation A process that assigns new absolute addresses to a computer program during execution so that the program may be executed from a different area of main storage.

enabled interrupt A condition, usually created by the operating system, during which the processor will respond to interrupt request signals of a specified class.

encryption The conversion of plain text or data into unintelligible form by means of a reversible mathematical computation.

execution context Same as *process state*.

external fragmentation Occurs when memory is divided into variable-size partitions corresponding to the blocks of data assigned to the memory (e.g., segments in main memory). As segments are moved into and out of the memory, gaps will occur between the occupied portions of memory.

field (1) Defined logical data that are part of a record. (2) The elementary unit of a record that may contain a data item, a data aggregate, a pointer, or a link.

file A set of related records treated as a unit.

file allocation table (FAT) A table that indicates the physical location on secondary storage of the space allocated to a file. There is one file allocation table for each file.

file management system A set of system software that provides services to users and applications in the use of files, including file access, directory maintenance, and access control.

file organization The physical order of records in a file, as determined by the access method used to store and retrieve them.

first come first served (FCFS) Same as *FIFO*.

first in first out (FIFO) A queueing technique in which the next item to be retrieved is the item that has been in the queue for the longest time.

frame In paged virtual storage, a fixed-length block of main memory that is used to hold one page of virtual memory.

gang scheduling The scheduling of a set of related threads to run on a set of processors at the same time, on a one-to-one basis.

hash file A file in which records are accessed according to the values of a key field. Hashing is used to locate a record on the basis of its key value.

hashing The selection of a storage location for an item of data by calculating the address as a function of the contents of the data. This technique complicates the storage allocation function but results in rapid random retrieval.

hit ratio In a two-level memory, the fraction of all memory accesses that are found in the faster memory (e.g., the cache).

indexed access Pertaining to the organization and accessing of the records of a storage structure through a separate index to the locations of the stored records.

indexed file A file in which records are accessed according to the value of key fields. An index is required that indicates the location of each record on the basis of each key value.

indexed sequential access Pertaining to the organization and accessing of the records of a storage structure through an index of the keys that are stored in arbitrarily partitioned sequential files.

indexed sequential file A file in which records are ordered according to the values of a key field. The main file is supplemented with an index file that contains a partial list of key values; the index provides a lookup capability to quickly reach the vicinity of a desired record.

instruction cycle The time period during which one instruction is fetched from memory and executed when a computer is given an instruction in machine language.

internal fragmentation Occurs when memory is divided into fixed-size partitions (e.g., page frames in main memory, physical blocks on disk). If a block of data is assigned to one or more partitions, then there may be wasted space in the last partition. This will occur if the last portion of data is smaller than the last partition.

interrupt A suspension of a process, such as the execution of a computer program, caused by an event external to that process and performed in such a way that the process can be resumed.

interrupt handler A routine, generally part of the operating system. When an interrupt occurs, control is transferred to the corresponding interrupt handler, which takes some action in response to the condition that caused the interrupt.

job A set of computational steps packaged to run as a unit.

job control language (JCL) A problem-oriented language that is designed to express statements in a job that are used to identify the job or to describe its requirements to an operating system.

kernel A portion of the operating system that includes the most heavily used portions of software. Generally, the kernel is maintained permanently in main memory. The kernel runs in a privileged mode and responds to calls from processes and interrupts from devices.

kernel mode A privileged mode of execution reserved for the kernel of the operating system. Typically, kernel mode allows access to regions of main memory that are unavailable to processes executing in a less-privileged mode, and also enables execution of certain machine instructions that are restricted to the kernel mode. Also referred to as *system mode* or *privileged mode*.

last in first out (LIFO) A queueing technique in which the next item to be retrieved is the item most recently placed in the queue.

lightweight process A thread.

livelock A condition in which two or more processes continuously change their state in response to changes in the other process(es) without doing any useful work. This is similar to deadlock in that no progress is made, but it differs in that neither process is blocked or waiting for anything.

locality of reference The tendency of a processor to access the same set of memory locations repetitively over a short period of time.

logical address A reference to a memory location independent of the current assignment of data to memory. A translation must be made to a physical address before the memory access can be achieved.

logical record A record independent of its physical environment; portions of one logical record may be located in different physical records or several logical records or parts of logical records may be located in one physical record.

macrokernel A large operating system core that provides a wide range of services.

mailbox A data structure shared among a number of processes that is used as a queue for messages. Messages are sent to the mailbox and retrieved from the mailbox rather than passing directly from sender to receiver.

main memory Memory that is internal to the computer system, is program addressable, and can be loaded into registers for subsequent execution or processing.

malicious software Any software designed to cause damage to or use up the resources of a target computer. Malicious software (malware) is frequently concealed within or masquerades as legitimate software. In some cases, it spreads itself to other computers via e-mail or infected disks. Types of malicious software include viruses, Trojan horses, worms, and hidden software for launching denial-of-service attacks.

memory cycle time The time it takes to read one word from or write one word to memory. This is the inverse of the rate at which words can be read from or written to memory.

memory partitioning The subdividing of storage into independent sections.

message A block of information that may be exchanged between processes as a means of communication.

microkernel A small privileged operating system core that provides process scheduling, memory management, and communication services and relies on other processes to perform some of the functions traditionally associated with the operating system kernel.

mode switch A hardware operation that occurs that causes the processor to execute in a different mode (kernel or process). When the mode switches from process to kernel, the program counter, processor status word, and other registers are saved. When the mode switches from kernel to process, this information is restored.

monitor A programming language construct that encapsulates variables, access procedures, and initialization code within an abstract data type. The monitor's variable may only be accessed via its access procedures and only one process may be actively accessing the monitor at any one time. The access procedures are *critical sections*. A monitor may have a queue of processes that are waiting to access it.

monolithic kernel A large kernel containing virtually the complete operating system, including scheduling, file system, device drivers, and memory management. All the functional components of the kernel have access to all of its internal data structures and routines. Typically, a monolithic kernel is implemented as a single process, with all elements sharing the same address space.

multilevel security A capability that enforces access control across multiple levels of classification of data.

multiprocessing A mode of operation that provides for parallel processing by two or more processors of a multiprocessor.

multiprocessor A computer that has two or more processors that have common access to a main storage.

multiprogramming A mode of operation that provides for the interleaved execution of two or more computer programs by a single processor. The same as multitasking, using different terminology.

multiprogramming level The number of processes that are partially or fully resident in main memory.

multitasking A mode of operation that provides for the concurrent performance or interleaved execution of two or more computer tasks. The same as multiprogramming, using different terminology.

mutex Similar to a binary semaphore. A key difference between the two is that the process that locks the mutex (sets the value to zero) must be the one to unlock it (sets the value to 1). In contrast, it is possible for one process to lock a binary semaphore and for another to unlock it.

mutual exclusion A condition in which there is a set of processes, only one of which is able to access a given resource or perform a given function at any time. See *critical section*.

nonprivileged state An execution context that does not allow sensitive hardware instructions to be executed, such as the halt instruction and I/O instructions.

nonuniform memory access (NUMA) multiprocessor A shared-memory multiprocessor in which the access time from a given processor to a word in memory varies with the location of the memory word.

object request broker An entity in an object-oriented system that acts as an intermediary for requests sent from a client to a server.

operating system Software that controls the execution of programs and that provides services such as resource allocation, scheduling, input/output control, and data management.

page In virtual storage, a fixed-length block that has a virtual address and that is transferred as a unit between main memory and secondary memory.

page fault Occurs when the page containing a referenced word is not in main memory. This causes an interrupt and requires that the proper page be brought into main memory.

page frame A fixed-size contiguous block of main memory used to hold a page.

paging The transfer of pages between main memory and secondary memory.

physical address The absolute location of a unit of data in memory (e.g., word or byte in main memory, block on secondary memory).

pipe A circular buffer allowing two processes to communicate on the producer–consumer model. Thus, it is a first-in-first-out queue, written by one process and read by another. In some systems, the pipe is generalized to allow any item in the queue to be selected for consumption.

preemption Reclaiming a resource from a process before the process has finished using it.

prepaging The retrieval of pages other than the one demanded by a page fault. The hope is that the additional pages will be needed in the near future, conserving disk I/O. Compare *demand paging*.

priority inversion A circumstance in which the operating system forces a higher-priority task to wait for a lower-priority task.

privileged instruction An instruction that can be executed only in a specific mode, usually by a supervisory program.

privileged mode Same as *kernel mode*.

process A program in execution. A process is controlled and scheduled by the operating system. Same as *task*.

process control block The manifestation of a process in an operating system. It is a data structure containing information about the characteristics and state of the process.

process descriptor Same as process control block.

process image All of the ingredients of a process, including program, data, stack, and process control block.

process migration The transfer of a sufficient amount of the state of a process from one machine to another for the process to execute on the target machine.

process spawning The creation of a new process by another process.

process state All of the information that the operating system needs to manage a process and that the processor needs to properly execute the process. The process state includes the contents of the various processor registers, such as the program counter and data registers; it also includes information of use to the operating system, such as the priority of the process and whether the process is waiting for the completion of a particular I/O event. Same as *execution context*.

process switch An operation that switches the processor from one process to another, by saving all the process control block, registers, and other information for the first and replacing them with the process information for the second.

processor In a computer, a functional unit that interprets and executes instructions. A processor consists of at least an instruction control unit and an arithmetic unit.

program counter Instruction address register.

program status word (PSW) A register or set of registers that contains condition codes, execution mode, and other status information that reflects the state of a process.

programmed I/O A form of I/O in which the CPU issues an I/O command to an I/O module and must then wait for the operation to be complete before proceeding.

race condition Situation in which multiple processes access and manipulate shared data with the outcome dependent on the relative timing of the processes.

real address A physical address in main memory.

real-time system An operating system that must schedule and manage real-time tasks.

real-time task A task that is executed in connection with some process or function or set of events external to the computer system and that must meet one or more deadlines to interact effectively and correctly with the external environment.

record A group of data elements treated as a unit.

reentrant procedure A routine that may be entered before the completion of a prior execution of the same routine and execute correctly.

registers High-speed memory internal to the CPU. Some registers are user visible — that is, available to the programmer via the machine instruction set. Other registers are used only by the CPU, for control purposes.

relative address An address calculated as a displacement from a base address.

remote procedure call (RPC) A technique by which two programs on different machines interact using procedure call/return syntax and semantics. Both the called and calling program behave as if the partner program were running on the same machine.

rendezvous In message passing, a condition in which both the sender and receiver of a message are blocked until the message is delivered.

resident set That portion of a process that is actually in main memory at a given time. Compare *working set*.

response time In a data system, the elapsed time between the end of transmission of an enquiry message and the beginning of the receipt of a response message, measured at the enquiry terminal.

reusable resource A resource that can be safely used by only one process at a time and is not depleted by that use. Processes obtain reusable resource units that they later release for reuse by other processes. Examples of reusable resources include processors, I/O channels, main and secondary memory, devices, and data structures such as files, databases, and semaphores.

round robin A scheduling algorithm in which processes are activated in a fixed cyclic order; that is, all processes are in a circular queue. A process that cannot proceed because it is waiting for some event (e.g., termination of a child process or an input/output operation) returns control to the scheduler.

scheduling To select jobs or tasks that are to be dispatched. In some operating systems, other units of work, such as input/output operations, may also be scheduled.

secondary memory Memory located outside the computer system itself; that is, it cannot be processed directly by the processor. It must first be copied into main memory. Examples include disk and tape.

segment In virtual memory, a block that has a virtual address. The blocks of a program may be of unequal length and may even be of dynamically varying lengths.

segmentation The division of a program or application into segments as part of a virtual memory scheme.

semaphore An integer value used for signaling among processes. Only three operations may be performed on a semaphore, all of which are atomic: initialize, decrement, and increment. Depending on the exact definition of the semaphore, the decrement operation may result in the blocking of a process, and the increment operation may result in the unblocking of a process. Also known as a **counting semaphore** or a **general semaphore**.

sequential access The capability to enter data into a storage device or a data medium in the same sequence as the data are ordered, or to obtain data in the same order as they were entered.

sequential file A file in which records are ordered according to the values of one or more key fields and processed in the same sequence from the beginning of the file.

server (1) A process that responds to request from clients via messages. (2) In a network, a data station that provides facilities to other stations; for example, a file server, a print server, a mail server.

session A collection of one or more processes that represents a single interactive user application or operating system function. All keyboard and mouse input is directed to the foreground session, and all output from the foreground session is directed to the display screen.

shell The portion of the operating system that interprets interactive user commands and job control language commands. It functions as an interface between the user and the operating system.

spin lock Mutual exclusion mechanism in which a process executes in an infinite loop waiting for the value of a lock variable to indicate availability.

spooling The use of secondary memory as buffer storage to reduce processing delays when transferring data between peripheral equipment and the processors of a computer.

stack An ordered list in which items are appended to and deleted from the same end of the list, known as the top. That is, the next item appended to the list is put on the top, and the next item to be removed from the list is the item that has been in the list the shortest time. This method is characterized as last in first out.

starvation A condition in which a process is indefinitely delayed because other processes are always given preference.

strong semaphore A semaphore in which all processes waiting on the same semaphore are queued and will eventually proceed in the same order as they executed the wait (P) operations (FIFO order).

swapping A process that interchanges the contents of an area of main storage with the contents of an area in secondary memory.

symmetric multiprocessing (SMP) A form of multiprocessing that allows the operating system to execute on any available processor or on several available processors simultaneously.

synchronous operation An operation that occurs regularly or predictably with respect to the occurrence of a specified event in another process, for example, the calling of an input/output routine that receives control at a precoded location in a computer program.

synchronization Situation in which two or more processes coordinate their activities based on a condition.

system bus A bus used to interconnect major computer components (CPU, memory, I/O).

system mode Same as *kernel mode*.

task Same as *process*.

thrashing A phenomenon in virtual memory schemes, in which the processor spends most of its time swapping pieces rather than executing instructions.

thread A dispatchable unit of work. It includes a processor context (which includes the program counter and stack pointer) and its own data area for a stack (to enable subroutine branching). A thread executes sequentially and is interruptible so that the processor can turn to another thread. A process may consist of multiple threads.

thread switch The act of switching processor control from one thread to another within the same process.

time sharing The concurrent use of a device by a number of users.

time slice The maximum amount of time that a process can execute before being interrupted.

time slicing A mode of operation in which two or more processes are assigned quanta of time on the same processor.

trace A sequence of instructions that are executed when a process is running.

translation lookaside buffer (TLB) A high-speed cache used to hold recently referenced page table entries as part of a paged virtual memory scheme. The TLB reduces the frequency of access to main memory to retrieve page table entries.

trap An unprogrammed conditional jump to a specified address that is automatically activated by hardware; the location from which the jump was made is recorded.

trap door Secret undocumented entry point into a program, used to grant access without normal methods of access authentication.

trojan horse Secret undocumented routine embedded within a useful program. Execution of the program results in execution of the secret routine.

trusted system A computer and operating system that can be verified to implement a given security policy.

user mode The least-privileged mode of execution. Certain regions of main memory and certain machine instructions cannot be used in this mode.

virtual address The address of a storage location in virtual memory.

virtual memory The storage space that may be regarded as addressable main storage by the user of a computer system in which virtual addresses are mapped into real addresses. The size of virtual storage is limited by the addressing scheme of the computer system and by the amount of secondary memory available and not by the actual number of main storage locations.

virus Secret undocumented routine embedded within a useful program. Execution of the program results in execution of the secret routine.

weak semaphore A semaphore in which all processes waiting on the same semaphore proceed in an unspecified order (i.e., the order is unknown or indeterminate).

word An ordered set of bytes or bits that is the normal unit in which information may be stored, transmitted, or operated on within a given computer. Typically, if a processor has a fixed-length instruction set, then the instruction length equals the word length.

working set The working set with parameter Δ for a process at virtual time t, $W(t, \Delta)$ is the set of pages of that process that have been referenced in the last Δ time units. Compare *resident set*.

worm Program that can travel from computer to computer across network connections. May contain a virus or bacteria.

REFERENCES

In matters of this kind everyone feels he is justified in writing and publishing the first thing that comes into his head when he picks up a pen, and thinks his own idea as axiomatic as the fact that two and two make four. If critics would go to the trouble of thinking about the subject for years on end and testing each conclusion against the actual history of war, as I have done, they would undoubtedly be more careful of what they wrote.

—*ON WAR*, CARL VON CLAUSEWITZ

ABBREVIATIONS

ACM	Association for Computing Machinery
IEEE	Institute of Electrical and Electronics Engineers

ABRA06 Abramson, T. "Detecting Potential Deadlocks." *Dr. Dobb's Journal*, January 2006.

AGAR89 Agarwal, A. *Analysis of Cache Performance for Operating Systems and Multiprogramming.* Boston: Kluwer Academic Publishers, 1989.

ANAN92 Ananda, A., Tay, B., and Koh, E. "A Survey of Asynchronous Remote Procedure Calls." *Operating Systems Review*, April 1992.

ANDE80 Anderson, J. *Computer Security Threat Monitoring and Surveillance.* Fort Washington, PA: James P. Anderson Co., April 1980.

ANDE89 Anderson, T., Laxowska, E., and Levy, H. "The Performance Implications of Thread Management Alternatives for Shared-Memory Multiprocessors." *IEEE Transactions on Computers*, December 1989.

ANDE04 Anderson, T., Bershad, B., Lazowska, E., and Levy, H. "Thread Management for Shared-Memory Multiprocessors." In [TUCK04].

ANDR83 Andrews, G., and Schneider, F. "Concepts and Notations for Concurrent Programming." *Computing Surveys*, March 1983.

ANDR90 Andrianoff, S. "A Module on Distributed Systems for the Operating System Course." *Proceedings, Twenty-First SIGCSE Technical Symposium on Computer Science Education, SIGSCE Bulletin*, February 1990.

ANDR04 Andrews, M., and Whittaker, J. "Computer Security." *IEEE Security and Privacy*, September/October 2004.

ANTE06 Ante, S., and Grow, B. "Meet the Hackers." *Business Week*, May 29, 2006.

APPL09 Apple. Inc. "Grand Central Dispatch: A Better Way to Do Multicore." *Technology Brief*, August 2009.

ARDE80 Arden, B., editor. *What Can Be Automated?* Cambridge, MA: MIT Press, 1980.

ARTS89a Artsy, Y., ed. Special Issue on Process Migration. *Newsletter of the IEEE Computer Society Technical Committee on Operating Systems*, Winter 1989.

ARTS89b Artsy, Y. "Designing a Process Migration Facility: The Charlotte Experience." *Computer*, September 1989.

ATLA89 Atlas, A., and Blundon, B. "Time to Reach for It All." *UNIX Review*, January 1989.

723

AXFO88 Axford, T. *Concurrent Programming: Fundamental Techniques for Real-Time and Parallel Software Design.* New York: Wiley, 1988.

AYCO06 Aycock, J. *Computer Viruses and Malware.* New York: Springer, 2006.

BACH86 Bach, M. *The Design of the UNIX Operating System.* Englewood Cliffs, NJ: Prentice Hall, 1986.

BACO03 Bacon, J., and Harris, T. *Operating Systems: Concurrent and Distributed Software Design.* Reading, MA: Addison-Wesley, 2003.

BAER80 Baer, J. *Computer Systems Architecture.* Rockville, MD: Computer Science Press, 1980.

BARB90 Barbosa, V. "Strategies for the Prevention of Communication Deadlocks in Distributed Parallel Programs." *IEEE Transactions on Software Engineering*, November 1990.

BARK89 Barkley, R., and Lee, T. "A Lazy Buddy System Bounded by Two Coalescing Delays per Class." *Proceedings of the Twelfth ACM Symposium on Operating Systems Principles*, December 1989.

BAYS77 Bays, C. "A Comparison of Next-Fit, First-Fit, and Best-Fit." *Communications of the ACM*, March 1977.

BECK97 Beck, L. *System Software.* Reading, MA: Addison-Wesley, 1997.

BELA66 Belady, L. "A Study of Replacement Algorithms for a Virtual Storage Computer." *IBM Systems Journal*, No. 2, 1966.

BELL94 Bellovin, S., and Cheswick, W. "Network Firewalls." *IEEE Communications Magazine*, September 1994.

BEN82 Ben-Ari, M. *Principles of Concurrent Programming.* Englewood Cliffs, NJ: Prentice Hall, 1982.

BEN06 Ben-Ari, M. *Principles of Concurrent and Distributed Programming.* Harlow, England: Addison-Wesley, 2006.

BERS96 Berson, A. *Client/Server Architecture.* New York: McGraw-Hill, 1996.

BIEB05 Bieberstein, N., et al. "Impact of Service-Oriented Architecture on Enterprise Systems, Organizational Structures, and Individuals." *IBM Systems Journal*, Vol. 44, No. 4, 2005.

BIH06 Bih, J. "Service Oriented Architecture (SOA): A New Paradigm to Implement Dynamic E-Business Solutions." *ACM Ubiquity*, August 2006. acm.org/ubiquity/views/v7i30_soa.html

BIRR89 Birrell, A. *An Introduction to Programming with Threads.* SRC Research Report 35, Compaq Systems Research Center, Palo Alto, CA, January 1989. http://www.research.compaq.com/SRC

BLAC90 Black, D. "Scheduling Support for Concurrency and Parallelism in the Mach Operating System." *Computer*, May 1990.

BOLO89 Bolosky, W., Fitzgerald, R., and Scott, M. "Simple but Effective Techniques for NUMA Memory Management." *Proceedings, Twelfth ACM Symposium on Operating Systems Principles*, December 1989.

BONW94 Bonwick, J. "An Object-Caching Memory Allocator." *Proceedings, USENIX Summer Technical Conference*, 1994.

BORG90 Borg, A., Kessler, R., and Wall, D. "Generation and Analysis of Very Long Address Traces." *Proceedings of the 17th Annual International Symposium on Computer Architecture*, May 1990.

BOVE06   Bovet, D., and Cesati, M. *Understanding the Linux Kernel.* Sebastopol, CA: O'Reilly, 2006.

BREN89   Brent, R. "Efficient Implementation of the First-Fit Strategy for Dynamic Storage Allocation." *ACM Transactions on Programming Languages and Systems,* July 1989.

BREW97   Brewer, E. "Clustering: Multiply and Conquer." *Data Communications,* July 1997.

BRIA99   Briand, L., and Roy, D. *Meeting Deadlines in Hard Real-Time Systems: The Rate Monotonic Approach.* Los Alamitos, CA: IEEE Computer Society Press, 1999.

BRIN01   Brinch Hansen, P. *Classic Operating Systems: From Batch Processing to Distributed Systems.* New York: Springer-Verlag, 2001.

BRIT04   Britton, C. *IT Architectures and Middleware.* Reading, MA: Addison-Wesley, 2004.

BROW03   Brown, A., Johnston, S., and Kelly, K. *Using Service-Oriented Architecture and Component-Based Development to Build Web Service Applications.* IBM Rational Software Technical Report, 2003. ibm.com/developerworks/rational/library/510.html

BROW72   Browne, P. "Computer Security—A Survey." *ACM SIGMIS Database,* Fall 1972.

BUHR95   Buhr, P., and Fortier, M. "Monitor Classification." *ACM Computing Surveys,* March 1995.

BULM79   Bulmer, M. *Principles of Statistics.* New York: Dover, 1979.

BUON01   Buonadonna, P.; Hill, J.; and Culler, D. "Active Message Communication for Tiny Networked Sensors." *Proceedings, IEEE INFOCOM 2001,* April 2001.

BURR04   Burr, W., Dodson, D., and Polk, W. *Electronic Authentication Guideline.* Gaithersburg, MD: National Institute of Standards and Technology, Special Publication 800-63, September 2004.

BUTT99   Buttazzo, G. "Optimal Deadline Assignment for Scheduling Soft Aperiodic Tasks in Hard Real-Time Environments." *IEEE Transactions on Computers,* October 1999.

BUYY99a   Buyya, R. *High Performance Cluster Computing: Architectures and Systems.* Upper Saddle River, NJ: Prentice Hall, 1999.

BUYY99b   Buyya, R. *High Performance Cluster Computing: Programming and Applications.* Upper Saddle River, NJ: Prentice Hall, 1999.

CABR86   Cabrear, L. "The Influence of Workload on Load Balancing Strategies." *USENIX Conference Proceedings,* Summer 1986.

CAO96   Cao, P., Felten, E., Karlin, A., and Li, K. "Implementation and Performance of Integrated Application-Controlled File Caching, Prefetching, and Disk Scheduling." *ACM Transactions on Computer Systems,* November 1996.

CARE08   Carey, M. "SOA What?" *IEEE Computer,* March 2008.

CARR81   Carr, R., and Hennessey, J. "WSClock—A Simple and Efficient Algorithm for Virtual Memory Management." *Proceedings of the Eighth Symposium on Operating System Principles,* December 1981.

CARR84   Carr, R. *Virtual Memory Management.* Ann Arbor, MI: UMI Research Press, 1984.

CARR89   Carriero, N., and Gelernter, D. "How to Write Parallel Programs: A Guide for the Perplexed." *ACM Computing Surveys*, September 1989.

CARR01   Carr, S., Mayo, J., and Shene, C. "Race Conditions: A Case Study." *The Journal of Computing in Small Colleges*, October 2001.

CARR05   Carrier, B. *File System Forensic Analysis.* Upper Saddle River, NJ: Addison-Wesley, 2005.

CASA94   Casavant, T., and Singhal, M. *Distributed Computing Systems.* Los Alamitos, CA: IEEE Computer Society Press, 1994.

CASS01   Cass, S. "Anatomy of Malice." *IEEE Spectrum*, November 2001.

CHAN85   Chandy, K., and Lamport, L. "Distributed Snapshots: Determining Global States of Distributed Systems." *ACM Transactions on Computer Systems*, February 1985.

CHAN90   Chandras, R. "Distributed Message Passing Operating Systems." *Operating Systems Review*, January 1990.

CHAP97   Chapin, S., and Maccabe, A., eds. "Multiprocessor Operating Systems: Harnessing the Power." Special issue of *IEEE Concurrency*, April–June 1997.

CHEN92   Chen, J.; Borg, A.; and Jouppi, N. "A Simulation Based Study of TLB Performance." *Proceedings of the 19th Annual International Symposium on Computer Architecture*, May 1992.

CHEN94   Chen, P., Lee, E., Gibson, G., Katz, R., and Patterson, D. "RAID: High-Performance, Reliable Secondary Storage." *ACM Computing Surveys*, June 1994.

CHEN96   Chen, S., and Towsley, D. "A Performance Evaluation of RAID Architectures." *IEEE Transactions on Computers*, October 1996.

CHEN04   Chen, S., and Tang, T. "Slowing Down Internet Worms." *Proceedings of the 24th International Conference on Distributed Computing Systems*, 2004.

CHU72   Chu, W., and Opderbeck, H. "The Page Fault Frequency Replacement Algorithm." *Proceedings, Fall Joint Computer Conference*, 1972.

CLAR85   Clark, D., and Emer, J. "Performance of the VAX-11/780 Translation Buffer: Simulation and Measurement." *ACM Transactions on Computer Systems*, February 1985.

CLAR98   Clarke, D., and Merusi, D. *System Software Programming: The Way Things Work.* Upper Saddle River, NJ: Prentice Hall, 1998.

CHER05   Cherbacko, L., et al. "Impact of Service Orientation at the Business Level." *IBM Systems Journal*, Vol. 44, No. 4, 2005.

CHES97   Chess, D. "The Future of Viruses on the Internet." *Proceedings, Virus Bulletin International Conference*, October 1997.

CHIN05   Chinchani, R., and Berg, E. "A Fast Static Analysis Approach to Detect Exploit Code Inside Network Flows." *Recent Advances in Intrusion Detection, 8th International Symposium*, 2005.

COFF71   Coffman, E., Elphick, M., and Shoshani, A. "System Deadlocks." *Computing Surveys*, June 1971.

COHE94   Cohen, F. *A Short Course on Computer Viruses.* New York: Wiley, 1994.

COME79   Comer, D. "The Ubiquitous B-Tree." *Computing Surveys*, June 1979.

CONR02   Conry-Murray, A. "Behavior-Blocking Stops Unknown Malicious Code." *Network Magazine*, June 2002.

CONW63   Conway, M. "Design of a Separable Transition-Diagram Compiler." *Communications of the ACM*, July 1963.

CONW67   Conway, R., Maxwell, W., and Miller, L. *Theory of Scheduling.* Reading, MA: Addison-Wesley, 1967. Reprinted by Dover Publications, 2003.

CORB62   Corbato, F., Merwin-Daggett, M.; and Dealey, R. "An Experimental Time-Sharing System." *Proceedings of the 1962 Spring Joint Computer Conference*, 1962. Reprinted in [BRIN01].

CORB68   Corbato, F. "A Paging Experiment with the Multics System." *MIT Project MAC Report MAC-M-384*, May 1968.

CORB96   Corbett, J. "Evaluating Deadlock Detection Methods for Concurrent Software." *IEEE Transactions on Software Engineering*, March 1996.

CORM09   Cormen, T., et al. *Introduction to Algorithms.* Cambridge, MA: MIT Press, 2009.

COST05   Costa, M., et al. "Vigilante: End-to-End Containment of Internet Worms." *ACM Symposium on Operating Systems Principles*, 2005.

COX89   Cox, A., and Fowler, R. "The Implementation of a Coherent Memory Abstraction on a NUMA Multiprocessor: Experiences with PLATINUM." *Proceedings, Twelfth ACM Symposium on Operating Systems Principles*, December 1989.

CUST94   Custer, H. *Inside the Windows NT File System.* Redmond, WA: Microsoft Press, 1994.

DALE68   Daley, R., and Dennis, R. "Virtual Memory, Processes, and Sharing in MULTICS." *Communications of the ACM*, May 1968.

DALT96   Dalton, W., et al. *Windows NT Server 4: Security, Troubleshooting, and Optimization.* Indianapolis, IN: New Riders Publishing, 1996.

DASG92   Dasgupta, P., et al. "The Clouds Distributed Operating System." *IEEE Computer*, November 1992.

DATT90   Datta, A., and Ghosh, S. "Deadlock Detection in Distributed Systems." *Proceedings, Phoenix Conference on Computers and Communications*, March 1990.

DATT92   Datta, A.; Javagal, R.; and Ghosh, S. "An Algorithm for Resource Deadlock Detection in Distributed Systems." *Computer Systems Science and Engineering*, October 1992.

DELL00   Dekker, E., and Newcomer, J. *Developing Windows NT Device Drivers: A Programmer's Handbook.* Reading, MA: Addison-Wesley, 2000.

DENN05   Denning, P. "The Locality Principle." *Communications of the ACM*, July 2005.

DENN68   Denning, P. "The Working Set Model for Program Behavior." *Communications of the ACM*, May 1968.

DENN70   Denning, P. "Virtual Memory." *Computing Surveys*, September 1970.

DENN71   Denning, P. "Third Generation Computer Systems." *ACM Computing Surveys*, December 1971.

DENN80a   Denning, P.; Buzen, J.; Dennis, J.; Gaines, R.; Hansen, P.; Lynch, W.; and Organick, E. "Operating Systems." In [ARDE80].

DENN80b   Denning, P. "Working Sets Past and Present." *IEEE Transactions on Software Engineering*, January 1980.

DENN84   Denning, P., and Brown, R. "Operating Systems." *Scientific American*, September 1984.

DENN87   Denning, D. "An Intrusion-Detection Model." *IEEE Transactions on Software Engineering*, February 1987.

DIJK65   Dijkstra, E. *Cooperating Sequential Processes.* Technological University, Eindhoven, The Netherlands, 1965. (Reprinted in *Great Papers in Computer Science*, P. Laplante, ed., IEEE Press, New York, NY, 1996.) Also reprinted in [BRIN01].

DIJK68   Dijkstra, E. "The Structure of 'THE' Multiprogramming System." *Communications of the ACM*, May 1968. Reprinted in [BRIN01].

DIJK71   Dijkstra, E. "Hierarchical Ordering of sequential Processes." *Acta informatica*, Vol. 1, No. 2, 1971. Reprinted in [BRIN01].

DIMI98   Dimitoglou, G. "Deadlocks and Methods for Their Detection, Prevention, and Recovery in Modern Operating Systems." *Operating Systems Review*, July 1998.

DONA01   Donahoo, M., and Clavert, K. *The Pocket Guide to TCP/IP Sockets.* San Francisco, CA: Morgan Kaufmann, 2001.

DOUG89   Douglas, F., and Ousterhout, J. "Process Migration in Sprite: A Status Report." *Newsletter of the IEEE Computer Society Technical Committee on Operating Systems*, Winter 1989.

DOUG91   Douglas, F., and Ousterhout, J. "Transparent Process Migration: Design Alternatives and the Sprite Implementation." *Software Practice and Experience*, August 1991.

DOWD93   Dowdy, L., and Lowery, C. *P.S. to Operating Systems.* Upper Saddle River, NJ: Prentice Hall, 1993.

DOWN08   Downey, A. *The Little Book of Semaphores.* www.greenteapress.com/semaphores/

DUBE98   Dube, R. *A Comparison of the Memory Management Sub-Systems in FreeBSD and Linux.* Technical Report CS-TR-3929, University of Maryland, September 25, 1998.

EAGE86   Eager, D.; Lazowska, E.; and Zahnorjan, J. "Adaptive Load Sharing in Homogeneous Distributed Systems." *IEEE Transactions on Software Engineering*, May 1986.

ECKE95   Eckerson, W. "Client Server Architecture." *Network World Collaboration*, Winter 1995.

ECOS07   eCosCentric Limited, and Red Hat, Inc. *eCos Reference Manual*, 2007. http://www.ecoscentric.com/ecospro/doc/html/ref/ecos-ref.html

EISC07   Eischen, C. "RAID 6 Covers More Bases." *Network World*, April 9, 2007.

ENGE80   Enger, N., and Howerton, P. *Computer Security.* New York: Amacom, 1980.

ESKI90   Eskicioglu, M. "Design Issues of Process Migration Facilities in Distributed Systems." *Newsletter of the IEEE Computer Society Technical Committee on Operating Systems and Application Environments*, Summer 1990.

FEIT90a   Feitelson, D., and Rudolph, L. "Distributed Hierarchical Control for Parallel Processing." *Computer*, May 1990.

FEIT90b   Feitelson, D., and Rudolph, L. "Mapping and Scheduling in a Shared Parallel Environment Using Distributed Hierarchical Control." *Proceedings, 1990 International Conference on Parallel Processing*, August 1990.

FERR83   Ferrari, D., and Yih, Y. "VSWS: The Variable-Interval Sampled Working Set Policy." *IEEE Transactions on Software Engineering*, May 1983.

FIDG96   Fidge, C. "Fundamentals of Distributed System Observation." *IEEE Software*, November 1996.

FINK88   Finkel, R. *An Operating Systems Vade Mecum.* Englewood Cliffs, NJ: Prentice Hall, 1988.

FINK89   Finkel, R. "The Process Migration Mechanism of Charlotte." *Newsletter of the IEEE Computer Society Technical Committee on Operating Systems*, Winter 1989.

FOLK98   Folk, M., and Zoellick, B. *File Structures: An Object-Oriented Approach with C++.* Reading, MA: Addison-Wesley, 1998.

FORR97   Forrest, S.; Hofmeyr, S.; and Somayaji, A. "Computer Immunology." *Communications of the ACM*, October 1997.

FOST91   Foster, L. "Automatic Generation of Self-Scheduling Programs." *IEEE Transactions on Parallel and Distributed Systems*, January 1991.

FRAN97   Franz, M. "Dynamic Linking of Software Components." *Computer*, March 1997.

FRAS97   Fraser, B. *Site Security Handbook.* RFC 2196, September 1997.

FRIE96   Friedman, M. "RAID Keeps Going and Going and..." *IEEE Spectrum*, April 1996.

GALL00   Galli, D. *Distributed Operating Systems: Concepts and Practice.* Upper Saddle River, NJ: Prentice Hall, 2000.

GANA98   Ganapathy, N., and Schimmel, C. "General Purpose Operating System Support for Multiple Page Sizes." *Proceedings, USENIX Symposium*, 1998.

GARG02   Garg, V. *Elements of Distributed Computing.* New York: Wiley, 2002.

GAUD00   Gaudin, S. "The Omega Files." *Network World*, June 26, 2000.

GAY03   Gay, D., et al. "The nesC Language: A Holistic Approach to Networked Embedded Systems." *Proceedings of the ACM SIGPLAN 2003 Conference on Programming Language Design and Implementation*, 2003.

GAY05   Gay, D.; Levis, P.; and Culler, D. "Software Design Patterns for TinyOS." *Proceedings, Conference on Languages, Compilers, and Tools for Embedded Systems*, 2005.

GEER06   Geer, D. "Hackers Get to the Root of the Problem." *Computer*, May 2006.

GEER09   Geer, D. "The OS Faces a Brave New World." *Computer*, October 2009.

GEHR87   Gehringer, E.; Siewiorek, D.; and Segall, Z. *Parallel Processing: The Cm* Experience.* Bedford, MA: Digital Press, 1987.

GIBB87   Gibbons, P. "A Stub Generator for Multilanguage RPC in Heterogeneous Environments." *IEEE Transactions on Software Engineering*, January 1987.

GING90   Gingras, A. "Dining Philosophers Revisited." *ACM SIGCSE Bulletin*, September 1990.

GOLD87   Goldberg, S. *Probability: An Introduction.* New York: Dover, 1987.

GOLD89   Goldman, P. "Mac VM Revealed." *Byte*, November 1989.

GOOD94   Goodheart, B., and Cox, J. *The Magic Garden Explained: The Internals of UNIX System V Release 4.* Englewood Cliffs, NJ: Prentice Hall, 1994.

GOPA85   Gopal, I. "Prevention of Store-and-Forward Deadlock in Computer Networks." *IEEE Transactions on Communications*, December 1985.

GORM04   Gorman, M. *Understanding the Linux Virtual Memory Manager.* Upper Saddle River, NJ: Prentice Hall, 2004.

GOYE99   Goyeneche, J., and Souse, E. "Loadable Kernel Modules." *IEEE Software*, January/February 1999.

GRAH72   Graham, G., and Denning, P. "Protection—Principles and Practice." *Proceedings, AFIPS Spring Joint Computer Conference*, 1972.

GRAN04   Grance, T.; Kent, K.; and Kim, B. *Computer Security Incident Handling Guide.* NIST Special Publication SP 800-61, January 2004.

GRAY97   Gray, J. *Interprocess Communications in UNIX: The Nooks and Crannies.* Upper Saddle River, NJ: Prentice Hall, 1997.

GRIM01a   Grimmett, G., and Stirzaker, D. *Probability and Random Processes.* Oxford: Oxford University Press, 2001.

GRIM01b   Grimmett, G., and Stirzaker, D. *One Thousand Exercises in Probability.* Oxford: Oxford University Press, 2001.

GRIM05   Grimheden, M., and Torngren, M. "What is Embedded Systems and How Should It Be Taught?—Results from a Didactic Analysis." *ACM Transactions on Embedded Computing Systems*, August 2005.

GROS86   Grosshans, D. *File Systems: Design and Implementation.* Englewood Cliffs, NJ: Prentice Hall, 1986.

GROS09   Gross, D., and Harris, C. *Fundamentals of Queueing Theory.* New York: Wiley, 2009.

GUNT00   Gunther, N. *The Practical Performance Analyst.* New York: Authors Choice Press, 2000.

GUPT78   Gupta, R., and Franklin, M. "Working Set and Page Fault Frequency Replacement Algorithms: A Performance Comparison." *IEEE Transactions on Computers*, August 1978.

HALD91   Haldar, S., and Subramanian, D. "Fairness in Processor Scheduling in Time Sharing Systems." *Operating Systems Review*, January 1991.

HALL01   Hall, B. *Beej's Guide to Network Programming Using Internet Sockets*, 2001. http://beej.us/guide/bgnet

HALL10   Hall, B. *Beej's Guide to Unix IPC*, 2010. Document available in premium content section for this book.

HAMM91   Hamming, R. *The Art of Probability: For Scientists and Engineers.* Reading, MA: Addison-Wesley, 1991.

HARR06   Harris, W. "Multi-core in the Source Engine." bit-tech.net technical paper, November 2, 2006. bit-tech.net/gaming/2006/11/02/Multi_core_in_the_Source_Engin/1

HATF72   Hatfield, D. "Experiments on Page Size, Program Access Patterns, and Virtual Memory Performance." *IBM Journal of Research and Development*, January 1972.

HENN07   Hennessy, J., and Patterson, D. *Computer Architecture: A Quantitative Approach.* San Mateo, CA: Morgan Kaufmann, 2007.

HENR84   Henry, G. "The Fair Share Scheduler." *AT&T Bell Laboratories Technical Journal*, October 1984.

HERL90   Herlihy, M. "A Methodology for Implementing Highly Concurrent Data Structures." *Proceedings of the Second ACM SIGPLAN Symposium on Principles and Practices of Parallel Programming*, March 1990.

HILL00   Hill, J., et al. "System Architecture Directions for Networked Sensors." *Proceedings, Architectural Support for Programming Languages and Operating Systems*, 2000.

HOAR74   Hoare, C. "Monitors: An Operating System Structuring Concept." *Communications of the ACM*, October 1974.

HOAR85   Hoare, C. *Communicating Sequential Processes.* Englewood Cliffs, NJ: Prentice-Hall, 1985.

HOFR90   Hofri, M. "Proof of a Mutual Exclusion Algorithm." *Operating Systems Review*, January 1990.

HOLL02   Holland, D.; Lim, A.; and Seltzer, M. "A New Instructional Operating System." *Proceedings of SIGCSE 2002*, 2002.

HOLT72   Holt, R. "Some Deadlock Properties of Computer Systems." *Computing Surveys*, September 1972.

HONE05   Honeynet Project. *Knowing Your Enemy: Tracking Botnets.* Honeynet White Paper, March 2005. http://honeynet.org/papers/bots

HONG89   Hong, J.; Tan, X.; and Towsley, D. "A Performance Analysis of Minimum Laxity and Earliest Deadline Scheduling in a Real-Time System." *IEEE Transactions on Computers*, December 1989.

HOWA73   Howard, J. "Mixed Solutions for the Deadlock Problem." *Communications of the ACM*, July 1973.

HP96   Hewlett Packard. *White Paper on Clustering*, June 1996.

HUCK83   Huck, T. *Comparative Analysis of Computer Architectures.* Stanford University Technical Report Number 83-243, May 1983.

HUCK93   Huck, J., and Hays, J. "Architectural Support for Translation Table Management in Large Address Space Machines." *Proceedings of the 20th Annual International Symposium on Computer Architecture*, May 1993.

HUTC08   Hutchinson, J., et al. "Migrating to SOAs by Way of Hybrid Systems." *IT Pro*, January/February 2008.

HWAN99   Hwang, K., et al. "Designing SSI Clusters with Hierarchical Checkpointing and Single I/O Space." *IEEE Concurrency*, January–March 1999.

HYMA66   Hyman, H. "Comments on a Problem in Concurrent Programming Control." *Communications of the ACM*, January 1966.

IBM86   IBM National Technical Support, Large Systems. *Multiple Virtual Storage (MVS) Virtual Storage Tuning Cookbook.* Dallas Systems Center Technical Bulletin G320-0597, June 1986.

INSO02a   Insolvibile, G. "Inside the Linux Packet Filter." *Linux Journal*, February, 2002.

INSO02b   Insolvibile, G. "Inside the Linux Packet Filter, Part II." *Linux Journal*, March, 2002.

ISLO80   Isloor, S., and Marsland, T. "The Deadlock Problem: An Overview." *Computer*, September 1980.

IYER01   Iyer, S., and Druschel, P. "Anticipatory Scheduling: A Disk Scheduling Framework to Overcome Deceptive Idleness in Synchronous I/O." *Proceedings, 18th ACM Symposium on Operating Systems Principles*, October 2001.

JACK10   Jackson, J. "Multicore Requires OS Rework, Windows Architect Advises." *Network World*, March 19, 2010.

JACO98a   Jacob, B., and Mudge, T. "Virtual Memory: Issues of Implementation." *Computer*, June 1998.

JACO98b   Jacob, B., and Mudge, T. "Virtual Memory in Contemporary Microprocessors." *IEEE Micro*, August 1998.

JAIN91   Jain, R. *The Art of Computer Systems Performance Analysis: Techniques for Experimental Design, Measurement, Simulation, and Modeling.* New York: Wiley, 1991.

JANS01   Jansen, W. *Guidelines on Active Content and Mobile Code.* NIST Special Publication SP 800-28, October 2001.

JHI07   Jhi, Y., et al. "Proactive Containment of Fast Scanning Worms through White Detection." *Proceedings of 3rd International Conference on Security and Privacy in Communication Networks*, September 2007.

JOHN91   Johnston, B.; Javagal, R.; Datta, A.; and Ghosh, S. "A Distributed Algorithm for Resource Deadlock Detection." *Proceedings, Tenth Annual Phoenix Conference on Computers and Communications*, March 1991.

JOHN92   Johnson, T., and Davis, T. "Space Efficient Parallel Buddy Memory Management." *Proceedings, Third International Conference on Computers and Information*, May 1992.

JONE80   Jones, S., and Schwarz, P. "Experience Using Multiprocessor Systems—A Status Report." *Computing Surveys*, June 1980.

JONE97   Jones, M. "What Really Happened on Mars?", 1997. http://research.microsoft. com/~mbj/Mars_Pathfinder/Mars_Pathfinder.html

JUL88   Jul, E.; Levy, H.; Hutchinson, N.; and Black, A. "Fine-Grained Mobility in the Emerald System." *ACM Transactions on Computer Systems*, February 1988.

JUL89   Jul, E. "Migration of Light-Weight Processes in Emerald." *Newsletter of the IEEE Computer Society Technical Committee on Operating Systems*, Winter 1989.

JUNG04   Jung, J., et al. "Fast Portscan Detection Using Sequential Hypothesis Testing." *Proceedings, IEEE Symposium on Security and Privacy*, 2004.

KANG98   Kang, S., and Lee, J. "Analysis and Solution of Non-Preemptive Policies for Scheduling Readers and Writers." *Operating Systems Review*, July 1998.

KAPP00   Kapp, C. "Managing Cluster Computers." *Dr. Dobb's Journal*, July 2000.

KATZ89   Katz, R.; Gibson, G.; and Patterson, D. "Disk System Architecture for High Performance Computing." *Proceedings of the IEEE*, December 1989.

KAY88   Kay, J., and Lauder, P. "A Fair Share Scheduler." *Communications of the ACM*, January 1988.

KENT00   Kent, S. "On the Trail of Intrusions into Information Systems." *IEEE Spectrum*, December 2000.

KEPH97a   Kephart, J.; Sorkin, G.; Chess, D.; and White, S. "Fighting Computer Viruses." *Scientific American*, November 1997.

KEPH97b   Kephart, J.; Sorkin, G.; Swimmer, B.; and White, S. "Blueprint for a Computer Immune System." *Proceedings, Virus Bulletin International Conference*, October 1997.

KESS92   Kessler, R., and Hill, M. "Page Placement Algorithms for Large Real-Indexed Caches." *ACM Transactions on Computer Systems*, November 1992.

KHAL93   Khalidi, Y.; Talluri, M.; Williams, D.; and Nelson, M. "Virtual Memory Support for Multiple Page Sizes." *Proceedings, Fourth Workshop on Workstation Operating Systems*, October 1993.

KILB62   Kilburn, T.; Edwards, D.; Lanigan, M.; and Sumner, F. "One-Level Storage System." *IRE Transactions*, April 1962.

KLEI75   Kleinrock, L. *Queueing Systems, Volume I: Theory.* New York: Wiley, 1975.

KLEI76   Kleinrock, L. *Queueing Systems, Volume II: Computer Applications.* New York: Wiley, 1976.

KLEI95   Kleiman, S. "Interrupts as Threads." *Operating System Review*, April 1995.

KLEI96   Kleiman, S.; Shah, D.; and Smallders, B. *Programming with Threads.* Upper Saddle River, NJ: Prentice Hall, 1996.

KLEI04   Kleinrock, L. *Queuing Systems, Volume Three: Computer Applications.* New York: Wiley, 2004.

KNUT71   Knuth, D. "An Experimental Study of FORTRAN Programs." *Software Practice and Experience*, Vol. 1, 1971.

KNUT97   Knuth, D. *The Art of Computer Programming, Volume 1: Fundamental Algorithms.* Reading, MA: Addison-Wesley, 1997.

KNUT98   Knuth, D. *The Art of Computer Programming, Volume 3: Sorting and Searching.* Reading, MA: Addison-Wesley, 1998.

KOOP96   Koopman, P. "Embedded System Design Issues (the Rest of the Story). *Proceedings, 1996 International Conference on Computer Design*, 1996.

KRIS94   Krishna, C., and Lee, Y., eds. "Special Issue on Real-Time Systems." *Proceedings of the IEEE*, January 1994.

KUPE05   Kuperman, B., et al. "Detection and Prevention of Stack Buffer Overflow Attacks." *Communications of the ACM*, November 2005.

LAI06   Lai, A., and Nieh, J. "On the Performance of Wide-Area Thin-Client Computing." *ACM Transactions on Computer Systems*, May 2006.

LAMP71   Lampson, B. "Protection." Proceedings, *Fifth Princeton Symposium on Information Sciences and Systems*, March 1971; Reprinted in *Operating Systems Review*, January 1974.

LAMP74   Lamport, L. "A New Solution to Dijkstra's Concurrent Programming Problem." *Communications of the ACM*, August 1974.

LAMP78   Lamport, L. "Time, Clocks, and the Ordering of Events in a Distributed System." *Communications of the ACM*, July 1978.

LAMP80   Lampson, B., and Redell D. "Experience with Processes and Monitors in Mesa." *Communications of the ACM*, February 1980.

LAMP86   Lamport, L. "The Mutual Exclusion Problem." *Journal of the ACM*, April 1986.

LAMP91   Lamport, L. "The Mutual Exclusion Problem Has Been Solved." *Communications of the ACM*, January 1991.

LAMP04   Lampson, B. "Computer Security in the Real World." *Computer*, June 2004.

LARM05   Larmour, J. "How eCos Can Be Shrunk to Fit." *Embedded Systems Europe*, May 2005. www.embedded.com/europe/esemay05.htm

LARO92   LaRowe, R.; Holliday, M.; and Ellis, C. "An Analysis of Dynamic Page Placement an a NUMA Multiprocessor." *Proceedings, 1992 ACM SIGMETRICS and Performance '92*, June 1992.

LEBL87   LeBlanc, T., and Mellor-Crummey, J. "Debugging Parallel Programs with Instant Replay." *IEEE Transactions on Computers*, April 1987.

LEE93   Lee, Y., and Krishna, C., eds. *Readings in Real-Time Systems.* Los Alamitos, CA: IEEE Computer Society Press, 1993.

LELA86   Leland, W., and Ott, T. "Load-Balancing Heuristics and Process Behavior." *Proceedings, ACM SigMetrics Performance 1986 Conference*, 1986.

LEON07   Leonard, T. "Dragged Kicking and Screaming: Source Multicore." *Proceedings, Game Developers Conference 2007*, March 2007.

LERO76   Leroudier, J., and Potier, D. "Principles of Optimality for Multiprogramming." *Proceedings, International Symposium on Computer Performance Modeling, Measurement, and Evaluation*, March 1976.

LETW88   Letwin, G. *Inside OS/2.* Redmond, WA: Microsoft Press, 1988.

LEUT90   Leutenegger, S., and Vernon, M. "The Performance of Multiprogrammed Multiprocessor Scheduling Policies." *Proceedings, Conference on Measurement and Modeling of Computer Systems*, May 1990.

LEVE10   Leventhal, A. "Triple-Parity RAID and Beyond." *Communications of the ACM*, January 2010.

LEVI00   Levine, J. *Linkers and Loaders.* San Francisco: Morgan Kaufmann, 2000.

LEVI03a   Levine, G. "Defining Deadlock." *Operating Systems Review*, January 2003.

LEVI03b   Levine, G. "Defining Deadlock with Fungible Resources." *Operating Systems Review*, July 2003.

LEVI05   Levis, P., et al. "T2: A Second Generation OS for Embedded Sensor Networks." Technical Report TKN-05-007, Telecommunication Networks Group, Technische Universitat Berlin, 2005. http://csl.stanford.edu/~pal/pubs.html

LEVI06   Levine, J.; Grizzard, J.; and Owen, H. "Detecting and Categorizing Kernel-Level Rootkits to Aid Future Detection." *IEEE Security and Privacy*, May–June 2006.

LEVY96   Levy, E., "Smashing the Stack for Fun and Profit." *Phrack Magazine*, File 14, Issue 49, November 1996.

LEWI96   Lewis, B., and Berg, D. *Threads Primer.* Upper Saddle River, NJ: Prentice Hall, 1996.

LHEE03   Lhee, K., and Chapin, S. "Buffer Overflow and Format String Overflow Vulnerabilities." *Software—Practice and Experience*, Vol. 33, 2003.

LI10   Li, Y.; Li, W.; and Jiang, C. "A Survey of Virtual Machine Systems: Current Technology and Future Trends." *Proceedings, Third International Symposium on Electronic Commerce and Security*, 2010.

LIED95   Liedtke, J. "On μ-Kernel Construction." *Proceedings of the Fifteenth ACM Symposium on Operating Systems Principles*, December 1995.

LIED96   Liedtke, J. "Toward Real Microkernels." *Communications of the ACM*, September 1996.

LIGN05   Ligneris, B. "Virtualization of Linux Based Computers: The Linux-VServer Project." *Proceedings of the 19th International Symposium on High Performance Computing Systems and Applications*, 2005.

LIND04   Lindsley, R. "What's New in the 2.6 Scheduler." *Linux Journal*, March 2004.

LIU73   Liu, C., and Layland, J. "Scheduling Algorithms for Multiprogramming in a Hard Real-time Environment." *Journal of the ACM*, February 1973.

LIU00   Liu, J. *Real-Time Systems.* Upper Saddle River, NJ: Prentice Hall, 2000.

LIVA90   Livadas, P. *File Structures: Theory and Practice.* Englewood Cliffs, NJ: Prentice Hall, 1990.

LOVE04   Love, R. "I/O Schedulers." *Linux Journal*, February 2004.

LOVE10   Love, R. *Linux Kernel Development.* Upper Saddle River, NJ: Addison-Wesley, 2010.

LURI94   Lurie, D., and Moore, R. *Applying Statistics.* U.S. Nuclear Regulatory Commission Report NUREG-1475. (Available from the Government Printing Office, GPO Stock Number 052-020-00390-4.)

LYNC96   Lynch, N. *Distributed Algorithms.* San Francisco, CA: Morgan Kaufmann, 1996.

MAEK87   Maekawa, M.; Oldehoeft, A.; and Oldehoeft, R. *Operating Systems: Advanced Concepts.* Menlo Park, CA: Benjamin Cummings, 1987.

MAJU88   Majumdar, S.; Eager, D.; and Bunt, R. "Scheduling in Multiprogrammed Parallel Systems." *Proceedings, Conference on Measurement and Modeling of Computer Systems*, May 1988.

MARW06   Marwedel, P. *Embedded System Design.* Dordrecht, The Netherlands: Springer, 2006.

MASS03   Massa, A. *Embedded Software Development with eCos.* Upper Saddle River, NJ: Prentice Hall, 2003.

MAUE08   Mauerer, W. *Professional Linux Kernal Architecture.* New York: Wiley, 2008.

MCDO06   McDougall, R., and Laudon, J. "Multi-Core Microprocessors are Here." *login*, October 2006.

MCDO07   McDougall, R., and Mauro, J. *Solaris Internals: Solaris 10 and OpenSolaris Kernel Architecture.* Palo Alto, CA: Sun Microsystems Press, 2007.

MCHU00   McHugh, J.; Christie, A.; and Allen, J. "The Role of Intrusion Detection Systems." *IEEE Software*, September/October 2000.

MCKU05   McKusick, M., and Neville-Neil, J. *The Design and Implementation of the Free-BSD Operating System.* Reading, MA: Addison-Wesley, 2005.

MEE96a   Mee, C., and Daniel, E. eds. *Magnetic Recording Technology.* New York: McGraw Hill, 1996.

MEE96b   Mee, C., and Daniel, E. eds. *Magnetic Storage Handbook.* New York: McGraw Hill, 1996.

MENA05   Menasce, D. "MOM vs. RPC: Communication Models for Distributed Applications." *IEEE Internet Computing*, March/April 2005.

MILE92   Milenkovic, M. *Operating Systems: Concepts and Design.* New York: McGraw-Hill, 1992.

MILO00   Milojicic, D.; Douglis, F.; Paindaveine, Y.; Wheeler, R.; and Zhou, S. "Process Migration." *ACM Computing Surveys*, September 2000.

MIRK04   Mirkovic, J., and Relher, P. "A Taxonomy of DDoS Attack and DDoS Defense Mechanisms." *ACM SIGCOMM Computer Communications Review*, April 2004.

MORG92   Morgan, K. "The RTOS Difference." *Byte*, August 1992.

MORR79   Morris, R., and Thompson, K. "Password Security: A Case History." *Communications of the ACM*, November 1979.

MOSB02   Mosberger, D., and Eranian, S. *IA-64 Linux Kernel: Design and Implementation.* Upper Saddle River, NJ: Prentice Hall, 2002.

MS96   Microsoft Corp. *Microsoft Windows NT Workstation Resource Kit.* Redmond, WA: Microsoft Press, 1996.

MUKH96   Mukherjee, B., and Karsten, S. "Operating Systems for Parallel Machines." In *Parallel Computers: Theory and Practice.* Edited by T. Casavant, P. Tvrkik, and F. Plasil. Los Alamitos, CA: IEEE Computer Society Press, 1996.

NACH97   Nachenberg, C. "Computer Virus-Antivirus Coevolution." *Communications of the ACM*, January 1997.

NACH02   Nachenberg, C. "Behavior Blocking: The Next Step in Anti-Virus Protection." *White Paper*, SecurityFocus.com, March 2002.

NAGA97   Nagar, R. *Windows NT File System Internals.* Sebastopol, CA: O'Reilly, 1997.

NEHM75   Nehmer, J. "Dispatcher Primitives for the Construction of Operating System Kernels." *Acta Informatica*, Vol. 5, 1975.

NELS88   Nelson, M.; Welch, B.; and Ousterhout, J. "Caching in the Sprite Network File System." *ACM Transactions on Computer Systems*, February 1988.

NELS91   Nelson, G. *Systems Programming with Modula-3.* Englewood Cliffs, NJ: Prentice Hall, 1991.

NEWS05   Newsome, J.; Karp, B.; and Song, D. "Polygraph: Automatically Generating Signatures for Polymorphic Worms." *IEEE Symposium on Security and Privacy*, 2005.

NG98   Ng, S. "Advances in Disk Technology: Performance Issues." *Computer*, May 1989.

NING04   Ning, P., et al. "Techniques and Tools for Analyzing Intrusion Alerts." *ACM Transactions on Information and System Security*, May 2004.

NIST95   National Institute of Standards and Technology. *An Introduction to Computer Security: The NIST Handbook.* Special Publication 800-12, October 1995.

NIST10   National Institute of Standards and Technology. *NIST/SEMATECH e-Handbook of Statistical Methods*, 2010. http://www.itl.nist.gov/div898/handbook

NRC91   National Research Council. *Computers at Risk: Safe Computing in the Information Age.* Washington, DC: National Academy Press, 1991.

NUTT94   Nuttal, M. "A Brief Survey of Systems Providing Process or Object Migration Facilities." *Operating Systems Review*, October 1994.

OGOR03   O'Gorman, L. "Comparing Passwords, Tokens and Biometrics for User Authentication." *Proceedings of the IEEE*, December 2003.

OUST85   Ousterhout, J., et al. "A Trace-Drive Analysis of the UNIX 4.2 BSD File System." *Proceedings, Tenth ACM Symposium on Operating System Principles*, 1985.

OUST88   Ousterhout, J., et al. "The Sprite Network Operating System." *Computer*, February 1988.

PAI00   Pai, V.; Druschel, P.; and Zwaenepoel, W. "IO-Lite: A Unified I/O Buffering and Caching System." *ACM Transactions on Computer Systems*, February 2000.

PANW88   Panwar, S.; Towsley, D.; and Wolf, J. "Optimal Scheduling Policies for a Class of Queues with Customer Deadlines in the Beginning of Service." *Journal of the ACM*, October 1988.

PAPO02   Papoulis, A., and Unnikrishna, P. *Probability, Random Variables, and Stochastic Processes.* New York: McGraw-Hill, 2002.

PARZ06   Parziale, L., et al. *TCP/IP Tutorial and Technical Overview.* IBM Redbook GG24-3376-07, 2006. http://www.redbooks.ibm.com/abstracts/gg243376.html

PATT82   Patterson, D., and Sequin, C. "A VLSI RISC." *Computer*, September 1982.

PATT85   Patterson, D. "Reduced Instruction Set Computers." *Communications of the ACM*, January 1985.

PATT88   Patterson, D.; Gibson, G.; and Katz, R. "A Case for Redundant Arrays of Inexpensive Disks (RAID)." *Proceedings, ACM SIGMOD Conference of Management of Data*, June 1988.

PATT09	Patterson, D., and Hennessy, J. *Computer Organization and Design: The Hardware/Software Interface.* San Mateo, CA: Morgan Kaufmann, 2009.
PAZZ92	Pazzini, M., and Navaux, P. "TRIX, a Multiprocessor Transputer-Based Operating System." In *Parallel Computing and Transputer Applications.* Edited by M. Valero et al., Barcelona: IOS Press/CIMNE, 1992.
PERR03	Perrine, T. "The End of crypt() Passwords...Please?" *login,* December 2003.
PETE77	Peterson, J., and Norman, T. "Buddy Systems." *Communications of the ACM,* June 1977.
PETE81	Peterson, G. "Myths About the Mutual Exclusion Problem." *Information Processing Letters,* June 1981.
PHAM96	Pham, T., and Garg, P. *Multithreaded Programming with Windows NT.* Upper Saddle River, NJ: Prentice Hall, 1996.
PHIL99	Phillips, J. *How to Think About Statistics.* New York: Freeman, 1999.
PIZZ89	Pizzarello, A. "Memory Management for a Large Operating System." *Proceedings, International Conference on Measurement and Modeling of Computer Systems,* May 1989.
POPE85	Popek, G., and Walker, B. *The LOCUS Distributed System Architecture,* Cambridge, MA: MIT Press, 1985.
PROV99	Provos, N., and Mazieres, D. "A Future-Adaptable Password Scheme." *Proceedings of the 1999 USENIX Annual Technical Conference,* 1999.
PRZY88	Przybylski, S.; Horowitz, M.; and Hennessy, J. "Performance Trade-offs in Cache Design." *Proceedings, Fifteenth Annual International Symposium on Computer Architecture,* June 1988.
RADC04	Radcliff, D. "What Are They Thinking?" *Network World,* March 1, 2004.
RAJA00	Rajagopal, R. *Introduction to Microsoft Windows NT Cluster Server.* Boca Raton, FL: CRC Press, 2000.
RAMA94	Ramamritham, K., and Stankovic, J. "Scheduling Algorithms and Operating Systems Support for Real-Time Systems." *Proceedings of the IEEE,* January 1994.
RASH88	Rashid, R., et al. "Machine-Independent Virtual Memory Management for Paged Uniprocessor and Multiprocessor Architectures." *IEEE Transactions on Computers,* August 1988.
RAYN86	Raynal, M. *Algorithms for Mutual Exclusion.* Cambridge, MA: MIT Press, 1986.
RAYN88	Raynal, M. *Distributed Algorithms and Protocols.* New York: Wiley, 1988.
RAYN90	Raynal, M., and Helary, J. *Synchronization and Control of Distributed Systems and Programs.* New York: Wiley, 1990.
REAG00a	Reagan, P. *Client/Server Computing.* Upper Saddle River, NJ: Prentice Hall, 2000.
REAG00b	Reagan, P. *Client/Server Network: Design, Operation, and Management.* Upper Saddle River, NJ: Prentice Hall, 2000.
REIM06	Reimer, J. "Valve Goes Multicore." ars technica, November 5, 2006. arstechnica.com/articles/paedia/cpu/valve-multicore.ars
RICA81	Ricart, G., and Agrawala, A. "An Optimal Algorithm for Mutual Exclusion in Computer Networks." *Communications of the ACM,* January 1981 (Corrigendum in *Communications of the ACM,* September 1981).

RICA83   Ricart, G., and Agrawala, A. "Author's Response to 'On Mutual Exclusion in Computer Networks' by Carvalho and Roucairol." *Communications of the ACM*, February 1983.

RIDG97   Ridge, D., et al. "Beowulf: Harnessing the Power of Parallelism in a Pile-of-PCs." *Proceedings, IEEE Aerospace*, 1997.

RITC74   Ritchie, D., and Thompson, K. "The UNIX Time-Sharing System." *Communications of the ACM*, July 1974.

RITC78   Ritchie, D. "UNIX Time-Sharing System: A Retrospective." *The Bell System Technical Journal*, July–August 1978.

RITC84   Ritchie, D. "The Evolution of the UNIX Time-Sharing System." *AT&T Bell Labs Technical Journal*, October 1984.

ROBB04   Robbins, K., and Robbins, S. *UNIX Systems Programming: Communication, Concurrency, and Threads.* Upper Saddle River, NJ: Prentice Hall, 2004.

ROBE03   Roberson, J. "ULE: A Modern Scheduler for FreeBSD." *Proceedings of BSDCon '03*, September 2003.

ROBI90   Robinson, J., and Devarakonda, M. "Data Cache Management Using Frequency-Based Replacement." *Proceedings, Conference on Measurement and Modeling of Computer Systems*, May 1990.

ROME04   Romer, K., and Mattern, F. "The Design Space of Wireless Sensor Networks." *IEEE Wireless Communications*, December 2004.

ROSE78   Rosenkrantz, D.; Stearns, R.; and Lewis, P. "System Level Concurrency Control in Distributed Database Systems." *ACM Transactions on Database Systems*, June 1978.

ROSS10   Ross, S. *First Course in Probability.* Upper Saddle River, NJ: Prentice Hall, 2010

RUBI97   Rubini, A. "The Virtual File System in Linux." *Linux Journal*, May 1997.

RUDO90   Rudolph, B. "Self-Assessment Procedure XXI: Concurrency." *Communications of the ACM*, May 1990.

RUSS11   Russinovich, M.; Solomon, D.; and Ionescu, A. *Windows Internals: Covering Windows 7 and Windows Server 2008 R2.* Redmond, WA: Microsoft Press, 2011.

SALT75   Saltzer, J., and Schroeder, M. "The Protection of Information in Computer Systems." *Proceedings of the IEEE*, September 1975.

SAND94   Sandhu, R., and Samarati, P. "Access Control: Principles and Practice." *IEEE Communications Magazine*, February 1996.

SAND96   Sandhu, R., et al. "Role-Based Access Control Models." *Computer*, September 1994.

SATY81   Satyanarayanan, M. and Bhandarkar, D. "Design Trade-Offs in VAX-11 Translation Buffer Organization." *Computer*, December 1981.

SAUE81   Sauer, C., and Chandy, K. *Computer Systems Performance Modeling.* Englewood Cliffs, NJ: Prentice Hall, 1981.

SAUN01   Saunders, G.; Hitchens, M.; and Varadharajan, V. "Role-Based Access Control and the Access Control Matrix." *Operating Systems Review*, October 2001.

SCAR07   Scarfone, K., and Mell, P. *Guide to Intrusion Detection and Prevention Systems.* NIST Special Publication SP 800-94, February 2007.

SELT90   Seltzer, M.; Chen, P.; and Ousterhout, J. "Disk Scheduling Revisited." *Proceedings, USENIX Winter Technical Conference*, January 1990.

SHA90   Sha, L.; Rajkumar, R.; and Lehoczky, J. "Priority Inheritance Protocols: An Approach to Real-Time Synchronization." *IEEE Transactions on Computers*, September 1990.

SHA91   Sha, L.; Klein, M.; and Goodenough, J. "Rate Monotonic Analysis for Real-Time Systems." In [TILB91].

SHA94   Sha, L.; Rajkumar, R.; and Sathaye, S. "Generalized Rate-Monotonic Scheduling Theory: A Framework for Developing Real-Time Systems." *Proceedings of the IEEE*, January 1994.

SHAN77 Shanker, K. "The Total Computer Security Problem: An Overview." *Computer*, June 1977.

SHEN02 Shene, C. "Multithreaded Programming Can Strengthen an Operating Systems Course." *Computer Science Education Journal*, December 2002.

SHIV92 Shivaratri, N.; Krueger, P.; and Singhal, M. "Load Distributing for Locally Distributed Systems." *Computer*, December 1992.

SHOR75 Shore, J. "On the External Storage Fragmentation Produced by First-Fit and Best-Fit Allocation Strategies." *Communications of the ACM*, August, 1975.

SHOR97 Short, R.; Gamache, R.; Vert, J.; and Massa, M. "Windows NT Clusters for Availability and Scalability." *Proceedings, COMPCON Spring 97*, February 1997.

SHUB03 Shub, C. "A Unified Treatment of Deadlock." *Journal of Computing in Small Colleges*, October 2003. Available through the ACM digital library.

SILB04 Silberschatz, A.; Galvin, P.; and Gagne, G. *Operating System Concepts with Java.* Reading, MA: Addison-Wesley, 2004.

SING94 Singhal, M. "Deadlock Detection in Distributed Systems." In [CASA94].

SINH97 Sinha, P. *Distributed Operating Systems.* Piscataway, NJ: IEEE Press, 1997.

SIRA09 Siracusa, J. "Grand Central Dispatch." *Ars Technica Review*, 2009. http://arstechnica.com/apple/reviews/2009/08/mac-os-x-10-6.ars/12

SMIT82 Smith, A. "Cache Memories." *ACM Computing Surveys*, September 1982.

SMIT85 Smith, A. "Disk Cache—Miss Ratio Analysis and Design Considerations." *ACM Transactions on Computer Systems*, August 1985.

SMIT88 Smith, J. "A Survey of Process Migration Mechanisms." *Operating Systems Review*, July 1988.

SMIT89 Smith, J. "Implementing Remote *fork()* with Checkpoint/restart." *Newsletter of the IEEE Computer Society Technical Committee on Operating Systems*, Winter 1989.

SMIT05 Smith, J., and Nair, R. "The Architecture of Virtual Machines." *Computer*, May 2005.

SOLT07 Soltesz, S., et al. "Container-Based Operating System Virtualization: A Scalable High-Performance Alternative to Hypervisors." *Proceedings of the EuroSys 2007 2nd EuroSys Conference, Operating Systems Review*, June 2007.

STAI10 Staimer, M. "Alternatives to RAID." *Storage Magazine*, May 2010.

STAL08 Stallings, W., and Brown L. *Computer Security: Principles and Practice.* Upper Saddle River, NJ: Prentice Hall, 2008.

STAL10 Stallings, W. *Computer Organization and Architecture*, 8th ed. Upper Saddle River, NJ: Prentice Hall, 2010.

STAL11 Stallings, W. *Data and Computer Communications.* Upper Saddle River: NJ: Prentice Hall, 2011.

STAN89 Stankovic, J., and Ramamrithan, K. "The Spring Kernel: A New Paradigm for Real-Time Operating Systems." *Operating Systems Review*, July 1989.

STAN93 Stankovic, J., and Ramamritham, K., eds. *Advances in Real-Time Systems.* Los Alamitos, CA: IEEE Computer Society Press, 1993.

STAN96 Stankovic, J., et al. "Strategic Directions in Real-Time and Embedded Systems." *ACM Computing Surveys*, December 1996.

STEE95 Steensgarrd, B., and Jul, E. "Object and Native Code Mobility Among Heterogeneous Computers." *Proceedings, 15th ACM Symposium on Operating Systems Principles*, December 1995.

STER99 Sterling, T., et al. *How to Build a Beowulf.* Cambridge, MA: MIT Press, 1999.

STON93 Stone, H. *High-Performance Computer Architecture.* Reading, MA: Addison-Wesley, 1993.

STRE83 Strecker, W. "Transient Behavior of Cache Memories." *ACM Transactions on Computer Systems*, November 1983.

SUMM84 Summers, R. "An Overview of Computer Security." *IBM Systems Journal*, Vol. 23, No. 4, 1984.

SUZU82 Suzuki, I., and Kasami, T. "An Optimality Theory for Mutual Exclusion Algorithms in Computer Networks." *Proceedings of the Third International Conference on Distributed Computing Systems*, October 1982.

SWAI07 Swaine, M. "Wither Operating Systems?" *Dr. Dobb's Journal*, March 2007.

SYMA01 Symantec Corp. *The Digital Immune System.* Symantec Technical Brief, 2001.

TAKA01 Takada, H. "Real-Time Operating System for Embedded Systems." In *Asia South-Pacific Design Automation Conference.* Edited by M. Imai and N. Yoshida. 2001.

TALL92 Talluri, M.; Kong, S.; Hill, M.; and Patterson, D. "Tradeoffs in Supporting Two Page Sizes." *Proceedings of the 19th Annual International Symposium on Computer Architecture*, May 1992.

TAMI83 Tamir, Y., and Sequin, C. "Strategies for Managing the Register File in RISC." *IEEE Transactions on Computers*, November 1983.

TANE78 Tanenbaum, A. "Implications of Structured Programming for Machine Architecture." *Communications of the ACM*, March 1978.

TANE85 Tanenbaum, A., and Renesse, R. "Distributed Operating Systems." *Computing Surveys*, December 1985.

TANE06 Tanenbaum, A., and Woodhull, A. *Operating Systems: Design and Implementation.* Upper Saddle River, NJ: Prentice Hall, 2006.

TAY90 Tay, B., and Ananda, A. "A Survey of Remote Procedure Calls." *Operating Systems Review*, July 1990.

TEL01 Tel, G. *Introduction to Distributed Algorithms.* Cambridge: Cambridge University Press, 2001.

TEVA87 Tevanian, A., et al. "Mach Threads and the UNIX Kernel: The Battle for Control." *Proceedings, Summer 1987 USENIX Conference*, June 1987.

THOM01 Thomas, G. "eCos: An Operating System for Embedded Systems." *Dr. Dobb's Journal*, January 2001.

THOM84 Thompson, K. "Reflections on Trusting Trust (Deliberate Software Bugs)." *Communications of the ACM*, August 1984.

TILB91 Tilborg, A., and Koob, G., eds. *Foundations of Real-Time Computing: Scheduling and Resource Management.* Boston: Kluwer Academic Publishers, 1991.

TIME90 Time, Inc. *Computer Security, Understanding Computers Series.* Alexandria, VA: Time-Life Books, 1990.

TIME02 TimeSys Corp. "Priority Inversion: Why You Care and What to Do About It." *TimeSys White Paper*, 2002. http://www.techonline.com/community/ ed_resource/tech_paper/21779

TUCK89 Tucker, A., and Gupta, A. "Process Control and Scheduling Issues for Multiprogrammed Shared-Memory Multiprocessors." *Proceedings, Twelfth ACM Symposium on Operating Systems Principles*, December 1989.

TUCK04 Tucker, A. ed. *The Computer Science Handbook.* Boca Raton, FL: CRC Press, 2004.

VAHA96 Vahalia, U. *UNIX Internals: The New Frontiers.* Upper Saddle River, NJ: Prentice Hall, 1996.

VENU09 Venugopal, K. Files Structures Using C++. New York: McGraw-Hill, 2009.

WAGN00 Wagner, D., and Goldberg, I. "Proofs of Security for the UNIX Password Hashing Algorithm." *Proceedings, ASIACRYPT '00*, 2000.

WALK89 Walker, B., and Mathews, R. "Process Migration in AIX's Transparent Computing Facility." *Newsletter of the IEEE Computer Society Technical Committee on Operating Systems*, Winter 1989.

WARD80 Ward, S. "TRIX: A Network-Oriented Operating System." *Proceedings, COMPCON '80*, 1980.

WARR91 Warren, C. "Rate Monotonic Scheduling." *IEEE Micro*, June 1991.

WARE79 Ware, W., ed. *Security Controls for Computer Systems.* RAND Report 609-1, October 1979. http://www.rand.org/pubs/reports/R609-1/index2.html

WEIZ81 Weizer, N. "A History of Operating Systems." *Datamation*, January 1981.

WEND89 Wendorf, J.; Wendorf, R.; and Tokuda, H. "Scheduling Operating System Processing on Small-Scale Microprocessors." *Proceedings, 22nd Annual Hawaii International Conference on System Science*, January 1989.

WHIT99 White, S. *Anatomy of a Commercial-Grade Immune System.* IBM Research White Paper, 1999.

WIED87 Wiederhold, G. *File Organization for Database Design.* New York: McGraw-Hill, 1987.

WOOD86 Woodside, C. "Controllability of Computer Performance Tradeoffs Obtained Using Controlled-Share Queue Schedulers." *IEEE Transactions on Software Engineering*, October 1986.

WOOD89 Woodbury, P., et al. "Shared Memory Multiprocessors: The Right Approach to Parallel Processing." *Proceedings, COMPCON Spring '89*, March 1989.

WORT94 Worthington, B.; Ganger, G.; and Patt, Y. "Scheduling Algorithms for Modern Disk Drives." *ACM SiGMETRICS*, May 1994.

WRIG95 Wright, G., and Stevens, W. *TCP/IP Illustrated, Volume 2: The Implementation.* Reading, MA: Addison-Wesley, 1995.

ZAHO90   Zahorjan, J., and McCann, C. "Processor Scheduling in Shared Memory Multiprocessors." *Proceedings, Conference on Measurement and Modeling of Computer Systems*, May 1990.

ZAJC93   Zajcew, R., et al. "An OSF/1 UNIX for Massively Parallel Multicomputers." *Proceedings, Winter USENIX Conference*, January 1993.

ZEAD97   Zeadally, S. "An Evaluation of the Real-Time Performance of SVR4.0 and SVR4.2." *Operating Systems Review*, January 1977.

ZOU05   Zou, C., et al. "The Monitoring and Early Detection of Internet Worms." *IEEE/ACM Transactions on Networking*, October 2005.

Index

Note: letters "A" and "B" followed by locators refers to Appendix page numbers. Green colored locators refers to online chapter page numbers.

A

Absolute loading, 334–336
Absolute scalability, 699
Access
  efficiency, 44
  matrix, 552
  methods for file systems, 526
  rights for file sharing, 540–541, 553
  time, 487
  token, 668–669
Access control, 146, 646–653
  categories of, 646–647
  commands, 650
  discretionary, 646, 647–651
  function of, 649
  lists, 553, 559–560
  mandatory, 646–647
  matrix of, 648
  protection and, 66
  role-based, 647, 651–653
  security scheme, 668
  security threats and, 646–653
  structures of, 552–553
  UNIX systems, 558–559
Access control lists
  discretionary, 670
  file system security, 553
  system, 670
  UNIX systems, 559–560
Accountability for computer security, 610
Accounting information, 109
Accumulator (AC), 12
Action field, 656
Active attacks, 615
Active Directory, 80
Active secondary, 700, 701
Address binding, 336
Addresses. *See also* Address translation; Virtual addresses
  executable, space protection, 666
  logical, 320, 323
  physical, 320
  read, 67
  real, 341
  registers, 9, 10
  relative, 320
  space, 187, 341
  space randomization, 667
Addressing, 68, 235–236
  direct, 235
  indirect, 235
  indirect process communication, 235–236
  Linux virtual memory, 384–385
  many-to-one relationship, 235
  message passing, 235–236
  one-to-many relationship, 235
  one-to-one relationship, 235
  for process, requirements of, 308
  translation of, 324
  virtual memory, 384–385

Address translation
  for paging system, 347, 348
  in segmentation, 357, 358
Advanced local procedure call (ALPC) facility, 84
Advertisement add-ons, 631
Alignment check, 132
All users class, 541
AMD64, 81
Amdahl's law, 171
Analyzers for intrusion detection, 145
Anomaly detection, 655
Anticipatory input/output scheduler, 511–512
Antivirus approaches, 657–661
  behavior-blocking software, 659–661
  digital immune system, 658–659
  generic decryption, 657–658
Anys state → exit process, 124
Aperiodic tasks, 443, 451
Appending access rights, 540
Application binary interface (ABI), 50, 75
Application layer, 17-8
Application programming interface (API), 50, 75, 679, 17-16
Architecture, 582
  client/server application, three-tier, 680, 685–686
  client/server model, 85–86
  cluster, 703–704
  file management systems, 525–526
  Linux VServer, 101
  microkernel, 71
  Microsoft Windows, 82–85
  Microsoft Windows Vista, 82
  middleware, 688–689
  UNIX systems, 91
  virtual machines (VM), 75–76
ARPANET, 17-6
Assets of computer system, threats to, 613–616
Assignment of processes to processors, 433–434
Associative lookup for page table, 353
Associative mapping, 351
Asynchronous input/output, Windows, 513–514
Asynchronous procedure call (APC), 514
Asynchronous processing, 161–162
Asynchronous remote procedure calls (RPC), 698
Asynchronous service, 691
Atomic bitmap operations, 286, 287
Atomic integer operations, 286–287
Atomic operations, 200, 285–287
AT&T, 90, 93
Attacks on computer system
  threats, 610–612
  types of, 610–611
Attribute definition table, 567
Audit records for intrusion detection, 655–657
Authentication, 145–146, 640–646
  biometric, 645–646
  computer security, 145–146, 640–646
  password-based, UNIX system, 640–643
  steps of, 145
  token-based, 643–645

Authentication (*continued*)
  of user's identification, 145, 146
  verification step of, 145
Authenticity of information, 69, 610
Autocovariance, 19-16
Automatic allocation, 66
Automatic management, 66
Automatic teller machine (ATM), 644
Auto-rooter, 620
Auxiliary carry flag, 132
Auxiliary memory, 27
Availability, 18-3
Availability of information, 69, 72, 609, 610
Available state, 388
Avoidance approaches for operating systems, 265
Awareness, degrees of, 205
Axiomatic definition of probability, 19-2–5

B
BACI (Ben-Ari Concurrent Interpreter), B-7
Backdoor, 619–621, 620
Background work, 161
Balancing resources, 401
Banker's algorithm, 271
Barbershop problem, A-15–21
Basic buffer overflow, 327
Basic file systems, 522
Basic input/output supervisor, 525
Basic spinlocks, 287–288
Batch systems
  multiprogrammed, 56–58
  simple, 53–56
Bayes's Theorem, 19-6–8
Behavior-blocking software, 659–661
Bell Labs, 90
Beowulf clusters, 706–708
  configuration of, 707
  features of, 706–707
Beowulf distributed process space (BPROC), 708
Beowulf Ethernet channel bonding, 708
Beowulf software, 707–708
Berkeley Sockets Interface, 17-16
Berkeley Software Distribution (BSD), 94
Best fit strategy, 315, 544
_bh, 288
Bias, 20-41
Binary semaphores, 213, 215, 221, 223, 224, 289–290
Biometric authentication, 645–646
Bitmap operations, Linux atomic, 286, 287
Bitmap scheduler, 587
Bit tables, 548–549
Blended attack, 622
Block device drivers, 100
Block diagram, 36, 479
Blocked → blocked/suspend process, 123
Blocked → exit process, 119
Blocked process, 122–123
Blocked → ready process, 119
Blocked state, 119, 147–148
Blocked/suspend → blocked process, 124
Blocked/suspended process, 123
Blocked/suspend → ready/suspend process, 123
Blocked/waiting process state, 117
Blocking, 234
  fixed, 541
  nonblocking, 695

permanent, 259
record, 541–543
Block operation, 162
Block-oriented device, 484
Blocks, 28, 189–190, 544
  boot, 557
  data, 557
  defined, 189
  dispatched, 190
  function of, 190
  process control, 109–110
  scheduled, 190
  size of, 30
Boot block, 557
Boot sector infector, 626
Bots, 631–633
  botnet, 631
  botnet attack, construction of, 632–633
  remote control facility, 632
  use of, 631–632
Bottom half code, 288
Bottom-half kernel threads, 463
Bounded-buffer monitor code, 231
Bounded-buffer producer/consumer
    problem, 229, 238
Brownian motion process, 19-19–22
Browser helper objects (BHOs), 631
B-trees, 532–535
  characteristics of, 533
  definition of, 533
  nodes into, insertion of, 535
  properties of, 533
  rules for, 534
Buddy system, 317–319
  algorithms of, 318
  example of, 318
  tree representation of, 319
Buffer cache, UNIX system, 507–508
Buffering, 369, 483–487
Buffer overflow
  basic, example of, 327
  stack values, 328
Buffer overflow attacks, 326–330
  compile-time defenses, 663–666
  dealing with, 663–667
  defending against, 330
  run-time defenses, 666–667
Buffer overrun. *See* Buffer overflow
Buffer registers
  input/output buffer register (I/OBR), 10
  memory buffer register (MBR), 9–10
Buffer swapping. *See* Double buffer
Busy waiting technique, 212, A-2

C
Cache consistency, 687
Cache levels, 30
Cache manager, 83, 513, 568
Cache memory, 27–31, 502–503. *See also* Disk cache
  blocks, 28
  block size, 30
  cache size, 30
  categories of, 30
  design of, 29–31
  main memory and, 28–29
  mapping function, 31

motivation, 27
principles of, 28–29
read operation of, 29–30
replacement algorithm, 31
slots, 28
write policy, 31
Cache operation, 353
Cache size, 30, 369–370
CalmRISC, 579
Canary value, 665
Capability tickets, 553
Carry flag, 132
Centralized algorithm, 18-18–19
Centralized control, 18-34
Central processing unit (CPU), 8
Certain event, 19-3
Chained allocation, 546–547
Chained free portions, 549
Chain pointer, 349
Challenge-response, 644
Changing protection access rights, 540
Channel, 18-12
Character device drivers, Linux, 100
Character queue, UNIX SVR4, 508
Chbind, 101
Chcontext, 100–101
Checkpointing, 704
Child process, 115
Chip multiprocessor, 35–36
Chroot, 100
CIA triad for security, 609
C implementation of UNIX systems, 90
Circular buffer, 486
Circular SCAN (C-SCAN) policy, 493
Circular wait condition, 18-31
Circular wait process, deadlock prevention using, 267, 269
Clandestine user, 143
Classes
    all users, 541
    of client-server applications, 683–685
    of interrupts, 14
    kernel (99-60), 462
    objects, 86
    priority, 463, 467
    real time (159-100), 461–462
    real-time priority, 467
    specific user, 541
    time-shared (59-0), 462
    user groups, 541
    variable priority, 467
Classification by target, 626
Cleaning policy, 376–377
Client, 678, 679. *See also* Client/server computing
Client-based processing, 684
Client machines, 678
Client/server applications, 680–687
    classes of, 683–685
    database applications, 681–683
    file cache consistency, 686–687
    three-tier architecture of, 685–686
Client/server binding, 697
Client/server computing, 678–689. *See also* Client/server
    applications
    architecture of, 680
    concept of, 678
    definition of, 678–680

middleware, 687–689
network for, 679
servers in, 678–679
terminology of, 679
Client-server model, 85–86
Clock algorithm, 367, 381, 386
Clock interrupt, 137
Clock page, 368
Clock replacement policy, 365, 366
Cloned () process, 188
Closing files, 522
Clouds, 171
Cluster bit map, 567
Clusters, 431, 565, 699–704
    architecture of, 703–704
    benefits of, 701
    Beowulf, 706–708
    configurations of, 699–701
    limitations of, 701
    Linux, 706–708
    methods of, 701
    multiprocessor system, 431
    objectives of, 699
    operating system design issues with, 702–703
    parallelizing computation, 702–703
    requirements of, 699
    sizes of, 566
    SMP, 704
    in symmetric multiprocessor, 704
Cluster service, 704
Coarse-grained services, 690
Coarse parallelism, 432–433
Coarse threading, 174
Codecs, 10
Coefficient of variation, 20-20
Commands, TinyOS, 598
Commercial operating systems, 578
Committed state, 388
Common Object Request Broker Architecture
    (CORBA), 690, 698
Communication
    architecture, 17-2–3
    cooperation among processes by, 208–209
    datagram, 17-16, 17-18
    deadlock, in distributed system, 18-44
    devices, 476
    indirect process, 235–236
    interprocess, 233
    lines, security of, 509, 615–616
    message, 18-38–44
    performance, 18-3
    socket, 17-18
    stream, 17-18
Compaction of memory, 314
Compare&swap instruction, 210–212
Compatible Time-Sharing System (CTSS), 60–61
Competition, 205
Compile-time defenses, 663–666
    language extensions, safe libraries and, 664–665
    programming language choices, 663–664
    safe coding techniques, 664
    stacking protection mechanisms, 665–666
Complement, 19-3
Completion deadline, 448
Compression viruses, 625
Computer-aided design (CAD), 40

Computer communications, 17-4
Computer emergency response teams (CERTs), 618
Computer network, 17-4
Computer systems. *See also* Operating systems (OS)
  assets of, threats to, 613–616
  attacks, types of, 610–611
  basic elements of, 8–10
  cache memory, 27–31
  direct memory access, 31–32
  instruction execution, 11–13
  interrupts, 14–23
  memory hierarchy, 24–27
  microprocessor, 10, 33–36
  overview of, 7–36
  threats, 610–612
  top-level components of, 9
Concurrency, 198–244, 258–298, A-1–20
  barbershop problem, A-15–21
  contexts of, 199–200
  deadlock, 259–278
  dining philosophers problem, 279–281
  example of, 201–203
  Linux kernel, mechanisms of, 285–292
  message passing, 233–239
  monitors, 226–232
  mutual exclusion, 209–213
  operating systems, concerns of, 204
  principles of, 201–209
  process interaction, 205–209
  race conditions of, 204, A-8–15
  readers/writers problems, 239–243
  semaphores, 213–226, A-8–15
  Solaris thread synchronization, primitives of, 292–294
  terms related to, 200
  UNIX, mechanisms of, 281–285
  Windows 7, mechanisms of, 294–297
Concurrent process, simultaneous, 77
Concurrent threads, simultaneous, 77
Conditional probability, and independence, 19-6
Condition codes, 132
Condition variables, 213, 227, 294, 297
  eCos, 590–591
  monitors, 227
Confidentiality, of information, 69, 609, 610
Configurability, 577, 579–582
Configuration database manager, 706
Configuration manager, Windows, 84
Connection-oriented protocol, 17-19
Consistency, 686
Consistent distributed global states, 18-13
Consumable resources, deadlock and, 264–266
Containment, 661–662
Context data, 109
Contiguous allocation, 545–546
Continuous-time stochastic process, 19-14
Continuous-value stochastic process, 19-15
Continuous variable, 19-8
Control, 11
  bits, 132, 349
  complexity of, 476
  load, 377–379
  mode, 135
  with multiple interrupts, transfer of, 22
  objects, Windows, 88
  operating system, structures of, 126–128
  process, 134–139

scheduling and, 482–483
  status registers and, 130, 131
  user, 444
Control bits, 132, 349
Control mode, 135
Control objects, Windows, 88
Cooperation, 205
Cooperative processing, 684
Copy-on-reference strategy, 18-6
Cores, 10, 35
Coroutines, 247, 283, A-4
Correlation coefficient, 19-13, 19-16
Corruption, 612
Counting (general) semaphores, 215, 222, 289–290
Covariance variables, 19-13
CPU emulator, 657
Create file operation, 537
Creation of files, 522
Criminal intruders, 618
Critchley, Adam, B-4
Critical resource, 206
Critical sections, 200, 206, 296–297
C-SCAN (circular SCAN) policy, 493
Csignal (c), 227
Currency mechanisms, 213
Cutler, Dave, 80
Cwait (c), 227

D
Data
  block, 557
  confidentiality, 609
  Context, 109
  integrity, 69, 609
  memory, external fragmentation of, 314
  processing, 11
  rate, 476
  security threats to, 614–615
  semaphores and, 219
  set of, 109
  SIMD techniques, 10
  streams, multiple, 565
  table entry, page frame, 380–381
  transfer capacity, RAID level 0 for high, 498–499
Database, 523
  client/server applications, 681–683
  configuration database manager, 706
  relational, 679
  server, 20-24–25
Datagram communication, 17-16, 17-18
DDR3 (double data rate) memory controller, 35
Deadlines, 401
Deadline scheduler, 510–511
Deadline scheduling, 448–452
  design issues, 449
  real-time scheduling, 448–452
  for tasks, 448–451
Deadlocks, 64, 200, 206, 213
  communication, in distributed system, 18-44
  conditions for, 267–268
  consumable resources, 264–266
  distributed, 18-30–44
  errors in process, 64
  example of, 261
  execution paths of, 262
  free, 18-26

illustration of, 260
integrated strategy for, 278
no, example of, 263
phantom, 18-31
principles of, 259–268
resource allocation graphs, 266–267
reusable resources, 263–264
store-and-forward, 18-42
Deadlock avoidance, 268, 270–275, 18-33–34
logic of, 275
process initiation denial, 270–271
resource allocation denial, 271–275
restrictions of, 274
Deadlock detection, 265, 268, 276–278
algorithm of, 276–277, 18-34–38
recovery, 277–278
Deadlock prevention, 265, 268–275,
18-32–33, 18-43
circular wait condition, 269
hold and wait condition, 269
mutual exclusion, 269
no preemption condition, 267, 269
Deception, security threats of, 612
Decision mode, 404
Dedicated processor assignment, 440–441
Dedicated resources, 601–602
Default ACL, 669
Default owner, 669
Defense Advanced Research Projects Agency
(DARPA), 17-6–7
Deferred service routines (DSRs), 584–585
Degrees of awareness, 205
Dekker's algorithm, A-2–7
Delay variable, 383–384
Delete access, 671
Delete file operation, 537
Deletion access rights, 540
Deletion of files, 522
Demand cleaning policy, 376
Demand paging, 361
Denial of service attacks, 615–616
Denning, Dorothy, 655
Density function, 19-8–9
Dentry object, Linux, 562, 564
*deps, 97
Design issues
with deadline scheduling, 449
of disk cache, 503–505
for embedded operating systems, 577
of input/output, 480–483
with multiprocessor scheduling, 433–435
Destination network address, 17-14
Detection of virus, 657
Detection-specific audit records, 655
Determinism, 443–444
Deterministic behavior, 583
Device driver interface to eCos kernel,
585–586
Device drivers, 83, 525
Device input/output, 482
Device list, 507
Die, 35
Differential responsiveness, 69
Digital Equipment Corporation, 80
Digital immune system, 658–659
Digital Signal Processors (DSPs), 10

Dining philosophers problem, 279–281
dining arrangement, for philosophers, 279
monitors, solutions using, 280–281
semaphores, solutions using, 280
Direct addressing, 235
Direct (hashed) file, 532
Direction flag, 132
Direct lookup for page table, 353
Direct memory access (DMA), 31–32
block diagram, 479
configurations for, alternative, 480
input/output operations, techniques for,
31–32, 477–480
Directories
attributes, 567
file, 553–554
management, 483
UNIX, 557
Disabled interrupts, 22–23
Discoverable services, 691
Discrete variable, 19-8
Discrete-time stochastic process, 19-14
Discrete-value stochastic process, 19-15
Discretionary access control (DAC),
646, 647–651
Discretionary access control list (DACL), 670
Disk allocation tables, 547
Disk block descriptors, 380–381
Disk cache, 40, 502–506
design issues of, 503–505
performance issues of, 505–506
Disk drives, 509
Disk duplexing, 515
Disk performance parameters, 487–489
rotational delay, 488–489
seek time, 488
timing comparison, 489
Disk scheduling
algorithms for, 491–492
anticipatory input/output scheduler,
511–512
deadline scheduler, 510–511
disk performance parameters, 487–489
elevator scheduler, 510
input/output management and, 474–516
policies for, 490–494
Disk storage, 565–566
Dispatched blocks, 190
Dispatcher objects, 88, 295–296
Dispatcher program, 111
Dispatching discipline, 20-13
Dispatch queues, 462
Disruption, security threats of, 612
Distributed algorithm, 18-19
Distributed control, 18-34
Distributed data processing (DDP), 17-2
Distributed deadlock, 18-30–44
in message communication, 18-38–44
in resource allocation, 18-30–38
Distributed denial-of-service (DDoS) attacks, 631
Distributed global states, 18-10–16
consistent, 18-13
distributed snapshot algorithm, 18-14–16
example of, 18-12
inconsistent, 18-13
process and channel graph, 18-15

Distributed message passing, 691–695
    blocking, differentiating between nonblocking and, 695
    middleware, 693
    primitives of, basic, 694
    reliability, differentiating between unreliability and, 694–695
Distributed multiprocessor system, 431
Distributed mutual exclusion, 18-16–30
    concepts of, 18-17–20
    distributed queue, 18-24–27
    distributed system, ordering of events in, 18-20–23
    token-passing approach, 18-28–30
Distributed operating systems, 73, 17-3
Distributed processing, 199
    Beowulf clusters, 706–708
    client/server computing, 678–689
    clusters, 699–704
    distributed message passing, 691–695
    Linux clusters, 706–708
    Microsoft Windows cluster server, 704–706
    remote procedure call (RPC), 695–698
    service-oriented architecture (SOA), 689–691
Distributed process management, 18-1–45
    distributed deadlock, 18-30–44
    distributed global states, 18-10–16
    distributed mutual exclusion, 18-16–30
    process migration, 18-2–10
Distributed queue, 18-24–27
    first version, 18-24–26
    second version, 18-26–27
Distributed snapshot, 18-13
Distributed snapshot algorithm, 18-14–16
Distributed system, ordering of events in, 18-20–23
Distribution function, 19-8–9
Distributions, 19-9–12
    exponential, 19-9–11
    normal, 19-12
    poisson, 19-11–12
DMA. *See* Direct memory access (DMA)
Domain Name System (DNS) database, 17-15
Dormant phase, 624
Double buffer, 486
Downloaders, 620
Driver input/output queue, 507
Dynamic allocation, 543–544
Dynamically linked libraries (DLLs), 705
Dynamic best effort scheduling, 447, 448
Dynamic biometrics, 146
Dynamic linker, 338–339
Dynamic linking, Linux, 95, 338–339
Dynamic link libraries (DLLs), 84, 339
Dynamic partitioning for memory, 314–317
    effect of, 315
    placement algorithm, 315–317
    replacement algorithm, 317
Dynamic password generator, 644
Dynamic planning-based scheduling, 447, 448
Dynamic run-time loading, 337
Dynamic scheduling, 442

E
Eager strategy, 18-5
ECos. *See* Embedded Configurable Operating System (eCos)
Efficiency, 69, 480
EFLAGS register, Pentium, 131–132

Electronic mail facility, 629
Elevator scheduler, 510
E-mail, security threats to, 622
E-mail viruses, 628
Embedded Configurable Operating System (eCos), 579–594. *See also* specific types of
    components of, 582–586
    configurability, 579–582
    hardware abstraction layer, 582–583
    input/output system, 584–586
    scheduler, 587–588
    standard C libraries, 586
    thread synchronization, 589–594
Embedded Configurable Operating System (eCos) kernel, 583–584
    device driver interface to, 585–586
    objectives of, 583
Embedded operating systems, 573–603
    characteristics of, 576–579
    commercial operating systems, adapting to existing, 578
    definition of, 574
    design issues for, 577
    eCos (Embedded Configurable Operating System), 579–594
    elements of, 576
    examples of, 575
    organization of, 576
    purpose-built, 578–579
    requirements/constraints of, 574–575
    TinyOS, 594–603
Emerald system, 171
Emulation control module, 657
Encapsulation, 86
Encrypted viruses, 626
Encryption, volume, 515
Energy efficiency, Microsoft Windows 7, 89
Enforcing priorities, 401
EnFuzion, 708
Engineering improvements, Microsoft Windows 7, 89
Ensemble averages, 19-25
Enterprise Edition (J2EE platform), 173
Environmental subsystems, Windows, 84
Ergodicity, 19-24–26
Errors in process, causes of, 63–64
    deadlocks, 64
    mutual exclusion, failed, 63–64
    program operation, nondeterminate, 64
    synchronization, improper, 63
Event, 19-2
Event flags, 213, 591–592
Event object, Windows, 296, 514
Event processor, 706
Events, TinyOS, 598
Eviction, 18-9–10
Exception-condition field, 656
Exchange instruction, 212
Executable address space protection, 666
Executable program, 64
Executables (EXEs), 84
Execution
    access rights, 540
    context (process state), 64
    modules of, 83–84
    of object-oriented design, 87
    paths of deadlock, 262
    phase, 624

of process, 158
process control, modes of, 134–136
of Solaris threads, 184–185
speed of, 162
stack, 160
state, 186
Executive stage, 12–13
Exit process state, 117
Exploits, 620
Exponential averaging, 410, 412
Exponential distributions, 19-9–11
Exponential population, means for, 20-40
Exponential smoothing coefficients, 411
Exposure, 610–611
External fragmentation of memory data, 314

F
Facial characteristics, 645
Facilities request, 17-14
Failback, 702
Failover, 702
Failover manger, 706
Fail-soft operation, 444–445
Failure management, clusters, 702
Fairness, 69, 401, 18-26
Fair-share scheduling, 420–422
False negatives/positives, 653
Falsification, 612
Fatal region, 262
Fat client, 684
Faulting processing, 378
Faults, 100
Fault tolerance, 78
Feedback, 413–415
Feedback scheduling, 414
Fetches, 11
Fetch policy, 361–362
Fetch stage, 12–13
Field, input/output files, 522–523
File allocation, 543–547
dynamic allocation *vs.* preallocation,
543–544
methods of, 545–547
portion size, 544–545
UNIX, 556–557
File allocation table (FAT), 543
File directories, 535–539
contents of, 535–536
elements of, 536
naming, 538–539
structure of, 537–538
tree-structured, 538, 539
working, 539
File infector, 626
File management systems, 520–569
architecture of, 525–526
B-trees, 532–535
elements of, 526
file sharing, 540–541
functions of, 526–527
Linux virtual file system (VFS), 560–564
objectives of, 524
overview of, 522–527
record blocking, 541–543
requirements of, minimal, 524–524
secondary storage management, 543–551

security (*See* File system security)
UNIX, 553–560
File object, Linux, 514, 562, 564
File organization/access, 527–532
criteria for, 527–528
direct file, 532
hash file, 532
indexed file, 531–532
indexed sequential file, 530–531
performance, grades of, 529
pile, 529–530
sequential file, 530
types of, common, 528–529
Files, 522
allocation (*See* File allocation)
cache consistency, 686–687
closing, 522
creation of, 522
deletion of, 522
direct, 532
directories (*See* File directories)
field, input/output, 522–523
hashed, 532
indexed, 531–532
indexed sequential, 530–531
large, support for, 565
links, 554
log, 567
long-term existence of, 522
management (*See* File management systems)
MFT2, 567
naming, 538–539
object, Linux, 514, 562, 564
opening, 522
operations performed on, 522
ordinary, 553
organization/access (*See* File organization/access)
performance, grades of, 529
pile, 529–530
properties of, 522
reading, 522
regular, 553
sequential (*See* Sequential files)
sharing, 207–208, 309, 522, 540–541
special, 554
structure, 522–524, 565–567
symbolic links, 554, 565
systems (*See* File systems)
tables, 127, 543, 567
tree-structured, 538, 539
UNIX, 553–555
UNIX FreeBSD, structure of, 555
writing, 522
File systems, 100, 187, 483, 522, 567
drivers, 513
isolation, 100
Windows, 564–569
File system security, 551–553
access control lists, 553
access control structures, 552–553
capability tickets, 553
File tables, 127
allocation table (FAT), 543
volume master, 567
File transfer, architecture for, 17-6
File Transfer Protocol (FTP), 17-15

Filter-based worm containment, 661
Fine-grained parallelism, 433
Fine-grained threading, 174
Fingerprinting, 632, 645
Finish operation, 162
Finite circular buffer, for producer/consumer problem, 225
Firewalls, 146–147
First-come-first-served (FCFS), 407, 438, 20-13
First fit strategy, 315–316, 544
First-in-first-out (FIFO) policy, 216, 364, 490
First-order statistics, 19-15–17
Five-state process model, 116–120
    states of, 117
    transitions of, 118–119
Fixed allocation
    local page, 367
    local scope, 371
    replacement policy, 370
Fixed blocking, 541
Fixed function units, 10
Fixed partitioning for memory, 310–314
    partition size, 310–312
    placement algorithm, 312–314
Flags, 97, 669
Flexibility of input/output devices, 577
Flooders, 620
Flushing strategy, 18-6
Foreground work, 161
FORTRAN programs, 40
Four page replacement algorithm,
    behavior of, 364
Frame, 307, 321, 322
Frame locking, 363
Free block list, 549–550
Free frame, 322
Free list, 507
Free Software Foundation (FSF), 94
Free space management, 547–550
    bit tables, 548–549
    chained free portions, 549
    free block list, 549–550
    indexing, 549
FREE state, 184
Frequency-based replacement, 504
FSCAN policy, 493–494
Functionally specialized multiprocessor
    system, 431
Functions
    access control, 649
    blocks, 190
    file management systems, 526–527
    kernel (nucleus), 135
    linking, 338
    loading, 334
    MAC OS Grand Central Dispatch (GCD), 192
    mapping, 30, 31
    Microsoft Windows input/output, 513
    operating systems (OS), 48–52
    processor, 9
    resource management in OS, scheduling and, 70
    selection, 403
    support, 135
    threads, 162–164
    wait, 295
    worms, 629
Fuzzing, 329

G

Gang scheduling, 439
GCC (GNU Compiler Collection), 665
Generality, 481, 661
General message format, 236–237
General semaphores, 215, 222
Generic_all access bits, 671
Generic decryption (GD), 657–658
Generic_execute access bits, 671
Generic_read access bits, 671
Generic_write access bits, 671
Global coverage, 661
Global replacement policy, 371
Global scope, 372
Global state, 18-13
Grand Central Dispatch (GCD), 78–79
Granularity, 432–433. *See also* Parallelism
Graphical Processing Units (GPUs), 10
Graphic user interface (GUI), 681
Group
    concept of, 705
    resources, 705
    SIDs, 669
Guard pages, 667
Gupta Corp, 684

H

Hackers, 616–618
Hamming code, 500
Hand geometry, 645
Handspread, 381
Hard affinity process, 181
Hard links, 565
Hard real-time task, 443
Hardware
    device drivers, 513
    interrupt processing, 19–20
    mutual exclusion, 209–213
    RAID, 514
    relocation, 320
    security threats to, 613
    simple batch systems, 55–56
    virtual memory (paging), 348–360
Hardware abstraction layer (HAL), 83, 582–583
Hashed file, 532
Hashed passwords, 641–642
Hash table, 507–508
Hexadecimal digit, 12
Hierarchical control, 18-34
High availability, 699
Highest response ratio next (HRRN), 413
High-level language (HLL), 50
High Performance Computing and Communications
    (HPCC), 706
Hit list scanning, 633
Hit ratio *(H)*, 25
Hold and wait condition, 18-31
Hold and wait process, deadlock prevention
    using, 267, 269
Host-based intrusion detection, 654–655
Host-based processing, 683
Hosting platform, 101
Hot-based IDS, 144
Human readable devices, 475
Hybrid threading, 174–175
Hypervisor, 74

I

IBM personal computer (PC), 60, 80, 94
Identification flag, 132
Identification of virus, 657
Identification step of authentication, 145
Identifiers, 109, 186
Idle user, 463
IDS. *See* Intrusion detection systems (IDS)
If statements, 231
Incapacitation, 612
In-circuit emulator (ICE), B-3
Inconsistent distributed global states, 18-13
Incremental growth, 72
Incremental scalability, 699
Independence, and conditional probability, 19-6
Independent events, 19-6
Independent increments, 19-19–24
    Brownian motion process, 19-19–22
    poisson counting process, 19-22–24
Independent parallelism, 432
Independent variables, 19-13
Indexed allocation, 547
Indexed files, 531–532
Indexed sequential files, 530–531
Indexing, 549
Index register, 64–65
Indirect addressing, 235
Indirect process communication, 235–236
Individual processors, 434–435
Infection from viruses, 626
Infection mechanism (vector), 623
Infection vector, 623
Inference, 611
Infinite buffer for producer/consumer problem,
    220, 221, 223, 224
Information, 68–69, 186
Information protection. *See* Security threats
Inheritance, 86–87
Initial infection from viruses, 626
Inode object, 562, 563
Inodes, UNIX, 554–556
    elements of, 554–555
    FreeBSD, structure of, 555
Inode table, 557
Input/output (I/O)
    address register (I/OAR), 10
    address registers, 10
    anticipatory scheduler, 511–512
    asynchronous, Windows, 513–514
    basic, 513
    buffering (*See* Input/output (I/O) buffering)
    channel, 478
    completion ports, 514
    design issues with, 480–483
    devices (*See* Input/output (I/O) devices)
    direct memory access, 478–480
    disk cache, 502–506
    disk scheduling, 474–516
    driver queues, 507
    eCos, 584–586
    evolution of, 477–478
    field files, 522–523
    file system, logical, 481–483, 526
    function, organization of, 477–480
    interrupt, 32, 137, 477
    Linux, 509–512

logical structure of, 481–483
management, 135
manager, 83, 513, 568
model of, 482
modules, 9, 10
organization of, 477–480
performing, techniques for, 31–32, 477
physical, 522, 525
processor, 11, 478
program/programmed, 14, 31–32, 477
RAID, 494–502, 499
scheduling, 396
space, single, 704
status information, 109
supervisor, basic, 525
tables, 127
three-level interrupt mode for, 584–585
UNIX SVR4 input/output, 506–509
Windows, 512–515
Input/output (I/O) buffering, 483–487
    circular buffer, 486
    double buffer, 486
    single buffer, 484–486
    utility of, 486–487
Input/output buffer register (I/OBR), 10
Input/output (I/O) devices
    data rates of, 476
    flexibility of, 577
    types of, 475–477
Insider attacks, 618–619
Instantiation of objects, 86
Instruction cycle, 11, 15–18
Instruction execution, 11–13. *See also* Direct
    memory access (DMA)
    categories of, 11
    characteristics of, 12
    executive stage of, 11
    fetch stage of, 11
    partial program execution, 12–13
    steps of, 11
Instruction register (IR), 11
Instruction set architecture (ISA), 50
Instructor's Resource Center (IRC), A-23–24
Integer operations, atomic, 286–287
Integrated mail systems, 658
Integrated strategy for deadlock, 278
Integrity of information, 609–610
Intel Core i7, 35, 36
Intel IA32, 579
Intel IA64, 81
Interactive scoring, 464–466
Interactive threads, 464
Interception, 611
Interface-based design, 690
Interface calls, 17-16–20
Interfaces
    application binary, 50, 75
    application programming, 50, 75, 679
    device driver interface to eCos kernel,
        585–586
    graphic user interface, 681
    native system, 84
    resource, 603
    single user, 704
    TinyOS resource, 601–603
    of typical operating systems, 50

Interfaces (*continued*)
  user, in intrusion detection systems, 145
  user/computer, 48–50
Internal fragmentation, 343, 354
Internal registers of processor, 9–10
Internal resources, 278
Internet Activities Board (IAB), 17-7
Internet Engineering Task Force (IETF), 17-10
Internet Protocol (IP), 17-8
  addresses, 17-16
  datagram, 17-14
  IPv6 and, 17-10–11
Interprocess communication (IPC), 71, 186, 233
Interrupt-driven input/output, 32, 477
Interruptible state, 187
Interrupt processing, 19–21
  hardware events of, sequence of, 19–20
  memory for, changes in, 20–21
  operations of, 20
  registers for, changes in, 20–21
  simple, 19
Interrupts, 14–23, 56, 100, 137. *See also* specific types of
  classes of, 14
  direct use of, 577–578
  disabled/disabling, 22–23, 210
  enable flag, 132
  handler, 17
  and instruction cycle, 15–18
  multiple, 21–23
  processing (*See* Interrupt processing)
  program flow of control with/without, 14–15
  request, 15
  Solaris threads, 185–186
  stage, 16
  WRITE call, 14–15, 18
  WRITE instruction, 15
Interrupt service routine (ISR), 23, 584
Intersection, 19-3
Intruders, 143–144, 616–619
  behavior patterns of, 616–619
  criminals, 618
  hackers, 616–618
  insider attacks, 618–619
Intrusion, 612, 616, 619
Intrusion detection, 144–145, 653–657
  audit records, 655–657
  host-based, techniques for, 654–655
  principles of, 653–654
  sensors for, 145
Intrusion detection systems (IDS), 144–145
  analyzers, 145
  hot-based, 144
  network-based, 144–145
  user interface, 145
Inverted page tables, 349, 350
I/O. *See* Input/output (I/O)
IOPL (I/O privilege level), 132
IP. *See* Internet Protocol (IP)
IPng. *See* Internet Protocol (IP)
IPv4 header, 17-11
IPv6, Internet Protocol and, 17-10–11
IRC (Internet Relay Chat) chat networks, 631
Iris, 645
_irq, 287
_irqsave, 287

Itanium, 81
Item population, 20-13

J
Jacketing, 168
Jackson's Theorem, 20-34–35
Java Application Server, 173
Java 2 Platform, 173
Java VM, 75
Job, serial processing, 52
Job control language (JCL), 54
Joint progress diagram, 260–261
Journaling, 565

K
Kendall's notation, 20-18–21
Kernel-level threads (KLT), 168–169
Kernel memory allocation
  Linux, 386
  Solaris, 379, 382–384
  UNIX, 379, 382–384
Kernels, 51, 83
  class (99-60), 462
  control objects, 88
  eCos, 585–586
  functions of, 135
  input/output manager, 513
  Linux (*See* Linux kernels)
  memory allocation (*See* Kernel memory allocation)
  microkernels, 71
  Microsoft Windows, 83–84
  mode, 56, 135
  mode rootkit, 633
  modules, 96
  monolithic, 71
  nonprocess, 140–141
  UNIX systems, 92–93
Key field for sequential files, 530
Keylogging, 620, 631
Kit (virus generator), 620
Knowledge access rights, 540

L
Language extensions, 664–665
Large disks, 565
Large files, 565
Largest process, 378
Last-in-first-out (LIFO) implementation, 128, 130, 20-13
Last process activated, 378
Lazy buddy system algorithm, 383–384
Least frequently used policy (LFU), 386, 503
Least recently used (LRU) policy, 31, 363–364, 503–504
Lightweight processes (LPW), 182, 183. *See also* Threads
Lines of memory, 28
Linkage editor, 337–338
Linking, 337–339
  dynamic linker, 338–339
  function of, 338
  linkage editor, 337–338
Links, 186
Links file, 554
Linux, 94–100, 384–386. *See also* Linux virtual file system
  (VFS); Linux VServer
  character device drivers, 100
  clone () flags, 189

clusters, 706–708
dentry object, 562, 564
dynamic linking, 95, 338–339
file object, 514, 562, 564
history of, 94–95
input/output, 509–512
loadable modules, 95–97, 336
memory barrier operations, 291
modular structure of, 95–97
page cache, 512
real-time tasks, 461
scheduling (*See* Linux scheduling)
semaphores, 290
spinlocks, 288
tasks, 186–188
threads, 188–189
2.4, 459
2.6, 95, 459
virtual machine process scheduling, 468–469
virtual memory (*See* Linux virtual memory)
Linux kernels
components of, 97–100
components of TCP/IP protocol, 17-20
concurrency mechanisms, 285–292
memory allocation, 386
Linux networking, 17-21–22
Linux scheduling, 457–461
non-real-time scheduling, 459–461
real-time scheduling, 457–458
Linux virtual file system (VFS), 560–564
concept of, 562
context of, 561
dentry object, 564
file object, 564
inode object, 563
object types in, 562
superblock object, 562–563
Linux virtual memory, 384–386
page allocation, 385–386
page replacement algorithm, 386
virtual memory addressing, 384–385
Linux VServer
applications running on, 101
architecture of, 101
chbind, 101
chcontext, 100–101
chroot, 100
file system isolation, 100
hosting platform, 101
network isolation, 101
process isolation, 101
root isolation, 101
token bucket filter (TBF), 468–469
virtual machine architecture, differentiating
    between, 100–101
virtual platform, 101
virtual servers, 100–101
List directory operation, 537
Livelocks, 200, A-5
Loadable modules, Linux, 95–97, 336
absolute, 336
characteristics of, 95
kernel modules, 96
module table, elements of, 96–97
Load balancing, clusters, 702

Load control, 377–379
Loading, 334–337
absolute, 334–335
addressing binding, 336
approaches to, 334
dynamic run-time, 337
function of, 334
modules, 336
relocatable, 335–336
Load sharing, 437–439, 18-3
Load-time dynamic linking, 338
Local coverage, 661
Locality of references, 26, 40–42, 344–345
principle of, 344
spatial, 42
temporal, 42
Local organization, 309
Local procedure call (LPC) facility, 696
Local replacement policy, 371
Local scope, 372–376
Local subnet scanning, 633
Lock-free synchronization, 297
Log file, NTFS, 567
Log file service, 568
Logical address, 320, 323
Logical input/output file system, 481–483, 526
Logic bomb, 620, 621
Long memory process, 19-17
Long-term existence of files, 522
Long-term scheduling, 396, 397–399
Long-term storage, 66
Loosely coupled multiprocessor system, 431
Loosely coupled service, 691
Lost calls cleared, 20-37
Lost calls delayed, 20-37
Lost calls held, 20-37
Lotus Domino, 173
Lowest-priority process, 378
Low interrupt latency, 583
Low task switching latency, 583

M
Mach 3.0, 94
Machine problems (MPs), B-5
Machine readable devices, 476
MAC OS Grand Central Dispatch (GCD), 189–192
blocks, 189–190
codes for, 191
functions of, 192
purpose of, 189
Mac OS X, 94
Macro viruses, 626, 627–628
Mailboxes, 213, 235, 592–593
Main memory, 9, 10, 28–29, 278
Main memory cache, 40
Maintenance hook, 619
Malicious programs, 620
Malicious software, 144, 619–623. *See also*
    Malware defense
backdoor, 619–621
logic bomb, 621
mobile code, 622
multiple-threat malware, 622–623
spreading new, 631
Trojan horse, 621–622

Malware defense, 657–663
  antivirus approaches, 657–661
  rootkit, countermeasures for, 662–663
  worms, countermeasures for, 661–662
Mandatory access control (MAC), 646–647
Many-to-many relationships, 169–170
Many-to-one relationships, 235
Mapping function, cache memory, 30, 31
Marker, 18-14
Masquerade attacks, 612, 615
Masquerader, 143
Master file table (MFT), 567
Matrix of access control, 648
Mean residence time, 20-11
Mean residence time for single-server queues, 20-22
Mean value, 19-9
Medium-grained parallelism, 433
Medium-term scheduling, 396, 399–400
Memory
  auxiliary, 27
  cache, 27–31, 502–503
  cards, 643–644
  compaction of, 314
  dynamic partitioning for, 314–317
  fault, 137–138
  for interrupt processing, changes in, 20–21
  layout for resident monitor, 53, 54
  Linux virtual, 384–386
  main, 9, 10, 28–29, 278
  physical, 100
  pointers, 109
  processor, 11
  protection, 55
  real, 343
  rootkit, 633
  secondary, 27
  shared, 283
  tables, 126–127
  two-level, 39–45
  virtual, 40, 67, 98, 340–389
Memory address register (MAR), 9
Memory buffer register (MBR), 9–10
Memory hierarchy, 24–27
  auxiliary memory, 27
  hit ratio, 25
  levels of, 24–26
  locality of reference, 26
  secondary memory, 27
  in software, 27
  two-level memory, 25–26, 39–45
Memory management, 58, 77, 135, 305–330
  buffer overflow, 326–330
  definition of, 306
  formats for, typical, 346
  Linux, 384–386
  memory partitioning, 310–321
  in OS, 66–68
  paging, 321–325
  read address, 67
  requirements of, 307–310
  security issues, 326–330
  segmentation, 325–326
  Solaris, 379–384
  storage management responsibilities of, 66
  terms associated with, 307
  UNIX, 379–384

UNIX SVR4, parameters of, 380–381
virtual address, 67
virtual memory, 67–68
Windows, 386–389
Memory management unit (MMU), 666
Memory partitioning, 310–321
  buddy system, 317–319
  dynamic partitioning, 314–317
  fixed partitioning, 310–314
  relocation, 319–321
Mesa monitors, 231
Message buffers, unavailability of, 18-41–44
Message communication
  deadlock in, 18-40
  distributed deadlock in, 18-38–44
Message passing, 233–239
  addressing, 235–236
  blocking, 234
  distributed (*See* Distributed message passing)
  implementation of, 234
  for interprocess communication, design
    characteristics of, 233
  message format, 236–237
  mutual exclusion, 237–239
  nonblocking, 234
  producer/consumer problem using, solution
    to bounded-buffer, 238
  queuing discipline, 237
  synchronization, 233–235
Messages, 237, 283, 18-6–7. *See also* Mailboxes
  contents attack, release of, 615
  format, 236–237
  modification of, 615
  mutual exclusion, 237
Metamorphic technique, 630
Metamorphic viruses, 627
MFT2 files, 567
Micro-electromechanical sensors (MEMS), 594
Microkernels, 71
Microprocessor
  cores, 10
  Digital Signal Processors (DSPs), 10
  evolution of, 10
  Graphical Processing Units (GPUs), 10
  multicore computer (chip multiprocessor), 35–36
  and multicore organization, 33–36
  Single-Instruction Multiple Data (SIMD)
    techniques, 10
  sockets, 10
  symmetric (SMP), 33–35
  System on a Chip (SoC), 10
Microsoft
  Common Language Infrastructure, 75
  DOS, 80
  Xenix System V, 93
Microsoft Windows. *See also* Microsoft Windows 7
  architecture of, 82–85
  asynchronous input/output, 513–514
  Azure, 81
  CE, 81
  client-server model, 85–86
  cluster server, 704–706
  file system, 564–569
  history of, 80–81
  input/output, 512–515
  kernel-mode components of, 83–84

Me, 80
memory management, 386–389
98, 80
95, 80
NT (3.1), 80
object-oriented design, 86–88
operating system for, modern, 81
overview of, 80–89
scheduling, 466–468
Server 2008, 80–81
symmetric multiprocessing (SMP),
  threads for, 86
3.0, 80
3.1, 80
2000, 80
Vista, 80, 82
XP, 80
Microsoft Windows 7, 81, 88–89
  characteristics of, 176
  concurrency mechanisms of, 294–297
  energy efficiency, 89
  engineering improvements, 89
  features of, 89
  object-oriented design of, 177–179
  performance improvements, 89
  processes of, 176–179
  reliability improvements, 89
  resources of, 176
  security, 89, 667–672
  subsystems of, support for, 181
  thread objects, 177–179
  threads, 89, 176–181
Middleware, 679, 687–689
  architecture of, 688–689
  distributed message passing, 693
Migrated process, 18-5–6
Migration scenario, 18-7
Migration, initiation of, 18-3–5
Minimal denial-of-service costs, 661
MIPS, 81, 579
Misappropriation, 612
Misfeasor, 143
Misuse, 612
Mobile code, 620, 622
Mobile-program systems, 658
Model parameters, estimating, 20-38–41
  sampling, 20-38–41
  sampling errors, 20-41
Modern operating systems (OS)
  development leading to, 71–73
  distributed operating system, 73
  microkernel architecture, 71
  monolithic kernel, 71
  multiprocessing, 72–73
  multiprogramming, 72–73
  multithreading, 71–72
  object-oriented design, 73
  process, 72
  symmetric multiprocessing (SMP), 72–73
Modes
  control, 135
  decision, 404
  kernel, 56, 135
  nonpreemptive, 404
  preemptive, 404
  switching, 138–139

system, 135
user, 56, 135
Modification of messages, 615
Modular programming, 66
Modular program structure, 162
Modular structure of Linux, 95–97
Modules. *See also* specific types of
  emulation control, 657
  of execution, 83–84
  input/output, 9, 10
  kernel, 96
  loadable, Linux, 95, 336
  loading, 336
  rendering, 174–175
  stackable, 95
  table, elements of, 96–97
Monitor point of view, 53–54
Monitors, 53, 213, 226–232
  alternate model of, with notify and
    broadcast, 230–232
  bounded-buffer producer/consumer
    problem, 229
  characteristics of, 227
  concurrency, 226–232
  condition variables, 227
  dining philosophers problem, solutions using, 280–281
  Mesa, 231
  resident, 53, 54
  security reference, 84
  with signal, 227–230
  simple batch systems, 53
  structure of, 228
  virtual machine, 74
Monolithic kernel, 71
Motivation, 27, 183, 18-2–3
MS-DOS, 80
Multicore computer, 35–36
  DDR3 (double data rate) memory controller, 35
  Intel Core i7, example of, 35–36
  multithreading of, 171–175
  operating systems, 77–79
  QuickPath Interconnect (QPI), 35–36
  software on, 171–174
  support, 464–466
  valve game software, application example, 174–175
Multicore organization, 33–36
Multics, 90
Multiexploit, 630
Multiinstance applications, 174
Multilevel feedback, 414
Multilevel queue scheduler, 587
Multipartite virus, 622
Multiplatform, 630
Multiple applications, 199
Multiple data streams, 565
Multiple interrupts, 21–23
  approaches to, 22–23
  control with, transfer of, 22
  disable interrupt, 22–23
  interrupt service routine (ISR), 23
  time sequence of, 23
Multiple random variables, 19-12–14
Multiple-threat malware, 622–623
Multiprocess applications, 173
Multiprocessing, 72–73, 199
Multiprocessor operating system, 77–79

Multiprocessor scheduling, 431–442, 468
   design issues, 433–435
   granularity, 432–433
   process scheduling, 435–436
   thread scheduling, 437–442
Multiprocessor system, 431
Multiprogrammed batch systems, 56–58
   example of, 57
   memory management, 58
   multiprogramming (multitasking), 56
   program execution attributes of, sample, 57
   on resource utilization, effects of, 58
   system utilization of, 56
   time-sharing systems, differentiating between, 60
   uniprogramming, 58
   utilization histograms, 58, 59
Multiprogramming, 56, 72–73, 199
   processors, 434–435
Multiprogramming levels, 377–378
Multiserver approach, 20-27
Multiserver model, 20-28–30
Multiserver queues, 20-22–24
   assumptions of, 20-18–19
   calculations for, 20-30
   formulas for, 20-23
   multiserver model, 20-28–30
   problems with, 20-28–30
   queuing models, 20-16
   queuing relationships, basic, 20-16–18
   single-server model, 20-28
Multitasking. *See* Multiprogramming
Multithreading, 71–72, 159–162
   Microsoft Windows 7, 179
   of multicore computer, 171–175
   native applications, 173
   process models, 160
   on uniprocessor, 164
Mutex, 213, 215–216, 589. *See also* Mutual exclusion
Mutex object, 296
Mutual exclusion, 200, 206, 237–239, 267, 269, 18-26,
   18-31, A-2–8
   attempts for, A-3
   Dekker's algorithm, A-2–7
   failed, 63–64
   hardware support for, 209–213
   illustration of, 207
   interrupt disabling, 210
   lock, 292–293
   Peterson's algorithm, A-7–8
   requirements for, 209
   semaphores, 218–219
   software approaches, A-2–8
   special machine instructions, 210–213
   using messages, 237
Mutually exclusive, 19-3
Mutual waiting, 18-38–41

N
*name, 96
Named pipes, 554
Naming files, 538–539
NASA, 706
National Institute of Standards and Technology (NIST),
   326, 651
Native audit records, 655
Native system interfaces (NT API), 84

Ndeps, 97
Nearest fit strategy, 544
NEC V8xx, 579
Negatively correlated, 19-13
Negotiation of process migration, 18-7–9
Nested task flag, 132
.NET, framework of, 75
Network access layer, 17-7–8
Network-based IDS, 144–145
Network operating system, 17-3
Network protocols, 17-1–23
   architecture of, 17-3–6
   definition of, 17-4
   elements of, 17-4–5
   Linux networking, 17-21–22
   sockets, 17-15–20
   tasks performed for, 17-3–4
   TCP/IP protocol architecture, 17-6–15
Networks, 615–616, 679. *See also*
   specific networks
   device drivers, 100
   drivers, 513
   isolation, 101
   protocols, 100
   vehicles for worms, 629
Networks of queues, 20-32–37
   Jackson's Theorem, 20-34–35
   packet-switching network, application
     to, 20-35–37
   partitioning, 20-33
   queues in tandem, 20-33
   traffic streams, merging of, 20-33
New process state, 117
New → ready process, 118
New → ready/suspend and new → ready process, 124
New Technology File System (NTFS)
   cluster sizes, 566
   components of, 568
   directory attributes, types of, 567
   disk storage, concepts of, 565–566
   examples of, 564
   features of, 564–565
   file structure, 565–567
   hard links, 565
   journaling, 565
   large disks, support for, 565
   large files, support for, 565
   multiple data streams, 565
   partition sizes, 566
   recoverability, 564–565, 568–569
   security, 565
   symbolic links, 565
   volume, 565–567
*next, 96
Next-fit, 316
Nimda attack, 622–623
No access rights, 540
Node, 699
No deadlock, 263
Node manager, 705
Nodes into B-trees, insertion of, 535
No-execute bit, 666
Nonblocking, 234, 695
Nonpersistent binding, 697
Nonpreemptive mode, 404
Nonprocess kernel, 140–141

Non-real-time scheduling, 459–461
　disadvantages of, 459
　priorities, calculating, 460–461
　real-time tasks, relationship to, 461
　timeslices, calculating, 460–461
Nonuniform memory access (NUMA), 362
No preemption condition, 18-31
No preemption deadlock prevention, 267, 269
Nonpreemptive transfers, 18-10
Normal distributions, 19-12
Normalized response time, 417–418
Notation for queuing systems, 20-14
Notify and broadcast, 230–232
N-step-SCAN policy, 493–494
Nsyms, 97
NTFS. *See* New Technology File System (NTFS)
Nucleus. *See* Kernels
Null Fork, 168
Null → new process, 118

O

Object-oriented design, 73
　categories of, 88
　concepts of, 86–88
　Executive of, 87
　kernel control objects, 88
　of Microsoft Windows 7, 177–179
　Security Descriptor (SD) of, 87
Object-oriented mechanisms, 698
Objects
　access rights, 553
　browser helper, 631
　classes, 86
　control, Windows, 88
　dentry, Linux, 562, 564
　dispatcher, 88, 295–296
　event, Windows, 296, 514
　field, 656
　file, Linux, 514, 562, 564
　inode, 562, 563
　instance, 86
　instantiation of, 86
　kernel control, 88
　manager, 83
　mutex, 296
　owner of, 670
　request broker, 693, 698
　semaphore, 296
　superblock, 562–563
　thread, 177–179
　types, 562
　waitable timer, 296
Obstruction, 612
One-to-many relationships, 170–171, 235
One-to-one relationship, 235
Online polls/games, manipulating, 632
Online resources, 705
ONPROC state, 184
Opcode, 12
Opening files, 522
Open-source Tomcat, 173
Operating mode bits, 132
Operating systems (OS). *See also* Modern operating
　systems (OS)
　achievements of, major, 62–70
　aspects of, 48–51

avoidance approaches for, 265
central themes of, 199
commercial, 578
concurrency, concerns of, 204
development of, 62–63
distributed, 73
eCos (*See* Embedded Configurable Operating
　System (eCos))
embedded (*See* Embedded operating systems)
evolution of, 52–62
functions, 48–52
information in, protection and security of, 68–69
interfaces of, typical, 50
Linux (*See* Linux)
Mac OS X, 94
memory management in, 66–68
Microsoft (*See* Microsoft Windows)
modern, development leading to, 71–73
multiprocessor/multicore, 77–79
objectives/functions of, 48–52
organization of, 82–84
overview of, 46–101
process-based, 142–143
processes, 62–66, 140–143
real-time, 443–447, 577
resource management in, 50–51, 69–70
services provided by, 49
structure, 200
symmetric multiprocessor, considerations of, 77–78
TinyOS (*See* TinyOS)
UNIX (*See* UNIX systems)
as user/computer interface, 48–50
virtual machines (VM), 74–76
Operating systems (OS) control
　file tables, 127
　input/output tables, 127
　memory tables, 126–127
　process tables, 127–128
　structures of, 126–128
Operating systems (OS) software
　cleaning policy, 376–377
　fetch policy, 361–362
　load control, 377–379
　placement policy, 362
　policies for, 361
　replacement policy, 362–370
　resident set management, 370–376
　virtual memory, 360–379
Optimal (OPT) replacement policy, 363
Oracle, 173
Ordinary file, 553
OS. *See* Operating systems (OS)
OS/161, B-2–3
Outcome, 19-2
Overall normalized response time, 417
Overflow flag, 132
Owner of object, 670

P

Packet-switching network, application to, 20-35–37
Page/paging, 307, 321–325
　address translation in system for, 347, 348
　allocation, 385–386
　behavior, 345, 354
　buffering, 369
　cache, Linux, 512

Page/paging (*continued*)
  characteristics of, 343
  demand, 361
  directory, 384
  fault, 350
  fault frequency (PFF), 375
  frame data table entry, 380–381
  logical addresses, 323
  middle directory, 385
  numbers, 349
  prepaging, 361
  replacement, 381–382
  replacement algorithm, 386
  segmentation and, combining, 357–359
  simple, 343
  size, 354–356
  system, 379–381
  table entry, 380–381
  translation lookaside buffer (TLB), 349–354
  virtual memory, 343, 345–356
  Windows, 388–389
Page tables, 321, 385
  direct *vs.* associative lookup for, 353
  inverted, 349, 350
  structure of, 347–349
  two-level hierarchical, 348
Parallelism, 78–79, 432–433
  coarse, 432–433
  fine-grained, 433
  independent, 432
  medium-grained, 433
  synchronization, 432
  very coarse-grained, 432–433
Parallelized application, 702
Parallelizing compiler, 702
Parallelizing computation, clusters, 702–703
Parameter passing, 697
Parameter representation, 697
Parametric computing, 702–703
Parasitic, 144
Parbegin, A-7
Parent process, 115
Parity flag, 132
Partial program execution, 12–13
Partition/partitioning, 20-33
  boot sector, 566–567
  dynamic, 314–317
  fixed, 310–314
  memory, 310–321
  size, 310–312, 566
Passive attacks, 615
Passive standby, 700, 701
Password, 146
Password-based authentication, 640–643
Pathname, 538
Payload, 623
Payload-classification-based worm
   containment, 662
Pentium EFLAGS Register bits, 132
PeopleSoft, 173
Percentiles, calculating, 20-25–26
Performance
  disk cache, issues of, 505–506
  files, grades of, 529
  improvements in Microsoft Windows 7, 89
  of software on multicore computer, 171–174

Performance comparison, 415–420
  queuing analysis, 415–418
  simulation modeling, 418–420
Periodic tasks, 443, 450
Permanent blocking, 259
Persistent binding, 697
Persistent rootkit, 633
Personal identification number (PIN), 146, 644
Peterson's algorithm, A-7–8
Phantom deadlock, 18-31
Physical address, 320
Physical input/output, 522, 525
Physical layer, 17-7
Physical memory, Linux, 100
Physical organization, 309–310, 483
Pile files, 529–530
Pipes, UNIX, 283
Placement algorithm for memory, 312–317
Placement policy, 361, 362
Plain spinlocks, 287
Platform, 582
Plug-and-play manager, Windows, 83
Poisson arrival rate, 416
Poisson counting process, 19-22–24
Poisson distributions, 19-11–12
Poisson increment process, 19-24
Polymorphic technique, 630
Polymorphic viruses, 627
Polymorphism, 87
Portion, 543, 544
Portion size, 544–545
Ports, 17-13
Ports, microkernels and, 71
Positively correlated, 19-13
POSIX, 80, 84, 188
Posix Programming Interface, B-5
PowerBuilder, 684
Power manager, Windows, 84
PowerPC, 81, 579
Power spectrum. *See* Spectral density
Preallocation, 543–544
Precleaning, 376
Precopy strategy, 18-5
Predictability, 401
Preempted process, 119
Preemptive mode, 404
Preemptive smallest number of threads first, 438
Preemptive transfers, 18-10
Prepaging, 361
Pre-thread static storage, 160
Printer interrupt service routine (ISR), 23
Printers, 509
Priorities, 449
  ceiling, 457
  classes, 463, 467
  enforcing, 401
  inheritance, 456–457
  level, 109
  Linux, calculating, 460–461
  policy, 490
  priority queuing, 402
  process, 466–468
  queues, 20-30–32
  queuing, 402
  thread, 466–468
  use of, 402–403

Priority inversion, 455–457
  priority ceiling, 457
  priority inheritance, 456–457
  unbounded, 455
Privacy, 609
Privileged instructions, batch systems, 55
Privileges, 669
Probability, 19-2–8
  axiomatic definition of, 19-2–5
  Bayes's Theorem, 19-6–8
  classical definition of, 19-5–6
  conditional, and independence, 19-6
  definition of, 19-2–6
  relative frequency definition of, 19-5
Problem statement, A-8
Procedure call, asynchronous, 514
Process and channel graph, 18-15
Process-based operating systems, 142–143
Process control, 134–139
  execution, modes of, 134–136
  information, 129–130, 131, 133
  operating system, structures of, 126–128
  process attributes, 129–133
  process creation, 136
  process location, 128–129
  process switching, 137–139
  structures of, 128–134
  UNIX System V Release 4 (SVR4), 151–152
Process control blocks, 109–110
  elements of, 129–130
  role of, 133–134
  simplified, 110
Process(es), 72, 98, 106–152
  for addressing, requirements of, 308
  affinity, 464, 466
  attributes of, 129–133
  characteristics of, 158
  components of, 64
  concept of, 62–66, 108–109, 158
  control (*See* Process control)
  creation of, 114–115, 136
  definition of, 62, 108–110
  description of, 126–134
  dispatching, 435
  elements of, 109, 128
  errors in, causes of, 63–64
  execution of, mechanisms for interrupting, 137
  identification, 129–130, 131
  identifier, 349
  image, 128, 149–150
  implementation of, 65
  initiation denial, deadlock avoidance
    strategy, 270–271
  input/output, 11
  isolation, 66, 101
  with largest remaining execution window, 378
  location of, 128–129
  management of, 64–65
  memory, 11
  migration, 704
  of operating systems (OS), 62–66, 140–143
  priorities, 466–468
  process control blocks and, 109–110, 133–134
  processing time, 449
  processor affinity, 177
  queues, 242

resources, 278
scheduling, 404, 435–436
security issues, 143–147
with smallest resident set, 378
spawning, 115
state of (*See* Process state)
state transitions, 396
structure, 183
suspension, 378–379
switching, 137–139
synchronization, 432
table entry, 150
tables, 127–128
termination of, 115–116
threads and, 66, 158–164, 169, 182
traces of, 111–113
UNIX SVR4 process management, 147–152
virtual machines (VM), 75
Process interaction, 205–209
  awareness, 205
  communication, 208–209
  resources, 206–207
  sharing, 207–208
Process migration, 18-2–10
  eviction, 18-9–10
  mechanisms, 18-3–7
  motivation, 18-2–3
  negotiation of, 18-7–9
  nonpreemptive transfers, 18-10
  preemptive transfers, 18-10
Process migration mechanisms, 18-3–7
  messages, 18-6–7
  migrated process, 18-5–6
  migration scenario, 18-7
  migration, initiation of, 18-3–5
  signals, 18-6–7
Process operation latencies (µs), 168
Processors, 8. *See also* Central processing
    unit (CPU); specific types of
  functions of, 9
  internal registers of, 9–10
  point of view, 53–54
  scheduling, types of, 397–400
  specific context, 187
  state information, 129–130, 131
  utilization, 401
Process state, 65, 110–125
  changing of, 139
  five-state model, 116–120
  suspended processes, 121–125
  two-state process model, 112–114
  ULT, relationship with, 166
  UNIX System V Release 4 (SVR4),
    147–149
Process-thread manager, Windows, 84
Producer/consumer problem
  bounded-buffer, 229, 238
  semaphores, 219–224
Profile based detection, 655
Program code, 109
Program counter (PC), 11, 20, 109
Program execution attributes, 57
Program flow of control with/without
    interrupts, 14–15
Programmed input/output, 31–32, 477
Programming language, 663–664

Programming projects, B-4–B-6
  additional, B-5
  small, B-5–B-6
  textbook-defined projects, B-4–B-5
Program operation, 64
Program status word (PSW), 19
Project MAC, 60, 90
Propagation phase, 624
Protection, 308–309
  access control and, 66
  sharing and, 359–360
Protocol, 17-4
Protocol data units (PDUs), 17-13
Pseudocodes, 5
Pthread libraries, 188
Pull mechanism, 466
Purpose-built embedded operating systems, 578–579
Push mechanism, 466
Pvmsync, 708

Q
Quality of service (QoS), 20-13
Queues
  behaviors, 20-3–7
  character, UNIX SVR4, 508
  dispatch, 462
  driver input/output, 507
  in tandem, 20-33
  networks of, 20-32–37
  parameters, 20-11–12
  process, 242
  single-server, formulas for, 416
  size, 20-13
  structure, 464
  with priorities, 20-30–32
Queuing
  diagram for scheduling, 399
  discipline, 237
  priority, 402
Queuing analysis, 415–418, 20-1–41
  examples of, 20-24–30
  importance of, 20-8–10
  model parameters, estimating, 20-38–41
  multiserver queues, 20-22–24
  queue behaviors, example of, 20-3–7
  queues, 20-30–37
  queuing models, 20-10–19, 20-37
  single-server queues, 20-20–22
Queuing models, 20-10–19, 20-37
  assumptions, 20-18–19
  multiserver queue, 20-16
  queuing relationships, basic, 20-16–18
  single-server queue, 20-10–15
Queuing networks, elements of, 20-34
Queuing relationships, basic, 20-16–18
Queuing systems, notation for, 20-14
QuickPath Interconnect (QPI), 35–36

R
Race conditions, 200, 204, A-8–15
  problem statement, A-8
RAID (redundant array of independent disks), 494–502
  characteristics of, 494
  for high data transfer capacity, 498–499
  for high input/output request rate, 499
  level 0, 495–499

level 1, 499–500
level 2, 500
level 3, 500–501
level 4, 501–502
level 5, 502
level 6, 502
proposal for, 495
software, 514–515
Random process. *See* Stochastic processes
Random scanning, 632
Random scheduling, 490
Random variables, 19-8–14
  density function, 19-8–9
  distribution function, 19-8–9
  distributions, 19-9–12
  multiple, 19-12–14
Rate halting, 662
Rate limiting, 662
Rate monotonic scheduling, 452–454
Ratio close to 1, 20-20
Ratio greater then 1, 20-21
Ratio less than 1, 20-20
Raw sockets, 17-16
Reactive operation, embedded systems, 577
Read address, 67
Read_control access, 671
Readers/writers
  lock, 294
  mechanisms, 239–243
  priorities of, 240–243
  process queues, state of, 242
  semaphores, 290
  spinlocks, 288–289
  using semaphores, solution to, 240, 241
Reading access rights, 540
Reading assignments, B-6
Reading files, 522
Read operation, 29–30
Ready → exit process, 119
Ready process state, 122
Ready → ready/suspend process, 123
Ready → running process, 118
Ready state, 117, 179
Ready/suspend process, 123
Ready/suspend → ready process, 123
Ready time, 448
Real address, 341
Real memory, 343
Real time
  class (159-100), 461–462
  operating systems, 443–447, 577
  priority classes, 467
  tasks, Linux, 461
  user, 463
Real-time scheduling, 430–470
  algorithms for, 447
  deadline scheduling, 448–452
  history of, 442–443
  Linux, 457–458
  and multiprocessor, 430–470
  priority inversion, 455–457
  rate monotonic scheduling, 452–454
  real-time operating systems,
    characteristics of, 443–447
  types of, 448
Receive primitive, 233–235

Record blocking, 541–543
  fixed blocking, 541
  methods of, 542
  variable-length spanned, 541
  variable-length unspanned, 542
Records, 523
  audit, for intrusion detection, 655–657
  detection-specific audit, 655
  native audit, 655
Recoverability, 564–565, 568–569
Recovery, 277–278
Redundant array of independent disks. *See* RAID
  (redundant array of independent disks)
*refs, 97
Registers
  address, 9, 10
  context, 150
  control and status, 130, 131
  index, 64–65
  input/output address, 10
  instruction, 11
  internal, of processor, 9–10
  for interrupt processing, changes in, 20–21
  memory address, 9
  memory buffer, 9–10
  Pentium EFLAGS, 131–132
Regular file, 553
Relational database, 679
Relative address, 320
Relative frequency definition of probability, 19-5
Release of message contents attack, 615
Reliability, 78, 89, 444, 551, 694–695
Relocatable loading, 335–336
Relocation, 307–308, 319–321
Remote control facility, 632
Remote execution capability, 629
Remote login (rlogin), 17-15
Remote login capability, 629
Remote procedure call (RPC), 163, 695–698
  advantages of, 695
  asynchronous, 698
  client/server binding, 697
  mechanism for, 696
  object-oriented mechanisms, 698
  parameter passing, 697
  parameter representation, 697
  synchronous, 698
Removal of virus, 657
Rendering module, 174–175
Replacement, frequency-based, 504
Replacement algorithms, 30, 31, 317, 363–369
  clock page, 368
  clock policy, 365–366
  first-in-first-out (FIFO) policy, 364
  fixed-allocation, local page, 367
  four page, behavior of, 364
  least recently used (LRU) policy, 363–364
  optimal policy, 363
Replacement policies, 361, 362–370. *See also*
  specific types of
  algorithms for, basic, 363–369
  and cache size, 369–370
  concepts of, 362
  frame locking, 363
  page buffering, 369
Replacement scope, 371

Replay attacks, 615
Report assignments, B-6
Repudiation, 612
Research projects, B-6
Reserved state, 388
Resident monitor, 53, 54
Resident set, 342
  size, 370
Resident set management, 362, 370–376
  fixed allocation, local scope, 371
  replacement scope, 371
  resident set size, 370
  variable allocation, 372–376
Resiliency, 661
Resource allocation, distributed deadlock in, 18-30–38
  deadlock avoidance, 18-33–34
  deadlock detection, 18-34–38
  deadlock prevention, 18-32–33
Resources, 704–705
  balancing, 401
  competition among processes for, 206–207
  configure interface, 603
  interface, 603
  manager, 50–51, 706
  of Microsoft Windows 7, 176
  ownership, 158 (*See also* Process/processes)
  requested interface, 603
  requirements, 449
  utilization, 58
Resources, allocation of
  denial, 271–275
  graphs, 266–267
Resources, management of, 69–70
  elements of, major, 69–70
  factors of, 69
  functional description of, 70
  round-robin, 70
Resource-specific interface, 603
Resource-usage field, 656
Response time, 401
  normalized, 417–418
  overall normalized, 417
  projected *vs.* actual, 20-9
Responsiveness, 444
Resume flag, 132
Retinal pattern, 645
Reusable resources, deadlock and, 263–264
Robot. *See* Bots
Role-based access control (RBAC),
  647, 651–653
Root isolation, 101
Rootkits, 620, 633–635
  classification of, 633
  countermeasures for, 662–663
  installation of, 633–634
  system-level call attacks, 634–635
Rotational delay, 487, 488–489
Rotational positional sensing (RPS), 488
Round-robin techniques, 70, 116, 407–410
Router, 17-8
RSX-11M, 80
Running → blocked process, 119
Running → exit process, 118
Running process state, 109, 117, 180, 184, 187
Running → ready process, 118–119
Running → ready/suspend process, 124

Run-time defenses, 666–667
  address space randomization, 667
  executable address space protection, 666
  guard pages, 667
Run-time dynamic linking, 339

S
Safe coding techniques, 664
Safe libraries, 664–665
Safe states, resource allocation, 271–272
Salt value of passwords, 641
Sample space, 19-3
Sampling, 20-38–41
  distribution of the mean, 20-38
  errors, 20-41
Saved thread context, 160
Scaling, 72
Scanning, 632
SCAN policy, 493
Scanrate, 381
Scheduled blocks, 190
Scheduler, 98
Scheduling, 52, 77, 158
  control and, 482–483
  criteria for, 401
  deadline, 448–452
  disk, 474–516
  dynamic, 442
  dynamic best effort, 448
  dynamic planning-based, 448
  feedback, 414
  gang, 439
  input/output, 396
  levels of, 398
  Linux, 457–461
  Linux virtual machine process, 468–469
  long-term, 396, 397–399
  medium-term, 396, 399–400
  multiprocessor, 431–442
  non-real-time, 459–461
  process, 404, 435–436
  processor, types of, 397–400
  and process state transitions, 396
  queuing diagram for, 399
  random, 490
  rate monotonic, 452–454
  real-time, 430–470
  short-term, 396, 400
  static priority-driven preemptive, 448
  static table-driven, 447
  thread, 437–442
  types of, 396
  uniprocessor, 395–425
  UNIX, traditional, 422–424
  UNIX FreeBSD, 463–466
  UNIX SVR4, 461–463
  Windows, 466–468
Scheduling algorithms, 400–422
  fair-share scheduling, 420–422
  performance comparison, 415–420
  priorities, use of, 402–403
  scheduling policies, alternative, 403–415
  short-term scheduling criteria, 400–402
Scheduling policies, 403–415
  feedback, 413–415
  first-come-first-served (FCFS), 407

  highest ratio next, 413
  round robin, 407–410
  shortest process next, 410–411
  shortest remaining time, 411–413
S.count value, 219
Search operation, 537
Secondary memory, 27
Secondary storage management, 543–551
  file allocation, 543–547
  free space management, 547–550
  reliability, 551
  volumes, 550
Second moment, 19-9
Second-order statistics, 19-15–17
Sector, 565
Security Descriptor (SD), 87
Security ID (SID), 668
Security reference monitor, 84
Security Requirements for Cryptographic Modules, 651
Security requirements triad, 609
Security systems
  concepts of, 608–610
  in Microsoft Windows 7, 89
  scope of, 613
  threats to, 607–635
Security threats, 607–635, 639–672
  access control, 646–653
  assets and, 613–616
  attacks and, 610–612
  authentication, 640–646
  bots, 631–633
  buffer overflow attacks, 663–667
  countermeasures for, 144–147
  intruders, 616–619
  intrusion detection, 616, 619, 653–657
  malicious software, 619–623
  malware defense, 657–663
  memory management, 326–330
  New Technology File System (NTFS), 565
  of process, 143–147
  rootkits, 633–635
  system access threats, 143–144
  viruses, 623–628
  Windows 7 security, 667–672
  worms, 628–630
Seek time, 487, 488
Segmentation, 325–326
  address translation in, 357, 358
  advantages of, 356
  characteristics of, 343
  implications of, 356
  organization of, 356–357
  paging and, combining, 357–359
  segments, protection relationship between, 359
  simple, 343
  virtual memory, 343, 356–357
Segment pointers, 307, 325, 359
Selection function, 403
Semaphores, 213–226, 283–284, 289–290, 293
  binary, 213, 215, 289–290
  counting, 215, 222, 289–290
  currency mechanisms, common, 213
  definition of, consequences of, 214–215
  dining philosophers problem, solutions using, 280
  eCos thread synchronization, 589

first-in-first-out (FIFO) process, 216
general, 215, 222
implementation of, 224–226
Linux, 290
mechanism of, example of, 217
mutex, 215–216
mutual exclusion, 218–219
object, Windows, 296
producer/consumer problem, 219–224
readers/writers, 240, 241
reader-writer, 290
s.count, value of, 219
shared data protected by, process accessing, 219
strong, 216
as variable, operations of, 214
weak, 216
Semantics, 17-4
Semaphores, A-8–15
Sensors for intrusion detection, 145
Separate servers, 701
Sequential files, 530
indexed, 530–531
key field for, 530
processing of, 523–524
Sequential search, 530
Serial processing, 52–53
Server-based processing, 683
Servers
client/server computing, 678–679
connected to disks, 701
share disks, 701
Service-oriented architecture (SOA), 689–691
Service(s)
broker, 690
processes, Windows, 84
provider, 690
requestor, 690
Set of data, 109
Setup time, 52–53
Shadow copies, volume, 515
Shared data protected, 219
Shared disk approach, 701
Shared memory multiprocessor, 283
Shared nothing, 701
Shared resources, 602
Sharing files, 207–208, 309, 522
Shortest process next (SPN) scheduling,
410–411
Shortest remaining time (SRT) scheduling,
411–413
Shortest-service-time-first (SSTF) policy, 490–493
Short memory process, 19-17
Short-term scheduling, 396, 400–402
Siebel CRM (Customer Relationship Manager), 173
Signaling/signals, 98, 284, 18-6–7
event object, 514
file object, 514
monitors with, 227–230
Signal-Wait, 168
Signature, 646
Signature-based worm scan filtering, 661
Signature detection, 655
Sign flag, 132
Simple batch systems, 53–56
hardware features of, 55–56
job control language (JCL), 54

kernel mode, 56
monitor, 53
points of view of, 53–54
user mode, 56
Simple interrupt processing, 19
Simple Mail Transfer Protocol (SMTP),
17-14–15
Simple paging, 343
Simple segmentation, 343
Simulation modeling for scheduling, 418–420
Simulation result, 419
Simulations, B-3–B-4
Simultaneous access for file sharing, 541
Simultaneous concurrent process, 77
Simultaneous concurrent threads, 77
Single buffer, 484–486
Single control point, 703
Single entry point, 703
Single file hierarchy, 703
Single input/output space, 704
Single instance service, 691
Single-Instruction Multiple Data (SIMD)
techniques, 10
Single job-management system, 704
Single memory space, 703
Single process space, 704
Single-server approach, 20-27
Single-server model, 20-28
Single-server queues, 416, 20-20–22
characteristics of, 20-13–15
features of, 20-12–13
formulas for, 20-19
mean residence time for, 20-22
parameters for, 20-10
queue parameters of, 20-11–12
queuing models, 20-10–15
queuing system structure for, 20-10
Single-system image, 703
Single-threaded process models, 160
Single user interface, 704
Single-user multiprocessing system, 161–162
Single virtual networking, 703
Size, 96
Slab allocation, 386
SLEEP state, 184
Slim read-writer locks, 297
Slots of memory, 28
Smallest number of threads first, 438
Small memory footprint, 583
Small programming projects, B-5–B-6
Smart cards, 644–645
SMP. See Symmetric multiprocessor (SMP)
Snapshot, 18-13
example of, 18-16
Sniffing traffic, 631
Sockets, 10, 17-15–20
application programming interface (API), 17-16
communication, 17-18
concept of, 17-15
connection, 17-17–18
datagram, 17-16
interface calls, 17-16–20
programming, 17-15
raw, 17-16
setup, 17-17
stream, 17-16

Sockets interface calls, 17-16–20
　for connection-oriented protocol, 17-19
　socket communication, 17-18
　socket connection, 17-17–18
　socket setup, 17-17
Soft affinity policy, 181
Soft real-time task, 443
Software
　behavior-blocking, 659–661
　Beowulf, 707–708
　malicious, 144, 619–623
　memory hierarchy in, 27
　RAID, 514–515
　security threats to, 613–614
　valve game, 174–175
Solaris
　memory management, 379–384
　process structure of, 183
　10, 94
　three-level thread structure of, 183
Solaris threads
　SMP management of, 182–186
　states of, 184–185
　synchronization primitives, 292–294
Spammer programs, 620
Spamming, 631
Spanned blocking, variable-length, 541–542
SPARC, 579
Sparks, Matt, B-5
Spatial locality, 42
Spawn state, 162
Special capabilities, utilization of, 18-3
Special file, 554
Special machine instructions, 210–213
　compare&swap instruction, 210–212
　disadvantages of, 212–213
　exchange instruction, 212
　properties of, 212–213
Special reader, 644
Special system processes, Windows, 84
Specific user class, 541
Spectral density, 19-17–19
Spinlocks, 213, 287–289
　basic, 287–288
　eCos thread synchronization, 593–594
　Linux, 288
　plain, 287
　reader-writer, 288–289
Spin waiting, 212, A-2
Sprite, 686–687
SQL Windows, 684
SSH (Secure Shell), 17-15
Stackable modules, Linux, 95–96
Stacking protection mechanisms, 665–666
Stack overflow, 327
Stack values, 328
Standard C Libraries, 586
Standard deviation, 19-9
Standby state, 179–180
Starting deadline, 448
Starvation, 200, 206, 213
Starvation free, 18-26
States, 271, 18-13. *See also* specific states
　available, 388
　blocked, 119, 147–148
　blocked/waiting process, 117

committed, 388
　execution, 186
　exit process, 117
　FREE, 184
　interruptible, 187
　new process, 117
　ONPROC, 184
　process, 65, 110–125
　of processes, 65, 110–125
　ready, 117, 179
　ready process, 122
　reserved, 388
　running process, 109, 117, 180, 184, 187
　safe, resource allocation, 271–272
　SLEEP, 184
　spawn, 162
　standby, 179–180
　stopped, 184, 188
　terminated, 180
　thread, 162–164
　thread execution, 160
　transition, 180
　uninterruptible, 187
　unsafe, 271
　waiting, 180
　zombie, 184, 188
Static biometrics, 146
Static priority-driven preemptive
　　scheduling, 447, 448
Static protocol, 644
Static table-driven scheduling, 447
Stationary stochastic processes, 19-17
Stealth viruses, 627
Stochastic processes
　elementary concepts of, 19-14–26
　ergodicity, 19-24–26
　first-order statistics, 19-15–17
　independent increments, 19-19–24
　second-order statistics, 19-15–17
　spectral density, 19-17–19
　stationary, 19-17
Stopped state, 184, 188
Storage management, 66
　access control, protection and, 66
　automatic allocation/management, 66
　long-term storage, 66
　modular programming, support of, 66
　process isolation, 66
Store-and-forward deadlock, 18-42
Stream communication, 17-18
Streamlined protection mechanisms, 577
Stream-oriented device, 484
Stream sockets, 17-16
Stripe, 498
Strong semaphores, 216
Structured applications, 199
Structured programming (SAL), 40
Structured query language (SQL),
　　679, 682, 688
Subject access rights, 553
Subject field, 655
Subtask structure, 449
Sun Microsystems, 93, 94
SunOS, 93
Superblock object, 562–563
Superblocks, 557

Superior price performance, 699
Supervisor call, 138
Support functions, 135
Suspended processes states, 121–125
   characteristics of, 124–125
   purposes of, 125
   states of, 122–123
   swapping, 121–124
   transitions of, 122, 123–124
SVR4. *See* UNIX System V Release 4 (SVR4)
Swap, 211
Swappable space, 278
Swapping process states, 121–124
Swap-use table entry, 380–381
Switching process, 137–139
Sybase Inc., 684
Symbolic links file, 554, 565
Symmetric multiprocessor (SMP),
     33–35, 72–73
   advantages of, 33–34
   availability, 72
   characteristics of, 33
   cluster, differentiating between, 704
   definition of, 33
   incremental growth, 72
   multicore support and, 464–466
   organization of, 34–35
   OS considerations of, 77–78
   scaling, 72
   threads for, 86
*syms, 97
Synchronization, 77, 234–235
   design characteristics of, 233
   eCos thread, 589
   granularity, 432
   improper, 63
   lock-free, 297
   message passing, 233–235
   processes, 432
   Solaris, thread primitives, 292–294
   of threads, 164
Synchronized access, 670
Synchronous input/output, Windows, 513–514
Synchronous RPC, 698
Syntax, 17-4
System call table
   modification of, 634
   redirecting, 635
   targets, 634
System-level call attacks, 634–635
System-level context, 150
System on a Chip (SoC), 10
System oriented, other criteria, 401
System oriented, performance related criteria, 401
System(s)
   access control list (SACL), 670
   access threats, 143–144
   bus, 9
   calls, Linux, 98
   files, 567
   integrity, 609
   ISA, 50
   mode, 135
   response time, 63
   utilization of, 56
   virtual machines (VM), 76

T
Tape drives, 509
Tasks, 598. *See also* Process/processes
   aperiodic, 451
   deadline scheduling for, 448–451
   hard real-time, 443
   Linux, 186–188
   periodic, 450
   real-time, Linux, 461
   soft real-time, 443
TCP header, 17-9
TCP segment, 17-14
TCP/IP protocol architecture, 17-6–15
   applications of, 17-14–15
   concepts of, 17-12
   Internet Protocol (IP), and IPv6, 17-10–11
   layers, 17-7–8
   Linux kernel components of, 17-20
   operation of, 17-12–14
   protocol data units (PDUs) in, 17-13
   User Datagram Protocol (UDP) and, 17-8–10
TELNET, 17-15
Temporal locality, 42
Terminals, 509
Termination of process states, 180
Textbook-defined projects, B-4–B-5
Thin client, 685
Thrashing, load control, 344
Threading granularity options, 174
Threads, 66, 157–192, 585. *See also* specific types of
   benefits of, 161
   bottom-half kernel, 463
   execution state, 160
   functionality of, 162–164
   interactive, 464
   kernel-level (KLT), 168–169, 182
   Linux process and, management of, 186–189
   MAC OS Grand Central Dispatch (GCD), 189–192
   management of, 186–189
   many-to-many relationships of, 169–170
   Microsoft Windows 7, improvements in, 89
   migration, 466
   multithreaded process models, 160
   multithreading, 159–162, 171–175
   objects, 177–179
   one-to-many relationships of, 170–171
   operations associated with change in, 162
   priorities, 466–468
   processes and, 158–164, 169, 182
   process operation latencies (µs), 168
   processor affinity, 177
   remote procedure call (RPC) using, 163
   single-threaded process models, 160
   in single-user multiprocessing system, 161–162
   for SMP, 86
   Solaris, and SMP management, 182–186
   states of, 162–164
   synchronization, 164, 589–594
   top-half kernel, 463
   types of, 164–171
   user-level (ULT), 164–168, 182
   Windows 7, and SMP management, 176–181
Thread scheduling, 437–442
   approaches to, 437
   dedicated processor assignment, 440–441
   dynamic scheduling, 442

Thread scheduling (*continued*)
    gang scheduling, 439
    load sharing, 437–439
Thread states, 162–164
    of Microsoft Windows 7, 179–180
    of Solaris, 184–185
Three-level interrupt mode, 584–585
Three-level thread structure, Solaris, 183
Three-tier client-server architecture, 685–686
Threshold detection, 655
Threshold random walk (TRW) scan detection, 662
Throughput, 401
Tightly-coupled multiprocessor, 20-26–27
Tightly coupled multiprocessor system, 431
Time average, 19-25
Time, creation of, 187
Timeliness, 661
Timer interrupts, 89, 587
Timers, batch systems, 55, 187
Time sequence of multiple interrupts, 23
Time-shared (59-0) class, 462
Time sharing, 60
Time-sharing systems, 58–62
    batch multiprogramming, differentiating between, 60
    Compatible Time-Sharing System (CTSS), 60–61
    memory requirements of, 60–61
    time sharing, 60
    time slicing, 60
Time-sharing user, 463
Timeslices/timeslicing, 60, 137, 407, 460–461
Time-stamp field, 656
Timestamping algorithm, 18-22–23
Timing, 17-4
Timing comparison, 489
TinyOS, 594–603
    components of, 596–599
    configurations for, examples of, 600–601
    goals of, 595–596
    resource interface, 601–603
    scheduler, 599–600
    wireless sensor networks, 594–595
TLB. *See* Translation lookaside buffer (TLB)
Token, 146
Token-based authentication, 643–645
Token bucket filter (TBF), 468–469
Token loss, 644
Token-passing algorithm, 18-29
Token-passing approach, 18-28–30
Top-half kernel threads, 463
Topological scanning, 633
Torvalds, Linus, 94
Trace of process, 111
Traffic analysis attacks, 615
Traffic streams, merging of, 20-33
Transfer time, 487
Transition of process state, 180
Translation lookaside buffer (TLB), 349–354
    cache operation and, 353
    operation of, 352
Transparency, 661
Transport layer, 17-8
Transport vehicles, 630
Trapdoor. *See* Backdoor
Trap flag, 132
Traps, 100, 138

Tree representation of buddy system, 319
Tree-structured file directory, 538, 539
Trial, 19-5
Trigger, 623
Triggering phase, 624
Trivial File Transfer Protocol (TFTP), 17-5
TRIX, 170
Trojan horse, 620, 621–622
Turnaround time (TAT), 401, 404, 419
Two-handed clock algorithm, 381
Two-level hierarchical page table, 348
Two-level memory
    characteristics of, 39–45
    locality, 40–42
    operation of, 42
    performance of, 25–26, 42–45
Two-priority categories, 416
Two-state process model, 112–114

U
U area, 150–151
ULT. *See* User-level threads (ULT)
Ultrafast spreading, 630
Unauthorized disclosure, 610
Unblock state, 162
Unbounded priority inversion, 455
Unbuffered input/output, 508–509
Uncorrelated, 19-13
Underlying distribution, 20-38
Uninterruptible state, 187
Union, 19-3
Uniprocessor
    multithreading on, 164
    scheduling, 395–425
Uniprogramming systems, 58
University of California at Berkeley, 495
University of Illinois at Urbana-Champaign, B-5
UNIX BSD (Berkeley Software Distribution), 90
UNIX FreeBSD, 94
    files, structure of, 555
    inodes, structure of, 555
    scheduling, 463–466
UNIX systems, 90–92, 553–560. *See also* specific systems
    access control lists, 559–560
    architecture of, 91
    Berkeley Software Distribution (BSD), 94
    buffer cache, organization of, 508
    C implementation of, 90
    concurrency mechanisms of, 281–285
    description of, general, 91–92
    devices, types of, 509
    directories, 557
    file access control, 558–559
    file allocation, 556–557
    files, 553–555
    history of, 90
    inodes, 554–556
    input/output, structure of, 507
    kernel, 92, 93
    license for, 90
    memory management, 379–384
    modern, 92–94
    password-based authentication in, implementation of, 642–643
    process structure of, 183

scheduling, traditional, 422–424
signals of, 285
Solaris 10, 94
System III, 90
System V, 90
traditional, 90–92
traditional, file access control, 558–559
Version 6, 90
Version 7, 90
volume structure, 557
UNIX System V Release 4 (SVR4), 93–94
  buffer cache, 507–508
  character queue, 508
  devices, types of, 509
  dispatch queues, 462
  input/output, 506–509
  parameters of, 380–381
  process control of, 151–152
  process description of, 149–151
  process image of, 149–150
  process management, 147–152
  process states of, 147–149
  process table entry of, 150
  scheduling, 461–463
  U area, 150–151
  unbuffered input/output, 508–509
Unreliability, 694–695
Unsafe state, resource allocation, 271, 274
Unspanned blocking, variable-length, 542–543
Update directory operation, 537
Updating access rights, 540
Usecount, 96
User applications, Windows, 84
User control, 444
User Datagram Protocol (UDP), 17-8–10
User dissatisfaction, 644
User groups class, 541
User identification (ID), 558
User interfaces, 48–50, 145
User ISA, 50
User-level context, 149–150
User-level threads (ULT), 164–168
  advantages of, 167–168
  and KLT, combined with, 169
  occurrences of, 165, 167
  process states, relationship with, 166
User mode, 56, 135
User-mode processes, 84–85
  environmental subsystems, 84
  execution within, 141–142
  service processes, 84
  special system processes, 84
  user applications, 84
  in virtual memory, 133
User mode rootkit, 633
User-oriented, other criteria, 401
User-oriented, performance related criteria, 401
User's identity authentication, 146
User-visible registers, 130
Usurpation, security threats of, 612
Utilization histograms, 58, 59

V
Valve game software, 174–175
Variable, operations of, 214

Variable-allocation replacement
  policy, 370
  global scope, 372
  local scope, 372–376
Variable-interval sampled working set
  (VSWS) policy, 375–376
Variable-length spanned, 541
Variable-length unspanned, 542
Variable priority classes, 467
Variant, 582
Variance, 19-9
VAX/VMS, 80
Venn diagrams, 19-4
Verification step of authentication, 145
Very coarse-grained parallelism, 432–433
VFS. *See* Linux virtual file system (VFS)
Virtual addresses
  map, 387–388
  memory management, 67
  space, 160, 341
Virtual interrupt flag, 132
Virtual interrupt pending, 132
Virtualization, 74–75
Virtualized resources, 602
Virtual machine monitor (VMM), 74
Virtual machines (VM), 74–76
  application of, 75
  architecture of, 75–76
  concept of, 74
  definition of, 341
  hosted, 76
  Java, 75
  Linux VServer architecture, differentiating
    between, 100–101
  multicore computer, OS considerations of, 79
  operating system, 75
  process, 75
  system, 76
  terminology of, 341
  and virtualization, 74–75
  virtual machine monitor (VMM), 74
Virtual memory, 40, 67, 98, 340–389
  addressing, 68, 384–385
  concepts of, 67
  hardware/control structures of, 348–360
  locality and, 344–345
  management, 384–389
  manager, 84, 568
  operating system software, 360–379
  paging, 343, 345–356
  protection, sharing and, 359–360
  segmentation, 356–357
  user-mode processes in, 133
Virtual 8086 mode, 132
Virtual platform, 101
Virtual servers, 100–101
Viruses, 620, 623–628
  classification of, 626–627
  compression, 625
  e-mail, 628
  encrypted, 626
  initial infection, 626
  macro, 626, 627–628
  metamorphic, 627
  nature of, 623–624

Viruses (*continued*)
    phases of, 624
    polymorphic, 627
    simple, 625
    stealth, 627
    structure of, 623, 624–626
    virus kits, 627
Virus kits, 627
Virus signature scanner, 657
VM. *See* Virtual machines (VM)
Voice, 646
Volume, 550, 565–567
    encryption, 515
    layout, 566–567
    master file table, 567
    shadow copies, 515
    structure, UNIX, 557
    volume layout, 566–567

W

Waitable timer object, Window, 296
Wait-die method, 18-33
Wait functions, Windows, 295
Waiting state, 180
Waiting time, 419
Weak semaphores, 216
Web clients, 623
Weblogic, 173
Web resources, 4–6
Web servers, 623
Websphere, 173
While loops, 231
Wide sense stationary, 19-17

Win32, 84
Windowing/graphics system, 83
Windows. *See* Microsoft Windows
Windows shares, 623
Wireless sensor networks (WSN), 594–595
Working directories, 539
Working set strategy, 372
Worms, 620, 628–630
    countermeasures for, 661–662
    functions of, 629
    network vehicles for, examples of, 629
    propagation model, 629
    technology for, state of, 630
    worm propagation model, 629
Wound-wait method, 18-33
WRITE call, 14–15, 18
Write_DAC access, 671
WRITE instruction, 15
Write_owner access, 670
Write policy, cache memory, 30, 31
Writing Across the Curriculum (WAC), B-6
Writing assignments, B-6–B-7
Writing files, 522

X

XML (Extensible Markup Language), 689–690

Z

Zero, 20-20
Zero-day exploit, 630
ZF (zero flag), 132
Zombies, 620. *See also* Bots
Zombie state, 184, 188